Pearson BTEC National

Applied Psychology
Book 2
Extended Certificate Units

**Cara Flanagan, Dave Berry,
Rob Liddle, Jock McGinty**
Advisor: Mark Walsh

Acknowledgements

The team who manage and produce this book are simply the best.

Illuminate Publishing, with the psychology list headed by the unique Rick Jackman, and assisted by Clare Jackman, Peter Burton, Saskia Burton and Vikki Mann, represent the best in educational publishing – always looking out for their authors and also for the people who buy the books.

Nic Watson, our editor, puts nothing short of love into ensuring our final product is as perfect as can be. We couldn't do it without her.

The third part of our team is design, fitting the text and pictures on each page. The design came from the gloriously talented Nigel Harriss and then Sarah Clifford of Kamae Design had the job of implementing this and has done a fabulous job of it.

Finally Cara, the lead author, owes much to Rob for the huge amount of work he has done (and always with such grace) and to both Dave and Jock for their excellent chapters and willingness to work to a tight schedule with downright cheerfulness! We also appreciate the invaluable advice from Mark.

A very special thank you to all of you.

The authors

Cara has written many books for A Level Psychology, and she speaks at and organises student conferences. In addition to books, she is senior editor of *Psychology Review*. In a previous life she was a teacher probably for more years than you have been alive and also an examiner for an equally long time. Her spare time (what there is of it) involves travelling with her husband and/ or children (all now 25+). She lives in the Highlands of Scotland (despite being American by birth) and loves a long walk in the mountains and night in a bothy.

Dave is Head of Psychology at Oldham Hulme Grammar School. When not teaching or writing he divides his time between his beloved wife and son, football, politics and *Come Dine With Me*. He does not share his wife's enthusiasm for shopping but will go if he is guaranteed a coffee every half hour. He has an unfortunate – but nevertheless lifelong – commitment to Leeds United Football Club.

Rob was an A Level Psychology teacher for more than 20 years, before turning to writing. He ventured back into teaching again recently and would like to give a big shout out to his ex-colleagues at Winstanley College. In his spare moments, Rob likes nothing better than to pluck away skill-lessly at his guitar. He is enthusiastically looking forward to *Frozen 2* coming out, even though his granddaughters couldn't care less.

Jock is Head of Psychology and Head of Sixth Form at Watford Grammar School for Boys. He has taught Psychology for over 15 years and is a senior A Level examiner and CPD presenter. He is Chair of the Association for the Teaching of Psychology. Jock is interested in positive psychology, specifically the role of character strengths in student satisfaction and academic success.

Mark is a teacher, writer and mental health worker when he's not baking bread or playing football. He currently works with students in further and higher education, teaching sociological psychology and providing mental health support. He has written many textbooks, course specifications and exam papers over the last 25 years, usually whilst listening to long, slow albums of electronic music.

Published in 2019 by Illuminate Publishing Ltd, P.O. Box 1160, Cheltenham, Gloucestershire GL50 9RW

Orders: Please visit www.illuminatepublishing.com or email sales@illuminatepublishing.com

© Cara Flanagan, Dave Berry, Rob Liddle, Jock McGinty, Mark Walsh

The moral rights of the authors have been asserted.

British Library Cataloguing in Publication Data

A catalogue record for this book is available from the British Library

ISBN 978-1-912820-05-4

Printed by Cambrian Printers, Aberystwyth

09.19

Editor: Nic Watson

Design: Nigel Harriss

Layout: Kamae Design

Contents

References

A full set of references are available for download from the Illuminate Publishing website.
Please visit www.illuminatepublishing.com/btecpsychreferences2

Extended certificate in Applied Psychology BTEC Level 3

Structure of the qualification

Unit	Unit title	Type	How assessed	GLH Guided learning hours	TQT Total qualification time
1	Psychological approaches and applications	Mandatory	External exam 1.5 hours 72 marks	90	475 hours total
2	Conducting psychological research	Mandatory and synoptic	Internal	90	235 hours should be spent in total across Units 1 and 2:
3	Health psychology	Mandatory	External exam 2 hours 70 marks	120	Unit 1: 90 GLH + about 25 hours revising and taking the exam.
	Optional units		Internal	60	Unit 2: 90 GLH + about 30 hours writing three reports and conducting the pilot study.
4	Criminal and forensic psychology				240 hours should be spent across Unit 3 and the optional unit:
5	Promoting children's psychological development				Unit 3: 120 GLH + about 35 hours revising and taking the exam.
6	Introduction to psychopathology				Optional unit: 60 GLH + about 25 hours writing the required reports.
7	Applied sport psychology				

How to use this book

Each unit opens with a spread which has:

- A set of questions to start you thinking about the content to come.
- A detailed table of contents.

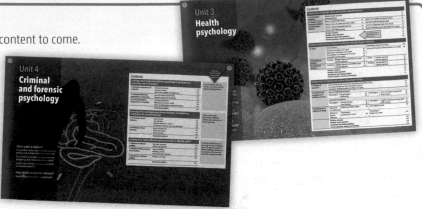

Content areas or learning aims

Unit 3 is divided into content areas A, B and C (because it is externally assessed).

Units 4, 5, 6 and 7 are divided into learning aims A, B and C (because they are internally assessed).

Main spreads

The specification content is covered on spreads such as the one on the facing page.
They all contain a similar pattern of boxes.

Extra material

Unit 3

Content areas A, B and C end with:

Summaries to revise from.

Multiple-choice questions to test yourself.

Assessment guidance to help supply the right material in your exam answers.

Revision guidance.

Practice questions, answers and feedback to see how student answers are marked.

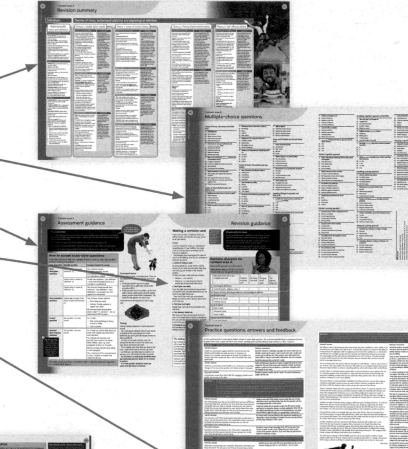

Units 4, 5, 6 and 7

Learning aims A, B and/or C end with:
Assessment guidance to guide you in writing your internally assessed report.

A beginning

Each spread begins with something we hope will grab your interest – it represents the nub of the topic to be studied on the spread.

Description

Assessment objective 1 (AO1) is concerned with your ability to report ***detailed*** descriptions of psychological knowledge and demonstrate your ***understanding*** of this knowledge.

We have generally presented the AO1 material just on the left-hand side of each spread, though sometimes it is on both sides.

Evaluation

Assessment objective 3 (AO3) is concerned with your ability to ***evaluate*** (***assess***, ***analyse***) the concepts and studies you have learned about.

On most spreads in this book we have presented some AO3 material on the right-hand side. Some topics don't require evaluation so there isn't any on the spread.

Special note

Each evaluation point is divided into three **PET** paragraphs because this is a great way to ensure you explain your point well:

1. **POINT** State the point simply.
2. **ELABORATION** The point is now Explained, using Evidence and/or Examples.
3. **THIS** shows that ... Finish with a conclusion often beginning 'This suggests' or 'This shows' or 'Therefore ...'.

That's your PET evaluation.

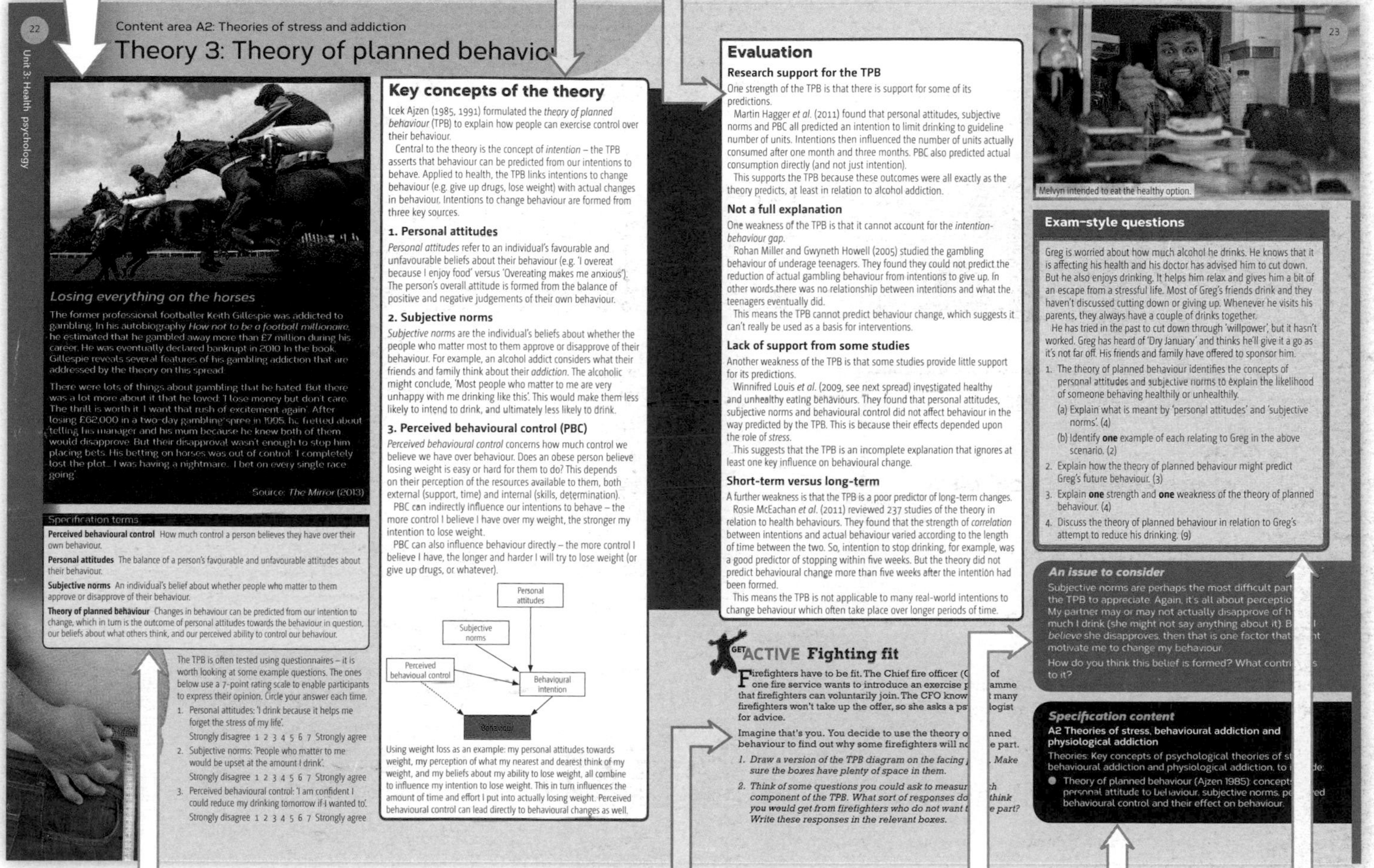

22

Unit 3: Health psychology

Content area A2: Theories of stress and addiction

Theory 3: Theory of planned behaviour

Losing everything on the horses

The former professional footballer Keith Gillespie was addicted to gambling. In his autobiography *How not to be a football millionaire*, he estimated that he gambled away more than £7 million during his career. He was eventually declared bankrupt in 2010. In the book, Gillespie reveals several features of his gambling addiction that are addressed by the theory on this spread.

There were lots of things about gambling that he hated. But there was a lot more about it that he loved: 'I lose money but don't care. The thrill is worth it. I want that rush of excitement again'. After losing £62,000 in a two-day gambling spree in 1995, he fretted about telling his manager and his mum because he knew both of them would disapprove. But their disapproval wasn't enough to stop him placing bets. His betting on horses was out of control: 'I completely lost the plot... I was having a nightmare... I bet on every single race going'.

Source: *The Mirror* (2013)

Specification terms

Perceived behavioural control How much control a person believes they have over their own behaviour.

Personal attitudes The balance of a person's favourable and unfavourable attitudes about their behaviour.

Subjective norms An individual's belief about whether people who matter to them approve or disapprove of their behaviour.

Theory of planned behaviour Changes in behaviour can be predicted from our intention to change, which in turn is the outcome of personal attitudes towards the behaviour in question, our beliefs about what others think, and our perceived ability to control our behaviour.

The TPB is often tested using questionnaires – it is worth looking at some example questions. The ones below use a 7-point rating scale to enable participants to express their opinion. Circle your answer each time.

1. Personal attitudes: 'I drink because it helps me forget the stress of my life'.
   Strongly disagree 1 2 3 4 5 6 7 Strongly agree
2. Subjective norms: 'People who matter to me would be upset at the amount I drink'.
   Strongly disagree 1 2 3 4 5 6 7 Strongly agree
3. Perceived behavioural control: 'I am confident I could reduce my drinking tomorrow if I wanted to'.
   Strongly disagree 1 2 3 4 5 6 7 Strongly agree

Key concepts of the theory

Icek Ajzen (1985, 1991) formulated the *theory of planned behaviour* (TPB) to explain how people can exercise control over their behaviour.

Central to the theory is the concept of *intention* – the TPB asserts that behaviour can be predicted from our intentions to behave. Applied to health, the TPB links intentions to change behaviour (e.g. give up drugs, lose weight) with actual changes in behaviour. Intentions to change behaviour are formed from three key sources.

1. Personal attitudes

Personal attitudes refer to an individual's favourable and unfavourable beliefs about their behaviour (e.g. 'I overeat because I enjoy food' versus 'Overeating makes me anxious'). The person's overall attitude is formed from the balance of positive and negative judgements of their own behaviour.

2. Subjective norms

Subjective norms are the individual's beliefs about whether the people who matter most to them approve or disapprove of their behaviour. For example, an alcohol addict considers what their friends and family think about their *addiction*. The alcoholic might conclude, 'Most people who matter to me are very unhappy with me drinking like this'. This would make them less likely to intend to drink, and ultimately less likely to drink.

3. Perceived behavioural control (PBC)

Perceived behavioural control concerns how much control we believe we have over behaviour. Does an obese person believe losing weight is easy or hard for them to do? This depends on their perception of the resources available to them, both external (support, time) and internal (skills, determination).

PBC can indirectly influence our intentions to behave – the more control I believe I have over my weight, the stronger my intention to lose weight.

PBC can also influence behaviour directly – the more control I believe I have, the longer and harder I will try to lose weight (or give up drugs, or whatever).

Personal attitudes → Behavioural intention; Subjective norms → Behavioural intention; Perceived behavioual control → Behavioural intention; Behavioural intention → Behaviour; Perceived behavioual control ⇢ Behaviour

Using weight loss as an example: my personal attitudes towards weight, my perception of what my nearest and dearest think of my weight, and my beliefs about my ability to lose weight, all combine to influence my intention to lose weight. This in turn influences the amount of time and effort I put into actually losing weight. Perceived behavioural control can lead directly to behavioural changes as well.

Evaluation

Research support for the TPB

One strength of the TPB is that there is support for some of its predictions.

Martin Hagger *et al.* (2011) found that personal attitudes, subjective norms and PBC all predicted an intention to limit drinking to guideline number of units. Intentions then influenced the number of units actually consumed after one month and three months. PBC also predicted actual consumption directly (and not just intention).

This supports the TPB because these outcomes were all exactly as the theory predicts, at least in relation to alcohol addiction.

Not a full explanation

One weakness of the TPB is that it cannot account for the *intention-behaviour gap*.

Rohan Miller and Gwyneth Howell (2005) studied the gambling behaviour of underage teenagers. They found they could not predict the reduction of actual gambling behaviour from intentions to give up. In other words there was no relationship between intentions and what the teenagers eventually did.

This means the TPB cannot predict behaviour change, which suggests it can't really be used as a basis for interventions.

Lack of support from some studies

Another weakness of the TPB is that some studies provide little support for its predictions.

Winnifred Louis *et al.* (2009, see next spread) investigated healthy and unhealthy eating behaviours. They found that personal attitudes, subjective norms and behavioural control did not affect behaviour in the way predicted by the TPB. This is because their effects depended upon the role of *stress*.

This suggests that the TPB is an incomplete explanation that ignores at least one key influence on behavioural change.

Short-term versus long-term

A further weakness is that the TPB is a poor predictor of long-term changes.

Rosie McEachan *et al.* (2011) reviewed 237 studies of the theory in relation to health behaviours. They found that the strength of *correlation* between intentions and actual behaviour varied according to the length of time between the two. So, intention to stop drinking, for example, was a good predictor of stopping within five weeks. But the theory did not predict behavioural change more than five weeks after the intention had been formed.

This means the TPB is not applicable to many real-world intentions to change behaviour which often take place over longer periods of time.

GET ACTIVE Fighting fit

Firefighters have to be fit. The Chief fire officer (C... of one fire service wants to introduce an exercise p...amme that firefighters can voluntarily join. The CFO know... many firefighters won't take up the offer, so she asks a ps...logist for advice.

Imagine that's you. You decide to use the theory o... nned behaviour to find out why some firefighters will n... e part.

1. *Draw a version of the TPB diagram on the facing ... Make sure the boxes have plenty of space in them.*
2. *Think of some questions you could ask to measur... h component of the TPB. What sort of responses do ... think you would get from firefighters who do not want t... e part? Write these responses in the relevant boxes.*

23

Melvyn intended to eat the healthy option.

Exam-style questions

Greg is worried about how much alcohol he drinks. He knows that it is affecting his health and his doctor has advised him to cut down. But he also enjoys drinking. It helps him relax and gives him a bit of an escape from a stressful life. Most of Greg's friends drink and they haven't discussed cutting down or giving up. Whenever he visits his parents, they always have a couple of drinks together.

He has tried in the past to cut down through 'willpower', but it hasn't worked. Greg has heard of 'Dry January' and thinks he'll give it a go as it's not far off. His friends and family have offered to sponsor him.

1. The theory of planned behaviour identifies the concepts of personal attitudes and subjective norms to explain the likelihood of someone behaving healthily or unhealthily.
   (a) Explain what is meant by 'personal attitudes' and 'subjective norms'. (4)
   (b) Identify **one** example of each relating to Greg in the above scenario. (2)
2. Explain how the theory of planned behaviour might predict Greg's future behaviour. (3)
3. Explain **one** strength and **one** weakness of the theory of planned behaviour. (4)
4. Discuss the theory of planned behaviour in relation to Greg's attempt to reduce his drinking. (9)

An issue to consider

Subjective norms are perhaps the most difficult part... the TPB to appreciate. Again, it's all about perceptio... My partner may or may not actually disapprove of h... much I drink (she might not say anything about it). B... *believe* she disapproves, then that is one factor that ... motivate me to change my behaviour.

How do you think this belief is formed? What contri... to it?

Specification content

A2 Theories of stress, behavioural addiction and physiological addiction

Theories: Key concepts of psychological theories of s... behavioural addiction and physiological addiction, to i... de:

- Theory of planned behaviour (Ajzen 1985): concept... personal attitude to behaviour, subjective norms, pe... ed behavioural control and their effect on behaviour.

Specification terms

We have defined the terms in the specification box for this spread. Other terms are defined in the index/glossary starting on page 310.

Application

Assessment objective 2 (AO2) is concerned with being able to ***apply*** your psychological knowledge and evaluation.

On each spread there is at least one '***Get active***' which gives you a chance to practise this AO2 skill of application.

In addition many of the topics you study are applied and therefore involve AO2.

An issue to consider

An opportunity to reflect on the issues discussed on the spread.

Exam-style questions

Questions similar to those in the exam provide some exam practice.

In Units 4, 5, 6 and 7 these boxes are called **Assessment practice**, and aim to help you practise skills for writing your internally-assessed reports.

Specification content

Tells you what you are required to study on this topic.

What are assessment objectives?

At the end of your studies you hope to have gained a qualification – this means someone has to assess your work.

To assist this process there are three assessment objectives (AOs): AO1, AO2 and AO3.

The course is designed so you can include all these AOs in what you learn. Each involves slightly different skills:

- AO1 involves reporting the knowledge coherently and including key terminology (details).
- AO2 involves PET skills (see top right).
- AO3 requires you to use what you have learned to explain a real-world situation.

What is psychology?

Psychologists study everything about people – and what could be more interesting than people? Just look in any newspaper or on Facebook – full of stories about people's behaviour.

These stories tell us about what people are doing and try to explain why they do the things they do – for example, reporting that someone had been married for 60 years, and offering an explanation about why their marriage was so successful. Or reporting that a person had committed a terrorist act and trying to explain that.

But psychology is more than just everyday interest in people...

Studying people (and animals).

Health psychology

Criminal and forensic psychology

Child psychology

Sport psychology

... Psychology is a science

This means it is a systematic investigation of what people do and why. This systematic investigation involves two things:

1. Developing theories to explain why people do things. In Unit 1 you studied the main approaches (theories) in psychology.
2. Conducting research studies to collect evidence of what people actually do. In Unit 2 you studied the research process.

Science is not perfect. Science takes small steps towards gradually getting at the 'truth'. This is where evaluation comes in – at all times scientists must question and retest their ideas.

But science is more than knowledge and evaluation...

... Science is applied

We depend on science to govern our world. Without science we could not develop safe and effective methods to treat disease, build bridges or buildings that don't fall down, try to forecast dangerous weather conditions, develop successful methods to deal with criminal behaviour and so on.

Psychological theory and research have a very large number of applications.

→ **Physical health** – advising the medical profession about, for example, how to best explain treatments to patients so they will remember what to do.

In Unit 3 you will be studying **Health psychology**.

→ **Mental health** – developing treatments for depression or anorexia and so on. This involves testing both psychological therapies and physical treatments such as the use of drugs.

For the extended certificate you will have the option to study an **Introduction to psychopathology** which is concerned with mental health.

The following three branches of psychology are also options for the extended certificate.

→ **Criminal and forensic psychology** Theories and approaches in psychology are applied to explain why some people become criminals. Psychological approaches are also used to develop successful methods to reduce reoffending and to research strategies to help the police solve crimes.

→ **Child psychology** is concerned with explaining how and why people change as they develop from birth through to adolescence.

→ **Sport psychology** Any sportsperson will tell you that winning is all in the mind. Yes, you do have to have certain skills but in the end it is the winning mindset that makes the difference between success and failure.

Professions using psychology

The BTEC course is a vocational one – which means it is concerned with the world of work. Therefore, a focus of the course is how the academic study of psychology is applied to the world of work. Someone who is a professional psychologist is likely to have a degree in psychology and then has gone on to do a postgraduate degree.

On the left we have mentioned some of these vocational areas, such as **criminal and forensic psychology** and **sport psychology** but there are jobs in these fields (and the ones further down this page) that don't require a degree in psychology or even a degree, but do benefit from knowledge of psychology, such as the ones below:

- Healthcare practitioner (nurse, radiographer, dietician, paramedic, physiotherapist, social care worker).
- Social worker.
- Teacher (understanding cognitive development).
- Counsellor (bereavement, drugs).
- Chaplain.
- Town planner.
- Police (dealing with people, not just crime).
- Crime scene investigator.
- Working with animals (zoo keeper, veterinarian, trainer).
- Law (solicitor, judge, court clerk).
- Military psychologist.
- Sports coach.
- Advertising and marketing.

Specialist branches of psychology

Clinical psychology

Psychologists are often confused with psychiatrists – a psychiatrist is first of all qualified as a medical doctor and then specialises in psychiatry. Psychiatrists study mental disorders, diagnose patients and provide treatments.

Clinical psychologists, counselling psychologists and other therapists are concerned with health issues – both physical and mental (psychopathology). Like psychiatrists, they may research, diagnose and treat clients. However, only a psychiatrist can prescribe medicine.

Educational psychology

Educational psychologists may be involved in designing, implementing and evaluating educational programmes for children with autism or dyslexia. They may also advise on how to deal with problem behaviour and may work directly with children who challenge the educational system. They are often involved in using psychological tests, such as intelligence tests, to help diagnose educational or behavioural problems.

Organisational psychology

Also sometimes called industrial psychology, occupational psychology or business psychology – using psychological theory and research in the world of commerce, addressing the needs of employers, employees and consumers. An organisational psychologist might help human resources departments to interview applicants and find the best person–organisation fit. An organisational psychologist might also advise on strategies to improve sales by addressing customer needs or how to assess consumer satisfaction. The 'organisation' does not have to be commercial – the focus of the organisational psychologist is on how any organisation functions.

Environmental psychology

Environmental psychology studies the interaction between people and their environment, i.e. their surroundings. The physical and human environment affects our behaviour, feelings, health and performance. Environmental psychologists might advise on the design of cities or buildings or office work spaces, including schools and hospitals as well as businesses. They are also concerned with ways to encourage people to care more for the environment.

Research psychology

Many psychologists work in universities, teaching students but also pursuing their own research interests.

Any job involving people involves psychology – even **mind reading**. But psychology does not teach you to actually read minds, it teaches you about what people are likely to think and do.

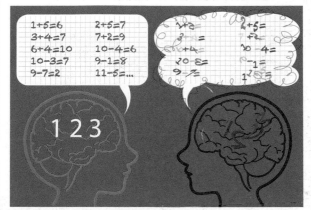

Dyscalculia – trouble with numbers. Perhaps a psychologist can help.

What's the ethics of using psychology to boost sales or win more votes? All practising psychologists must be registered with the British Psychological Society (BPS) and must show respect, competence, responsibility and integrity. So they can use psychology to make more money as long as they behave ethically in doing so.

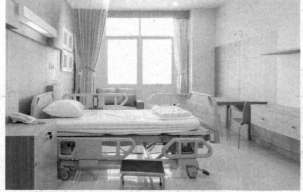

Designed by a psychologist? Research shows people recover more quickly if they have a nice view from their hospital room (Ulrich 1984).

Unit 3
Health psychology

These strange structures might look like weird mushrooms, but they're not.

They are your own cells, doing the important job of keeping you alive.

They are cells of your immune system, fighting off life-threatening bodily invaders like viruses.

They usually do a great job. But not always, otherwise we wouldn't get ill.

Ever had a cold at exam time?

How does stress affect your health?

What does it do to your immune system?

Contents

Defining health and stress

Changing views of health and ill health

A visit to your doctor 40 or so years ago would have been very different from a visit today. It's not just the fashions that have changed, or the technology.

Imagine it's 1975 and you are talking to your doctor about some stomach pains you've been having. He asks you questions about the recent history of the pain and whether stomach problems run in your family. He examines your stomach, takes your blood pressure and temperature and maybe even refers you for some tests. His main interest is in your physical symptoms.

Fast forward to today. Now your doctor still asks the same questions and gives you the same examination. But she also wants to know about your lifestyle, your diet, how much you exercise, whether you smoke or drink much alcohol. She is very interested in any stress you've been under recently.

These days, a diagnosis is based on social and psychological factors as well as physical ones.

Specification terms

Health and ill health Health is a positive state, in which we can face the challenges of life, overcome stress, achieve our goals and fulfil our potential. This applies to our whole lives and not just our physical state. Ill health is any deviation from this.

Stress A physiological and psychological state of arousal that arises when we believe we do not have the ability to cope with a perceived threat (stressor).

Stressor Any feature of the environment that causes a stress response, including factors associated with work, everyday minor hassles and major changes in our lives.

Exercise is an essential part of a healthy lifestyle.

Health and ill health

According to the World Health Organization (WHO 1948), *health* is 'A state of complete physical, mental and social well-being and not merely the absence of disease or infirmity'. *Ill health* is therefore any deviation from this healthy state.

There are two other definitions of health/illness that have dominated conversations and research on health and ill health (illness) – the *biomedical* and *biopsychosocial* definitions.

Biomedical definition

The biomedical definition views health/illness in terms of physical or biological factors. It defines illness as 'physical disease' which is diagnosed by a medical professional (doctor) from a person's symptoms. The illness is treated (often in a hospital) with physical methods (such as drugs or surgery) which aim to address the physical/biological causes.

The approach tends to define health as 'the absence of illness'. A healthy person is therefore someone who is free from disease, pain and disability. When we become ill, the aim of treatment is not really to enhance our health but to return us to our pre-illness condition. The focus is on biological functioning rather than on, for instance, social and psychological causes of illness.

The biomedical approach is closely associated with medical science and technological advances (e.g. brain scanning, chemotherapy) and is the dominant view of health/illness in the healthcare systems of Western countries.

Biopsychosocial definition

George Engel (1977) was one of the first medical practitioners to argue that the biomedical definition does not take into account all of the factors that play a role in health and illness. He proposed a biopsychosocial approach instead.

This definition suggests that health/illness is the result of several interacting factors. Biological characteristics (e.g. *genes*, *neurochemistry*) are just one set of factors, alongside psychological/behavioural characteristics (e.g. stress, attitudes) and social environment (e.g. family, *culture*). Treatment takes into account all three factors.

The approach aims to enhance the person's health rather than just make them 'not ill'. It also focuses on prevention. This has led to the development of educational programmes designed to promote healthy lifestyles (e.g. exercising, losing weight, stopping smoking, reducing alcohol intake, etc.).

The biopsychosocial approach has been very influential in the treatment of mental disorders. Mental ill health is not just a matter of faulty biological functioning. There is more to treatment than just correcting this fault.

Health as a continuum

The biomedical approach has tended to dominate our view of health, and therefore, health and ill health have traditionally been viewed as two categories – you are either healthy or you are ill.

The biopsychosocial approach has a more complex view. Health exists on a continuum and varies between two extremes. Over time a person can be very healthy, very ill or anywhere in between. This is true of mental health as much as it is of physical health.

| Extremely good health | Good health | Average health | Poor health | Extremely poor health |

As we have seen, 'health' under the biopsychosocial definition includes many social, physical and psychological factors. This means that someone in extremely good health is functioning well in all or most of these areas. Someone with extremely poor health has more than just a physical disease. They could be experiencing great stress and difficulties in their lives at the same time (e.g. relationship issues, facing job redundancy, etc.).

Stress

Stress is an emotional response to situations of threat. Such threats are called *stressors*. They may be physical (a lion is attacking) or psychological (you are worried about your exams). In both cases your body produces a response – a response which is affected by your perceived ability to cope.

Stressors

A stressor is the threat that creates stress.

Physical stressors There are many things in the environment that create stress, such as temperature, noise and overcrowding.

Psychological stressors Later in this unit (content area B) we will be looking closely at four very important and common psychological stressors – major events in our lives (e.g. getting married or divorced, coping with bereavement), everyday niggles and annoyances ('hassles' such as sitting in a traffic jam), the workplace and our own personalities.

The stress response

It is useful to distinguish between physiological and psychological stress.

Physiological stress refers to how the body physically responds to a stressor. We are all familiar with the bodily symptoms of a stressful experience (e.g. increased heart rate, sweating, sick feeling in your stomach, etc.). We look at this in more detail on page 46.

Psychological stress is the emotion you experience when a stressor occurs.

Perceived ability to cope

Just because a stressor happens to you, this does not mean you will experience psychological stress. It depends on how you think about the stressor and about your ability to cope with it.

To put it technically, psychological stress occurs when the perceived demands of your environment are greater than your perceived ability to cope with them.

Consider a common example of 'perceived demands': You must have noticed that students can respond very differently to the stressor of an exam. Most people experience some 'stress' when they think about an upcoming exam – feeling anxious, their heart rate increases, they feel sick. But other students find the thought of exams bothers them very little.

The different responses occur because of different perceptions of the exam – some think of it as a threat, others feel very confident, some even see it as a challenge. It is these *perceptions* of the stressor that affect the response itself.

Of course, whether you become stressed by the demands of your environment depends on another factor...

Perception of available resources This refers to how we think about our ability to deal with stressors. The key feature of coping is our *perception* of the resources we have available to combat the stressor.

Resources can be internal or external. *Internal coping resources* are psychological and include resilience (the ability to persist and to 'bounce back' after a setback), as well as *self-efficacy* (discussed on page 26). *External coping resources* include social support, the networks of friends, family and other people who we can call upon when we experience stressors that threaten to overwhelm us.

In both types of resource, perception is crucial. You may not actually have many friends, or you never really stick to a task for more than five minutes. But what matters is that you *believe* your coping resources are enough to overcome the stressor. So, a student who knows they have revised thoroughly for an exam is likely to cope better than someone who fears they have done very little. But someone who manages to kid themselves they have revised will probably also cope fairly well (although they may experience more stress when the results come out).

Stress isn't all negative – the term *eustress* describes positive stress. Some people enjoy the adrenaline rush of a bungee jump. Personally, we prefer to limit our flying to the inside of an aluminium tube.

Exam-style questions

Meera is her mother's main carer and has been doing this for two years with hardly any time off. She finally had to give up a job she enjoyed to continue caring for her mother. Meera tells her doctor that she keeps getting headaches and is feeling depressed. The doctor takes Meera's blood pressure and says she could have a chemical imbalance in her brain. He prescribes some antidepressants to put it right. Meera then tells the doctor that her partner has left her. The doctor says that Meera might benefit from some psychological therapy as well as antidepressants.

1. What are the stressors in this situation? (2)
2. Meera is suffering from psychological stress. Explain what this means in the context of her situation. (2)
3. Explain **one** definition of health/ill health. (2)
4. Explain what is meant by 'health as a continuum'. (2)
5. Explain **one** aspect of Meera's conversation with her doctor in terms of the biomedical definition and **one** in terms of the biopsychosocial definition. (2 + 2)
6. Meera is worried that she cannot cope with her situation. Explain how Meera's perceived ability to cope may affect her stress levels. (3)

> **You can read about assessment issues on pages 34, 70 and 108.**

An issue to consider

How we perceive a stressor (and our coping abilities) is what really matters. Does that explain why two people can face the same stressor and respond completely differently?

How could you apply that to a common stressor such as getting divorced?

Specification content

A1 Psychological definition of health and ill health, addiction and stress

Definitions and characteristics of health and ill health, addiction and stress.

- Health and ill health: biomedical, biopsychosocial, health as a continuum.
- Stress: definition of a stressor, psychological stress, stress and perceived ability to cope.

GET ACTIVE Health, stress and sleep

Sleep is increasingly seen as a crucial part of being healthy. We need decent quality sleep in order to feel well. When we are ill we often cannot sleep properly, and this makes us feel worse. Stress can also prevent or disrupt sleep. The *Pittsburgh sleep quality index* (PSQI) will help you assess your sleep quality: tinyurl.com/y2l9vtwl

1. *Fill in the PSQI. Is your score what you expected?*
2. *How does stress affect your sleep patterns?*
3. *How do you feel when you don't get enough sleep?*

Defining addiction

Adrian's story

The World Health Organization recognises two *behavioural* addictions (as opposed to addictions involving substances such as heroin). One is gambling, which we cover in detail later in this unit. The other is video gaming.

At the height of his addiction, Adrian was playing online multiplayer games for up to 16 hours each day. At the time he was 25 years old with a job and a family. He worked from home as a software developer, so he could easily find the time to play games. But as he was paid by the hour, Adrian found himself getting into deeper and deeper financial trouble.

He and his partner argued frequently about his behaviour. Each time, Adrian promised to change and for a while reduced his playing time. He became moody and depressed, so always went back to his old ways, preferring the short-term rush over any improvements in his relationship. 'When I wasn't playing games, I was thinking about playing games.'

(Based on various case studies.)

Specification terms

Addiction A mental health problem in which an individual takes a substance or engages in a behaviour that is pleasurable but eventually becomes compulsive with harmful consequences.

Behavioural addiction Occurs when someone compulsively continues a behaviour and experiences withdrawal when they stop it.

Conflict When two or more things have competing demands, creating a clash.

Dependence (salience) is indicated either by a compulsion to keep taking a drug/continue a behaviour (psychological dependence) or indicated by withdrawal symptoms (physical dependence).

Mood alteration Changing a person's emotional state. May be caused by addictive drugs and behaviour.

Physiological addiction Dependence on a substance, shown when an addict gives it up and experiences withdrawal symptoms.

Relapse Reverting to addiction after a period of giving up.

Tolerance A reduction in response to a drug, so that the addicted individual needs more to get the same effect.

Withdrawal A set of symptoms that develop when the addicted person abstains from or reduces their drug use.

Physiological and behavioural addiction

We are all familiar with a range of addictions, such as drug addiction and gambling addiction. But what is *addiction*? For example, can you be addicted to your mobile phone or to sunbeds? Addiction is a complex mental health disorder. People can become addicted to a substance (such as heroin) or to a behaviour (such as gambling) because it produces pleasurable experiences. People persist despite the harmful consequences.

Classifying addiction

There are several different kinds of addiction, which are usually grouped into two main categories – *physiological* and *behavioural*.

What counts 'officially' as an addiction in the UK is determined by the *International classification of diseases* (ICD). The current edition (at the time of writing) is the ICD-11 which has a large category called 'Disorders due to substance use or addictive behaviours'.

'Substance use' refers to drugs such as cocaine, alcohol, caffeine and many others. Only two *behavioural addictions* are officially recognised – gambling and gaming. The ICD-11 also identifies several behavioural addictions that might one day be included, such as internet use, shopping and sex.

Physiological addiction

The key aspect of addiction is its physiological effect (physiological means 'of your body'). There are two signs that indicate when a person is physically/physiologically addicted to a substance:

1. When a person stops taking the substance (or engaging in the behaviour) they experience *withdrawal* effects. This is likely to lead to relapse.
2. Over time, the person needs a bigger dose of the substance to get the same effect (known as *tolerance*).

We cover two examples of *physiological addiction* later in this unit – smoking and alcohol. But what about chocolate? People who eat chocolate may well show psychological signs of withdrawal if they are deprived (e.g. cravings). But psychologists believe that chocolate 'addiction' is not a true addiction because tolerance does not occur.

Chocolate does contain mood-altering chemicals, but only in very small amounts. So, chocolate 'addiction' is probably more cultural than physiological.

Behavioural addiction

A person can become addicted to a behaviour (such as gambling) rather than a chemical substance (such as smoking). They are judged to be addicted because the behaviour produces the same physical effects as a chemical substance, including tolerance and withdrawal. Two examples we cover later in the unit are shopping and gambling. But what about mobile phone use? Is that a *behavioural addiction*?

Many people show signs of being dependent on using their mobiles. There is withdrawal – cravings and signs of negative emotional states such as anger, irritability and *anxiety*. There is even tolerance, the need to use a mobile progressively more often and in more situations. This is why mobile overuse is very likely to become an officially recognised addiction in the near future.

Can a person be addicted to chocolate?

The salience of an addiction refers to its importance in our lives. When we're not doing it, we're thinking about it.

Griffiths' six components of addiction

As we have seen, withdrawal and tolerance are two signs of addiction. But Mark Griffiths (2005) argues that there are actually six key components that should be required for a diagnosis of behavioural addiction.

1. Physical and psychological dependence (salience) occurs when it becomes impossible to lead a normal life without the substance or behaviour. *Salience* means that the addictive behaviour comes to dominate the individual's life. It is their most important activity, at the centre of their thinking, feelings and behaviour, and it takes up most of their time. Other behaviours (e.g. social ones) are neglected and deteriorate. When the person is not engaging in the behaviour they are preoccupied with thoughts about it and crave it in its absence.

2. Tolerance occurs when an individual requires increased doses of the substance in order to achieve effects originally produced by lower doses. Someone who repeatedly takes a drug such as cocaine finds that eventually they get less of a 'buzz' from their normal dose. The same process occurs in behavioural addictions – increasing 'amounts' of the activity are needed to get the earlier effects. For example, an addicted gambler may need to place bigger and bigger bets to get the 'rush' they used to get from placing smaller bets.

3. Withdrawal refers to the effects that occur when an individual suddenly reduces or ceases the addictive activity. These can be divided into physiological ones (such as headaches, nausea, loss of appetite and insomnia) and psychological ones (such as irritability and low mood). There is some evidence that addicted gamblers can experience stronger withdrawal effects than people who are physiologically dependent on drugs (Rosenthal and Lesieur 1992).

4. Relapse happens when a person repeatedly reverts to their earlier dependent patterns of behaviour after having given them up. This can happen even after a very long period of abstinence. For example, when someone takes up gambling or smoking again having stopped years earlier.

5. Conflict A person's addictive behaviour almost inevitably gives rise to *conflict. Inter*personal conflict occurs *between* an addicted person and other people. The addict frequently chooses short-term pleasure and ignores the consequences of their behaviour, creating conflict in their relationships, work, education and/or social lives. *Intra*personal conflict occurs *within* the addicted individual. The person experiences a loss of control because they want to stop behaving in ways that are damaging but cannot do so.

6. Mood alteration An addictive activity such as gambling produces various positive and negative subjective experiences. For example, the person may feel a 'high' or 'rush', or in other cases a feeling of 'numbness'. The same substance or activity can produce different mood-altering effects on different occasions, probably due to expectations (e.g. smokers experience arousal in the morning but more relaxing effects at other times of day).

Exam-style questions

Marcus spends at least five hours each day playing on his Xbox. This means he is neglecting his homework and has found himself in trouble at school. When he can't play, he is thinking about playing most of the time. He pays little attention in class and his work is suffering. Marcus' behaviour causes a lot of arguments at home. Sometimes his parents ban him, and he becomes irritable and moody. He once tried to reduce his playing time to one hour a day but it didn't last. If anything, he is spending longer than ever playing.

1. Define what is meant by 'behavioural addiction'. (2)

2. Explain **one** difference between physiological addiction and behavioural addiction. (2)

3. Griffiths identified six characteristics of addiction. Give **two** of these. (2)

4. Identify **two** features of the scenario above that suggest Marcus has an addiction. Explain **one** of these features in more detail. (3)

5. Define what is meant by 'tolerance'. What evidence is there that Marcus is experiencing tolerance? (2)

6. Psychology helps us to understand addiction in terms of relapse and mood alteration. Define both of these terms with reference to Marcus. (4)

An issue to consider

Not everyone is equally likely to try drugs (or gambling) and not everyone is equally likely to become addicted to them. What are the factors that increase (or decrease) the risk of addiction?

For teenagers, peer influences are perhaps the most important factor. Some people may have genes that make them more vulnerable to addiction (so not all risk factors are environmental).

Can you think of any others?

GET ACTIVE I am not addicted

Daryl tells his girlfriend that he is not addicted to cigarettes even though he has been smoking for several years. He says he can quit any time he wants.

His girlfriend is not so sure because Daryl always seems to want to have a cigarette and gets irritated when he can't. She also knows he has tried to give up several times in the past. He carries on smoking even though he's well aware that it could give him cancer. In fact he seems to be smoking more than ever. She is reluctant to push him too hard to quit because he says smoking is the most important thing in his life, even more important than her.

Identify Griffiths' six components of addiction in Daryl's behaviour. Write **one** *sentence for each component.*

Specification content

A1 Psychological definition of health and ill health, addiction and stress

Definitions and characteristics of health and ill health, addiction and stress.

● Behavioural and physiological addiction.
● Griffiths' six components of addiction: physical and psychological dependence (salience), tolerance, withdrawal, relapse, conflict, mood alteration.

Theory 1: Health belief model

Cervical
CANCER
Awareness

Beliefs about health screening

Almost 1000 women die each year in the UK from cancer of the cervix. But there is a test that can detect abnormal cells at an early stage. It used to be called the *smear test*, but even the name was putting women off having it. So now it's known as *cervical screening*.

Every woman in the UK is invited for their first test when they reach 25. But still 29% of women do not take up the offer (in some parts of the UK it's over 40%). That's partly due to embarrassment and issues concerning body image. But for some women, it's because they don't believe they are likely to get cervical cancer. Others don't realise exactly how devastating the disease can be.

But screening makes early detection of cell abnormalities much more likely, and this has huge benefits for young women such as Anna Crib. She broadcast her cervical screening test live on Channel Mum. You can see it here: tinyurl.com/y6pe6rz9

All of the factors involved in deciding to have a test are explored in the health belief model on this spread.

Specification terms

Cost-benefit analysis An individual weighs up the balance between the perceived benefits of changing behaviour and the perceived barriers (obstacles to change).

Demographic variable The characteristics of a population and an individual, such as age, sex, education level, income level, marital status, occupation, religion.

Health belief model Predicts the likelihood of behaviour change. The key factors are perceived seriousness, perceived susceptibility, cost-benefit analysis, demographic variables, cues to action and self-efficacy.

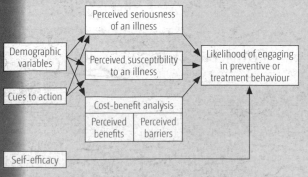

The health belief model.

Key concepts of the model

The *health belief model* (HBM), first developed by Irwin Rosenstock (1966), is a psychological theory that tries to explain why people do or do not engage in healthy behaviour. Rosenstock related the behaviour to the person's beliefs.

The essence of the model can be summed up in three questions that an individual might ask themselves:

1. How serious are the consequences (perceived seriousness)?
2. How likely am I to get the disease or illness (perceived susceptibility)?
3. What are the advantages versus disadvantages of taking this action (*cost-benefit analysis* which weighs up perceived benefits versus perceived barriers)?

1. Perceived seriousness

Whether a person changes their behaviour or not depends partly on how severe they think the consequences will be if they do not change. For example, condoms can help avoid sexually transmitted diseases such as *chlamydia*. Some people might think this is not serious enough to start using a condom regularly. On the other hand, contracting HIV is a more severe outcome so condom use is more likely if the person perceives this as a likely consequence.

Perceived seriousness is not just about health. It includes other outcomes as well, for example the effects on family, work and social relationships.

2. Perceived susceptibility

Consider the example of condom use. Someone having unprotected sex has to believe that they are personally and realistically vulnerable (susceptible) to the illness or disease that condoms protect against. If the person considers themselves exclusively heterosexual and believes HIV/AIDS is a 'gay disease', they will probably not perceive themselves as susceptible ('HIV only affects gay men, I'm not a gay man, therefore I can't get HIV and I don't need to use a condom').

3. Cost-benefit analysis

The perceived benefits of a health-related action are balanced against obstacles that stop the person taking that action.

Perceived benefits In order to start using condoms during sex, the person has to believe that this action will bring them benefits. The main benefit is that a condom is an effective way of protecting themselves (and their partners) from disease. Another is that using one shows a partner that protecting their health is important.

Perceived barriers In our example, perceived barriers might include the inconvenience of using condoms during sex, the belief that they reduce pleasure, the suggestion of a lack of trust in a relationship and so on.

Modifying factors

Demographic variables The central elements of the HBM are influenced by several *demographic variables* – your characteristics such as your age, gender, culture and so on. This helps to explain how it is that two people who experience the same health-related challenges differ in their perceptions of seriousness, susceptibility, benefits and barriers – and therefore one changes their behaviour and the other might not.

Cues to action Information that is presented to an individual may predispose them to 'readiness to act' and affect their perceived seriousness/susceptibility. According to Godfrey Hochbaum (1958), such information (cues) can be internal (e.g. experience of symptoms such as pain) or external (e.g. media campaigns, awareness of other people with the disease, advice from medical professionals). These cues are crucial in shifting the person from thinking about changing their behaviour to actually changing it.

Self-efficacy (a person's belief in their own competence) This was a later addition to the HBM (Rosenstock *et al.* 1988), referring to the person's expectation that they are capable of making a behavioural change. This is closely related to perception of skill. For example, being able to use a condom effectively and sensitively (and asking a partner to do so) takes some skill. If a person has a low sense of self-efficacy in relation to condom use this will directly affect the likelihood that they engage in this health behaviour.

Evaluation

Effectiveness and practical applications

One strength of the HBM is its use in developing practical interventions to change health-related behaviour.

Sara Willamson and Jane Wardle (2002) used the HBM to devise a programme to increase the number of people seeking screening for bowel and colon cancers. This and other studies have found such interventions to be reasonably or moderately successful in changing health-related behaviours.

This suggests that the HBM is a *valid* explanation of how people can shift their behaviour in a more healthy direction.

Strong credibility

Another strength of the HBM is it was developed by health researchers and practitioners.

The health researchers worked directly with people who wanted to change their health-related behaviours. Therefore, the model is based on real-life experiences of health problems.

This makes the HBM a credible explanation that is accepted by people who want to change their behaviour and the professionals who want to help them.

How many models?

One weakness is that changes made to the HBM have not been welcomed by everyone.

For instance, Rick Zimmerman and Dee Vernberg (1994) argued that once self-efficacy and demographic factors (and other variables) are added, the HBM becomes a different model altogether. This is reflected in Chris Carpenter's (2010) study (next spread) which focused only on the original four variables (susceptibility, severity, benefits and barriers).

This suggests the HBM may not be one single model and is attempting to be 'all things to all people'.

How rational are we?

Another weakness is that the model is based on the assumption that people make rational decisions about their health behaviours.

We supposedly weigh up the costs and benefits of a behaviour before deciding how to act. We consider this analysis logically alongside our perceptions of seriousness and susceptibility. We work out how well-equipped we are to make a change. Do we do all this when we decide to have salad for tea instead of chips? Or do we often make our choices out of habit? Or because we respond emotionally rather than rationally (and that's why we have just one more piece of chocolate)?

This suggests there may be other psychological factors that are more important in behaviour change than those in the HBM.

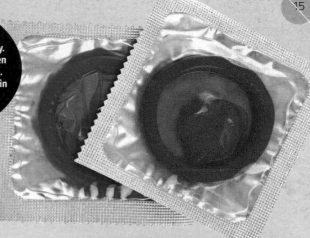

On this spread, and many other spreads, we have supplied four criticisms of the theory. You would not need all of these when answering a 9-mark essay question. However, you may be asked to explain two strengths or two weaknesses so we have generally covered two of each.

Men are more likely to use these if they see the relevance and that there's something in it for them.

Exam-style questions

Guz is eight years old and has Type I diabetes which means he has to be injected with insulin every day. He has lived with the condition for several years. Because he is young, his parents have done this for him but now he has to learn to inject himself.

They have explained to Guz very clearly that if he does not inject himself then he will become very ill. Guz understands that the injections will make him feel much better and will avoid unpleasant symptoms. Guz is very sensible, but sometimes he is busy doing other things and worries that he might easily forget. He doesn't like how injecting sometimes draws attention to himself.

1. In terms of the health belief model explain how cost-benefit analysis could be applied to Guz's behaviour. (2)

2. Explain **one** strength and **one** weakness of the health belief model. (4)

3. The health belief model identifies several concepts that can explain the likelihood of someone behaving healthily or unhealthily.

   (a) Explain how the concept of perceived seriousness could predict Guz's behaviour. (2)

   (b) Explain how the concept of perceived susceptibility could predict Guz's behaviour (2).

4. Identify **one** internal **or** external cue and explain how it might affect Guz's behaviour. (3)

5. Discuss the health belief model as an explanation of Guz's behaviour. (9)

An issue to consider

The word 'perceived' features a lot in the health belief model. Some people are definitely at risk of an illness but don't take any action to reduce that risk. Why is that?

Is it possible that what one person perceives as a 'benefit' someone else might see as a 'barrier'? Can you think of any examples?

GET ACTIVE Alys changes her mind

Alys did not go for her last cervical screening. She believes she is very unlikely to get the disease because no one in her family has ever had it and anyway she's too young (she's 32). She's read about the procedure being uncomfortable and other reports about it just confuse her so she just decided to 'forget it'. And anyway she doesn't like that 'medical stuff' and doesn't even know the phone number of her surgery. However, Alys changed her mind and finally booked an appointment after hearing how reality TV star Jade Goody had died from cervical cancer when she was just 27.

Use the HMB to explain Alys' behaviour in terms of: perceived seriousness, susceptibility, benefits and barriers, demographic variables, cues to action and self-efficacy.

Specification content

A2 Theories of stress, behavioural addiction and physiological addiction

Theories: Key concepts of psychological theories of stress, behavioural addiction and physiological addiction, to include:

● Health belief model (Rosenstock 1966): concepts of perceived seriousness, susceptibility, cost-benefit analysis, how demographic variables such as age, gender, culture and external/internal cues affect behaviour.

Studies related to theory 1: The health belief model

I don't want to know

Some people with a serious illness refuse treatment that could save their lives. How can we explain this?

Consider cancer of the pancreas. Surgery is the only treatment that can potentially cure a person with this cancer. But only one-third of patients who could benefit decide to undergo surgery. Manuel Castillo-Angeles (2017) and his co-researchers applied the health belief model (HBM) to find out why.

Some patients do not appreciate the seriousness of their condition because they have deliberately closed their eyes to it (typically patients say 'There were a lot of things I chose not to know').

For some patients there were two key barriers preventing them from choosing surgery – poor communication with their surgeon and confusion caused by online information.

Lack of self-efficacy was also an issue. Some patients did not believe they could cope with life after the surgery ('My family has to help take care of me and... I'm incapacitated a lot').

Becker *et al.* (1978) Compliance with a medical regimen for asthma

Aims

Marshall Becker and his colleagues wanted to use the health belief model (HBM) to explain mothers' compliance with *asthma* treatment for their children.

Procedure

The participants were 111 mothers of children diagnosed with asthma and who attended an emergency clinic to treat an asthma attack. Each mother was interviewed about their attitudes towards health-related matters, such as seriousness of asthma, and whether they complied with the treatment plan. Blood samples were taken from the children to check for presence of asthma medication.

Findings

There were *positive correlation*[...] between mothers' compliance with giving prescribed medicine and:

- Perception of the serious[...]ild's asthma.
- Beliefs about their child[...] attacks.
- Beliefs about seriousn[...] with their child's education).

There were four perceive[...] with the schedule for giving the drug, children com[...]veryday activities.

Only two *demograp*[...]thers were more likely to comply.

Conclusions

The HBM is usef[...] cases of long-term conditions such[...]ponent of the HBM as predictors of h[...]

Not needed

Carpe[...] the effe[...] variables in predicti[...]

Aims

Chris Carpenter (2010) conducted a *meta*-[...] to investigate the effect of time on the relationships between measurement of variab[...]haviour change.

Procedure

18 *longitudinal studies* were selected, each measuring at least two HBM variables. Carpenter analysed the studies in terms of the time between measurement of variables and measurement of outcome health-related behaviour. He also looked at whether each study's outcome was a treatment (e.g. taking a medicine) or a preventative behaviour.

Findings

Seriousness – relationship with behaviour change was positive but weak. The effect of seriousness was greatest when time between initial measurement and outcome was short.

Susceptibility – no relationship with behaviour change. The exception was compliance with drug treatment, where there was a consistently positive effect.

Benefits – a positive relationship with behaviour change but this weakened over time.

Barriers – the strongest predictor of behaviour change (less so for treatment than prevention), but time almost no effect.

Conclusions

This review offered little support for the HBM. HBM variables appear to differ in how strongly they predict behaviour. Perceived barriers and benefits may be the only two components of the HBM that consistently predict behaviour.

Becker *et al.* found that some of the mothers were so concerned about their child's health that they gave the treatment when it wasn't needed. Strangely, the mothers who followed the medical advice most closely were the ones who trusted the doctors least.

GET ACTIVE Measuring the model

On the previous spread, the *health belief model* (HBM) is illustrated with the example of practising safe sex by using condoms. Imagine you are carrying out research into this issue. You want to see if the HBM predicts condom use, so you need to ask questions that will measure each component of the model. Bear in mind that your participants are not psychology students and have never heard of this model.

1. *Draw seven squares and write the name of one component of the HBM in each square (e.g. perceived barriers, etc.).*

2. *In each square, add a question (or two) that is relevant to that component of the model.*

3. *Cut out the boxes and arrange them into the shape of the model (see the diagram on the previous spread).*

Becker *et al.* interviewed mothers after their children had been through a life-saving procedure in an emergency department, like this one. Perhaps that's not the best time for a research interview.

Evaluation

Subjective and objective measurements

One strength was the researchers collected two types of data.

They asked each mother whether they had complied with the asthma treatment plan (a subjective *self-report*). They also took blood samples from the children to test for presence of the asthma medication (an objective measure). Because there was a very strong positive correla[...] the two measures, this suggests there was no need to confirm [...] subjective self-reports with an objective measure.

This showed that simply asking mothers whether they h[...] valid measure that could be easily used in this and other [...]

Nature of data collection

One weakness is that the researchers conducted intervie[...] stressful conditions.

The participants were visiting hospital during an emerg[...] having asthma attacks). The researchers themselves note[...] responses under these conditions may have been differe[...] circumstances. For instance, in a less stressful interview [...] may have been more rational.

This means that the influences of the four component[...] over- or underestimated in this study.

Evaluation

Future directions and applications

One strength is that this study can give researchers and practitioners valuable suggestions about what to do next.

This review clarified the 'state of play' regarding the HBM. It highlighted the components of the model that 'work' (benefits, barriers) and those that are not effective (seriousness, susceptibility), providing a focus for further research. It also indicated the conditions in which the model is most effective (e.g. prescribed drug treatment) which has implications for practitioners in terms of how to try to change behaviour.

This means that new approaches may give a greater chance of changing health-related behaviour.

Outdated health belief model

One weakness is that this review analysed a number of different studies.

The HBM has since evolved into a more complex model of health-related behaviour that was not analysed in this study. For example, the central variables of *self-efficacy* and cues to action were not included. This was because these variables had not been tested in research studies at the time. This in itself suggests a wider problem – that development of the model has outrun testing of it in research.

Therefore, Carpenter reviewed and analysed an outdated version of the HBM.

Exam-style questions

Agnes has been told by her GP that she is 'pre-diabetic' and needs to make changes to her diet to lose weight. The GP explains that if she does not change her behaviour, then Agnes will soon become diabetic and risk several complications as a result, such as losing a limb and problems with her hearing and vision.

Changing her diet will avoid all of these negative consequences and improve her overall health as well. However, Agnes knows that [...] because she has been on several [...]

[...] study by Carpenter (2010). Refer to [...]

[...] out a study testing the health belief [...]

[...] (3)

[...] and use it to explain whether Agnes [...]

[...] nter (2010). Refer to Agnes in your [...]

[...] odel as an explanation of Agnes' [...] **two** research studies in your answer. (9)

An issue to consider

Here is an issue for lots of theories and models in psychology. If research shows that a part of a theory is wrong, does that undermine the whole theory?

If barriers and benefits are more important than susceptibility and seriousness, should we abandon the health belief model or try to change it?

Specification content

A2 Theories of stress, behavioural addiction and physiological addiction

Studies: Key principles and critical evaluation of studies investigating psychological theories, to include critique of assumptions, methodology and ethics.

- Health belief model:
  - Becker *et al.* (1978) Compliance with a medical regimen for asthma.
  - Carpenter (2010) A meta-analysis of the effectiveness of health belief model variables in predicting behaviour.

Theory 2: Locus of control and Rotter (1966)

Spot the difference

My friend Joe has just one testicle.

Joe is the sort of person who has to be in control. He tries to keep in charge of as many aspects of his life as he can – his diet, exercise, sleeping, etc. He had heard about how important it is for men to examine their testicles regularly. So that is what he was doing when he found an unusual lump. Joe was diagnosed with testicular cancer at the age of 31. Like 95% of all men with this diagnosis, he survived. His left testicle was surgically removed 20 years ago now.

My friend Sandro nearly had a heart attack.

He noticed he was getting occasional chest pain, and was much shorter of breath than he used to be and his arms sometimes went numb. But Sandro was the sort of person who didn't want to face up to the possibility he was ill. He didn't want to make a fuss. His attitude was one of 'It'll all come out in the wash'. Fortunately for Sandro, his partner was not in denial and made him visit his GP before it was too late. Now he has a different attitude.

Specification term

Locus of control Refers to the sense we each have about what directs events in our lives. Internals believe they are mostly responsible for what happens to them (internal locus of control). Externals believe it is mainly a matter of luck or the influence of other people or other outside forces (external locus of control).

Teenagers with an internal locus of control may be better able to resist the influence of their friends.

Key concepts of the theory

Internal and external locus of control (LoC)

Julian Rotter (1966) proposed that some people believe the things that happen to them are largely under their own control. They have an *internal locus of control* (and are called *internals*). An internal would explain success in terms of their own efforts – they succeeded because they worked hard. On the other hand, internals believe that if they fail it's because they didn't work hard enough.

People with an external LoC (called *externals*) tend to believe that the things that happen to them are out of their control and occur because of luck, circumstance, other people, bad weather, etc. So, an external who is promoted at work might believe their manager was in a good mood that day.

In reality, people are not simply either fully internal or fully external. LoC is more of a continuum than a type, with high internal at one end and high external at the other.

Attributions and health behaviour

You learned about *attribution* in an earlier part of your course (page 16 in our Year 1 'Certificate' book). Attribution is the process of explaining other people's behaviour – and also explaining our own behaviour. We explain our own (and other people's) behaviour in terms of internal and external causes. Internals and externals attribute their own health-related behaviours to different causes.

Take *addiction* as an example. Internals view their behaviour as under their own control. They avoid some of the risk factors that make them vulnerable to addiction, such as resisting influence from their peers and avoiding situations of *stress*. An external who believes their behaviour is more a matter of luck or 'it's down to my genes and that's all there is to it' is less likely to take control. They may feel there is nothing they can do to avoid risk. Therefore, their way of explaining the causes of their behaviour (internal or external) increases or decreases the likelihood that they become addicted.

Rotter (1966) Generalised expectancies for internal versus external control of reinforcement

Aims

Julian Rotter (1966) aimed to review research into internal/external LoC and behaviour and to devise a questionnaire to measure LoC.

Procedure

Rotter reviewed several published and unpublished studies that investigated the links between LoC and other psychological variables (e.g. the *need to achieve*).

He also reviewed questionnaires designed to measure LoC including his own, the *Internal-External scale* (I-E scale). This consists of 29 pairs of statements, one internal and one external (e.g. 'Sometimes I can't understand how teachers arrive at the grades they give' and 'There is a direct connection between how hard I study and the grades I get'). LoC is measured by participants choosing one statement in each pair that most closely reflects their beliefs.

Findings

Rotter found that the I-E scale is a *reliable* and *valid* measure of LoC.

He also found, from his review of research, that internals are more likely than externals to act to improve their environment, to resist attempts to influence them and to be concerned with skill and ability.

Non-smokers were significantly more internal than smokers. Males who read an anti-smoking message and then gave up smoking were more likely to be internals than people who did not give up (despite accepting the anti-smoking message).

Conclusions

Rotter concluded that LoC is a powerful predictor of a wide variety of behaviours in many situations.

LoC can be validly and reliably measured in adults and children using several methods including the I-E scale. Rotter suggested that LoC is affected by factors such as type of parenting, culture and socioeconomic influences.

Evaluation

Research support for LoC

One strength is evidence to support the link between LoC and conformity.

Theo Avtgis (1998) conducted a review of studies into this link. He found that high externals were more persuadable and conformist than high internals. The overall effect was significant but not strong.

This suggests that LoC may make externals more vulnerable to risk factors for addiction – they may be relatively easily influenced by smoking or drinking peers or by advertising, for example.

Practical application

Another strength is that the link between an internal LoC and health is useful.

Catharine Gale *et al.* (2008) measured the LoC of 7551 children aged 10 years. By the time they were 30, those who were internals were less likely than the externals to be obese or experience psychological stress. An internal LoC in childhood seems to offer some protection against poor health in adulthood.

This suggests that interventions aimed at developing an internal LoC could be one way of helping people to gain health benefits later.

Limited role for LoC in health-related behaviours

One weakness is that the role of LoC in resisting influence may be exaggerated.

As Rotter (1982) himself later pointed out, LoC is only relevant in novel situations. It has little effect on our behaviour in familiar situations where previous experience is always more important. This means that someone who has been influenced in specific situations in the past (e.g. persuaded to have a drink in the pub) are likely to be persuaded again, even if they are highly internal.

This limits the power of LoC to predict changes in health-related behaviours.

Role of LoC is complex

Another weakness is that the link between LoC and stress is not simple.

The traditional view is that extreme internals cope better with stress than extreme externals. However, Neal Krause (1986, see next spread) found that extreme internals respond to unavoidable events by becoming stressed, just as externals do (but for different reasons – internals experience stress because they blame themselves). So being internal does not automatically protect you from stress.

This shows that it is too simplistic to suggest that LoC can account for *individual differences* in health-related behaviours.

Evaluation

Comprehensive review

One strength is that Rotter's review was one of the earliest and most comprehensive investigations into the role of LoC.

His review explained why studies gave different findings about the effects of key variables (e.g. stress) on behaviour. It was because internals and externals respond differently to certain variables, but the studies did not take account of this.

This 'discovery' triggered an avalanche of research clarifying the role of LoC, ultimately creating a strong research base for the concept.

Issues of reliability

One weakness of Rotter's study was variability in the studies used.

Any weaknesses in these studies would reduce the validity of the conclusions drawn by Rotter. For instance, *social desirability bias* may have affected the validity of questionnaire studies because people are not truly representing their experience. In short, Rotter's review is only as valid as the studies he reviewed. There was no measure of the quality of the studies, whereas more modern reviews of research do check this.

This means we cannot rely on the conclusions Rotter draws about LoC.

GET ACTIVE Measuring LoC

A psychology student produces an LoC questionnaire. Each item has two statements, one reflecting an internal LoC and the other reflecting an external LoC. For example: 'It is ridiculous to say that teachers are unfair to students' and 'Most students don't know how much their marks are affected by teachers' moods'.

1. *Which statement is internal and which is external?*

2. *The student believes that this is the best way to measure locus of control reliably. Explain how the study by Rotter (1966) supports her belief.*

Exam-style questions

Patrick and Arthur are both trying to lose weight. Patrick has replaced a lot of foods in his diet with healthier alternatives, he exercises every day and has reduced his alcohol intake. He has also taken a much greater interest in what might happen to him if he continues an unhealthy lifestyle.

Arthur feels his life is a chaotic mess. He is stressed and thinks there is nothing he can do to lose weight. Everything he does just seems to make things worse.

1. Explain what is meant by the term 'locus of control'. (2)

2. Explain how attributions can determine health-related behaviour. (3)

3. State whether Patrick has an internal or external locus of control and explain your answer. (3)

4. Describe **one** conclusion of the study by Rotter (1966) and use it to explain Patrick's behaviour. (4)

5. Discuss the locus of control theory as an explanation of Patrick's and Arthur's behaviour. Refer to at least **one** research study in your answer. (9)

An issue to consider

Do you see yourself as an internal or an external? How do you think other people see you?

The issue is whether it matters who is making the judgement.

Specification content

A2 Theories of stress, behavioural addiction and physiological addiction

Theories: Key concepts of psychological theories of stress, behavioural addiction and physiological addiction, to include:

● Locus of control (Rotter 1966): internal and external locus of control, the role of attributions in determining health behaviour.

Studies: Key principles and critical evaluation of studies investigating psychological theories, to include critique of assumptions, methodology and ethics:

● Locus of control: Rotter (1966) Generalised expectancies for internal versus external control of reinforcement.

Studies related to theory 2: Locus of control

Tips for stressed-out students

Everyone agrees that students are stressed. For example, a survey by the National Union of Students in 2015 found that 77% of university students experienced stress-related anxiety. There are many sources of support to help students who are stressed. Most of the tips offered by websites have one thing in common. They are all ways of helping you to gain more control over your life, on the (reasonable) assumption that this will reduce stress. Advice includes: find ways to relax, watch your diet, get enough sleep, exercise regularly, find ways of studying more effectively, think positively.

Following these tips will help a lot of students. But evidence on this spread suggests there will always be a small proportion of students who need more support.

But will becoming more 'internal' always protect you from stress?

Getting married and being married – like all life events they have their ups and downs, both of which may be stressful (just ask these two).

Other major life events include parenthood, divorce and even Christmas. They all use 'psychic energy' and even if the event is a happy one, the outcome is stress.

Abouserie (1994) Sources and levels of stress in relation to locus of control and self-esteem in university students

Aims

Reda Abouserie aimed to identify academic sources of *stress* in students, investigate gender differences and examine links between sources of stress, *locus of control* (LoC) and *self-esteem*.

Procedure

675 students (70% females) completed four questionnaires:

- *Academic stress* ... 84 causes of stress related to learning and social factors.
- *Life* ... ms divided participants into low/moderate/serious/very serious lev...
- *LoC* ... s and 12 related to failure, producing a total score indicating degree of i...
- *Rose* ... ms measuring self-esteem.

Findings

Academ... ssful (e.g. exams, too much to do). In terms of life stress, 77.6% of students ... % serious stress and 12% reported 'no problem'.

Academ... vels were both significantly higher in females.

There w... tion between LoC and academic stress, but no significant correlation between ... significant *negative correlations* between self-esteem and both academic...

Conclusions

The maj... oderate levels of stress generally related to academic studies. But we can ex... need professional help to improve their coping resources or reduce academic s... arther research is needed to discover why female students appear to be less resistant to academic and life stressors.

Counselling could focus on helping students to change their LoC in a more internal direction. The same argument applies to self-esteem – raising it could help students to cope with stress.

Krause (1986) Stress and coping: Reconceptualising the role of locus of control beliefs

Aims

Neal Krause aimed to see if older adults with an extreme *internal* or *external LoC* will experience stressful life events more strongly than people with a moderate internal or external LoC.

Procedure

351 retired people aged over 65 were interviewed and completed questionnaires to measure *depression*, stressful life events and LoC. The life events questionnaire concerned the major life events that we do not experience very often, but which are stressful. The questionnaire included both closed and open items (participants could add whatever responses they wanted).

Findings

Participants with extreme internal control beliefs experienced fewer stressful life events (mean = 1.53) than extreme externals (mean = 2.2). However, extreme internals and extreme externals were both more vulnerable (than moderates) to becoming depressed when they were stressed.

The participants who believed in the effects of chance (externals) were more vulnerable to the effects of stress than participants who did not believe in the effects of chance (internals).

Conclusions

Krause suggests that having an internal LoC is a 'mixed blessing'. Compared to externals, extreme internals are more likely to avoid stressful events, but they respond just as negatively (self-blame) to unavoidable events.

So, the view that internals are better than externals at coping with stress is too simplistic and should be replaced with more complex models of how older adults cope.

 GET ACTIVE Changing views of LoC

Krause's argument (see facing page) is that we need to change the way we view locus of control. An internal LoC has traditionally been seen as desirable and an external LoC as undesirable. This is because externals were thought to be vulnerable to stress and internals resistant to it. But, as we have seen, Krause disputes this.

1. Draw a bar chart to represent the findings of Krause's study on the facing page. You do not need to use figures. The vertical axis is 'stress/depression', low to high. Write four labels on the horizontal axis, from left to right: extreme external, moderate external, moderate internal, extreme internal. Read the findings and decide where you should plot the four vertical bars corresponding to these labels.

2. How does this view of LoC differ from the traditional view?

Learning to manage your time effectively is a good way of helping you to feel in control of your life.

Evaluation

Applications of the research

One strength is that the study potentially has vocational applications.

As Abouserie concluded, students who experience serious stress may have their academic progress undermined. Counselling can help such students by shifting their LoC from external to internal. Sessions could [...] to change beliefs about the effects of their abilities and develop [...] controlling the environment (e.g. time management).

This is valuable because it presents a way of improv[...] life of students.

Biased questionnaires

One weakness of the study is that it used [...] may have been biased.

For instance, there was no attempt in the s[...] of *social desirability bias*. In other words, stude[...] the questionnaires in a way intended to make t[...] even possible that this might explain the gender [...] study, if males were less likely to admit to experienc[...]

This means that the findings of the study may not b[...] and therefore the conclusions drawn should be treated [...]

Evaluation

Changed our view of LoC

One strength of this study is that it presents a nuanced, complex a[...] more accurate view of LoC than the traditional concept.

Research before this study tended to assume that people with an extreme internal locus of control are more or less immune from the effects of stress. Krause showed that this was a simplistic interpretation because it ignores the self-blame that extreme internals experience when they fail to cope with unavoidable *stressors*.

The findings of this study suggest that older people with an extreme internal LoC may also need help to cope with some stressors.

Biased sample

One weakness is that the sample of participants was biased.

The ethnic mix of the sample did not reflect the ethnicity of retired people in the USA at the time. For example, 90% of the retired US population in 1985 was white, and 8% was black/African American (US Department of Health and Human Services 1987). The sample in the study was 64% white and 27% black/African American (and 9% other). So, white people were under-represented in the study and black/African American people were over-represented.

This means the study's findings cannot be generalised to the wider population of retired people.

Exam-style questions

Rom is a university student who is always very busy. He is a hard work[...] he currently has four essays and a practical on the go. He [...]rt-time job and has to make time for planning meals, [...]od and looking after the house.

[...]e is organised and on top of everything he needs [...]s with his studies, unlike his friend Marina. She is [...]d by all her work and also trying to run her life. [...] that nothing she does makes a difference so [...]nakes Marina feel bad about herself.

[...]d out the study 'Sources and levels of [...]s of control and self-esteem in university

[...] this study. (3)

[...]e study. (2)

[...]ether Rom or Marina will

[...]ion of the study by Krause (1986). (2)

[...]ause (1986). Refer to the [...]n your answer. (4)

[...]ocus of control as an explanation of [...]s and Marina's behaviour. Refer in your answer to the study by Abouserie (1994). (9)

You should by now have a fair idea of the kind of exam questions that can be asked – try to think of a few more of your own.

An issue to consider

The two studies on this spread used very different samples of participants – students and retired people. Do you think it is possible to draw conclusions about everybody from these studies?

Specification content

A2 Theories of stress, behavioural addiction and physiological addiction

Studies: Key principles and critical evaluation of studies investigating psychological theories, to include critique of assumptions, methodology and ethics:

- Locus of control:
  - Abouserie (1994) Sources and levels of stress in relation to locus of control and self-esteem in university students.
  - Krause (1986) Stress and coping: Reconceptualising the role of locus of control beliefs.

Theory 3: Theory of planned behaviour

Losing everything on the horses

The former professional footballer Keith Gillespie was addicted to gambling. In his autobiography *How not to be a football millionaire*, he estimated that he gambled away more than £7 million during his career. He was eventually declared bankrupt in 2010. In the book, Gillespie reveals several features of his gambling addiction that are addressed by the theory on this spread.

There were lots of things about gambling that he hated. But there was a lot more about it that he loved: 'I lose money but don't care. The thrill is worth it. I want that rush of excitement again'. After losing £62,000 in a two-day gambling spree in 1995, he fretted about telling his manager and his mum because he knew both of them would disapprove. But their disapproval wasn't enough to stop him placing bets. His betting on horses was out of control: 'I completely lost the plot... I was having a nightmare... I bet on every single race going'.

Source: *The Mirror* (2013)

Specification terms

Perceived behavioural control How much control a person believes they have over their own behaviour.

Personal attitudes The balance of a person's favourable and unfavourable attitudes about their behaviour.

Subjective norms An individual's belief about whether people who matter to them approve or disapprove of their behaviour.

Theory of planned behaviour Changes in behaviour can be predicted from our intention to change, which in turn is the outcome of personal attitudes towards the behaviour in question, our beliefs about what others think, and our perceived ability to control our behaviour.

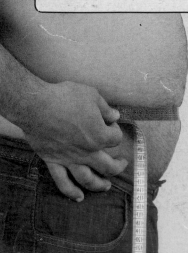

The TPB is often tested using questionnaires – it is worth looking at some example questions. The ones below use a 7-point rating scale to enable participants to express their opinion. Circle your answer each time.

1. Personal attitudes: 'I drink because it helps me forget the stress of my life'.
   Strongly disagree 1 2 3 4 5 6 7 Strongly agree

2. Subjective norms: 'People who matter to me would be upset at the amount I drink'.
   Strongly disagree 1 2 3 4 5 6 7 Strongly agree

3. Perceived behavioural control: 'I am confident I could reduce my drinking tomorrow if I wanted to'.
   Strongly disagree 1 2 3 4 5 6 7 Strongly agree

Key concepts of the theory

Icek Ajzen (1985, 1991) formulated the *theory of planned behaviour* (TPB) to explain how people can exercise control over their behaviour.

Central to the theory is the concept of *intention* – the TPB asserts that behaviour can be predicted from our intentions to behave. Applied to health, the TPB links intentions to change behaviour (e.g. give up drugs, lose weight) with actual changes in behaviour. Intentions to change behaviour are formed from three key sources.

1. Personal attitudes

Personal attitudes refer to an individual's favourable and unfavourable beliefs about their behaviour (e.g. 'I overeat because I enjoy food' versus 'Overeating makes me anxious'). The person's overall attitude is formed from the balance of positive and negative judgements of their own behaviour.

2. Subjective norms

Subjective norms are the individual's beliefs about whether the people who matter most to them approve or disapprove of their behaviour. For example, an alcohol addict considers what their friends and family think about their *addiction*. The alcoholic might conclude, 'Most people who matter to me are very unhappy with me drinking like this'. This would make them less likely to intend to drink, and ultimately less likely to drink.

3. Perceived behavioural control (PBC)

Perceived behavioural control concerns how much control we believe we have over behaviour. Does an obese person believe losing weight is easy or hard for them to do? This depends on their perception of the resources available to them, both external (support, time) and internal (skills, determination).

PBC can indirectly influence our intentions to behave – the more control I believe I have over my weight, the stronger my intention to lose weight.

PBC can also influence behaviour directly – the more control I believe I have, the longer and harder I will try to lose weight (or give up drugs, or whatever).

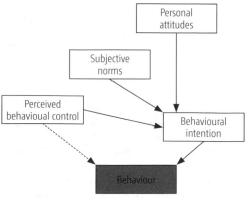

Using weight loss as an example: my personal attitudes towards weight, my perception of what my nearest and dearest think of my weight, and my beliefs about my ability to lose weight, all combine to influence my intention to lose weight. This in turn influences the amount of time and effort I put into actually losing weight. Perceived behavioural control can lead directly to behavioural changes as well.

Evaluation

Research support for the TPB

One strength of the TPB is that there is support for some of its predictions.

Martin Hagger et al. (2011) found that personal attitudes, subjective norms and PBC all predicted an intention to limit drinking to guideline number of units. Intentions then influenced the number of units actually consumed after one month and three months. PBC also predicted actual consumption directly (and not just intention).

This supports the TPB because these outcomes were all exactly as the theory predicts, at least in relation to alcohol addiction.

Not a full explanation

One weakness of the TPB is that it cannot account for the *intention-behaviour gap*.

Rohan Miller and Gwyneth Howell (2005) studied the gambling behaviour of underage teenagers. They found they could not predict the reduction of actual gambling behaviour from intentions to give up. In other words there was no relationship between intentions and what the teenagers eventually did.

This means the TPB cannot predict behaviour change, which suggests it can't really be used as a basis for interventions.

Lack of support from some studies

Another weakness of the TPB is that some studies provide little support for its predictions.

Winnifred Louis et al. (2009, see next spread) investigated healthy and unhealthy eating behaviours. They found that personal attitudes, subjective norms and behavioural control did not affect behaviour in the way predicted by the TPB. This is because their effects depended upon the role of *stress*.

This suggests that the TPB is an incomplete explanation that ignores at least one key influence on behavioural change.

Short-term versus long-term

A further weakness is that the TPB is a poor predictor of long-term changes.

Rosie McEachan et al. (2011) reviewed 237 studies of the theory in relation to health behaviours. They found that the strength of *correlation* between intentions and actual behaviour varied according to the length of time between the two. So, intention to stop drinking, for example, was a good predictor of stopping within five weeks. But the theory did not predict behavioural change more than five weeks after the intention had been formed.

This means the TPB is not applicable to many real-world intentions to change behaviour which often take place over longer periods of time.

GET ACTIVE Fighting fit

Firefighters have to be fit. The Chief fire officer (CFO) of one fire service wants to introduce an exercise programme that firefighters can voluntarily join. The CFO knows that many firefighters won't take up the offer, so she asks a psychologist for advice.

Imagine that's you. You decide to use the theory of planned behaviour to find out why some firefighters will not take part.

1. *Draw a version of the TPB diagram on the facing page. Make sure the boxes have plenty of space in them.*

2. *Think of some questions you could ask to measure each component of the TPB. What sort of responses do you think you would get from firefighters who do not want to take part? Write these responses in the relevant boxes.*

Melvyn intended to eat the healthy option.

Exam-style questions

Greg is worried about how much alcohol he drinks. He knows that it is affecting his health and his doctor has advised him to cut down. But he also enjoys drinking. It helps him relax and gives him a bit of an escape from a stressful life. Most of Greg's friends drink and they haven't discussed cutting down or giving up. Whenever he visits his parents, they always have a couple of drinks together.

He has tried in the past to cut down through 'willpower', but it hasn't worked. Greg has heard of 'Dry January' and thinks he'll give it a go as it's not far off. His friends and family have offered to sponsor him.

1. The theory of planned behaviour identifies the concepts of personal attitudes and subjective norms to explain the likelihood of someone behaving healthily or unhealthily.
   (a) Explain what is meant by 'personal attitudes' and 'subjective norms'. (4)
   (b) Identify **one** example of each relating to Greg in the above scenario. (2)
2. Explain how the theory of planned behaviour might predict Greg's future behaviour. (3)
3. Explain **one** strength and **one** weakness of the theory of planned behaviour. (4)
4. Discuss the theory of planned behaviour in relation to Greg's attempt to reduce his drinking. (9)

An issue to consider

Subjective norms are perhaps the most difficult part of the TPB to appreciate. Again, it's all about perception. My partner may or may not actually disapprove of how much I drink (she might not say anything about it). But if I *believe* she disapproves, then that is one factor that might motivate me to change my behaviour.

How do you think this belief is formed? What contributes to it?

Specification content

A2 Theories of stress, behavioural addiction and physiological addiction

Theories: Key concepts of psychological theories of stress, behavioural addiction and physiological addiction, to include:

● Theory of planned behaviour (Ajzen 1985): concepts of personal attitude to behaviour, subjective norms, perceived behavioural control and their effect on behaviour.

Studies related to theory 3:
Theory of planned behaviour

Making resolutions

The road to hell is paved with good intentions (proverb, author unknown).

New Year is traditionally the time for resolutions. And one of the most common is 'I must exercise more'. Mid-January is traditionally the time when New Year's resolutions are dropped, forgotten and abandoned for another year. The theory of planned behaviour can help explain why this is.

Let's assume that most people really do intend to exercise more when they make their resolutions. Where does this intention come from? I (Rob) make the resolution because, although I know exercising more will be hard in lots of ways, I also know my health will benefit. So overall, I have a positive attitude towards what exercise can do for me personally. Other people whose opinions I respect have been telling me for ages that I really need to make the effort (my partner, doctor, mum...). Can I do it? I believe I can, because I'm determined, I've joined a gym and my friends and family are behind me.

So, I sit down and make a plan... which lasts all of two weeks.

On this spread we look at two studies of the theory of planned behaviour as it has been applied to two resolutions – eating more healthily and drinking less alcohol.

We work out subjective norms from the opinions of other people who matter to us. Many parents reduce their smoking and drinking if they realise that their children disapprove of their behaviour. Not these two though.

Louis *et al.* (2009) Stress and the theory of planned behaviour: Understanding healthy and unhealthy eating intentions

Aims

Winnifred Louis *et al.* aimed to test the *theory of planned behaviour* (TPB) as an explanation of health decision-making and its relationship with *stress*.

Procedure

154 male and female students completed a questionnaire to measure the following related to healthy eating behaviour: *personal attitudes*, *subjective norms*, *perceived behavioural control* and intentions to eat healthily or unhealthily.

The researchers also measured the participants' degree of life stress and their perceptions of body image.

Findings

Personal attitudes towards he[alth]y ... [inten]tion to eat healthily but subjective norms did not.

There was a small ef[fect] ... eating intentions.

Subjective norm[s] ... [predic]ted intentions to eat unhealthily, but only at low lev[els] ...

Conclu[sions]

The ... [p]erceived control predicted intentions to e... [effe]ct of attitudes, norms and control on inten... the theory.

Cooke [et al. ... do]es the theory of planned [behaviour predict alcoh]ol consumption? A system[atic review and meta-a]nalysis

Aims

Richard Cooke and colleag[ues ...] [in]to the *correlations* between TPB variables, intentions to consu[me and] [al]cohol consumption.

Procedure

The researchers reviewed 40 studies [measur]ing intentions to consume alcohol. The studies had also directly measured personal attitudes, subjective norms and perceived control.

In addition, some of the studies measured *self-efficacy* (a person's confidence in their ability to reduce or give up drinking).

Alcohol consumption was defined as falling into one of five categories including 'getting drunk' (drinking just to get drunk) and 'heavy episodic drinking' (more than 56 g of ethanol in a single session).

Findings

Positive correlations were found between: intentions to consume and actual consumption, intentions and attitudes, subjective norms and perceived control (in descending order of strength).

Episodic drinking predicted intentions to drink more strongly than other types of drinking.

Self-efficacy positively correlated with both intention to drink and actual consumption (more strongly than perceived control).

Conclusions

The TPB appears to be useful in understanding intentions to drink alcohol. The findings suggest that interventions to reduce drinking should target personal attitudes and intentions rather than control and subjective norms.

Self-efficacy is a useful variable to measure in studies and to target in interventions, even though it is not directly part of the TPB.

Evaluation

Practical applications

One strength is that the findings show how interventions should be structured.

The study highlights the best ways to target scarce resources to increase healthy eating. Healthy-eating programmes should seek to increase perceived control and reduce stress. However, as subjective norms were not influential, interventions should not focus on social pressure to eat healthily.

This is ultimately the aim of any research – to produce a useful application based on a theory.

Self-report measures

One weakness is that this study, like most research into the TPB, was based on questionnaire (*self-report*) data.

Self-reports are subjective measures of the variables in the TPB, and suffer from limitatio[ns] such as *social desirability bias* whereby participants respond to questions in a way [that] they think makes them 'look good'. There w[as] no objective measures in this study, such [as] amount of actual healthy eating particip[ants] engaged in.

This means the study is measuring in[tentions] but not behaviours, and intentions m[ay not lead] to changes in behaviour (the *intentio[n-behaviour] gap* discussed on the previous sprea[d]).

Evaluation

Relatively large number of studies

One strength is that a large number of studies (40 of them) were included in this review.

Therefore, the researchers considered a large amount of data. 40 studies compares very favourably with the *median* number of studies in other reviews, which is three (Davey *et al.* 2011).

This means we can have more confidence in the conclusions of the review and it meant the researchers could generate *credible* hypotheses to be tested in future research.

Not cause-and-effect

One weakness is that the data reviewed in this study is almost entirely correlational.

The TPB is supported by many studies that show positive correlations between intention to consume alcohol on the one hand and planned behaviour variables (attitudes, norms, control) on the other, as well as between intentions and actual behaviour in some cases. However, only *experimental* studies can demonstrate cause-and-effect relationships, and as Falko Sniehotta *et al.* (2014) point out, 'We do not need any more correlational studies of the TPB'.

This suggests that we cannot conclude, from this research, that intentions can *cause* changes in alcohol consumption.

GET ACTIVE Marsha's night out

Marsha likes a drink and is planning to have quite a few this weekend. She associates drinking with having a fun time with her friends and quite likes the idea of losing control a bit. It can be expensive to go out drinking but she can afford it, and fortunately she doesn't really suffer from hangovers. She has been an enthusiastic drinker for a few years now, ever since her parents let her have a few sips of wine on special family occasions.

1. Identify **one** example each of personal attitudes, subjective norms, perceived behavioural control and intentions in this scenario.

[obscured text] Cooke et al. (2016), if Marsha [obscured] her drinking, which **two** [obscured] be targeted?

[obscured] re healthily. He likes crisps, sweets, chips, [obscured] diet because he needs to lose weight. That [obscured] big stumbling block for Stefan is drinking. He [obscured] so he needs to cut down drastically. Stefan's [obscured] and he drinks more than they do as well. He has [obscured] ore. This time he needs more help so he has been [obscured] is also under a lot of stress at work and he knows [obscured] lthy things and drinks to cope.

[obscured] by Louis *et al.* (2009). (3)

[obscured] by Louis *et al.* (2009). Use this finding to explain [obscured] more healthy diet. (4)

3. For the [obscured] (2016):
   (a) Give **one** aim.
   (b) Give **one** conclusion and use it to explain Stefan's behaviour. (2)
   (c) Explain **one** strength and **one** weakness of the study. (4)

4. With reference to **two** research studies, discuss the theory of planned behaviour as an explanation of Stefan's attempt to eat more healthily. (9)

(Note card reads: "Not needed :)")

An issue to consider

It's the New Year's resolution problem. You reach the point where you definitely decide you're going to work harder, get up earlier, eat more healthily, be more organised or whatever. But nothing comes of it. What in your own experience has prevented you from converting intentions into behaviours?

What could you do to overcome these barriers (and don't answer with 'try harder')?

Specification content

A2 Theories of stress, behavioural addiction and physiological addiction

Studies: Key principles and critical evaluation of studies investigating psychological theories, to include critique of assumptions, methodology and ethics:

- Theory of planned behaviour:
  - Louis *et al.* (2009) Stress and the theory of planned behaviour: Understanding healthy and unhealthy eating intentions.
  - Cooke *et al.* (2016) How well does the theory of planned behaviour predict alcohol consumption? A systematic review and meta-analysis.

Theory 4: Self-efficacy theory

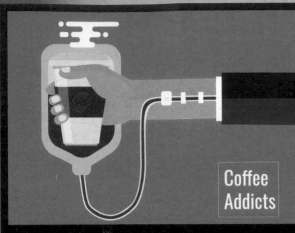

Coffee Addicts

Can you give it up?

Do you smoke? If you decided to give up, would you find it a hard or easy thing to do?

I (Rob) know two people who have stopped after years of smoking. One struggled for months, gradually reducing her daily dose of cigarettes to zero, relapsing several times. Even now she vapes instead of smokes. The other person just decided one day she would stop, and she did.

What about caffeine? Do you drink coffee or energy drinks? Is it hard or easy for you to give them up? Social media – hard or easy?

According to *The Guardian* (2018), teenagers are leaving Facebook, Instagram and Snapchat in small but significant numbers. Some find it easy. Others, like Kanye West, keep quitting and returning. The one thing above all others that prevents them from finally leaving is FOMO, fear of missing out. FOMO bothers some young people greatly, so they feel they can't give up. Others don't care – they know they can leave and they do.

Specification terms

Self-efficacy A person's confidence in being able to do something. Such confidence generates expectations and these act as self-fulfilling prophecies.

Vicarious reinforcement Occurs when a learner observes a model's behaviour being reinforced (rewarded).

A good gym trainer will set his or her students achievable targets, such as being able to walk sideways up a wall.

Key concepts of the theory

Self-efficacy refers to the belief we have in our ability to carry out an action or task. Albert Bandura (1977) suggested that self-efficacy is central to our motivation to change behaviour.

People with high self-efficacy believe they will be successful and therefore are more strongly motivated to tackle difficult tasks. They are more likely to persist in a challenging task and increase their effort to ensure success. But people with low self-efficacy believe they will fail and therefore avoid such challenges (or they give up quickly if the task cannot be avoided).

In order to judge whether we are capable of tackling a task successfully, we need an accurate perception of our level of self-efficacy. According to Bandura, this awareness comes from four main sources of self-efficacy information.

1. Mastery experiences

The most important source of self-efficacy is the experience of performing a task successfully. This is not just because we get practice, but also because we learn that we are capable of performing the task or improving our skills – we feel more competent and are more likely to perform well at the task in the future (or at a similar one). On the other hand, failing at a task reduces our self-efficacy, perhaps catastrophically if it happens before self-efficacy has developed.

For example, children with *Type I diabetes* have to learn how to inject insulin correctly. Practice develops the skill but it also increases self-efficacy, so the person has increasingly greater confidence in their ability.

A person's self-efficacy can be developed by giving them opportunities to complete tasks successfully. The task therefore has to be carefully matched to the person's current skill level. In fact it should be a little bit beyond their current skill level to provide a challenge but there is no point in providing a task that is so challenging that failure is guaranteed.

2. Vicarious reinforcement

Self-efficacy is affected by observing another person (*model*) performing a task. If you observe the person being successful, your self-efficacy increases (obviously it decreases if they fail). The other person is especially influential if you perceive them to be similar to yourself (*identification*).

Group-based health programmes (e.g. WeightWatchers or Alcoholics Anonymous) provide both mastery and *vicarious experiences*. Observing others in the same position as you losing weight or abstaining from alcohol enhances your belief that 'If they can do it, so can I'.

3. Social persuasion

Encouragement and discouragement from others can have a profound impact on our self-efficacy. Bandura focused on verbal persuasion (using words is a form of social persuasion). For instance, a person spending time at the gym after recovering from a heart attack can be greatly motivated by a trainer telling them 'You can do it!'. Used correctly, social/verbal persuasion adds to the person's belief they can succeed.

The effects of social persuasion depend on the perceived credibility of the persuader. So, if the trainer is qualified and experienced, and the person doing the exercise trusts them, then the trainer's social persuasion will enhance self-efficacy even further. Social persuasion is less influential than mastery and vicarious experiences, but it is much easier to provide.

4. Emotional states

Self-efficacy is influenced by the person's emotional state. *Stress, anxiety* and fear can all reduce self-efficacy. For instance, someone new to exercising in a gym may well experience one or more of these arousal states because they believe they are being observed and evaluated. As a result, they expect to 'fail', and because their self-efficacy is reduced that is exactly what happens.

A good trainer will remove these emotional obstacles (e.g. through relaxation and social persuasion), allowing the person to focus on the task at hand.

Evaluation

Support from research

One strength is the large body of research supporting the predictions of self-efficacy theory.

Victor Strecher *et al.* (1986) reviewed many studies of self-efficacy and health-related behaviour. They found strong relationships between self-efficacy beliefs and behaviour change in the areas of weight control, contraception use, exercise, etc. Furthermore, the *experimental* studies they reviewed showed that self-efficacy can be increased and lead to behaviour change.

This shows that self-efficacy is a consistent and *reliable* predictor of short-term and long-term health-related behaviour change.

Effective practical applications

Another strength is that the theory offers several strategies that interventions can use to produce behaviour change.

For example, the theory suggests that opportunities to perform a task successfully have to be structured very carefully. The target behaviour should be broken down into achievable elements, with the earlier ones easier than later ones. Also, *relaxation training* can be used to reduce anxiety (emotional states), improving self-efficacy and making change more likely. Many of these strategies are quite different from those suggested by other behaviour change models.

Therefore, the theory provides many useful practical suggestions.

Definition and measurement issues

One weakness is that there is huge variation in how concepts of the theory are defined and measured.

For instance, self-efficacy has sometimes been confused with *self-esteem* and self-confidence. This means that what is being measured by research studies is not self-efficacy at all. Furthermore, Clive Eastman and John Marzillier (1984) argue that the questionnaires used to measure self-efficacy (including Bandura's own) are unclear, open to interpretation and in many cases not measuring self-efficacy at all.

This means that supposed evidence for the benefits of self-efficacy may not be *valid*.

Backfire effects

Another weakness is that Bandura's theory assumes that high self-efficacy is universally a positive thing, but there is evidence that it can backfire.

In one study, Jeffrey Vancouver *et al.* (2002) increased students' self-efficacy by giving them positive feedback (social persuasion) as they played a puzzle-based game. This increased the performance of many students on the current game, but lowered it on the next. The researchers then withheld feedback, which lowered the students' self-efficacy but increased their performance. The researchers argued that high self-efficacy may lead to overconfidence, which means the individual makes less effort the next time they perform the task.

This suggests the model is flawed because it does not predict some of the negative effects of high self-efficacy.

^{GET}ACTIVE Design the perfect exercise programme

People recovering from a heart attack are strongly advised to take part in physical exercise. Most of these clients will have exercised very little over recent years. They believe and expect that they will fail to get any benefit. This is why it is really important to 'start small' and build up gradually. Imagine you are a fitness instructor devising a programme for these clients.

1. *Make a list of specific mastery experiences – remember to 'start small' and build up.*

2. *How would you use vicarious experiences to help your clients achieve mastery?*

3. *Think of some specific verbal persuasion phrases (individually tailored).*

4. *What could you do to encourage the right emotional state in your clients?*

Smug? Overconfidence may be an undesirable outcome of self-efficacy.

Exam-style questions

Vee has joined Alcoholics Anonymous, a support group for people who are addicted to alcohol and want to do something about it. She likes the idea that there are people at the meetings who can explain their own experiences with alcohol. It means she doesn't feel on her own. She has already picked up quite a few tips about how to stay off the booze. Vee finds the other people very encouraging and it does her good to see that other people have been successful. One person in the group has been sober for two years. The weekly meeting has a very relaxed atmosphere and is like an 'oasis of calm' in Vee's otherwise fairly hectic life.

1. In terms of self-efficacy theory, explain what is meant by 'mastery experiences'. (2)

2. Self-efficacy theory claims that social persuasion and emotional states influence self-efficacy. Define these terms and for each **one** give an example from Vee's experience. (4)

3. Explain how vicarious reinforcement affects Vee's self-efficacy. (2)

4. Explain **one** strength and **one** weakness of self-efficacy theory as an explanation of Vee's behaviour. (4)

5. Discuss self-efficacy theory in relation to Vee's attempts to stop drinking. (9)

An issue to consider

Do you have a particular talent or skill? Can you play a musical instrument? Drive a car? Dance? Cook? Play a sport? Recite pi to 100 decimal places? You can do these things to a certain standard. But you also *know* you can do them. That is the essence of self-efficacy.

So, is self-efficacy an 'overall' characteristic? Or do we have self-efficacies for different things?

Specification content

A2 Theories of stress, behavioural addiction and physiological addiction

Theories: Key concepts of psychological theories of stress, behavioural addiction and physiological addiction, to include:

● Self-efficacy theory (Bandura 1977): mastery experiences, vicarious reinforcement, the effect of social persuasion and emotional state on self-efficacy and likelihood of behavioural change.

Studies related to theory 4: Self-efficacy theory

Are you dentophobic?

Some people are so afraid of the dentist that they would literally rather their teeth fall out than go to the dentist. Or perhaps you don't like going to the dentist but you 'grit your teeth' and get on with it (pun intended). You associate the dentist with pain, needles, unpleasant sounds and smells. You may feel the whole business is so unpleasant that you wouldn't be able to cope with it.

According to self-efficacy theory, one reason for this is probably because the thought of visiting the dentist is emotionally arousing (i.e. it makes you stressed and anxious). As emotional arousal reduces self-efficacy, you are likely to avoid the dentist. Good news for your mental health (but only temporarily), bad news for your dental health.

Who knew the power of self-efficacy theory?

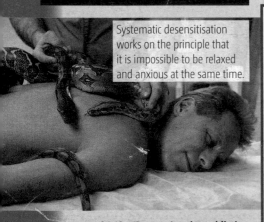

Systematic desensitisation works on the principle that it is impossible to be relaxed and anxious at the same time.

Types of self-efficacy related to addiction

Resistance self-efficacy A person's belief about their ability to prevent an addictive behaviour from starting.

Harm-reduction self-efficacy A person's belief about their ability to keep the harmful effects of their addiction to a minimum.

Coping self-efficacy A person's belief about their ability to avoid relapse.

Recovery self-efficacy A person's belief about their ability to overcome relapses once they occur.

Bandura and Adams (1977) Analysis of self-efficacy theory of behavioural change

Aims

Albert Bandura and Nancy Adams investigated the role of *self-efficacy* in the treatment of snake phobia. The treatment they used was *systematic desensitisation* (SD), in which a *client* identifies increasingly fearful situations that produce fear, ranging from the lowest level (e.g. seeing a small snake at a distance) to the highest level (e.g. handling a big snake). At each level the client focuses on relaxation before moving on to the next level.

The researchers wanted to see if reducing emotional arousal through relaxation would enhance self-efficacy and reduce avoidance of snakes.

Procedure

Ten people with a chronic snake phobia were assessed for:

- Degree of avoidance – successful performance of 29 tasks involving a large snake.
- Fear arousal – amount of fear experienced (measured by rating from 1 to 10) when the 29 tasks were described to them and again when they carried them out.
- Efficacy expectations – participants rated how strongly they believed they could perform the 29 tasks, on a scale from 0 to 100.

SD was given individually. The tests used before treatment were repeated within one week of the treatment ending.

Findings

There were higher levels of self-efficacy after treatment compared with before. There was a strong *positive correlation* between ⟨...⟩ level and approach behaviour towards the snake. Finally, there was a substantial reducti⟨...⟩ fter treatment.

Conclusions

The treatment inc⟨...⟩ ⟨...⟩ with a phobia), supporting Bandura's self-efficacy theory and con⟨...⟩ ⟨...⟩ntral role in behaviour change.

Marl⟨...⟩ and addictive beha⟨...⟩

Aims

Alan Marlatt and his c⟨...⟩ ⟨...⟩ered how self-efficacy can prevent the onset of *addic⟨...⟩*

Procedure

The researchers identified a wide ran⟨...⟩ ⟨...⟩ween different types of self-efficacy (see left) and a variety of addictions.

Findings of the review

1. Low resistance self-efficacy plus peer influence predicts alcohol and nicotine use by adolescents.
2. Harm-reduction self-efficacy can be increased in adolescents who are already drinking and smoking.
3. Low coping self-efficacy means alcoholics stay longer in treatment.
4. Recovery self-efficacy, established after *relapse*, helps addicts 'bounce back' from relapse. Interventions help the addict recognise relapse triggers.

Conclusions

Self-efficacy influences smoking and alcohol addiction at the initiation, maintenance and relapse stages. Interventions can therefore target self-efficacy in a variety of ways to:

- Increase self-efficacy through meeting achievable targets.
- Identify people at greater risk of addiction or relapse (extra support).
- Reduce the self-harm associated with the drug.
- Identify 'triggering' situations that can be coped with to avoid relapse.

Evaluation

Standardised procedures

One strength is that the researchers used several *standardised procedures*.

For example, the 29 snake-related tasks were the same for everyone. Also, the SD treatment was conducted identically for each participant. Therefore, the experience of the study did not vary much from one participant to another. This means the outcomes could not be due to differences in how the procedure was conducted.

This means that important *confounding variables* were controlled and meant that the study could be *replicated*.

Self-reports

One weakness is that *self-report methods* were used to measure key variables.

For example, fear arousal was assessed on a scale of 1 to 10 and self-efficacy on a scale of 1 to 100. The participants may have under-reported their level of fear and over-reported their level of self-efficacy in order to 'look good' (*social desirability bias*). Also, the subjective nature of the scales means it is impossible to know if the values (1, 2, 3, etc.) had the same meaning for every participant (actually very unlikely).

This means that the role of self-efficacy may have been over- or und[er-estim]ated.

Part of self-efficacy is the ability to 'bounce back' from setbacks and relapses.

Evaluation

Comprehensive and thorough

One strength of the review was that it covered a wide v[ariety of]
several types of self-efficacy.

Resistance, coping and recovery self-efficacy are a[...]
stages of the addiction process. Therefore, it make[...]
cover research into each of these aspects, espe[...]
learned for practical interventions.

This means that we can draw conclusion[...]
efficacy can be created and can contribut[...]

Subjective selection of studi[es]

One weakness is that a review of research i[...]

This is because the researchers had to decide wh[...]
the review. This is a key decision because it strongly in[...]
can be drawn. The researchers included a large number of st[...]
no indication in their review of the criteria or process they used t[...]

This means it is unclear how much *credibility* we can give to the co[...]
because they may be based on a biased selection of studies.

(handwritten note: Not Need)

GET ACTIVE Jamal's self-efficacy

Jamal started smoking when he was 12. A friend offered him a cigarette and he didn't want to look uncool so he accepted it. Eventually he was smoking a lot each day. But he knew it was harming his health so he decided to reduce his daily intake. Now Jamal smokes about half of what he used to. He tried to give up completely a few times but after the first couple of goes he sort of knew it wouldn't work. Each time he would always find himself in situations where he enjoyed smoking.

1. *Marlatt* et al. *(1995) identified four types of self-efficacy. Give an example of each one from Jamal's behaviour.*

2. *Explain* **two** *ways in which Jamal's self-efficacy could be increased to help him combat his addiction.*

Exam-style questions

Mani first started gambling on fruit machines at an arcade with a friend who kept encouraging him to play and he didn't feel he could refuse. Gambling soon became more important to him than a bit of fun. Eventually Mani got help and he now knows how to avoid the situations that trigger his craving to gamble. He started by reducing his visits to the [bett]ing shop until he gave up altogether. Mani now feels he [has the s]kills to cope, which means that he isn't attracted to [gambling as] he used to be. He has had a couple of 'slips' [but manages] to bounce back.

[...Mar]latt et al. (1995):
[...] (3)
[...] (2)
[...] explain Mani's behaviour. (2)
[...] of the study by Bandura and Adams
[... to] explain Mani's behaviour. (2)
[...stu]dies by Bandura and Adams (1977)
[...] et al. (1995), discuss self-efficacy as an
[... explanatio]n of Mani's behaviour. (9)

Issue to consider

[Hav]e you ever thought to yourself, 'I could never do [th]at'? Think about something you 'could never do'.

What is stopping you? Is it just your low level of self-efficacy? Is it because you wouldn't know how to go about doing it?

If so, how could you apply Bandura's self-efficacy theory to help you?

Specification content

A2 Theories of stress, behavioural addiction and physiological addiction

Studies: Key principles and critical evaluation of studies investigating psychological theories, to include critique of assumptions, methodology and ethics.

● Self-efficacy theory:
  ○ Bandura and Adams (1977) Analysis of self-efficacy theory of behavioural change.
  ○ Marlatt *et al.* (1995) Self-efficacy and addictive behaviour.

Revision summary

Definitions

Theories of stress, behavioural addiction and physiological addiction

Defining health, stress and addiction

Health and ill health

General definition Complete physical, mental and social well-being, not just absence of disease.

Biomedical definition Physical/biological factors, illness is physical disease, health is absence of disease.

Associated with technological advances (e.g. brain scanning, chemotherapy).

Biopsychosocial definition An interaction between biological, psychological and social factors.

Aims to enhance health, focus on prevention. Influential in treating mental disorders.

Health as a continuum Health/ill health are two extremes with many states in between.

Stress

Defining stress An emotional response to situations of threat.

Stressors create stress

Physical stressors (environmental), e.g. temperature, noise.

Psychological stressors, e.g. life events and daily hassles.

The stress response

Physiological stress: bodily symptoms, e.g. increased heart rate, sweating, feeling sick.

Psychological stress: emotion you experience when a stressor occurs.

Perceived ability to cope People react differently to the same stressors.

Stress occurs when perceived demands of environment are greater than perceived ability to cope (e.g. exams).

Response affected by our perception of internal (e.g. resilience) and external (e.g. social support) coping resources.

Addiction

Defining addiction Complex mental health disorder, pleasurable despite harmful consequences.

Classifying addiction ICD-11 substance use or addictive behaviours. Physiological (e.g. cocaine, caffeine) or behavioural (gambling, gaming).

Physiological addiction Physical effects:

Withdrawal: experienced when substance/behaviour stops.

Tolerance: higher dose needed for same effect.

Behavioural addiction Produces same physical effects as substance addiction (withdrawal, tolerance), e.g. gambling, mobile use.

Griffiths' six components of addiction

1. Physical and psychological dependence (salience): addiction dominates addict's life.
2. Tolerance: more needed for same effect.
3. Withdrawal: when stopping drug or addictive behaviour.
4. Relapse: after abstinence.
5. Conflict: within self and with others.
6. Mood alteration: positive and negative subjective experiences.

Theory 1: Health belief model

Key concepts of the HBM

Rosenstock (1966) developed HBM to explain why people engage in healthy behaviour (or not). Three key questions:

1. Perceived seriousness Change depends on how we perceive outcomes of not changing (e.g. condoms may prevent chlamydia but is seriousness enough to warrant use?).

2. Perceived susceptibility Only change (use condoms) if we see ourselves as realistically vulnerable to illness (chlamydia, HIV/AIDS, etc.).

3. Cost-benefit analysis Balance of...

Perceived benefits: advantages of changing behaviour.

Perceived barriers: obstacles preventing us changing.

Modifying factors

Demographic variables (age, gender, religion etc.) affect likelihood of change.

Cues to action: internal (e.g. pain) and external (e.g. doctor's advice).

Self-efficacy: change more likely if we believe we have ability to do it.

Becker et al. (1978)

Aims Use HBM to explain mothers' compliance with treatment for asthma in their children.

Procedure 111 mothers of children with asthma interviewed when attending emergency clinic for asthma attack. Blood samples taken from children to check for presence of asthma medication.

Findings

Positive correlations between mothers' compliance to giving medication and:

- Perceived seriousness of asthma.
- Perceived susceptibility to asthma.
- Beliefs about seriousness (e.g. interference with child's education).

Four perceived barriers, e.g. getting prescriptions, child disliking taste.

Only two demographic variables mattered: mothers being married and educated.

Conclusions Each HBM component useful in predicting treatment compliance even in long-term conditions.

Carpenter (2010)

Aims Meta-analysis of studies into effect of time on HBM variables and behaviour change.

Procedure Selected 18 longitudinal studies.

Analysed in terms of time between measuring variables and behaviour change.

Also whether each study's outcome was a treatment or a preventative behaviour.

Findings

Seriousness: relationship with behaviour change was positive but weak.

Susceptibility: no link with behaviour change, except positive effect on compliance with drug treatment.

Benefits: positive relationship with behaviour change.

Barriers: strongest predictor of behaviour change.

Conclusions Little support for HBM. Barriers and benefits were the only components to consistently predict behaviour change.

Evaluation

Effectiveness and practical applications Use of HBM shown to increase uptake of bowel and colon screening (Williamson and Wardle 2002).

Strong credibility Devised by health researchers and practitioners working with real-life behaviour change, so well accepted.

How many models? Not one single model, and research studies often involve different combination of elements (Zimmerman and Vernberg 1994).

How rational are we? Model assumes decisions are rational (e.g. cost-benefit analysis) but emotions and habits are important.

Evaluation

Subjective and objective measurements Mothers' self-reports and blood samples were in agreement, confirms self-report as a valid measure.

Nature of data collection Mothers' responses may have been different under less stressful conditions. Challenges validity.

Evaluation

Future directions and applications Review provided focus for future research, showed which parts of HBM most effective.

Outdated health belief model HBM has evolved and now more complex and different model from the one analysed in this review (e.g. self-efficacy and cues to action were not included in the studies in this analysis), so the study is outdated.

Theory 2: Locus of control theory

Key concepts of LoC theory

Rotter (1966) proposed locus of control (LoC) theory.

Internal and external LoC

Internals: believe that events are under own control, e.g. either success or failure at work is due to their own efforts.

Externals: believe that events are outside own control, and explained by e.g. luck, other people, etc.

LoC is a continuum.

Attributions and health behaviour

Attribution is the process of explaining other people's behaviour and also explaining our own behaviour.

Internals and externals attribute own health-related behaviours differently, e.g. addiction could be explained by ability to avoid risk factors (internal) or explained by genes (external).

Rotter (1966)

Aims Review research into internal/external LoC and devise questionnaire to measure LoC.

Procedure Reviewed studies into LoC and other variables (e.g. need to achieve).

Reviewed questionnaires of LoC, including his own I-E scale with 29 pairs of statements.

Findings

I-E scale was reliable and valid measure of LoC.

Studies found internals more likely to act to improve environment, non-smokers more likely to be internals.

Conclusions LoC is a powerful predictor of many behaviours, affected by factors such as culture and parenting.

Abouserie (1994)

Aims Study academic sources of stress in students, gender differences and links between sources of stress, LoC and self-esteem.

Procedure 675 students completed: Academic stress questionnaire (ASQ), Life stress questionnaire (LSQ), LoC scale and Rosenberg self-esteem scale.

Findings

Academic sources (e.g. exams) most stressful for students, but 12% reported no problem.

Higher stress in females.

Positive correlation between LoC and academic stress but not life stress. Negative correlation between self-esteem and academic and life stress.

Conclusions Most students moderately stressed (academic) but about 10% need professional help.

Krause (1986)

Aims Test hypothesis that older adults with extreme internal and external LoC experience stressful life events more strongly than moderate internals and externals.

Procedure 351 retired people over 65 interviewed and completed questionnaires to measure depression, stressful life events and LoC (open and closed questions).

Findings

Extreme internals had fewer stressful life events than extreme externals.

Both more vulnerable to stress-related depression than moderates.

Those who believed in chance (externals) more vulnerable to the effects of stress than internals.

Conclusions Internal LoC is a mixed blessing, extreme internals stressed by unavoidable events. Simplistic to think internals cope better.

Evaluation

Research support for LoC High externals found to be more conformist, so vulnerable to addiction risk factors (Avtgis 1998).

Practical application By age 30 those who were assessed as internal at 10 were less likely to be obese or stressed than externals. Internal LoC protects against stress (Gale et al. 2008).

Limited role for LoC in health-related behaviours LoC only relevant in new situations, otherwise previous experience more important. So LoC role exaggerated.

Role of LoC is complex Extreme internals stressed by unavoidable events, LoC more complex than once thought (Krause 1986).

Evaluation

Comprehensive review Explained why studies produced different findings when looking at same variables (e.g. stress) – because internals and externals respond differently. Useful contribution.

Issues of reliability Selected studies may have weaknesses (e.g. social desirability bias), Rotter did not check quality.

Evaluation

Applications of the research Counselling can help students shift from external to internal, can improve academic progress.

Biased questionnaires Students may answer questionnaires to make themselves 'look good' (social desirability bias), may explain gender difference because males less likely to admit stress.

Evaluation

Changed our view of LoC Extreme internals not immune from stress (self-blame), so study presents complex and more accurate view of LoC.

Biased sample Ethnic mix not representative of retired people in USA. White under-represented, black/African American over-represented. Cannot generalise to all retired people or people generally.

Theory 3: Theory of planned behaviour

Key concepts of the TPB

Ajzen (1985, 1991) proposed the TPB to explain how people control voluntary behaviours.

Intention is the central concept, which is affected by three sources:

1. Personal attitudes Balance of the person's favourable and unfavourable attitudes towards own behaviour.

2. Subjective norms Person's beliefs about whether people who matter to them approve or disapprove of their behaviour.

3. Perceived behavioural control (PBC) How much control we believe we have over own behaviour.

Indirect influence on intentions, e.g. the more control I believe I have over my weight, the stronger my intention to lose weight.

Direct influence on intentions, e.g. the more control I believe I have, the longer and harder I will try to lose weight.

Evaluation

Research support for the TPB Research showed that attitudes, norms and PBC influenced intentions, which then influenced actual alcohol consumption (Hagger et al. 2011).

Not a full explanation Gambling behaviour of teenagers not predicted by intentions, and TPB not useful for interventions (Miller and Howell 2005).

Lack of support from some studies Attitudes, norms and PBC all affected by stress, so do not predict behaviour in way TPB suggests (Louis et al. 2009).

Short-term versus long-term Intention is a good predictor of not drinking within 5 weeks but not over longer period. So TPB not applicable to real-life behaviour change (McEachan et al. 2011).

Louis et al. (2009)

Aims Test TPB to explain health decision-making and stress.

Procedure Questionnaires measured 154 male and female students' healthy-eating behaviour in terms of personal attitudes, subjective norms, perceived behavioural control and intentions to eat healthily or unhealthily.

Life stress and perceptions of body image also measured.

Findings

Attitudes and control predicted intentions to eat healthily but norms did not.

Small effect of perceived control on healthy-eating intentions.

Subjective norms favouring healthy eating did predict intentions to eat unhealthily, but only at low levels of stress.

Conclusions Only partial support for TPB: effects of attitudes, norms and control on intentions depended on stress. Not part of theory.

Evaluation

Practical applications Shows best way to target resources: increase control and reduce stress, ignore social pressure.

Self-report measures Questionnaire data, subjective measures of intentions but not objective measures of behaviour.

Cooke et al. (2016)

Aims Review research into links between TPB, intention to consume alcohol and actual alcohol consumption.

Procedure Reviewed 40 studies of intentions to drink alcohol, personal attitudes, norms and perceived control.

Some studies measured self-efficacy.

Five categories of consumption (e.g. getting drunk, heavy episodic drinking).

Findings Positive correlation between:

- Intentions to consume and consumption.
- Intentions and attitudes (especially for episodic drinkers).
- Subjective norms and perceived control.
- Self-efficacy and both intention to drink and actual consumption (more strongly than perceived control).

Conclusions TPB is useful to understand intentions to drink. Interventions should target attitudes and intentions.

Evaluation

Relatively large number of studies 40 studies much better than median for most reviews (usually about three studies), gives confidence in conclusions.

Not cause-and-effect Many correlations between elements of the TPB but very few experimental studies. 'We do not need any more correlational studies of the TPB' (Sniehotta et al. 2014).

Theory 4: Self-efficacy theory

Key concepts of the theory

Self-efficacy is the belief in one's own ability to perform a task successfully, central to behavioural change.

Awareness of self-efficacy comes from four sources:

1. Mastery experiences Experience of performing task successfully means you learn about your own capability and feel confident performing future tasks.

2. Vicarious reinforcement Your self-efficacy increases when you observe someone else performing a task successfully.

Especially if you perceive them as similar to you.

3. Social persuasion Encouragement from others (using words) increases self-efficacy, adds to belief we can succeed.

Source has to be credible (e.g. qualified).

4. Emotional states Stress and anxiety reduce self-efficacy (e.g. being 'evaluated'), we expect to fail and do.

Evaluation

Support from research Self-efficacy linked to several health behaviours, can be increased leading to change (Strecher et al. 1986).

Effective practical applications Break target behaviour into achievable tasks (easiest first), use relaxation training to reduce stress.

Definition and measurement issues Some self-efficacy scales are unclear and do not measure self-efficacy. Or self-efficacy confused with confidence or self-esteem (Eastman and Marzillier 1984).

Backfire effects Increasing self-efficacy lowered performance on next task, led to over-confidence and less effort (Vancouver et al. 2002).

Bandura and Adams (1977)

Aims To investigate role of self-efficacy in the treatment of snake phobia, by using systematic desensitisation (reducing emotional arousal) which should enhance self-efficacy and reduce avoidance of snakes.

Procedure Ten people with snake phobias assessed on 29 tasks with a snake:

- Avoidance.
- Fear arousal, self-rating on scale of 1 to 10.
- Self-efficacy, self-rating on scale of 0 to 100.

Given treatment and assessed again.

Findings

Higher self-efficacy and lower arousal after treatment.

Positive correlation between self-efficacy and avoidance.

Conclusions The treatment helped participants increase self-efficacy, supports predictions of Bandura's theory.

Evaluation

Standardised procedures Same tasks for everyone, experience of procedure identical, so findings not due to confounding variables.

Self-reports Subjective measures of fear and self-efficacy, may be influenced by social desirability bias and therefore over- or under-reported the role of self-efficacy.

Marlatt et al. (1995)

Aims Review research into links between self-efficacy and aspects of addiction.

Procedure Wide range of studies identified which had investigated link between types of self-efficacy and various addictions.

Findings of the review

- Resistance self-efficacy: when low and combined with peer influence, predicts alcohol and nicotine use by adolescents.
- Harm-reduction self-efficacy: can be increased if adolescent already drinking/smoking.
- Coping self-efficacy: when low means alcoholics stay longer in treatment.
- Recovery self-efficacy: helps addicts 'bounce back' from relapse.

Conclusions Interventions should target self-efficacy to reduce self-harm of drug through achievable targets, extra support, and identifying triggering situations.

Evaluation

Comprehensive and thorough Wide variety of studies, several types of self-efficacy considered at different stages of addiction process.

Subjective selection of studies Researchers decided which studies to include but did not describe the selection criteria used. Conclusions could be based on biased selection.

Content area A
Multiple-choice questions

Defining health and stress

1. 'Health is the absence of illness' is part of the _____ definition.
(a) WHO.
(b) Continuum.
(c) Biopsychosocial.
(d) Biomedical

2. The biomedical definition focuses on _____ causes of illness.
(a) Biological.
(b) Social.
(c) Psychological.
(d) Cultural.

3. Increased heart rate is part of:
(a) Perceived coping ability.
(b) Psychological stress.
(c) Physiological stress.
(d) Long-term stress.

4. Social support is an example of:
(a) An internal coping resource.
(b) A stressor.
(c) An environmental demand.
(d) An external coping resource.

Defining addiction

1. An example of a behavioural addiction is:
(a) Gambling.
(b) Caffeine dependency.
(c) Smoking.
(d) Alcoholism.

2. The most important risk factor in adolescence is:
(a) Stress.
(b) Genes.
(c) Family.
(d) Peers.

3. Griffiths says there are _____ components of addiction.
(a) 2.
(b) 3.
(c) 5.
(d) 6.

4. Term that means that addictive behaviour comes to dominate the individual's life:
(a) Tolerance.
(b) Conflict.
(c) Salience.
(d) Relapse.

Theory 1: Health belief model

1. Believing you might be vulnerable to becoming ill is:
(a) Perceived susceptibility.
(b) Perceived seriousness.
(c) A perceived barrier.
(d) Not part of the model.

2. An example of an internal cue to action is:
(a) Pain.
(b) Advice from your doctor.
(c) Media campaigns.
(d) Knowing people with the illness.

3. Belief in your ability to change your own behaviour is:
(a) A cue to action.
(b) Perceived seriousness.
(c) Self-efficacy.
(d) A demographic variable.

4. Bowel and colon cancer screening was investigated by:
(a) Rosenstock *et al.*
(b) Zimmerman and Vernberg.
(c) Carpenter.
(d) Williamson and Wardle.

Studies related to theory 1

1. Becker *et al.*'s participants were:
(a) Children with asthma.
(b) Children with type I diabetes.
(c) Mothers of children with asthma.
(d) Fathers of children with asthma.

2. Becker *et al.*'s measurements were:
(a) Subjective only.
(b) Objective only.
(c) Both subjective and objective.
(d) Neither subjective nor objective.

3. Carpenter concluded that the two key components of the HBM are:
(a) Perceived susceptibility and seriousness.
(b) Perceived seriousness and barriers.
(c) Perceived barriers and benefits.
(d) Perceived susceptibility and benefits.

4. Carpenter's review did not include studies of:
(a) Self-efficacy.
(b) Perceived susceptibility.
(c) Perceived benefits.
(d) Perceived barriers.

Theory 2: Locus of control and Rotter (1966)

1. Internals generally do not:
(a) Take responsibility for their failures.
(b) Blame themselves.
(c) Feel they have control over events.
(d) Attribute their successes to chance.

2. Rotter's questionnaire:
(a) Has 29 pairs of statements.
(b) Has 14 'internal' and 15 'external' statements.
(c) Is an unreliable measure.
(d) Is called the 'Locus of Control Scale'.

3. Avtgis investigated locus of control and:
(a) Exams.
(b) Conformity.
(c) Drinking.
(d) Obesity.

4. In his review, Rotter did not check the:
(a) Number of studies.
(b) Quality of studies.
(c) Reliability of his scale.
(d) Validity of his scale.

Studies related to theory 2

1. Abouserie's participants were:
(a) Office workers.
(b) Police officers.
(c) Nurses.
(d) Students.

2. Students can improve their academic progress by:
(a) Becoming more external.
(b) Becoming more internal.
(c) Ignoring environmental demands.
(d) Studying less.

3. The questionnaire in Krause's study included:
(a) Both open and closed items.
(b) Just open items.
(c) Just closed items.
(d) Just multiple-choice items.

4. Krause found that extreme internals blame themselves for failing to cope with:
(a) Controllable stressors.
(b) Predictable stressors.
(c) Unavoidable stressors.
(d) All of the above.

Theory 3: Theory of planned behaviour

1. According to the theory of planned behaviour, the key influence on behaviour is:
(a) Subjective norms.
(b) Intentions.
(c) Personal attitudes.
(d) Perceived behavioural control.

2. Only _____ affect/affects behaviour both directly and indirectly:
(a) Personal attitudes.
(b) Subjective norms.
(c) Perceived behavioural control.
(d) Intentions.

3. Hagger *et al.* (2011) studied:
(a) Drinking behaviour.
(b) Smoking.
(c) Gambling.
(d) Cocaine use.

4. McEachan *et al.* (2011) found the TPB was poor at predicting change more than _____ after intentions formed.
(a) 5 days.
(b) 5 years.
(c) 5 months.
(d) 5 weeks.

Studies related to theory 3

1. Louis *et al.* (2009) studied intentions to:
(a) Drink less.
(b) Give up smoking.
(c) Eat healthily.
(d) Stop gambling.

2. The questionnaires in Louis *et al.*'s study:
(a) Collected objective data.
(b) Measured intentions.
(c) Measured actual behaviours.
(d) Avoided social desirability bias.

3. Cooke *et al.* (2016) concluded that interventions should target:
(a) Just personal attitudes.
(b) Subjective norms.
(c) Both attitudes and intentions.
(d) Perceived behavioural control.

4. According to Sniehotta *et al.*, we do not need any more studies of the theory of planned behaviour that are:
(a) Studies of cause and effect.
(b) Experimental studies.
(c) Correlational studies.
(d) Observational studies.

Theory 4: Self-efficacy theory

1. People with low self-efficacy:
(a) Give up easily.
(b) Know they can perform a task successfully.
(c) Like a challenge.
(d) Are good at overcoming obstacles.

2. Having a trainer say to you 'You can do it!' is an example of:
(a) A new experience.
(b) Vicarious reinforcement.
(c) An emotional state.
(d) Social persuasion.

3. Strecher *et al.*'s review found that self-efficacy:
(a) Does not predict weight loss.
(b) Can be increased.
(c) Has no correlation with contraceptive use.
(d) Cannot predict long-term behaviour change.

4. Vancouver *et al.* found that self-efficacy can:
(a) Lower performance on the current task.
(b) Lead to more effort next time.
(c) Lower confidence.
(d) Backfire.

Studies relating to theory 4

1. Bandura and Adams investigated the effect of self-efficacy on:
(a) Weight loss.
(b) Treatment for snake phobia.
(c) Reducing alcohol intake.
(d) Condom use.

2. Bandura and Adams measured self-efficacy on a scale of:
(a) 1 to 10.
(b) 0 to 10.
(c) 0 to 100.
(d) 1 to 100.

3. Marlatt *et al.* studied _____ types of self-efficacy.
(a) 5.
(b) 4.
(c) 3.
(d) 2.

4. Marlatt *et al.*'s study included:
(a) Criteria for selecting studies.
(b) Their own data.
(c) Just a few studies.
(d) Explanations of what previous studies found.

And here is a word search for you!

You have ten terms from content area A to find!

B	X	G	I	N	T	E	N	T	I	O	N	S	P	L
L	Y	T	I	F	X	K	Q	Z	X	G	X	N	H	W
W	A	Y	Z	O	B	G	B	K	L	A	G	G	L	M
R	X	B	C	J	F	P	T	C	G	V	P	K	M	B
T	L	J	O	T	D	N	Z	V	T	V	R	F	K	I
U	S	F	J	U	V	B	A	N	D	U	R	A	F	Z
D	Y	T	V	Y	S	H	Y	U	S	B	X	J	U	R
M	S	B	R	Q	Z	E	N	B	U	I	Z	Z	W	R
D	H	E	I	E	B	Z	R	J	Q	O	P	Z	P	E
X	X	B	L	N	S	D	C	I	B	M	X	Z	M	L
J	M	B	W	F	T	S	Z	N	E	E	M	A	B	A
U	O	A	F	P	E	E	O	Q	H	D	E	C	M	P
X	B	R	G	B	J	F	R	R	N	I	S	J	A	S
C	K	R	L	B	Y	N	F	N	Z	C	H	T	S	E
V	O	I	Z	Q	F	B	G	I	A	A	M	X	T	L
J	D	E	L	T	O	C	A	N	C	L	T	N	E	G
L	U	R	J	I	X	N	V	P	P	A	Z	O	R	W
I	H	S	K	R	K	G	U	Q	P	S	C	M	Y	P
I	K	G	A	O	K	I	Q	X	M	R	L	Y	A	G
D	X	S	R	W	M	X	V	K	Z	A	S	Q	O	X
I	K	H	X	H	A	D	D	I	C	T	I	O	N	V

Word search answers

INTENTIONS
SELFEFFICACY
BARRIERS
BANDURA
MASTERY
ADDICTION
STRESSOR
INTERNAL
BIOMEDICAL
RELAPSE

"How are you not seeing this? Of course doughnuts are a hole food!"

MCQ answers

Defining health and stress 1D, 2A, 3C, 4D
Defining addiction 1A, 2D, 3D, 4C
Theory 1: Health belief model 1A, 2A, 3C, 4D
Studies related to theory 1 1C, 2C, 3C, 4A
Theory 2: Locus of control and Rotter (1966) 1D, 2A, 3B, 4B
Studies related to theory 2 1D, 2B, 3A, 4C
Theory 3: Theory of planned behaviour 1B, 2C, 3A, 4D
Studies related to theory 3 1C, 2B, 3C, 4C
Theory 4: Self-efficacy theory 1A, 2D, 3B, 4D
Studies related to theory 4 1B, 2C, 3B, 4D

Content area A
Assessment guidance

Note that the Unit 3 exam is slightly different from the Unit 1 exam.

The examination

Unit 3 (Health psychology) is externally assessed by one examination. You will be awarded a mark for the whole paper – Distinction (D), Merit (M), Pass (P), Near Pass (NP) or Unclassified (U).

The exam is 2 hours. The total number of marks for the paper is 70.

The paper is divided into three sections (A, B and C), each with up to 30 marks.

Each section may contain material from all content areas A, B and C.

How to answer exam-style questions

On the next spread we provide some examples of student answers to exam-style questions but here is some general guidance.

Type of question	Example question	Example structure for answer
Short description questions	Define what is meant by 'addiction'. (1)	One-sentence answer. Description required, include psychological terms to provide detail, e.g. dependence, relapse.
	Explain what is meant by 'addiction'. (2)	Provide two sentences – your definition + some extra information (such as an example or a justification).
	Explain what is meant by 'addiction'. (3)	This time you should provide three sentences – your definition + some elaboration + an example. See next spread for an illustration.
Short evaluation questions	Explain **one** strength of the theory of planned behaviour. (2)	Two-sentence answer required: • Point: State your point. • Evidence: Provide evidence to support your point. We have presented all evaluation points using P + E and also T – see our explanation of PET on page 5.
Context questions	See question 2 on next spread.	For 2 marks: • State some psychology (a theory, concept or study). • Link to scenario.
Extended open-response questions	See question 4 on next spread.	For 9 marks you should write about 450 words with roughly equal description and evaluation. You will help the examiner, and yourself, if you construct an answer which follows a plan, e.g. seven paragraphs of about 50–70 words. Before you begin, identify what will go in each paragraph. Plus a conclusion if the command word is *assess*, *compare* or *evaluate* (not needed for *discuss*).

Information on how your answers are marked is given on the next Assessment page at the end of content area B, page 70.

! **Health warning** The material on assessment advice is not from the exam board. It is our interpretation of the 'rules of the game'.

Command terms

All questions contain a *command term*. There are two key pieces of information in the command term:
1. It tells you whether you must supply description (AO1), application (AO2) and/or evaluation (AO3).
2. It tells you how much to provide, e.g. the term *define* means a brief answer whereas *explain* means provide some further explanation. The marks for the question are also a clue.

Command terms are explained in full on page 108.

Timing

Timing is always important in exams because it is fixed.

You must spend sufficient time on each answer in relation to the marks but not too much (otherwise you don't give full enough answers to other questions).

As there are 70 marks and you have 120 minutes for the Unit 3 exam, that means you have about 1¾ minutes per mark.

This is slightly more time than you have for the Unit 1 exam which was 1¼ minutes per mark – we think you can write about 35 words in 1¼ minutes so for 1¾ minutes it's about 50 words.

So, for Unit 3 a 9-mark essay should be about 450 words and you have about 16–20 minutes to write it.

A 6-mark question should be about 300 words and take about 10 minutes.

Revision guidance

Making a revision card

If you used our Year 1 'Certificate' book, you will be familiar with the idea of using cues to recall information.

A cue

A cue is a thing that serves as a reminder of something else. If I say 'Griffiths' that might serve as a cue for you to recall there are six features of addiction.

Psychologists have investigated the value of cues in remembering. They act as a reminder of what else you know.

1. Construct revision cards

For every spread you study, create a card for revision (if you wish you can create more than one card, e.g. one for each of the research studies).

On the card draw a table with two columns:

- Column 1 = cue word(s).
- Column 2 = a small amount of text to remind you of important information.

2. See if your cues work

Cover the right-hand column on your revision card and for each cue write down what you can recall for the right-hand side.

Then check how much you remembered. Maybe you need to add a word or date to your cue to help you.

3. Test your recall again

Repeat step 2 and see if you remember more next time.

4. Test memory using cues

This time see if you can just recall the list of cues. In the exam all you need to remember is the cues and then the rest should be available to you from your memory.

Psychological research shows that cues are the best way to enhance recall – and also that testing enhances memory – see below.

There's more on revision cards on page 71.

And effective revision is discussed on page 109.

Preparing for the exam

Exams mean revising – but the secret is that revising should happen now. Start revising as you go along.

We have divided this book into spreads. Each spread represents one chunk of the specification.

When you are studying each spread you should prepare a revision card for the content of that spread.

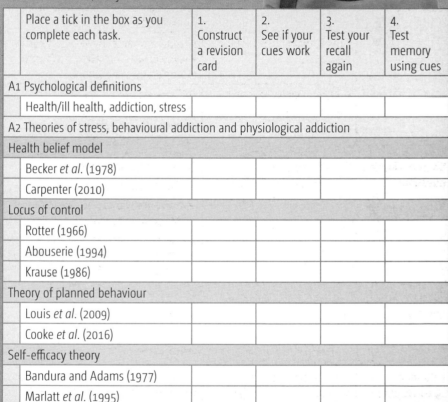

Revision checklist for content area A

Below are the key topics for content area A.

Follow the four steps on the left for successful revision. Do it now, not just before the exams.

Place a tick in the box as you complete each task.	1. Construct a revision card	2. See if your cues work	3. Test your recall again	4. Test memory using cues
A1 Psychological definitions				
Health/ill health, addiction, stress				
A2 Theories of stress, behavioural addiction and physiological addiction				
Health belief model				
Becker *et al.* (1978)				
Carpenter (2010)				
Locus of control				
Rotter (1966)				
Abouserie (1994)				
Krause (1986)				
Theory of planned behaviour				
Louis *et al.* (2009)				
Cooke *et al.* (2016)				
Self-efficacy theory				
Bandura and Adams (1977)				
Marlatt *et al.* (1995)				

The testing effect

Your memory is stored in cells in your brain. There are links made in your brain between different memories. Each time you travel down these links, they become stronger.

Therefore, each time you try to recall something your memory is strengthened.

In one study (Roediger and Karpicke 2006) there were two groups of participants.

The testing group read a passage of text and then closed their book and tested how much they remembered.

The studying group read the same passage of text and then reread it a few times.

Both groups then took a test after one week. You can see which group remembered most.

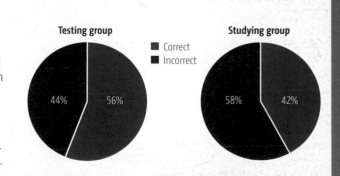

Testing group — Correct 56%, Incorrect 44%

Studying group — Correct 42%, Incorrect 58%

Content area A
Practice questions, answers and feedback

On this spread we look at some typical student answers to exam-style questions. The comments provided from an experienced teacher (in green) show what is good and bad in each answer. Learning how to provide effective exam answers is a SKILL. Practise it.

Question 1: Explain what is meant by 'health as a continuum'. (2)

Hamid's answer

Health as a continuum suggests that the concept has two ends (health and ill health) and really everyone is somewhere in between. For example, most people are towards the healthy end because they have maybe one illness. Very few people have total good health.

Teacher comments

Questions asking for a definition may begin with *give* or *define* (or even *identify* or *state*) and be worth 1 mark. In such cases even a single word answer may be sufficient. But if the question starts with *explain* that means define it and give some further information, such as an example.

Hamid has done just that, so the full 2 marks.

Jacob's answer

Health as a continuum means health is on a continuum, something that goes from one end to another with shades of grey in between.

Jacob's and Bronwen's answers are similar in length but Jacob has really wasted the first part of his answer with repetition, and the second part explains a continuum but not health as a continuum. Altogether there isn't enough for any marks.

Bronwen's answer

A continuum means there aren't just two categories, health and ill health. It's not one or the other.

Bronwen's answer is worth 1 out of 2 marks. The second sentence just restates the first one.

Question 2: Greg is worried about how much alcohol he drinks. He knows that it is affecting his health but he also enjoys drinking. Most of his friends drink and they haven't discussed cutting down or giving up.

He has tried in the past to cut down through 'willpower', but it hasn't worked. Greg has heard of 'Dry January' and thinks he'll give it a go as it's not far off. He might even get people to sponsor him.

The theory of planned behaviour identifies several concepts that can explain the likelihood of someone behaving healthily or unhealthily.

Explain how **one** of these concepts could help predict Greg's future behaviour. (2)

Hamid's answer

The TPB basically says that we can predict how someone will behave if we know what their intentions are. If we know their intentions are strong then they are likely to change. Intentions are the result of things like your personal attitudes or your beliefs about what other people think. These all impact on what you decide you want to do. Without intentions your behaviour won't change.

Students quite often write lengthy answers when they are not clear what they want to say. Perhaps they hope that the examiner will find something worthwhile in their answer.

Hamid has spotted that the question is about the TBP and just written anything he can remember, giving a very basic explanation of the TPB. He has actually identified three concepts in the theory (only one was asked for) and failed to apply it to Greg, so a very generous 1 mark out of 2.

Jacob's answer

One concept in the TPB is beliefs about what other people think. In Greg's case his friends do drink. This would affect Greg's intentions to change his behaviour because he knows they are not anti-drinking and don't intend giving up.

By contrast Jacob responds directly to the question by identifying one appropriate concept and giving an example from the scenario and then predicts Greg's behaviour. A full 2 marks.

Bronwen's answer

Intentions are the key concept in the TPB, which is basically the expression of what a person decides they are going to do. In this case, Greg has decided to stop drinking.

Bronwen's answer shows knowledge of the TPB but the link to the scenario is weak. So only 1 mark. Always link your answer to the scenario if the question asks for it. If you don't then you will limit the amount of marks you can gain.

Question 3: Describe the procedure of the study by Krause (1986) Stress and coping: Reconceptualising the role of locus of control beliefs. (3)

Hamid's answer

About 350 retired people were tested for depression, life events and locus of control. The aim was to see if locus of control was a better predictor of stress than life events.

Hamid's answer starts well with some good details but the second sentence focuses on aims so is not relevant, 1 out of 3 marks.

Jacob's answer

The participants in the study were retired people over the age of 65. They were given various questionnaires to answer on depression, life events and locus of control. The questions had open as well as closed questions so that data could be collected beyond the researchers' expectations.

It looks like Jacob has made a point when revising of ensuring he has three points to make. He has made these clear to the examiner who thus has no trouble in awarding the full 3 marks.

Bronwen's answer

This study aimed to investigate whether locus of control was related to how much stress people feel. Krause studied older people using a questionnaire and did find that internal LoC helped some of the time.

Bronwen has failed to focus on the question which asked only for the procedure used in the study. Therefore, only a small part of her answer is creditworthy. However, this part is so minimal ('Krause studied older people using a questionnaire') that Bronwen would gain no marks.

Question 4: Laurence runs a weight loss class. He is a firm believer in helping his students to relax so they get the most out of his classes. He asks people who have lost weight in the previous week to stand up and explain how they did it. Laurence is as encouraging as possible, but he also knows that his students need targets to help them lose weight.

Discuss self-efficacy theory to explain why Laurence's students are likely to lose weight. (9)

Hamid's answer

Self-efficacy theory (by Bandura) states that people who have confidence in their ability to do something, are more likely to be able to do it. It sounds like Laurence is someone who believes in this because his approach with his students aims to boost their confidence, i.e. boost their self-efficacy. For example, he asks them to stand up and explain why they were successful at losing weight and this will help the individual be more self-confident. This also provides vicarious reinforcement for the others because they see someone else can be successful which encourages them to try.

There are three other key factors that can increase our self-efficacy – mastery experiences is one of them. This may explain why Laurence tells students to set targets because that means they have opportunities to achieve something definite, which will enhance their self-efficacy.

Another factor is social persuasion which links to Laurence being as encouraging as he can. For social persuasion to be successful it is important that the source of the message has perceived credibility so that's why it's very important that Laurence does this to raise his students' confidence in their own abilities.

The fourth factor is emotional state. If someone is feeling stressed or anxious this reduces confidence and leads a person to start to expect failure. Laurence recognises this in his attempts to help his students relax so they can get the most out of his classes.

There is research support for the success of self-efficacy theory. A review by Strecher *et al.* showed that there was a strong correlation between people who had high self-efficacy and those who changed their behaviour, e.g. in controlling weight (as in Laurence's case). In particular, experimental studies showed that increasing self-efficacy did cause changes in health-related behaviours. This research is important in showing that it is not just a theory but has proven practical use.

Another strength is that the theory suggests different ways to change behaviour. As outlined above there are four recommendations of things to do. Breaking a task down into these components helps an instructor like Laurence to improve the self-efficacy of his clients to lose weight. It is a key aim of any psychological theory that it should be useful in practice.

One weakness is that, even though there are these clear factors, they are not specific to self-efficacy theory. It may be that self-efficacy is little more than increased self-confidence or increased self-esteem. This means that you don't really need the concept of self-efficacy at all. Studies that assess it may be measuring other things.

Another weakness with the concept of self-efficacy (and also self-confidence) is that sometimes too much may be a negative thing. Vancouver *et al.* found that when they increased self-efficacy on playing a game, participants then played better on the current game but later actually did worse. Whereas if they withheld positive feedback this initially resulted in lower self-efficacy but actually led to improved performance. This suggests that trying to boost self-efficacy may lead to over-confidence.

The take-home message is that probably some form of increased self-confidence helps people tackle hard-to-achieve targets (such as weight loss) but there is a danger that people think being confident is all that is needed whereas the bottom line is that it is hard work.

548 words

Teacher comments

Hamid has written a beautifully structured essay with a clear plan. Don't be afraid to make your essay plan really obvious because it helps an examiner identify the points you are making.

There are three important things Hamid has achieved. (1) There is a good balance between description and evaluation, (2) there are clear and sustained links throughout to the scenario/context, (3) the key criteria in the mark scheme (see page 70) are demonstrated, e.g. the knowledge is *detailed* and the evaluation is *well-developed*.

It is always tempting to write too much description – on each page in this book we have written about 600 words in the main panel on description. The most you need in an essay for description is maybe 200 words. We have *explained* the information to help you understand it, but you must select it carefully in an essay. It is important not to make your essay too descriptive as there are an equal amount of marks for description, links to the scenario and evaluation points. An imbalanced essay will reduce the overall amount of marks you can gain.

That said, it is important to include detail in your description (AO1) and demonstrate your understanding – so always develop any point you make. For example, the sentence in the first paragraph, 'This also provides vicarious reinforcement for the others...' could have ended here but the addition of '...because they see someone else can be successful which encourages them to try' is a key element in displaying understanding.

The application (AO2) is demonstrated with specific references and even quotes from the scenario, e.g. 'students relax so they can get the most out of his classes'. It is not enough just to mention 'Laurence', you need to engage with the elements in the scenario. If you just write a description of a theory without applying it, you will lose marks.

In the evaluation (AO3) you should notice the PET rule in action (described on page 5) and also notice there are no dates for the research. We provide dates in the book but you don't have to include them.

Finally, there is a conclusion here – though the command term *discuss* doesn't require one. It still can be evidence of analysis (AO3) as long as you don't just give a summary.

As it stands this essay is unrealistically long. If we removed the final two paragraphs it is still definitely a distinction essay and very nearly full marks (it might be seen as a little imbalanced without the penultimate paragraph).

Practice

No athlete would dream of running a race without doing many practice runs of the right distance and within a set time. Always write exam answers in the allotted time – allow yourself about 20 minutes for a 9-mark essay (it is precisely 15¾ minutes but it pays to spend a bit of extra time on the essays). You should prepare before starting to write your answer and maybe even write a few notes but then write the answer with the clock ticking.

See pages 72–73 and 110–111 for more student answers with comments on what is good and bad.

Causes of stress: Life events and Rahe *et al.* (1970)

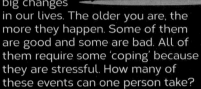

Luckiest man alive

We've all experienced big changes in our lives. The older you are, the more they happen. Some of them are good and some are bad. All of them require some 'coping' because they are stressful. How many of these events can one person take?

Frane Selak is a Croatian man who has been called 'the world's unluckiest lucky man'. This is mostly because he has escaped death seven times – a train crash, a plane crash, a bus crash, exploding cars (twice), run over by a bus, another car accident. 40 people died in these accidents. Selak was incredibly unlucky to be involved, but incredibly lucky to survive.

Then in 2003 he won the equivalent of £700,000 in the Croatian national lottery. Perhaps his luck was turning. He bought two houses and a boat. But he found that he couldn't stand the pressure of having a lot of money, so he gave most of the rest away.

Specification terms

Stress See page 10.

Life events Significant and relatively infrequent experiences/occasions in people's lives that cause stress. They are stressful because we have to expend psychological energy coping with changed circumstances.

Why did Rahe *et al.* choose to study sailors aboard ships? Because a ship is a 'closed' environment where everyone experiences the same stressors and viruses, etc. So if some people become ill and some don't, that's because of differences between them as individuals, not because of differences in their environment.

Role of life events in stress

What are life events?

For most of us, the main sources of *stress* in our lives are the big events, the important things that happen from time to time – getting married or divorced, someone close to us dying, a change in our financial situation (for better or worse), a new addition to the family.

These *life events* are not everyday happenings. We experience them as stressful because we have to make a significant psychological adjustment to cope with the changed situation – sometimes life events are referred to as 'life changes'. The bigger the event, the more we need to adjust, so the more stressful it is. This is just as true for positive events (getting married) as it is for negative ones (getting divorced).

The effects of life events are additive. If two major life events occur together you have to make an even bigger psychological adjustment.

Measuring life events

Thomas Holmes and Richard Rahe (1967) were the first to focus on the importance of life events and, in order to conduct research on the effects, they created the *Social readjustment rating scale* (SRRS) to measure life events. You can learn more about this by doing the Get active on the facing page.

The SRRS is a list of 43 life events, each one being given a number of life change units (LCUs). This number reflects the amount of adjustment needed to adapt to the life event. For example, divorce has 73 LCUs associated with it, marriage has 50 and death of a close friend 37. To obtain an overall score a person has to indicate all the events they have experienced over a set period of time and the level of stress is calculated by adding up the LCUs for these events.

Life events and illness

Researchers have tried to find out whether illnesses (physical and psychological) are associated with stressful life events. The SRRS has been used to do this. Most studies work out a total LCU score for each participant from their life events over the previous six or 12 months. Rahe (1972) suggested that a person scoring under 150 has a 30% probability of experiencing a stress-related illness in the following year. That probability increases to 50% for someone scoring between 150 and 299 LCUs. It increases again to 80% for someone who scores over 300 LCUs.

Rahe *et al.* (1970) Prediction of near-future health change from subjects' preceding life changes

Aims

Richard Rahe *et al.* wanted to see if scores on a life events questionnaire predicted the onset of illness.

Procedure

The researchers studied 2664 US Navy personnel aboard three ships (aircraft carriers). The participants completed a questionnaire called the *Schedule of recent experiences* (SRE) which was the forerunner to the SRRS. They were asked to identify every life event experienced in the six months before they went on a tour of duty overseas. A total LCU score was calculated for each participant for this six-month period.

During the tour of duty aboard ship, every illness (including trivial ones) was reported to the ship's medical unit. After returning from the tour of duty, an independent researcher reviewed all the medical records and calculated an illness score for each participant. Neither the participants nor the medical staff onboard the ships were aware of the purpose of the study.

Findings

There was a small but significant *positive correlation* (+.118) between the LCU scores and the illness scores. The participants who had the most stressful life events in the six months before active service also had the most illnesses in the subsequent six months aboard ship.

Conclusions

Rahe *et al.* concluded that life events are a reasonably robust predictor of later stress-related illness. Most of the reported illnesses were minor (because the participants were generally very fit and healthy). However, it is important not to overstate the influence of life events because the correlation was relatively weak.

GET ACTIVE Find out your stress score

We have seen that life events are measured with Holmes and Rahe's (1967) SRRS. Research suggests there should be a link between stress measured by the SRRS and physical/psychological symptoms.

You can complete the SRRS yourself online: tinyurl.com/y37ulj7q. You will get a score reflecting life event stress. This is the total number of life change units (LCUs) for the events you have experienced in the past 12 months.

1. *Do you think your score truly represents the stress you feel you have experienced over that time?*

2. *Having completed the SRRS, can you identify any problems with it as a measure of stress?*

Getting married is usually a joyful event. But it's still stressful because it's a big change that you have to adjust to.

Evaluation

Support from research

One strength is a large body of evidence showing that life events are linked to illness.

For example, Raija Lietzén *et al.* (2011) followed nearly 17,000 healthy people. At the start of the study none of them had *asthma* but, after two years, 192 had developed it. Life events were measured over the same two-year period. There was a moderate but significant positive correlation between life event stress and onset of asthma. This link could not be explained by other influences such as the presence of smokers in the home.

This is a particularly powerful finding because the study is *prospective* – it predicted future illness from past life events.

Positive and negative life events

One weakness of the life events approach is that it assumes all change is stressful, so it muddles together both positive and negative events.

Many psychologists have questioned this assumption. They suggest that positive and negative events have different effects. Jay Turner and Blair Wheaton (1997) found that negative events accounted for most of the stress measured by the SRRS. Therefore, the life events scale may not be *valid* because it gives us a global (overall) measure of stress.

This means a better approach might be to look at the effects of specific life *stressors*, especially negative ones.

Evaluation

Large sample size

One strength of the study was the large number of participants.

There were 2664 participants in this study. This is a large number by the standard of most psychological research. A large sample is not necessarily a strength in itself. But it does mean the participants are more likely to be representative of the population. In this case, the sailors came from three different ships and varied in age, rank, educational level and degree of naval experience.

This means the conclusions drawn about the links between life events, stress and illness have greater validity and are generalisable to the wider population.

Self-report method

One weakness of the study is that it used a *self-report method*.

Items on scales such as the SRE and SRRS are more like general categories than specific events. For example, 'divorce' is not a single event but a process involving several events. This means items are open to different interpretations by participants. Bruce Dohrenwend *et al.* (1990) found that 'serious illness and injury' was interpreted in a variety of ways from 'sprained arm' to 'life-threatening heart attack'. People who are under severe stress when they complete a stress scale usually place the most negative interpretation on the items.

This means that scales such as the SRRS may not give us a valid assessment of the stress people are experiencing.

Exam-style questions

Gaby and Jules moved in together last year after going out with each other for two years. Not long afterwards Gaby became pregnant. When the baby was born, Gaby and Jules were very happy even though they had to make a lot of changes. But gradually the two of them started having more and more arguments. Gaby went back to work but they still had some financial problems. Even Christmas was more stressful than usual. Worst of all, just a couple of months ago, Gaby's dad died. Throughout all this time Gaby has been getting more headaches and feeling anxious. She is finding that she cannot sleep very well and has had to take a few days off work because of illness.

1. Gaby and Jules have been experiencing several life events in the past year.

   Explain what is meant by 'life events'. (2)

2. Identify **two** life events experienced by Gaby and/or Jules. (2)

3. Explain the role of life events in the stress Gaby is experiencing. (3)

4. Rahe *et al.* (1970) carried out a study into life events.

   (a) Describe the procedure of this study. (3)

   (b) Give **one** finding from the study and use it to explain Gaby's behaviour. (2)

   (c) Explain **one** conclusion Rahe *et al.* came to. (2)

5. With reference to Gaby's experience, assess the role of life events in stress. Refer to at least **one** research study in your answer. (9)

You can read about assessment and revision issues on pages 34–35, 70–71 and 108–109.

An issue to consider

Before you move on to the next spread, think about this. Life events are the big things that happen to us. But do you think that perhaps they are not the main causes of stress?

What about the little things? Why might they be more stressful?

Specification content

B1 Stress

Causes of stress:

● Definition and role of life events in stress.

● Rahe *et al.* (1970) Prediction of near-future health change from subjects' preceding life changes.

● Including the strengths and weaknesses of using self-reports in measurement of stress.

Causes of stress: Daily hassles and Kanner *et al.* (1981)

What a load of... hassles!

Have any of the following happened to you in the last month? For each one that has, how severe was it (somewhat, moderately or extremely)?

- Misplacing or losing things.
- Too many responsibilities.
- Caring for a pet.
- Preparing meals.
- Don't like fellow workers.
- Too many interruptions.
- Physical illness.
- Not getting enough sleep
- Too many things to do.
- Concerns about weight.
- The weather.
- Transport problems.

These are from the Hassles scale by Kanner *et al.* (1981). The full scale is here: tinyurl.com/y5ohmtzu.

Specification term

Daily hassles The relatively minor but frequent aggravations and annoyances of everyday life that combine to cause us stress, such as forgetting where you have put things and niggling squabbles with other people.

Had to happen sometime didn't it? One more hassle.

Role of daily hassles in stress

What are daily hassles?

Richard Lazarus *et al.* (1980) was one of the first psychologists to argue that big infrequent *life events* are not the main sources of *stress*. After all, the research we looked at on the previous spread shows that life events have only a moderate link with illness. Instead, it is the everyday irritations and frustrations that can get on top of us and cause us to feel stressed. These are called *daily hassles*.

Primary and secondary appraisal

According to Lazarus, when we experience a hassle we first carry out a *primary appraisal*. We think about how threatening the hassle is to our psychological *health*.

If we conclude it is a threat, then we perform a *secondary appraisal* and think about how well-equipped we are to cope. This is important because it means the concept includes the idea that we *interpret* the meaning hassles have for us. They are not necessarily stressful in and of themselves. What matters is how we think about them and how we think of our ability to cope.

Measuring daily hassles

Allen Kanner *et al.* (1981) developed the *Hassles scale*. It has 117 daily hassles from seven categories: work, health, family, friends, environment, practical considerations and chance occurrences (see examples on left). Each day you select all the hassles you have experienced that day and also indicate the severity of the hassle on a scale of 1 to 3 (somewhat, moderately or extremely severe). Finally, you add up the severity scores to get a total score for that day or period of time.

Kanner *et al.* (1981) also produced the *Uplifts scale*. Uplifts are small daily 'boosts' that make us feel a bit better (e.g. enjoying spending time with friends, getting enough sleep). They counteract the effects of hassles to some extent.

Daily hassles and illness

Daily hassles threaten our health because we experience a lot of them and their effects add up. They can also make us ill through their link with life events because a life event can disrupt our normal daily routines. Life events are indirect sources of stress which affect us by creating lots more hassles. The hassles themselves are stressful because we experience them directly.

Kanner *et al.* (1981) Comparison of two modes of stress measurement: Daily hassles and uplifts versus major life events

Aims

Allen Kanner *et al.* (1981) investigated the question of whether daily hassles or life events were a better predictor of psychological *ill health*.

Procedure

The researchers devised the *Hassles and uplifts scale* (see left). A total of 100 participants (aged 45 to 64 years) completed the scale every month for nine consecutive months. At the same time they completed the *Hopkins symptom checklist*. This measured psychological symptoms of *anxiety* and *depression*. They also completed a measure of life events on two occasions – one month before the study began (to cover the previous six months) and in the tenth month.

Findings

There were significant *positive correlations* between hassle frequency and psychological symptoms at the start and end of the study (for men and women). Hassles were a significantly stronger predictor of symptoms than life events, at both the start and end of the study.

Conclusions

Kanner *et al.* concluded that daily hassles are a more reliable predictor of psychological symptoms of illness than life events. Daily hassles overlap considerably with life events. But the contribution of hassles to symptoms was strong even when the effects of life events were removed statistically.

GET ACTIVE It's the little things

The problem with hassles scales is that they are very general. Because they are designed to be completed by everyone, they include a huge range of hassles. This means that many items do not apply to – for instance – students. One solution is to devise a scale specifically to measure hassles for students. In an inspired burst of creativity, we could call it the *Student hassles scale*.

1. *Think about your day-to-day life. Make a list of the hassles you could experience (it doesn't mean you have experienced them). Have a look at the original Hassles scale for inspiration.*

2. *You could get together with other students from your class and pool your hassles.*

3. *And while we're at it, is there a better way to measure severity than just a three-point scale of somewhat/moderately/ extremely?*

'What do you mean we're a hassle?'

Evaluation

Supporting research evidence

One strength is that the role of daily hassles is supported by many studies.

For example, John Ivancevich's (1986) participants completed the Hassles scale and the *Schedule of recent experiences* (forerunner of the SRRS). Hassles were stronger predictors of poor health, poor job performance and absence from work than life events. So, in the context of work and jobs, it is everyday *stressors* that have the greatest impact on health.

There is now overwhelming evidence that daily hassles play a more significant role in illness (and therefore presumably stress) than life events.

Retrospective research

One weakness is that many of the studies into daily hassles involve *retrospective* recall.

Participants complete checklists by recalling the hassles they have experienced over a certain time period (e.g. the past month). But how accurate are participants' memories? This is an issue especially for hassles research because daily hassles are, by definition, minor and frequent. Therefore, they are easily forgotten or, alternatively magnified, so people may well under- or overestimate how many they experience.

This means that research might not accurately reflect the impact of hassles on stress or health.

Evaluation

Self-report method

One strength of the study is the use of the Hassles scale.

This is a *self-report method*, which makes sense because asking people to report their hassles is the most direct way of assessing them. An alternative would involve observing participants over a certain period of time, which would not be as practical or convenient as using a self-report measure. Self-reports also encourage openness and honesty, because participants note their responses on a *questionnaire* rather than give them face-to-face to another person.

These factors increase the *validity* of our measurements of stress.

Response bias

One weakness is that the Hassles scale may have suffered from *response bias*.

117 items makes the scale very lengthy, and participants had to complete this every month (in Kanner *et al.*'s study), plus completing the other scales as well. The items on the Hassles scale are scored in one 'direction' only. That is, for every item, 1 is always 'somewhat', 2 is always 'moderately' and 3 is always 'extremely'. It is too easy for participants to automatically choose the same response each time.

This means that the Hassles scale may not be a valid measure of the stress of daily hassles.

Exam-style questions

Anya got a new job in a different town a couple of months ago. It was a promotion so it meant she had more money. But she had to move house and her usual daily routines were disrupted. Anya used to walk to work but now she has to take the car and she often gets stuck in traffic. She feels she isn't on top of her game like she used to be. She is more disorganised, has trouble finding things when she needs them and just generally has too much to do. Anya has started getting colds more often as well as niggling muscle pains. When she measured her blood pressure it was a bit on the high side. She feels anxious and even sometimes a bit down.

1. Explain what is meant by 'daily hassles'. (2)
2. Identify **two** daily hassles experienced by Anya. (2)
3. Explain **two** differences between a life event and a daily hassle. Refer to Anya in your answer. (4)
4. Describe **one** finding of the study by Kanner *et al.* (1981). Use it explain Anya's behaviour. (3)
5. Explain how self-report is a problem when measuring stress. Refer to the study by Kanner *et al.* in your answer. (3)
6. Some psychologists argue that Anya gets ill because major life events cause her stress. Others believe that the cause is the daily hassles she faces.

   Discuss the role of daily hassles in Anya's experience of stress. In your answer, refer to life events as well as daily hassles. (9)

An issue to consider

Hassles are not stressful in themselves. They become stressful if we perceive them to be stressful and if we believe we can't cope with them.

Do you think this is true? Are there any examples from your own daily life to support this idea?

Specification content

B1 Stress

Causes of stress:

- Definition and role of daily hassles in stress.
- Kanner *et al.* (1981) Comparison of two modes of stress measurement: Daily hassles and uplifts versus major life events.
- Including the strengths and weaknesses of using self-reports in measurement of stress.

Causes of stress: The workplace and Johansson *et al.* (1978)

Specification term

Role conflict Occurs when an employee (e.g. middle manager) faces competing demands as a result of their responsibilities in the workplace. This causes stress and can lead to dissatisfaction, illness and absenteeism.

Office chair races – could be a good way of taking back control in the workplace.

Role of the workplace in stress

Role conflict

There are two major types of *role conflict*. Intra-role conflict occurs when an employee's role in the workplace presents competing demands. This could happen when roles are poorly defined and the employee has to report to two managers. Or the managers may insist that an employee performs incompatible tasks (e.g. two projects that cannot be completed at the same time).

Inter-role conflict occurs when a person has two roles with competing demands. Often, one role is work-related and the other is outside the workplace. For example, a parent may find it stressful to combine childcare with their work responsibilities (if they often have to work late hours). Or a student with a part-time job could find their employer insisting on certain hours that conflict with college time.

Effects of the work environment

Two common *stressors* arising from the work environment are temperature and noise.

Temperature Hot workplaces are associated with negative outcomes such as stress and aggressive behaviour (Parsons 2014). Being too cold is also stressful because it is a negative stimulus leading to distress/stress.

Noise Workplaces full of loud sounds can be stressful because noise is unpleasant. In particular, uncontrollable noises are particularly stressful because of lack of control, which, as we will see in the study below, is a key factor in *stress*.

Level of control

There are many aspects of the workplace related to control or lack of it. Having control of a situation allows a person to feel they have a choice. As we saw on the previous spread, in relation to *daily hassles*, stress is felt negatively when we appraise a situation as something we cannot cope with. Therefore, something that cannot be controlled (such as noise) is experienced negatively.

Johansson *et al.* (1978) Social psychological and neuroendocrine stress reactions in highly mechanised work

Aims

Gunn Johansson *et al.* (1978) wanted to compare the stress responses of two very different groups of workers in a Swedish sawmill.

Procedure

One group of participants were high-risk workers: 14 sawyers, edgers and graders whose jobs involved preparing timber. The jobs were repetitive and the workers were cut off from others in the sawmill. They had little control over their work because the pace was dictated by machine. The jobs were demanding because the task was complex and carried a lot of responsibility.

The other group were low-risk workers: 10 maintenance workers, matched with the first group in terms of education level and job experience. They had more control, greater flexibility, more contact with other workers and less responsibility.

The researchers measured illness and absenteeism levels from personnel records. To measure levels of stress hormones (*adrenaline* and *nonadrenaline*), they took urine samples from the workers four times each day for two days (once before they left home in the morning and three times during the working day). Body temperature and self-reported levels of alertness and mood at the time of urine collection were also recorded.

Findings

Levels of stress hormones were higher in the high-risk group overall. The first sample each day showed that they had higher levels even before they left home. Levels in the high-risk group increased over the day, whereas levels decreased in the low-risk group. There were more illnesses and a higher absenteeism rate among the high-risk workers and lower levels of well-being.

Conclusions

The demands of a job (in this case work overload and responsibility) interact with a lack of control to create high levels of physiological arousal in the body. This leads to the production of stress hormones (e.g. adrenaline) which may cause higher levels of illness and other negative consequences.

Evaluation

Research support for control

One strength of job control is that research confirms its importance in the experience of stress.

For instance, Hans Bosma et al. (1997) studied 10,000 British civil servants in a wide range of job grades. They found that workload was not a significant workplace stressor, but lack of control was. Employees who reported low job control at the start of the study were more likely to have heart disease five years later. This was true even after lifestyle factors were accounted for.

These findings show that lacking job control is a significant stressor that can lead to serious stress-related illnesses.

Cultural differences

One weakness is that the role of job control depends upon *culture*.

Christina Györkös et al. (2012) reviewed earlier research studies and found that a lack of job control is considered stressful in *individualist cultures* (e.g. the USA and UK). But control was seen as less desirable (and a lack of control as less damaging) in *collectivist cultures* (e.g. China). Therefore, the concept of job control may be limited to Western societies, reflecting cultural ideals of personal rights and fairness.

This suggests that lack of control is not a universally undesirable feature of the workplace that contributes to stress in all circumstances.

Evaluation

Practical application

One strength of Johansson et al.'s research is that it can help reduce stress in the workplace.

The study clearly demonstrated that a lack of control has potentially severe negative outcomes for individuals (e.g. illness) and the organisation (e.g. absenteeism). Giving workers some control over their jobs can help to remove some of these consequences. For instance, a job that involves a variety of tasks rather than following a monotonous 'production line' process can be less stressful. Interaction with other employees can also be built into jobs (perhaps by minimising the use of emails).

This shows how research can lead to changes that improve the well-being and quality of life of employees.

Not a causal effect

One weakness of the study was that it was not a 'true' *experiment*.

In a true experiment, the researchers place participants into the groups (*conditions* of the *independent variable*). This helps to cancel out any pre-existing differences between participants that might explain the findings. But Johansson et al. could not do this in the sawmill, because the employees were already assigned to their roles. So, the two groups could have differed in ways that had an effect on the outcome. For example, perhaps people in the high-risk group were more ambitious than those in the low-risk group.

This means that the *validity* of the study is low because the findings may be explained by factors other than lack of job control.

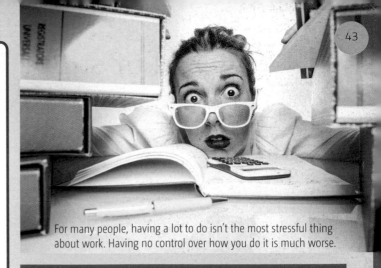

For many people, having a lot to do isn't the most stressful thing about work. Having no control over how you do it is much worse.

Exam-style questions

Kim is a full-time BTEC student who also has a part-time job in the kitchen of a well-known pizza delivery and takeaway shop. He works at the weekends and sometimes works extra shifts on a couple of evenings during the week, depending if he's needed. His boss asks him to take on these extra shifts at very short notice. Kim doesn't like the kitchen because it's very hot.

There are two people he works with who are constantly shouting. Kim has never made a whole pizza by himself. He has to produce the bases for the others. They're always criticising him for being too slow, so Kim feels the pressure is on him all the time.

1. Some psychologists believe role conflict is a source of stress in the workplace.

   (a) Explain what is meant by 'role conflict'. (2)

   (b) Identify **one** example of role conflict in Kim's workplace. (1)

   (c) Identify **two** other sources of stress Kim is experiencing at work. (2)

2. Explain the role of the workplace in stress. (3)

3. Johansson et al. (1978) studied stress reactions. For this study:

   (a) Give **one** aim. (1)

   (b) Describe **one** conclusion from this study and use it to explain Kim's behaviour. (2)

4. Evaluate the role of the workplace in Kim's level of stress. Refer to at least **one** research study in your answer. (9)

An issue to consider

Consider why role conflict could be stressful. Could it be caused by pressure from too many roles? Or could it be lack of control?

Specification content

B1 Stress

Causes of stress:

● Role of the workplace in stress: role conflict, effect of the environment, level of control.

● Johansson et al. (1978) Social psychological and neuroendocrine stress reactions in highly mechanised work.

GET ACTIVE Too much or too little?

Is having control more stressful than not having it? Students are in an interesting position of having control over some things but not over others. For example, your class timetable is out of your hands. You are told where to go, at what time and generally what to do when you get there. But you have a lot of control over your 'free' time in school or college and at home.

1. Which do you find more stressful – controlling your own time or being told how to spend it?

2. Imagine you have a deadline to meet (you probably won't have to think too hard to imagine this). You have complete control over how you meet the deadline. Make a list of the factors that determine whether you will feel stressed or not.

Causes of stress: Personality and two studies

The worn-out chairs of Meyer Friedman

There is an entertaining story of how one of the personality types on this spread (Type A) was discovered.

Meyer Friedman and Ray Rosenman were cardiologists (heart doctors) with a thriving practice. Their secretary noticed that the patients who had a certain kind of heart problem (coronary heart disease) were always on time, never missed an appointment and always sat on the more upright chairs rather than the comfy sofas.

One day, a number of the chairs had to be re-upholstered because the fabric had worn out. These were the upright chairs and the repairman apologised for the size of the bill. It was expensive because all of the seat fabric had to be replaced, even though only the front edge was worn.

Friedman had a lightbulb moment. These people were so busy and impatient that they were literally sitting on the edge of their seats.

Specification terms

Hardy personality A personality factor used to explain why some people seem able to thrive in stressful circumstances. It consists of commitment, challenge and control.

Type A personality Describes someone who is competitive, time-urgent (e.g. impatient) and hostile in most situations. Research has linked this personality type to coronary heart disease (CHD).

Type B personality Describes someone who is laid-back, relaxed and tolerant of others in most situations (i.e. the opposite of Type A).

Type A personality.

Role of personality in stress

People do not all respond to *stressors* in the same way – we say there are *individual differences*. Two personality differences have been identified, as discussed below.

Hardy personality

Suzanne Kobasa (1979) proposed that a *hardy personality* (or 'hardiness') can protect against *stress* and *ill health*. She described three key components (the 3Cs):

- *Commitment* Hardy people throw themselves into life and have a strong sense of purpose.
- *Challenge* Hardy people welcome change as an opportunity rather than as a threat. They enjoy change as an opportunity for development.
- *Control* Hardy people prefer to make things happen rather than sitting back. They actively try to influence their environment even in times of stress.

Type A and B personality

Meyer Friedman and Ray Rosenman were two cardiologists who noticed their heart patients shared a similar pattern of behaviour. They called this pattern *Type A personality* and suggested it was closely associated with the development of *coronary heart disease* (CHD), such as heart attacks.

Friedman (1996) suggested that people with Type A personalities have high levels of:

- *Competitiveness* They are ambitious, motivated by achievement and view life in terms of goals, challenges and targets.
- *Time urgency* They are fast-talking, impatient and view artistic and creative activities as a waste of time.
- *Hostility* They are aggressive, intolerant of others and are easily angered.

Freidman and Rosenman also identified another type of personality which they called *Type B*. This type contrasts in every way with Type A. Type B people are more relaxed, 'laid back', tolerant and less competitive and hostile than Type As.

Studies of the effect of personality on stress

Maddi (1987) Hardiness training at Illinois Bell Telephone

Salvatore Maddi, who worked with Kobasa, studied managers and supervisors at the Bell Telephone Company in the USA during an extremely stressful reorganisation.

About two-thirds of the participants suffered ill health and poor work performance. But the rest were not affected. Instead, their health remained stable and they felt happier and more fulfilled at work than they had ever been.

These managers who fared best scored highly on measures of the 3Cs of hardiness.

Rosenman *et al.* (1976) Multivariate prediction of coronary heart disease during 8½ year follow-up in the Western collaborative group study

The *Western collaborative group study* classified over 3000 men in California as Type A or Type B at the start of the study (in the 1960s). All the men were free from coronary heart disease (CHD) at this point.

After 8½ years, 257 men had developed CHD. 70% of these had been classified as Type A at the start of the study, twice as many as the Type Bs who developed CHD. Type As also had higher levels of stress hormones (e.g. *adrenaline*) and higher blood pressure and cholesterol levels (both risk factors for CHD).

This supports the view that a Type A personality makes individuals more vulnerable to stressors.

GET ACTIVE Testing time!

Time to have a go at some more tests. You can find one to measure Type A/B personality here: tinyurl.com/mqvcb. There is a hardiness questionnaire you can complete here: tinyurl.com/y59rbae5. As we have seen, Type A has been linked with illness. Hardiness, on the other hand, gives some protection against illness.

1. Are you surprised by your scores? Do they reflect your own views about your personality?

2. Looking at individual items on these questionnaires, make a list of ways in which someone could reduce their risk of illness and/or increase their resistance to it.

3. Having completed the scales, can you identify any problems with them?

This is the sort of thing that hardy people like to do. Not literally, but they do like a challenge.

Evaluation

Two Cs or three?

One weakness is that the 3Cs don't contribute equally to hardy personality.

Hardiness researchers assume that commitment, challenge and control are independent of each other. But other researchers believe they overlap significantly. There seems to be an element of control involved in commitment and challenge. Other psychological research (e.g. *internal locus of control*) suggests that a sense of control is central to well-being. Therefore, Jay Hull *et al.* (1987) argued that researchers should focus on control and commitment and abandon challenge altogether.

This means that the traditional theory of hardy personality lacks *validity* and may not be as practically useful as once thought.

Research support for Type A

One strength of Type A is that there is support from research into its role in illness.

José Egido *et al.* (2012) studied 150 Spanish men and women who had had a stroke. Compared with a matched *control group*, these participants were more likely to have Type A personalities. The difference could not be explained by traditional lifestyle factors such as smoking and diet. This study is more recent than many in this area.

This support for the link between Type A and *cardiovascular disorder* suggests that personality is a valid predictor of stress-related illness.

Evaluation

Self-report

One weakness of hardiness studies is that they use *self-report methods*.

These scales suffer very much from *social desirability bias*. This is because the components of hardiness (the 3Cs) are generally seen as positive characteristics to have. Therefore, participants are likely to exaggerate the extent to which they have these characteristics. There are no objective measures which confirm these subjective states.

The self-report measures of hardiness rely on the subjective views that participants have about themselves and are not confirmed by objective measures of behaviour.

Contradictory evidence

One weakness of the Type A concept is that there is some evidence showing that it is less important than Type B.

David Ragland and Richard Brand (1988) followed up some of the men from the original study by Friedman and Rosenman. They had all survived a heart attack. The researchers found that after several years, Type B survivors were more likely to die than Type As. It seems that Type As were more motivated to make positive lifestyle changes after a first heart attack, reducing their risk of a second one.

This shows that the relationships between Type A/B, stress and illness are complex and not yet fully understood.

Exam-style questions

Leo is the sort of person who likes to get the most out of life. He 'works hard and plays hard'. He likes to be in control and sees every problem as a challenge to be overcome. Leo is facing a lot of changes at work but he is really enjoying it. He rarely gets ill and has never had a day off work.

Flora is always rushing about, trying to get lots of things done. She is very ambitious at work and wants to get to the top as soon as possible. She can't stand waiting for anything and can be quite aggressive. She recently saw her doctor about chest pains.

Kelly is an incredibly laid back person who enjoys painting and writing. She has time for everyone. She likes to relax and nothing seems to bother her.

1. Identify the personality types of Leo, Flora and Kelly. (3)

2. In relation to stress, explain what is meant by:
   (a) Type A personality. (2)
   (b) Type B personality. (2)
   (c) Hardy personality. (2)

   > You should by now have a fair idea of the kind of exam questions that can be asked – try to think of a few more of your own.

3. Explain **one** strength or **one** weakness of the role of personality in stress. Refer to any combination of Leo, Flora and Kelly in your answer. (3)

4. Psychologists have found that people who are hostile and impatient are more likely to become ill than people who are 'laid back'. People who enjoy a challenge and take control are also healthier. But other psychologists disagree.

   With reference to Leo, Flora and Kelly, assess the role of personality in stress. (9)

An issue to consider

Perhaps it is locus of control that really determines how affected you are by stress.

How does this factor relate to hardiness and Type A/B personality?

Specification content

B1 Stress

Causes of stress:
● Definition and role of personality in stress: hardy personality, Type A/B personality.

Physiological responses to stress

It was a dark night

Are you sitting comfortably? Then I'll begin.

You and a friend are walking home through the local woods. You walk past the tree trunks that have reminded you of screaming faces since you were a child. A sense of dread suddenly rises from your stomach. You put your hand in your pocket...

And fail to find the phone you thought was there. You borrow your friend's phone and call yours. Someone seems to answer. You hear breathing. You swear they're chuckling to themselves. Oh well, bye-bye phone.

You get home safe and sound and go up to your bedroom. Where you see your phone on your desk exactly where you left it. Your heart is bursting out of your chest, you're breathing heavily and sweat breaks out all over. You feel cold and sick.

Let's find out why...

Specification terms

Acute stress A threat requiring an immediate response.

Adrenaline A hormone produced by the adrenal glands which is part of the human body's acute stress response. It is also a neurotransmitter.

Chronic stress A threat that continues over weeks and months.

General adaptation syndrome Selye's explanation of stress – the body responds in the same way to any stressor: alarm reaction, resistance and exhaustion.

Hypothalamic-pituitary-adrenal (HPA) system The body's response to a chronic (long-term) stressor. The hypothalamus triggers the pituitary gland to release the hormone ACTH which in turn stimulates release of cortisol from the adrenal cortex.

Sympathomedullary (SAM) system The body's response to an acute (short-term) stressor. The hypothalamus triggers the sympathetic nervous system which causes the adrenal medulla to release adrenaline and noradrenaline. This is the fight or flight response.

Supercalifragilisticexpialidocious. Stop being scared of long words.

The body's response

The general adaptation syndrome (GAS)

Hans Selye (1936) was the first to use the term *stress* in a psychological way. He experimented with rats, subjecting them to various *stressors* (e.g. extreme cold, surgical injury). He found that it didn't matter what the stressor was, the responses were the same.

Selye concluded that 'stress' is a general response of the body to any stressor. He called this response the *general adaptation syndrome* because it is *general* (a reaction to all stressors), *adaptive* (it helps the body cope with a stressor) and a *syndrome* (it includes a group of symptoms/responses).

In fact the response is only adaptive in the short-term. Selye described how the stress response progresses:

Stage 1 – Alarm reaction When the threat or stressor is recognised the *hypothalamus* in the brain triggers the production of *adrenaline/noradrenaline* in readiness for fight or flight.

Stage 2 – Resistance When the threat/stressor ends, functioning returns to normal levels. However, if the stressor continues, a longer-term stress response starts using up the body's resources (e.g. sugars, hormones). The body appears to be coping, whereas in reality, physiologically speaking, things are deteriorating, e.g. the *immune system* becomes less effective.

Stage 3 – Exhaustion The resources needed to resist the stressor are depleted. The individual begins to re-experience the initial symptoms (e.g. sweating, raised heart rate). The adrenal glands may become damaged and the immune system compromised. Stress-related illnesses or 'diseases of adaptation' (as Selye called them) are now likely, such as *coronary heart disease*.

A more modern approach

A better understanding of *physiology* has led to a more precise version of what is happening in the body in response to stress (see diagram at bottom of facing page).

Acute stress: The SAM system Controls the body's immediate response to an *acute* (immediate) stressor, the *fight or flight response*. SAM stands for *sympathomedullary*. This word looks complicated, but let's break it down.

- *Sympatho* refers to the *sympathetic branch* of the *autonomic nervous system* (ANS), which controls the body's 'automatic' responses that we don't have to think about. When a stressor is perceived by the hypothalamus, the sympathetic branch is triggered.

- *Medullary* refers to the middle (medulla) of our two *adrenal glands* (just above each kidney). The hypothalamus signals the *adrenal medullas* to release the hormone adrenaline (and noradrenaline) into the bloodstream. These hormones circulate in the blood and stimulate target organs, e.g. the heart, diversion of blood (oxygen) to the muscles, sweating etc.

When the threat/stressor stops the ANS returns to a relaxed state – the *parasympathetic branch* takes over. This generally has opposite effects to the sympathetic branch, returning the body to the *rest and digest* state.

Chronic stress: The HPA system At the same time as the SAM system begins a slower response starts, the *hypothalamic-pituitary-adrenal system*:

- *Hypothalamic* refers to the hypothalamus which activates the HPA system alongside activating the SAM system. It does this by releasing into the bloodstream a hormone called *corticotropin releasing factor* (CRF).

- *Pituitary gland* detects CRF which responds by releasing a hormone called *adrenocorticotrophic hormone* (ACTH) into the bloodstream.

- *Adrenal glands* are again involved, but this time it is the outer portion of the gland, called the *adrenal cortex* which releases *cortisol*.

Cortisol is central to the body's *chronic stress* response. For example, it affects the metabolism of glucose, a source of energy for the body which fuels the stress response. But it also has damaging effects on the body. It suppresses the immune system, which we explore in more detail in the next spread.

The HPA is self-regulating via a negative feedback loop. The hypothalamus and pituitary both monitor levels of cortisol in the bloodstream. When levels exceed a set point, CRF and ACTH are reduced. These lower levels are detected by the adrenal cortex, which in turn reduces cortisol.

Note – if the threat disappears the whole HPA response stops.

Evaluation

Gender differences in the physiological responses

One weakness is that the physiological stress response is different for males and females.

Shelley Taylor (2006) argued that the fight or fight response applies only to males. Fight or fight would be risky for our distant female ancestors because running away would have left offspring defenceless. A more adaptive response for females would have been *tend and befriend*. A stressor (e.g. threat) is met with protection and nurturing (tending) of offspring and befriending of other females to provide social support.

This suggests that explanations of stress in terms of the GAS, SAM and HPA are biased towards male physiology.

More than two responses

Another weakness is that there is more to the acute response than fight or flight.

Fight or flight involves either confronting a stressor or running away from it. However, another response has been observed in which an individual 'freezes'. Animals (e.g. rabbits) faced with a predator become paralysed. Humans report becoming 'dissociated', as if they were somehow 'distant', rooted to the spot but not really part of what is happening. This may be adaptive because a predator could lose interest in a non-responsive prey.

This suggests that fight or flight is just part of a more complex response to acute stressors.

Fight or flight response is maladaptive

A further weakness is that the physiological response does not help us cope with many modern stressors.

The fight or flight response would have been adaptive in our evolutionary past. It was a useful response to a stressor such as confronting a hungry animal. But this doesn't work if you are stuck in a traffic jam or at a desk in an exam room (examples of modern stressors). Though it does help if a car honks at you when you are crossing a road – you jump out of the way.

Also, stressors in our evolutionary past were nearly always acute – they would end quickly one way or another (either you survived or you got eaten). Modern stressors are often chronic and the physiological response can cause damage to the body (e.g. CHD).

This means that the physiological stress response is actually maladaptive in the modern world because it can do us harm.

Role of perception

Another weakness is that focusing on physiological responses overlooks the role of psychological factors.

Richard Lazarus (1991) pointed out that we *cognitively* appraise a stressor by working out if it is a threat and whether we have the resources to cope with it. Our perception of a stressor affects how we physiologically respond to it. We may not respond at all if we don't interpret something as a stressor. As non-human animals do not do this, Selye's research with rats does not present a full picture of the human stress response.

This suggests that our response to stress can only be fully understood by considering cognitive factors alongside physiology.

GET ACTIVE Costs v. benefits

We have seen that Selye carried out his initial research on rats. Every university psychology department has an ethics committee. Its members carry out a *cost-benefit analysis*.

1. Imagine you are a member of such a committee. What do you think are the main ethical issues raised by Selye's research?

2. Costs and benefits can be ethical and they can be practical. What are the practical costs and benefits of Selye's research? What are the ethical costs and benefits?

Exam-style questions

Ash was asleep when he heard a really loud bang from downstairs. He jumped out of bed and made his way down the stairs with a heavy vase in his hand. His heart was racing and he felt sick. When he got to the living room he saw that a big picture had fallen off the wall. He calmed down quickly and went back to sleep.

Deena is in a job she hates. Every morning she wakes up dreading the day ahead. She knows it will be stressful and it always is. This has been going on for months and she feels trapped. She has made an appointment with her doctor because she is getting chest pains.

1. Identify **one** stressor in Ash's life and **one** in Deena's life. (2)

2. Use the general adaption syndrome to explain the physiological responses of both Ash and Deena. (4)

3. Explain **one** limitation of viewing Deena's stress as a purely physiological response. (3)

4. Explain Ash's stress response in terms of **one** physiological system. (2)

5. Explain Deena's stress response in terms of **one** physiological system. (2)

6. Discuss Ash's and Deena's physiological responses to stress. (9)

An issue to consider

Addison's disease is a disorder of the adrenal glands which means cortisol is not produced.

How would this affect a person with Addison's disease? Why might this be a problem?

SAM system — HPA system

Hypothalamus — Hypothalamus

CRF

Sympathetic branch of ANS — Pituitary gland

ACTH (through blood)

Adrenal medulla — Adrenal cortex

Adrenaline/ Noradrenaline — Cortisol

Specification content

B1 Stress

Physiological responses to stress, to include:

● General adaptation syndrome (GAS).

● Role of the sympathomedullary (SAM) and the hypothalamic-pituitary-adrenal (HPA) system in chronic and acute stress.

● Role of adrenaline in the stress response.

Limitation of viewing stress as a purely physiological response:

● Gender differences in physiological responses.

● More than two responses, the 'freeze' response and role of cognitions.

● Fight or flight response is maladaptive in modern society.

● Role of personality, variation in level and type of hormones released.

Stress and ill health and Kiecolt–Glaser *et al.* (1984)

I always get ill just before exams

We're used to thinking of stress as always a bad thing. But it can be good for us.

Phil Evans and his colleagues (1994) studied students who had to give a presentation to an audience. Students who were particularly stressed by the experience showed increases in *secretory immunoglobulin A* (sIgA). This substance does a protective job.

Suzanne Segerstrom and Greg Miller (2004) reviewed 30 years' worth of studies into stress and the immune system:

- Acute stressors (short-term ones lasting minutes) can sometimes boost the immune system, preparing it to fight infections.
- Chronic stressors (long-term ones lasting longer) suppress the immune system. These include exams, which may be why so many students get ill at certain times of the year.

Specification terms

Cardiovascular disorder Any disorder of the heart (cardio) or blood vessels (vascular), including blood vessels in the brain (e.g. stroke).

Immune system The body's defence against invading antigens ('foreign bodies'). Its activity can be suppressed by stress, reducing its activity and effectiveness.

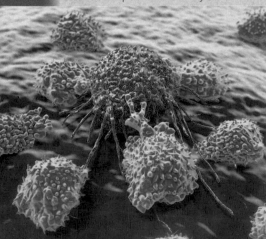

Lymphocytes surround a cancer cell and begin to attack it. But Kiecolt-Glaser *et al.*'s research shows this response is affected by stress.

Stress and ill health

Immune system

The *immune system* is the body's defensive barrier against *antigens* (invading germs and other foreign bodies). There are two main lines of defence:

- Innate immunity – a general immune response to any antigen. This is a relatively fast response involving white blood cells (*leucocytes*) and *natural killer* (NK) cells that destroy tumour cells and cells infected with viruses.
- Acquired immunity – involves *lymphocytes* that recognise and destroy specific antigens. *B cells* produce antibodies that destroy antigens in the bloodstream. There are also *memory T cells* which recognise antigens, and *killer T cells* which destroy cells infected with antigens.

Suppression of the immune system

Stress can cause illness by preventing the immune system from working efficiently (*immunosuppression*).

Stress can suppress the immune system directly. For example, *cortisol* produced by the HPA response (discussed on the previous spread) inhibits production of lymphocytes, disrupting acquired immunity.

Stress also suppresses the immune system indirectly. For example, it influences lifestyle behaviours (e.g. smoking, drinking, sleep) that in turn affect immunity.

Stress and cardiovascular disorders (CVDs)

We have seen that stress affects CHD (*coronary heart disease*) but it has a wider effect on the cardiovascular system which includes the heart (cardio) and also blood vessels (vascular system).

Stress hormones (e.g. *cortisol* and *adrenaline*) can cause *atherosclerosis* (narrowing of arteries) by increasing the formation of fatty clumps (plaques) on artery walls.

Stress can have immediate (*acute*) and longer-term (*chronic*) effects on *cardiovascular disorders* (CVDs). For example, the effects of acute stress were studied by Ute Wilbert-Lampen *et al.* (2008). They found that cardiac emergencies trebled during some football matches in the 1996 World Cup.

Kiecolt–Glaser *et al.* (1984) Psychosocial modifiers of immunocompetence in medical students

Aims

Janice Kiecolt-Glaser *et al.* sought to study the effects of a naturally-occurring *stressor* (exams) on the immune systems of human participants (students).

Procedure

75 medical students gave blood samples twice – one month before an exam period and on the day of the final exam week (after two exams were taken).

On both occasions the participants completed the *Brief symptom inventory* (BSI), a 53-item checklist giving a score for 'distress'. At the first blood sample, they also completed the SRRS (see page 38) to measure the stress of *life events* over the previous year. This was used to divide participants into 'high-stress' and 'low-stress' groups. They also filled in the *UCLA loneliness scale* which was used to divide them into 'high-loneliness' and 'low-loneliness' groups.

Findings

There was significantly lower NK cell activity in:

- The second blood sample compared with the first.
- The high-stress (more life events) group compared with the low-stress group.
- The high-loneliness group compared with the low-loneliness group.

Greater distress (as assessed by the BSI) was reported during the exams than one month before.

Conclusions

The findings show that a relatively mild chronic stressor (exams) has a significantly direct suppressive effect on the immune system, even in a young and healthy sample (medical students). The build-up of many stressful life events can have negative effects on health.

Evaluation

Support for stress effects on the immune system

One strength is studies showing that stress suppresses the immune system.

For example, Diedre Pereira *et al.* (2003) studied women who were HIV-positive. HIV is a virus that reduces immune system activity. Women who experienced many stressful life events were more likely to develop pre-cancerous lesions of the cervix than women who experienced fewer events. Stress reduced immune functioning further in some women.

This finding shows that stress may have direct suppressive effects on the immune system and lead to diseases other than just CVDs.

Short-term versus long-term effects

One weakness with this explanation is that stress can enhance the immune system rather than suppress it.

Firdaus Dharbhar (2008) subjected rats to mild short-lived stressors and found that this stimulated a significant immune response. So, the immune system can actually give some protection against acute stressors. But long-term stressors are damaging to the immune and cardiovascular systems. Timo Heidt *et al.* (2014) found that a chronic stressor caused an immune inflammation response which damaged the hearts of mice.

This shows that the relationship between stress, the immune system and *ill health* is complex and not yet fully understood.

Evaluation

Valuable contribution

One strength is that the study demonstrated a link in humans between stress and immune functioning.

This was a valuable finding because most of the previous research used non-human animals. This study was able to confirm that earlier findings about the reduction of NK cell activity also apply to humans.

This study stimulated a lot of further research to establish the effects of stress on immune functioning and demonstrate a link with illness.

Unclear link with illness

One weakness is that the study did not show how stress affected illness.

Kiecolt-Glaser *et al.* did not collect data on changes in drug or alcohol use, sleep patterns or diet. So, these lifestyle-related factors could account for immune suppressive effects.

This means that the study could not draw conclusions about the specific causal link between the immune system and illness without further research.

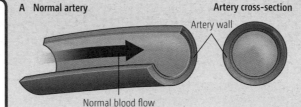

There are several cardiovascular disorders, one of which is atherosclerosis. An artery becomes progressively narrowed by cholesterol forming a plaque on its wall. Eventually the artery becomes completely blocked and this can cause a heart attack or stroke depending on which artery is affected.

Exam-style questions

Sanj is a student in the middle of an important exam period. Everyone is on study leave and he is shut away revising hard. He has hardly seen anyone for weeks. He still has a nasty cold that started over two weeks ago and he can't seem to shake it off.

Jana has a stressful job as a manager in a big company. There are times when she feels in a panic and she can feel her heart beating very fast. She visited her doctor because of chest pains and is having further tests. She worries she might have a heart attack.

1. Explain what is meant by 'suppression of the immune system'. (3)
2. Explain how stress could account for the ill health of:
   (a) Sanj. (3)
   (b) Jana. (3)
3. In relation to Jana, assess the role of stress in cardiovascular disorders. (4)
4. Explain **one** strength and **one** weakness of knowing about the link between stress and suppression of the immune system. (4)
5. Kiecolt-Glaser *et al.* (1984) conducted a study on 'Psychosocial modifiers of immunocompetence in medical students'.
   (a) Describe the procedure of this study. (3)
   (b) Explain what **one** finding of this study can tell us about Sanj's experience. (2)
   (c) Explain **one** conclusion of this study. (2)
6. Discuss the link between stress and illness in Sanj and Jana. Refer in your answer to at least **one** research study. (9)

An issue to consider

Kiecolt-Glaser did further research looking at the links between stress, the immune system and wound healing. Given the information on this spread, what do you think she found?

GET ACTIVE Measuring distress in the key study

Kiecolt-Glaser *et al.* used a questionnaire called the *brief symptom inventory* (Derogatis 1983) to assess their participants' levels of 'distress'. You can find the BSI here: tinyurl.com/y2td4mwb (the questionnaire itself is on page 42). It is useful to have a look at the items to get an idea of what the researchers were measuring.

1. The researchers found that the participants reported more distress during the exams than one month earlier. Look at each item and think about the impact exams would have. Have exams ever affected you like this?

2. What do you think of the scale as a measure of distress? What kind of distress is being measured?

Specification content

B1 Stress

The link between stress and ill health, to include:
- Suppression of the immune system.
- Role of stress in cardiovascular disorders.
- Kiecolt-Glaser *et al.* (1984) Psychosocial modifiers of immunocompetence in medical students.

Smoking: Biological approach and Vink *et al.* (2005)

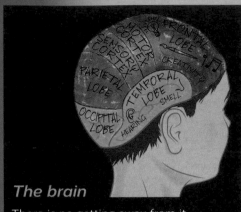

The brain

There is no getting away from it – understanding the structure of the brain is very helpful for your psychological studies. Here are two suggestions:

1. Get a white bathing cap and ask your friend to wear it. Draw on the cortical areas of the brain. (The cortex is the thin layer over the top of the whole brain, like an orange peel. It is where all your thinking happens.)

2. Get a cauliflower. Slice it in half and identify the subcortical areas of the brain as shown in the diagram on the facing page. (The subcortical areas are the ones 'under' the cortex, in the middle of your brain, and these deal with stress, emotion and memory.)

Specification terms

Addiction See page 12.

Dopamine A neurotransmitter that generally has an excitatory effect and is associated with the sensation of pleasure. Unusually high levels are associated with schizophrenia and unusually low levels are associated with Parkinson's disease.

This is how twin studies help us understand the genetics of smoking: identical twins (monozygotic, MZ) share 100% of their genes, whereas non-identical twins (dizygotic, DZ) share only 50% of their genetic material. Therefore, if MZ twins behave more like each other (e.g. they both smoke) than DZ twins do, then their greater genetic similarity could be responsible.

Biological explanation of smoking addiction

The *biological approach* can explain initiation, maintenance and relapse of smoking addiction.

Initiation

A person may start smoking because of biological factors related to nicotine (which is addictive).

Genetic predisposition *Genes* may be a risk factor for nicotine *addiction*. Dorit Carmelli *et al.* (1991) found that genetic influences contribute about 53% to the risk of taking up smoking. This is a widely accepted figure, with other studies ranging from 11% to 75% (Lodhi *et al.* 2016). Another source of evidence for genes comes from the twin study described by Vink *et al.* below.

Dopamine receptors *Neurons* in the area of the brain called the *ventral tegmental area* (VTA) have receptors on their surfaces which respond to *dopamine* molecules (see diagram on facing page). Dopamine is the brain's 'pleasure and reward' chemical. ✓ACH

Nicotine molecules are also able to attach to these ~~dopamine~~ receptors. When a smoker first takes a drag of a cigarette, nicotine molecules reach these receptors very quickly (in seconds). This triggers release of dopamine in a nearby brain area called the *nucleus accumbens* (NA). The feelings of pleasure (the 'buzz') the smoker receives are rewarding because of the dopamine release – in the majority of cases, the first-time smoker is on the way to being 'hooked'.

Maintenance and relapse

Role of dopamine Smokers continue to smoke because nicotine molecules continue to attach to receptors in the VTA and dopamine is released in the NA. The pleasure from the dopamine release rewards the smoking behaviour, so the smoker is compelled to continue.

Nicotine regulation The *nicotine regulation model* (Schachter 1977) argues that people continue smoking to regulate nicotine in their bloodstream, to keep continually activating dopamine neurons and maintain the 'buzz'. In other words, smokers continue smoking to avoid *withdrawal* symptoms (an example of *negative reinforcement*).

Withdrawal symptoms A short time after finishing a cigarette, withdrawal symptoms appear (e.g. feeling of anxiety, craving). Smokers become skilled at avoiding these symptoms by smoking again at the earliest signs. This brings their blood nicotine levels back up.

Tolerance Over time, the constant stimulation of dopamine receptors reduces their sensitivity. The person has to smoke more in order to restimulate receptors to previous levels and achieve the sensations they used to get, i.e. *tolerance*, including tolerance to mood-changing effects (less buzz) and tolerance to the negative effects of nicotine (fewer headaches).

Vink *et al.* (2005) Heritability of smoking initiation and nicotine dependence

Aims

Jacqueline Vink *et al.* wanted to see if genetic risk factors contribute separately to smoking initiation and nicotine *dependence*.

Procedure

The researchers gathered smoking-related data from the *Netherlands twin register* on five occasions between 1991 and 2000. The data came from 868 *monozygotic* (MZ) twin pairs and 704 *dizygotic* (DZ) twin pairs. In the final survey (2000), smokers and ex-smokers completed the *Fagerström test for nicotine dependence* (FTND).

Findings

For smoking initiation, 44% of the variation between individuals was explained by genetic factors (56% by environmental). For nicotine dependence, 75% of the variation between individuals was explained by genetic factors (25% by environmental).

Conclusions

Genetic factors make a substantial contribution to both the initiation of smoking and ongoing nicotine dependence. The genetic factors contributing to the two behaviours are not independent of each other (there is overlap).

GET ACTIVE Smoking and biology

Daphne and Velma are discussing why so many people smoke and why these people find it hard to give up. Daphne thinks smoking is a 'lifestyle choice' and most people could give up if they just tried. But Velma disagrees. She says, 'Smoking is an addiction and there are biological reasons why people start smoking, keep smoking and can't give up. It runs in families, and brain chemicals and nicotine in the bloodstream are both involved. And then there's the withdrawal symptoms'.

1. For each of the factors Velma mentions, write **one** sentence explaining it.

2. Can you think of any non-biological reasons why smoking is addictive?

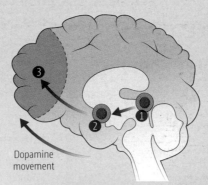

Dopamine movement

The arrows show the movement of dopamine in the brain during smoking. Dopamine is the rewarding 'feel-good' chemical responsible for the elation associated with most addictive drugs. In smoking, nicotine first attaches to dopamine receptors in the ventral tegmental area (1). This stimulates release of dopamine in the nucleus accumbens (2) and finally the frontal cortex (3).

Evaluation

Research support for nicotine regulation

One strength is that there is evidence for the regulation theory.

Stanley Schachter (1977) gave light and heavy smokers cigarettes containing lower-than-usual amounts of nicotine. This meant the smokers would have lower levels of nicotine in their bloodstream than they were used to. As predicted by the nicotine regulation model, heavy smokers increased their smoking (by 25%) more than the light smokers did (by 18%), in order to make up the bigger nicotine deficit.

Therefore, the *validity* of the theory was supported because the finding matched a prediction of the theory.

Evidence against nicotine regulation

One weakness is the evidence that not everyone regulates their nicotine levels.

Saul Shiffman *et al.* (1995) studied 'chippers', people who smoke regularly but do not become dependent on nicotine. Chippers who smoked an average of five cigarettes a day showed no withdrawal symptoms when they abstained and no compulsion to smoke again. They may have learned to smoke through observation of *models* (see next spread) rather than because of the rewarding dopamine hit associated with nicotine.

This finding is hard for the regulation theory to explain because it suggests some people smoke for non-biological reasons.

Evaluation

Practical application

One strength of the study is that it may have practical benefits.

The researchers found a 56% contribution by environmental factors to variation in smoking initiation. This implies that starting to smoke is by no means inevitable and steps can be taken to make it less likely. The environmental component is probably explained by *social learning* (i.e. *modelling* by parents). Interventions targeting parents to stop could have an additional benefit in removing a common and powerful *role model* for children to imitate.

This shows that Vink *et al.'s* findings about the genetic basis of smoking could lead to benefits by targeting an environmental factor.

Problems with self-report

One weakness with the study is that the researchers used *self-report methods* such as the FTND to collect data.

The FTND produces a score for nicotine dependence ranging from 0 (none) to 10 (high). The participants responded to items such as, 'Do you find it difficult to refrain from smoking in places where it is forbidden?' Some participants may have given responses that present them in a more positive light, because they don't want to be perceived as 'addicts'.

This means the scale demonstrated *social desirability bias* and the findings may not reflect the true behaviours of smokers and ex-smokers in the study.

Exam-style questions

Emer started smoking when he was 14, following in the footsteps of his parents, brother and sister. His whole family smokes, not just his parents and brother but his grandparents, aunties and so on. He enjoyed the 'rush' he got the first time he smoked and the way it seemed to make him feel more alert. He still finds that cigarettes give him a buzz but not as much as they once did and he smokes more these days. He doesn't like it when he can't smoke because he feels bad and really wants a cigarette. Sometimes he feels a headache coming on but when he has a cigarette he feels better.

1. Psychologists explain addiction in terms of initiation, maintenance and relapse. Define what is meant by 'maintenance'. (1)

2. Identify **one** reason why genetic predisposition may play a role in Emer's smoking. (1)

3. Explain the role of dopamine receptors in initiation of Emer's smoking. (2)

4. Assess the role of nicotine regulation in maintaining Emer's smoking. (4)

5. Emer finally managed to give up smoking and hasn't had a cigarette for a week.

   Using the biological approach, explain why Emer might relapse. Refer in your answer to both tolerance and withdrawal symptoms. (3)

6. Give **one** finding of the study by Vink *et al.* (2005) and use it to explain Emer's behaviour. (4)

7. With reference to Emer, discuss the biological approach to smoking. Refer to at least **one** research study in your answer. (9)

An issue to consider

It used to be assumed that MZ twins and DZ twins both shared very similar environments – but now it is recognised that MZ twins shape their environment similarly (e.g. their genes affect their taste in music). This means MZ twins don't just have more similar genes, they also have more similar environments.

How does this affect our interpretation of twin studies?

Specification content

B2 Physiological addiction

Smoking – biological approach:

- Initiation: genetic predisposition to addiction, dopamine receptors, Vink *et al.* (2005) Heritability of smoking initiation and nicotine dependence.

- Maintenance and relapse: role of dopamine, nicotine regulation, tolerance, withdrawal symptoms.

Smoking: Learning approach

Too much of a good thing?

The problem with smoking is that smokers enjoy it too much. Perhaps if they disliked it they might quit more easily. But how do you get a smoker to dislike smoking?

A smoker learns to enjoy smoking because it is rewarding, i.e. they are conditioned to like it. Therefore, the solution is to countercondition – make smoking unpleasant.

One way of doing this is to use a technique called *rapid smoking*. The smoker takes a draw on a cigarette every five or six seconds. Once that cigarette is done with, they go onto the next one, and the next. They keep going and soon feel sick (and some actually are sick). This is all done in a supportive environment of course.

This is a form of aversion therapy – which you'll read about on page 88.

Specification terms

Classical conditioning Learning by association. Occurs when two stimuli are repeatedly paired together – an unconditioned (unlearned) stimulus (UCS) and a new 'neutral' stimulus (NS). The neutral stimulus eventually produces the same response that was first produced by the unlearned stimulus alone.

Negative reinforcement In operant conditioning, a stimulus that increases the probability that a behaviour will be repeated because it leads to escape from an unpleasant situation and is experienced as rewarding.

Positive reinforcement In operant conditioning, a stimulus that increases the probability that a behaviour will be repeated because it is pleasurable.

Role models People who have qualities we would like to have and we identify with, thus we model or imitate their behaviour and attitudes.

Self-efficacy A person's confidence in being able to do something. Such confidence generates expectations and these act as self-fulfilling prophecies.

Cue for a cigarette.

Learning explanation of smoking addiction

The *learning approach* can explain initiation, maintenance and relapse of smoking addiction.

Initiation

Parental and peer role models The origins of smoking lie in *social learning* (explained in Unit 1 of our Year 1 'Certificate' book). Typically, a child or adolescent observes parents and peers smoking, who provide *role models* to imitate.

As smokers usually gain satisfaction and pleasure from smoking, this is also observed and experienced by the young person as *vicarious reinforcement*. This makes it more likely that they will also begin smoking, as they expect to experience the same rewards.

Positive reinforcement is a component of *operant conditioning*, which states that if a consequence of a behaviour is desirable then it will be repeated (this was also in Unit 1 of your course). *Positive reinforcement* refers to a pleasurable reward.

Nicotine is a powerful reinforcer through its physiological effects on the *dopamine* reward system (see previous spread). The enjoyable sensations reward the smoking behaviour, so a second cigarette is more likely, and so on.

Maintenance

Negative reinforcement is another operant conditioning concept. With *negative reinforcement*, the consequence is still desirable but it involves escape from something unpleasant. This can explain continuing *dependence* on nicotine.

There are times when a smoker cannot smoke (e.g. they are asleep or have no access to cigarettes). After a relatively short time they may become impatient and anxious, i.e. they experience mild but unpleasant *withdrawal* symptoms (the main sign of physical dependence). They relieve symptoms by smoking again. This is negatively reinforcing because it stops unpleasant sensations.

Classical conditioning also plays a role in continuing dependence on nicotine. This is because the smoker learns an association between the sensations involved in smoking and its pleasurable effects. Sensations include the smell of smoke, the 'catch' at the back of the throat, the feel of a cigarette between the lips and fingers. Each of these is initially a *neutral stimulus*, but after being paired with cigarettes they become *conditioned stimuli*. Each is capable of triggering a response without delivery of nicotine to the brain.

Relapse

Conditioned cues (classical and operant conditioning) The pleasurable effect of smoking is called a *primary reinforcer* (operant conditioning). It is rewarding in itself (not learned) through its effects on the brain's dopamine reward system.

However, smoking a cigarette is accompanied by lots of other things – objects, people, places. These stimuli are called *secondary reinforcers* (or *conditioned cues*) because they become associated (through *classical conditioning*) with the primary reinforcer. This means that they become rewarding in their own right, without the need to smoke.

Conditioned cues are partly the reason why smokers who have quit end up relapsing back into their *addiction*. Whenever the ex-smoker encounters an object, person or place they associate with smoking, they experience some of the pleasurable response they used to get from a cigarette. This triggers a craving, which often becomes impossible to resist.

Self-efficacy in this context refers to a person's confidence in their ability to stop smoking and continue to abstain.

The reason why low *self-efficacy* is potentially central to *relapse* is because of the impact it has on the person's attitudes, beliefs and behaviours. For example, someone with low self-efficacy will make relatively less effort to quit, be more reluctant and negative in doing so, expect to relapse, fail to seek support and revert to smoking at the first sign of difficulty.

Evaluation

Support for conditioned cues

One strength is evidence to support the role of conditioned cues in nicotine addiction.

Brian Carter and Stephen Tiffany (1999) reviewed 41 studies. These studies typically presented smokers and non-smokers with images of smoking-related cues (e.g. lighters, ashtrays, packets). Smokers reacted strongly to these images, showing increased physiological arousal and reporting high levels of craving.

These findings are consistent with predictions about conditioned cues, showing that nicotine addicts do respond to such cues which predisposes them to relapse.

Real-life practical applications

Another strength is that the learning approach has practical benefits.

Several treatment programmes are based on the learning approach. For example, *aversion therapy* (see beginning of spread) *counterconditions* nicotine addiction by associating the pleasurable effects of smoking with an unpleasant stimulus (e.g. electric shock). Some research studies have found this to be an effective treatment. Edward Smith and Linda Caldwell (1989) found that 52% of participants in such a programme were still abstaining one year later (compared with 25% who abstained without treatment).

These treatments have real benefits in reducing NHS spending and improving quality of life.

A limited explanation

One weakness of the learning approach is that it cannot explain all nicotine addiction.

The approach claims that *observational learning* and vicarious reinforcement are powerful initiators of smoking. Yet many young people who observe parents, siblings and peers smoking do not go on to take up smoking themselves. Only about 50% of adolescents who smoke cigarettes become addicted to nicotine. Others smoke occasionally without experiencing withdrawal when they stop.

This shows that there must be several causes of smoking initiation and maintenance, which is hard for any one approach to explain in terms of a few processes or factors.

Role of self-efficacy

Another weakness is evidence that self-efficacy is not central to quitting and relapsing.

For example, Chad Gwaltney *et al.* (2009) reviewed 54 studies of the relationship between self-efficacy and quitting. They found a consistent but only 'modest' effect for individuals who felt very confident at the outset that they could quit. Self-efficacy predicted later abstinence from smoking but the effect was much smaller than they expected.

The researchers concluded that low self-efficacy plays a small role in risk of relapse, but this is only one of many relevant factors.

On this spread, and many other spreads, we have supplied four criticisms of the theory. You would not need all of these when answering a 9-mark essay question. However, you may be asked to explain two strengths or two weaknesses so we have generally covered two of each.

Thankfully, not a common sight now.

Exam-style questions

Sandy started smoking because his parents and friends smoked and they seemed to enjoy it. He did too once he started. He still enjoys the buzz but also finds it relaxing, especially when he hasn't been able to have a cigarette for a while. He likes playing with his lighter and the cigarette packet. Sandy enjoys the sensations of the cigarette and everything that goes with the experience of smoking.

1. In the context of addiction, explain what is meant by 'initiation of smoking'. (2)
2. In relation to initiation of Sandy's smoking, explain the roles of:
   (a) Parental and peer influences. (2)
   (b) Positive reinforcement. (2)
3. Using the concepts of negative reinforcement and classical conditioning, explain how Sandy's smoking is maintained. (4)
4. Sandy stopped smoking recently although he still has cravings for a cigarette. These are quite strong when he meets friends and they go out for a drink or they come round to watch the footy. Sandy doesn't really believe he has the willpower to stay off cigarettes.

   Use the concept of self-efficacy to explain why Sandy might relapse. (3)
5. Explain **two** weaknesses of the learning approach as an explanation of Sandy's smoking. (4)
6. Assess the learning approach as an explanation of Sandy's smoking. Refer to **one** other approach in your answer. (9)

An issue to consider

We have seen that conditioned cues can contribute to risk of relapse.

But can some cues be more 'personal' than others and therefore more powerful and risky?

Specification content

B2 Physiological addiction

Smoking – learning approach:

- Initiation: parental and peer role models, positive reinforcement.
- Maintenance: negative reinforcement, i.e. removal of withdrawal symptoms, classical conditioning and association between sensory information and nicotine effects.
- Relapse: classical conditioning, conditioned cues, self-efficacy.

ᵍᵉᵗ ACTIVE Cue to relapse

Cues associated with smoking can be relapse triggers for people who have quit. Addiction researcher Cynthia Conklin (2006) showed that cues are not just objects and people – they can also be environments. She found that smokers experienced intense cravings when looking at images of smoking-related environments (e.g. pubs), even when all the usual cues were removed from the image.

1. *Make a list of all the smoking-related cues you can think of.*
2. *What form of learning makes an environment become a secondary reinforcer of smoking? Write down step-by-step how this happens.*
3. *What is the relevance of these findings for helping smokers quit?*

Alcohol: Cognitive approach

Cheers?

In 2006 the Mental Health Foundation published a report called *Cheers? Understanding the relationship between alcohol and mental health*. This report uncovered the extent of alcohol use amongst the adult population of the UK, and the reasons why people use and abuse alcohol and become dependent upon it. Here are some stats:

➤ 63% said drinking made them feel happier.

➤ 66% of 18- to 24-year-olds said alcohol made them feel more confident.

➤ 46% of people in full-time work said alcohol made them less anxious. These people also said they drank every day and would find it very hard to give up.

➤ Alcohol consumption has doubled in the last 50 years (up to 2006, probably even more so by now).

The idea that people drink alcohol to make themselves feel better (or feel less bad) is a widely accepted one and is the basis of the theory covered on this spread. Here's one more statistic for you. One-third of adults say they rely on alcohol to 'get through Christmas'.

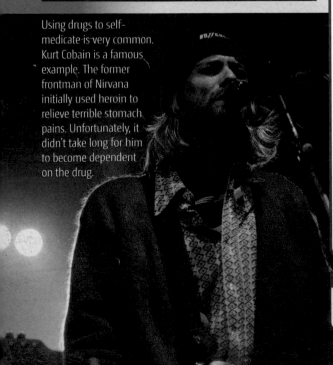

Using drugs to self-medicate is very common. Kurt Cobain is a famous example. The former frontman of Nirvana initially used heroin to relieve terrible stomach pains. Unfortunately, it didn't take long for him to become dependent on the drug.

Self-medication model of alcohol addiction

This explanation focuses on how an individual thinks about or perceives past traumatic experiences and current feelings of distress – a *cognitive approach*.

Initiation

Mitigation for current issue According to Edward Khantzian (1985), *addiction* to alcohol and other drugs can be explained by early experiences of *trauma*. Someone who was traumatised in childhood through abuse or neglect (or perhaps the loss of a parent) may well develop a mental disorder (e.g. *depression*, *anxiety*).

The disorder is accompanied by emotional distress and the person may turn to drugs such as alcohol to relieve their symptoms. This *self-medication* has a soothing function. The person uses alcohol to manage their anxiety and psychological pain and to become emotionally stable.

Specific effects Because self-medication is used to manage negative emotional states, the choice of drug is not random. Khantzian believed there is a link between the specific state and the drug used to relieve it. He called this *specificity*.

Alcohol is often used by people who experience anxiety because it has relaxing effects (and is widely and easily available). Someone with depression on the other hand may use cocaine or amphetamines because they are stimulants that can boost *self-esteem*. This choice is often the outcome of experimentation with various drugs. Someone addicted to alcohol may have tried out other drugs first.

Maintenance

Assumptions about managing the problem Early trauma and current distress means the individual is not in a position to look after themselves and they experience low self-esteem. For example, they may lack the skills to cope with *stress* or to cope in social situations.

Khantzian describes addiction as a 'self-regulation disorder'. People self-medicate because they cannot control their self-esteem, relationships or self-care. An individual uses alcohol to help overcome these problems (e.g. it allows them to be more sociable and friendly). This is how the user progresses from use to addiction. Alcohol has a powerful short-term ability to relieve lack of self-care, the distress of low self-esteem and poor relationships. This *reinforces* the individual's *dependence* on alcohol as they quickly learn they can't get by without it.

Stress relief The person cannot soothe themselves because of their experience of trauma, especially when they are stressed. They have not developed confidence in themselves so cannot judge their true value or worth.

Relapse

Counterproductive Using alcohol to self-medicate is ultimately counterproductive and self-defeating. It creates a *rebound effect*, causing symptoms to worsen or provoking a *relapse*.

Increase of stress levels A person dependent on alcohol who reduces or ceases their use will experience *withdrawal* symptoms which in turn creates stress.

'Solving' problem causes relapse The risk at this point is that the stress of withdrawal added to the person's current distress makes their existence unbearable. His or her solution is to drink again or even use other drugs to manage their symptoms.

Khantzian called this the paradox of self-medication. It is the start of a self-perpetuating cycle of distress, use, addiction, more distress, relapse and so on. This is why he argued that the underlying mental disorder should be treated, not the alcohol addiction. The addiction resolves after the emotional distress is dealt with, so the person no longer needs to self-medicate.

Specification term

Self-medication model Views addiction as a way of relieving current feelings of distress caused by past experiences of trauma. How we perceive or think about the trauma and distress is a cognitive process.

Evaluation

Trauma and distress

One strength of the self-medication model is overwhelming evidence to support the role of early trauma.

An influential study by Vincent Felitti *et al.* (1998) investigated adverse childhood experiences (ACEs) in almost 10,000 people. Participants reported their experiences of sexual, emotional and/or physical abuse when they were children. An ACE score was derived for each participant to reflect the amount and severity of abuse. The researchers found a strong relationship between ACE scores and later addiction (especially to alcohol) and other health-risk behaviours.

This shows that childhood trauma is linked to addiction in adulthood, as predicted by the model.

Self-medication and addiction

Another strength is research confirming a link between self-medication and risk of addiction.

Samuel Lazareck *et al.* (2012) studied the drug use of more than 34,000 American adults over a three-year period. Some of the participants were diagnosed with a *mood disorder* (e.g. depression). Some participants self-medicated with drugs (including alcohol) and some did not. The self-medicating participants were up to seven times more likely to develop an addiction to the drug over the three years.

This finding shows that the model is correct in predicting that self-medication is a substantial risk factor for the development of alcohol addiction.

Role of specificity

One weakness is a lack of evidence for the role of specificity in the model.

Anna Lembke (2012) points out that in most cases, people who are dependent on one drug also use at least one other equally often. She also argues that many young people with mental disorders prefer drugs that are used by their peers. So, relief from emotional distress is not the main motivator of drug choice in this group.

This means that the model may be wrong in claiming that people self-medicate with a drug that best addresses their specific symptoms.

Cause and effect

Another weakness is evidence showing that underlying mental disorder does not cause addiction.

This is a basic argument of the model. For it to be correct, the disorder has to develop first followed by the addiction. David Fergusson *et al.* (2009) showed that this is not the case. They assessed depression and alcohol dependence in over 1000 participants when they were aged 18, 21 and 25 years. They concluded that depression did not cause alcohol abuse. Instead, alcohol abuse caused a greater risk of depression.

This means that alcohol addiction cannot be the result of self-medication for symptoms of a disorder.

Pink Floyd's lyrics to 'Comfortably Numb' echo the self-medication theory. Watch here at tinyurl.com/ad56mqd.

GET ACTIVE It makes me feel OK

Enid is a 50-year-old doctor who drinks two bottles of wine every evening. This is how she describes her drinking: 'It started as a way of coping with the stress of my job. And I also think I have some unresolved issues from a long time ago. I drink to get into a state of numbness where I don't have to worry about anything, not even how much I drink. It's the only time I really feel OK. I know I'm dependent, I can't imagine how I would get by without it'.

1. Give **two** examples of how Enid is using alcohol to self-medicate.

2. How does the self-medication model explain the initiation and maintenance of Enid's dependence on alcohol?

3. If Enid tried to stop drinking, what does the model predict is likely to happen?

Exam-style questions

Janine developed feelings of deep anxiety in her adolescence which she still experiences almost daily. She attributes this to abuse she suffered when she was a young child. She grew up in a dysfunctional household. Her father often physically assaulted her mother. Neither of them looked after Janine properly and she was often left to fend for herself and her younger sister. Now that she is an adult, many areas of Janine's life are in a mess. She drinks at least a bottle of vodka every day to make herself feel better.

1. Explain how the cognitive approach might account for the initiation of Janine's alcohol addiction. (4)

2. Explain what is meant by 'self-medication' in relation to alcohol use. (2)

3. Explain **one** strength and **one** weakness of the self-medication model of alcohol addiction. (4)

4. Explain the role of self-medication in the maintenance of Janine's alcohol addiction. (3)

5. Janine has just stopped drinking but she is worried that she can't cope with her life if she doesn't have alcohol.

   Use the self-medication model to explain why Janine is at risk of relapse. (3)

6. Assess the cognitive approach to Janine's alcohol addiction. (9)

An issue to consider

The self-medication model has been described as the most compassionate, kind or humane explanation of addiction. Can you explain why?

Specification content

B2 Physiological addiction

Alcohol – cognitive approach:

Self-medication model:

- Initiation – use of alcohol as mitigation for current issue, use of substances for specific effects.

- Maintenance – assumption about management of the problem, stress relief.

- Relapse – counterproductive, increase of stress levels, 'solving' problem causes relapse.

Alcohol: Learning approach

The dark side of addiction

Eva is a 65-year-old woman who was once a successful lawyer. When she was 35 a former client began legal proceedings against her because he believed Eva had been professionally negligent. The case was settled in Eva's favour but it took two years. All Eva can remember now about that time is fear, stress and that it was when she began to drink.

Since then Eva has been through a never-ending cycle. She drinks as much as a bottle of vodka each day. She has sometimes blacked out and woken up in hospital. She manages to stay sober for a while (her record is two months). But in that time, even once the terrible withdrawal symptoms have gone, she is always thinking about the drink. Her life falls to pieces, she gets stressed, hits the bottle again and the cycle continues.

For Eva, alcohol seems to make her life a chaotic mess and to offer a solution at the same time. George Koob (2009) calls this 'the dark side of addiction'. It is what makes giving up drugs (including alcohol) so hard for most people. It is the outcome of negative reinforcement, which features prominently on this spread.

Specification terms

See page 52.

For many people who drink too much, alcohol is an escape from a stressful life. But withdrawal symptoms prevent them from stopping because they are so unpleasant. This is how negative reinforcement works.

Operant conditioning of alcohol addiction

The *learning approach* (*operant conditioning*) can explain initiation, maintenance and relapse of alcohol addiction.

Initiation

Positive reinforcement This may be direct or indirect. Alcohol activates the brain's *dopamine* reward system relatively quickly – alcohol molecules attach to dopamine receptors on *neurons* in the *ventral tegmental area* (VTA). Dopamine is released in a nearby area called the *nucleus accumbens* (NA) and in *frontal areas* of the brain (see diagram on page 51). This creates a sense of pleasure.

The consequence is that the drinker experiences *positive reinforcement*. In addition, they may be in an environment where they receive rewards for drinking. For example, friends may praise them for engaging in drinking games. The pleasurable sensations positively reinforce the behaviour of drinking alcohol – making drinking likely to be repeated.

Indirect effects are related to parental and peer *role models*, as discussed in relation to smoking *addiction* (page 52). A young person observes others enjoying alcohol, becoming more sociable, confident and friendly. They experience these rewarding effects 'second-hand' (*vicarious reinforcement*). So, even before taking their first drink, a young person may learn that alcohol will produce positive consequences.

Negative reinforcement Initiation of drinking also partly comes about through *negative reinforcement*. Some people experience drinking alcohol as a way of escaping stressful lives. People learn this from watching films where the characters have a drink to unwind or to avoid pain. This can be a strong motivator for taking a first drink.

Maintenance

Positive reinforcement Drinking alcohol provides ongoing rewards which make drinking likely to be repeated (positive reinforcement as described above). A related feature of maintenance is *motivational toxicity*. The rewards from drinking exceed those from previously rewarding activities (relationships, sex, hobbies) because drinking becomes central to the person's life. Drinking eventually becomes the alcoholic's only source of reward.

Negative reinforcement Drinking is maintained over time to avoid or reduce *withdrawal* symptoms. When someone dependent on alcohol stops drinking, they experience unpleasant and sometimes disturbing withdrawal symptoms. These include physiological responses such as sweating, heart palpitations and trembling. There are also psychological symptoms such as craving, *anxiety*, irritability and low mood.

These symptoms can be avoided by drinking again. Relief from withdrawal symptoms is *negatively reinforcing* – it strengthens drinking behaviour (e.g. drinking alcohol the morning after a binge to reduce a hangover). In some cases, the *fear* of withdrawal symptoms can be enough to trigger drinking before symptoms occur.

Relapse

Negative reinforcement The learning processes that initiate and maintain drinking can also cause *relapse* when a drinker has stopped. As we have seen, withdrawal symptoms can be unpleasant enough to prevent someone from giving up drinking. At any point in the process of abstaining, the relief gained from drinking again can be strong enough to provoke a relapse.

Even when withdrawal is over and relief is no longer a motivator, alcohol may still be an attractive escape from reality. If this is what initiated drinking in the first place, the chances are that drinking has made the problems worse. There is now even more reason for using alcohol to avoid the *stress* of everyday life.

In CERP (left), a drinker has to fully experience their cravings for alcohol (with support) instead of avoiding them by drinking again.

Evaluation

Research support for negative reinforcement

One strength is evidence to support negative reinforcement as an explanation of relapse.

According to George Koob (2009), drinking again to relieve the symptoms of withdrawal may be controlled by a brain structure called the *amygdala*. This becomes hyperactive during withdrawal, activating the *hypothalamic-pituitary-adrenal (HPA) system* (see page 46). This also makes the ex-drinker vulnerable to *stressors* (such as *life events*), making a relapse highly likely. So, withdrawal from alcohol resembles a severe stress response and relapsing is a way of calming it.

This research suggests that the negative reinforcement responsible for maintenance and relapse has a biological reality in the brain.

Practical applications

Another strength is that the learning approach has opened up several possibilities for treating alcoholism.

One approach has been to counteract the negatively reinforcing effects of alcohol. Drinkers often use alcohol to avoid unpleasant consequences. *Cue exposure with response prevention* (CERP) treatment (Laberg 1990) forces drinkers to confront these consequences. In cue exposure, the therapist presents the drinker with alcohol-related cues (e.g. glasses, bottles, smells, an actual drink). The drinker experiences the physiological and psychological effects associated with their addiction (e.g. increased heart rate, cravings). But in response prevention they are not allowed to drink to relieve these symptoms.

This shows how understanding the processes that create addiction can lead to potentially successful treatments.

Note that *classical conditioning* can also be applied, see page 88.

Mixed evidence for dopamine

One weakness is evidence that suggests dopamine is not critical to the effects of alcohol.

Destroying the nucleus accumbens of a rat eliminates dopamine release. But the rat will still press a lever at a high rate to receive alcohol (Koob 1992), implying that dopamine is not necessary to motivate the behaviour. Also, Jennifer Mitchell *et al.* (2012) showed that drinking in humans is associated with the release of chemicals called *endorphins* (the brain's natural painkillers) from the same areas as dopamine.

This suggests dopamine may not be the key biochemical factor at all stages of alcohol addiction and that endorphins play an important role.

Narrow explanation

Another weakness is that operant conditioning (reinforcement) cannot explain the transition from use to abuse of alcohol.

Most people try alcohol at some point and many will enjoy alcoholic drinks on a regular basis, perhaps even daily. But few of them become dependent (that is, experience withdrawal symptoms when they abstain). This is hard to explain if the effects of alcohol are positively and negatively reinforcing and based on a biological reward system in the brain.

This suggests that other non-conditioning factors are crucial in alcohol addiction, the most obvious and probably most influential of these being *genes*.

GET ACTIVE Measuring alcohol use

Researchers need to be able to measure alcohol-related behaviours in their studies. Health practitioners sometimes need to quickly screen patients for their alcohol use. Both often use the *Alcohol use disorders identification test* (AUDIT). This is a ten-item assessment produced by the World Health Organization (WHO). You can see it for yourself here: tinyurl.com/j7vm372.

1. How many of the items are about the effect of alcohol intake on behaviour?

2. How might the AUDIT be used by addiction researchers in studies?

3. How would health practitioners such as GPs, nurses and psychologists use the AUDIT?

Exam-style questions

Maisie started drinking because her friends and family did and they seemed to really like it. She and her friends would play drinking games round each other's houses. She drank more and more because she enjoyed it and wanted to block out a lot of bad things in her life. Whenever she goes without a drink for a few hours she feels depressed and anxious. Maisie has tried to stop but always feels terrible so it never works. One time, she got better but life was so unbearable she started drinking again.

1. Psychologists suggest that Maisie's alcohol addiction may have begun through operant conditioning. Explain the roles of the following in initiation of Maisie's alcohol addiction:

   (a) Role models. (2)

   (b) Positive reinforcement. (2)

   (c) Dopamine. (2)

2. Use the concept of negative reinforcement to explain the maintenance of Maisie's alcohol addiction. (3)

3. Recently, Maisie managed to stop drinking. She still has some bad withdrawal symptoms. But the worst thing is that she misses her friends because they all used to drink together.

   Using the learning approach, explain why Maisie might relapse. (3)

4. Explain **one** strength and **one** weakness of the learning approach as an explanation of Maisie's alcohol addiction. (4)

5. Assess the learning approach as an explanation of Maisie's alcohol addiction. Refer to **one** other approach in your answer. (9)

Don't forget assessment and revision issues on pages 34–35, 70–71 and 108–109.

An issue to consider

Although this spread is about alcohol abuse (or addiction), the mechanisms described here (dopamine reward, etc.) also explain typical alcohol use. So, what do you think is the difference?

Specification content

B2 Physiological addiction

Alcohol – learning approach:

Operant conditioning:

● Initiation – positive reinforcement, positive consequences such as relaxation, increased dopamine; negative reinforcement, relief from stress, influence of role models.

● Maintenance – negative reinforcement, relief from withdrawal symptoms.

● Relapse – reduction of withdrawal symptoms, negative reinforcement.

Gambling: Cognitive approach and Griffiths (1994)

FOBTs

Simon Perfitt drove a Porsche. He earned a lot of money but spent it (and more) on the 'crack cocaine of gambling' – fixed odds betting terminals (FOBTs). He reckons his habit cost him £200,000.

As far as he was concerned work was getting in the way of his gambling. One of them had to go, so he chose to say goodbye to work. His girlfriend left him after he tried to blackmail her out of £5000. He stopped brushing his teeth and had to have five of them removed.

Simon became irrational. He would behave superstitiously, parking in certain places because he believed this improved his chances of winning. He dropped huge amounts of money on the number of the table he had breakfast at in his hotel.

When on the FOBTs Simon entered a trance-like state in which he would play almost automatically with hardly any conscious awareness of what he was doing. 'You don't keep track and there's an element of self-deception. You just remember the wins and forget the losses.'

Source: *The Guardian* (2013)

Specification terms

Cognitive bias A distortion of attention, memory and thinking. It arises because of how we process information about the world, especially when we do it quickly. This can sometimes lead to irrational judgements and poor decision-making.

Cost-benefit analysis An individual weighs up the balance between the perceived benefits of changing behaviour and the perceived barriers (obstacles to change).

Illusion of control The mistaken belief of having a special ability to influence the operation of chance outcomes.

Irrational thoughts Ideas and beliefs that do not have logical basis in reality.

Recall bias A self-serving memory that exaggerates the benefits of a behaviour and minimises the costs.

It could be you ... but in reality it almost certainly won't be.

Expectancy theory of gambling addiction

The *cognitive approach* focuses on explanations about the way we think. In expectancy theory, the 'thinking' is expectations people have about what will happen if they gamble.

Initiation – cost-benefit analysis

A person's decision to gamble depends upon their expectations of the future costs and benefits of their behaviour. The potential costs of betting include financial losses and *anxiety*. The potential benefits include enjoyment, financial gain and a feeling of control. If a person expects the benefits to outweigh the costs, they are likely to gamble.

Maintenance

Expectations are not rational or logical because our cognitions can be biased and distorted.

Irrational thoughts Addicted gamblers are guided by *irrational thoughts* about how probability, chance and luck operate. For example, *gambler's fallacy* is the mistaken belief that, if something happens more frequently than normal during a given period (five heads tossed in a row), it will happen less frequently in the future (or vice versa).

Cognitive biases An addicted gambler's thinking is biased towards perceiving favourable outcomes. An example is the 'near miss' bias. Imagine a gambler bets on several horses to win their races, but they all come second or third. The horses have clearly lost and the gambler has lost his or her bets (and money). But the gambler interprets these outcomes as near misses, so instead of constantly losing they are 'constantly nearly winning' (Griffiths 1994). The near miss provides rewards (tension, excitement) that maintain gambling behaviour.

Illusions of control and exaggeration of ability An addicted gambler may believe they can influence a gambling outcome. They might consider that some superstitious behaviour (touching an item of clothing) alters the odds in their favour. Others think they have a special knowledge that makes them experts in selecting race horses.

Relapse

Recall bias and overestimation of success An addicted gambler who quits is at risk of *relapse* because their memory is self-serving. In other words, they recall wins/successes and overestimate the benefits of gambling. But they forget losses/failures and underestimate the costs. This bias makes a recovering gambler vulnerable because their distorted *cost-benefit analysis* makes gambling seem more attractive than it was.

Griffiths (1994) The role of cognitive bias and skill in fruit machine gambling

Aims

Mark Griffiths wanted to compare the thought processes of regular gamblers (RGs) and non-regular gamblers (NRGs).

Procedure

Griffiths used the 'thinking aloud' method with 30 RGs and 30 NRGs in a fruit machine arcade (they spoke their thoughts out loud as they gambled). These verbalisations were recorded and Griffiths used *content analysis* to place them in rational and irrational categories. He also assessed the participants' perceptions of their skill levels.

Findings

RGs made almost six times as many irrational verbalisations as the NRGs (14% to 2.5%). RGs were prone to the *illusion of control* ('I'm going to bluff this machine') and to *personification* of the machine ('This machine likes me'). RGs also assessed themselves as more skilful on fruit machines than the NRGs.

Conclusions

Cognitive factors may play a significant role in maintaining gambling behaviour.

GET ACTIVE Distorted thinking

Rosanna Michalczuk *et al.* (2011) studied 30 addicted gamblers who attended the UK National Problem Gambling Clinic. Compared with non-gambling participants, the addicted gamblers showed more and stronger gambling-related cognitive distortions of all types. Here are some examples: 'Now we're motoring, we'll be here all night'; 'These cards are definitely not my friends'; 'I'm going for red, it's my lucky colour'; 'Now I've won there's no stopping me'; 'At last my happy time is here'.

1. Draw up a table with the following headings: *'Illusions of control (superstitious beliefs/rituals)', 'Personification', 'Inability to stop', 'Expecting gambling to bring relief'.*

   Look at the statements above and decide which headings they go under. Write them in.

2. Think of some more examples and add them to your table.

Griffiths argues that the 'near miss' is such a powerful maintainer of gambling that it should really be renamed the 'near win'.

Evaluation

Practical applications

One strength is that there are effective treatments based on the cognitive approach.

These directly address the addicted gambler's *cognitive biases* and irrational thoughts, replacing them with more rational ways of thinking about gambling. Cognitive-based treatments have had some success in reducing addicts' gambling behaviour. For example, Robert Ladouceur *et al.* (2001) found that correcting pathological gamblers' perceptions of randomness reduced their gambling behaviour even 12 months later.

This supports the view that cognitive distortions underlie addicted gambling behaviour because tackling them reduces it.

Problems explaining initiation and maintenance

One weakness is that expectancy theory cannot fully explain the link between cognitions and gambling.

For instance, there are many people who have irrational thoughts and distorted cognitions about gambling. But very few people ever start gambling in the first place. Of those who do, even if they gamble occasionally, only about 1–3% have difficulty controlling their behaviour (Ladouceur 1996). If expectancy theory is correct, it is surprising there are not many more addicted gamblers.

This suggests that cognitive factors are not enough to explain why people start and continue to gamble.

Evaluation

Ecological validity

One strength of Griffiths' study is its high level of *ecological validity*.

Griffiths studied gamblers' cognitive distortions in a real-life gambling situation. He wanted to avoid the artificiality of a lab-based procedure. This is important because the findings from lab studies and real-life studies are different. For example, George Anderson and Iain Brown (1984) found that the heart rates of gamblers in a lab did not increase. But they did increase when they gambled in a casino.

This means that Griffiths' findings and conclusions can be applied to real-life situations in which people actually gamble.

Sampling issues

One weakness is that his participants may have been unusual.

Griffiths recruited participants using a method called *snowball sampling*. A small number of already-recruited participants recommend other gamblers. But because they are known to each other, the participants may share certain characteristics (e.g. they might have similar levels of *addiction*). Therefore, they may not be representative of most gamblers.

This means that Griffiths' findings may tell us little about the cognitive distortions of the majority of the gambling population.

Exam-style questions

When Sol first saw people placing bets on horses he said, 'I think I'd enjoy that and I might win'. He always wears his lucky socks before he places a bet. He loves the excitement of betting and likes celebrating even if his horse comes third. Sol also plays the fruit machines in the betting shop. He believes he wins because he's good at pressing the right buttons at the right time.

1. Using the concept of cost-benefit analysis, explain the initiation of Sol's gambling. (2)

2. Cognitive psychologists believe that several factors help to maintain gambling. Use the concepts of 'cognitive bias' and 'illusion of control' to explain why Sol continues to gamble. (4)

3. Psychology can help explain why people who try to give up gambling may relapse. Define what is meant by 'relapse'. (1)

4. Sol is taking a break from gambling. When he things about it, he remembers he used to be quite good at it and won a fair bit of money.

   Use the cognitive approach to explain why Sol is at risk of relapse. (3)

5. Explain the role of irrational thoughts in gambling addiction. (2)

6. Griffiths (1994) carried out a study on gambling.

   (a) Describe the procedure. (3)

   (b) Give **one** finding that helps to explain Sol's gambling. (1)

7. Discuss how the cognitive approach explains Sol's gambling. Refer to at least **one** research study in your answer. (9)

An issue to consider

Griffiths wanted to include non-gamblers in his study but his university's ethics committee wouldn't let him.

Why do you think this was? Can you think of any ways in which his study might be considered unethical?

Specification content
B3 Behavioural addiction

Gambling – cognitive approach:

Expectancy theory:
- Initiation – cost-benefit analysis.
- Maintenance – irrational thoughts, cognitive biases, illusions of control, exaggeration of ability.
- Griffiths (1994) The role of cognitive bias and skill in fruit machine gambling.
- Relapse – recall bias and overestimation of success.

Gambling: Learning approach

Another true story

Ranjit Bolt is a playwright who visited 'tacky' and 'seedy' betting shops to play blackjack gaming machines. He loved the 'adrenaline rush' or hitting 20 or 21 – 'Few things can match it'. He has gambled in lots of environments but particularly enjoys the atmosphere of betting shops.

His addiction began after he was introduced to online poker by a friend. He thought he was making money. But when he checked his bank account after a few weeks he was already down by £4000. Then he would play three days straight without sleep until he was hallucinating. Bolt writes of gambling: 'Like all addictive activities, it offers astonishing highs – highs as high as the lows are low'. Such as the time he turned his last £2000 into £82,000 over a three-week period. And then lost it all in ten minutes.

When he wrote this article, Bolt had not gambled for several months. But he describes walking down the road, noticing the many betting shops and getting a strong urge to go in one and gamble once again on the machines.

Source: *The Guardian* (2012)

Specification terms

Cue reactivity Cravings and arousal can be triggered in, for example, gambling addicts when they encounter cues related to the pleasurable effects of gambling (e.g. sounds of a fruit machine).

Variable reinforcement schedule In operant conditioning when a reward is delivered at intervals that change each time rather than, for example, every tenth trial.

Gambling websites are busy, flashy, colourful, noisy and exciting. A bit like me.

Learning explanation of gambling addiction

The *learning approach* (*learning theory*) includes *social learning*, *classical conditioning* and *operant conditioning*.

Initiation

Social learning Many people begin gambling by observing *models* and experiencing *vicarious reinforcement*. Seeing others rewarded for their gambling (their pleasure and enjoyment) is a powerful initiator.

Observation is not just direct but can be indirect through media reports and presentations of excited lottery winners, the glamour of horse racing, etc. This could trigger a desire for the same reinforcement in someone who hasn't gambled before.

Classical conditioning is also influential in the early stages of gambling. The first-time gambler enjoys the intense external (flashing lights, bustling crowds, noise, etc.) and internal (excitement, tension) sensations they experience. These quickly become associated with the gambling activity (they become *conditioned stimuli*).

Maintenance

Operant conditioning can explain how gambling behaviour continues over time.

Positive reinforcement Gambling provides occasional opportunities to win money as well as an exciting 'buzz'. Both reward a gamble and make it likely to be repeated. Some addicted gamblers experience a 'big win' not long after they start gambling. This memorable reward has great significance for the gambler and they continue to gamble to repeat it.

Near misses are also positively reinforcing, even though the gambler loses money. Near misses provide a short-lived burst of excitement and tension (like hitting a goalpost in football). Gambling games often include built-in near misses (like spinning the bonus wheel in *Candy Crush Saga* and not quite getting the jackpot).

Negative reinforcement Gambling can also be an escape from reality for some people. The temporary relief from everyday *anxiety* is negatively reinforcing and again strengthens gambling behaviour.

Partial reinforcement occurs when only some instances of a behaviour are rewarded. This is exactly what happens in most gambling. For example, fruit machines operate on a *partial reinforcement schedule*. They are programmed to pay out only on some bets, so the gambler's behaviour is only reinforced sometimes. B.F. Skinner (1948) showed that this schedule causes the learned behaviour to persist for a longer time than *continuous reinforcement*.

Variable reinforcement is a type of partial reinforcement in which only a certain proportion of gambles are rewarded. A *variable reinforcement schedule* creates the most persistent gambling behaviours. For example, a fruit machine might pay out after an average of 10 spins but not on every 10th spin (too predictable). Instead, the first payout might come after two spins, the second after seven spins, the third after 15 spins and so on.

This is a highly unpredictable pattern of reinforcement. The gambler cannot be sure when the reward will appear so they continue to feed a fruit machine or place bets even when they do not win for a long time.

Relapse

Cue reactivity explains how gambling can be reinstated after the gambler has quit. Experienced gamblers encounter many *conditioned cues* (or *secondary reinforcers*, see page 52). These are stimuli that become reinforcing because they are associated with physiological and emotional arousal. They include adverts for gambling, the colourful look of lottery scratchcards, the noisy and flashy environment of a casino, the crowded and busy look of a gambling website. They cue the arousal that the ex-gambler associates with gambling and most likely still craves.

Conditioned cues are hard for the ex-gambler to avoid because they are everywhere in the social and media environment (e.g. walking past a betting shop). They are continuous low-level reminders of the pleasures of gambling and significant risk factors for *relapse*.

Evaluation

Research support

One strength is evidence to support the learning approach.

For example, Mark Dickerson (1979) observed gamblers in two betting offices in Birmingham. High-frequency gamblers (HFGs, who placed most bets on horses) consistently placed their bets in the last two minutes before the start of a race. If low-frequency gamblers (LFGs) had not placed a bet by this point, they were more likely to bet on the next race instead. It is likely that the HFGs delayed their bets to prolong the rewarding excitement they felt.

This shows that *positive reinforcement* can explain gambling behaviour in a real-life environment (rather than just in a contrived study of behaviour).

Role of partial reinforcement

Another strength is support from research evidence for the role of partial reinforcement.

Rachel Horsley *et al.* (2012) compared high-frequency gamblers (HFGs) and low-frequency gamblers (LFGs) in their sensitivity to partial reinforcement on a computer game. Some participants received reinforcement every time they successfully solved a puzzle (continuous reinforcement). Others received the reinforcement only on some occasions (partial reinforcement). Eventually no rewards were provided. But the HFGs continued to play for significantly longer than the LFGs even though reinforcement had stopped.

This finding shows how partial reinforcement may specifically influence addicted gamblers to continue gambling even when they are losing.

Role of individual differences

One weakness is that conditioning does not occur in the same way in every gambler.

Mark Griffiths and Paul Delfabbro (2001) note that responses to identical stimuli differ from person to person, as do motivations. Some people gamble to relax, others to experience arousal. Some people quit and never gamble again even though they experience the same conditioned cues (*cue reactivity*) as people who relapse.

These findings are difficult for learning theory to explain without including some *cognitive* features of gambling such as *irrational thoughts*.

Lacks explanatory power

Another weakness is that learning theory cannot explain all types of gambling.

Some gambling outcomes are due entirely to chance or luck (e.g. scratch cards, fruit machines) so the gambler has no opportunity to influence them (even if they think they can). Other gambles benefit more from the skill of the gambler (e.g. sports betting). Also, for some gambles there is little delay between the bet and the outcome (fruit machines). For others the delay is much longer (sports betting). It is hard for learning theories to explain *addiction* to gambles requiring skill in which there is a delay between bet and outcome.

This means that the learning approach lacks explanatory power because it cannot provide a general explanation of all gambling addiction.

To be fair, not all betting offices are this glamorous.

Exam-style questions

Louis started betting on online fruit machines when a friend introduced him to a website. He immediately enjoyed the flashing colours and the 'busy' appearance of the site. He had quite a big win almost as soon as he started. He has had a few small wins since, but nothing like that first one. He has noticed how it's hard to work out when he'll get a win. He can go a long time without winning anything, and then two payouts come along close together. He was spending up to six hours a day on gambling websites, but it was better than his everyday life. He has stopped gambling for now, but it's hard for him because he has to use the internet every day.

1. Explain how the learning approach accounts for the initiation of Louis' gambling addiction. (3)

2. Explain the role of variable reinforcement in maintaining Louis' gambling addiction. Give specific examples in your answer. (3)

3. Using the concept of cue reactivity, explain why Louis might relapse. (3)

4. Explain **one** strength and **one** weakness of the learning approach as an explanation of gambling. (4)

5. Evaluate the learning approach as an explanation of Louis' gambling behaviour. Refer to **one** other approach in your answer. (9)

An issue to consider

You have now looked at two approaches to gambling behaviour. In what ways are they similar and how are they different?

Could they be combined in some way to produce a better explanation?

GET ACTIVE A friend in need

A friend wants your advice because until recently he was spending several hours every day down the arcade playing the slot machines. He wants to know how he can keep off the machines. Before you can help, you need to know if social learning and classical conditioning were involved in your friend starting to gamble. Likewise, you want to know if he continued to play the machines because of *negative reinforcement* and *variable reinforcement*.

1. *Write four questions you could ask your friend to gather this information, bearing in mind he is not a psychology student.*

2. *Based on the learning approach, what **two** pieces of advice would you give to help your friend avoid relapse?*

Specification content

B3 Behavioural addiction

Gambling – learning approach:

● Initiation – association between gambling and pleasure/excitement therefore behaviour strengthened.

● Maintenance – variable reinforcement schedules, behaviour strengthened due to variable success.

● Relapse – cue reactivity, cues associated with behaviour increase likelihood of relapse, i.e. walking past betting shops, gambling advertisements.

Shopping: Learning approach

Shop til you drop?

Are you a shopaholic? Do you often need some retail therapy? Here's what shopping addict Isabella Fels says about her behaviour:

'...the thing about shopping that most appeals to me is the social aspect of it. Shop assistants act like they're your best friends, other shoppers make chitchat as they shop themselves, and with everything you buy, there's a promise that it could change your life somehow' (bodyandsoul.com.au).

So, Isabella is addicted to shopping because she finds it rewarding.

An interesting aspect of shopping addiction is how women's and men's behaviours are so often perceived differently. A woman whose shopping is out of control is a shopaholic, an addict (and often seen as 'typical' in our culture). But a man who buys compulsively is a 'collector'. He often won't even be considered a shopper, because in many cultures that's not a 'man thing'.

Specification terms

See pages 52 and 60.

It is said that Lindsay Lohan spent $5000 a day in online shopping binges – and this was when she was in rehab.

Learning explanation of shopping addiction

There is some debate about whether *out-of-control shopping* is actually an *addiction*. However, most psychologists do recognise it is a problem, so they prefer to use the phrase *compulsive shopping*. This term has become widespread, so we use this term interchangeably with addiction on this spread.

Initiation

According to the *learning approach*, most people shop at some time so the beginning of an addiction may simply be from direct experience of having a good time shopping! Rewards may also be experienced indirectly.

Role models and vicarious reinforcement Someone who observes *role models* enjoying shopping and its outcomes is likely to experience *vicarious reinforcement*. That is, they indirectly experience the rewarding effects of shopping such as enjoyment and pleasure. This may be enough to trigger a desire for the same rewards in someone who hasn't shopped to the same extent before.

Celebrities and advertisements Characters in adverts are a significant source of vicarious reinforcement. Consumer goods are presented as bringing pleasure to those who buy them. Adverts suggest that buying can give us pleasure and gain success or status.

Celebrities are effective models because of their association with a glamorous lifestyle based (in this context) on shopping. If the observer identifies with the celebrity then imitation of their behaviour is even more likely. Identification occurs when the observer perceives the celebrity is similar to themselves in some way. 'Down-to-earth' celebrities in everyday situations are especially powerful models for this reason.

Maintenance

Positive reinforcement Shopping becomes compulsive because of its rewarding effects, which include excitement, pleasure and fun. But the role of *positive reinforcement* extends further than the immediate shopping experience. Friends may shop together and discuss purchases afterwards, gaining status or praise for buying. Several features of the shopping environment are also positively reinforcing such as the sounds, colours and smells of shops, or the enjoyable feedback from online stores.

Adrenaline rush and rewards The brain's *dopamine* reward system is assumed to be involved in motivating people to shop compulsively (although this is a very under-researched area). This is because *behavioural addictions* are thought to trigger the same biochemical processes underlying reinforcement as drugs do. Dopamine is released from the *nucleus accumbens* into the *frontal areas* of the brain. This is where the rewarding 'rush' (feeling of elation) comes from when we buy something (people often refer to it as an 'adrenaline rush').

Negative reinforcement Many people experience the aftermath of a shopping binge as a feeling of emptiness. They may have been using shopping to block out negative feelings that they now find resurfacing. This motivates the compulsive shopper to shop again, as relief from feelings they find unpleasant or from a reality they don't want to face.

Relapse

Cues associated with shopping Once a compulsive shopper has gained some control over their behaviour they are still vulnerable to shopping-related cues. These are hard to avoid because they are everywhere in the day-to-day environment. They include shops on the high street, adverts on TV and social media, websites, etc. These trigger the arousal that the shopper associates with their compulsion and still craves (*cue reactivity*).

Relief from withdrawal symptoms (negative reinforcement) A recovering compulsive shopper experiences negative emotions (*anxiety*, *depression*, emptiness, boredom, guilt) that can be relieved by shopping again. But this relief is only temporary, so compulsive shopping becomes a cycle of destructive behaviour, recovery and *relapse*.

Evaluation

Role of shopping

One strength is research support for advertising as a cue to shopping.

Johannes Knoll and Jörg Matthes (2017) reviewed 46 studies into the effects of celebrities in adverts. Shoppers' attitudes were significantly more positive towards products when they were endorsed by celebrities than when they were not. Some of the reviewed studies concluded that participants often perceived a celebrity as 'someone they like'.

This shows that identification plays an important role in how adverts featuring celebrities influence attitudes towards products.

Gender differences

Another strength is that learning processes can explain gender differences in shopping addiction.

Most research indicates that male and female compulsive shoppers buy different categories of products (Dittmar 2005). Women compulsively shop for clothes, shoes, cosmetics and jewellery. Men shop for electronic goods, CDs and 'hardware' (e.g. tools). These items match stereotypical gender roles (at least in Western *cultures*) and buying them attracts positive reinforcement from others (making it more likely that similar items will be bought again).

This supports the view that *operant conditioning* plays a key role in shopping addiction.

Self-report

One weakness is that research studies use *self-report methods*.

Participants indicate the extent of their shopping compulsion by completing *questionnaires*. There is a high degree of *social desirability bias* built into these scales. This is because most people are reluctant to admit to an addiction or compulsive behaviour (which is seen as socially undesirable). They would rather project a more positive impression. Studies depend on participants' subjective interpretations of their own behaviour, with no objective confirmation (e.g. observations of their behaviour).

This suggests that, if anything, research findings may underestimate the extent of shopping addiction.

Cognitive factors

Another weakness is that there is a greater role for *cognitive* factors in compulsive shopping than the learning approach recognises.

It is hard to explain several features of shopping addiction on the basis of reinforcement alone without cognitive factors. For example, Patrick Trotzke *et al.* (2015) investigated online shopping. They found that the positive reinforcement of excitement was not enough to explain compulsive shopping as opposed to non-compulsive shopping. Other factors were necessary, including anonymity and the expectation that online shopping would satisfy specific goals and desires.

This suggests that the most satisfactory explanation of shopping addiction could be one that combines cognitive and behavioural factors.

GET ACTIVE A shopping quiz

Have a go at the compulsive shopping quiz here: tinyurl.com/yxlb6sql.

It's really just a bit of fun rather than a serious assessment, and some of the questions probably won't even apply to you. As you answer the questions, think about the elements of compulsive shopping they are assessing. When you get your score at the end, you'll be able to see all the questions and your responses.

1. *What do you think of your score? Does it surprise you or not?*

2. *Have a look again at all the questions. Which ones are assessing the roles of positive and negative reinforcement? What about the 'adrenaline rush'? Is there anything about relief from withdrawal symptoms?*

Shopping online is certainly easier but not necessarily more compulsive than other shopping. Which indicates that an addiction to shopping must involve more than just convenience. Perhaps shopping in stores offers more excitement and distraction.

Exam-style questions

As a child Misha joined her mum and dad to go shopping and it was always great fun. Now she does the same with her friends who share her love of shopping. She shops online as well, enjoying all the colours of the websites. She gets a real 'rush' when she clicks the 'Buy' button. Misha follows a few celebrities on Instagram and is really interested in what they are buying and advertising. Most of Misha's friends shop like she does, in fact that's all they talk about. They share what they've been buying on social media. Misha gets so bored and lonely when she isn't shopping.

1. Psychology can help explain the initiation of Misha's shopping addiction. Define what is meant by 'initiation'. (1)

2. In the context of Misha's shopping addiction, explain the role of vicarious reinforcement. (2)

3. Explain the role of operant conditioning in the maintenance of Misha's shopping addiction. Give an example in your answer. (3)

4. Misha has decided to cut back on her shopping. But she doesn't get as many 'Likes' on social media, and hasn't seen her friends and is feeling anxious.

   Explain how cues and negative reinforcement might cause Misha to relapse. (3)

5. Assess the learning approach to Misha's shopping addiction in terms of strengths and weaknesses. (6)

6. The learning approach claims that addiction initiation, maintenance and relapse can be explained through learning processes such as operant conditioning. Discuss the learning approach to explaining Misha's behaviour. (9)

An issue to consider

Some researchers do not believe that compulsive shopping is actually an addiction.

What are the arguments for and against it as an addiction?

Specification content

B3 Behavioural addiction

Shopping – learning approach:

- Initiation – role models guide on how to behave, vicarious reinforcement, role of celebrity and advertisements.

- Maintenance – association with excitement and pleasure, adrenaline rush and rewards, positive reinforcement.

- Relapse – cues associated with shopping are seen, advertisements, need to shop, relief from withdrawal symptoms/negative reinforcement.

Shopping: Cognitive approach

Madame Bovary syndrome

A typical compulsive shopper will buy things they don't need and then just add them to the pile. Clothes, shoes and jewellery never worn, make-up never used, books never read. Tools that never see any DIY.

In a way it is like a form of collecting (which is how men's compulsive shopping is often seen). Accumulating things doesn't begin to fill the empty hole that the compulsive shopper feels. But the process of buying provides the escape.

In Gustave Flaubert's classic novel, Madame Bovary leads a dull and frustrating life as a country doctor's wife. But she is ambitious and wants to experience more – more beauty, passion, luxury. She fills the void in herself by shopping. She buys so much that she runs up a huge debt she cannot repay.

This is why compulsive shopping is sometimes called *Madame Bovary syndrome*.

Specification term

Self-esteem The feelings that a person has about their self-concept.

See also page 54.

Graceful, elegant, untroubled. But only on the surface. Below the water, the swan's legs are paddling for all they're worth. People who use shopping to self-medicate often have a lot going on 'below the surface'.

Self-medication model of shopping addiction

Self-medication is an example of the *cognitive approach*. It means that shopping is potentially a way to treat other problems. People even call it 'retail therapy' maybe as a kind of joke. But for some people it is a way of dealing with serious personal issues.

Initiation

Excitement and relief from boredom A person may find shopping is an exciting and easily-accessed activity to relieve boredom. Anyone can look around shops or go online. There is even no cost in buying things as virtually everything can be returned. This means a shopping habit may begin.

Psychological problems, distress and lack of self-esteem Self-medication theory argues that shopping is sometimes used in the same way as alcohol (see page 54) – that is, as relief from emotional distress and low *self-esteem* that may be associated with mental disorders (such as *depression*).

Edward Khantzian (1985) claimed issues such as emotional distress originate in childhood *trauma* (e.g. from abuse, neglect and loss). The trauma may have been buried but is brought back to the surface by the *stress* of a major life event (e.g. divorce, bereavement).

'Trauma' is a strong word and may give the impression that only extremely harsh experiences matter. However, parental criticism, for example, can also give rise to later distress.

Maintenance

Reduction of anxiety *Compulsive shopping* means spending money which leads many people into serious financial problems, specifically debts that cannot easily be repaid. A compulsive shopper experiences *anxiety* when they consider the true consequences of their *addiction*. They may face cues that trigger this anxiety (e.g. bank statements, comments from others).

The anxiety can be relieved by behaviours that disguise the shopper's reality (e.g. hiding bank statements, avoiding friends). But the simplest method is to continue shopping.

However, using shopping to self-medicate emotional distress is counterproductive. Compulsive shoppers often get into serious debt because they spend huge amounts of money. This adds to the stress, which in turn creates greater anxiety.

Continuation of boredom/anxiety relief Compulsive shoppers often report that they think of nothing else when they are shopping. Their attention is very narrowly focused on what they are doing. Shopping relieves their anxiety, provides excitement and allows them to forget their everyday lives. Richard Elliott (1994) called this the 'mood repair' function of shopping.

But once the online 'Buy' button is clicked or the high-street spree is over, the usual anxieties come flooding back for an addict. But now there is more to be anxious about (more products to hide, more secrets to keep, more debt).

The anxiety can be immediately relieved by shopping again. In cases of severe compulsive shopping this destructive maintenance cycle can go on for years or even decades.

Relapse

Effects of withdrawal A compulsive shopper who decides to stop is vulnerable to the feelings of distress, boredom and loneliness that they were trying to relieve by shopping. They also may experience anxiety due to financial worries.

Breakdown of coping strategies The shopping is a coping strategy to deal with the other problems. As we saw with alcohol addiction, this is the paradox of self-medication. Edward Khantzian (1985) believed the addiction cycle could only be overcome by treating the underlying emotional distress (or *co-morbid* mental disorder).

In other words, the compulsive shopper needs to find a different way to deal with the underlying problems. For example, increasing self-esteem emotionally stabilises the person, so they would have no need to self-medicate. Therapy would help them to focus on other areas of their lives where self-esteem could be boosted. For example, by making friends or getting more out of existing relationships, seeking fulfilment at work or in hobbies, activities, etc.

Evaluation

Support for early trauma

One strength is research support for the role of early trauma in shopping addiction.

Gilles Valence *et al.* (1988) compared the family histories of compulsive shoppers and non-compulsive control participants. They found that the compulsive shoppers reported significantly more experiences of family dysfunction in their childhoods (e.g. they had parents with anxiety, depression and alcoholism). Wayne DeSarbo and Elizabeth Edwards (1996) linked childhood abuse and neglect with later emotional distress and compulsive shopping.

This shows that shopping may well be a behaviour that self-medicates distress arising out of early trauma and neglect.

Link to mental disorders

Another strength is there is evidence to link compulsive shopping with mental disorders.

Donald Black (2007) points out that compulsive shopping is co-morbid with several disorders (i.e. they often occur together). For example, research shows that between 41% and 80% of compulsive shoppers also have an *anxiety disorder* (e.g. a phobia, diagnosed or undiagnosed). Between 21% and 100% have a *mood disorder* (e.g. depression).

This suggests that self-medication theory is correct in claiming that current emotional distress arises out of mental disorders. This is significant support when combined with the research into early trauma.

Non-cognitive factors important

One weakness of self-medication theory is that it ignores or minimises the role of non-cognitive factors.

We have noted research linking compulsive shopping with early trauma (see above). One interpretation of these findings is that parents with mental disorders create a dysfunctional home environment which causes trauma in children. However, another interpretation is that mental disorders such as depression and anxiety have a significant *genetic* component (as confirmed by other research, see Unit 6, page 230).

This would help to explain why these children grow up to develop depression and/or anxiety as well as shopping addiction – because they share common genetic roots, not because the depression/anxiety is the outcome of trauma.

Cause and effect

Another weakness is that the nature of the links between compulsive shopping and other factors is unclear.

Unlike in alcohol addiction, this is a very under-researched area. As we have seen, there is evidence of links between trauma, mental disorders, emotional distress and compulsive shopping. Self-medication theory predicts that mental disorders should occur before compulsive shopping develops. There is little evidence to confirm this. It is just as likely that people who shop compulsively eventually become depressed and anxious.

This shows that more research is needed to establish the direction of cause and effect.

'What have I done?' Seeing an item, buying it, getting it home (or delivered) and opening the packaging is all exciting. But almost immediately for a shopping addict, this is replaced by anxiety and emptiness.

Exam-style questions

When Saj went through a painful relationship break-up he felt very stressed. The stress brought up all sorts of past issues, including memories of the neglect he suffered as a child. Saj had always felt bad about himself and this made him depressed. So one day he went online to buy some clothes and things he wanted just to feel better. But he ended up spending a small fortune on things he didn't need. Saj did feel a lot better for a short while, then he found he got bored very quickly. He was also lonely since the break-up so he bought more stuff. This pattern continued for a year before he decided to just quit shopping for good. Saj hasn't bought anything for a week but he can feel the issues coming back again.

1. Explain how the cognitive approach can account for initiation of Saj's shopping addiction. (3)

2. Explain the role of self-esteem in Saj's shopping addiction. (3)

3. Explain the role of self-medication in the maintenance of Saj's shopping addiction. Refer to specific examples in your answer. (3)

4. Use the cognitive approach to shopping addiction, to explain why Saj might relapse. (3)

5. Explain **one** strength and **one** weakness of self-medication as an explanation of Saj's shopping addiction. (4)

6. Assess the cognitive approach as an explanation of Saj's shopping addiction. Refer to **one** other approach in your answer. (9)

An issue to consider

If compulsive shopping is a form of self-medication, what do you think are the problems that are being medicated?

GET ACTIVE Comparing approaches

Justene has been caught yet again for shoplifting and this time she has appeared in the magistrates' court. At the end of the trial, the magistrate addresses Justene: 'We have heard submissions from two psychologists. Dr Lecter says you are motivated by a strong feeling of pleasure in shopping, an 'adrenaline rush'. But Dr Kildare points to your troubled childhood and family background, and your history of depression and anxiety'. The magistrate is concerned Justene will shoplift again, so he asks Dr Lecter and Dr Kildare for their views.

1. *Based on what the two psychologists have already said, how would they each explain the risk of Justene relapsing?*

2. *What are the main points of difference between the two explanations?*

Specification content

B3 Behavioural addiction

Shopping – cognitive approach:

Self-medication:

● Initiation – relief from boredom, psychological problem, distress, lack of self-esteem, excitement.

● Maintenance – reduction of anxiety associated with spending, continuation of boredom/anxiety relief.

● Relapse – withdrawal causes lack of excitement/boredom, increase of anxiety (due to financial worries), breakdown of coping strategies.

Content area B
Revision summary

Stress

Causes of stress

Life events

What are life events? Major changes, relatively infrequent, cause stress because readjustment needed. Include positive (e.g. getting married) and negative (e.g. getting divorced).

Measuring life events Social readjustment rating scale (SRRS, Holmes and Rahe 1967), 43 events with life change units (e.g. divorce is 73 LCUs). Add up LCUs over set period (e.g. 12 months).

Life events and illness Under 150 LCUs = 30% chance stress-related illness in following year. Between 150 and 299 LCUs = 50% chance. Over 300 LCUs = 80% chance (Rahe 1972).

Evaluation

Support from research Life events predicted asthma within two year follow-up period (Lietzén et al. 2011).

Positive and negative life events Negative are more stressful. Better to look at specific stressors not overall score (Turner and Wheaton 1997).

Rahe et al. (1970)

Aims Would LCU scores predict illness?

Procedure 2664 US Navy personnel completed SRE (like SRRS). Identified all events in six months before tour of duty. Total LCU score for each participant. All illnesses reported on tour of duty.

Findings Small but significant positive correlation (+.118). Sailors with most stressful life events also had most illness aboard ship.

Conclusions Life events are reasonable predictors of later illness.

Evaluation

Large sample size 2664 participants. Sample representative, so generalise conclusions to population.

Self-report method SRRS/SRE items open to interpretation (e.g. 'serious illness'), reduces validity.

Daily hassles

What are daily hassles? Minor everyday frustrations and irritations that cause stress (e.g. difficult neighbours, planning meals).

Primary and secondary appraisal
(1) Think about how threatening hassle is to our health (primary).
(2) Think about how well we can cope (secondary). We interpret meaning of hassles.

Measuring daily hassles Hassles scale, 117 items from seven categories. Choose all hassles that day and rate severity (1 to 3).
Also Uplifts scale to measure events that counteract stress (Kanner et al. 1981).

Daily hassles and illness Effects add up. Also a life event creates many hassles (disruption).

Evaluation

Supporting research evidence Hassles better predictor of job-related illness than life events (Ivancevich 1986).

Retrospective research Complete scales by recalling hassles but may be inaccurate. Research over- or underestimates impact of hassles on stress/health.

Kanner et al. (1981)

Aims Compare hassles and life events as predictors of illness.

Procedure 100 participants completed Hassles and uplifts scale every month for 9 months, plus measures of life events and anxiety/depression.

Findings Positive correlations between number of hassles and anxiety/depression at start and end of study. Greater than for life events.

Conclusions Hassles are more reliable predictor of psychological symptoms than life events.

Evaluation

Self-report method Hassles scale a direct assessment, practical unlike observation. More honest responses than face-to-face.

Response bias Hassles scale very long and items scored in just one direction. Respondent may choose rating automatically.

The workplace

Role conflict
Intra-role: competing demands within the same role.
Inter-role: competing demands between different roles.

Effects of work environment
Temperature: too hot/cold creates stress and aggression.
Noise: unpleasant stimulus especially if no control.
Level of control Lack of control reduces choices, negative experience.

Evaluation

Research support for control Civil servants' workload not a stressor but low control = heart disease later (Bosma et al. 1997).

Cultural differences Lack of control stressful in individualist cultures but not in collectivist. Western concept (Györkös et al. 2012).

Johansson et al. (1978)

Aims Compare stress of two groups of sawmill workers.

Procedure Measured illness, absenteeism, stress hormones, alertness, mood in:
High-risk group (sawyers): repetitive, isolated, low control but complex.
Low-risk group (maintenance): more control and flexibility.

Findings Higher hormones in high-risk group, and increased during day. Also more illness, absenteeism.

Conclusions Job demands and lack of control create stress, physiological arousal and illness.

Evaluation

Practical application Giving control can reduce stress (e.g. task variety, interaction with others), improves well-being.

Not a causal effect Participants not placed into groups, already existing jobs. Differences between groups may explain findings (not lack of control).

Personality

Hardy personality Kobasa (1979):
Commitment (sense of purpose).
Challenge (welcome change).
Control (active not passive).
Protects against stress.

Type A and B personality Friedman and Rosenman: Type A people are competitive, hostile, time-urgent, risk of heart disease. Type B are the opposite (laid back).
Risk factor for stress and illness.

Evaluation

Two Cs or three? Control important in commitment/challenge. Remove 'challenge' (Hull et al. 1987).

Research support for Type A People who had a stroke more likely to be Type A, recent link with cardiovascular disorders (Egido et al. 2012).

Maddi (1987)

Aims Are there links between stress, hardiness and illness?

Procedure Interviewed managers at Bell Telephone in US during major reorganisation.

Findings About ⅓ did not become ill, scored high on 3Cs.

Conclusions Hardiness protects against effects of stress at work.

Evaluation

Self-report Social desirability bias in hardiness scales. The 3Cs are positive characteristics, so participants exaggerate them.

Rosenman et al. (1976)

Aims Does personality type predict CHD?

Procedure 3000+ men free from CHD assessed as Type A or B.

Findings 8½ years later, 257 men had CHD. 70% had been assessed as Type A. Higher stress hormones, higher cholesterol than Type Bs.

Conclusions Personality type is a risk factor for CHD, more vulnerable to stressors.

Evaluation

Contradictory evidence Type B heart attack survivors more likely to have second heart attack later and die than Type A survivors – because they make lifestyle changes to avoid heart attack (Ragland and Brand 1988).

Physiological responses to stress

The body's response

The general adaptation syndrome (GAS)
Selye (1936): Stress is body's general response to any stressor.
Alarm reaction: adrenaline and fight or flight response triggered by hypothalamus.
Resistance: continuing stressor means long-term response uses body's resources.
Exhaustion: resources depleted, initial stress symptoms reappear, immune system damaged.

A more modern approach
Acute stress: The SAM system. Immediate response, fight or flight. Sympathetic branch of ANS triggered. Adrenal medullas release adrenaline. Parasympathetic branch restores to normal (rest and digest).
Chronic stress: The HPA system. Hypothalamus releases CRF. Detected by pituitary gland which releases ACTH. Stimulates adrenal cortexes to release cortisol.
Cortisol central to stress response but long-term damage.
HPA self-regulates via negative feedback loop.

Evaluation

Gender differences in the physiological responses These responses apply to males (biased), fight or flight risky for females (would abandon offspring), tend and befriend better (Taylor 2006).

More than two responses Freeze response, e.g. animals become paralysed, humans 'disassociate'. Predator ignores unresponsive prey.

Fight or flight response is maladaptive SAM/fight or flight damaging in more chronic stress situations (e.g. traffic jams).

Role of perception In humans, perception of stressor affects physiological response. Different for animals, so Selye's theory (based on rats) is not a full picture.

Stress and ill health

Stress and ill health

Immune system Defence against antigens.
• Innate immunity: general, fast response involving leucocytes and NK cells.
• Acquired immunity: specific, lymphocytes (e.g. B cells, memory T cells, killer T cells).

Suppression of the immune system Stress has direct effect (cortisol reduces lymphocytes) and indirect (lifestyle).

Stress and cardiovascular disorders (CVDs) Stress hormones cause atherosclerosis in blood vessels.
Chronic and acute effects, e.g. cardiac incidents during World Cup (Wilbert-Lampen et al. 2008).

Evaluation

Support for stress effects on the immune system HIV+ women with high stress more likely to develop cervical cancer (Pereira et al. 2003).

Short-term versus long-term effects Short-term stressor enhanced the immune response (Dharbhar 2008) but long-term damaged heart in mice (Heidt et al. 2014).

Kiecolt-Glaser et al. (1984)

Aims Effects of exams (acute stressor) on immune system.

Procedure Blood samples from 75 medical students one month before exams and during exams. Also measured life events, distress and loneliness.

Findings Lower NK cell activity: during exams, in high-stress group and in high-loneliness group. More distress reported during exams.

Conclusions Chronic stressor (exams) directly suppresses immune system in healthy people.

Evaluation

Valuable contribution Showed direct stress effects in humans, previous research in animals.

Unclear link with illness No link with illness shown, could be lifestyle factors (indirect) because they weren't controlled.

Physiological addiction

Smoking

Biological approach

Biological explanation

Initiation

Genetic: 53% risk of starting to smoke (Carmelli et al. 1990).

Dopamine receptors: neurons in VTA respond to nicotine, stimulates dopamine release in NA.

Maintenance and relapse

Role of dopamine: smoking releases dopamine in NA, pleasure maintains addiction.

Nicotine regulation: smoke to maintain blood nicotine level, avoid withdrawal symptoms.

Withdrawal symptoms: anxiety, smoke to avoid.

Tolerance: dopamine receptors have reduced sensitivity so more nicotine needed for same effect.

Evaluation

Research support for nicotine regulation Heavy smokers given nicotine-reduced cigarettes smoked more to maintain blood nicotine level (Schachter 1977).

Evidence against nicotine regulation Chippers (regular smokers) smoke but do not become dependent, so not biological (Shiffman et al. 1995).

Vink et al. (2005)

Aims Search for genetic risk factors in initiation and nicotine dependence.

Procedure Smoking data from Netherlands twin register on five occasions. MZ and DZ twins completed FTND test for nicotine dependence.

Findings Genes explain 44% risk of initiation, 75% of nicotine dependence.

Conclusions Genes make large contribution to smoking initiation and nicotine dependence.

Evaluation

Practical application Smoking initiation mostly environmental, likely social learning. So interventions should target parents who also act as role models.

Problems with self-report Participants may not want to appear as 'addicts' on FTND, social desirability bias.

Learning approach

Learning explanation

Initiation

Parental/peer role models (social learning): child observes parents and peers enjoy smoking, vicarious reinforcement.

Positive reinforcement: pleasure from nicotine (dopamine) leads to repeat smoking

Maintenance

Negative reinforcement: smoking continues because avoids unpleasant withdrawal of stopping.

Classical conditioning: association learned between smoking sensations and pleasurable effects.

Relapse

Conditioned cues: pleasure from smoking (primary reinforcer) is associated with cues (e.g. lighters) that become secondary reinforcers. Cues then trigger cravings.

Self-efficacy: confidence in ability to quit and abstain. If this is low, person makes less effort.

Evaluation

Support for conditioned cues Smokers react strongly to smoking cues (e.g. ashtrays), arousal and craving (Carter and Tiffany 1999).

Practical application Aversion therapy counterconditions addiction, learn to associate smoking with unpleasant stimulus (e.g. shock). 52% abstaining one year later (Smith and Caldwell 1989).

A limited explanation Many who observe others smoking do not imitate. Only 50% who try cigarettes become regular smokers. Other factors involved.

Role of self-efficacy Review of 54 studies found other factors more important (Gwaltney et al. 2009).

Alcohol

Cognitive approach

Self-medication model

Initiation

Mitigation for current issue: experience of early trauma causes current emotional distress. Relieved by addiction (Khantzian 1985). Specific effects: choice of drug matched to emotional state (e.g. alcohol relieves anxiety).

Maintenance

Assumptions about managing the problem: distress causes low self-esteem. Drug allows self-regulation (short-term).

Stress relief: trauma stops self-soothing when stressed, because no confidence.

Relapse

Counterproductive: drug use creates rebound effect, problems worse.

Increase stress levels: withdrawal symptoms create stress.

'Solving' problem causes relapse: stress of withdrawal plus current distress = relapse or new drugs. Paradox of self-medication is the cycle of addiction.

Evaluation

Trauma and distress Strong link between adverse childhood experiences (ACEs) and later addictions (Felitti et al. 1998).

Self-medication and addiction People who self-medicated mood disorders with alcohol seven times more likely to be dependent in three years (Lazareck et al. 2012).

Role of specificity Many people use more than one drug. Often follow peer choices rather than select drug for specific effect (Lembke 2012).

Cause and effect Mental disorder does not lead to addiction. Alcohol abuse is more likely as cause of depression (Fergusson et al. 2009).

Learning approach

Operant conditioning

Initiation

Positive reinforcement: alcohol activates neurons in VTA so dopamine released in NA, creates pleasure. Positive reinforcement from pleasure and rewards in environment (e.g. friends). Indirect effects from observing peers and parents, vicarious reinforcement.

Negative reinforcement: drinking to escape stress (seen in films).

Maintenance

Positive reinforcement: ongoing rewards, plus motivational toxicity (rewards from drinking).

Negative reinforcement: drinking reduces withdrawal symptoms (unpleasant physiological and psychological effects). Relief from symptoms (or fear of them) strengthens drinking.

Relapse

Negative reinforcement: during abstinence, relief from withdrawal symptoms from drinking is strong enough for relapse.

Evaluation

Research support for negative reinforcement Amygdala hyperactive in withdrawal, stimulates HPA. Relapse calms this stress response (Koob 2009).

Practical applications CERP counteracts negative reinforcement effects. Alcoholic is exposed to alcohol cues but cannot relieve them by drinking (Laberg 1990).

Mixed evidence for dopamine Rats with no NA (no dopamine) still press lever for alcohol (Koob 1992). Drinking in humans releases endorphins (Mitchell et al. 2012).

Narrow explanation Many people drink without dependence. Must be other factors apart from biological reward system.

Behavioural addiction

Gambling

Cognitive approach

Expectancy theory

Initiation – cost-benefit analysis Decide to gamble if expect future costs (losses, anxiety) outweigh benefits (enjoyment, control).

Maintenance

Irrational thoughts, e.g. gambler's fallacy.

Cognitive biases, e.g. near miss is 'nearly winning'.

Illusions of control and exaggeration of ability: falsely believe can influence a gamble though special skill.

Relapse Recall bias and overestimation of success: recovering gamblers forget losses and recall benefits.

Evaluation

Practical applications Replace distortions with rational thinking, reduces gambling (Ladouceur et al. 2001).

Problems explaining initiation and maintenance Many people with distorted cognitions don't gamble. Only 1–3% of gamblers cannot control behaviour (Ladouceur 1996).

Griffiths (1994)

Aims Compare thinking of regular (RG) and non-regular gamblers (NRG).

Procedure Thinking aloud while playing fruit machines. Content analysis placed comments into 'rational' and 'irrational'.

Findings RGs six times more irrational verbalisations than NRGs. Prone to illusion of control and personification.

Conclusions Cognitive factors may play major role.

Evaluation

Ecological validity Real-life gambling has different responses (e.g. heart rate) than artificial lab (Anderson and Brown 1984).

Sampling issues Gamblers recommended other gamblers (snowball sampling), all participants similar.

Learning approach

Learning explanation

Initiation

Social learning: observe models rewarded (vicarious reinforcement), triggers desire.

Classical conditioning: external and internal stimuli (pleasurable) associated with gambling.

Maintenance

Positive reinforcement: continued gambling, winning and 'buzz' are rewarding.

Negative reinforcement: escape from reality, temporary relief.

Partial reinforcement: fruit machines pay only on some bets, so behaviour persists longer than continuous reinforcement (Skinner 1948).

Variable reinforcement: fruit machine pays every 10th spin on average, e.g. on 2nd, 7th, 15th, etc. Gambling persists after rewards stop.

Relapse

Cue reactivity: gambler quits but encounters many conditioned cues (e.g. scratch cards). High risk of relapse.

Evaluation

Research support High-frequency gamblers (HFGs) placed bets just before race, enjoying the delay (Dickerson 1979).

Role of partial reinforcement HFGs partially reinforced then gambled longer than LFGs after rewards stopped (Horsley et al. 2012).

Role of individual differences Some people gamble to relax or for arousal, some never relapse, others do despite same conditioned cues (Griffiths and Delfabbro 2001).

Lacks explanatory power Hard to explain some gambling, e.g. gambling on pure chance or gambling with a delay between bet and outcome. No single general explanation.

Shopping

Learning approach

Learning explanation

Initiation

Role models and vicarious reinforcement: observe model shopping and indirectly experience enjoyment.

Celebrities and advertisements: products bring status associated with celebrities.

Maintenance

Positive reinforcement: excitement of shopping experience, praise and status from friends.

Adrenaline rush and rewards: dopamine reward system provides 'rush' (like drugs).

Negative reinforcement: shopping blocks negative feelings, resurface and then more shopping.

Relapse

Cues associated with shopping: hard to avoid (TV adverts), trigger cravings.

Relief from withdrawal symptoms (negative reinforcement): negative emotions can be relieved through shopping again but only temporarily.

Evaluation

Role of shopping More positive attitudes toward products endorsed by celebrities (Knoll and Matthes 2017).

Gender differences Men and women buy different products. Attracts positive reinforcement from others, so buy similar products again.

Self-report Social desirability bias: people reluctant to admit to addiction, give more positive impression. Findings may underestimate compulsion.

Cognitive factors Reinforcement not enough to explain compulsive online shopping. Cognitive factors also involved (Trotzke et al. 2015).

Cognitive approach

Self-medication model

Initiation

Relief from boredom: shopping is easy way.

Psychological problems, distress and lack of self-esteem: shopping used as relief from distress from early 'trauma'. Stress brings feelings to surface (Khantzian 1985).

Maintenance

Reduction of anxiety: spending money leads to debt. Shopper feels anxiety, but relieved by more shopping.

Continuation of boredom/anxiety relief: narrow focus of attention while shopping reduces anxiety (mood repair). But worse afterwards, so more shopping.

Relapse

Effects of withdrawal: boredom, distress, anxiety.

Breakdown of coping strategies: paradox because shopping helps cope with problems but also makes them worse. Treat underlying problem (e.g. low self-esteem), not addiction.

Evaluation

Support for early trauma Compulsive shoppers report family dysfunction (e.g. alcoholism, Valence et al. 1988). Childhood abuse linked to later distress and shopping (DeSarbo and Edwards 1996).

Link to mental disorders Compulsive shopping is co-morbid with other disorders, e.g. 41–80% also have anxiety disorder (Black 2007).

Non-cognitive factors important Dysfunctional home (trauma) may lead to shopping addiction. Alternatively mental disorders may be inherited from parents.

Cause and effect Little evidence disorders occur before compulsive shopping. Could be that shopping causes anxiety and depression rather than vice versa.

Multiple-choice questions

Causes of stress: Life events and Rahe *et al.*

1. Life events are:
(a) Very common.
(b) Minor sources of stress.
(c) Quite easy to cope with.
(d) Relatively infrequent.

2. Life events are measured with the Social _____ _____ Scale.
(a) Retrospective Review.
(b) Readjustment Rating.
(c) Redirection Review.
(d) Relationship Rating.

3. Rahe *et al.* (1970) found _____ between the LCU and illness scores.
(a) A negative correlation.
(b) A weak but significant positive correlation.
(c) No correlation.
(d) A strong positive correlation.

4. Which statement is most accurate?
(a) Both positive and negative life events are stressful.
(b) Only negative life events are stressful.
(c) Positive life events are more stressful than negative ones.
(d) There are no positive life events.

Causes of stress: Daily hassles and Kanner *et al.*

1. Thinking about the threat of a hassle is called:
(a) Initial appraisal.
(b) Primary appraisal.
(c) Secondary appraisal.
(d) Final appraisal.

2. Hassle severity is measured on a scale of:
(a) 1 to 3.
(b) 1 to 5.
(c) 1 to 7.
(d) 1 to 9.

3. Kanner *et al.* concluded that daily hassles:
(a) Do not predict illness.
(b) Are less useful predictors than life events.
(c) Are better predictors than life events.
(d) Do not exist.

4. Ivancevich studied hassles in the context of poor health and:
(a) Work/jobs.
(b) Revising for exams.
(c) Shopping for food.
(d) Going on holiday.

Causes of stress: The workplace and Johansson *et al.*

1. Two main types of role conflict are:
(a) Primary and secondary.
(b) Alpha and beta.
(c) Intra and inter.
(d) High and low.

2. Workplace stress is often due to a lack of:
(a) Knowledge.
(b) Noise.
(c) Control.
(d) Role conflict.

3. Johansson *et al.*'s study took place in a:
(a) Swedish sawmill.
(b) Danish dairy.
(c) Norwegian nursery.
(d) Finnish fishmarket.

4. Györkös *et al.* found that job control depended on:
(a) Job type.
(b) Job level.
(c) Gender.
(d) Culture.

Causes of stress: Personality and two studies

1. One component of hardy personality is:
(a) Commitment.
(b) Consistency.
(c) Continuation.
(d) Constancy.

2. Type B people are usually:
(a) Hostile.
(b) Laid back.
(c) Competitive.
(d) Time-urgent.

3. Rosenman *et al.* followed up participants after:
(a) 8½ days.
(b) 8½ weeks.
(c) 8½ months.
(d) 8½ years.

4. Hull *et al.* argued we should abandon:
(a) Control.
(b) Commitment.
(c) Challenge.
(d) All hope.

Physiological responses to stress

1. The second stage of the GAS is:
(a) Exhaustion.
(b) Resistance.
(c) Alarm reaction.
(d) Fight or flight.

2. Adrenaline release is part of the:
(a) Parasympathetic branch.
(b) SAM system response.
(c) HPA system response.
(d) Chronic stress response.

3. The pituitary gland releases:
(a) Noradrenaline.
(b) Cortisol.
(c) CRF.
(d) ACTH.

4. Fight or flight is:
(a) Useful for chronic stressors.
(b) Adaptive in today's world.
(c) Mostly a female response.
(d) Mostly a male response.

Stress and ill health and Kiecolt-Glaser *et al.*

1. Innate immunity includes:
(a) Lymphocytes.
(b) Killer T cells.
(c) NK cells.
(d) B cells.

2. Wilbert-Lampen *et al.* (2008) studied:
(a) An acute stressor.
(b) A chronic stressor.
(c) A long-term stressor.
(d) The immune system.

3. Kiecolt-Glaser *et al.*'s participants completed:
(a) The SSRS.
(b) The BSI.
(c) The UCLA loneliness scale.
(d) All of the above.

4. Acute stressors can:
(a) Strengthen the heart.
(b) Enhance the immune system.
(c) Improve the blood vessels.
(d) Suppress the cardiovascular system.

Smoking: Biological approach and Vink *et al.*

1. Carmelli *et al.* found a genetic contribution of _____ to smoking.
(a) 11%.
(b) 53%.
(c) 75%.
(d) 85%.

2. Nicotine causes dopamine to be released in the:
(a) Nucleus accumbens.
(b) Ventral tegmental area.
(c) Genes.
(d) Receptors.

3. Vink *et al.* (2005) studied:
(a) MZ and DZ twins.
(b) MZ twins only.
(c) DZ twins only.
(d) Identical twins only.

4. The FTND suffers from:
(a) Gender bias.
(b) Cognitive bias.
(c) Social response bias.
(d) Social desirability bias.

Smoking: Learning approach

1. Observing someone enjoying smoking leads to:
(a) Positive reinforcement.
(b) Classical conditioning.
(c) Negative reinforcement.
(d) Vicarious reinforcement.

2. Withdrawal symptoms are:
(a) Positive reinforcers.
(b) Negative reinforcers.
(c) Vicarious reinforcers.
(d) Secondary reinforcers.

3. Low self-efficacy explains:
(a) Smoking initiation.
(b) Smoking maintenance.
(c) Smoking relapse.
(d) Withdrawal symptoms.

4. _____ of adolescents who try cigarettes become regular smokers.
(a) 25%.
(b) 40%.
(c) 50%.
(d) 75%.

Alcohol: Cognitive approach

1. People self-medicate with drugs because they cannot self-regulate:
(a) Their self-esteem.
(b) Their relationships.
(c) Their own care.
(d) All of the above.

2. Which statement is most accurate?
(a) It is best to treat the addiction.
(b) Self-medication reduces risk of relapse.
(c) Rebound explains initiation.
(d) Self-medication is counterproductive.

3. ACE (Felitti et al.) stands for:
(a) Advanced childhood events.
(b) Adverse childhood experiences.
(c) Addictive cognitive experiences.
(d) Adjusted childhood events.

4. Lembke (2012) questioned the role of:
(a) ACEs.
(b) Specificity.
(c) Depression.
(d) Trauma.

Alcohol: Learning approach

1. Alcohol activates release of dopamine in the:
(a) Nucleus accumbens.
(b) Ventral tegmental area.
(c) Frontal areas of the brain.
(d) Both (a) and (c).

2. Negative reinforcement explains:
(a) Initiation only.
(b) Maintenance only.
(c) Initiation, maintenance and relapse.
(d) Relapse only.

3. According to Koob, the amygdala controls:
(a) Dopamine release.
(b) Withdrawal symptoms.
(c) Positive reinforcement.
(d) Vicarious reinforcement.

4. One treatment is called:
(a) Response exposure with cue prevention.
(b) Cue and response prevention.
(c) Cue and response exposure.
(d) Cue exposure with response prevention.

Gambling: Cognitive approach and Griffiths

1. 'Near miss bias' is an example of:
(a) Cognitive bias.
(b) Cost-benefit analysis.
(c) Gambler's fallacy.
(d) Illusion of control.

2. Griffiths used the _____ method.
(a) Typing out.
(b) Writing down.
(c) Thinking aloud.
(d) Keeping thoughts to yourself.

3. RGs made _____ times more irrational comments than NRGs.
(a) 6.
(b) 5.
(c) 4.
(d) 3.

4. About _____ of gamblers have trouble controlling their behaviour.
(a) 0.5–1%.
(b) 1–3%.
(c) 10–30%.
(d) 50%.

Gambling: Learning approach

1. Classical conditioning explains:
(a) Gambling relapse.
(b) Gambling maintenance.
(c) Gambling initiation.
(d) All of the above.

2. Maintenance is positively reinforced by:
(a) Anxiety.
(b) Withdrawal symptoms.
(c) Near misses.
(d) Escape from bad situation.

3. Horsley et al. found _____ strongly motivated gambling.
(a) Partial reinforcement.
(b) Vicarious reinforcement.
(c) Negative reinforcement.
(d) Continuous reinforcement.

4. Griffiths and Delfabbro found that all people gamble:
(a) To relax.
(b) To win money.
(c) To experience arousal.
(d) There is no single reason.

Shopping: Learning approach

1. Celebrities have influence on shoppers through:
(a) Initiation.
(b) Identification.
(c) Negative reinforcement.
(d) Cues.

2. Shopping to eliminate a feeling of emptiness is an example of:
(a) Vicarious reinforcement.
(b) Classical conditioning.
(c) Positive reinforcement.
(d) Negative reinforcement.

3. Knoll and Matthes studied the role of:
(a) Conditioned cues.
(b) Celebrity endorsement.
(c) Relapse.
(d) Gender.

4. Trotzke et al. investigated:
(a) Supermarket shopping.
(b) Catalogue shopping.
(c) Online shopping.
(d) High street shopping.

Shopping: Cognitive approach

1. Compulsive shopping starts as a response to:
(a) Emotional distress.
(b) Early trauma.
(c) Boredom.
(d) Any of the above.

2. According to the self-medication model, shopping:
(a) Has a mood repair function.
(b) Has a genetic element.
(c) Begins through positive reinforcement.
(d) Is maintained by social learning.

3. Khantzian argues therapy should:
(a) Remove the addiction.
(b) Reduce the emotional distress.
(c) Ignore the mental disorder.
(d) Ignore self-esteem.

4. Self-medication theory minimises:
(a) Cognitive factors.
(b) The role of anxiety.
(c) Genetic factors.
(d) The role of emotional distress.

MCQ answers

Causes of stress: Life events 1D, 2B, 3B, 4A
Causes of stress: Daily hassles 1B, 2A, 3C, 4A
Causes of stress: The workplace and Johansson et al. 1C, 2C, 3A, 4D
Causes of stress: Personality and two studies 1A, 2B, 3D, 4C
Physiological responses to stress 1B, 2B, 3D, 4D
Stress and ill health and Kiecolt-Glaser et al. 1C, 2A, 3D, 4B
Smoking: Biological approach and Vink et al. 1B, 2A, 3A, 4D
Smoking: Learning approach 1D, 2B, 3C, 4C
Alcohol: Cognitive approach 1D, 2D, 3B, 4B
Alcohol: Learning approach 1D, 2C, 3B, 4D
Gambling: Cognitive approach and Griffiths 1A, 2C, 3A, 4B
Gambling: Learning approach 1C, 2C, 3A, 4D
Shopping: Learning approach 1B, 2D, 3B, 4C
Shopping: Cognitive approach 1D, 2A, 3B, 4C

Hovland-Yale theory of persuasion and Hovland and Weiss (1951)

Specification term

Hovland-Yale theory of persuasion
Whether a message persuades people to change their behaviour depends not just on the message itself (the communication) but on who gives it (the communicator) and who receives it (the recipients).

This message is quite clear, but it is only one side of the argument.

Time to quit
SMOKING

Hovland-Yale theory of persuasion

Carl Hovland and his colleagues Irving Janis and Harold Kelley (1953) argued that there are three main factors that contribute to whether a message persuades people to change their attitudes or behaviour.

The communicator (source)

Credibility is a key factor. A communicator is more persuasive when he or she is perceived as credible (i.e. believable). They have greater credibility when they are thought to be experts. For example, a highly qualified medical doctor would be a good choice to communicate health-related information (e.g. an anti-smoking campaign).

Credibility is also derived from personal experience. Someone who used to take drugs could speak persuasively to young people about their dangers.

The communication (message)

There are two key factors. The first is emotional appeal. Health messages that include a fear-related threat can change behaviour. But the recipient has to believe negative outcomes can be avoided. For example, a message about the dangers of smoking is more persuasive if it also explains how to quit.

The second key factor is whether the argument presented is two-sided or not. An anti-smoking message could just contain the information that smoking is dangerous to health. Or it could point out that smoking brings pleasure and other benefits as well.

Furthermore there is an interaction between the communication and the recipient – a well-informed audience, familiar with both sides of an argument, would find a one-sided presentation biased and therefore less persuasive.

The recipients (audience)

Highly intelligent people are less easy to persuade than people of lower intelligence. This is because they have the *cognitive* resources to process even complex messages, so they resist persuasion. People of lower intelligence are persuadable because they do not fully understand the message or pay full attention to it.

People lacking *self-esteem* are more easily persuaded than people who have high levels (who tend to resist persuasive messages). This means that health campaigns should target people with low self-esteem for greater success.

Hovland and Weiss (1951) The influence of source credibility on communication effectiveness

Aims

Carl Hovland and Walter Weiss investigated how the credibility of a source (trustworthy or untrustworthy) affected the likelihood of opinion change. They also wanted to see whether the impact of credibility changed over time.

Procedure

Two groups of Yale University American students were presented with the same information (both positive and negative articles) relating to four topics (including antihistamine drugs). For one group the information came from high-credibility sources (e.g. an academic journal). The other group's information came from low-credibility sources (e.g. a tabloid newspaper). The students' own opinions were measured before the presentation, immediately afterwards and four weeks later.

Findings

The participants changed their minds significantly more often with high-credibility sources. Low-credibility sources were almost always seen as presenting unfair arguments. Over time, agreement with high-credibility sources decreased (on average by 10.7%) as agreement with low-credibility sources increased (on average by 7.4%).

Conclusions

Persuasive communications are more likely to change opinions if they come from credible sources. However, the study demonstrated the role of the *sleeper effect*. People who are initially not persuaded by low-credibility sources eventually forget where the information came from. They then may change their opinions in line with the information because they no longer recall that it had low credibility. Over time, agreement with high- and low-credibility sources ends up about the same.

The impact of a health-related message depends partly on whether the recipient thinks it applies to them.

Evaluation

Research support

One strength is evidence supporting the theory's predictions concerning the message.

James Sturges and Ronald Rogers (1996) presented 15- and 20-year-olds with messages about the dangers of smoking. The messages varied in how threatening they were (high or low threat, e.g. 'You might get cancer' or 'People are not as likely to die'). Another variation was whether the messages suggested it was easy or hard to give up (e.g. 'It is easy for you to keep away from tobacco' or 'It is hard work to stay away from tobacco'). Different groups of participants heard different messages. The most persuasive message was the one that combined high threat with the suggestion that it is possible to quit smoking.

This shows the theory is correct in predicting that emotional appeal is only persuasive when recipients believe they can cope with change.

Role of self-esteem

One weakness is that research does not support the theory's view of self-esteem.

Roy Baumeister and Martin Covington (1985) found that people with high self-esteem were actually more easy to persuade than those with low self-esteem. However, the people with high self-esteem were less willing to admit to being persuaded. William McGuire (1968) argued that the relationship between persuasion and self-esteem is a curve rather than a straight line (*curvilinear correlation*). That is, people with moderate levels of self-esteem are less easy to persuade than people with high and low levels.

Therefore, this prediction about characteristics of the recipients has been overturned, partly undermining the *validity* of the theory.

Evaluation

Practical application

One strength is that the study can make health campaigns more effective.

The findings suggest that the credibility of the source only really matters if a short-term change of behaviour or attitudes is required. So, a short-term intervention should emphasise credibility. Credibility is less important for long-term changes than other factors such as emotional appeal, the content of the message and features of the recipients. Long-term interventions should therefore focus on these.

The study is useful because scarce resources can be targeted more efficiently to gain the greatest change.

Lack of generalisability

One weakness is that the findings are difficult to *generalise*.

The participants were all students from Yale University. Students are not very representative of the wider population because they are younger and more educated than the majority. The participants were also a 'captive audience'. They were exposed to sources that were created by the researchers. These may be quite different from naturally-occurring encounters with sources in reality (e.g. other people).

This means the findings are limited to fairly narrow circumstances and may tell us little about how health-related messages persuade most people in the real world.

GET ACTIVE You tell me

Sanjay is a student nurse who asks you for a favour. He is struggling to understand the behaviour of one of his patients. Mr Johnson is diabetic, a heavy smoker, eats a very poor diet and does no exercise. He understands the risks to his health because he has been given all the available information. But Mr Johnson still continues his unhealthy behaviour, and now one of his feet has been amputated. Sanjay cannot believe that people can know all the facts about their health and yet ignore them.

Sanjay knows you have studied psychology and emails you, asking you to explain some of the reasons why patients do or do not take notice of health-related information. Write an email back to him.

Exam-style questions

Each Christmas, the government funds a media campaign against drink-driving. A central element is a TV advert that tries to persuade viewers that drinking and driving isn't worth it. The 2018 advert featured a police officer describing her experiences of attending road traffic accidents. She talked about the terrible things she had seen over footage of wrecked cars and people in distress. She said, 'I know people like to have a drink at Christmas, so do I. But you don't have to get into your car afterwards.'

The advert was broadcast nationally and one person who saw it was Paulo. He had been looking forward to the festive season and drinking large amounts of alcohol as he usually did. His partner said as they watched the advert, 'I sometimes worry that could be you one day.' This made Paulo wonder if he should give up drinking altogether.

1. According to the Hovland-Yale theory, persuasion depends on the communicator, the communication and the recipient. Identify all **three** in the scenario. (3)

2. Explain what is meant by the 'recipient'. (2)

3. In Paulo's decision to stop drinking, explain the roles of:
   (a) The communicator. (2)
   (b) The communication. (2)

   Don't forget assessment and revision issues on pages 34–35, 70–71 and 108–109.

4. Evaluate the Hovland-Yale theory of persuasion. Refer to Paulo in your answer. (6)

5. Give **one** aim and explain **one** conclusion of the study by Hovland and Weiss (1951). (4)

6. Discuss how the Hovland-Yale theory could help persuade Paulo to stop drinking. Refer to at least **one** research study in your answer. (9)

An issue to consider

'Persuasion' is about trying to change people's beliefs, attitudes and behaviours.

To what extent is it ethical to use psychological research to 'persuade' people?

Specification content

C1 Theories of persuasion

Hovland-Yale theory of persuasion:

● The role of the communicator, communication and the recipient in persuasion.

● Hovland and Weiss (1951) The influence of source credibility on communication effectiveness.

Elaboration-likelihood model and Petty *et al.* (1981)

My daddy works on this site
Charlie aged 5

Please drive carefully

Make it personal

If we want to get people to change their attitudes or behaviour, what should our message look like? Should it be scary, as we saw on the previous spread? Should it be friendly? The theory on this spread says it should be personal.

Have you ever been through a motorway roadworks at 50 mph? The speed limit is there to protect drivers. But the roadworks are also a building site where people work, so the limit protects them too. But how do you get drivers to respect the speed limit?

One solution is to personalise the speed limit. At some roadworks, signs are put up with an image of children and text such as the picture above. As lots of drivers have children, or know children, this message is highly personalised and relevant.

A student hearing that his university is planning to introduce another exam.

The elaboration-likelihood model

Richard Petty and John Cacioppo's (1981) *elaboration-likelihood model* (ELM) suggests there are two ways a message can persuade someone to change their attitude or behaviour (dual process).

Process 1: Central route

I might be persuaded by the message itself after I process its content in detail. I do this because I am interested in the issue and motivated by it (it has personal relevance). This is 'high elaboration' because I thoroughly evaluate (elaborate) the message content.

Process 2: Peripheral route

I might be persuaded by factors other than the message's content (e.g. the attractiveness of the source). I do not process the content, perhaps because I don't have enough time or I don't have the ability. This is 'low elaboration' because my evaluation of the content is minimal.

Factors of influence

It is possible to be persuaded via the *central* or *peripheral routes*. So, what determines which route is used? The ELM suggests several factors, such as relevance of the message and need for cognition.
 Another issue is where the source is pointing – if a celebrity or person who is attractive is associated with the message then the route of influence is peripheral whereas if a celebrity actually highlights the content, encouraging the audience to pay attention to it, then the route is central.

Individual differences

People differ in their ability and motivation to process a message centrally. The key difference is *need for cognition* (NFC). People high in NFC are motivated to think about many issues – they enjoy analysing arguments. Therefore, they will be most persuaded through the central route.

Petty *et al.* (1981) Personal involvement as a determinant of argument-based persuasion

Aims

Does high involvement lead to attitude change through persuasion by the central route, and low involvement by the peripheral route?

Procedure

American university students heard a message suggesting a new 'comprehensive exam' should be introduced which all students would have to pass in order to graduate.
 Each student was given a further message which differed in these ways:

- Some were told the exam would be introduced the following year (high personal relevance), others were told ten years (low relevance).
- Some were told the message was produced by an expert, others by someone who was not an expert.
- For some the message contained strong arguments (facts, statistics) and for others weak arguments (opinions).

The students' attitudes were measured by rating the concept of a comprehensive exam and the extent to which they agreed with it.

Findings

When personal involvement was high, the main factor influencing attitude was the quality of the argument (the strong argument produced a very favourable attitude). The expertise of the source had little influence. However, for low involvement the quality of the argument had no significant effect on attitude, but expertise did (attitude was favourable when the source was an expert).

Conclusions

When an issue is personally relevant, attitude change occurs through thoughtful processing of the message (central route). When an issue is not relevant, peripheral cues are more influential.

Evaluation

Practical application

One strength of the ELM is that it can make health messages more persuasive.

Health campaigners might be tempted to use the peripheral route, for example by involving celebrities. However, the ELM shows that this is self-defeating because attitude or behaviour change would be short-lived. A better solution is to use both central and peripheral routes. For example, in a school context, start by getting the attention of an unmotivated audience by using someone with personal experience (e.g. an ex-drug user). Then help the audience to process the message more actively (e.g. using role-play to personalise it).

This shows that the ELM is useful because it suggests practical ways of making health messages appeal to 'hard-to-reach' groups such as adolescents.

Poor explanatory power

One weakness of the model is that it does not really explain *how* persuasive messages affect attitudes and behaviour.

The ELM offers a thorough, detailed and complex *description* of the two routes to persuasion. But it does not *explain* how this happens because it lacks an underlying theory of the psychological processes involved. Also, the complexity of the model works against it. For example, it proposes a large number of factors influence the choice of processing route (source attractiveness, relevance, need for cognition, etc.).

This makes it hard to use the ELM to predict actual behaviour change (e.g. which processing route is most persuasive in a given situation).

Evaluation

Influential study

One strength of Petty *et al.*'s study is that it had a huge influence on the field of persuasion research.

It sparked a torrent of research studies into how persuasive messages could be framed for maximum impact in terms of behaviour and attitude change. The findings were highly relevant in the area of health promotion. For example, Anke Oenema *et al.* (2005) matched messages about healthy eating to recipients by making them more personal, which increased central processing and led to greater behavioural change.

This shows the study had real value as the ultimate aim of scientific research is to produce information that will improve the world.

Sample issues

One weakness of the study is that the participants were university students.

It is reasonable to assume that students have greater *cognitive* abilities (such as need for cognition) than other groups of people in the population (they generally enjoy learning about new things). This may explain why attempts to *replicate* Petty *et al.*'s (1981) findings have not been very successful. For example, Tali Te'eni-Harari *et al.* (2007) tried to replicate the study with younger participants. They found that involvement made no difference to children's attitudes, a very different finding from Petty *et al.*'s.

This suggests that the unrepresentative nature of the participants may mean that the findings can't be generalised to other groups such as younger people.

GET ACTIVE Changing views on health

The governing members of a Health Trust are concerned about the latest figures on sexually transmitted diseases, HIV and unwanted pregnancies. They decide to start a campaign to promote safe sex targeted at older teenagers. This will include posters, flyers and a brief video to be shown in schools. The Trust knows from past experience that it is difficult to get this group to change their behaviour, so they ask a clinical psychologist for help in designing the campaign.

The psychologist decides that the elaboration-likelihood model offers the best way of getting results. Based on this, what advice do you think she should give the Trust?

Ed Sheeran supports World Mental Health Day each year. Would a celebrity endorsement persuade you to take more care of your mental health?

Exam-style questions

Rona goes out and binge-drinks at least twice a week. At the weekends she spends most of the time with a hangover. Rona's friends decide to try and persuade her to stop.

Amelia tries first and explains to Rona the dangers of her behaviour along with some statistics about binge drinking. But Rona finds her arguments 'boring' and says she is way too busy to think about them and they don't apply to her anyway.

Liam has a go next. He knows that Rona is a big fan of the Hollywood star Lindsay Lohan. So, he explains how Lindsay managed to overcome her alcohol addiction. Rona was very interested and said she would look into it further.

1. The elaboration-likelihood model states that there are two routes to persuasion, central and peripheral. Which route did Amelia's argument take? (1)

2. Explain **one** difference between the peripheral and central routes to persuasion. (2)

3. Explain Rona's responses to Amelia and Liam in terms of the elaboration-likelihood model of persuasion. (4)

4. Petty, Cacioppo and Goldman (1981) conducted a study on persuasion:

   (a) Explain the procedure. (3)

   (b) Give **one** finding and use it to explain Rona's behaviour. (3)

5. In terms of the elaboration-likelihood model of persuasion, discuss how Rona might be persuaded to change her behaviour. Refer to at least **one** research study in your answer. (9)

An issue to consider

Have you ever changed your mind about an issue? What influenced you? Was it the quality of the argument or something about the person presenting it?

Specification content

C1 Theories of persuasion

Elaboration-likelihood model of persuasion:

● Use of peripheral or central route to persuasion.
● Factors of influence (role of celebrity).
● Individuals' differences in influence.
● Petty, Cacioppo and Goldman (1981) Personal involvement as a determinant of argument-based persuasion.

Physiological stress management techniques: Drug therapies

Flyoffthehandle and friends

There is a thread on the website *Reddit* where people who suffer from severe stress and anxiety describe what it is like. Many of them focus on body sensations (heart rate, stomach butterflies, etc.).

The body sensations 'make the anxiety worse because they're telling you there's something to be worried about'.

A post from StressSuperStar described her anxiety as 'that feeling you get when you trip and you don't know if you are going to catch yourself or not, all day long.'

RacingHeart said, 'It's like you're driving and a cop's flying past you, your heart's racing, you're kinda shaky and sweaty, and it's all in the back of your head the rest of the day.'

For KeepItReal it's '...a feeling of panic in your body, your stomach turns, you get hot and your heart pounds, like what happens when you think something went very wrong.'

Flyoffthehandle has a piece of advice: '...for you to have a chance of sorting out your physical well-being, you must eradicate the source of the external forces which cause the problems in your head.'

Maybe if you could manage the body sensations, the stress and anxiety would go away.

Source: Reddit (names changed)

Specification terms

Benzodiazepines (BZs) Drugs used to reduce anxiety. They attach to receptors of the neurotransmitter GABA, enhancing its effects.

Beta blockers (BBs) Drugs used to reduce anxiety. They attach to beta-receptors in the cells of the heart and other parts of the body that are usually stimulated during sympathetic arousal. They prevent adrenaline having such a strong effect.

Drug therapy Treatment involving drugs, i.e. chemicals that have a particular effect on the functioning of the brain or some other body system. In the case of mental disorders such drugs usually affect neurotransmitter levels.

Drug therapies

Anxiety is the main psychological symptom of *stress*. This is accompanied by many unpleasant physiological sensations produced by the arousal of the *sympathetic nervous system* (the *fight or flight response*, see page 46), such as increased heart rate and sweating.

Anti-anxiety drugs (*anxiolytics*) can relieve these sensations. By reducing the physiological symptoms of stress, drugs can provide a person with emotional stability and a chance to assess what is causing the stress.

Two types of drug are usually recommended to help manage anxiety.

Benzodiazepines (BZs)

This class of anti-anxiety drug includes *diazepam* (Valium) and *alprazolam* (Xanax). They are among some of the most commonly prescribed drugs in Western countries. A high dose induces sleep, but a moderate dose has an anti-anxiety effect.

Benzodiazepines (BZs) are relatively fast-acting in reducing physiological arousal in the *central nervous system* (CNS).

Mode of action BZs work by boosting one way in which the body naturally combats anxiety. They interact with a *neurotransmitter* called *GABA* (gamma-aminobutyric acid). GABA's main function is to reduce (inhibit) the activity of *neurons* in most areas of the brain. It does this by making it less likely that electrical signals are passed from one *neuron* to another (see diagram below left). The overall effect is to 'calm' activity in the CNS.

BZs work by enhancing the inhibiting effects of GABA. Neurons have receptors on their surfaces that GABA molecules attach to. When this happens, channels open in the receptors to allow chemicals into the neuron (see diagram below left). This changes the chemical composition of the neuron and slows its activity.

BZ molecules can also attach to GABA receptors but without blocking them. Instead, they open the channels even more, so more chemicals get into the neuron. This means that there is even less neural activity in the CNS. The individual feels less anxiety as a result.

BZs have a secondary effect on another neurotransmitter, *serotonin*. The usual function of serotonin is to increase the activity of neurons. BZs disrupt this function, contributing to the overall calming of the CNS.

Beta blockers (BBs)

Beta-adrenergic blockers (or *beta blockers*, BBs) act on the *sympathetic branch* of the *autonomic nervous system* (ANS) which plays a key role in increasing the body's arousal in preparation for the fight or flight response.

Beta blockers (e.g. *atenolol, propranolol*) counteract this effect, reducing the physiological arousal that accompanies the stress response – for example, BBs reduce heart rate and blood pressure. In fact they are often prescribed for people with various heart problems.

Mode of action There are receptors located in the heart and blood vessels – these are called *beta-adrenergic receptors*. Molecules of the hormones *adrenaline* and *noradrenaline* attach to these receptors. As we saw on page 46, these neurotransmitters/hormones are produced by the adrenal medulla as part of the body's stress response. This explains why heart rate and blood pressure increase in times of stress.

BBs work by blocking the receptors in the heart and blood vessels so they cannot be stimulated by adrenaline and noradrenaline. This slows heart rate and reduces blood pressure. The heart pumps less intensely so needs less oxygen. Some BBs enhance these effects because they block receptors in the lungs and blood vessels as well as in the heart.

Most BBs do not affect the brain directly, so they reduce anxiety without altering consciousness. This means they are often used by people such as surgeons and performers. They want to remove the physical symptoms of stress (e.g. hand tremors) but stay alert. BBs are banned from sporting competitions because they are performance-enhancing (e.g. improve hand-eye coordination).

This diagram shows a GABA molecule and a BZ molecule attached to a receptor on a neuron. This opens a channel for chemicals to enter the neuron (see text for more details).

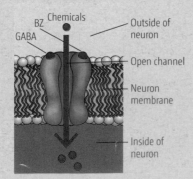

Evaluation

Support for effectiveness

One strength of drug treatment is the supporting evidence from many research studies.

David Baldwin *et al.* (2013) reviewed studies of BZs and found that they were significantly more effective in treating acute anxiety than a *placebo* (an inactive 'pretend' version of the drug). However, some BZs were more effective than others. A review of BB research by Desmond Kelly (1980) concluded that these drugs helped to treat everyday anxieties associated with a number of *stressors* including public speaking and exams.

These findings show that BZs and BBs are consistently useful treatments of stress-related anxiety. Research also suggests they may work even better in combination (Hayes and Schulz 1987).

Convenient and safe

Another strength is that drugs are a much easier therapy than the psychological therapies covered later in this unit.

In terms of convenience, a real benefit of any drug is that a person just has to remember to take it. Unlike with psychological therapies, no major effort, commitment or motivation is needed. Another benefit is that both BZs and BBs have relatively few serious side effects compared with other drugs (Erdmann 2009). The exception to this is when they are taken with alcohol or other specific anti-anxiety drugs (but patients are warned against this).

These advantages make drugs an attractive short-term treatment as long as side effects and *dependence* can be avoided.

Does not treat underlying problem

One weakness of drugs is that they treat the symptoms of stress but not the causes.

BZs and BBs reduce anxiety and its physiological symptoms. They can help a person manage *acute stress* by proving short-term relief. This is valuable because it helps the person assess their options in an emotionally stable state. But as there is a serious risk of dependence (see below) and of side effects (e.g. confusion, trembling, dizziness), drug treatment for *chronic stress* can do more harm than good.

This suggests that a psychological therapy (such as stress inoculation training, see page 84) might be a better approach to treating longer-term stress.

Dependence

Another weakness of using drugs to treat stress is the risk of dependence.

BBs are generally not physically addictive. But they can create a psychological dependence in people who feel they cannot function without them. In the case of BZs, both physical and psychological dependence is not uncommon. Some people experience *withdrawal* effects when they try to stop taking the drugs. The main symptoms are anxiety, *depression*, headaches and sleep disturbances. Guidelines recommend that BZs should be prescribed for no longer than two to four weeks. But some people take them for much longer than this.

This is a problem because sometimes dependence can be more harmful for a person than the stress being treated in the first place.

Researching drug effectiveness

When drugs are tested for effectiveness, some participants take a 'placebo'. This is a version of the drug that contains no active substance. If participants taking the placebo recover just as well as those taking the drug, then the apparent effectiveness of the drug is due to believing it will do you good.

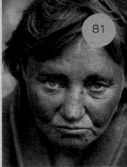

GET ACTIVE Seeking advice

Jess is homeless and lives on the streets. Her lifestyle is extremely chaotic, unpredictable and stressful. She does not know where she will sleep each night and her personal safety is always in danger. It has been hard for her to get medical care. She is terrible at keeping appointments. But she is so stressed that her blood pressure is out of control.

Eduardo is a BTEC student who suffers from exam stress. Whenever the exam period comes round, he finds it very hard to sit down in an exam room. But he also panics when he thinks about exams. This makes it hard for him to revise. He plans to go to university and eventually do a postgraduate degree. So that's at least another four years of exams then.

1. *Explain why drug therapy would be a good treatment for Jess and Eduardo. Use specific examples from their experiences to support your explanations.*
2. *Is there anything in their experience to suggest that drug therapy would not be a good treatment and an alternative might be better?*

Exam-style questions

Kirsty is a farmer who has to work very hard. She noticed her heart had a strange rhythm and she felt dizzy and short of breath. She went to her doctor who took her pulse and measured her blood pressure. Both were very high. Kirsty also said she felt so anxious she couldn't concentrate on anything.

Leo is a musician who plays violin in an orchestra. Although he is a talented player, he gets very anxious and his hands start to shake when he is performing on stage. This affects the quality of his sound and he is worried that he will have to leave the orchestra. But some of the other musicians tell him there are drugs he can take to reduce his anxiety.

1. Give **two** types of drug therapy for stress management. (2)
2. Explain what is meant by 'physiological stress management techniques'. (2)
3. Explain how benzodiazepines could help Kirsty. (3)
4. Explain how beta blockers could help Leo. (3)
5. In terms of its strengths and weaknesses, evaluate drug therapy as a method of managing Kirsty's and/or Leo's stress levels. (6)
6. Discuss **one** physiological stress management technique Leo could use. (9)

An issue to consider

Drug therapy has costs and benefits so its use is a matter of balance.

Where do you think the balance lies? At what point is drug therapy beneficial and at what point does it stop being beneficial?

Specification content

C2 Treatment and management of addiction and stress

Physiological stress management techniques:
● Drug therapy – benzodiazepines (BZs), beta blockers.

Physiological stress management techniques: Biofeedback

Biofeedback beginnings

The story of the stress management method on this spread began in the 1960s with some rats.

Neal Miller and Leo DiCara paralysed the rats with a drug called *curare*. Normally this would have been fatal because curare prevents the muscles involved in breathing from working. But Miller and DiCara kept the animals alive using an artificial respirator.

In this state, half of the rats were rewarded whenever their heart rates slowed. The other half were rewarded whenever their heart rates increased. The researchers used an electrode implanted in the rats' brains to stimulate their 'pleasure centre'. This created a 'sense of pleasure', which was the reward.

Miller and DiCara discovered that heart rates became faster in the rats rewarded for 'speeding up' and became slower in the rats rewarded for 'slowing down'.

This might not sound very surprising. But the point is that the change in heart rate was completely involuntary. The rats had no 'conscious' control over it because they were paralysed. It was learned through operant conditioning – a permanent change in behaviour occurred because it was reinforced.

But...

Leo DiCara continued to do research into biofeedback and could not replicate his and Miller's original findings. When other researchers asked him to share his data, and continued to press him for it, DiCara committed suicide. It now appears he may have invented the data, and so there is a sizeable question mark over the scientific origins of biofeedback.

Specification term

Biofeedback A method of stress management that turns physiological processes (such as heart rate) into signals that a client then learns to control. Clients do this by applying the techniques they have learned, such as relaxation and breathing exercises.

There's more to relaxation training than chilling out with a beer you know.

Biofeedback

We saw on the previous spread that physiological *stress management* targets the effects of an *acute stressor* on the *sympathetic nervous system*. This produces several physiological changes in our bodies such as increased heart rate, faster breathing and muscular tension. If we can minimise the physiological changes with, for example, drugs, then we would reduce the *anxiety* that comes with them. However, drugs do not provide a safe or long-lasting solution.

If we could control the internal changes that might help, in the same way as we control what our arms or legs are doing. The problem is the physiological changes are involuntary – they are controlled 'automatically' by the *sympathetic branch* of the autonomic nervous system.

The aim of *biofeedback* is to enable us to take control of these automatic and unconscious processes by presenting them to us in a form that is obvious. Biofeedback uses technology to let us see and hear our physiological functioning.

Thomas Budzynski *et al.* (1973) identified three main phases to biofeedback training.

Phase 1: Awareness and physiological feedback

For *physiological* feedback a client is connected to a machine that converts physiological activities into signals that can be seen and heard. For example, electrodes are placed on the client's fingertips to monitor heart rate. The signal is amplified and presented on a screen for the client to see. Rises and falls in heart rate are shown in the image.

Other physiological activities can also be fed back to the client. Muscular tension can be measured using an *electromyogram* (EMG). The electrical activity of the muscles is converted into a tone that can be heard through earphones. The tone varies in pitch depending on how tense or relaxed the muscles are.

A trained therapist explains what is happening to the client at every stage of the process. Therefore, the feedback provided by the machines is meaningful to the client.

Phase 2: Relaxation training and control

In *relaxation training* feedback is used to take control of responses. A client learns how to adjust their breathing, for example, to make the signal move in the desired direction. This could mean lowering the line of a graph on a screen, or lowering the pitch of a tone heard through earphones. In recent years biofeedback has started to use game-based interfaces to motivate clients. For instance, every time a client lowers their heart rate they get closer to completing an on-screen puzzle.

Some physiological responses can be controlled through relaxation. This requires training because it is 'deeper' relaxation than the everyday type most of us experience. A therapist will help the client to tense a specific muscle group for a few seconds and then relax them. This is repeated several times before moving on to another muscle group until most or all of the body is covered. Training also includes deep breathing exercises to slow heart rate and visualisation to help a client imagine relaxing and calming scenes.

Role of operant conditioning The machine gives the client feedback that confirms their responses are moving in the right direction. Achieving this goal is rewarding for the client, as is praise from the therapist. *Positive reinforcement* means that, in future, the behaviour is repeated without any conscious behaviour on the client's part. This makes further success more likely.

Phase 3: Transfer

Training takes place in relaxing and stress-free settings such as a therapy room. The outside world is very different, so it is crucial that the client is able to transfer their skills to everyday life. Portable biofeedback machines are available (you can even get mobile apps). The client can use one to apply their relaxation skills in stressful situations as they arise.

Evaluation

Support for biofeedback

One strength is research evidence that shows biofeedback is effective.

Jane Lemaire *et al.*'s (2011) participants were medical doctors. After training, they used a biofeedback device three times a day for a 28-day period. They also completed *questionnaires* at various points to measure their perception of how stressed they were. The *mean* stress scores for these participants fell significantly over the course of the 28 days. There was a *control group* of people who did not receive biofeedback. Their stress scores also fell, but by a much smaller amount.

These findings suggest that biofeedback is effective in improving the psychological state of someone experiencing stress.

Long-term benefits

Another strength is that biofeedback is a longer-term technique than, for example, drugs.

Biofeedback training gives the client a set of skills to help them cope with stressors in the future. It is not just for immediate short-term relief from anxiety (although it is effective for this as well). Repeated use of biofeedback may reduce arousal of the sympathetic nervous system over time. Relaxation also gives the client a chance to think more clearly about the stressors themselves and what they can do to reduce or remove them.

Therefore, biofeedback is not a 'quick fix' to manage stress and does have benefits beyond short-term relief from symptoms.

Inconsistent outcomes

One weakness is that biofeedback does not have consistently positive results.

In the study by Lemaire *et al.* mentioned above, the researchers also measured heart rate, blood pressure and levels of stress hormones. There were no *significant changes* in these measures over the course of the study. Biofeedback had no effect on the physiological indicators of stress over a 28-day period.

This shows that the effectiveness of biofeedback depends on what is being treated. It makes the individual person 'feel better', which is a positive outcome. But biofeedback may be less beneficial for reducing physiological risk factors associated with stress.

Not suitable for everyone

Another weakness of biofeedback is that it requires a lot of effort and motivation from the client.

This is especially true of the transfer phase when the client needs to apply the skills they have learned in real-world situations. Ironically the stress that drove them to seek biofeedback in the first place can be so demotivating they may give up using it. There is also an educational element to biofeedback in the first phase. This means the client has to make some effort to understand the relationship between their physiological functioning and the signals they receive.

This suggests that the convenience of *drug therapy* would be better suited to some clients than the commitment of biofeedback.

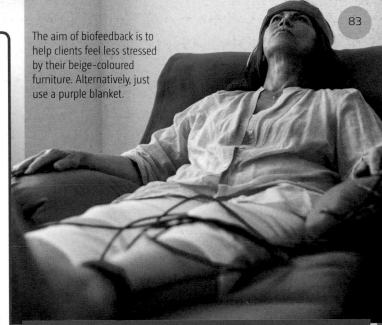

The aim of biofeedback is to help clients feel less stressed by their beige-coloured furniture. Alternatively, just use a purple blanket.

Exam-style questions

Larry is a full-time carer for his mum. She has dementia and he looks after her 24 hours a day. Although he is well-organised, he feels out of control with a lot of things. This means Larry is often stressed. Apart from feeling anxious all the time, he has a lot of physical symptoms. He can never relax and his muscles are tense so he gets headaches. His heart races and he gets 'butterflies' in his stomach.

He found the time to see his GP, who discovered that Larry's blood pressure was too high. She thought his other symptoms were stress-related too. She said she would prescribe some tablets but also wondered if Larry would be interested in other ways of coping.

1. In the context of biofeedback, explain what is meant by:
   (a) Physiological feedback. (2)
   (b) Relaxation training. (2)
2. Explain **two** physiological stress management techniques Larry could use. (4)
3. Explain **one** strength and **one** weakness of biofeedback as a stress management technique. (4)
4. Evaluate stress management techniques Larry could use. Include biofeedback and **one** other physiological technique in your answer. (9)

> You should by now have a fair idea of the kind of exam questions that can be asked – try to think of a few more of your own that could be asked on each spread.

An issue to consider

What is it about biofeedback that makes people feel less stressed? Is it the physiological feedback or the relaxation training? How could you find out?

Specification content

C2 Treatment and management of addiction and stress

Physiological stress management techniques:

● Biofeedback – physiological feedback, relaxation training.

GET ACTIVE Outlining the steps

Jussi found a biofeedback therapist through a website. Jussi suffers from severe anxiety brought about by the stress in her life. Medication from her doctor gave her some temporary help, but she wants a better long-term solution. Jussi has made her first appointment but she is wondering what to expect. The website gives her a few ideas. She knows that there will be three main phases to biofeedback. Apparently she will learn to relax. Jussi didn't realise you had to learn to do this. There's also something about a machine and being able to use biofeedback in real life.

It's important to understand the practical steps involved in biofeedback training and use. Therefore, explain to Jussi what will happen in each phase of biofeedback training. Write your explanation as a step-by-step bullet-pointed list.

Psychological stress management techniques: SIT

Coping with stage fright

Stage performers are doing a job, and great ones make it look easy.

But a surprising number suffer from stage fright, when overwhelming anxiety hits them as they're about to go on stage. The actor Laurence Olivier had to be physically pushed onto the stage for his scenes. The singer Barbra Streisand was so afflicted with stage fright that she didn't perform live for 27 years.

The singers Lorde (above) and Adele (see below) both suffer from anxiety. But it doesn't stop either of them from being brilliant performers. They have ways of dealing with stage fright that are similar to the method described on this spread.

Lorde talks aloud to herself. In the language of this spread, she uses 'coping self-statements' such as 'You are in the zone'. The positivity of her talk replaces the negativity in her head. As her appearance at Glastonbury in 2016 showed, Adele manages her anxiety by swearing a lot and joking.

Most performers emphasise that stage fright never really disappears. But you can learn to cope with it enough for you to still perform at your best.

Specification term

Stress inoculation training (SIT) A stress management technique which helps individuals develop coping skills and then exposes the individual to moderate amounts of anxiety to enable the practice of coping.

Even the world's most successful singers can become extremely stressed. Adele has often explained how she is sick before performances (she even projectile vomited on someone once).

Stress inoculation training (SIT)

Many *stressors* are things we have no control over, such as traffic jams on the way to work or an unpleasant boss. But we can control the way we *think* about a stressor. Thinking about a stressful situation positively rather than negatively changes how we feel and respond. This is a *cognitive behavioural approach* to treatment – it is *cognitive* because it is about how we think and it is *behavioural* because the ultimate aim is to change our behaviour (how we feel and respond).

Don Meichenbaum and Roy Cameron (1973) created a form of CBT specifically to target *stress* and, in addition, to give people protection (inoculation) against future stressors by helping them to learn how to cope in advance (like a physical 'inoculation' gives protection against a disease).

Meichenbaum and Cameron divided *stress inoculation training* (SIT) into three phases, each focused on practical ways to help the stressed client. In practice there is some overlap between the phases and clients sometimes have to work backwards to an earlier phase to refresh before moving forwards again.

Duration of therapy depends on the client but typically lasts for nine to twelve sessions in a two to three month period. Each session is between one and one-and-a-half hours. One or two sessions are for follow-up after several weeks or months.

Phase 1: Cognitive preparation

SIT starts with the client and the therapist identifying and understanding the stressors faced by the client. Meichenbaum (2007) states that the relationship between client and therapist is important to success in SIT – there should be warm collaboration (i.e. not the therapist telling the client what to do). The therapist is supportive but it is the client who is responsible for their own progress. They are the expert on their own experiences.

The client learns that stressors can be overcome by seeing them as challenges rather than as threats. Also, a stressor that might seem overwhelming can often be broken down into smaller elements that are easier to cope with.

Phase 2: Skill acquisition

The client learns skills they need to cope with stress. The therapist has a 'toolbox' of skills, such as relaxation, social skills, time management, communication and cognitive restructuring (thinking about stressful situations more positively).

The choice of skills is tailored to the client's specific needs, but most benefit from learning to use self-talk effectively. This includes using coping self-statements such as, 'You've got a plan, stick to it' and 'You're in control here, so don't worry'. These replace negative and anxious internal dialogue with positive thoughts.

There is a behavioural element to SIT because the client practises these skills in the safe environment of the therapy clinic. They imagine using the skills, watch the therapist model them and then act them out in role plays.

Phase 3: Application and follow-through

Personal experiments The client gradually transfers their skills to the real world by conducting personal experiments. These are homework tasks set by the therapist so the client can apply their coping skills in situations that become increasingly stressful. They discuss the experience in therapy sessions and work on skill development further if necessary. As the client's control over their *anxiety* increases, the therapist's role becomes less important.

Relapse prevention SIT accepts that setbacks are inevitable, so the client learns how to cope with them before they happen. The client learns to view setbacks as temporary learning opportunities and not permanent failures. The therapist helps the client see that success is down to their own skills and not due to luck or chance or other people (i.e. they develop an *internal locus of control*).

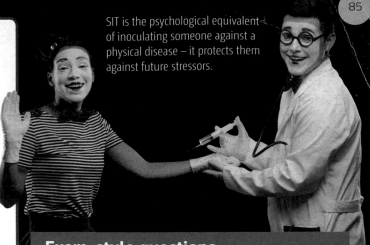

SIT is the psychological equivalent of inoculating someone against a physical disease – it protects them against future stressors.

Evaluation

Evidence of effectiveness

One strength of SIT is that it has received support from several studies.

For example, Richard Sheehy and John Horan (2004) used SIT with first-year university law students. This group included students who scored highly on measures of stress and were predicted to perform badly in exams. The therapy course was relatively short (four 90-minute sessions, one per week). These students showed lower levels of stress after SIT, compared with a *control group* of students placed on a waiting list. All participants experiencing SIT (including the controls) showed lower levels of anxiety. Participants predicted to be in the bottom 20% of exam performance showed substantial improvements.

These findings show that a practical and manageable SIT course can help students cope with stress and improve academic performance.

Flexibility

Another strength of SIT is that it is tailored to a client's needs.

SIT can involve a wide range of stress management techniques in the skills acquisition phase. Some of these are more suitable for elderly people or people with learning difficulties. It is used with individuals, couples, small and large groups and in different settings (work, home, etc.). SIT has even been adapted for online use (Litz *et al.* 2004). Michael Spiegler (2012) argues that SIT is so flexible it can potentially help to manage any kind of stress, including stress associated with racism and homophobia.

This flexibility means that it has the potential to be increasingly applied to new situations.

A demanding therapy

One weakness is that SIT places great demands on clients.

SIT requires high levels of commitment and motivation (e.g. time, effort). Training can be lengthy and involve a lot of self-reflection, learning of new skills and practice. Follow-through is especially demanding. For example, some people are less able than others to use coping self-statements when they are experiencing anxiety in a stressful situation. Although SIT prepares clients to face *relapse*, it is so demanding that some people do not continue therapy.

This means that research studies may well underestimate the effectiveness of SIT because early leavers are counted as 'unsuccessful'.

Too complex

Another weakness of SIT is that it is unnecessarily complicated.

SIT uses lots of different cognitive and behavioural techniques to target a wide variety of stressors and situations. The different techniques are unlikely to all be equally effective, but it is hard to pinpoint exactly what it is about SIT that works. For instance, clients are encouraged to develop a sense of control over stress. Countless other studies show that control is crucial to psychological well-being. Or perhaps SIT is little more than 'positive thinking', with skill acquisition playing a secondary role.

This means that the benefits of SIT might be achieved much more easily.

GET ACTIVE Medics in the army

Stress inoculation is used as a therapy to treat people whose stress levels are so high they could suffer harm. For some people, extreme stress is an unavoidable part of their job. A good example is medical staff in the military, who have to confront exceptionally stressful situations on and away from the battlefield. Therefore, the British Army has used 'virtual' SIT to help develop stress coping skills. In the follow-through phase, medics apply their learned skills in a virtual environment that is as realistic as possible but also 'safe' because they cannot be harmed.

For each phase of SIT, explain how it could be used to help train medical staff to be better at coping with the stress arising from work with injured soldiers.

Exam-style questions

Dermot works as a waiter in a restaurant. For him it is a stressful job because he feels he isn't very good at talking to people. This makes him anxious and is affecting his performance at work. Every time he takes an order he thinks he is going to panic. He doesn't like to make eye contact with customers and can't wait until the conversation is over. Even worse, Dermot believes that every time he interacts with a customer it will go badly and there's nothing he can do about it. It doesn't help that he is quite disorganised and sometimes late for work.

1. Explain **one** difference between psychological and physiological stress management techniques. (2)

2. Stress inoculation training is a stress management technique that has three phases: cognitive preparation, skill acquisition and application/follow-through.

   (a) Explain what is meant by 'cognitive preparation'. (3)

   (b) Using examples, explain how skill acquisition could help Dermot. (4)

   (c) In the context of stress inoculation training, explain how application and follow-through can help Dermot to manage his stress. (4)

3. Assess stress inoculation training as a method of Dermot managing his stress. Refer to both strengths and weaknesses of the therapy in your answer. (6)

4. Discuss how stress inoculation training could help Dermot to manage his stress levels. Refer in your answer to **one** physiological technique of stress management. (9)

An issue to consider

You might find that you use coping self-statements to 'gee yourself up' when feeling stressed (out loud or to yourself).

What do they do for you?

Specification content

C2 Treatment and management of addiction and stress

Psychological stress management techniques:

● Stress inoculation training – cognitive preparation, skill acquisition, application and follow-through.

Psychological stress management techniques: Social support

This shed saves lives

There is an epidemic of loneliness among elderly people in the UK, according to a report in 2019 by the charity *Ageing well without children.*

There are over a million people aged over 65 years who have no children. This group of people are more lonely, more isolated, in poorer health and less able to access healthcare than any other group of people in the country. And yet they are almost invisible. The charity says they are 'dangerously unsupported' (McNeil and Hunter 2014).

Some older people are doing something about this. *The UK Men's Sheds Association* is a charity that supports the development of and promotes access to over 500 'Men's Sheds' across the UK. These are community spaces (including sheds) where men can meet up, use their practical skills and be with others.

This is one example of how people can support each other, and in doing so reduce loneliness and stress.

Specification terms

Emotional support Focused on what a person is feeling – the anxiety associated with stress and trying to find ways to reduce those feelings.

Esteem support Helping someone to attach greater value to themselves so they view their abilities with greater confidence.

Instrumental support Practical help such as lending money, cooking a meal, providing information.

Self-esteem The feelings that a person has about their self-concept.

Social support People cope with stressful situations by seeking help from their friends, family and acquaintances.

'You OK hun?' <concerned emoji> It has become a bit of a cliché, but there are many ways to offer emotional and esteem support on social networks.

Social support

Most of us have a social network, a collection of people we interact with to varying degrees. This includes family members, friends (face-to-face and online) and work colleagues – all are potential sources of *social support*.

Some networks are bigger than others, and some offer more support in times of *stress* than others. For example, someone with a relatively small social network may get a lot of support from just a few close friends. On the other hand, people who have large networks may find the relationships within them are not close enough to provide much support. So, the quality of the network may be more important than the size of it.

Catherine Schaefer *et al.* (1981) identified at least three different types of social support.

Instrumental support This is practical help (an 'instrument' is something which is useful practically). *Instrumental support* could be in the form of physically doing something to help (e.g. giving someone a lift to hospital, cooking a meal, providing money). Or it could involve giving information (e.g. telling someone how they can cope with stress, providing bus times or details of recipes).

Emotional support This is about feelings. We provide *emotional support* when we express warmth, concern, affection, empathy or love for someone ('I'm sorry you're going through such a tough time', 'I'm really worried about you'). This type of support is not meant to be practical. We offer it to comfort the recipient, to help make them feel better and to lift their mood, especially when they are stressed.

Esteem support We give *esteem support* when we feel someone needs to have more faith in themselves and their abilities. We might express our confidence in them ('You're so good, I know you can do this'). This increases their feelings of *self-esteem* (belief in themselves), their *self-efficacy* (confidence in their abilities) and in turn reduces their levels of stress.

Explaining the benefits

Buffering hypothesis Sheldon Cohen and Thomas Wills (1985) argue that social support protects us against the negative effects of stress by creating psychological distance (a 'buffer zone').

This is a *cognitive* process – our support network gives us a 'breathing space' and a chance to think about the *stressor* differently. The support acts as a 'reserve' that dampens the impact of stressors and allows us to cope better. However, this means that such support doesn't really help at other times (and can in fact backfire – see evaluation).

Direct effects hypothesis This states that social support is beneficial at all times, not just during stress. It has positive effects on our health and well-being, perhaps through helping us to relax and reducing physiological arousal of the nervous system.

Other issues

The three types of support are not independent of each other. They overlap considerably and we usually use more than one of them at a time (and perhaps all three). For example, if you are a 'shoulder to cry on', you are probably offering all three types of support – you are there as a practical helper, you make the person feel better (hopefully) and you increase their confidence.

Instrumental support, although helpful, can sometimes appear a bit 'business-like' and lacking emotional engagement. But even this can provide emotional support because it is a sign that the provider cares.

All three types can also be given without the supporter being physically present. Emotional and esteem support are offered all the time on online social networks such as Facebook and Instagram. Different types of network can provide different types of support.

Evaluation

Research support

One strength is research evidence for social support.

Sheldon Cohen *et al.* (2015) studied the effects of giving hugs on the likelihood of becoming ill during stress (hugging is a behavioural form of emotional support). Participants were deliberately exposed to the common cold virus and monitored. Those who believed they had greater social support had a significantly reduced risk of becoming ill, even if they were highly stressed. Hugs accounted for about one-third of the protective effect of support. Participants who had the most hugs were less likely to become ill and their symptoms were less severe if they did.

These findings show that emotional support can provide some protection against the negative effects of stress.

Practical application

Another strength is that the types of support can be applied to different *cultures*.

Shelley Taylor *et al.* (2004) compared uses of social support in Americans of European and Asian origins. They found that Asian-Americans were less likely than European-Americans to seek and use social support in times of stress. This was because they did not want to disrupt their communities by appearing to impose their problems on everyone else. Later research by Taylor *et al.* (2007) suggested that social support is more effective for Asian-Americans if it does not make too many demands of other people (i.e. not emotional support).

This shows that social support is related to cultural preferences.

Backfire effects

One weakness of social support is that it can backfire and have negative effects.

Social support is not always beneficial – it depends on who provides it and when. For example, we appreciate practical help from family and friends. But sometimes information from the same sources can be inaccurate and counterproductive. Even emotional support from a relative can be unhelpful. For instance, they might insist on coming with us to a hospital appointment, but that makes us feel more anxious than if we had gone on our own. Sometimes support may be given to make the supporter feel better.

This suggests that social support is more beneficial when it is requested by the person undergoing stress than when it is imposed by a well-meaning supporter.

Gender differences

Another weakness is that men and women benefit differently from social support.

Men appear to have larger social networks than women. But what really matters is whether the person under stress seeks out their network and uses its support. Lisa Tamres *et al.* (2002) reviewed studies of gender differences. Most studies found that women used emotional support to cope with stress significantly more than men. However, men did frequently use instrumental support.

This shows that social support may not always be helpful unless it takes individual differences such as gender into account.

Pets can be great sources of support, especially for someone who is lonely. It just goes to show that support doesn't always need words. Unless there's something you know that I don't know.

GET ACTIVE Supporting vulnerable clients

Imagine you are a social worker and Jannik is one of your clients. He is in his 70s and has lived on his own since his partner Phil died two years ago. He has no children and the rest of his family live some distance away. Jannik is showing signs of dementia and he is now having trouble looking after himself. His sister pops in from time to time but there is a limit to what she can do to help. You are worried that Jannik is vulnerable without social support. You have some contacts with charities in the local community that might be able to help.

1. Write a list of Jannik's likely support needs and group them into the three categories of instrumental, emotional and esteem.

2. What support could local charities provide to meet these needs?

Exam-style questions

Frankie was going through a very stressful time. Her relationship was breaking up and she had to go to hospital for several appointments and an operation. Understandably she felt anxious and depressed a lot of the time, and found it hard to motivate and organise herself.

Fortunately, Frankie had many friends and family members who helped her. Her brother made sure Frankie got to her appointments on time and helped her pack for her stay in hospital. Her best friend was a 'shoulder to cry on', which Frankie sometimes did over a glass of wine. Her boss always made sure Frankie knew when she had produced good work.

1. In the context of Frankie's experience:

   (a) Identify **one** example of instrumental support and explain how it could help her manage stress. (3)

   (b) Identify **one** example of emotional support and explain how it could help her manage stress. (3)

   (c) Identify **one** example of esteem support and explain how it could help her manage stress. (3)

2. Name **one** physiological stress management technique Frankie could also use. Explain **one** difference between using this technique and getting social support. (3)

3. Explain **one** strength and **one** weakness of social support as a method of managing Frankie's stress levels. (4)

4. Discuss how at least **one** psychological stress management technique could help reduce Frankie's stress. (9)

An issue to consider

Think of your own experiences in receiving support at times of stress. Which kinds of support did you find the most helpful? Did you find that some kinds of support were just annoying?

Specification content

C2 Treatment and management of addiction and stress

Psychological stress management techniques:

● Social support – instrumental (practical), emotional (comfort), esteem (self-esteem).

Physiological treatments for addiction: Aversion therapy

Don't read this while you're eating

What's the worst thing you've ever smelled? When I (Rob) went on holiday once, the electricity in my home went off. This tripped the fuses so the electricity didn't come back on when the power was restored. Everything in the freezer defrosted. It was summer. The smell was indescribably disgusting. It seemed to permeate everything. It was so thick you could taste it.

Here's what it reminded me of – the members of the band *Slipknot* used to keep a decomposing crow in a jar. They would inhale big breaths of it so they could throw up on stage. The lengths some people go to for Art.

Some smells are so strong that you can be put off anything that you associate with them. Even the thought of it can make you feel ill. That's why you were warned at the start of this panel.

And that's why smells are sometimes used to stop addictions, along with electric shocks and drugs that make you vomit. Yes, this spread has it all...

Specification term

Aversion therapy A behavioural treatment based on classical conditioning. A maladaptive behaviour is paired with an unpleasant stimulus such as a painful electric shock. Eventually, the behaviour is associated with pain without the shock being used. In covert sensitisation the aversive stimulus is not real but imagined.

Some say traditional aversion therapy strips the alcoholic of their dignity. But then again so does alcoholism.

Aversion therapy

Aversion therapy is based on the *classical conditioning* explanation of addiction (see page 52). We learn to associate two stimuli with each other if they frequently occur at the same time. Addiction, for example, can develop when taking a drug (*neutral stimulus*) and experiencing pleasure (*unconditioned response*) become associated with each other through frequent pairing.

If this process can be reversed, then perhaps the addiction can be removed. In *counterconditioning*, the drug is associated with a new unconditioned response – this time an unpleasant state such as feeling sick or uncomfortable. The unpleasant state is aversive (we usually want to avoid it), so the client gradually loses the desire for the drug (or behaviour).

Aversion therapy for alcohol addiction

A client is given a drug called an *emetic* because it causes vomiting (emesis). He or she quickly feels ill and starts vomiting after about five or ten minutes. But before they do, they are also given an alcoholic drink to hold, smell and (if they can) taste. Therefore, alcohol is associated with an aversive stimulus.

This process is repeated several times using higher doses of the emetic drug and other alcoholic drinks. For real-life application, a capsule can be placed under the skin for slow release of the drug (e.g. *disulfiram*, brand name Antabuse).

The end result should be that the client has learned a new stimulus-response and stops drinking.

Aversion therapy for gambling addiction

Another aversive stimulus is electric shocks. These have been used instead of drugs for treating *behavioural addictions*. Shock is also useful with clients who have medical conditions which make frequent vomiting dangerous, such as high blood pressure. The shocks are not damaging but, as they are meant to be aversive, they have to be painful. The level of shock is usually chosen by the client themselves. They select a shock that is uncomfortable but not distressing or unbearable.

The client chooses images that are linked to their gambling addiction (e.g. betting shops, fruit machines, betting slips, horses, etc.). Non-gambling images are also included. The client looks at each image in turn. Every time a gambling-related picture is displayed, they receive a two-second electric shock.

After repeated pairings an association is formed between the unpleasant experience (the shock) and the gambling behaviour. The end result should be cessation of gambling.

A new form of aversion therapy – Covert sensitisation

Aversion therapy raises *ethical issues* (see evaluation). Therefore, traditional aversion therapy has mostly been replaced by *covert sensitisation*. The client imagines how the unpleasant symptoms would feel rather than experiencing them for real. An association is still formed between the behaviour and the (imagined) unpleasant symptoms. The result is a reduced desire for the drug (or behaviour) of addiction.

Covert sensitisation for nicotine addiction

Therapy begins with the client relaxing as the therapist reads from a script describing an aversive situation. The client imagines themselves smoking a cigarette. The description lingers on the sensations involved so the client can experience them fully (almost as if they were really smoking). The client then imagines extremely unpleasant consequences, the feeling of nausea and vomiting for example.

Because this imaginary scene needs to be vivid, the therapist goes into graphic detail about all the sights, sounds, smells, physical movements and feelings involved. For instance, the client may be instructed to imagine their cigarette and fingers covered in faeces.

As the session ends, the client imagines a scene in which they 'turn their back' on cigarettes and experience feelings of relief.

Evaluation

Research support

One strength is evidence to support the effectiveness of aversion therapy.

For example, Helmut Niederhofer *et al.* (2003) used aversion therapy with alcohol-dependent adolescents. The treatment group received 200 mg of *disulfiram* every day for 90 days. Compared with a *placebo control group*, these participants abstained for *significantly* longer (average 68.5 days, against 29.7 for the placebo group). There were also no differences between the two groups in terms of side effects (apart from occasional diarrhoea in the treatment group).

Therefore, aversion therapy may be an effective treatment for alcoholism, extending the period before *relapse* without significant side effects.

Chronic addiction

Another strength is that aversion therapy is useful for chronic addiction.

Aversion has been used with patients who have not benefitted from other treatments. Given that these patients have proven 'hard to treat', the effectiveness rates of aversion are surprisingly high. Treatment is based on changing behaviours that are learned 'automatically' through classical conditioning. In a sense the client does not have to 'do' anything except tolerate the unpleasant treatment. Unlike with psychological therapies, the client does not have to self-reflect, learn difficult skills or even make major lifestyle changes.

This is why aversion therapy may be less challenging for chronic alcoholics than other treatments.

Ethical issues

One weakness is that aversion therapy raises serious ethical issues.

Clients experience extreme nausea, some pain and perhaps loss of dignity. These are all forms of physical and psychological harm. They are not just unfortunate results of aversion therapy – they are 'built in', necessary elements of the treatment. Letting clients choose their own shock level was an attempt to address ethical issues. A more satisfactory solution was the preference for covert sensitisation. This does not use shocks or vomiting and poses fewer medical risks. It also allows clients to retain their dignity and is less likely to lower their *self-esteem*.

This suggests that aversion does not need to be abandoned as a treatment for addiction, as long as it is the more ethically acceptable covert sensitisation version that is used.

Lack of long-term effectiveness

A further weakness is that aversion therapy only seems to work in the short-term.

A study by McConaghy *et al.* (1983) found that reductions in gambling behaviour and cravings were much greater after one month than after one year. McConaghy *et al.* (1991) followed up these participants over a two- to nine-year period. They found that aversion therapy was no more effective than placebo. Most participants had reverted to their earlier behaviour. The study did find that, once again, covert sensitisation was a more effective long-term treatment.

This suggests that any benefits from aversion therapy are lost relatively quickly and other treatments might be more effective.

On this spread, and many other spreads, we have supplied four criticisms of the theory. You would not need all of these when answering a 9-mark essay question. However, you may be asked to explain two strengths or two weaknesses.

Down in one? Imagine getting your tongue in there and chewing on that lot. Just one of the things you might think about in covert sensitisation.

Exam-style questions

Harry is addicted to alcohol. He drinks excessively every day because he enjoys how it makes him feel. He likes the smell and taste of many alcoholic drinks. He often gets really bad hangovers but this is not enough to make him stop. He drinks on his own and whenever he is socialising with other people.

Greta is addicted to online gambling. She plays fruit machines for hours at a time. She likes the colours and the flashing lights of the websites. They give her a great 'buzz' which she enjoys. But she also likes the social interaction with other people playing online.

Ash smokes more than 20 cigarettes a day. He loves the 'hit' from the first cigarette of the day. He thinks smoking helps him to relax. He even enjoys playing with his lighter and he always fancies a cigarette when he sees someone else get their lighter out and start smoking.

1. Explain how aversion therapy could be used to treat:
   (a) Harry's alcohol addiction. (3)
   (b) Greta's gambling addiction. (3)
   (c) Ash's nicotine addiction. (3)
2. Many psychologists have concerns over the use of aversion therapy. Explain possible ethical issues in using aversion therapy to treat Harry's alcohol addiction. (4)
3. Explain **one** other weakness of aversion therapy with reference to either Greta or Ash. (3)
4. Discuss **one** physiological treatment for addiction. Refer in your answer to at least **two** of the people in the scenario, Harry, Greta and Ash. (9)

GET ACTIVE Trying to give up

Sally knows she is addicted to nicotine because she can't stop smoking. She enjoys the pleasure of smoking and gets very irritable and restless when she can't smoke. She really wants to stop but she has failed many times in the past. This time she is going to need help. Sally has heard of a treatment where you get electric shocks when you smoke a cigarette. But she doesn't fancy the sound of that. She would like to get the same effect but without the pain. Sally is also interested in the psychological theory behind the treatment.

1. Suggest a treatment that would be suitable for Sally.

2. Explain how the treatment would be carried out and how it works.

An issue to consider

Aversion therapy is considered unethical by many people.

What do you think? Consider costs and benefits to both the individual and wider society.

Specification content

C2 Treatment and management of addiction and stress
Physiological treatments for addiction:
● Aversion therapy.

Physiological treatments for addiction:
Drug therapies

The nose has it

Imagine you're addicted to something, let's say chocolate.

You know a little bit is divine, but too much is bad for you. But like all chocoholics, you just can't help yourself. So, you reach for the bar of chocolatey heaven and... your hand picks up a spray, you stick it up your nose and press. Suddenly you don't feel like eating the chocolate anymore.

If this seems far-fetched, the reality is possibly even more impressive. Researchers in Finland, led by Professor Hannu Alho, are testing a nasal spray that could stop people gambling. The spray contains *naloxone*, a drug which is already used in a spray to reverse some of the effects of a heroin overdose.

The idea is that an addicted gambler who feels a craving to gamble will have a shot of naloxone instead.

It has an almost instant effect on the brain, unlike tablets which take about an hour because they have to be processed through the digestive system.

On this spread we'll see why this might just work.

Specification term

Drug therapy Treatment involving drugs, i.e. chemicals that have a particular effect on the functioning of the brain or some other body system. In the case of mental disorders such drugs usually affect neurotransmitter levels.

'Wow, I didn't realise nicotine patches were that big.'

Drug therapies

Types of drug therapies for addiction

Aversives produce unpleasant (*aversive*) consequences such as vomiting. As we saw on the previous spread, *disulfiram* treats alcoholism by creating hypersensitivity to alcohol.

Agonists are basically drug substitutes. *Agonists* attach to receptors on *neurons* and activate them, producing a similar effect to a drug of *addiction*. They satisfy cravings but are less harmful than addictive drugs. They can be administered medically and allow a gradual reduction of dose.

Antagonists attach to neuron receptors and block them. This means an addictive drug cannot attach and produce its usual effects. So, antagonists do not provide the euphoric feelings many addicts crave.

Drug therapies for nicotine addiction

Nicotine replacement therapy is the most common treatment for nicotine addiction. Nicotine is the addictive substance in tobacco smoke and NRT provides it using gum, inhalers and patches. The dose is more controlled and 'cleaner' because tobacco smoke also contains other more harmful chemicals which are absent in NRT.

Nicotine delivered via *nicotine replacement therapy* (NRT) operates biochemically in the same way we have seen before (page 50). Molecules attach to receptors in neurons in the *ventral tegmental area* (VTA) of the brain. This stimulates release of *dopamine* in the *nucleus accumbens*.

The nicotine dose can be reduced gradually over time using smaller patches, for example. This means the *withdrawal* symptoms can be managed over a period of two or three months, improving the chances of avoiding *relapse*.

Bupropion (trade name e.g. Wellbutrin) started life as a treatment for *depression* (an *antidepressant*). Its biochemical effects are unclear but it appears to work in the opposite way to nicotine. According to Huibert Mansvelder *et al.* (2007) *bupropion* molecules attach to the neuron receptors in the VTA, blocking them and so reducing dopamine release in the nucleus accumbens. This is associated with reduced cravings and fewer withdrawal symptoms. Bupropion is often used on its own but sometimes alongside NRT to support smokers in their attempts to quit.

Drug therapies for gambling behaviour

Currently in the UK, no drug is officially approved to treat gambling addiction. But research is ongoing into several possibilities. The two most promising candidates are opioid antagonists and antidepressants.

Opioid antagonists An *antagonist* drug is one that blocks another drug or a brain biochemical (e.g. a neurotransmitter such as dopamine or *serotonin*). It does this by attaching to the receptors on neurons that the neurotransmitter would normally attach to. This means the neurotransmitter cannot have its usual effect.

Opioid antagonists such as *naltrexone* and *naloxone* have an indirect effect on gambling addiction. The *dopamine reward system* we outlined above does not work in isolation. It is affected in turn by another reward system in the brain, the opioid system. Opioid antagonists block the opioid system. The result is that gambling does not produce a rewarding dopamine release, so the gambler's cravings are dampened down. Some researchers have linked this to a reduction in actual gambling behaviour (e.g. Kim and Grant 2001).

Evaluation

Research support for nicotine treatment

One strength is that evidence shows some drugs can be effective.

John Hughes (2011) conducted a review of 66 trials of several drug treatments for nicotine addiction (including 49 trials of bupropion). He concluded that bupropion used on its own *significantly* increased long-term abstinence compared with *placebo*. Its effectiveness was similar to that of NRT but the two treatments combined produced no further benefits. A similar review by Lindsay Stead *et al.* (2012) found that all forms of NRT were more effective than placebo (nasal spray was the most effective method).

These findings show that drug treatments are potentially very useful for helping people to stop smoking, increasing quality of life and making huge savings for the NHS.

Further research support

Another strength is that drug treatment is effective in gambling addiction.

Jon Grant *et al.* (2008a) gave the opioid antagonist naltrexone to addicted gamblers every day over an 18-week period. The gamblers were *randomly allocated* to low-, medium- and high-dose groups. This was a placebo-controlled trial in which neither the participants nor the researchers knew who was taking the drug. Compared with placebo, the gamblers experienced significantly lower gambling urges/cravings and a reduction in gambling behaviour. There were no differences between men and women and the strength of dose had no effect on outcomes.

This suggests that even a low dose of an opioid antagonist is enough to treat a gambling addiction.

Individual differences

One weakness is that drugs are not equally effective for all addicted people.

Even small *genetic* variations between people can have a major impact on drug treatments. For instance, Tammy Chung *et al.* (2012) concluded that the effects of naltrexone on alcoholism depend on variations in a single gene. Alcoholics who had one version of this gene responded better to treatment than those with the other version. Grant *et al.* (2008b) found addicted gamblers with a family history of alcoholism benefitted most from an opioid antagonist. This suggests a genetic factor is involved.

This shows that researchers urgently need to discover the factors that make drug treatments more effective for some gamblers than for others.

Side effects

Another weakness of drugs is the risk of harmful side effects.

These range from the relatively trivial to much more serious. For instance, the side effects of NRT are usually mild and include dizziness, stomach problems and sleep disturbances. But the doses of naltrexone and naloxone needed to improve gambling addiction are relatively high. Therefore, the risk of serious side effects is greater (e.g. suicidal thoughts). Although minor side effects can be tolerated, severe ones mean clients may stop taking medication.

Therefore, the benefits of a drug treatment need to be carefully weighed up against the risk of side effects, which might make another treatment a better option.

Many people have noticed the irony of using drugs to treat addictions.

Exam-style questions

Lucia would love to kick her smoking habit. She likes the 'hit' she gets from her first drag. She has tried in the past to stop by using willpower, but it has never worked. She finds smoking is too enjoyable to stop for long. Lucia wonders if there is another way she could give up.

Amir is addicted to gambling on horse races. He can't stop himself because he craves the 'rush' he gets when he places a bet. He loves the build-up, the environment of the betting shop and even writing down his horses on the betting slip. He tries to stop but he keeps coming back to it again and again.

1. Apart from drug therapies, name **one** other physiological treatment for addiction. (1)
2. Explain **one** difference between this treatment and drug therapies. (2)
3. Explain **two** physiological treatments that could be used to help Lucia. (2 + 2)
4. Explain how drug therapies could be used to help Amir. (3)
5. Explain **one** strength and **one** weakness of using drug therapies to treat Amir's gambling addiction. (4)
6. You have also studied psychological treatments for addiction.

   Compare psychological treatments for addiction with physiological treatments for addiction. (9)
7. Discuss how **two** physiological treatments for addiction could help Lucia and/or Amir. (9)

An issue to consider

Some people feel that taking drugs to help beat an addiction is 'cheating'.

What do you think?

Specification content

C2 Treatment and management of addiction and stress

Physiological treatments for addiction:
● Drug therapies.

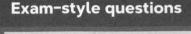 GET ACTIVE Hooked

Having been smoking since the first year of secondary school, Lin is well and truly hooked. She really wants to give up but nothing has worked in the past. Lin knows some smokers enjoy the feel of the cigarette, the lighter and the packet. But all she really enjoys is the 'buzz', and she doesn't mind how she gets it.

Kane's addiction to online poker is out of control. He too is hooked. When he can't play, he gets strong and horrible cravings that can't be satisfied until he's back online again. The feeling of relief is massive and he reckons this has stopped him giving up in the past.

Which drug treatments might Lin and Kane benefit from? Explain how each treatment would work to help combat Lin and Kane's addictions.

Psychological treatments for addiction: CBT

Surprising beliefs about smoking

- Exercising makes smoking less harmful.
- Smoking makes me attractive and/or thin.
- The filter on my cigarette is all the protection I need.
- Giving up smoking will make no difference to my health.
- I eat lots of fruit and veg, so I'll be OK.
- My grandad smoked 60 a day all his life and he lived to 153, so that just shows you.
- Nicotine patches and vaping are just as bad as smoking.
- I smoke, but I've got a lower risk of getting lung cancer than the average smoker.

The final one comes from a study by Christine McMaster and Christina Lee (1991) and is perhaps the most worrying of them all. Can you see why?

The therapy we look at on this spread argues that false beliefs like these should be the starting point for tackling addictions. If we can change the distorted ways in which people think about gambling, shopping, smoking, drinking and taking other drugs, then their behaviour will change as well.

Specification term

Cognitive behavioural therapy (CBT) A method for treating mental disorders based on both cognitive and behavioural techniques. From the cognitive viewpoint the therapy aims to deal with thinking, such as challenging irrational thoughts. The therapy also includes behavioural techniques such as skills training and using reinforcement.

Can you resist the cues?

Cognitive behavioural therapy (CBT)

Cognitive explanations focus on the way we think. Such explanations assume that irrational ways of thinking lead to drugs/shopping/gambling being used (inappropriately) to cope with *stress* and this leads to *addiction*. The *learning approach* (behavioural) focuses on learning and therefore unlearning.

Cognitive behavioural therapies (CBT) vary but they all have two indispensable elements:

- The cognitive element aims to change the irrational thinking underlying addictions (cognitive restructuring).
- The behavioural element aims to help a client learn to avoid high-risk situations or to cope better in them if they cannot be avoided.

Functional analysis

CBT usually starts with the client and therapist working together to identify high-risk situations. They both try to work out which distorted thoughts and irrational beliefs trigger the client's cravings and addiction-related behaviours. Client and therapist both reflect on what the client is thinking before, during and after. The client may keep a 'thought diary'.

Functional analysis is an ongoing process which is useful later in therapy as well as at the beginning. This is because it can help identify why a client is still having problems coping, or why they are relapsing and what skills they need to develop further.

Cognitive restructuring

The client's distorted cognitions are confronted and challenged by the therapist. The client may not even be aware of how their irrational (or 'faulty') thinking affects their behaviour. Or they may believe that they have been successfully coping up until now.

By asking for evidence of this, the therapist forces the client to rethink their irrational beliefs. It is important that the client 'owns' their awareness and is not just told by the therapist that their thinking is distorted.

Behaviour change

Clients learn new skills that will replace their main way of coping (i.e. their addiction). The therapist can use a range of *skills training* techniques such as assertiveness training, anger management and social skills training (see next spread).

The therapist provides opportunities for the client to practise these skills in a safe environment and also in the real world through homework tasks.

Relapse prevention

The client learns techniques to help avoid *relapse*. In high-risk situations there are cues that trigger the addictive behaviour. It may not be possible to avoid high-risk situations and therefore it is important to identify the cues and learn to cope.

For example, an alcoholic may try to avoid some high-risk situations such as a party with lots of free alcohol. However, it may be difficult to avoid situations where people are drinking so the addict needs to become aware of the cues that trigger their addictive behaviour. The cue is lots of people drinking and having fun, and this triggers an irrational thought (e.g. 'Drinking now will make me attractive, clever, happy, etc.'). The client learns to identify such thoughts and challenge them – this removes the trigger. The client can then use their skills to cope appropriately with the situation, such as using assertiveness to refuse a drink politely but firmly. (This use of cues is described on page 57 – CERP.)

It is important for the client to understand that the situation does not *make* them drink (in this example). To believe it does is a distorted way of thinking.

L - U - C - K - Y   Addicted gamblers often believe (irrationally) that their own skill increases their probability of winning a game of pure chance. Or they have a special ability to predict the outcome of events. Therapy aims to make the addict aware of the irrationality of their thinking. They then need to learn skills to help them cope with the high-risk situations identified in the functional analysis (e.g. walking past a betting shop, seeing a gambling website). Thoughts and feelings that may trigger relapse are also challenged (how does feeling bored, unhappy or stressed 'make' you gamble?).

Evaluation

Research support

One strength is research evidence that CBT is effective in treating drug addictions.

Molly Magill and Lara Ray (2009) reviewed 53 trials of CBT involving people with substance use disorders including alcohol. The studies selected for the *review* all compared CBT treatment with *control groups*. These varied but included other treatments and 'treatment as usual' (TAU), i.e. the treatment the client would normally receive. There was a small but significant benefit for CBT. Shorter CBT programmes were more effective than longer ones, and women benefitted more than men. The researchers estimated that 58% of the CBT clients had better outcomes than clients in comparison groups.

These findings are strong evidence that CBT is effective in treating a wide range of substance addictions.

Relapse prevention

Another strength is that CBT is especially effective at preventing relapse in clients who stick with therapy.

Most people dependent on drugs or gambling have a cycle of addiction which involves alternating periods of use, abstinence and relapse. Unlike some treatments, CBT has a realistic view of relapse which is built into the therapy. Relapse is viewed as a temporary setback rather than as a permanent failure. It is an opportunity for further cognitive restructuring and behavioural change.

This suggests that the combination of cognitive and behavioural strategies is particularly effective.

Short-term and long-term effects

One weakness of CBT is the evidence suggesting it has few long-term benefits.

Magill and Ray's study (see above) found that the benefits of CBT for substance addiction tailed off after six to nine months and reduced even further after one year. Sean Cowlishaw *et al.* (2012) reviewed 11 studies and showed that CBT is very effective in reducing gambling behaviour for up to three months. But after 12 months there were no differences between CBT and comparison groups. They concluded that 'the durability of therapeutic gain is unknown'.

This is a consistent but puzzling finding, given that CBT is thought to be especially useful for preventing relapse.

What works?

Another weakness of CBT is that it is too flexible to evaluate.

CBT uses a wide variety of different techniques and is delivered in many ways, with and without a therapist physically present. This makes CBT highly flexible, allowing it to be tailored to individual needs. But this benefit also makes it hard for researchers to identify which elements of CBT are most useful in treating addictions. One study may find a certain CBT programme is effective, but another study of a different programme comes to another conclusion.

This suggests that the lack of a standard CBT protocol for addictions is a disadvantage for research into its effectiveness.

GET ACTIVE Challenging gambling beliefs

Tammy bets a lot on horse races, but only when she is wearing her lucky hat. She tells her friends that she is very good at choosing the best horses and this means she has to bet on them. Her friends in the betting shop have noticed that Tammy celebrates even if her horse doesn't quite win.

1. *Functional analysis would identify high-risk situations. Make a list of potential situations that could trigger Tammy's gambling cravings.*

2. *Gamblers have irrational thoughts and beliefs about chance, luck and probability. Write down some distorted cognitions that Tammy might experience in these high-risk situations.*

3. *Tammy's therapist would challenge her distorted cognitions. Make a list of questions the therapist could ask to do this.*

Exam-style questions

Theo believes that shopping makes him happy. If he sees something he likes in a shop, it's as if he can't help himself. It's the same online. He explains to his friends that he has no choice, he has to buy the item.

His friends think Theo does this to make himself feel better, because he has a stressful life. Theo works in an office on the high street, so he walks past shops every day. He has a few friends who enjoy shopping as much as he does. They have noticed that Theo never refuses an invitation to go to the shops. He sometimes works from home and has to use his laptop all day.

1. Cognitive behavioural therapy is a psychological treatment for addiction. Name **one** physiological treatment. (1)

2. Explain **one** difference between this physiological treatment and cognitive behavioural therapy. (2)

3. Explain how cognitive behavioural therapy could be used to treat Theo's addiction. (3)

4. Explain **one** strength and **one** weakness of using cognitive behavioural therapy to treat Theo's addiction. (4)

5. Discuss cognitive behavioural therapy as a treatment for Theo's addiction. In your answer refer to **one** physiological treatment for addiction. (9)

You should by now have a fair idea of the kind of exam questions that can be asked – try to think of a few more of your own.

An issue to consider

CBT changes the distorted thinking and maladaptive behaviours of clients.

Which is more important? Could one be successful without the other?

Specification content

C2 Treatment and management of addiction and stress

Psychological treatments for addiction:
- Cognitive behavioural therapy (CBT).

Psychological treatments for addiction: Skills training

Social skills or gaming skills?

The psychologist Mark Griffiths (2010), who we encountered on page 13, investigated the social skills of university students addicted to computer gaming. Students who played a lot reported they were more anxious about social situations than students who played only occasionally.

There are a couple of explanations for this finding. It could be that young people whose social skills are not especially developed gravitate towards computer gaming – it is an attractive and exciting solo activity that offers an escape from stressful social interaction.

Alternatively, these young people have spent quite a lot of time gaming from a young age. So, they have not learned the social skills most of us acquire in childhood and adolescence.

Griffiths' research points towards a potential treatment for addiction. What if the lack of social skills is not just an unfortunate side effect of addiction but is actually central to it? A lack of skills means game players cope with life the only way they know how – by gaming. Perhaps these skills can be learned through training programmes? The treatment on this spread suggests they can.

Specification term

Skills training A form of therapy in which clients learn specific abilities to help them cope with high-risk situations. Such abilities include assertiveness, verbal and non-verbal social skills and anger management. Training uses a range of techniques including group discussion, modelling and role play.

In skills training, the therapist models the skills clients need to learn to cope with their lives. Perhaps one of these skills is actually modelling. Wouldn't that be a coincidence? I'm confused now. I'm going for a lie down.

Skills training

Skills training basics

Skills training can be used as part of *CBT* (see previous spread) or as a standalone treatment for *addiction*. It can be used independently because it does not necessarily assume that the client has irrational beliefs. As a separate programme, skills training is relatively specific and narrow.

As the client practises his or her skills, their self-efficacy increases so they learn they are capable of controlling their own behaviour successfully. Coping in a high-risk situation is not down to luck or chance but the result of their own actions (i.e. an *internal locus of control*).

There are several skills often grouped together under the heading of 'life skills'. These include assertiveness, anger management and social skills training (SST).

Assertiveness training

Conflict in relationships is a common *stressor* that triggers *relapse* in many addicts. Disagreements can quickly escalate into arguments that become manipulative or aggressive. Or the client avoids any kind of confrontation for fear it develops into conflict.

Assertiveness training helps a client to cope with conflicts in a controlled and rational way (including clients who are over-assertive). This minimises the chances they will turn to drugs, shopping or gambling to relieve negative feelings associated with conflict.

Anger management

Some addicts find it hard to control their emotions. Arousal can often be expressed as anger, especially in situations that provoke *anxiety* or are seen as threatening. Clients may be carrying anger from childhood experiences that led to the addiction (as suggested by *self-medication theory*, see pages 54 and 64). Training can help a client express emotions more constructively (e.g. channelled into creative activity).

Social skills training (SST)

Most clients can benefit from developing skills that help them cope with anxiety in social situations. Griffiths' research described on the left suggests that addicted gamers may lack such skills (as a cause or effect of their game-playing).

A recovering alcoholic will encounter situations where alcohol is available (weddings, parties) or gambling cravings are cued (standing outside a betting shop).

SST focuses on improving both verbal and nonverbal communication skills such as tone of voice (firm but not angry) and appropriate eye contact.

Skills training techniques

Group discussion Skills training usually takes place in small groups. Everyone can share experiences and ideas and discuss what could work and why something has not worked. Discussion might identify common high-risk situations to be explored further in training (e.g. how to refuse a drink without becoming angry).

Modelling and role play The therapist demonstrates (*models*) a skill (e.g. using eye contact in refusing a drink) to the group (or they may call upon someone in the group who has mastered the skill). Clients then try to imitate the skill in a role play with each other. This might be recorded for playback later, when the whole group can watch and discuss the interaction. An individual client gets feedback from the therapist or group, probably highlighting areas for improvement but hopefully also identifying successes. The therapist positively reinforces the client's behaviour with praise and encouragement.

Homework Tasks are set so the client practises their developing skills in the real world. These are carefully planned so that the early tasks are achievable and the client works up to more challenging situations over time. The client might keep a diary of his or her experiences for discussion and feedback in sessions.

Visualisation The client imagines situations in which they have to be assertive (e.g. turning down the offer of a cigarette). They mentally work through all the steps involved in the interaction before they role-play it. This helps the client to feel better prepared in a real-life situation.

Evaluation

Research support

One strength of skills training is evidence showing it is effective.

Tony Toneatto (2016) *randomly allocated* 'problem gamblers' to one of four treatments. These included CBT (with *cognitive* restructuring) and *behavioural therapy* (skills training with no cognitive element). The participants in all groups gambled less and spent less money immediately after treatment and after one year. There were no *significant* differences in outcomes between the four treatments.

This study shows that a six-session skills training programme without cognitive restructuring was just as effective as CBT in treating gambling addiction.

Long-term effectiveness

Another strength is that there are long-term benefits to skills training.

In the study by Toneatto (above), the significant improvements gained from skills training (and the other treatments) were maintained after 12 months. Although there was some tail-off, participants were still gambling less and spending less money than they were before training. This is because skills training is 'future-focused'. The aim is to provide clients with skills they can use in any high-risk situations they will encounter at some point – they are better prepared to cope, so relapse is less likely.

This is a desirable outcome because the real problem is finding solutions that work permanently.

Lack of treatment adherence

One weakness of skills training is that it can be very demanding for clients.

Many find it hard to 'stick with it' (adherence is lacking) because it requires a lot of motivation, effort and commitment. Some clients drop out, others continue but take it less seriously. For example, they attend fewer sessions and fail to complete homework tasks. Many people who are addicted to drugs or gambling seek skills training because of some crisis in their lives. Once the crisis is resolved or not so important, they stop coming to sessions before training is complete.

This means it is hard for researchers to work out exactly how effective skills training is.

Role of cognitive factors

Another weakness is that skills training lacks a cognitive element.

Skills training assumes that people with addictions can be helped without addressing underlying cognitive distortions and irrational beliefs. However, there is some evidence that CBT is more effective than skills training. For example, according to Nick Heather *et al.* (2006) social skills training benefits moderately-dependent drinkers, whereas CBT benefits the whole range of clients up to severely-dependent.

This suggests that skills training may be more effective when used as the behavioural component of CBT rather than as a separate treatment for addiction.

Get the message? Hopefully, without anyone having to get angry. Assertiveness is a useful skill for addicted people and it helps to make relapse less likely.

Exam-style questions

Deshi goes out a lot and can never say no when someone offers him a drink. Refusing makes him stressed, so he gives in to make himself feel better.

He was neglected and abused when he was a child. He has grown up with strong emotions that he cannot express properly and drinking helps him cope.

Deshi always forgets that it will only take a couple of drinks before he loses control of himself. His friends don't like the way he gets aggressive when he's been drinking. He sits in a corner avoiding talking to other people or even looking them in the eye. It's probably an escape so he doesn't have to interact with anyone.

1. Deshi's addiction is being maintained by his fear of being stressed. In the context of addiction, explain what is meant by 'maintenance'. (2)

2. Some psychologists believe that learning new skills can help to treat addictions.
   Explain how skills training could help treat Deshi's addiction. (4)

3. Skills training is a psychological treatment. Name **one** physiological treatment for addiction. (1)

4. Explain **one** difference between this treatment and skills training in terms of Deshi's addiction. (2)

5. Explain **one** strength and **one** weakness of using skills training to treat Deshi's addiction. (4)

6. Discuss how treatments for addiction could help Deshi. In your answer you should include **one** physiological treatment and **one** psychological treatment. (9)

GET ACTIVE Coping without booze

Imagine you are a counsellor who works at a treatment centre for ex-professional footballers who have addictions. Several of your clients are alcoholics. You have noticed that most of them seem to lack the skills they need to cope with a pressurised life without turning to alcohol. Some find it impossible to refuse a drink, or they react to an offer of a drink with anger. Most of them find it hard to interact with other people.

1. *Make a list of the skills you could work on with your clients. Choose **one** of these skills.*

2. *How could you use group discussion to start developing this skill?*

3. *You will model this skill for the group to imitate. Write down how you will do this, step-by-step in bullet-point format.*

4. *Describe **one** homework task that you could ask your clients to carry out.*

An issue to consider

Do you think skills training could bring benefits apart from helping to reduce addictive behaviours? What might they be?

Specification content

C2 Treatment and management of addiction and stress
Psychological treatments for addiction:
● Skills training.

Reasons for non-adherence and Bulpitt and Fletcher (1988)

Farouq's story

Patients who are prescribed medicines but don't take them are thought to cost the NHS more than half a billion pounds every year. But when you read that statistic, perhaps your first thought wasn't 'That's a lot of money', but 'Why would anyone not take their medication?'.

Failing to follow medical advice, including not taking medication, is called non-adherence. Here is a real-life case study:

Farouq is 63 and has had Type II diabetes for ten years. He gets free health care including prescriptions and a monthly visit to a clinic.

People with diabetes need to watch what they eat because it affects their blood glucose (sugar) level and their body can no longer control such increases. Lack of control may lead to more serious illness.

But Farouq ignores dietary advice and eats what he likes. Farouq frequently doesn't take his medication because the different packages confuse him. His general attitude is, 'When your time is up there's nothing you can do about it'.

As a result he often has hypoglycaemic attacks and his overall health is poor. He developed severe ulcers on both feet. And these got worse because Farouq would not go to the specialist centre to get them properly treated.

(Based on an article by Agabna 2014)

Specification terms

Cost-benefit analysis An individual weighs up the balance between the perceived benefits of changing behaviour and the perceived barriers (obstacles to change).

Non-adherence Patients sometimes do not follow ('stick to') medical advice. If they decide to do this after careful consideration, this is rational non-adherence.

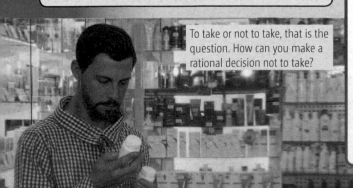

To take or not to take, that is the question. How can you make a rational decision not to take?

Rational non-adherence

It makes sense, for the benefit of our health, to follow medical advice carefully, i.e. to adhere (stick) to it. However, in the developed world only about 50% of patients follow treatment according to instructions (Brown and Bussell 2011). In other words, people often do not adhere to medical advice (*non-adherence*). Sometimes patients choose non-adherence after thinking about it logically and rationally (i.e. rational non-adherence). This spread looks at rational non-adherence.

Cost-benefit analysis

This approach assumes patients make a deliberate decision to follow or not follow medical advice after weighing up the costs and benefits (*cost-benefit analysis*).

The main benefit of taking prescribed medication is that it will reduce or eliminate the symptoms of an illness, disease or injury. However, psychologists have identified several potential costs. These include:

Potential side effects as explained in the study below.

Financial barriers For example, people with private medical insurance that covers treatment are more likely to adhere to medication because they are less sensitive to the cost (Laba *et al.* 2012). When people have to pay for an element of their treatment costs when they previously did not pay, they are then more likely to opt for non-adherence instead (López-Valcárcel *et al.* 2017).

Patient-practitioner relationship The level of trust the patient has in their medical practitioner affects non-adherence. The greatest influence on trust is the practitioner's relationship style. A practitioner-centred approach emphasises professional distance from the patient. The practitioner has all the authority and power in the relationship and views treatment as non-negotiable. This style is more likely to lead to non-adherence than a more friendly and personal patient-centred approach.

Lack of understanding Patients may not fully understand medical advice because it is complex. This means they may not even remember what the practitioner has told them to do. A patient who has to take multiple medications at different times of the day may decide non-adherence is a rational response.

Bulpitt and Fletcher (1988) Importance of well-being to hypertensive patients

Aims

Chris Bulpitt and Astrid Fletcher wanted to *review* research studies into adherence to medical treatments in people with *hypertension* (high blood pressure).

Procedure

The researchers selected more than 40 studies that looked at why hypertensive patients did not adhere to treatment plans (i.e. taking prescribed drugs). Bulpitt and Fletcher analysed these studies to identify the effects of treatment on physical and psychological well-being as well as on work and leisure activities. They compared the symptoms of treated and untreated patients.

Findings

Unacceptable side effects (e.g. unsteadiness, dizziness, diarrhoea) were a major reason why patients stopped taking medication. In a study by David Curb *et al.* (1985), 23% of patients withdrew from treatment – 8% were male patients who experienced sexual problems. There was also some evidence of a decline in work performance because of side effects, for example some hypertension medications led to memory problems.

Conclusions

Most patients adhere to medication treatment plans for hypertension. But adherence is less likely if the costs (side effects) outweigh the benefits (symptom improvement).

Some patients have to take a lot of medication. The drugs come in all sorts of different packages which may change from one prescription to another. It's easy to get confused and end up not taking the right medication.

Evaluation

Supporting evidence

One strength is that research confirms the influence of several factors on non-adherence.

For example, Joyce Cramer *et al.* (1989) found that adherence in patients who had to take one drug dose per day was 88%. But for two doses it was 77% and for three it was 39%. Complexity of treatment can lead to non-adherence, despite the patient's best efforts. Beatriz González López-Valcárcel *et al.* (2017) studied what happened in Spain when older patients had to start paying a share of medication costs in 2012. They found that adherence declined significantly for expensive drugs, but not for cheaper ones.

These studies show that non-adherence is increased by financial barriers and the complexity of the treatment plan, suggesting it has a rational basis.

Unjustified assumptions

One weakness is that the approach is based on a questionable view of the patient.

Rational non-adherence implies that the patient has weighed up the costs and benefits of following medical advice in a cool and calm way before making a decision in their best interests. However, Patrick Corrigan *et al.* (2014) point out that health decisions are not often made rationally. They conclude that many decisions are made without a plan, and that the patient's current stressful situation is often more important than a cost-benefit analysis. Also, the rational approach ignores the crucial role of emotional factors.

This suggests that portraying non-adherence as a rational process cannot explain all health-related decision-making.

Evaluation

Practical application

One strength of the study is that it highlights a major reason why patients do not adhere to treatment.

The side effects of medication can be so uncomfortable or disturbing that the patient decides to stop taking it, even when it reduces their symptoms. A key feature of side effects is that they impact negatively on the patient's everyday functioning as well as on their physical and psychological well-being, so the effects are very immediate and influence the daily decision about what to do.

This illustrates how important it is for research to continue developing effective drugs with fewer side effects. Patients also need to be made aware of how the benefits of a drug outweigh the negative effects.

Issue of validity

One weakness of the study is that it is *secondary research*.

In other words, Bulpitt and Fletcher did not carry out their own original study (*primary research*). Instead they reviewed studies that had already been conducted. The problem with this is that if those studies lacked *validity*, then these weaknesses would be reflected in the review's conclusions. This would not be an issue if the reviewers had some method of establishing the quality of the studies. However, the researchers do not include any details of this in their report.

This means that Bulpitt and Fletcher may have drawn conclusions based on poor quality studies.

GET ACTIVE Patients won't take their meds

One important risk factor for *cardiovascular disorder* (CVDs, such as heart disease and stroke) is level of blood cholesterol. Statins are drugs that reduce cholesterol. They are very effective and therefore significantly improve the outlook for patients at risk of CVDs. However, up to 80% of high-risk patients do not take statins in the prescribed doses. A group of exasperated GPs think this is just because patients can't be bothered. However, a health psychologist argues there may be good reasons why people don't take their drugs.

Write a short report explaining the reasons the health psychologist might present to the doctors. For added impact, refer to at least one research study.

Exam-style questions

Karine has severe back pain after a fall. Her doctor has given her a treatment plan. She has to take four different drugs every day, attend physiotherapy sessions, do exercises at home and go for an MRI scan. Karine knows that she will have to pay for her prescription and the nearest pharmacy is miles away. The last time she took medication for something she experienced bad side effects.

The doctor Karine saw isn't her usual one and she didn't like the way he spoke to her. He also seems quite inexperienced and Karine suspects he doesn't know what he's talking about. He didn't make much sense because he used a lot of fancy words and didn't explain them. Karine has heard that backs get better by themselves anyway.

1. Explain what is meant by 'rational non-adherence'. (2)

2. Karine is seriously considering ignoring her doctor's advice.

   Explain how a cost-benefit analysis might influence Karine's decision. (3)

3. Explain the roles of financial barriers and the patient-practitioner relationship in Karine's decision. (4)

4. Bulpitt and Fletcher (1988) conducted a study on the importance of well-being for hypertensive patients.

   (a) Describe **one** finding of the study and use it to explain Karine's behaviour. (3)

   (b) Explain **one** strength and **one** weakness of the study. (4)

5. Discuss possible reasons why Karine might not adhere to her doctor's professional advice. Refer in your answer to at least **one** research study. (9)

An issue to consider

Can you personally imagine ever making a rational decision not to follow medical advice? Or have you ever done so? What reasons might you have?

Specification content

C3 Maintenance of behavioural change

Reasons for non-adherence:

- Rational non-adherence, including cost-benefit analysis, financial barriers, patient-practitioner relationship, lack of understanding.

- Bulpitt and Fletcher (1988) Importance of well-being to hypertensive patients.

Reasons for non-adherence: Ley's cognitive model

Specification term

Ley's cognitive model The model suggests that patients may not adhere to treatment because they lack understanding of medical advice, cannot recall it accurately and/or they are dissatisfied with the interaction they have with their practitioner.

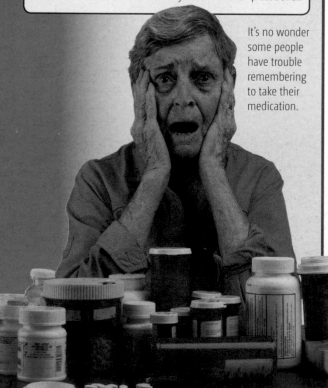

It's no wonder some people have trouble remembering to take their medication.

Ley's cognitive model

Basics of the model

Philip Ley (1988) devised a *cognitive* model of adherence, 'cognitive' because it emphasises the role of thinking in the patient's adherence to medical advice.

Adherence depends on three main factors:

- How much a patient understands the advice.

- How much they can recall (memory) of the advice.

- How satisfied they are with their interaction with the practitioner.

Understanding and memory can influence adherence directly or indirectly (through the patient's satisfaction). Understanding also influences memory – the more information a patient understands, the better their memory of it.

Understanding and adherence

Patients often do not understand the advice they are given. Because they usually realise this is the case, they become dissatisfied with the consultation/interaction. Ley's model predicts that this will lead to *non-adherence* in most cases.

However, even if the patient is satisfied, their lack of understanding is still likely to lead to non-adherence. This is because they think they are doing what is required when they are not (e.g. taking the wrong dose of a medication). Patients can sometimes even leave an appointment unsure whether another one has been agreed (Armstrong *et al.* 1990).

Reasons for lack of understanding One reason is the language used by the practitioner. Patients might not understand the meaning of technical terms (or their understanding of the meaning differs from the practitioner's professional understanding).

Another reason is that the practitioner could assume the patient knows more than they really do. For example, John Weinman *et al.* (2009) found that more than 50% of people did not know the locations of the liver, ovaries, thyroid, lungs, gallbladder, pancreas or kidneys. There was no improvement in understanding since research over 30 years earlier. This mismatch between what the patient knows and what the practitioner thinks the patient knows is responsible for a great deal of dissatisfaction.

Memory and adherence

Patients may feel they understand the advice they are given, and they may be satisfied with their consultation. But if they cannot remember the advice, then adherence is impossible.

For instance, John Bain (1977) asked patients to recall the details of their medicine prescription. 37% could not remember the name of the drug, 23% forgot the frequency of the dose and 25% did not recall the duration of the treatment. Such patients are at risk of failing to take the correct dose of a medicine at the right times. Patients are even more likely to forget the details of other advice, for example concerning lifestyle changes (Kravitz *et al.* 1993).

Roy Kessels (2003) concluded that between 40% and 80% of medical advice is immediately forgotten (and only about half of what is remembered is correct).

Reasons for forgetting One reason is *anxiety*. When a patient is anxious, their attention becomes narrower. They latch onto what they believe are key words and ignore the rest. For example, a very key word is 'cancer'. Once a patient hears this, they may not pay much attention to what follows, which might be more positive ('But it's at a very early stage and we can do something about it'). Other ignored information might concern follow-up appointments and medication, making adherence unlikely.

Another reason patients forget advice is because they do not appreciate its importance. For example, advice about treatment is often seen by patients as less important than the diagnosis. When advice is stated very generally ('You must rest') a patient may think it is not as important as a specific statement ('Do not go to work for three days').

Evaluation

Research support

One strength of Ley's model is evidence for the role of memory.

Lu Dong *et al.* (2017) studied treatment adherence in 48 people diagnosed with *depression*. Some were receiving therapy to improve their memories. The researchers found that these participants did demonstrate improved memory compared with a *control group* of participants who did not receive memory support. They were also more likely to take their medication correctly.

These findings suggest that the model is right in its prediction that improved memory leads to improved adherence.

Practical application

Another strength is that the model can improve adherence.

Patients' understanding can be improved by practitioners using clear language that is not open to interpretation (e.g. by using the word 'tablet' instead of 'dose'). Practitioners should also not assume too much existing knowledge. In addition, memory for advice can be improved – for instance, practitioners should give the most important advice first and make its importance explicit. Ensuring the patient is not extremely anxious also helps.

These are relatively easy ways that two factors identified by the model can be used to improve adherence.

Complex role of understanding

One weakness of the model is its simplistic view of patients' understanding.

The model assumes the relationship between understanding and adherence is linear. In other words, the better the patient's understanding the more they will adhere to advice. However, there is some evidence against this. Beatrix Hamburg and Gale Inoff (1982) looked at this relationship in *diabetic* adolescents at a summer camp. They found the best treatment adherence in adolescents with a moderate understanding of their diabetes. Those with the least and most understanding were less likely to adhere.

This suggests that the true relationship between understanding and adherence is *curvilinear*, and therefore more complex than the model suggests.

Correlational findings

Another weakness is that research into the model is mostly *correlational*.

The factors in Ley's model make *clinical* sense in that many practitioners recognise them as influencing adherence. Although adherence is undoubtedly linked to understanding and memory, the key question is what is the nature of the relationship? Most research finds *significant* correlations between the variables. But this does not mean that forgetting and lack of understanding *cause* poor adherence.

The *validity* of the model is limited by the lack of research into cause-and-effect relationships between factors.

When a patient gets bad news from a medical professional, they might not be listening to what he or she is saying.

Exam-style questions

Cas is in his 40s and is recovering from a heart attack. He also has diabetes and high blood pressure, which means he now has to take 16 tablets at different times of the day.

His doctor told Cas about the different drugs he will need to take and when Cas should take them. But there was a lot of information to take in and Cas remembers being quite anxious because he could have another heart attack. The doctor was also using some words Cas didn't recognise and talking in long sentences.

The doctor talked to Cas about his lifestyle, advice he had already heard from his physiotherapist. Cas has become very confused about his treatment and is worried that he isn't taking his tablets correctly.

1. Identify **two** factors that mean Cas may not take his medication correctly, according to Ley's cognitive model. (2)
2. For each factor, explain how they might affect Cas' adherence. (4)
3. Describe Ley's cognitive model of treatment adherence. (4)
4. In the context of Ley's cognitive model of adherence, explain the effects of:
   (a) Understanding. (2)
   (b) Memory. (2)
5. Explain **one** strength and **one** weakness of Ley's cognitive model of adherence as an explanation of Cas' behaviour. (4)
6. Assess Ley's cognitive model of adherence. Refer to Cas in your answer. (9)

GET ACTIVE You must remember this...?

This activity will help you appreciate how hard it can be to recall medical information. Use your favourite search engine to find 15 words relating to medical treatment and conditions (e.g. names of drugs and unusual diseases). Now find 15 words that are nothing to do with medical matters ('neutral' words), but they must be the same length as the medical words. Write down both sets of words in one list, all mixed up together. Hide the list for at least a couple of days. When you're ready, write down as many of the words as you can remember.

1. Look at the words you recalled. Is there a pattern to the words you recalled?
2. Did you remember fewer of the medical terms? If so, why do you think that is, bearing in mind that the neutral words were a similar length?

An issue to consider

To what extent do you think it is possible to increase patient adherence to their medication?
Which strategy would you identify as the most important one?

Specification content

C3 Maintenance of behavioural change
Reasons for non-adherence:
● Ley's cognitive model (1988) The effect of understanding and memory on adherence.

Physiological methods used to improve adherence and Lustman *et al.* (2000)

Take your medicine

Patients sometimes do not follow medical advice because they are depressed. Often this is because coping with their 'main' condition is so stressful. For instance, as many as 36% of people who have HIV/AIDS also have symptoms of depression (Gonzalez *et al.* 2011).

People who are depressed are less likely to take medication for other conditions (e.g. diabetes). This is because there is more to depression than just 'feeling down'. Depression affects not just how you feel, but how you think and how you behave. Here is a list of some symptoms of depression. What effects might they have on adherence?

- Lowered mood and self-esteem, feeling sad, empty, worthless.

- Poor concentration and decision-making.

- Reduced energy and activity levels.

Specification term

Antidepressant A group of drugs which increase the production of serotonin and/ or noradrenaline, and reduce symptoms of depression.

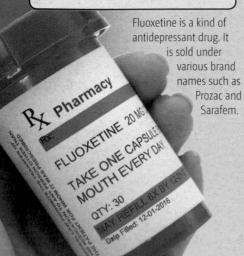

Fluoxetine is a kind of antidepressant drug. It is sold under various brand names such as Prozac and Sarafem.

Physiological methods

Physiological methods increase adherence by altering the body's *physical* functioning. They can be used with physical disorders (e.g. *diabetes*) or mental disorders (e.g. *depression*). They can also be used to detect if an addicted person is adhering to a treatment.

Biochemical tests

Testing samples of blood, saliva or urine can detect traces of a drug in a person's body. As the person knows they are going to be tested, they will adhere to treatment. Kevin Volpp *et al.* (2009) used this method to confirm that participants had stopped smoking. Testing on its own is unlikely to improve adherence much, so it is often used alongside psychological methods (see next spread).

Side effects management

Physiological side effects (e.g. dizziness, nausea, cramps) are a major obstacle to adherence. If these are reduced people are more likely to adhere, for example by using other medication. This is not without risk because the new medication used may have its own side effects.

Antidepressants

Many illnesses, disorders and diseases are *co-morbid* (i.e. they often occur together). For example, depression (mental disorder) is co-morbid with diabetes (physical disorder) and/or eating disorders. In these cases, patients with a physical condition may not take medication because depression robs them of their motivation.

Therefore, the solution is to reduce the depression and one way of doing this is to prescribe *antidepressant* drugs (such as *fluoxetine*, see study below). A patient who feels less depressed can think more clearly and is better motivated to pay attention to their physical condition. So, they are more likely to adhere to treatment.

Lustman *et al.* (2000) Fluoxetine for depression in diabetes: A randomised double-blind placebo-controlled trial

Aims

Patrick Lustman and colleagues used *fluoxetine* to treat depression in diabetic patients to see if reducing depression would improve adherence to diabetes medication (and thus improve health).

Procedure

60 volunteer patients with diabetes (26 with Type I and 34 with Type II) met diagnostic criteria for depression in the *Diagnostic and statistical manual of mental disorders* (DSM). Participants also scored 14 or above on the *Beck depression inventory* (BDI) or the *Hamilton rating scale for depression* (HAM-D).

Several were excluded because they had a history of other issues (e.g. suicidal behaviour, substance abuse, etc). Participants were *randomly allocated* to one of two groups:

- Treatment – received fluoxetine, one tablet per day for eight weeks (20 mg at start, but increased to 40 mg if minimal side effects).

- Control – received a *placebo*, one tablet per day, looked identical to the fluoxetine.

The study was *double-blind* (neither the researchers nor the participants knew who received the placebo or the fluoxetine). Depressive symptoms and glycaemic control (blood glucose level) were measured at the start and end of the eight weeks.

Findings

By the end of the study, there was a *significantly* greater reduction in depression symptoms in the treatment group than in the placebo group. There was an improvement in mean blood glucose level in both groups. The improvement was greater in the fluoxetine group but not significantly so.

Conclusions

The findings suggest that depression could be relieved through the use of a placebo drug. By relieving depression, participants were able to exert better control over their blood glucose levels – though even the placebo group improved. This suggests that just believing that your depression is being treated may help.

GET ACTIVE Measuring depression

The *Beck depression inventory* (BDI) is a very popular quick screening test for symptoms of depression. You can see the original version used by Lustman *et al.* here: tinyurl.com/ycfujfy5. The *Hamilton rating scale for depression* (HAM-D) was also used, and is here: tinyurl.com/yy8bthmp.

1. For each item on these scales, think about how it could affect someone's adherence. Will some items have a bigger impact than others?

2. Some of the participants completed the BDI and some completed the HAM-D. This could be a weakness of the study. Explain how.

Lustman *et al.*'s study had a placebo group. The participants were given an inactive version of the antidepressant, although they didn't know this. Blindfolds and spoons were not needed.

Evaluation

Supporting research

One strength is evidence to support the use of antidepressants.

Sarah Markowitz *et al.* (2011) conducted a *review* of eight studies using different types of antidepressant (including the study by Lustman *et al.* 2000). The benefits of antidepressants for improving adherence depended on the type used. Apart from fluoxetine (as demonstrated by Lustman *et al.*), a similar drug called *sertraline* was also effective, as was a more recent antidepressant called *buproprion*.

These were associated with improvements in glucose control in the diabetic patients, thus suggesting the patients were adhering to their diabetes treatment regime.

Alternatives may be better

One weakness of physiological methods is that they are not as effective as the alternatives.

It is hard to know exactly how effective antidepressants are because there is no evidence of long-term benefit. Alternatives include psychological methods (e.g. *CBT* – see next spread), which are associated with longer-lasting improvements in adherence. Having said this, a significant advantage of antidepressant treatment is its ease of use and convenience compared with most of the psychological alternatives (which require commitment and effort).

Therefore, on balance, physiological methods currently do not provide the long-term improvements that patients can get from alternatives but continue to appeal.

Evaluation

Sound methodology

One strength of the study is that it used a randomised, double-blind, placebo-controlled procedure (*randomised controlled trial*).

This is the 'gold standard' of treatment studies. Random placement of the participants into the two groups meant that any pre-existing differences between them would be balanced out. The double-blind procedure ensured that the researchers' and participants' expectations could not influence the findings (because no one know which tablet the participants were getting). The use of a placebo *condition* meant that a distinction could be made between the physiological benefits of the drug and the expectations of being treated.

This means we can be confident that the differences found between the treatment and control groups were genuine and not the result of poor methodology.

Short-term versus long-term

One weakness of the study is that the effects were only short-term.

This is because the participants were not followed up beyond the eight weeks the study lasted. We have no idea whether participants continued to adhere to diabetes treatment in the longer term. We do know that adherence in the treatment group was not significantly greater than in the placebo group (it was only a 'trend'). So even in the short term, the benefits were not that clear-cut.

This suggests that the benefits of treating co-morbid depression are not well-established and need further research.

Exam-style questions

Erika is a 31-year-old woman who has severe arthritis in her hands. She cannot use her fingers properly and is often in a lot of pain. This is making her very depressed because her everyday life is badly affected. Erika has to take several tablets every day and keep appointments each month. Unfortunately, being so down means she doesn't always do this. She decided to visit a psychologist who suggested a few ways to help. For example, Erika could have cognitive behavioural therapy and reminders on her mobile phone to take her medication. The psychologist also thought that prescribing antidepressants could be a solution.

1. Identify **one** physiological method the psychologist suggested that could improve Erika's treatment adherence. (1)

2. Explain how this method could improve Erika's adherence. (3)

3. Lustman *et al.* (2000) carried out the study on depression in diabetes. For this study:
   (a) Give **one** aim. (1)
   (b) Describe the procedure. (3)
   (c) Explain how **one** finding relates to Erika's experience. (2)

4. Evaluate **one** physiological method of improving Erika's treatment adherence. Refer to at least **one** research study in your answer. (9)

An issue to consider

To what extent is non-adherence the concern of health practitioners? If a person does not wish to take their medication, is that their decision? How far should a health practitioner go to help someone adhere to what the practitioner believes is best for them?

Specification content

C3 Maintenance of behavioural change

Methods used to improve adherence:
- Physiological methods: use of antidepressants.
- Lustman *et al.* (2000) Fluoxetine for depression in diabetes: A randomised double-blind placebo-controlled trial.

Psychological methods used to improve adherence and Volpp *et al.* (2009)

What do you treat first?

Arthritis is an extremely disabling condition which can affect people of any age, not just the elderly. It can affect the hands, knees, hips, spine and other joints, limiting movement and causing pain. It can also cause permanent muscle wasting, for example distorting the fingers so they become very difficult to use for everyday tasks.

A disease like arthritis can be hard to live with because it is painful and also may be experienced after many years of a person's life. It's not surprising that people with arthritis can become very depressed. When this happens there is a danger that they are not motivated to take medication to help their arthritis.

This can happen in lots of conditions, including diabetes and cardiovascular disorders. As we see on this spread, a sensible approach might therefore be to treat the person's depression first.

Specification terms

Adherence reminders Techniques of 'nudging' patients into following medical advice (e.g. box to organise pills).

Cognitive behavioural therapy (CBT) A method for treating mental disorders based on both cognitive and behavioural techniques. From the cognitive viewpoint the therapy aims to deal with thinking, such as challenging irrational thoughts. The therapy also includes behavioural techniques such as skills training and using reinforcement.

Randomised controlled trial Test of the effectiveness of a treatment in which participants are placed into the treatment or control group using a chance (*random*) technique to balance out pre-existing differences between them.

How much would it take to make you quit?

Psychological methods

Psychological methods improve adherence by changing a client's behaviour or the way they think about their treatment (or both).

Reinforcement/financial incentives

Financial incentives are powerful positive *reinforcers* of desired behaviour. Money was used in the Volpp *et al.* study below to improve smoking cessation rates.

Cognitive behavioural therapy (CBT)

CBT (see page 92) can increase adherence by addressing distorted cognitions about treatment. For example, a client may believe they will definitely experience a side effect even though the drug information leaflet lists the side effect as 'very rare'. CBT can help clients re-evaluate their negative view of the medication. This is combined with *skills training* (e.g. time management and organisational skills) to help clients keep appointments.

Adherence reminders

Reminder packages Physical devices may be used to organise medication and indicate when it should be taken. An example is a box divided into compartments, one for each day of the week. Such packaging helps to overcome unintentional *non-adherence* because a person forgets to take medication.

Phone calls and texts Pharmacies and GP surgeries are increasingly using automated phone calls and/or texts to remind people to take medication. Calls/texts also give reminders of appointments (e.g. to attend screening) or even of treatment goals at high-risk times.

Volpp *et al.* (2009) A randomised, controlled trial of financial incentives for smoking cessation

Aims

Kevin Volpp and colleagues aimed to see if a financial incentive of US$750 would improve long-term rates of smoking cessation.

Procedure

The study was a *randomised controlled trial* in a workplace. The participants were 878 employees of a large company in the US who each smoked at least five cigarettes every day. They were *randomly allocated* to one of two groups to receive information about:

- Smoking-cessation programmes (information-only group).
- Smoking-cessation programmes plus financial incentives (incentive group).

The structure of the incentives was: $100 to complete a smoking-cessation programme, $250 to stop smoking within six months from the start of the study (confirmed by a saliva/urine test) and a further $400 to abstain from smoking for a further six months (confirmed by another test).

Three months after the start of the study, all participants were asked if they had stopped smoking. Those who had stopped for at least one week were interviewed. Those who had not stopped were contacted after another three months for a full assessment (i.e. at six months). Every participant was *interviewed* again six months after their first interview (which was either at nine months or 12 months) and again after another six months (either at 15 months or 18 months after start of study).

Findings

After nine and 12 months, smoking cessation in the incentive group was 14.7% and 5% in the information-only group, a *significant* difference. After 15 and 18 months the figures were 9.4% (incentive) and 3.6% (information-only), also a significant difference. The incentive group also had significantly higher rates of joining a smoking-cessation programme (15.4% vs. 5.4%), completing the programme (10.8% vs. 2.5%) and cessation within the first six months (20.9% vs. 11.8%).

Conclusions

Offering financial incentives via the workplace appears to be a successful way to increase the number of people who stop smoking.

Evaluation

Research support

One strength is that there is evidence to support the effectiveness of psychological methods.

For example, the key study by Volpp *et al*. (facing page) concluded that cash payments had a positive effect on completing a smoking-cessation programme. Kamal Mahtani *et al*. (2011) reviewed studies into reminder packages. They had a moderate effect on increasing adherence and showed some benefit in improving blood pressure and other medical outcomes.

These are relatively easy methods of improving adherence and are cost-effective when compared with wasted resources, missed appointments and unused medication.

Long-term tail-off

One weakness is that psychological methods may be less effective for *chronic* conditions.

There is a lack of evidence about the long-term benefits of phone calls and texts. This is disappointing, as it is people with chronic disorders who stand to benefit most. The risk of daily reminders is that their usefulness 'tails off' after a relatively short time. The person becomes used to getting messages and/or calls, and may even start to see them as a nuisance. Tracy Ting *et al*. (2012) concluded that many of the adolescent patients they studied eventually ignored the texts.

Therefore, research is urgently needed into the long-term uses of these methods, especially as they are likely to become a bigger part of the 'health service of the future'.

Evaluation

Objective measures

One strength of the study is that it used an objective measure of cessation.

Previous studies relied mainly on *self-report*, that is participants indicating that they have stopped smoking (e.g. via *questionnaire*). The risk is that participants may give inaccurate information out of a desire to please the researchers and make the study 'work' (*social desirability bias*). Volpp *et al*. avoided this by using a biochemical saliva/urine test for the presence of *cotinine* (biochemically related to nicotine). This objectively confirmed that participants had stopped smoking.

This increased the *validity* of the study by making it more certain that participants really did stop smoking in response to financial incentives.

Generalisability issues

One weakness is that the study has limited *generalisability*.

The researchers recorded *socio-demographic* variables such as gender, age, education level and so on. Over 90% of the participants were ethnically white and the sample as a whole was better-educated with a higher income relative to national figures. Also, 235 of the 878 (27%) participants who started the study dropped out over the course of the study. It is unclear if these participants shared any characteristics that could have affected the final sample.

Therefore, the findings may not tell us much about the effectiveness of financial incentives in producing smoking cessation in the wider population.

Texts or calls can remind you to take medication or keep an appointment. They can even give you a boost when you have goals to meet.

Exam-style questions

Asha is an alcoholic. After a long struggle, she finally agreed a few months ago to attend meetings of Alcoholics Anonymous. This meant that she had to completely give up alcohol, which she did initially. But Asha has missed a few meetings and she definitely is not abstaining from the drink now.

Her psychologist is very concerned about Asha's non-attendance. He believes that the AA meetings will work but obviously that can only happen if Asha goes to them. He is wondering if there is anything that can help Asha to stick to the treatment they agreed on.

1. Identify **three** psychological methods that could be used to improve Asha's adherence to treatment. (3)

2. Select **two** of these methods and explain how they could improve Asha's treatment adherence. (4)

3. Explain **one** finding of the study by Volpp *et al*. (2009). Use it to explain Asha's behaviour. (4)

4. The psychologist remembers that there are other methods available, including physiological ones.

   Explain why a physiological method might be a better way of improving Asha's adherence to treatment. (3)

5. Discuss financial incentives and cognitive behavioural therapy as methods of improving Asha's treatment adherence. Refer in your answer to at least **one** research study. (9)

An issue to consider

How do you feel about paying people to give up their addictions? What are the arguments for and against?

GET ACTIVE Reminders

You work in a GP's surgery and have been asked to write some reminder text messages for patients. Usually these are standard messages sent to all patients they apply to. But the GPs at this surgery like the personal touch. Dan has Type II diabetes, arthritis and an *anxiety disorder*. For his diabetes he has to take a drug, 200 mg three times a day, after food. He has an appointment about his arthritis with a physiotherapist in four days' time. His CBT therapist is helping him to set goals and use positive 'self-talk' to help with his anxiety.

Write some personal text messages to remind Dan about these treatments.

Specification content
C3 Maintenance of behavioural change
Methods used to improve adherence:

- Psychological methods: use of reinforcements/financial incentives to improve.
- Volpp *et al*. (2009) A randomised, controlled trial of financial incentives for smoking cessation.
- Cognitive behavioural therapy, adherence reminder packages – telephone calls, SMS.

Revision summary

Persuasion

The theories

Hovland-Yale theory

The communicator (source) More persuasive when seen as credible (e.g. expert in anti-smoking campaign). Also personal experience (e.g. ex-drug taker).

The communication (message) Emotional appeal, e.g. message with threat works if recipient believes outcome can be avoided. One-sided presentation seen as biased by well-informed audience.

The recipients (audience) Intelligent people with cognitive resources are less persuadable. People with low self-esteem are more persuadable.

Evaluation

Research support Most persuasive anti-smoking message was high threat + 'possible to quit' (Sturges and Rogers 1996).

Role of self-esteem High self-esteem people easier to persuade, opposite to theory (Baumeister and Covington 1985).

Hovland and Weiss (1951)

Aims Does credibility affect opinion change over time?

Procedure Students given high- or low-credibility articles on four topics, opinions measured before, after and four weeks later.

Findings More opinion change with high-credibility sources. High-credibility agreement decreased over time, low-credibility agreement increased.

Conclusions Credible sources more persuasive. Sleeper effect: impact of low-credibility sources increases over time.

Evaluation

Practical application Short-term campaign should focus on credibility, long-term on other factors.

Lack of generalisability Participants were students, young and well-educated, captive audience not real-world arguments.

Fear arousal theory

Early theories of the effects of fear Dolland and Miller (1950) argued that fear creates unpleasant arousal (e.g. anti-smoking message), reduced by behaviour change (negative reinforcement).

Fear-behaviour relationship Janis and Feshbach (1953) suggest it is curvilinear. Weak fear = no arousal or change, moderate fear = most change. High fear is counterproductive, no behaviour change but denial instead (reduces arousal state).

Evaluation

Research support Fear arousal persuaded students to get vaccinated (Dabbs and Leventhal 1966).

Mixed evidence Fear does influence behaviour but link was not found to be curvilinear (Janis and Feshbach 1953).

Janis and Feshbach (1953)

Aims Do fear-arousing messages produce defensive reactions?

Procedure Groups of students saw presentation on oral hygiene which was either strongly, moderately or minimally fear-arousing. Changes in hygiene behaviour measured after one week.

Findings Changed behaviour: 36% minimal group, 22% moderate, 8% strong.

Conclusions No support for curvilinear, but challenges linear theory.

Evaluation

Measured behaviour change Not just attitudes or intentions.

Lack of replication Fear actually does change health-related attitudes, intentions and behaviours (Tannenbaum et al. 2015), challenges Janis and Feshbach.

Elaboration-likelihood model (ELM)

Process 1: Central route Petty and Cacioppo (1981) suggest message is persuasive if it's relevant and I am motivated to evaluate (elaborate) it.

Process 2: Peripheral route Persuaded by non-content factors, e.g. source attractiveness, little processing of message (low elaboration).

Factors of influence Celebrity makes message become associated with glamour (peripheral) or highlights content (central).

Individual differences People high in need for cognition (NFC) enjoy evaluating arguments: central route.

Evaluation

Practical application Short-term change with celebrities via peripheral route, so combine with central route (e.g. role play makes relevant).

Poor explanatory power Description not explanation, lacks psychological processes.

Petty et al. (1981)

Aims Does high involvement lead to central route, low involvement to peripheral route?

Procedure Students heard (1) new exam next year or in ten years, (2) message from expert or non-expert, (3) strong or weak arguments.

Findings Expertise most influential when involvement was low. When involvement was high, quality of argument was influential.

Conclusions Personally-relevant message changes attitudes via central route, less relevant via peripheral.

Evaluation

Influential study Sparked research into health-related behaviour change (Oenema et al. 2005).

Sample issues Students have greater need for cognition (NFC). Replication with children unsuccessful (Te'eni-Harari et al. 2007). Unrepresentative sample.

Treatment and management of addiction and stress

Stress management techniques

Physiological

Drug therapies

Anxiety is a psychological symptom of stress, linked to physical sensations (fight or flight). Relieved by anti-anxiety drugs.

Benzodiazepines (BZs) e.g. *diazepam* (Valium), anti-anxiety in moderate dose. Reduces CNS arousal quickly.

Mode of action: BZs boost GABA, increasing its inhibitory effects, calming CNS. BZs attach to GABA receptors without blocking them, opening channels further. Reduces serotonin activity and thus reduces neural activity.

Beta blockers Counteract ANS activity, reducing sympathetic arousal of fight or flight (e.g. heart rate).

Mode of action: BBs block beta-adrenergic receptors in heart and blood vessels, adrenaline cannot attach. Reduce anxiety without affecting alertness.

Evaluation

Support for effectiveness Review found BZs more effective than placebo. But some BZs less effective than others (Baldwin et al. 2013). Good for everyday anxiety (Kelly 1980).

Convenient and safe Easier than psychological therapy, little commitment or effort. Safe in overdose.

Does not treat underlying problem Drugs manage anxiety short-term, but long-term damage, therapy may be better.

Dependence BZs produce physical and psychological withdrawal effects, so take for no more than four weeks.

Biofeedback

Tackles stress by reducing ANS activity (sympathetic nervous system) – no conscious control over ANS.

Client learns to take control after seeing or hearing physiological responses.

Phase 1: Awareness and physiological feedback Machine converts client's arousal (e.g. heart rate, muscular tension) into signals that reflect changed activity. Therapist explains feedback.

Phase 2: Relaxation training and control Client learns to take control by changing the signal (e.g. slow heart rate). Relaxation training helps reduce arousal.

Role of operant conditioning: machine feedback and therapist's praise positively reinforce client control.

Phase 3: Transfer Portable devices help client transfer skills to real-life situations.

Evaluation

Support for biofeedback Doctors using biofeedback reduced stress scores over 28 days (Lemaire et al. 2011).

Long-term benefits Set of skills for future, arousal lowers over time, gives space to think more clearly about stressors.

Inconsistent outcomes Objective measures (e.g. heart rate) did not reduce in doctor study (Lemaire et al. 2011).

Not suitable for everyone Commitment and effort needed especially in transfer phase, stress may prevent this happening.

Psychological

SIT

(Stress inoculation training)

We control how we think about stressors: a cognitive behavioural approach, think positively.

Meichenbaum and Cameron (1973) devised SIT to give protection (inoculation) against future stressors. Learn to cope in advance.

Phase 1: Cognitive preparation Client and therapist identify stressors, learn to perceive them as challenges.

Supportive therapeutic relationship.

Phase 2: Skill acquisition Client learns skills (e.g. social skills, relaxation) to cope with future stressors.

Most benefit from use of 'self-talk', including coping self-statements.

Behavioural element: observe, model, practise skills.

Phase 3: Application and follow-through Personal experiments: homework tasks in increasingly stressful real-world situations.

Relapse prevention: setbacks are chances to learn, develop internal locus of control.

Evaluation

Evidence of effectiveness Short SIT course reduced stress in law students, improved exam performance of bottom 20% (Sheehey and Horan 2004).

Flexibility Lots of skills suitable for different groups (e.g. elderly), tailored to client (e.g. online).

A demanding therapy Needs commitment, ability to reflect, many leave which lowers effectiveness overall.

Too complex Broad range of skills for many stressors, not equally effective. May just be positive thinking and skill acquisition is only secondary importance.

Social support

Support networks can help during stress. Vary in size but quality more important.

Instrumental support Practical help, physical (e.g. lift to hospital), giving information (e.g. bus times).

Emotional support Expressing warmth, concern, etc., offers comfort and lifts mood.

Esteem support Express confidence in someone, increases self-efficacy and self-esteem.

Explaining the benefits Buffering hypothesis: support gives psychological distance from stressor ('buffer zone'). Only helps during stress (Cohen and Wills 1985).

Direct effects hypothesis: support helps at all times, reduces physiological arousal.

Other issues All three types overlap and are often provided together and without face-to-face contact.

Evaluation

Research support Belief in social support protected against common cold. Hugs provide 1/3 of effect (Cohen et al. 2015).

Practical application Benefit of social support types depends on culture (Taylor et al. 2004), less used by Asian-Americans.

Backfire effects Support not always beneficial, e.g. relative accompanying you to hospital may create anxiety.

Gender differences Women use emotional support more than men (Tamres et al. 2002).

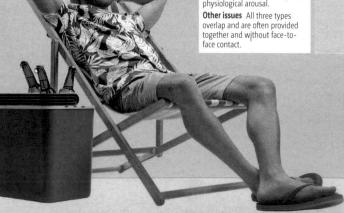

Maintenance of behavioural change

Treatments for addiction

Physiological

Aversion therapy

Based on classical conditioning. Counterconditioning associates drug with unpleasant UCR.

Aversion therapy for alcohol addiction Client takes emetic drug, vomits while smelling/tasting alcohol. Slow-release Antabuse used for real-life situations.

Aversion therapy for gambling addiction Client decides on level of electric shock while looking at self-selected gambling images.

A new form of aversion therapy: covert sensitisation Client imagines symptoms of aversion instead of experiencing them.

Covert sensitisation for nicotine addiction Client vividly imagines smoking with very unpleasant results. And imagines giving up and feelings of relief.

Evaluation

Research support Alcoholics given disulfiram had longer to relapse than placebo group (Niederhofer et al. 2003).

Chronic addiction Aversion therapy less challenging for 'hard-to-treat' clients because alters 'automatic' behaviours.

Ethical issues Psychological and physical harm is part of treatment. But covert sensitisation is more acceptable.

Lack of long-term effectiveness Long-term aversion therapy no better than placebo (McConaghy et al. 1991).

Drug therapies

Aversives: unpleasant consequences.

Agonists: mimic drug effects, satisfy cravings.

Antagonists: block drugs so addict experiences no pleasurable feelings.

Drug therapies for nicotine addiction NRT: clean dose of nicotine in gum or nasal spray. Reduce over time to manage withdrawal.

Bupropion: reduces dopamine release in nucleus accumbens, reduces cravings.

Drug therapies for gambling behaviour Opioid antagonists: *naltrexone* blocks opioid system, no dopamine release, reduces gambling cravings indirectly.

Evaluation

Research support for nicotine treatment Bupropion and NRT better than placebo in long-term (Hughes 2011).

Further research support Low dose of naltrexone reduced gambling cravings and behaviour (Grant et al. 2008).

Individual differences Responses to naltrexone depend on single gene, so don't work for all (Chung et al. 2012).

Side effects Some trivial but the serious ones (e.g. suicidal thoughts) may lead to ending treatment.

Psychological

CBT

(Cognitive behavioural therapy)

Irrational thinking leads to taking drugs as a way to cope with stress, and then leads to addiction.

Cognitive = change thinking.

Behavioural = learn coping skills.

Functional analysis Client and therapist identify high-risk situations and identify which thoughts trigger cravings, keep diary.

Cognitive restructuring Therapist challenges distorted thinking (e.g. client may erroneously believe they are coping).

Behaviour change Learn new skills for coping (e.g. anger management), practise in safe environment.

Relapse prevention Skills to avoid relapse. Identify cues triggering irrational thoughts, challenge them, learn to cope with situation.

Evaluation

Research support Small but significant benefit of CBT for substance addictions (Magill and Ray 2009).

Relapse prevention Learn a more realistic view of relapse, see as a chance for growth, breaks addiction cycle.

Short-term and long-term effects Good short-term but no benefit for gambling after 12 months (Cowlishaw et al. 2012).

What works? Many techniques which are flexible but therefore therapy lacks standard protocol, hard to evaluate.

Skills training

Self-efficacy increases through skills training, develop internal locus of control.

Assertiveness training Cope with conflict in controlled way.

Anger management Express emotions (e.g. from childhood) constructively.

Social skills training (SST) Improve communication to cope with anxiety in social situations.

Skills training techniques Group discussion: share ideas, thoughts.

Modelling and role-play: imitate therapist, record role play and get feedback.

Homework: real-world practice, keep diary.

Visualisation: imagine using skills, role-play.

Evaluation

Research support Skills training just as good as CBT to reduce gambling (Toneatto 2016).

Long-term effectiveness Benefits after 1 year (Toneatto 2016), future-focused treatment.

Lack of treatment adherence Demanding therapy and effort needed, high drop-out or quit when crisis over.

Role of cognitive factors CBT helps even severe alcoholics but skills training works only for moderate drinkers.

Reasons for non-adherence

Rational non-adherence

Making a logical decision not to follow medical advice.

Cost-benefit analysis Potential costs:

Side effects e.g. dizziness, memory problems.

Financial barriers e.g. cost of drugs.

Patient-practitioner relationship e.g. lack of trust, dislike style.

Lack of understanding e.g. advice can be complex.

Evaluation

Supporting evidence Complex drug treatments and cost lead to non-adherence (Cramer et al. 1989).

Unjustified assumptions Health decisions not usually made rationally. Often unplanned, under stress (Corrigan et al. 2014).

Bulpitt and Fletcher (1988)

Aims Review studies of adherence in hypertension patients.

Procedure Over 40 studies analysed, comparing treated and untreated patients.

Findings Side effects are a major reason for non-adherence.

Conclusions Non-adherence if costs outweigh benefits.

Evaluation

Practical application Develop drugs with fewer side effects, and make clear to patients that benefits outweigh side effects.

Issue of validity This is secondary research, issues with original studies reflected in this one.

Ley's cognitive model

Basics of the model Adherence depends on patient's understanding, memory and satisfaction. Effects of these three elements can be direct or indirect.

Understanding and adherence Patients who do not understand advice become dissatisfied or may believe they are following advice = non-adherence.

Reasons for lack of understanding: medical language, practitioner assumes too much knowledge of patient.

Memory and adherence Patients cannot follow advice if they forget it.

Reasons for forgetting: anxiety (focus on some words e.g. 'cancer'). Also don't realise importance of advice.

Evaluation

Research support Better adherence in depressed patients given memory support (Dong et al. 2017).

Practical application Use clear language, reduce anxiety, important advice should be given first.

Complex role of understanding Moderate understanding linked to highest level of adherence in diabetic teenagers (Hamburg and Inoff 1982).

Correlational findings Lack of understanding and forgetting may not *cause* non-adherence.

Methods to improve adherence

Physiological methods

Alter body's functioning and increase adherence.

Biochemical tests e.g. urine test for presence of drugs.

Side effects management Medicine to reduce side effects of other drugs.

Antidepressants Reduce co-morbid depression, increase motivation.

Evaluation

Supporting research Antidepressants (e.g. fluoxetine) improved adherence (Markowitz et al. 2011).

Alternatives may be better e.g. CBT may give longer-term benefits (but more effort).

Lustman et al. (2000)

Aims Does reducing depression improve adherence?

Procedure Depressed diabetic patients given fluoxetine or placebo for 8 weeks.

Findings Reduced depression in treatment group, better glucose control.

Conclusions Antidepressants offer a way to improve adherence to diabetic medication.

Evaluation

Sound methodology Participants randomly allocated, placebo control, double-blind.

Short-term versus long-term No follow-up so longer-term benefits unclear, more research needed.

Psychological methods

Improve adherence by changing behaviour and/or thinking.

Reinforcement/financial incentives Money is a powerful reinforcer (Volpp et al. 2009).

CBT Can deal with distorted thinking about treatment, improve skills (e.g. organisational skills to record appointments).

Adherence reminders Reminder packages e.g. box to organise medication.

Phone calls/texts e.g. daily reminders to take drugs and when appointments are.

Evaluation

Research support Reminders increase adherence (Mahtani et al. 2011).

Long-term tail-off Daily texts are eventually ignored by chronic patients (Ting et al. 2012).

Volpp et al. (2009)

Aims Would money improve long-term smoking quit rates?

Procedure Employees placed in a financial incentive ($750) or information-only (control group).

Findings Quitting after 9 and 12 months: 14.7% (incentive), 5% (control). After 15 and 18 months: 9.4% (incentive) and 3.6% (control).

Conclusions Financial incentives via workplace increase quitting.

Evaluation

Objective measures Used biochemical test not self-report, greater validity.

Generalisability issues Sample not representative in terms of ethnicity or education (white and better-educated and higher income).

Multiple-choice questions

Hovland-Yale theory of persuasion and Hovland and Weiss

1. Credibility comes from:
(a) Expertise.
(b) Personal experience.
(c) Both of the above.
(d) Neither of the above.

2. Well-informed audiences prefer:
(a) A two-sided argument.
(b) A one-sided argument.
(c) A low-credibility source.
(d) An amusing argument.

3. Hovland and Weiss supported the:
(a) Audience effect.
(b) Credibility effect.
(c) Sleeper effect.
(d) Waker effect.

4. McGuire studied:
(a) Credibility.
(b) Fear.
(c) Self-esteem.
(d) Intelligence.

Fear arousal theory of persuasion and Janis and Feshbach

1. An early theory was by:
(a) Tannenbaum *et al.*
(b) Dollard and Miller.
(c) Dabbs and Leventhal.
(d) Leventhal and Singer.

2. Janis and Feshbach argued the fear-behaviour relationship is:
(a) Curvilinear.
(b) Linear.
(c) A straight line.
(d) A negative correlation.

3. _____ of the minimal-fear group changed behaviour in Janis and Feshbach's study.
(a) 36%.
(b) 24%.
(c) 22%.
(d) 8%.

4. Dabbs and Leventhal studied:
(a) Drink-driving behaviour.
(b) Dental hygiene.
(c) Anti-smoking campaigns.
(d) Tetanus vaccination.

Elaboration-likelihood model and Petty *et al.*

1. Processing via the central route involves:
(a) Glamour of celebrities.
(b) High cognitive ability.
(c) Very little elaboration.
(d) Elaborating message content.

2. Petty *et al.* studied:
(a) Need for cognition.
(b) Self-esteem.
(c) Personal involvement.
(d) Celebrity attractiveness.

3. Health campaigns should use the:
(a) Younger people.
(b) Peripheral and central route.
(c) Central route only.
(d) Peripheral route only.

4. Te'eni-Harari *et al.* could not replicate Petty *et al.*'s findings with:
(a) Younger people.
(b) Older students.
(c) Teachers.
(d) Elderly people.

Physiological stress management techniques: Drug therapy

1. Benzodiazepines enhance:
(a) Adrenaline activity.
(b) Serotonin activity.
(c) GABA activity.
(d) ANS activity.

2. Beta blockers affect:
(a) The brain directly.
(b) The ANS.
(c) The CNS.
(d) GABA.

3. BZs and BBs are good for:
(a) Short-term stress.
(b) Long-term stress.
(c) Chronic stress.
(d) Depression.

4. BZs should not be prescribed for longer than:
(a) Four days.
(b) Four weeks.
(c) Four months.
(d) Four years.

Physiological stress management techniques: Biofeedback

1. The first phase of biofeedback is:
(a) Relaxation training.
(b) Awareness and feedback.
(c) Transfer.
(d) Control.

2. Biofeedback works through:
(a) Positive reinforcement.
(b) Negative reinforcement.
(c) Vicarious reinforcement.
(d) Variable reinforcement.

3. Biofeedback is:
(a) Good for short-term stress.
(b) Good for long-term stress.
(c) Both of the above.
(d) A quick fix.

4. Lemaire *et al.* found a reduction in:
(a) Stress hormones.
(b) Blood pressure.
(c) Heart rate.
(d) Feelings of stress.

Psychological stress management techniques: SIT

1. SIT is a form of:
(a) Biofeedback.
(b) Cognitive behavioural therapy.
(c) Drug treatment.
(d) Vaccination against viruses.

2. The second stage of SIT is:
(a) Application.
(b) Skill acquisition.
(c) Cognitive preparation.
(d) Follow-through.

3. SIT views relapse as:
(a) Unhelpful.
(b) A disaster.
(c) The end of therapy.
(d) A chance for learning.

4. Sheehy and Horan studied:
(a) Law students.
(b) Psychology students.
(c) BTEC students.
(d) Primary schoolchildren.

Psychological stress management techniques: Social support

1. The best kind of social support is:
(a) Instrumental.
(b) Emotional.
(c) Esteem.
(d) No one type is better than the others.

2. Expressing confidence in someone is _____ support:
(a) Mixed.
(b) Emotional.
(c) Instrumental.
(d) Esteem.

3. 'Support is only useful in times of stress' is a prediction of:
(a) The direct effects hypothesis.
(b) The indirect effects hypothesis.
(c) Instrumental support.
(d) The buffering hypothesis.

4. Cohen *et al.* investigated the protective effects of:
(a) Rugs.
(b) Hugs.
(c) Pugs.
(d) Kisses.

Physiological treatments for addiction: Aversion therapy

1. Aversion therapy is based on
(a) Classical conditioning.
(b) Operant conditioning.
(c) Vicarious reinforcement.
(d) Reverse reinforcement.

2. A popular drug used in aversion therapy is:
(a) Diazepam.
(b) Disulfiram.
(c) Benzodiazepines.
(d) Beta blockers.

3. A common aversive stimulus used in gambling addiction is:

(a) Emetic drug.

(b) Foul smell.

(c) Electric shock.

(d) Flowers.

4. Niederhofer *et al.* studied:

(a) Middle-aged smokers.

(b) Elderly gamblers.

(c) Adolescent alcoholics.

(d) Addicted shoppers.

Physiological treatments for addiction: Drug therapies

1. Agonist drugs:

(a) Activate neuron receptors.

(b) Block neuron receptors.

(c) Produce vomiting.

(d) Prevent dopamine release.

2. Naltrexone is:

(a) An aversive.

(b) An opioid agonist.

(c) An opioid antagonist.

(d) Also called bupropion.

3. Stead *et al.* found the most effective form of NRT was:

(a) Gum.

(b) Nasal spray.

(c) Patch.

(d) Inhaler.

4. The effect of naltrexone on alcoholism depends on:

(a) A single gene.

(b) Hundreds of genes.

(c) No known genes.

(d) Gender.

Psychological treatments for addiction: CBT

1. CBT usually starts with:

(a) Cognitive restructuring.

(b) Relapse prevention.

(c) Functional analysis.

(d) Behaviour change.

2. In CBT, a recovering addict can best reduce their relapse risk by:

(a) Avoiding people.

(b) Ignoring cues.

(c) Avoiding clues.

(d) Learning coping skills.

3. Magill and Ray carried out:

(a) A lab experiment.

(b) A review.

(c) A questionnaire survey.

(d) An interview study.

4. A weakness of CBT is:

(a) Few long-term benefits.

(b) Few short-term effects.

(c) Its approach to relapse.

(d) It is completely ineffective.

Psychological treatments for addiction: Skills training

1. Skills training:

(a) Decreases self-efficacy.

(b) Lowers self-esteem.

(c) Develops an external LoC.

(d) Increases self-efficacy.

2. An example of modelling is:

(a) Visualising social situations.

(b) Discussing targets and goals.

(c) Imitating the therapist.

(d) Keeping a homework diary.

3. In Toneatto's study, the improvements from skills training (and other treatments) lasted:

(a) 3 months.

(b) 6 months.

(c) 9 months.

(d) 12 months.

4. According to Heather, SST:

(a) Addresses cognitive distortions.

(b) Is better than CBT.

(c) Benefits severe drinkers.

(d) Benefits moderate drinkers.

Reasons for non-adherence and Bulpitt and Fletcher

1. About _____ of patients in the developed world follow treatment instructions.

(a) 25%.

(b) 50%.

(c) 75%.

(d) 100%.

2. Patients often do not follow medical advice because:

(a) They can't afford to.

(b) It is complex.

(c) Side effects are unacceptable.

(d) All of the above.

3. Bulpitt and Fletcher studied patients with:

(a) Heart disease.

(b) Diabetes.

(c) Hypertension.

(d) Arthritis.

4. Bulpitt and Fletcher's study is:

(a) Secondary research.

(b) Primary research.

(c) Original research.

(d) A laboratory experiment.

Reasons for non-adherence: Ley's cognitive model

1. Adherence is affected by:

(a) Satisfaction.

(b) Understanding.

(c) Memory.

(d) All of the above.

2. Kessels claimed between _____ and _____ of medical advice is forgotten.

(a) 10%, 30%.

(b) 40%, 80%.

(c) 50%, 70%.

(d) 60%, 90%.

3. Lu Dong *et al.* studied patients with:

(a) Dementia.

(b) Depression.

(c) Anxiety.

(d) Diabetes.

4. Hamburg and Inoff found most adherence was linked with:

(a) Most understanding.

(b) Least understanding.

(c) Moderate understanding.

(d) Memory.

Physiological methods used to improve adherence and Lustman *et al.*

1. One physiological measure is:

(a) CBT.

(b) Skills training.

(c) Antidepressants.

(d) Biofeedback.

2. Lustman *et al.*'s participants had:

(a) Diabetes.

(b) Asthma.

(c) Hypertension.

(d) Nicotine addiction.

3. Two disorders occurring together:

(a) Comatose.

(b) Coincidental.

(c) Correlational.

(d) Co-morbid.

4. Lustman *et al.*'s procedure was:

(a) Double-blind.

(b) Silver standard.

(c) Single-blind.

(d) Triple-blind.

Psychological methods used to improve adherence and Volpp *et al.*

1. Distorted cognitions are addressed by:

(a) CBT.

(b) Reminder packages.

(c) Financial incentives.

(d) Biochemical tests.

2. Volpp *et al.* offered:

(a) $1000.

(b) $100.

(c) $500.

(d) $750.

3. The longest follow-up was after:

(a) 9 months.

(b) 12 months.

(c) 15 months.

(d) 18 months.

4. Volpp *et al.*'s sample was:

(a) 50% white.

(b) 90% African American.

(c) 90% white.

(d) 90% Asian American.

MCQ answers

Hovland-Yale theory and Hovland and Weiss 1C, 2A, 3C, 4C

Fear arousal theory of persuasion and Janis and Feshbach 1B, 2A, 3A, 4D

Elaboration-likelihood model and Petty *et al.* 1D, 2C, 3B, 4A

Physiological stress management techniques: Drug therapy 1C, 2B, 3A, 4B

Physiological stress management techniques: Biofeedback 1B, 2A, 3C, 4D

Psychological stress management techniques: SIT 1B, 2B, 3D, 4A

Psychological stress management techniques: Social support 1D, 2D, 3D, 4B

Physiological treatments for addiction: Aversion therapy 1A, 2B, 3C, 4C

Physiological treatments for addiction: Drug therapies 1A, 2C, 3B, 4A

Physiological treatments for addiction: CBT 1C, 2D, 3B, 4A

Psychological treatments for addiction: Skills training 1D, 2C, 3D, 4D

Reasons for non-adherence: Bulpitt and Fletcher 1B, 2D, 3C, 4A

Reasons for non-adherence: Ley's cognitive model 1D, 2B, 3B, 4C

Methods used to improve adherence: Physiological methods 1C, 2A, 3D, 4A

Methods used to improve adherence: Psychological methods 1A, 2D, 3D, 4C

Assessment guidance

... it's how you use it

If you could go into the exam with all of your textbooks, you might not get top marks.

How can that be, we hear you ask? It's because exams are not just about knowing a set of facts – they require you to be able to explain these facts and to organise them in a meaningful way. It's not what you know, but how you use your knowledge.

Command terms

On page 34 we indicated some of the command terms associated with the three skills (AO1, AO2, AO3) that are assessed in both internal and external examinations. We will look at them in more detail here, based on the explanations provided in the specification.

AO1 Demonstrate psychological knowledge, be able to recall key assumptions, concepts and research.

- *Describe* Psychological knowledge needs to be developed, but justification is not required.
- *Give* Recall a feature or characteristic.
- *Give a reason why* A statement is provided and an explanation required.
- *Identify* Select a correct answer.
- *Name* Recall a feature or characteristic using the correct terminology.
- *State* Recall a feature or characteristic.

AO2 Demonstrate understanding by explaining the link between psychological assumptions, concepts and research to behaviour in society.

- *Describe* As above.
- *Explain* Requires a justification of a point or an example. Sentences should be linked to provide an element of reasoning.
- *Interpret* Recognise a pattern in a stimulus.
- *Justify* Give reasons/evidence to support a statement.

AO3 Apply and evaluate psychological assumptions, concepts and research to explain contemporary issues of relevance to society.

- *Analyse* A methodical and detailed examination, breaking down a topic or information.
- *Assess* Give careful consideration of varied factors that apply to a specific situation and identify the most important. Come to a conclusion.
- *Compare* Give careful consideration of varied factors and identify which are the most important or relevant. Come to a conclusion.

- *Discuss* Identify and investigate all aspects of an issue or situation.
- *Evaluate* Consider various aspects of a subject's qualities in relation to its context, such as strengths or weaknesses. Come to a judgement (conclusion), supported by evidence.
- *Explain* See above.

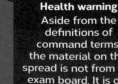

Health warning
Aside from the definitions of command terms, the material on this spread is not from the exam board. It is our interpretation of the 'rules of the game'.

Effective description

Effective description means adding details.

Question: *Define what is meant by the term 'stress'. (1)*

Answer: Stress is a physiological and psychological state that arises when we don't believe we can cope with a perceived threat.

> Detail is always important. Certain words (such as *physiological, psychological perceived*) add some depth (detail) to the definition.
>
> As you are revising underline these words in the text.

Effective application

Questions with a scenario or context aim to test your understanding because you have to try to use the information you have learned to explain something new. You can only do that if you understand the concepts.

Almost every sentence should be related to both the scenario/context and the theory/study you are using.

Effective evaluation

For effective evaluation you should do at least two of the following three things (the PET rule):

- **P**oint – state the point you wish to make.
- **E**xplain/**E**laborate/provide **E**vidence – provide some substance to support the claim you are making.
- **T**his suggests that ... end with a mini-conclusion. Sum up the point you have demonstrated.

If you look at every evaluation point in this book you will see this is what we have done.

Effective conclusions

Some 9-mark questions require a conclusion. A conclusion is not a summary, i.e. you are not just briefly repeating all your key points. You are seeking to write one or two sentences that offer a synthesis of what you wrote in the essay. What is the *take home message*?

This is a summary (the key points are identified):

> In conclusion we can see that the aversion therapy has had some success as a treatment for addiction but maybe not long-term and certainly not without ethical problems.

This is a conclusion:

> In conclusion aversion therapy does not come out well as a treatment for addiction because, from a client's point of view, it is unpleasant and doesn't offer a real promise of recovery.

Effective structure

Examiners are human. Yes, really. You need to help them award you marks. You can do this by organising your answer clearly. Look at the essay answers on pages 37, 73 and 111 and spot the organised ones.

A happy examiner who has just marked a well-organised answer.

Revision guidance

Focus on getting it back out

Many students focus on getting information *in* to their memory (memorising facts). However, exams are more about getting it back *out*.

If I show you your revision card, you say, 'Yes I remember all of that' (this is called *recognition memory*) but can you recall it in an exam?

Solution Follow step 3 on the right, test your recall repeatedly using cues (see *The testing effect* on page 35).

Once more with meaning

Of course you may have difficulty in recalling information. You may find that every time you try to recall something, even using the cues, nothing comes to mind.

Solution The testing effect is one strategy to improve recall. Another strategy is active revision. Our memories evolved to store important information and not waste time on unimportant information. Therefore, you have to do something to make the information more meaningful. Compose a song using the key words and sing them. Have a debate on the topic with friends. Make up a quiz for your friend. Anything more active than just making notes.

Persistence

Psychologists have shown that one of the key characteristics of students who do well is *delayed gratification*. They can control their impulses – for example, when you see a chocolate bar, do you find it hard to resist eating it straight away? Can you sit there with it on your desk and wait till after you have written that essay?

STICK WITH IT!

Solution Research has shown that trying to do just that (practise resisting) can boost your grades.

Confidence

You learned about *self-efficacy* in this unit (see page 26). If you believe in yourself, it boosts your performance. For example, research you studied in Unit 1 of our Year 1 'Certificate' book (Chatard *et al.*) showed that when girls are reminded of the gender stereotype that girls are less good at Maths than boys, the girls underestimated their maths ability.

Solution Have things above your desk which remind you of your successes. Before the exam, remind yourself how much studying you have done and again think of your successes. Raise your self-efficacy.

Trust us. We are psychologists. We know about the mind.

Psychologically informed

On pages 35 and 71, we explained an important technique – the REVISION CARD, which uses cues to trigger your recall of important information.

On the left of this page we look at a number of other strategies based on what we psychologists know about how the mind works.

All our advice is based on psychological research.

Revision checklist for content area C

Below are the key topics for content area C. For each topic you should:

1. Construct a revision card (see pages 35 and 71 for an explanation).
2. Test your recall using your cues. Check afterwards to see what you have forgotten.
3. Test your recall again using the cues.
4. Now test your memory of the cue words.

Place a tick in the box as you complete each task.	1. Construct a revision card	2. First test of recall	3. Second test of recall	4. Test memory using cues
C1 Theories of persuasion				
Hovland-Yale theory				
Hovland and Weiss (1951)				
Fear arousal theory				
Janis and Feshbach (1953)				
Elaboration-likelihood model				
Petty *et al.* (1981)				
C2 Treatment and management of addiction and stress				
Physiological stress management techniques				
Drug therapies				
Biofeedback				
Psychological stress management techniques				
Stress inoculation training (SIT)				
Social support				
Physiological treatments for addiction				
Aversion therapy				
Drug therapies				
Psychological treatments for addiction				
CBT				
Skills training				
C3 Maintenance of behavioural change				
Reasons for non-adherence				
Bulpitt and Fletcher (1988)				
Ley's cognitive model				
Methods to improve adherence				
Physiological: Lustman *et al.* (2000)				
Psychological: Volpp *et al.* (2009)				

Content area C
Practice questions, answers and feedback

On this spread we look at some typical student answers to exam-style questions. The comments provided from an experienced teacher (in green) show what is good and bad in each answer. Learning how to provide effective exam answers is a SKILL.

Question 1: Erroll was very upset about an incident at work and a friend offered to go out for a coffee with him to chat about how he was feeling.

Identify the type of support that Erroll might be receiving. (1)

Hamid's answer

Instrumental.

Bronwen's answer

Esteem support because the friend might have been trying to make him feel good.

Teacher comments

Although *identify* questions do not ask you to write in a lot of depth make sure you are clear in your answer – both answers are potentially correct but Hamid needed to give some extra detail. No marks for Hamid and 1 for Bronwen.

Question 2: Assess stress inoculation training as a method of managing stress in terms of its strengths and weaknesses. (6)

Hamid's answer

Stress inoculation training (SIT) works on the principle that a long-term solution for stress problems is to learn techniques to deal generally with stress situations and therefore this inoculates you against a bad stress response.

The first step is cognitive preparation where you learn to think about the situation differently. You change your mental framework. The 3Cs that are involved are challenge, commitment and control. So, the person is encouraged to recognise that stress can be reduced using these methods.

The second step is skill acquisition where the client is taught by the therapist how to use a variety of skills to cope with their stress in any situation. These skills include things such as relaxation, good communication, social skills and time management. The client can then practise these in the therapy clinic. They might also watch other people and model the behaviour as a way to learn how to cope.

Step three is application and follow-through where the client starts to try the skills out in everyday life (called 'personal experiments'). They report back to their therapist and discuss what they have done. It is important in the long term to also practise strategies to deal with inevitable setbacks and accept them as inevitable. The therapist can encourage their client to think of setbacks as learning opportunities so they don't get discouraged.

One criticism of SIT is its complexity. There is a lot to learn about and practise in order for stress inoculation to work. Many people don't have the time or inclination for such effort and prefer to just benefit from some elements of the model. In fact research suggests that learning to think more positively may reap many of the same benefits as SIT which could be achieved by learning a new skill such as relaxation. 299 words

A 6-mark question is marked using the same levels as for 9 marks. Level 1 = 1–2 marks, level 2 = 3–4 marks, level 3 = 5–6 marks.

For 6 marks, about 300 words in length is appropriate (see calculation on page 34).

Hamid has presented a good response with quite a bit of elaboration. There is one mistake at the start where he has confused the first stage of SIT with the steps involved in the hardy personality (the 3Cs) – though this is partly correct. Marks are never subtracted for errors but they contribute to the overall impression. Now the response can't be described as 'accurate'.

A second issue is the imbalance between description (AO1) and evaluation (AO3). It is much better to write one elaborated point than use Hamid's strategy of mentioning many points but explaining none of them.

Hamid's answer fits the level 2 descriptors: 'some accurate' knowledge and understanding with 'minor gaps' and the discussion is 'well-developed' but a 'range' of aspects is not considered. There is a brief conclusion at the end as appropriate for an *assess* question. A slightly generous 4 out of 6 marks.

Jacob's answer

SIT involves three stages which are: cognitive preparation (this involves changing the way you think and approach your health problems), skill acquisition (learning new skills) and application and follow-through (practising the skills in everyday life situations and also keep doing it). Stress inoculation training contains the word 'inoculation' which means that it is meant as a therapy that will prepare a person to deal with future situations that may be stressful rather than just being about learning to deal with a current or ongoing problem. This is a cognitive therapy which basically means it tries to deal with how a person thinks – quite often stressors can't actually be changed so it is a better approach to aim to change how you think about them. SIT adds to this cognitive aspect by also teaching new coping skills which will further reduce the problem. So, it's like a cognitive behavioural therapy.

One criticism of this model is that it is too complicated when it could just be thinking more positively. Another criticism is that it is too hard and long for many people so they give up. A positive is that it has shown to be effective in research studies. Another positive is that it is flexible for each individual's needs.

In conclusion, it is clear that this has been a very useful approach with lots of possible adaptations. 227 words

Jacob's answer starts with a rather brief description of the therapy. This is followed by a lot of waffle about inoculation and the cognitive approach – it is relevant but could all be said in one sentence.

The second paragraph squeezes in four evaluation points but none of them are developed, so would be described as 'limited' and 'generic' (see mark scheme on page 70).

At the end he has written 'In conclusion, ...' – but just writing 'In conclusion' doesn't mean you are writing a conclusion! This conclusion contains nothing of credit.

This is clearly a level 1 answer which basically has very little creditworthy content. None of the criteria for level 2 apply, so 1 out of 6 marks.

Question 4: Leo felt unwell at home so his partner helped him measure his blood pressure with a machine. It was through the roof. They both knew that Leo had been under a lot of stress recently because of work and other things in his life. They discussed what Leo could do about it.

Evaluate methods for managing levels of stress.

In your answer you should consider at least **one** physiological and **one** psychological method. (9)

Jacob's answer

There are many different psychological and physiological methods to help manage stress. Each has advantages and disadvantages which means it is up to individuals to decide which is best for them.

Leo has high blood pressure which suggests that it might be good to use drugs as a way to treat the stress and to lower his blood pressure. There is certainly evidence that drugs can reduce blood pressure and other physical effects. In a study by Baldwin *et al.* the use of a drug (BZs) was compared with a placebo. A placebo is a kind of pretend drug where someone thinks they are getting the real thing but aren't and therefore only their expectations can create a benefit. BZs were more effective in reducing stress than the placebo which show they do have a real effect on reducing anxiety.

However, some people prefer not to use drugs because of side effects. So, an alternative is to use something like biofeedback, though this has different advantages. It is quite a complex procedure and would require effort on Leo's part whereas taking drugs is easy – you just have to remember to take the tablet.

A downside of drugs are the side effects. BZs are known to cause problems and it is not recommended that they should be taken for more than a month. It depends a bit how serious he thinks his problem is because just relaxation might help to reduce his blood pressure.

An alternative approach is that Leo could consider psychological methods, especially as he seems to also have some psychological stressors (e.g. work). Stress inoculation training is one possibility though this again has the downside of being very complicated and requiring a lot of time to learn and practise various skills. There is research evidence suggesting it is effective even in rather short courses of four sessions.

There is the positive that once it is learned Leo could then use it when he encounters future stressors because it is an all-purpose method and is called an 'inoculation' because it aims to offer general protection. Not all people like to engage in this kind of therapy though because it does require effort.

Another psychological approach is social support – Leo can turn to his friends. In fact he probably does that. However, a drawback is that sometimes you can rely too much on advice from friends, which may be inaccurate, or your friends might even become too intrusive in your life. Another issue is that men tend to be less able to turn to others, so this approach may not work for Leo.

433 words

Teacher comments

Jacob starts with an introduction which, to be honest, is a waste of precious time.

He then focuses on evaluating the different methods and omits to include the important details of the methods. 'Evaluate' means both describe and evaluate. The question requires that Jacob covers at least one physiological method and at least one psychological method – but this means that one of each would be enough.

By covering all of the four methods in the specification for stress management, Jacob really misses the criteria in the top level (see mark scheme on page 70). In fact he has failed to satisfy many of the criteria in level 2. The knowledge and understanding is hinted at but is more 'isolated elements' than 'some'. There are major gaps, such as the individual steps for SIT. There is reference to the scenario/context but these are largely just mentioning the name 'Leo'. The discussion is at least 'partially-developed' and there is certainly some look at the interrelationships.

Therefore, this answer lies between level 1 and 2 and on balance is probably 3 marks.

The omission of description has had a serious effect on Jacob's mark. Sometimes it's better to concentrate on a few methods done well than try to do too many and only be able to mention them all briefly.

Bronwen's answer

These are the methods Leo might use:

1. Benzodiazepines (BZs) – reduce anxiety and are effective but they have side effects and shouldn't be used for a long time.

2. Beta blockers (BBs) – are good for blood pressure because they stop adrenaline stimulating the blood vessels. These are good for people who need to stay alert (e.g. surgeons) because they don't affect thinking but are not good for sportspeople.

3. Biofeedback – a system where you learn to control involuntary responses such as your blood pressure (in Leo's case) but it requires quite a bit of dedication to learn. It would not be good for things like work issues.

4. Stress inoculation training (SIT) might be better for the more psychological problems such as problems at work. You learn methods to control your feelings about stress rather than deal with the problem itself. It's good to learn such a technique because it lasts long-term but Leo may not feel he wants to spend time on a long course.

5. Social support is the final method, looking for emotional support (he might get that from his partner), instrumental support (he might get practical ideas from his work colleagues) or esteem support (either from his partner or work colleagues – they might make him feel better about himself).

In conclusion, Leo might best choose a combination of BZs for the blood pressure and try SIT for long-term management of his social problems.

236 words

Bronwen has also made the mistake of going for breadth rather than depth but, unlike Jacob she has included some description. However, the description lacks detail and what evaluation there is, is very underdeveloped.

Bronwen's answer is clearly organised but is tending to be rather list-like, which is not good. The evidence of your understanding is demonstrated in the extent to which you can explain the points you are making. For example, instead of just writing 'It's good to learn such a technique because it lasts long-term', Bronwen might have added an example, such as 'SIT includes, for example, learning time management techniques which are likely to come in useful at work or even when organising your home routine'.

There is only some occasional evaluation and again little real engagement with Leo's problems.

Bronwen is firmly at level 1 but gets 3 marks because of the conclusions. She knows quite a lot but just hasn't provided enough evidence that she understands it because she can't use her knowledge to explain how Leo may use these methods.

Unit 4

Criminal and forensic psychology

What makes a criminal?

Do you think crime is the result of biological factors, such as brain influences or genetics?

Or is it more to do with the way people are brought up, their immediate environment?

Is there such a thing as a criminal mind? Or a criminal personality?

How should society treat criminals?

Should they be punished or rehabilitated?

Pearson
recommended
assessment
approach

Contents

A report detailing different theories and research used to explain criminal behaviour.

A report exploring the effectiveness of different methods and punishments of criminal behaviour.

An offender profile based on a case study of a real or imagined event. This should include the different profiling methods and an evaluation of the methods used when creating the profile.

Inherited criminality

The first time Jeffrey Landrigan met his biological father was in prison – on death row in fact, whilst Landrigan Junior was serving time for murder. A fellow prisoner had pointed out how similar Jeffrey looked to another prisoner (his father), who, it turned out, was also on death row for murder.

And the coincidences didn't end there. The two men had led remarkably similar lives. Both had troubled childhoods (this was, in the case of Jeffrey, despite being adopted by a stable, loving family). Both engaged in early criminal behaviour. Both were drug addicts. Both were sentenced to death for the brutal murder of two people. Incredibly, Jeffrey was soon to discover that his biological grandfather was also a career criminal, killed by police during a robbery in 1961.

Landrigan's legal defence team tried to argue at appeal that Jeffrey was not responsible for his crimes, or should be seen as *less* responsible, as he had clearly been genetically predisposed to commit murder. The jury were unconvinced. Landrigan's appeal was rejected and he was executed by lethal injection in 2010.

Specification terms

Adoption studies Genetic factors are implicated if adopted children are more similar to their biological parents with whom they share genes (but not environment) than to their adoptive parents with whom they share environment (but not genes). Environmental factors are implicated if the reverse is true.

Diathesis-stress model Behaviour is explained as the result of an underlying vulnerability (diathesis) and a trigger, both of which are necessary for the behaviour to be shown.

Family studies A means of assessing the contribution made by genetic factors by comparing an individual to people closely related (such as parents) and less closely related (such as grandparents).

Inherited Passed to you from previous generations.

Twin studies If a particular behaviour is more genetic than environmental we would expect MZ twins to show a higher concordance rate than non-identical (DZ) twins (who share about 50% of their genes). MZ stands for *monozygotic* meaning 'one egg' whereas non-identical twins come from two eggs – *dizygotic*.

Can criminality be inherited?

Can someone be born a criminal? The case of Jeffrey Landrigan (on the left) suggests this could be true. There are two ways to explain this – the learning approach or the biological approach, both of which you studied in the approaches unit (see our Year 1 'Certificate' book).

- According to the *learning approach* children learn to become a criminal from their families through rewards and observation of others. We will look at this explanation in learning aim A3.
- According to the *biological approach* becoming a criminal might be something you inherit, so perhaps it is the case that crime could be 'passed on' biologically in the same way as hair or eye colour. This is the explanation we will look at now.

Family studies

Many psychological studies have tried to investigate the extent to which criminal behaviour might be *inherited*. One way of doing this is to analyse how often crime occurs within a family. A huge study by Thomas Frisell *et al.* (2010) looked at all the convictions for violent crime in Sweden over 30 years using a national register. This involved over 12 million individuals!

The headline figure was that violent criminals were about five times more likely to have a first-degree relative who had also been convicted of a violent offence. (A first-degree relative is a sibling, child or, in the case of Jeffrey Landrigan, a parent.) The researchers took this as strong evidence that violent crime may be influenced by *genes*. It would also provide an explanation for the Jeffrey Landrigan case.

Twin studies

Twin studies analyse *concordance rates*, the number of twin pairs who both display a particular characteristic – in this case, criminal behaviour.

If crime is genetic we should expect higher rates of concordance amongst identical twins than non-identical twins. A famous study by Karl Christiansen (1977) involved both types of twins from Denmark. In each case, one of each twin pair had a criminal conviction. The concordance rate for identical twins was 35% which was much higher than the 13% for non-identical twins, suggesting that crime might be genetic.

Adoption studies

Adoption studies are useful as they make it possible to separate *genetic* and *environmental* influences in crime. Another large study by Sarnoff Mednick *et al.* (1984) involved over 13,000 adopted Danish children and their families. Criminality was defined as having at least one court conviction which was checked against national police records.

Mednick *et al.* found that when adopted children had no family history of crime, the percentage of convicted criminals was about 13%. However, this rose to 20% in the *sample* of adoptees who had one or both biological parents with a criminal conviction.

The researchers concluded that this difference could only be explained by genetics, as the biological parents had had little or no influence on the child's upbringing.

If there was such a thing as a 'criminal gene', what would we do with those who carry it? Our legal system is based on the idea of moral responsibility – that each person has the responsibility for controlling their own behaviour.

Where does the possibility of a criminal gene leave the idea of criminal responsibility? Should 'genetic criminals' be seen as responsible for their crimes? Finally, would it even be possible to rehabilitate a genetic criminal, if offending behaviour is a 'natural' part of them?

Evaluation

Problems with family studies

One weakness of family studies is that family members learn from each other.

Family members do not only have genes in common, they also share experiences. Learning theories of crime, such as *social learning* and *differential association* (discussed later in the unit), would suggest that crime is transmitted between members of a family, not through genetic inheritance, but through learning processes.

This weakens the *validity* of the inheritance theory as there may be other explanations for why criminal behaviour runs in family.

Problems with twin studies

One weakness of twin studies is that the environment acts as a *confounding variable*.

As mentioned on the facing page, the fact that twins are raised in the same environment (have the same friends, go to the same school, etc.) is a major confounding variable in twin studies. We cannot be sure if high concordance rates are due to shared genetics or shared upbringing. Also, because of their *physical* similarity, *MZ twins* may be treated more similarly than *DZ twins*, and this may explain the higher concordance rates for MZ twins.

This suggests that twin study evidence which seems to support genetic links to crime should be treated with caution.

Problems with adoption studies

One weakness of adoption studies is that biological and environmental influences may not be completely separated.

Adoption studies are based on the idea that genetic influences in crime can be studied in isolation as there is no influence from the biological parents. However, this assumption may be false. First, some children may experience late adoption which means that much of their childhood could still be spent with their biological parents. Second, many adoptees continue to maintain regular contact with their natural parents despite being raised by another family.

This suggests that the biological parents might still have an environmental influence on their children despite not living with them, so conclusions from adoption studies should be treated with caution.

GET ACTIVE The diathesis-stress model

This model provides a way of combining inherited and learning factors.

Genetic inheritance is likely to play an important role in criminal behaviour – but the influence of an offender's experiences should not be ignored. Indeed, although a person's genetic make-up may *predispose* them to commit crime, such behaviour may only be triggered by the right (or in the case of crime, the wrong) conditions.

Interestingly, in the Mednick *et al.* study on the facing page, another finding was that if the adopted parents *and* the biological parents had criminal convictions, the rates of conviction in the adopted children increased still further – to 24.5%.

1. *How can this be explained by the diathesis-stress model?*

2. *How might you argue that the Landrigan case (top left of facing page) is evidence against the diathesis-stress model?*

Assessment practice

At the end of learning aim A you must write:

A report detailing different theories and research used to explain criminal behaviour.

This report must be related to a scenario or context. We have used a real-life context.

You can see the assessment criteria and an explanation of command terms on pages 130 and 131.

Ronnie and Reggie Kray were identical twins who became notorious gangsters in the East End of London during the 1950s and '60s. Known as 'The Firm', they ruled their criminal empire with vicious violence. They were eventually imprisoned for their involvement in two murders. Their older brother Charlie was also a criminal and was also imprisoned for his role in these murders. Their father Charlie Senior was occasionally involved in criminal activity, although nothing on the scale of his sons.

A1.1 Learning aim A1 – Task 1

The first part of your report for learning aim A will be concerned with biological explanations for criminality – these are covered on this spread and the next two spreads.

This activity will help you practise the skills required to write the report in response to your scenario/context.

1. **Explain** how the account of the Kray family supports the view that criminality can be inherited. (A.P1)

2. **Explain** how some research evidence supports the view that criminality in the Kray family was inherited. (A.P2)

3. **Discuss** the inherited criminality explanation with reference to criminality in the Kray family. (A.M1)

4. **Evaluate** the research evidence relating to the inherited criminality explanation with reference to criminality in the Kray family. (A.D1)

An issue to consider

Our legal system is based on the idea of moral responsibility – that each person has the responsibility for controlling their own behaviour.

Where does the possibility of a criminal gene leave the idea of criminal responsibility? Should 'genetic criminals' be seen as responsible for their crimes?

Specification content

A1 Biological explanations of criminality

● Inherited criminality, twin, family and adoption studies, and diathesis–stress model.

Low gene activity

Criminality in the genes?

In 2007, Abdelmalek Bayout was sentenced to nine years in prison by an Italian court for the brutal murder of Walter Perez. Perez had taunted Bayout, an Algerian national, for wearing eye make-up which Bayout later claimed was for religious reasons. Perez paid the ultimate price for his unkindness and was stabbed to death by Bayout in response to his comments.

Bayout was spared life imprisonment on account of the fact that he had a history of mental illness. However, Bayout's sentence was reduced still further on appeal – by a year. The circumstances of this were historic. Bayout's legal team presented evidence from a neuroscientist that their defendant was a 'genetic criminal', that he had abnormalities on five genes which explained his irrational behaviour.

One of these was the so-called 'warrior gene', MAOA. Bayout's legal team explained that the MAOA gene had been linked to increased aggression in a series of research studies. Bayout was therefore, it was argued, less responsible for his crime than someone without such genetic defects would be. The judge agreed – to some extent – and in a world first, reduced Bayout's sentence on the basis of the genetic evidence.

Could criminality be in someone's DNA? If you were a defence barrister representing a violent criminal in court, and you knew your client had low levels of MAO-A and CDH13, would you bring this to the court's attention? Does this justify their crimes? Or would it depend on the type of crime it was? Do 'genetic criminals' still have a choice to commit crime or not?

Low gene activity

If we accept that criminal behaviour is at least partly *inherited*, how might that happen? There is a growing body of research which indicates that some *genes* may be responsible for criminal behaviour, so that criminality may be written into someone's genes when they are born. This is not as far-fetched as it sounds!

Two genes in particular have received a fair bit of attention – *MAOA* and *CDH13*. We all have these genes but they come in different forms. Some people have forms of the genes which are low in activity and this has been linked to aggressive behaviour and violent crime.

MAOA – the 'warrior gene'

The *MAOA gene's* main function is to trigger production of a chemical called *monoamine oxidase A* (abbreviated as *MAO-A*).

This breaks down particular chemicals in the brain, known as *neurotransmitters*. As you know from your study of the *biological approach*, neurotransmitters allow nerve cells in the brain to communicate with each other. One important neurotransmitter is *serotonin*.

Abnormally high levels of serotonin have been linked to aggression. Some people have a form of the MAOA gene that causes low levels of MAO-A activity. This mean that serotonin is not broken down with the same efficiency, so levels of serotonin are too high and aggressive behaviour is more likely.

This has resulted in the MAOA gene being nicknamed the 'warrior gene' because of its association with increased aggression.

Evidence for the MAOA 'warrior gene'

One of the first studies of the MAOA gene was by Han Brunner *et al.* (1993), who did a genetic analysis of a Dutch family. Several of the male members of the family had engaged in violent criminal behaviour, such as rape and murder. Each of the men was found to have the low-activity form of MAOA. This suggests that low MAOA activity is involved in destructive behaviour, and many studies have supported this conclusion.

CDH13

Another potential 'warrior gene' is CDH13 (cadherin 13 gene). The job of this gene is to produce a protein adhesive (glue) that sits around membranes in the brain. Low levels of CDH13 have been linked to *substance abuse*, including alcoholism.

A major study of 900 criminals from Finland found that around 10% of the most violent offenders (some of whom had committed more than ten murders) carried a low-activity MAOA gene (Tiihonen *et al.* 2014). However, the same group also carried a variant of CDH13. This genetic pattern was not seen in a comparison group of non-violent offenders. Could it be that this genetic combination made criminal activity even more likely?

Specification terms

CDH13 gene Produces adhesive proteins in the brain. Low levels of CDH13 have been linked to substance abuse, and, in a small number of studies, to violent behaviour.

Genes A unit of inheritance. They consist of chemical instructions (DNA) which tell your body what proteins to manufacture – and basically that is what you are, a huge number of proteins. Genes are inherited from parents and contribute to the development of an individual's characteristics.

MAOA gene Regulates the production of monoamine oxidase A (MAO-A) which, amongst other things, regulates the breakdown of serotonin in the brain. People who have a low-activity MAOA gene have high levels of serotonin which is associated with aggressive behaviour.

Evaluation

Too simple

One weakness of the low-activity gene explanation is that it is too simple.

Crime is a complex social activity that is unlikely to be explained by genetic influences alone. There are all kinds of social reasons why people may be drawn to offending, such as poor education, social deprivation and poverty, and these are not addressed by genetic theories. Also, if crime does have a genetic basis, it may not be explained by a couple of genes working in isolation. For instance, a study by Richard Tremblay *et al.* (2005) found several possible genetic markers for aggression in mice. It is likely that human aggression is even more genetically complex.

This means that the influence of MAOA and CDH13 may be only one part of a very complex picture.

Limited number of crimes

Another weakness of the low gene activity explanation is that it tends to only account for violent crime.

Research into MAOA and CDH13 has suggested a link between low activity of these genes and aggressive behaviour. It is no coincidence then that studies have focused exclusively on very serious offences that are the result of extreme violence or a loss of control, like rape and murder. Other non-violent offences, such as financial and property crime (so-called 'white-collar crimes'), are not explained by low gene activity.

This weakens the extent to which a genetic explanation can be applied to criminal behaviour in general.

Gender differences

One strength of the MAOA explanation is that it can account for gender differences in crime.

The vast majority of criminal offences are committed by men. In 2017, nearly 81,000 UK prisoners were male compared to fewer than 4000 females, and this difference is even greater for violent crime. The explanation is that women have two copies of the MAOA gene whereas men have only one. In women, low activity of this gene can be overridden by the fact that they may possess one 'normal' MAOA gene which counteracts the low-activity form.

This means that the MAOA gene explanation makes an important contribution to our understanding of gender differences in crime.

Dave really wanted that promotion, but as he approached the interview room, his colleagues worried that he'd psyched himself up a little too much.

GET ACTIVE Born bad?

Waleed is a prison officer. He has just transferred from an adult prison to work at a Young Offender Institution (YOI) for young men aged 18–21. He decided to move jobs because he wants to help young people to improve their lives and put their offending behaviour behind them.

Dean has worked at the YOI for several years and when he heard Waleed say he wanted to improve lives, he laughed saying, 'Don't get your hopes up – they're born bad, mate'.

Dean went on to explain that despite providing the young offenders with education, job training, advice and life skills lessons many of them went on to reoffend and often continued to be violent. Some came back to the YOI multiple times and others ended up in adult prison. His advice to Waleed was, 'Get used to it, mate. I'm telling you, they're born bad. You can't change that'.

1. *Would you accept what Dean says or challenge his view of young offenders?*

2. *How could you use psychological theory or research to support your argument?*

Assessment practice

At the end of learning aim A you must write a report (see previous spread and page 130). This report must be related to a scenario or context. We have used a real-life context.

'What you must understand about the Kray twins, an old friend of theirs once told me, is that they were born to be criminals' (Pearson 2011).

The history of the Kray family points towards the possibility that criminality is genetically inherited. The hallmark of the Kray's criminal behaviour was that it was extremely violent. They were born into a boxing family (which included their Aunt Rose). Many family members (such as grandfather 'Mad' Jimmy Kray) often put their skills to use on the streets.

A1.2 Learning aim A1 – Task 2

The first part of your report for learning aim A will be concerned with biological explanations for criminality – these are covered on the previous spread, this spread and the next spread.

1. **Explain** how the account of the Kray family supports the view that criminality can be explained by low gene activity. (A.P1)

2. **Explain** how the research evidence supports the view that criminality in the Kray family was the result of low gene activity. (A.P2)

3. **Discuss** the 'low-activity gene' explanation with reference to criminality in the Kray family. (A.M1)

4. **Evaluate** the research evidence relating to low gene activity with reference to criminality in the Kray family. (A.D1)

An issue to consider

One major aim of putting people in prison is to reform or rehabilitate them (though some people might argue that prison is not the best way of doing this).

Where does the idea of a 'genetic criminal' leave the process of rehabilitation? If crime is part of the DNA of some people, can those people ever be truly reformed?

Specification content

A1 Biological explanations of criminality
● Low activity in genes MAOA and CDH13.

Role of the amygdala and aggression

The Texas shooter

On 1 August 1966, Charles Whitman, a former US Marine, took a pile of guns and ammunition to the top of a 300-foot tower at the University of Texas and proceeded to shoot 46 people, killing 15 and wounding 31. Whitman, who had murdered both his wife and mother the night before, was eventually shot by local police officers to end the carnage.

Forever known as the 'Texas Tower Sniper', Whitman had previously sought advice from five doctors and a psychiatrist to try to help him control his aggressive urges. The psychiatrist had described him as 'oozing with hostility' but found it difficult to explain Whitman's aggressive feelings. Whitman wrote of himself, 'I don't really understand myself these days. I am supposed to be an average reasonable and intelligent young man. However, lately (I can't recall when it started) I have been a victim of many unusual and irrational thoughts' (Whitman 1966).

In a letter, Whitman had suggested that, upon his death, his brain was examined to see if there was evidence of damage or abnormality. Doctors duly obliged, and the analysis revealed that Whitman had been living with a brain tumour that was pushing down on a small structure in the brain called the *amygdala*. Since Whitman's death many studies have revealed a link between the amygdala and aggressive behaviour in humans and animals.

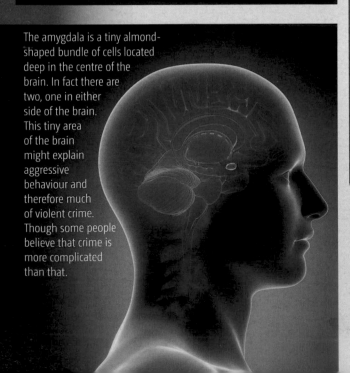

The amygdala is a tiny almond-shaped bundle of cells located deep in the centre of the brain. In fact there are two, one in either side of the brain. This tiny area of the brain might explain aggressive behaviour and therefore much of violent crime. Though some people believe that crime is more complicated than that.

Aggression and violent crime

Every day we encounter lots of situations that may 'wind us up' and cause us to experience *stress*. These situations might include getting stuck in traffic, losing something or being given too much homework! Our response to these events tends to vary depending on the mood we are in: we may feel frustrated, overwhelmed or perhaps even inspired to work harder to deal with the stressor.

However, for some people, their typical reaction – even to relatively mild situations – is anger and aggression. Could it be that people who have difficulty controlling their level of aggression are more likely to be involved in violent crime? And more likely to be serving prison sentences as a result?

Proactive and reactive aggression

Psychologists distinguish between different types of aggression. *Proactive aggression* is aggression that is designed to help a person achieve a particular goal. For instance, a footballer may need to become aggressive to tackle an opponent and help their team's chances of winning. Displaying aggression may enable a bully to steal another child's lunch money in the school playground.

By contrast, *reactive aggression* is a response to a real or perceived threat or to provocation. The key thing here is what the person *perceives* to be a threat. For people who are easily angered and have a 'short fuse', apparently trivial situations (such as being jostled or even simply being looked at in a bar) may produce deep and intense feelings of aggression. Reactive aggression tends to increase during adolescence (sounds familiar?!). In adulthood it is often associated with emotional immaturity.

The role of the amygdala

Can Charles Whitman's seemingly unexplained and murderous aggression be explained by the *amygdala* – a tiny structure deep within the brain? The amygdala is part of the *limbic system* and, along with the *hypothalamus*, contributes to the brain's 'shock response'. When functioning properly it promotes our survival instinct by allowing us to experience fear.

A case study of a woman born without an amygdala revealed that she was unable to feel fear, and showed no emotional response to snakes, spiders or horror films (Adolphs *et al.* 1994). In animal and human studies, structural damage or abnormal activity in the amygdala have been linked to aggressive behaviour.

Intermittent explosive disorder (IED)

The inability to control emotional outbursts can be so serious that it is classed as a mental disorder in some people. *Intermittent explosive disorder* is when an individual reacts in an aggressive way that is totally out of proportion to the threat posed. For instance, people with IED may cause serious damage to property, or even other people, in response to fairly minor incidents. People with IED may report feelings of tension or stress before the explosive 'attack'. They usually feel relief immediately afterwards which can give way to feelings of regret, guilt or shame when they realise the impact of the episode on others.

IED is rare, it occurs in around 2–3% of the population. For a diagnosis to be made, the individual has to experience the aggressive episodes quite regularly – around twice a week for a period of at least three months.

Specification terms

Amygdala A small region of the brain which is responsible for detecting fear and preparing an animal for emergency events. It is associated with memory, emotion, sleep, arousal and the fight or flight response.

Intermittent explosive disorder A type of control or conduct disorder characterised by explosive and destructive rages which are out of proportion to the situation at the time.

Reactive aggression Aggression that occurs as a response to a real or perceived threat. This is distinct from proactive aggression which is designed to achieve a particular goal.

GET ACTIVE Ollie's outbursts

Ollie cannot seem to control his temper. He is banned from the school football team, despite being a talented player, as he has been sent off four times since the beginning of the season. Following his last sending off, he walked into the changing rooms and damaged a sink by trying to kick it off the wall.

He has been involved in several fights at school, most recently when he punched another student who accidentally pushed him in the dinner queue. When called to the headmaster's office to explain himself, Ollie became upset. He described how he sometimes feels 'out of control', that he was 'really sorry' but could not explain why he had behaved in the way he had.

1. *Is Ollie's behaviour best described as proactive or reactive aggression? Why?*

2. *What signs are there that Ollie may have intermittent explosive disorder?*

3. *What is the possible role of the amygdala in Ollie's aggressive behaviour?*

Evaluation

Research evidence

One strength of the amygdala explanation is that there is evidence that links it to IED.

A study by Michael McCloskey *et al.* (2016) showed participants pictures of aggressive and 'neutral' (expressionless) faces. Twenty of the people tested had been diagnosed with IED, the other 20 were a non-IED *control group*. Amygdala activity in the IED group was much higher than the non-IED in response to the aggressive faces.

This suggests that reactive aggression is more intense in people with IED, and this may be because of abnormally high activity (*hyperactivity*) in the amygdala.

Gender differences

Another strength of the amygdala explanation is that it may explain gender differences in violent crime.

Much is known about the amygdala in relation to differences between the sexes (e.g. Hamann 2005). The amygdala is larger in males than females (except during adolescence). In addition the right amygdala (that is, the part of the amygdala that is found in the right *hemisphere* of the brain) is responsible for acting on negative emotions. This part of the amygdala is much more active in men. The left amygdala produces thought rather than action in response to stress, and tends to dominate in women.

This suggests that the much greater number of males serving prison sentences for violent crime could be because of a greater tendency to react violently when placed under stress.

Limited explanation

One weakness of the amygdala explanation is that it is too simple.

Evidence suggests that violent crime and aggression is probably not explained by one single area of the brain operating on its own. Even in the McCloskey *et al.* study above, hyperactivity in the amygdala was not the only finding. IED participants also showed less of a connection between the amygdala and another area of the brain (the *orbitofrontal cortex*, OFC) that has also been linked to aggressive and explosive behaviour.

This suggests there may be a whole series of circuits or pathways in the brain that contribute to aggression, and ultimately, violent offending.

Assessment practice

At the end of learning aim A you must write a report (see pages 115 and 130). This report must be related to a scenario or context. We have used a real-life context.

The Krays saw themselves as 'professionals' who used violence to get want they wanted. However, both brothers also had notoriously violent tempers. They carried out many assaults impulsively with an excessive and uncontrolled degree of violence. Their worst crimes were partly planned and partly improvised. For example, Reggie stabbed Jack 'The Hat' McVitie to death in a fit of temper when his gun failed to go off.

You can see the assessment criteria and an explanation of command terms on pages 130 and 131.

A1.3 Learning aim A1 – Task 3

The first part of your report for learning aim A will be concerned with biological factors, covered on the previous two spreads and this spread.

1. **Explain** how the account of the Kray twins supports the view that violent crimes can be explained by aggression. (A.P1)

2. **Explain** how the research evidence supports the view that aggression played a significant role in the Kray twins' criminality. (A.P2)

3. **Discuss** the view that aggression plays a role in violent crime with reference to the Kray twins' criminality. (A.M1)

4. **Evaluate** the research evidence relating to the role of aggression in violent crime with reference to the Kray twins' criminality. (A.D1)

An issue to consider

If it was possible for babies to have a prenatal test to assess whether their amygdala was functioning properly, would this be a good idea?

If it appeared that a child was likely to exhibit aggressive behaviour as a result of the test, should anything be done about it? And if so, what?

Specification content

A1 Biological explanations of criminality

● Role of the amygdala and aggression – intermittent explosive disorder and reactive aggression.

Eysenck's theory of criminality

The Joker

One of the scariest characters in recent cinema history is Batman's sworn enemy, The Joker.

The Joker, played chillingly and brilliantly by the late Heath Ledger, is the classic superhero villain. His appearance is striking, particularly his contorted grin which is forever fixed following an assault by his own father when The Joker was a child. However, it is his twisted behaviour and personality that makes The Joker such a compelling on-screen presence.

The Joker is irrational, unstable, unpredictable, and will stop at nothing to get what he wants. He shows no empathy for the victims of his crimes and is callous and calculating. A true psychotic.

The Joker is also a thrill-seeker, who possesses a warped, sadistic sense of humour and seems to get a 'kick' out of the suffering of others.

Specification terms

Extroversion Outgoing, externally-oriented people who enjoy risk and danger because their nervous systems are under-aroused.

Eysenck's theory of criminality A person who scores highly on measures of extroversion, neuroticism and psychoticism is cold and unfeeling, and is likely to engage in crime.

Neuroticism The degree to which a person experiences the world as distressing, threatening and unsafe. It is an overreactive response to threat.

Personality Patterns of thinking, feeling and behaving that differ between individuals. These are relatively consistent from one situation to another, and over time.

Psychoticism A personality characterised by aggressiveness, hostility and lack of empathy for others. May be related to high levels of testosterone.

The criminal personality

Hans Eysenck was a leading figure in psychological research in the 1950s and '60s. He was interested in how people engage with the world and claimed that each of us has a collection of stable characteristics that direct behaviour in different situations, such as kind, easy-going, talkative, restless, impulsive, controlled, quiet. These characteristics make up our *personality*.

Dimensions of personality and the criminal type

Eysenck's theory suggested that personality can be measured along three dimensions:

- **Extroversion–introversion** *Extroverts* crave excitement and stimulation. They are 'adrenaline junkies' who often get involved in dangerous, risk-taking behaviour. Extroverts do not readily respond to *conditioning* (*reinforcement* and *punishment*), i.e. they do not tend to learn from their mistakes. This is quite important when thinking about criminal behaviour because it means a person would not be affected as strongly by punishment.
- **Neuroticism–stability** *Neurotic* individuals are nervy and anxious. Their general instability means their behaviour is difficult to predict. Neurotics may be particularly prone to drug or alcohol problems and may be at risk of depression.
- **Psychoticism–normality** *Psychotics* are individuals who are self-centred, cold and lack empathy for other people.

Eysenck's criminal type is someone who scores highly on measures of E, N and P. Eysenck developed the *Eysenck personality questionnaire* (EPQ), a questionnaire which places respondents along E and N and P dimensions to determine personality type.

Biological basis

Eysenck suggested that there is a biological root to personality. The personality traits we develop are explained by the type of nervous system we inherit. The constant need for excitement that extroverts have is because of an underactive nervous system which needs unusually high levels of stimulation.

Neurotic individuals are unstable because their nervous system is overreactive. Therefore, they tend to be volatile and react strongly to situations others would find less stressful.

Psychoticism has been related to higher levels of *testosterone*, which means that men (who have higher levels of testosterone than women) are more likely to be found at this end of the spectrum.

The socialisation process

Despite the biological aspects of the theory, Eysenck did acknowledge that the way a person is brought up (the way they are *socialised*) will determine whether a person becomes law-abiding or not.

However, the fact that extroverts are natural reward-seekers makes them less affected by punishment for wrongdoing. Similarly, high neuroticism interferes with efficient learning which may relate to a difficulty taking on board social rules. So, a criminal personality affects the way in which the person responds to their upbringing, making crime more likely.

Eysenck's theory may have useful applications in preventing crime. The theory argues that criminal tendencies, such as the inability to learn from one's mistakes, can be identified in early childhood. This would suggest, if intervention comes early enough, it may be possible to change the socialisation experiences of high-risk children to prevent them becoming offenders. Such experiences may be best delivered in the home, or possibly at school.

Evaluation

Gender differences

One strength of Eysenck's theory is that it may account for gender differences in crime.

Marvin Zuckerman (1979) has suggested that a major component of extroversion is the personality trait of *sensation-seeking*. This is defined as the pursuit of danger and risk-taking to experience a variety of new sensations. Like Eysenck, Zuckerman drew a line connecting risk-taking to biology, claiming that sensation-seeking is linked to testosterone levels. This is supported by the fact that men tend to score higher on Zuckerman's own sensation-seeking scale.

This suggests that higher rates of crime amongst men may indeed be due to higher testosterone levels and a higher capacity for risk-taking.

Descriptive theory

One weakness of Eysenck's theory is that it does not really explain *why* people commit crime.

Some researchers, such as Dennis Howitt (2009), have argued that whilst Eysenck's theory can tell us that people who offend are likely to be extrovert, neurotic or psychotic, it cannot tell us how these traits motivate criminal behaviour. Therefore, the theory may be of little use to forensic psychologists as they are likely to be interested in what the motivation for crime is, in order to understand it and perhaps prevent it.

This suggests that the concept of the criminal personality may have little practical use in the real world.

Limited explanation

Another weakness of Eysenck's theory is that there may be more than one criminal type.

More recent models of the criminal personality have challenged Eysenck's model. The *five-factor model* of personality (Digman 1990) accepts Eysenck's concepts of extroversion and introversion, but also adds openness, conscientiousness and agreeableness. Of these, low levels of agreeableness and conscientiousness are related to criminality.

This research suggests that the criminal personality may be more complicated than Eysenck proposed.

GET ACTIVE Three criminals

A police chief inspector was dealing with the following three cases:

Janet Flynn A quiet and unassuming 45-year-old woman with few friends. Janet works in the finance department of a large company and has been quietly defrauding it for the last 20 years. She has made tens of thousands of pounds over that period.

Simon Simpson A family man with a highly paid job. Simon is well-liked by his colleagues and appears calm and well-adjusted to those who know him. His wife describes him as 'steady, someone who doesn't take risks'. Simon is also a serial killer who has murdered dozens of women whilst claiming to be away at weekends for work.

Jed Jackson A 22-year-old repeat criminal, Jed has already been in and out of prison several times. A self-confessed 'adrenaline junkie', he has a driving ban for speeding, and has stolen and written off several cars. Jed is receiving treatment for drug and alcohol addiction and receives support for depression.

1. Which of these cases most clearly illustrates Eysenck's criminal personality?

2. How could the other two cases be used to criticise the theory?

Assessment practice

At the end of learning aim A you must write a report (see pages 115 and 130). This report must be related to a scenario or context. We have used a real-life context.

John Wayne Gacy was an American serial murderer and rapist. He was convicted of the murders of 33 young men. He was known to the media as 'The Killer Clown' because he would dress up as a clown at children's parties.

Gacy tortured many of his victims, including some who survived. He took drugs, drank heavily and was involved in the local 'wife-swapping' scene. He was a businessman who was appointed to neighbourhood committees by people in his community.

According to his neighbours, Gacy's behaviour became increasingly erratic and unpredictable after he and his wife were divorced. On several occasions he was suspected by the police of involvement in several crimes (and even accused by survivors) but was always able to persuade them of his innocence.

Expressing no remorse, he was executed in prison in 1994.

A2.4 Learning aim A2 – Task 4

You can see the assessment criteria and explanation of command terms on pages 130 and 131.

The second part of your report for learning aim A will be concerned with individual differences explanations for criminality – these are covered on this spread and the next spread.

This activity will help you practise the skills required to write the report in response to your scenario/context.

1. **Explain** how the account of John Wayne Gacy's crimes supports Eysenck's theory of criminality. (A.P1)

2. **Explain** how the research evidence supports the view that John Wayne Gacy's criminality can be explained by Eysenck's theory of criminality. (A.P2)

3. **Discuss** Eysenck's theory of criminality with reference to John Wayne Gacy's criminal behaviour. (A.M1)

4. **Evaluate** the research evidence relating to Eysenck's theory of criminality with reference to John Wayne Gacy's criminal behaviour. (A.D1)

An issue to consider

Eysenck's theory was based on the idea that personality is something that can be measured using a questionnaire – but can it?

Is a person's personality fixed for all time? Or can it change depending on the situation or the experiences we have? Can criminal personalities be changed?

Specification content

A2 Individual differences explanations of criminality

● Eysenck's theory of criminality, including three dimensions/traits of personality – extroversion, neuroticism and psychoticism.

Cognitive factors and criminality

Heinz's moral dilemma

In Europe, a woman was near death from a special kind of cancer. There was one drug that the doctors thought might save her. It was a form of radium that a druggist in the same town had recently discovered. The drug was expensive to make, but the druggist was charging ten times what the drug cost him to make. He paid $400 for the radium and charged $4000 for a small dose of the drug. The sick woman's husband, Heinz, went to everyone he knew to borrow the money, but he could only get together about $2000, which was half of what the drug cost. He told the druggist that his wife was dying and asked him to sell it cheaper or let him pay later. But the druggist said, 'No, I discovered the drug and I'm going to make money from it'. So, Heinz got desperate and considered breaking into the man's store to steal the drug for his wife.

- Should Heinz steal the drug?

- Why?

- Does the druggist have the right to charge what he wants for the drug?

- Would it be a good husband's duty to steal the drug for his wife?

- What if the dying person were not his wife, but a stranger. Should Heinz steal the drug?

Source: Colby and Kohlberg (1987)

Kohlberg suggested that criminals have a 'childlike' way of viewing the world – they are only interested in what they can gain and what they can get away with (they're also really bad at drawing apparently).

Kohlberg's theory of moral development

Is there such a thing as a criminal mind? It is often suggested in the media that, in order to understand what drives some people to commit offending behaviour, we must 'get inside the mind of the criminal'.

Cognitive psychologists, who take the human mind to be their main object of study, might be able to help us with this. Some researchers within this approach have argued that criminals think in quite a different way from the rest of us – their sense of right and wrong is distorted. This makes them able to justify their crimes in a way that law-abiding citizens would not be able to, and certainly would not agree with.

One important psychologist who supported this view was Lawrence Kohlberg.

Kohlberg's stages of moral development

Kohlberg is best known for his *stages of moral development* (see bottom of facing page). A stage theory means that people change the way that they think as they get older. Kohlberg believed this applied to the way we think about moral issues of what is right and what is wrong.

The moral dilemma technique

Kohlberg tested his theory by asking children and adults to give their opinion on a series of moral dilemmas, such as the one about Heinz on the left.

A moral dilemma is a situation where a person must decide on their preferred course of action, though whichever option they choose will have some undesirable consequence. The most famous of Kohlberg's moral dilemmas is the Heinz dilemma where the options involve breaking the law or ending/prolonging his wife's suffering. In Kohlberg's research the answers that participants gave determined their level of *moral reasoning*. Kohlberg would assign them to a stage and level based on how sophisticated he thought their reasoning about the dilemma was.

Kohlberg was able to show that the way people think about moral issues changes as they get older, and also varies from person to person. For instance, not everyone will reach the later stages of moral reasoning (the post-conventional level).

Criminality and the pre-conventional level

The aim of Kohlberg's original stage theory was to describe moral reasoning in everybody, it was only later that he turned his attention to the criminal mind. He argued that criminals were more likely to reason at the lower ends of the model (the *pre-conventional level*) whereas non-criminals are more likely to have progressed to the conventional level and beyond.

This is because criminals tend to be concerned with what they might gain from situations, and what they can get away with (the pre-conventional level is based on avoiding *punishment* and obtaining rewards).

Specification terms

Kohlberg's stages of moral development A theory describing the way people think about right and wrong, and how this thinking changes as a child gets older. Kohlberg identified different levels of thinking based on people's answers to moral dilemmas.

Moral reasoning The process by which an individual draws upon their own value system to determine whether an action is right or wrong.

Pre-conventional level The first level of Kohlberg's stage theory. It is characterised by childlike immature reasoning which has also been observed in the adult criminal population.

Evaluation

Evidence to support

One strength of the cognitive approach to criminality is that it has research support.

A number of studies have supported Kohlberg's prediction that criminals reason at lower levels than non-criminals. For example, people who commit crime have been found to have a less mature, more self-centred perspective on the world, and often find it difficult to empathise with the views of others (Chandler 1973). A study by Emma Palmer and Clive Hollin (1998) compared male and female offenders with a non-criminal *control group* using 11 moral dilemma questions. The offending group showed less mature reasoning than the non-offending group.

This suggests that criminals may have a certain cognitive 'style' that makes them more likely to offend, which adds weight to Kohlberg's theory.

Type of crime

One weakness of the cognitive approach is that moral reasoning may depend on the type of crime.

A study by David Thornton (1982) found that criminals who have a financial motive, such as those who commit robbery, do indeed reason at less mature pre-conventional levels. However, those who are found guilty of more impulsive crimes, such as assault, do not. Pre-conventional reasoning is much more a feature of crimes where the offender believes they have a better chance of not being caught.

This limits the *validity* of the cognitive approach as it may not apply to every offence.

Gender differences

A further weakness of the cognitive approach is there may be gender differences in moral reasoning.

Carol Gilligan (1981), in her influential book *In a different voice*, was very critical of Kohlberg's research, pointing out that the *interviews* used to develop his stage theory had failed to include any female participants. As a result, Kohlberg's stage theory, which he assumed described moral reasoning in everyone, in fact may only apply to males. Male moral reasoning, Gilligan suggests, is based more on principles of law and justice (stage 4 of the model), whereas female reasoning is based more on compassion and care (stage 3). For Gilligan, this gives males a natural advantage even before they answer the questions about the moral dilemma.

This inbuilt bias may mean that Kohlberg's theory does not provide an adequate account of cognitive development, or indeed criminality, in females.

GET ACTIVE Kohlberg's stages of moral development (1976)

Here are brief descriptions of the three levels and six stages of moral development described by Kohlberg.

Level 1 Pre-conventional	Aged 4–10. Good (i.e. moral) behaviour determined by avoidance of punishment and getting rewards.
Stage 1 Punishment orientation	Unquestioning deference to a superior power. The physical consequence of an action determines its goodness or badness.
Stage 2 Instrumental orientation	'You scratch my back and I'll scratch yours'. Fairness is important as long as one's own needs are satisfied.
Level 2 Conventional	Child seeks to conform to the rules of family, social group or nation, and seeks to help maintain the rules.
Stage 3 Good boy/girl orientation	Child behaves well to please others. Behaviour judged by intention, 'He means well'.
Stage 4 Authority orientation	Respect for authority, fixed rules, doing one's duty. Seeking to maintain the social order.
Level 3 Post-conventional	Acts according to universal principles that exist apart from the authority of the groups who hold them.
Stage 5 Social contract orientation	A 'legal' point of view. Respect for democratic process of arriving at social rules, e.g. those who wrote the US Constitution.
Stage 6 Universal ethical principles	Decisions based on one's own conscience. Respect for the dignity of all humans.

1. *Consider your own answers to the Heinz dilemma. Which level/stage would you say you were in?*

2. *Is it straightforward to work out which stage your answers fit into?*

3. *Do you agree with Gilligan's argument (above) that males and females think about moral issues in a different way?*

Assessment practice

At the end of learning aim A you must write a report (see pages 115 and 130). This report must be related to a scenario or context. We have used a real-life context.

John Wayne Gacy's crimes were mostly sexually motivated. He found them intensely enjoyable, and this included the thrill of luring his victims to their deaths. His experiences of being questioned by the police without consequence convinced him that he had nothing to fear and could continue killing. When he was arrested he said to the police officers, 'Clowns can get away with murder'. Just before he was executed he claimed that killing him meant nothing because it would not compensate his victims' families for their losses.

A2.5 Learning aim A2 – Task 5

The second part of your report for learning aim A will be concerned with individual differences explanations for criminality – these are covered on the previous spread and this spread.

1. **Explain** how the account of John Wayne Gacy supports Kohlberg's theory of moral development as applied to criminality. (A.P1)

2. **Explain** how the research evidence supports Kohlberg's theory of moral development as an explanation of John Wayne Gacy's criminality. (A.P2)

3. **Discuss** Kohlberg's theory of moral development with reference to John Wayne Gacy's criminal behaviour. (A.M1)

4. **Evaluate** the research evidence relating to Kohlberg's theory of moral development with reference to John Wayne Gacy's criminal behaviour. (A.D1)

An issue to consider

Kohlberg used imaginary situations to try to find out about people's moral development. He asked people to explain their reasoning. What would be a better way of doing this? What might the problems be with interviewing criminals in particular?

Specification content

A2 Individual differences explanations of criminality

● Cognitive factors and criminality: Kohlberg stages of moral development – moral reasoning and lack of opportunity to develop moral thinking beyond the pre-conventional level.

Social learning theory

Copycats

You may have come across the phrase *copycat crime*. Occasionally, individuals may be 'inspired' by real-life or media depictions of crimes and want to replicate these. Grimly, the copycat effect is most commonly associated with violent murders or suicides which result in more of the same through imitation.

The term was first used in around 1916 due to the copycat crimes that were inspired by Jack the Ripper's murders in the Whitechapel area of London in the late 19th century. In modern times, the phrase has more often been applied to crimes that have been influenced by media representations in film and television.

The highly publicised and brutal murder of toddler James Bulger in 1993 by two ten-year-old boys shocked the nation. There was much made in the media coverage of the fact that James' murderers had imitated chilling details from a horror film they had recently seen, *Child's Play 3*.

There have been many other film-inspired murders over the years. This is *social learning* – learning by observing what others do. Should films that portray crime be banned because of such potential consequences?

Are children especially influenced by same-sex role models? This might explain why committing crime appears to run in families.

The social approach

Earlier in this unit we considered whether criminal behaviour is best explained by biological factors, such as *genetics*. The focus of the next few pages is quite different. 'Social' refers to the influence of other people on our behaviour – so explanations of crime emphasise external influences on offending rather than biology.

In the 1960s Albert Bandura introduced *social learning theory* (*SLT*) which argues that crime is a learned behaviour which arises principally through interaction with the society that the criminal is a part of. (You learned about SLT in the psychological approaches and applications unit which is covered in our Year 1 'Certificate' book.)

Social learning theory and crime

Bandura began by trying to explain why some people behave more aggressively than others. He acknowledged that the urge to aggress is biological but the way we express our aggression is learned. It is learned in two ways:

- **Directly** – if a child is praised for performing a behaviour (such as snatching their toy back from another child) this makes it more likely that the child will repeat the same action. Equally if the child was punished for the same behaviour or the other child snatched it back this makes it less likely that the behaviour will be repeated. Gradually the child learns what behaviours 'work' and what behaviours to avoid.

- **Indirectly** – Bandura's particular contribution was to point out that many behaviours are learned through *observation* and *imitation* of the behaviour of others. In particular, children are heavily influenced by the people they look up to and want to be like, such as parents, older siblings, even teachers (*some* teachers!). These are called *role models*. As children become teenagers their role models may change, they may identify more with sports stars or famous musicians, for instance.

If children are surrounded by criminal role models when they are growing up, then they are much more likely to go on and commit crime themselves.

This becomes even more likely if criminal behaviour is seen to be rewarded. This is called *vicarious reinforcement* – the term *reinforcement* means 'strengthened' and *vicarious* means 'second-hand'.

There are many ways in which crime may be rewarded, such as through financial gain or increased status and respect within a gang. This may have a big impact on some people, making a life of crime appear more glamorous and attractive.

Modelling

We learn how to behave by observing role models. There are two ways in which the term *modelling* is used in SLT:

1. When someone (like a role model) demonstrates a specific behaviour, such as an experienced criminal showing somebody how to break into a car, they are said to be modelling that behaviour.
2. When the observer imitates that behaviour, by breaking into a car themselves, they are also said to be modelling the behaviour.

Gender differences

SLT can be used to explain gender differences – why boys and girls (men and women) behave differently. This may partly be due to their biology but is also due to modelling. Boys are more likely to identify with male role models and therefore model the behaviour shown by the men around them and in films etc. The same is true for girls. In this way boys and girls learn the behaviours considered appropriate in their society.

Specification terms

Modelling Either an observer imitates the behaviour of a model or a model demonstrates a behaviour that may be imitated by an observer.

Social learning theory (SLT) A way of explaining behaviour that includes both direct and indirect reinforcement, combining learning theory with the role of cognitive factors.

Students (over)acting a dramatic scene in a PSHE lesson. The girl on the right received a BAFTA nomination.

GET ACTIVE PSHE

Imagine you are a trainee teacher and you've been given the task of designing some PSHE lessons (personal, social, health and economic education). The lessons will be aimed at Year 9 and 10 students and are to do with resisting social pressure to get into crime. Three of the topics are:

- Not carrying a knife.
- Not taking drugs.
- Not cyberbullying.

You've been reading about social learning theory recently and are keen to use some of Bandura's ideas in the classroom. You are also keen to make the lessons as interactive as possible and get the students working in groups.

1. *In your lessons, how could you use the idea of modelling to illustrate the topics above?*
2. *How could you use the idea of vicarious reinforcement to illustrate the topics above?*

Evaluation

Gender differences

One strength of SLT is that evidence supports gender differences in learning.

In Bandura's most famous piece of research, children saw adults attacking a life-size inflatable doll (a 'Bobo' doll) in a playroom setting. When given their own doll to play with, children imitated the aggression they had seen, especially when the adult model was the same sex as the child. This suggests that the sex of the model is key, and that children are more likely to identify and imitate the behaviour of same-sex role models.

This increases the *validity* of the SLT explanation of how we imitate role models and how gender differences in behaviour occur.

Wide application

Another strength of SLT is that it can be applied to different types of crime.

Although experimental evidence has tended to focus on aggressive behaviour, SLT could account for lots of different types of crime. Indeed, it is possible that an individual could learn any crime, from tax evasion to armed robbery, through the combined influence of the processes of observation, imitation and vicarious reinforcement. This is an advantage when compared to biological explanations which concern themselves more with impulsive, violence-based crimes.

This wider application increases the usefulness of the social learning approach.

Causal issues

One weakness of SLT is there may be an issue with cause and effect.

SLT is built on the idea that observing others (role models) contributes to the learning of criminal behaviour. However, it is also possible that young people already have criminal attitudes, and then seek out peers who are similar to themselves (Siegel and McCormick 2006). This would explain why not everyone who is exposed to criminal attitudes and behaviour goes on to commit crime.

This suggests that association with deviant role models may be an effect of criminal behaviour rather than the cause itself.

Assessment practice

At the end of learning aim A you must write a report (see pages 115 and 130). This report must be related to a scenario or context. We have used a real-life context.

The Kray twins' childhood featured a great deal of violent and criminal activity. Members of the Kray family going back a few generations were street fighters. The twins themselves fought with other children and eventually adults in their neighbourhood.

John Wayne Gacy grew up in a violent household. His father was an alcoholic who often physically abused Gacy's mother in front of the children. Although Gacy tried hard to make his father proud of him, he was constantly unsuccessful.

A3.6 Learning aim A3 – Task 6

The third part of your report for learning aim A will be concerned with social explanations for criminality – these are covered on this spread and the next two spreads.

This activity will help you practise the skills required to write the report in response to your scenario/context.

1. **Explain** how the account of the Krays (and/or John Wayne Gacy) supports the social learning theory of criminality. (A.P1)
2. **Explain** how the research evidence supports the view that the Krays' (and/or John Wayne Gacy's) criminal behaviour developed through social learning. (A.P2)
3. **Discuss** the social learning theory with reference to the Kray twins' (and/or John Wayne Gacy's) criminality. (A.M1)
4. **Evaluate** the research evidence relating to social learning theory with reference to the Kray twins' (and/or John Wayne Gacy's) criminality. (A.D1)

An issue to consider

Not all children and adults are influenced by what they see. Not everyone who watches a violent film, or plays a violent video game, goes out and commits acts of violence themselves.

What factors do you think make some people more likely to be influenced than others? Is there anything society could do about that?

Specification content

A3 Social psychological explanations of criminality

- Social learning theory – Bandura, modelling, gender differences, as applied to criminality.

125

Differential association model

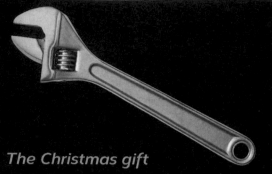

The Christmas gift

On Christmas Day 1969, four-year-old Bobby Bogle rushed downstairs to open the only gift he had received from his parents – a heavy metal wrench. That afternoon, Bobby and his brothers used the new present to break into a local store and steal soda. Bobby's father – a prolific criminal known locally as 'Rooster' – was delighted when he heard what his sons had done.

The children's lawbreaking was by no means a one-off for the Bogle family. The family's criminal activity spanned four generations and included the full range of offences, from burglary to insurance fraud, even murder!

Fox Butterfield, a psychologist who has studied the Bogles extensively, argues that the family breaks some popular myths about the causes of crime. For example, many researchers have suggested that people turn to crime through a lack of love, perhaps because of absent or neglecting parents. However, for the Bogles it was their strong family ties that lay at the heart of their offending. As Butterfield explains, when a Bogle broke the law, they did it out of love and respect for their parents, to make them proud and certainly not as an act of rebellion.

In the words of Tracey Bogle (one of Bobby's older brothers – yes, a brother), 'If I'd been raised in a family of doctors, I would probably be a doctor. But I was raised in a family of outlaws who hated the law'.

Source: *New York Post* (2018)

Key concepts of the model

Edwin Sutherland's (1939) *differential association model* of crime contains many of the same features as *social learning theory* (discussed on the previous spread). So much so that you could be forgiven for thinking that Sutherland was heavily influenced by the work of Bandura. In fact, Sutherland's theory predates Bandura's by about 35 years, so it may well be the other way around. Importantly, both theories share the belief that crime is a learned behaviour, rather than something that is influenced by biological factors.

Who – from whom is crime learned?

For Sutherland, crime is acquired in the same way as any other behaviour – through learning. In particular, individuals learn the values, attitudes, techniques and motives for criminal behaviour through associating with *different* people (therefore, *differential association*). These people tend to be 'significant others' who the child respects and looks up to, such as family members or a peer group. Note that this is very similar to the idea of children identifying with different *role models* in Bandura's theory.

Criminality comes about in two ways, through the learning of certain *attitudes* towards crime, and the learning of specific criminal *acts*.

How is crime learned?

When a person is socialised into a group they will be exposed to values and attitudes towards the law. In law-abiding families or peer groups, most of these attitudes are likely to be anti-criminal. However, in some circumstances (such as being raised in the Bogle family) a person may be exposed to many more pro-criminal attitudes than anti-criminal. When this happens, Sutherland argues, a person will go on to offend.

Indeed, Sutherland claimed that it is possible to predict exactly how likely it is that an individual will commit crime if we have knowledge of three things. These are the frequency (*how many*), intensity (*how strong*) and duration (*how long*) of pro-criminal attitudes the person has been exposed to. For example, if a teenager has been exposed to lots of strongly-held pro-criminal attitudes among family and friends, over a long period of time, then they are likely to see breaking the law as a reasonable thing to do.

What is learned?

Significant criminal others are not only a source of pro-criminal attitudes, they may also provide the novice offender with the techniques and skills for committing crime. This could include anything from picking a lock to fiddling financial accounts, to removing evidence from the scene of a crime!

Sutherland makes it clear that the learning of criminal acts may occur through *observation* and *imitation* on the part of the observer. Alternatively, criminal acts may be learned through deliberate, direct tuition on the part of the role model offender. This is like the two meanings of the term *modelling* discussed on the previous spread.

Specification term

Differential association model A social explanation for criminality which identifies what is learned (criminal attitudes as well as actual techniques), how it is learned (observation and imitation) and from whom (significant others, such as family members and friends).

In the aftermath of the devastation caused by Hurricane Katrina in 2005, most of the local residents were rehoused many miles away from where they grew up. David Kirk (2009) has studied how this affected those people who were ex-prisoners. Kirk was able to demonstrate how taking ex-prisoners out of the neighbourhood where they developed pro-criminal attitudes in the first place, made them significantly less likely to reoffend (reoffending rates reduced by 15% compared to national reoffending rates).

This study supports differential association theory and has important implications for how offenders might be dealt with.

Evaluation

Explanatory power

One strength of the differential association model is that it can account for crime in different sectors of society.

Sutherland recognised that some types of crime, such as burglary, may be more common in some communities, such as those where there are high levels of poverty (see the next spread). However, it is also the case that some forms of crime, such as financial crime, are found in particular social groups, such as the more wealthy sections of the population. Sutherland introduced the term 'white-collar crime' to describe middle-class crimes in this category.

This strengthens the theory as it can explain how shared norms and values can account for crime in many different contexts.

Alternative explanations

One weakness of the differential association model is that intergenerational crime could be explained by other theories.

Sutherland argues that the response of the family is crucial in how the child's value system develops. If the family makes crime seem more legitimate and reasonable then this could explain why offending seems to run in families so often. However, such intergenerational crime could just as easily be explained by the fact that family members share genetics, as well as learned values.

This means that it is very difficult to disentangle the influence of nature and nurture in relation to criminal behaviour.

Negative stereotyping

A further weakness is that the differential association model may lead to negative stereotyping of 'at-risk' children.

Not everyone who is exposed to pro-criminal attitudes goes on to commit crime. Similarly, the positive effect of being raised in a criminal family – in the sense of not wanting to follow in a parent's footsteps – should not be underestimated. Differential association risks stereotyping people who come from impoverished, offending families as inevitably criminal, when this may not be the case.

This means that the differential association model ignores the ability of people to make conscious decisions about their behaviour.

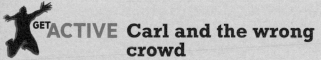

GET ACTIVE Carl and the wrong crowd

Carl's form tutor is talking to a fellow teacher about Carl's progress this year.

'Oh no, Carl's subject grades have fallen again. I'm dreading telling his mum and dad at parents' evening as they are so supportive and really want him to do well. I've taught both of Carl's brothers and they were brilliant A-star students.'

'I feel so sorry for Carl's parents. They've really tried to get him to change his friendship group who are such a bad influence. He's been hanging around with them for the last couple of years. They are local lads who don't go to this school.'

'Some of the lads in the form used to be friendly with Carl but aren't any more. They told me Carl's gang has been in trouble with the police, and that Carl has been caught shoplifting. I bet his parents were distraught.'

1. *Explain how Carl's behaviour could be interpreted as supporting differential association theory.*

2. *Why could it be argued that Carl's case is poor support for the genetic explanation of crime?*

Sutherland came up with the term 'white-collar crime' to refer to financial crimes, such as fraud, carried out by the middle classes. So, not necessarily people who go around stealing white collars then...

Assessment practice

At the end of learning aim A you must write a report (see pages 115 and 130). This report must be related to a scenario or context. We have used a real-life context.

Read again the accounts of the Kray twins on previous spreads.

From what you have read about the Kray twins, consider how aspects of their family background may be relevant to their later criminal activities. Think about: who the Krays most likely learned their criminal behaviour from, how they learned their pro-criminal attitudes and what they learned (as well as pro-criminal attitudes).

A3.7 Learning aim A3 – Task 7

The third part of your report for learning aim A will be concerned with social explanations for criminality – these are covered on the previous spread, this spread and the next spread.

1. **Explain** how the account of the Krays supports the differential association model. (A.P1)

2. **Explain** how the research evidence supports the view that the Kray's family background contributed to their criminality. (A.P2)

3. **Discuss** the differential association model with reference to the development of criminality in the Kray twins. (A.M1)

4. **Evaluate** the research evidence relating to the differential association model with reference to criminality in the Kray twins. (A.D1)

An issue to consider

In a typical prison, there will be a combination of young and inexperienced offenders surrounded by other, more experienced offenders.

Can you think why differential association theory would suggest this could be a problem? How might this influence how effectively prisoners can be reformed/rehabilitated?

Specification content

A3 Social psychological explanations of criminality

● Differential association model – what, how, and from whom criminal behaviour is learned.

Effects of upbringing on criminal behaviour

A tale of two homes

We referred on page 124 to the disturbing death of James Bulger in 1993. James was murdered by two ten-year-old boys, Jon Venables and Robert Thompson (pictured), after being led away from his mother at a busy shopping centre in Liverpool.

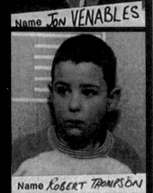

Name Jon VENABLES

Name Robert THOMPSON

There was much written, mostly by UK newspapers, about how these children had been 'born evil', the product of some innate, devilish influence.

Amid the outrage, relatively little attention was paid – until later in the boys' trial – to the upbringing that Thompson and Venables had experienced. Robert Thompson was part of what the judge described as a 'terribly dysfunctional family'. The fifth of seven children, Thompson's mother was an alcoholic who often left the children to fend for themselves (his father had left the family home five years earlier). An NSPCC case conference reported that the boys in the Thompson household grew up frightened of each other – they 'bit, hammered, battered and tortured each other' (*The Guardian*, 2000).

Jon Venables' parents lived in separate households but with shared responsibility for childcare. Jon's brother and sister both had learning difficulties and were taught in special schools (Venables himself was diagnosed with hyperactivity). His mother was severely depressed and sometimes violent. The court heard how Venables would pile up his toys around his bed as protection, fearful that his mother may attack him.

Prime Minister Tony Blair visits a Sure Start centre, a programme initiated by the Labour government in 1998 to offer support in early learning and childcare to economically disadvantaged families (as well as health support and links to local job centres). This initiative was based on psychological research that demonstrated the importance of emotional care, especially in relation to criminal behaviour.

The programme received considerable government and council finance until funding was cut by successive governments. Studies have suggested some positive outcomes for Sure Start though others claim that the programme did not run long enough for an accurate assessment to be made.

Upbringing and criminal behaviour

Social learning theory and the *differential association model* both support the view that criminal behaviour is learned within a social context. They point to key processes of *observation* and *imitation* as the reasons why crime can often run in families.

However, other commentators have drawn attention to other, less direct 'risk' factors that may make some children more vulnerable to committing crime. These are controversial views because there is a danger that children may be stereotyped as criminal purely on the basis of their family background.

Disrupted families

'Disruption' in this context may refer to a number of different factors and does not only describe those families where parents may have separated or divorced.

A detailed study by David Farrington *et al.* (1994), called the *Cambridge study in delinquent development* aimed to identify family risk factors in crime. Over 400 white working-class males were followed from age 8 to age 32 (a *longitudinal study*). At the end of the study 40% had criminal convictions. A minority (7%) were defined as 'chronic offenders' (i.e. persistent) and they were responsible for many of the crimes that were recorded.

It was observed that these chronic offenders had often been raised in 'disrupted families' which included, for example, a single parent, a delinquent sibling or a convicted parent.

Maternal deprivation

In the 1950s the *psychiatrist* John Bowlby proposed that healthy emotional development depends on receiving continuous care from your mother (or mother-figure) for the first two or three years of your life. Bowlby called this period the *critical period* to emphasise its importance in the child's development. He argued that the absence of a stable and secure loving bond *(attachment)* between the child and its mother during this critical period would lead to a range of emotional and behavioural consequences.

These consequences included delinquency (petty crime as a teenager or young adult), low intelligence, depression and the development of a personality type called *affectionless psychopathy* – characterised by a lack of guilt and empathy for other people. Bowlby claimed, controversially, that these consequences were irreversible, and would result in lifelong changes to the child's behaviour and character.

Poverty

The *Peterborough Youth Study* (Wikström 2003) was designed to investigate government figures which showed that the most deprived (poorest) 5% of the country were 100 times more likely to have multiple problems (police contact, alcohol abuse, etc) than those in the most advantaged 20%.

Over 1900 pupils (aged 14–15) from state schools in the Peterborough area completed *questionnaires*. They were asked to *self-report* on criminal activity including robbery and theft either of or from a car. It was revealed that a large percentage of males (45%) and a relatively large percentage of females (31%) had committed at least one of the crimes. Frequent offenders often came from economically-deprived backgrounds. They also tended to have other risk factors such as poor self-control, drink and drug problems, truancy and poor parental monitoring.

The study suggests that crime is complex and comes about because of a variety of home-based causes including poverty.

Evaluation

Demonising groups

One weakness of research into effects of upbringing is that it may demonise people because of their background.

As we have seen in the rest of this unit, crime is very complex and could be explained by a variety of different factors: biological, psychological and social. An over-focus on upbringing and family background risks stigmatising certain groups as potential criminals or 'bad apples'. There is no straightforward causal relationship between family background, social circumstances and crime, and to assume there is would be to oversimplify a very complicated problem.

This suggests that any sweeping generalisations should not be made.

Criticism of Bowlby

One weakness of the maternal deprivation theory is that it confuses a number of different factors.

Bowlby described separation between a child and their mother-figure which made it sound as if physical separation was the issue. Research has shown that physical separation may not have harmful effects if good substitute emotional care is offered (Robertson and Bowlby 1952).

Other research has shown that having an emotionally-disturbed parent (lack of emotional care but no physical separation) may have lasting consequences on development (Radke-Yarrow *et al.* 1985).

This suggests that Bowlby's concept of maternal deprivation was too simple.

Poverty and crime

Another weakness is that growing up in poverty does not inevitably lead to crime.

When crime and poverty are discussed, the typical debate is about whether poverty breeds criminality, and to what extent. In reality, according to Peter Cuthbertson (2018), the vast majority of people living in deprived circumstances are law-abiding and not engaged in criminal activity. As well as this, Cuthbertson argues that one of the worst aspects of poverty in the UK, is that poor people are far more likely to be the victims of crime. This produces fear amongst poor communities, something that is rarely acknowledged in research.

This means that the poverty and crime hypothesis may obscure some important facts about the lived experience of crime amongst the poor.

GET ACTIVE The diathesis-stress model

Having considered several theories of crime, it seems unlikely that crime can be fully explained by a single influence alone.

To take one example, you might assume that gene variations which produce low levels of MAO-A (see page 116) are very rare. However, research suggests that low gene activity is seen in approximately a third of the population. If this is true, why are there not many more violent criminals in society?

For a possible answer, we turn once again to the diathesis-stress model. Remember, this theory argues that criminal behaviour is best explained as the outcome of biological/genetic factors, plus some form of environmental or biological 'trigger'.

A study by Giovanni Frazzetto *et al.* (2007) looked at a group of adult males with the low-activity form of the MAOA gene. As we might expect, some of these males were violent and aggressive. However, this was only the case if they had experienced some sort of trauma during their upbringing, such as physical or sexual abuse.

1. *How does Frazzetto* et al.*'s study support the diathesis-stress model of crime?*

2. *Which theory of crime are you most persuaded by? Which is the least plausible?*

Do we tend to think that family members all behave the same as one another? Could that lead to stereotyping of people with criminal (or superhero) backgrounds?

Assessment practice

At the end of learning aim A you must write a report (see pages 115 and 130). This report must be related to a scenario or context. We have used a real-life context.

Read again the accounts of the Kray twins on previous spreads. Also consider the following:

The Kray family lived alongside some of Britain's poorest people in London's East End. Both boys contracted the (then often fatal) disease diphtheria at the age of three years. Reggie was in hospital for almost three months and Ronnie for at least six, separated most of that time from other family members, including their mother Violet.

A3.8 Learning aim A3 – Task 8

The third part of your report for learning aim A will be concerned with social explanations for criminality – these are covered on this spread and the previous two spreads.

This activity will help you practise the skills required to write the report in response to your scenario/context.

1. **Explain** how the account of the Kray family supports the view that upbringing has effects on criminality. (A.P1)

2. **Explain** how the research evidence supports the view that the Kray twins' upbringing affected their criminal behaviour. (A.P2)

3. **Discuss** the 'effects of upbringing' explanation with reference to the Kray twins' criminal behaviour. (A.M1)

4. **Evaluate** the research evidence relating to the effects of upbringing with reference to the Kray twins' criminality. (A.D1)

An issue to consider

It has often been said that crime is not the product of sick individuals but the product of a sick society.

To what extent do you agree with this statement?

Specification content

A3 Social psychological explanations of criminality

● The effects of upbringing on criminal behaviour:
  ○ Disrupted families.
  ○ Maternal deprivation.
  ○ Poverty.

Learning aim A

Assessment guidance

Learning aim A assessment

You are required to produce one or more reports (but not more than three) for the three learning aims in this unit.

You can, if you wish, combine the report for learning aim A with the report for learning aim B and/or C. No learning aim can be subdivided.

The specification recommends three reports for Unit 4.

The report can be written or presented as a poster, PowerPoint or other form.

The report for learning aim A can only be completed after you have studied the content of learning aim A as it is a synoptic assessment (see 'Synoptic assessment' on the facing page).

Recommended assessment approach

The *Delivery Guide for Unit 4* states that your report (or presentation, poster, etc.) for learning aim A:

- Is likely to be theoretical in nature and consider how theories and research are used to explain criminal behaviour.

Assignment briefs

The board supplies suggested assignment briefs which you can use – see *Unit 4 Authorised assignment brief for Learning aim A.*

Your centre can also devise their own assignment brief which should have a vocational scenario/context and a series of tasks to complete.

Vocational scenario	The task (from the assignment brief)
The *Delivery Guide for Unit 4* suggests that a scenario might present, for example, a case study with a request for a report from another professional, e.g. Probation Service, Judge, Prison Governor to explain an individual's, or group of individuals', behaviour.	Produce a detailed report that examines how psychological approaches and research can be used to explain criminal behaviour. Your report should include the following: • An **explanation** of the use of psychological approaches with supporting evidence in the explanation of criminal behaviour. (See pass criteria below.) • A **discussion** of the explanations of criminal behaviour utilising psychological research. (See merit criteria below.) • An **evaluation** of the use of psychological approaches and research to explain criminal behaviour. (See distinction criteria below.)

Assessment information

Your final report will be awarded a Distinction (D), Merit (M), Pass (P), Near Pass (N) or Unclassified (U).

The specification provides criteria for each level as shown below.

Pass	Merit	Distinction
A.P1 EXPLAIN the use of psychological approaches to examine criminal behaviour.		
A.P2 EXPLAIN research supporting psychological explanations of criminal behaviour.		
	A.M1 DISCUSS explanations of criminal behaviour using psychological research.	
		A.D1 EVALUATE the use of psychological approaches and research to explain criminal behaviour.

Marking factors The specification also provides information that an assessor will take into consideration when marking your assignment.

Marking factors	Pass	Merit	Distinction
Biological explanations of criminal behaviour will be ...	... investigated including inheritability of criminal behaviour.	... discussed ... ... and judgements made including the results and conclusions of the research ... ... and an evaluation of its methodological strengths and weaknesses.	... evaluated in terms of validity ... ... and will consider the strengths and weaknesses of each explanation.
Individual differences explanations of criminal behaviour will be ...	... investigated including traits of a criminal and cognitive factors.		
Social psychological explanations of criminal behaviour will be ...	... investigated.		
In addition ...	... learners will reference research on which these theories are based.	... judgements will include an appreciation of the different patterns of criminal behaviour.	... learners' evaluations will consider the impact of different crimes on society.

Self-review checklist

Writing a big report requires organisation and planning. You learned about time management as part of the unit on conducting psychological research (in our Year 1 'Certificate' book). Apply those skills to writing your report for this unit.

It is important to set yourself target dates at the outset.

It is also important to write at least two drafts.

First draft

Remember this is a *draft*. So you can write anything, just get thoughts on the page (see 'Blank page syndrome' on page 147). But do not copy anything, even at this stage (see 'Plagiarism' on the right).

Date to complete first draft:

	Date completed	Explain (A.P1)	Explain (A.P2)	Discuss (A.M1)	Evaluate (A.D1)
• In the first grey column enter the completion dates for each section of your report. • As you write each section tick the yellow boxes when you have explained, discussed and evaluated, as appropriate.					
A1 Biological explanations of criminality					
Inherited criminality					
Low gene activity					
Role of the amygdala and aggression					
A2 Individual differences explanations of criminality					
Eysenck's theory of criminality					
Cognitive factors and criminality					
A3 Social psychological explanations of criminality					
Social learning theory					
Differential association model					
Effects of upbringing on criminal behaviour					
References compiled					

Second draft

The next step is to revise your first document. Below is a checklist of things to consider.

Date to complete second draft:

	Date completed
I have checked that I have covered each of the four marking factors (grey column) in the table on the facing page.	
I have gone through and deleted any irrelevant material.	
I have checked that every point has some evidence to back it up.	
I have identified long sentences and rephrased them.	
I have checked that each paragraph deals with one idea.	
I have corrected any spelling mistakes.	
I have checked that each paragraph makes reference to the scenario/context.	

Final draft

Read through your completed second draft to polish the report.

Date to complete final draft:

Referencing

If you cite any research study or source (such as a website) you need to include this in a list of references at the end of your report.

The conventions for referencing are described on page 160.

Command terms used in this unit

The assessment criteria for learning aims A, B and C use the following command terms:

Assess = Consider factors that apply to a specific situation, come to a conclusion.

Discuss = Identify and investigate all aspects of an issue or situation.

Evaluate = Consider strengths/weaknesses, come to a conclusion.

Explain = State and then justify or give an example.

Produce = Apply knowledge to a plan or report.

Synoptic assessment

This assessment is synoptic. Synoptic refers to the ability to provide an overview of many different strands of information.

In your assessment you must demonstrate that you can identify and use effectively, in an integrated way, an appropriate selection of skills, techniques, concepts, theories and knowledge from across the whole unit as relevant to this task.

Plagiarism

Plagiarism means to use someone else's work without crediting the source. It means to steal and pass off the words (or ideas) of another as one's own.

All the work submitted as your internal assessments must be your own. We are lucky to have the internet at our fingertips when writing this book and we often cut and paste content into our notes – and it is very easy to forget we have done this. However, we know this can be easily checked and if we were found to have committed plagiarism in our book we would be accused of committing a crime and could be fined or receive a prison sentence for plagiarising someone else's work.

The same is true for you – it is tempting to use something written on a website or in this book and feel 'I can't say it as well as this' and therefore copy it exactly. You cannot do that unless the sentence is in quotes and attributed to the author.

We take great care to ensure that all of our sentences are our own. You must do the same or you will be disqualified from this exam.

Imprisonment

Police poster campaign criticised

Colin Joyce was a member of the notorious Manchester-based Gooch Gang. He received life imprisonment for his part in the murders of gangsters Ucal Chin and Tyrone Gilbert alongside a range of drug and gun offences.

The Manchester police created a poster with a picture of Colin Joyce alongside a computer-generated image of Joyce in 35 years' time. These were then displayed on huge billboards around the city. Chief Constable Peter Fahy believed the posters would deter would-be gangsters from committing a crime which would put them in prison until they were very old.

He said, 'I hope that these images will make those people thinking of embarking on this type of lifestyle think again – life is a very long time.'

However, human rights groups have criticised the poster campaign for sending out the wrong message about the aims of prison. They argue that the objective of prison is to rehabilitate and reform criminals rather than make an example of them.

Source: *The Telegraph* (2009)

What do high rates of recidivism suggest about the effectiveness of prison? Which of the aims of imprisonment are not being met?

Specification terms

Deterrence The act of discouraging offending through fear of the consequences.

Imprisonment Being held captive.

Incapacitation Preventing further crime by physically isolating an offender.

Institutionalisation A deficit in social and life skills that comes about after a long period in an institution such as a prison.

Punitive punishment A form of discipline that is intended to be harsh (even draconian) and it is the harshness that should discourage further criminal behaviour.

Recidivism When a convicted criminal reoffends.

Rehabilitation The reintegration of an offender into society.

The aims of imprisonment

The most common way of dealing with criminal behaviour is *imprisonment*. Offenders are punished by having their freedom taken away and must remain behind bars for a specified period, their sentence, which is determined by a judge.

People disagree about what prison is for. Some would argue that prison should be more than simply a *punishment* for wrongdoing, it should also aim to reform or *rehabilitate* the offender, so they are less likely to reoffend.

It may be that prison achieves both of these aims – punishment and rehabilitation. Or alternatively achieves neither! We will explore some of the arguments below.

Incapacitation

One aim that prison definitely achieves is that of *incapacitation*. The offender is removed from society with the intention of protecting the public. However, the need for this varies depending on the nature of the offence. For example, the public will obviously require more protection from a serial killer or child abuser than an individual who is refusing to pay their council tax.

Punitive punishment or rehabilitation

The *punitive punishment* model is based on the argument that an offender should suffer for what they have done, and one way of doing this is to deprive them of their liberty. In biblical terms, this is an 'eye for an eye', in the sense that society is taking its revenge on the offender, and the level of suffering should reflect the seriousness of the crime. A victim of the crime, or friends and family of the victim, may feel a need for revenge which is satisfied by punishment.

In contrast, others see *rehabilitation* as the main point of putting offenders in prison. When they are released, offenders should leave prison as 'better people' ready to take back their place in society. For this reason, an important part of prison is the opportunity to develop new skills, participate in education, and access training or treatment programmes. There should also be the opportunity for the offender to consider what drove them to commit crime in the first place.

Deterrence

Finally, the nature of the prison experience is designed to discourage the offender (or other would-be offenders) from participating in crime in the future. *Deterrence* works on two levels.

First, *general deterrence* aims to send a message to members of society that crime will not be tolerated, and an unpleasant consequence of prison is likely to occur as a result.

Second, *individual deterrence* is meant to ensure that the offender is less likely to commit crime again on their release, having experienced the 'short, sharp shock' of prison.

Recidivism

The main aim of deterrence is to prevent *recidivism*, which is another name for reoffending. High recidivism rates are a major problem. For instance, a Ministry of Justice report in 2013 stated that nearly 60% of UK offenders will reoffend within a year of release, and in 14 prisons in England and Wales, this is as high as 70%.

Rates of reoffending are not as high in other countries (for instance, in Norway rates were as low as 20% in 2017). However, what do high rates of recidivism suggest about the effectiveness of prison? Which of the aims of imprisonment are not being met?

Evaluation

Treatment and training

One strength of imprisonment is that it may provide opportunities for treatment and training.

Around half of violent criminals in UK prisons have a problem with *substance abuse*. Prisons may enable access to help. Also, on entry, many prisoners receive an individual learning plan to support the development of basic skills including literacy and computing. The availability of these courses may depend on factors such as the level of overcrowding in the prison, staff-to-prisoner ratios and prison funding.

The consequence is that access to treatment and training may contribute to offenders making positive changes in their lives.

Psychological effects of prison

One weakness of imprisonment is that it may affect mental health.

For many, the prison system can be a traumatic experience. In 2016, the National Audit Office reported that there were 40,161 incidents of self-harm in prisons and 120 suicides. Similarly, the Prison Reform Trust in 2014 found a significant proportion of prisoners reported symptoms of serious mental disorder (around 15% of male prisoners and 25% of females).

This suggests that imprisonment is not only ineffective in rehabilitating offenders but may end up making some situations much worse.

Institutionalisation

Another weakness of imprisonment is that prisoners may become *institutionalised*.

Some prisoners may become so accustomed to the routines associated with prison life that they struggle to readjust 'on the outside' once they are released. This is particularly likely for those who have experienced a long sentence. It is also the case that behaviours that are considered unacceptable in society are encouraged and rewarded in prison. This means that offenders may be ill-equipped to rebuild their lives after prison.

This therefore casts doubt on the ability of prison to reform and rehabilitate because repeat offences are more likely if prisoners struggle to adapt to non-prison life.

GET ACTIVE Summing up

A judge was summing up the case of a serial offender.

'Ladies and gentlemen of the jury, Nick Lotts stands before you today, a serial burglar who has caused devastation to the lives of others for many years. He has shown little remorse in this courtroom and I have no doubt he will offend again. Now it is his turn to pay.

For these reasons, I am passing a sentence of eight years in prison. The public need protecting from his crimes, and the defendant, like other people engaging in similar behaviour, must recognise that such actions will not be tolerated. Perhaps in prison the defendant will reflect on the distress he has caused and will learn to mend his ways.'

1. Which aims of imprisonment are identified in the judge's summing up above?

2. How effective do you think prison is in achieving these aims?

Assessment practice

At the end of learning aim B you must write:

A report exploring the effectiveness of different methods and punishments of criminal behaviour.

This report must be related to a scenario or context. We have used two real-life contexts.

The Kray twins' were sentenced in 1969 to life imprisonment, with a minimum of 30 years before consideration for parole (the longest sentences ever given for murder at the Central Criminal Court). As a Category A prisoner, Ronnie Kray was denied many everyday freedoms such as socialising with other prisoners. He was transferred to a secure hospital (Broadmoor) and died in 1995 without being released. Reggie was released on compassionate grounds and died of cancer in 2000.

John McVicar was an armed robber ('Britain's Most Wanted'). He was sentenced to 26 years' imprisonment in 1970, having already escaped from prison twice. He took advantage of the educational opportunities offered to him in prison by earning three A levels and a sociology degree. He was released on parole in 1978 and eventually became a writer, journalist and sociologist.

B1.1 Learning aim B1 – Task 1

The first part of your report for learning aim B will be concerned with methods of punishing criminal behaviour and the effectiveness of these methods – these are covered on this spread and the next three spreads.

This activity will help you practise the skills required to write the report in response to your scenario/context.

1. **Explain** how the experience of the Krays illustrates the use of imprisonment as a way of punishing criminal behaviour, with reference to psychological theory. (B.P4)

2. **Explain** how the experience of John McVicar illustrates the use of imprisonment as a form of rehabilitation, with reference to psychological theory. (B.P4)

3. **Assess** the effectiveness of imprisonment with reference to the experiences of both the Kray twins and John McVicar. (B.M2)

4. **Evaluate** the impact of imprisonment with reference to the experiences of both the Kray twins and John McVicar. (B.D2)

An issue to consider

We have seen how the problem of recidivism/reoffending is something that calls the effectiveness of the prison system into question.

What other ways of dealing with offending behaviour are you aware of? Are these methods more or less likely to deal with the problem of recidivism?

Specification content

B1 Punishing criminal behaviour

Effectiveness, and social and ethical implications of punishment methods.

● Imprisonment – incapacitation, punitive punishment or rehabilitation, deterrence, i.e. recidivism rates, effect of institutionalisation when released, mental health and suicide rates in prison.

Zero tolerance

Car trouble

In 1969, Philip Zimbardo conducted an unusual experiment. He arranged for two cars to be abandoned in two different neighbourhoods in the US. One was in the Bronx area of New York, a place where there are high rates of poverty and crime. The other was left in the affluent middle-class suburb of Palo Alto, California. The two cars were identical: the same make and model, both had their registration plates removed and the hoods (bonnets) were up.

In the Bronx, no more than ten minutes had passed before the car was attacked by vandals. Within twenty-four hours pretty much everything of value had been removed, including the radiator and battery. The car was smashed, the interior was destroyed, and it was quickly reduced to a pile of junk.

In Palo Alto, the car sat untouched for a week without even a scratch. That was until Zimbardo himself smashed part of the car with a sledgehammer. Shortly after, passers-by were joining in, wrecking the car with the hammer. Within hours, it lay on its roof, utterly demolished like its Bronx counterpart.

Specification terms

War on drugs A term first used by President Nixon in the 1970s. The *war on drugs* is a campaign, led by the US government, on drug prohibition, with the aim of reducing the illegal drug trade in America. The initiative includes a set of drug policies that are intended to discourage the production, distribution and consumption of illegal drugs.

Zero tolerance An approach to law enforcement that involves consistent and aggressive policing of what is sometimes referred to as 'petty crime'. The aim is to reduce antisocial behaviour and decrease fear of crime amongst the general public.

Zero tolerance

The term *zero tolerance* refers to a style of policing which tries to prevent the development of antisocial norms, i.e. where the community comes to accept that certain undesirable behaviours are usual and just have to be accepted.

Adopting this approach to dealing with criminal behaviour involves relentless attempts to maintain social order. Minor offences, such as littering, graffiti and vandalism, are subject to aggressive 'crackdowns' and harsh punishments in the same way that more serious crimes, such as assault or burglary, would be.

Broken windows theory

Zero tolerance has its origins in a theory developed by James Wilson and George Kelling in 1982. The *broken windows theory* suggests that if a particular area falls into disrepair, and it appears that no one cares about it, further and deliberate damage will follow (as in the abandoned cars experiment on the left).

This is an analogy for how social order can rapidly deteriorate within particular societies. For instance, if someone leaves graffiti on a wall this will lead others to do the same, as it appears no one is in charge of the situation, no one cares, and there are no consequences for acting in this way. Once a situation arises in which *prosocial* norms are bypassed and ignored, crime becomes more likely.

From this perspective, zero tolerance policing is seen as a preventative strategy which seeks to eliminate social disorder before it starts.

The US model

Although zero tolerance policies have been implemented in a number of places (parts of London, Hartlepool and Middlesbrough in the UK), they are most associated with the policing strategy of the New York Police Department (NYPD) in the 1990s.

The Police Commissioner at the time, Bill Bratton, was responsible for its introduction even though he has described zero tolerance as a 'troublesome' term that does not capture the full complexity of what went on in New York. Put simply, the NYPD strategy:

- Set clear goals and plans for crime reduction.
- Transferred policing responsibility from a national to a local level.
- Focused on quality of life and the targeting of crime 'hot-spots'.

Based on the broken windows model, low-level disorder was tackled quickly and punished harshly to prevent it escalating.

The 'war on drugs'

One significant example of zero tolerance policing was America's well-documented *war on drugs* in the 1980s and 1990s. The then president, Ronald Reagan, popularised a 'moralist' approach to recreational drugs with harsher punishments for users, leading to much higher rates of *imprisonment*. The number of people behind bars for drug offences in the US skyrocketed from 50,000 in 1980 to 400,000 by 1997.

The war on drugs focused its efforts on minimising drug use at street level rather than funding preventative measures such as education or treatment programmes. Thus, specific policing tactics targeted small-time dealers and raids on properties where individual drug use was known to be taking place – so-called 'crack houses' – were commonplace.

As part of the 'war on drugs', police used zero tolerance strategies to try to disrupt dealing of recreational drugs at street level.

GET ACTIVE Possibilities for system abuse

Zero tolerance hands the police new powers, such as the ability to 'stop and search' (known as 'stop and frisk' in America). The assumption is that the police will implement these powers in a fair and even-handed way. However, Lisa Moore and Amy Elkavich (2008) point out that the number of people serving prison time for drug offences is 13 times higher for black males than white males (despite the fact that black males are no more likely to take drugs than whites).

1. *What does this statistic suggest?*

2. *Why is this a problem for zero tolerance? And society more generally?*

Evaluation

Evidence of effectiveness

One strength of zero tolerance is that it has proved effective in reducing crime.

Analysis of the 1990s New York model of zero tolerance indicates that it had a positive impact on rates of serious crime. Franklin Zimring (2011) notes that between 1990 and 2009, rates of murder went down by 82% in New York, compared to a 56% drop across nine other similar-sized US cities during the same time frame.

This suggests policing based on the broken windows model may yield positive outcomes in the real world.

Other factors

One weakness is that crime may have reduced for other reasons.

The striking reduction in incidence of murder in New York in the 1990s would appear to lend support to the effectiveness of zero tolerance strategies. However, Benjamin Bowling (1999) questions whether it was necessarily a change in policing approach that made 'all the difference'. He points to an unprecedented 'murder spike' in the five years before 1990 due to widespread use of crack cocaine which decreased sharply in the early '90s. It may be that the apparent success of zero tolerance was because drug markets became more stable, and the crime rate was falling anyway.

This suggests that the success of zero tolerance, at least in New York, may have been oversold by its supporters.

Consequences of the drugs war

One weakness of the war on drugs policy is that it had negative consequences.

By the late 1990s, most of its proponents were forced to concede that the so-called 'war on drugs' had failed. Zero tolerance had resulted in the imprisonment of many, but street-level drug use was merely displaced to other areas, rather than reduced. Worse, the war on drugs has been blamed for an increase in the risk of HIV transmission as money from safe syringe and treatment programmes was diverted (Cooper *et al.* 2005). In 1993, the *National Institute on Drug Abuse* estimated that 2.5 million drug users could have benefited from treatment but less than half of those were – because the US government was spending three times more on drug law enforcement than treatment.

This suggests that the US government's war on drugs may have taken money away from other more effective strategies.

Assessment practice

At the end of learning aim B you must write a report (see pages 133 and 146). This report must be related to a scenario or context. We have used a real-life context.

Detective Superintendent Ray Mallon was head of Middlesbrough CID. The tabloid newspapers loved him and gave him the nickname 'Robocop' because of his 'hardline, no-nonsense' approach. In 1996 Mallon promised he would cut the crime rate in his area by 20% in 18 months, and if he failed he would resign. He fulfilled his promise through zero tolerance – uncompromising policing of 'trivial' offences, particularly burglary and street crimes such as drunkenness and disorder around nightclubs. Mallon's officers used 'stop and search' freely and he oversaw the introduction of CCTV across the city.

B1.2 Learning aim B1 – Task 2

The first part of your report for learning aim B will be concerned with methods of punishing criminal behaviour and the effectiveness of these methods – these are covered on the previous spread, this spread and the next two spreads.

1. **Explain** how the experience of Ray Mallon illustrates the use of zero tolerance as a way of punishing criminal behaviour, with reference to psychological theory. (B.P4)

2. **Assess** the effectiveness of zero tolerance with reference to the example of Ray Mallon. (B.M2)

3. **Evaluate** the impact of zero tolerance with reference to the example of Ray Mallon. (B.D2)

An issue to consider

Do you think zero tolerance policing is something that should be adopted more widely? Should the US model be a feature of policing in this country? Justify your argument.

Specification content

B1 Punishing criminal behaviour

Effectiveness, and social and ethical implications of punishment methods.

● Zero tolerance – US model, 'war on drugs', possibilities for system abuse.

Offender disclosure schemes

Sarah Payne

Sarah Payne of Hersham, Surrey was out playing with her two elder brothers and younger sister when she disappeared on 1 July 2000. Sarah was just eight years old at the time. A nationwide search failed to produce any clues as to the little girl's whereabouts, and Sarah's parents made several appeals on television in the hope of securing her safe return.

But Sarah never did come home and her body was subsequently discovered in a field in Pulborough, 15 miles away from where she had been playing a fortnight earlier. Seventeen months later, Sussex Police had gathered sufficient forensic evidence to charge Roy Whiting with Sarah's abduction and murder.

Whiting, who was on the sex offender registry, had already been questioned within 24 hours of Sarah's death. Following his conviction for her murder, he is currently serving a minimum 40-year jail term.

Specification term

Offender disclosure schemes Members of the community can apply to the police if they suspect someone they have come into contact with has a criminal record. Police may then disclose the information to the applicant. This covers child sexual offences to protect children at risk, as well as people who may be in danger of domestic violence.

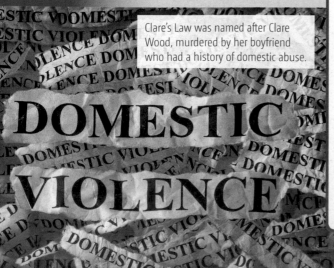

Clare's Law was named after Clare Wood, murdered by her boyfriend who had a history of domestic abuse.

Offender disclosure schemes

Offender disclosure is a collective term for schemes that allow members of the general public to access information about the criminal history of people they know or come into contact with.

There are two types of disclosure – the *Child sex offender disclosure scheme* (often called *Sarah's Law*) and the *Domestic violence disclosure scheme* (often called *Clare's Law*). Both are relatively recent additions to the statute book and are based on the same principle – that if someone is concerned about a person they have come into contact with, they should be able to know whether that person has been convicted of a crime in the past.

Offender disclosure schemes as a form of punishment

Offender disclosure schemes are a form of punishing criminal behaviour. Any *punishment* is designed to keep the public safe and protect them from harm. In this sense, giving the public access to information about past child sexual abuse or domestic violence shames the offender and is a 'pre-emptive strike' preventing similar incidents from happening in the future.

The child sex offender disclosure scheme

This scheme allows parents, carers or guardians to ask the police to tell them if someone has a criminal record for child sexual offences. The need for this arises when parents are concerned that someone who is having regular contact with their child may have a history of child abuse.

If police checks confirm this to be the case, the police will consider sharing this information. However, this will only occur if the police believe that disclosure is in the best interests of the child – that is, continued exposure to the person may place the child at risk.

In the event of a disclosure, the police will confidentially reveal details of past offences to the parents. Under the scheme, police are also able to warn parents if concerns have been raised by third parties, such as grandparents or neighbours.

Sarah's Law The child sex offender disclosure scheme was established following the death of Sarah Payne (see left). Sarah's mother and father, supported by the *News of the World* newspaper, subsequently campaigned for a change in the law, to allow access to the sex offender registry, so parents could know whether a convicted child sex offender was living in their area. The first pilot of Sarah's Law (as it became known) occurred in four areas of the UK in 2008. In 2010, the scheme was extended to cover the whole of England and Wales after the pilot was judged to be successful by the Home Office.

The domestic violence disclosure scheme

This scheme is very similar to Sarah's Law and allows people to find out from police if their partner has a history of domestic violence. This may be particularly relevant when someone begins a relationship and suspects their new partner may have violent tendencies. An application for disclosure can be made by the individual or might also be sought by the friends or relatives of the person embarking on the new relationship.

As with Sarah's Law, the police will check the criminal history of the partner and assess whether a disclosure needs to be made. Disclosures of this type cover all forms of relationship and are designed to protect people whether they are male or female, gay or straight, old or young, and so on.

Clare's Law The domestic violence disclosure scheme also came into force in the most tragic of circumstances. Mother-of-one Clare Wood was killed by her ex-boyfriend George Appleton who, it was later revealed, had a history of violence against women. In the weeks before she was murdered, Clare had contacted Greater Manchester Police several times explaining that she was being harassed by Appleton and that he was threatening to kill her. Sadly, Clare's calls were not acted upon and she was found dead at her Salford home in 2009, strangled by Appleton, just four months after ending their relationship.

As Sarah Payne's parents had done before him, Clare's grieving father, Michael Brown, campaigned for a change in the law. In 2014, the domestic violence disclosure scheme, or Clare's Law, was rolled out across the country as a result of Mr Brown's efforts.

GET ACTIVE Megan's Law

The US has its own version of Sarah's Law – it's called *Megan's Law* (following the murder of seven-year-old Megan Kanka in 1994). There are some key differences between Sarah's Law and Megan's Law. In the US, the public are given much more information about registered sex offenders than they are in the UK. Decisions on how much information is made available are governed by state law, but it is not unusual for sex offenders' names, addresses and photographs to appear on social media sites such as Facebook.

1. *Do you think Sarah's Law should more closely mirror Megan's Law in the US?*

2. *What do you think are the possible dangers associated with the US model of offender disclosure?*

Keeping Children Safe

Evaluation

Deterrent

One strength of offender disclosure schemes is that they may deter people from committing crime.

We saw how, in relation to custodial sentencing, one important role in punishing behaviour is that of *deterrence* – 'putting people off' committing crime due to fear of the consequences. Since the introduction of Sarah's Law and Clare's Law, offenders are now aware that they cannot easily leave their past crimes behind, as details of these may be disclosed in the future. Some critics, for instance Anne-Marie McAlinden (2005), have argued that this leads to the shaming and stigmatising of offenders and does not help them *rehabilitate*. That said, disclosure may prove to be an effective additional punishment for many offenders.

This suggests that Sarah's Law and Clare's Law may prevent some people from committing crime in the first place.

Hidden danger

One weakness of both Sarah's Law and Clare's Law is the hidden nature of the offences.

For offender disclosure schemes to work, police must have accurate records of past offences. However, critics have claimed many sexual offences against children and incidents of domestic violence do not feature on police statistics. Mark Williams-Thomas argues that there could be as many as 250,000 people in the UK with a sexual interest in children, but only around 30,000 currently appear on the sex offender registry (Sare 2008). Similarly, Kate Fitz-Gibbon and Sandra Walklate (2017) estimate that only around one in four domestic violence victims will report their experiences to the police.

This suggests that offender disclosure could lead to a false sense of security as police records may be inaccurate.

Removing responsibility

A further weakness of offender disclosure schemes is that they could remove responsibility from the police.

Critics have argued that both forms of offender disclosure would not actually have protected the people they were 'inspired' by. Sandra Horley, the Chief Executive of *Refuge* (a charity which supports abused women and their families), points out that Clare Wood was well aware her partner was violent prior to her death. Simply knowing that her partner was violent did not keep Clare safe – what she needed was swift and effective action by the police. Likewise, it is unlikely that Sarah's Law would have saved Sarah Payne. Whiting would have had to have raised suspicions in the local community and an application been made on Sarah's behalf – but these were not the circumstances in which she was murdered.

This suggests that it is important that offender disclosures are not seen as a substitute for strong protection from the police.

Assessment practice

At the end of learning aim B you must write a report (see pages 133 and 146). This report must be related to a scenario or context. We have provided a context for practice.

Gemma knew that her boyfriend had several convictions for assaulting his previous girlfriend. But she believed it could never happen to her because she was 'different'. Gemma's boyfriend punched her, put her head through a window and threatened to kill her. He was arrested but denied everything. Under the 'right to know' route of the domestic violence disclosure scheme, the police offered to give Gemma information about her boyfriend. She finally discovered the truth about him, and he was eventually jailed. Gemma used her 'right to ask' to request information about her new boyfriend.

B1.3 Learning aim B1 – Task 3

The first part of your report for learning aim B will be concerned with methods of punishing criminal behaviour and the effectiveness of these methods – these are covered on the previous two spreads, this spread and the next spread.

This activity will help you practise the skills required to write the report in response to your scenario/context.

1. **Explain** how Gemma's experience illustrates the use of offender disclosure schemes, with reference to psychological theory. (B.P4)

2. **Assess** the effectiveness of offender disclosure schemes with reference to Gemma's experience. (B.M2)

3. **Evaluate** the impact of offender disclosure schemes with reference to Gemma's experience. (B.D2)

> You can see an explanation of command terms and the assessment criteria on pages 131 and 146.

An issue to consider

It is perhaps difficult to consider the rights of an offender, but do you think they have any rights when disclosures are made (for instance, to object about the information that is being passed on)?

Or should offenders lose their rights as soon as they commit crimes of this nature?

Specification content

B1 Punishing criminal behaviour

Effectiveness, and social and ethical implications of punishment methods.

● Offender disclosure schemes.

Community sentences, fines and discharges

The Thirsk rail crash

In 1892, James Holmes was a signalman on the North Eastern railway. On the night of 2nd November, Holmes was operating a signal box about 3 miles from Thirsk. It was not a typical night for Holmes, he had been awake for 36 hours mourning the tragic death of his baby daughter. Holmes had begged the stationmaster to find a replacement for his shift, arguing that he was exhausted, distressed and unfit to work.

The replacement signalman never came, and Holmes was left to operate the signal box worrying about his grieving wife and the thick fog that was developing. Three hours into his shift, Holmes was advised of two express passenger trains due from the north. The first passed through Holmes' area, and Holmes was advised that an unexpected goods train was also due and he indicated it should proceed.

At this point, Holmes is said to have become overwhelmed by sleep. He awoke, confused, around 10 minutes later, assuming the goods train had passed through. It hadn't (it had stopped), and before Holmes realised what had happened the second express train hurtled into the stationary goods train at 60 miles per hour.

Although Holmes was found guilty of the manslaughter of nine passengers and the train guard, he was given an absolute discharge which meant he served no sentence. This was a decision that was strongly supported by the jury and the public at the time.

Alternatives to custodial sentences

Not all people who commit crime go to prison. A judge passing sentence also has other non-custodial options at his/her disposal. These are usually applied when a less serious, low-level crime has been committed that does not, in the judge's opinion, justify a period 'behind bars'.

Community sentences

A *community sentence* is a form of *punishment* which includes some kind of activity carried out in the local community. This generally takes the form of unpaid work such as removing graffiti or tidying up areas that are overgrown or abandoned. In the UK, the minimum penalty that can be imposed by the court is 40 hours and the maximum is 300 hours.

There are other conditions that come with community service. An offender may be required to attend treatment for drug or alcohol problems, or even support for mental health, provided they give their consent. The offender's movements are restricted too. They may have to observe a curfew and be home at a certain time for an agreed period.

In 2017 in the UK, just over eight per cent of offenders (about 95,000) were given community sentences. (All statistics from *The Sentencing Council for England and Wales*.)

Probation

It is possible that someone serving a community sentence may be on *probation*, a non-custodial sentence handed out by the court. Individuals on probation may have to engage in unpaid work and seek treatment for illness or addiction. As well as this, they may have to complete an education or training programme whilst having regular meetings with an *offender manager* (formerly called a *probation officer*).

Breaching the rules of probation, such as failing to attend meetings or committing another crime, is a serious matter and is likely to result in a prison sentence.

Fines

The most common type of non-custodial sentence is a *fine*. This is shown by the fact that, in 2017, 75% of sentences in the UK were fines. Fines can often be imposed without the offender having to be present in court, as is the case with a speeding or parking ticket. Since March 2015, there is no upper limit for a fine – it was formerly £5,000 – but larger fines can be applied alongside a custodial sentence, or instead of one.

For instance, fraud is sometimes punished with very large fines. A prison sentence is unnecessary as the fraudster is not considered to be a direct danger to the public. This is because they will have been removed from the position or profession in which the crime was committed in the first place.

Discharges

Discharges are sentences usually for the least serious cases, such as very minor thefts. There are two types: *absolute* and *conditional discharges*. An absolute discharge is when no punishment is given by the court, either because the experience of going to court is seen to be punishment enough or when the judge feels there are mitigating circumstances for the offender's behaviour – as in the case of James Holmes on the left.

A conditional discharge is more serious. The offender cannot commit another offence for anything up to three years. If another offence is committed, an individual on a conditional discharge will be returned to court and punished for both the original offence and the latest offence. Discharges accounted for four per cent of all sentences in the UK in 2017.

Community sentencing usually involves the offender 'giving back' to society in some way, for example, in the form of unpaid work.

Seeking justice for both the public and criminals. Prison may not be the best option.

GET ACTIVE You be the judge

The weblink below gives you the opportunity to pass sentence on criminal cases.

tinyurl.com/csd2yyh

Use the information on this spread, as well as your knowledge of custodial sentencing, to make judgements about what sentence is appropriate in each case.

Finally, see how your sentence compares to the sentence that a judge would hand out in a real-life context.

Evaluation

Economic benefit

One strength of non-custodial sentences is there is an economic benefit.

In purely financial terms, non-custodial sentences provide a net gain for society compared to prison. The UK has the largest prison population in Europe and the average cost of housing a single prisoner is around £38,000 per year, though this can be as much as £80,000 for very dangerous prisoners in maximum security institutions (statistics from GOV.UK). Community sentences, by contrast, cost a fraction of this – around £3,000 to £4,000, depending on the precise nature of the scheme. The money saved by the Criminal Justice System could be used to fund other *rehabilitative* services.

This suggests that keeping people out of prison is ultimately a preferable option, financially and in terms of rehabilitation.

Impact on offender

Another strength is the positive impact on offenders.

There are several ways in which offenders may benefit from non-custodial sentences. Supporters of community punishment argue that such schemes are more effective at reducing reoffending rates – around 36% compared to 60% for those who are released after serving a short sentence (Prison Reform Trust 2018). Outside prison walls, young offenders do not have the opportunity to learn negative behaviours and the 'tricks of the criminal trade' from older, more experienced offenders (a process referred to as *prisonisation*). Finally, the shame and stigma of serving a prison sentence which may damage an individual's job prospects and reputation within the community is removed.

This suggests that, for individuals who commit crime at least, there may be several benefits to community sentencing.

Impact on victim

One weakness is that victims of crime and the public at large may prefer prison.

Victims of crime may feel they want revenge for what they have been through and a prison sentence provides this. However, in 2006, the Lord Chief Justice expressed the view that community sentences do provide a visible demonstration of reparation to the community which prison sentences do not. Nevertheless evidence suggests that community sentences are viewed as 'soft options' compared to the perceived 'short, sharp shock' of the prison environment. For example, a YouGov poll (2010) found that two-thirds of respondents thought that community sentences were 'weak and undemanding'.

This suggests that the public prefers to see an offender receive a prison sentence.

Assessment practice

At the end of learning aim B you must write a report (see pages 133 and 146). This report must be related to a scenario or context. We have used a real-life context.

Chris Brown is most famous for assaulting his then-girlfriend Rihanna in 2009. He pleaded guilty and received a sentence combining community service, counselling and five years' probation. The sentence was criticised by many domestic violence campaign organisations for being 'soft' because it did not include an element of imprisonment. The sentence appeared to have worked when Brown and Rihanna resumed their relationship in January 2013 ('he's a different person'), but they split up again months later. In 2017 Brown was handed a five-year restraining order after threatening to kill his new girlfriend.

B1.4 Learning aim B1 – Task 4

The first part of your report for learning aim B will be concerned with methods of punishing criminal behaviour and the effectiveness of these methods – these are covered on the previous three spreads and this spread.

1. **Explain** how the case of Chris Brown and Rihanna illustrates the use of community sentences, with reference to psychological theory. (B.P4)

2. **Assess** the effectiveness of community sentences with reference to the case of Chris Brown and Rihanna. (B.M2)

3. **Evaluate** the impact of community sentences with reference to the case of Chris Brown and Rihanna. (B.D2)

An issue to consider

Do you agree with the final evaluation point that non-custodial sentencing is too lenient? Consider this from your own and from a victim's perspective.

In what situations, and for what crimes, do you think non-custodial sentences are appropriate?

Specification content

B1 Punishing criminal behaviour

Effectiveness, and social and ethical implications of punishment methods.

● Community sentences – effective alternative to custodial sentences, types of community sentences, i.e. probation, recidivism rates, reduction in stigma.

● Fines and discharges.

Anger management

Naomi Campbell

Naomi Campbell was one of a number of very famous supermodels in the 1980s and 1990s. Born in London, she has achieved worldwide fame and has appeared on the cover of more than 500 magazines. She was the first black model to feature on the cover of *TIME* magazine, as well as the UK, French and Russian versions of *Vogue*. Campbell has also had a successful career in pop music, film and television, and it was once reported that she said that she would not get out of bed 'for less than $10,000 a day' (though Campbell herself has disputed this).

Almost as well-documented as Naomi Campbell's glittering career though, are her problems in controlling her temper. She was convicted of assault four times between 1998 and 2009. Two of these occasions involved hitting people – first, her personal assistant (with a phone) and then her former housekeeper (also with a phone). In 2008, Campbell kicked and spat at two police officers at Heathrow Airport during an argument over lost luggage which led to her being banned for life by British Airways. She also assaulted a photographer the following year.

Campbell has attended anger management courses and completed community service as a result of her behaviour.

Specification terms

Anger management Therapy that involves identifying the signs that trigger anger as well as learning techniques to calm down and deal with the situation in a positive way. The aim of anger management is not to prevent anger but to recognise it and manage it.

Hostile attribution bias A tendency to assume that someone else's behaviour has an aggressive or antagonistic motive when it is actually neutral.

Stress inoculation training (SIT) A stress management technique which helps individuals develop coping skills and then exposes the individual to moderate amounts of anxiety to enable practice of coping.

The cognitive approach to criminal behaviour

Anger management is one of several *cognitive* approaches to dealing with crime. You learned about the cognitive approach earlier in your course – it is the approach that seeks to explain behaviour in terms of mental processes.

Some researchers suggest that cognitive factors are at the root of violent crime. There are people who have a style of thinking that predisposes them to react violently to events. Such thinking is irrational but could perhaps be modified through anger management techniques.

Cognitive bias

As part of the cognitive approach you studied errors in the way we process information (see our Year 1 'Certificate' book, page 16), such as *hostile attribution bias*. In general *cognitive biases* are good because they simplify social interactions and allow us to make decisions quickly (they are 'shortcuts' that help us process incoming information).

However, such biases are not rational, they enable us to bypass thinking and just react instantaneously. In the case of violent criminals, they may irrationally and rather too quickly judge other people's motives as aggressive and confrontational when they may not be. Someone with this bias may see other people as provoking them when they are not. Non-aggressive cues, such as being 'looked at', may be misread, triggering a disproportionate and aggressive response in the offender. The attribution is made that the other person is being hostile – but this is an incorrect assumption (in other words, a form of bias).

Anger management

Anger management is a way of dealing with irrational thoughts such as the hostile attribution bias that may underlie criminal behaviour. Raymond Novaco (1975) developed anger management as a therapy that combines cognitive principles with *learning theory* (called *cognitive-behaviourist*). He argues that:

1. Cognitive factors trigger emotional arousal, leading to a violent act.
2. Anger is *reinforced* by the individual's feelings of control in that situation.
3. Thus, the best way of *rehabilitating* an offender is by first changing their thoughts in a positive direction, then positive behaviour will follow.

Stress inoculation training

Stress inoculation training (SIT) is a specific type of anger management often used with violent offenders (though it was initially designed to deal with *stress*, see page 84). The idea of 'inoculation' is to expose the offender to a small amount of stress, and encourage them to change their natural reaction, in the hope that this will generalise to the rest of their behaviour. This is similar to inoculation in medicine when a person is given a small strain of a virus, so they can build up resistance to it.

SIT has three stages:

1. **Cognitive preparation** Working with a therapist, offenders identify the triggers to stress and anxiety that cause them to react violently. For instance, when they perceive someone to be staring at them (see above) or being nudged or jostled at a busy bar.
2. **Skills acquisition** Offenders are taught coping mechanisms to help them deal with triggers more effectively. For example, counting to ten or repeating calming words or phrases ('self-talk'). Techniques may also focus on reducing physical stress such as deep breathing and meditation.
3. **Application and follow-through** Finally, offenders practise the skills they have been taught in role-play situations. The success of therapy is determined by their ability to select appropriate and non-aggressive responses to a wide range of trigger events.

What triggers aggression?
Can violent offenders learn to control their anger when faced with different trigger events?

Evaluation

Supporting evidence

One strength of the concept of hostile attribution bias is there is supporting evidence.

A study by Michael Schönenberg and Aiste Jusyte (2014) showed 55 violent offenders images of emotionally ambiguous facial expressions. In other words, it was difficult to tell what emotion the person in the picture was feeling. The violent offenders were more likely to interpret the images as angry and hostile compared to a *control group* of non-violent offenders.

This suggests that violent offenders have a hostile attribution bias which could make them more likely to react aggressively to other people.

Recidivism

One weakness of anger management is that it has only a limited effect on *recidivism*.

Perhaps surprisingly, follow-up studies of released inmates suggest that anger management has little impact on long-term reoffending rates (e.g. Rice 1997). This is despite the fact that therapies like SIT are designed to tackle the root cause of offending, to try to reform the offender. According to Ronald Blackburn (1993) this may be because the application and follow-through phase – based on role play – can never completely replicate the kinds of aggressive cues and situations that an offender is likely to experience in real life.

This suggests that, although the offender may learn helpful techniques to control their anger during therapy, these do not always transfer to everyday life.

Root cause

A further weakness is that anger may not be the root cause of offending.

One possible explanation for the disappointing impact on recidivism rates may be that the rationale behind anger management is flawed, and anger is not the root cause of offending. A study by Wagdy Loza and Amel Loza-Fanous (1999) found no difference in anger levels between groups of violent and non-violent offenders. When the violent offender did *attribute* their criminality to anger, they tended to do so to excuse their behaviour, rather than being genuinely angry.

This suggests that anger management programmes are unlikely to be successful in all circumstances as they presume a link between anger and offending which may not be there in the first place.

A hostile aggressive expression. Though perhaps only those with a hostile attribution bias would interpret it in that way.

GET ACTIVE Al's aggression

Al Beatem is serving a six-month prison sentence for grievous bodily harm. He assaulted a stranger in a local pub because, in Al's words, 'He kept looking at me funny and couldn't take his eyes off the missus'.

In the past, Al has found it difficult to hold down a job as he struggles to interact with work colleagues. He also has a problem with authority and has found it difficult to follow instructions from his bosses.

Al has been assigned a therapist in prison who has suggested he follows a course of anger management.

1. *Explain how Al might benefit from anger management, and what steps the therapist might take to support him.*
2. *Using the information on this spread, explain how likely it is that Al will be able to change his behaviour.*

Restorative justice

The Woolf within

You could say that Peter Woolf and Will Riley met in unusual circumstances. Their first encounter was when Woolf attempted to burgle Riley's London home. Robbery was a commonplace activity for Woolf who was desperate to fund a heroin addiction he had had since the age of 15.

Riley's upmarket Islington residence was in stark contrast to Woolf's who, at the time, was living in a squat in the East End of London spending his nights wrapped in a curtain. When Riley came home and discovered Woolf on his premises, a fight between the pair ensued, and, despite several blows to the head with a griddle pan, Riley was able to detain his new acquaintance until the police arrived.

Traumatised, Riley agreed to a suggestion by police that he take part in a restorative justice programme to help him move on from the experience. This would involve meeting Woolf again face-to-face under police supervision. To Riley's surprise, Woolf appeared genuinely remorseful during the meeting, and the two of them were able to communicate openly with each other about their feelings.

Against all odds, the pair became firm friends. They even lecture together about the benefits of restorative justice, acceptance and forgiveness. Woolf has written a book about his experiences, *The Damage Done*, which discusses how the police programme ended up being the trigger that helped him turn his life around.

Source: *The Woolf Within*, tinyurl.com/la526ld

Specification term

Restorative justice An approach to justice which aims to reduce and atone for offending behaviour as well as address the needs of the victim. It involves reconciliation between offender and victim, as well as the wider community.

> Restorative justice gave me a chance to understand the harm I caused.

> It felt good to be heard.

> He did seem to be really sorry.

> I was able to understand it all and move on.

Restorative justice

Restorative justice (RJ) seeks to achieve justice by repairing the harm done by an offender rather than simply punishing them. Crime is not only about the person who commits it. Most criminal behaviour also involves a victim who is forced to live with the consequences of loss or trauma that crime so often brings with it. Restorative justice is an approach to modifying criminal behaviour that tries to shift emphasis away from the needs of the offender and more towards the needs of the victim.

In addition, restorative justice seeks to address some of the aims of *imprisonment* – to *rehabilitate* offenders so they do not commit crime again and to allow society to feel that the offender has 'paid' for his/her crime.

The process

The process usually involves communication between the offender and the victim. The offender may write a letter to a victim or may give payment to compensate for any loss. There may be an interaction between offender and victim, for example video conferencing or a face-to-face meeting between victim and offender. This needs to be carefully managed to ensure that both victim and offender benefit from the process, so there is always an impartial facilitator involved.

Victim's perspective

Someone who is subject to a crime may be living with all kinds of negative consequences: sleepless nights, emotional effects, repairing damage to themselves or property, coming to terms with the loss of a loved one and so on.

Victims are encouraged, wherever possible, to play an active part in the restorative justice process. The primary aim of the exercise is to enable victims to achieve some kind of closure from the incident and move on.

Therefore, an important aim of restorative justice is to empower the victim and help them cope with the aftermath of crime.

Rehabilitation of offenders

In addition to the victim's perspective, it is also hoped that getting the offender to see the real-life consequences of their actions is the first step towards their own rehabilitation.

Certainly, in the case of Peter Woolfe (left), understanding the emotional distress he had caused Will Riley led him to want to change his behaviour for the better. The attempted robbery of Will's home was his last. Peter was supported by the police, other agencies and even helped by Will. He went on to find a job and a new relationship. Although not all cases of restorative justice will be as successful as this one, if each party fully commits to the process, there may be positive outcomes for both victim and offender.

Therefore, the aim of the dialogue between offender and victim is to develop the offender's empathy so they will be less likely to commit crime in the future.

Atonement for wrongdoing

According to John Braithwaite (2004) 'crime hurts, justice should heal'. Restorative justice involves the offender and the victim working together in some way so that the offender can atone (make up) for what they have done.

When there is a supervised meeting between the two parties (as in the case on the left), the victim is invited to give their side of the story and explain how they were personally affected by the incident. The intention is that this should enable the offender to understand the consequences of their actions from the victim's point of view.

Restorative justice programmes can take many forms. If the victim is unable or unwilling to face the offender then there are alternative ways in which the offender can atone for their actions. For instance, they may pay for repairs to damaged property.

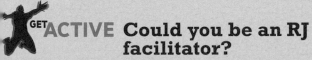

GET ACTIVE: Could you be an RJ facilitator?

Restorative justice (RJ) is quite a new approach and is becoming increasingly popular in different settings, not just as part of the criminal justice system. There are currently around 80 professional restorative justice practitioners employed in the UK. The role includes deciding whether a case is suitable for RJ, preparing the participants, managing the process and evaluating its success.

1. *What non-criminal settings do you think RJ has been used in?*
2. *What qualities/skills would a good RJ facilitator need?*

Evaluation

Recidivism

One strength of restorative justice programmes is there is some evidence they reduce *recidivism*.

A *meta-analysis* of 24 published studies by Kristin Bain (2012) investigated which aspects of restorative justice are most effective in reducing recidivism, as well as what offender characteristics make for the best restorative justice candidates. The main findings were that recidivism rates tend to decrease more for adults than juvenile offenders, especially when there is direct contact with the victim. That said, programmes where there is some involvement with the local community, and where there were high levels of victim satisfaction, actually saw slight increases in recidivism.

This suggests that some restorative justice programmes may be more successful at reducing reoffending rates than others.

Economic impact

One weakness of restorative justice programmes is the costs outweigh the benefits.

Joanna Shapland *et al.* (2008) conducted a government funded research project claiming that for every £1 spent on restorative justice there would be a saving of £8 for the criminal justice system through reduced reoffending (though, as the point below suggests, evidence for this is mixed).

However, there may be significant short-term costs with these schemes, such as the need for a highly trained mediator. Also, there tends to be a high dropout rate as the victim or the offender may decide that they cannot go through with the scheduled meeting, and so money is wasted.

This suggests that although restorative justice may save money in the long-term (compared to other options like prison), it may not always be financially viable in the short-term.

Offender must show remorse

A further weakness is that the offender must be genuinely sorry for what they have done.

The success of restorative justice programmes may hinge on the offender's intentions being honourable – that is, they must be taking part because they genuinely regret the hurt caused and want to make amends. This is complicated by the fact that some schemes come with an incentive, such as the offender getting time off a prison sentence, and it is this that may have influenced their decision to participate. In addition, the victim themselves may have other motives, such as wanting to satisfy a need for revenge.

This suggests that restorative justice must be carefully managed to make sure that both parties have signed up to the scheme for the right reasons.

Bringing the two sides together.

Assessment practice

At the end of learning aim B you must write a report (see pages 133 and 146). This report must be related to a scenario or context. We have used a real-life context.

Gareth Thomas is a rugby union legend, a former captain of Wales and the first international rugby player to come out as gay. He was assaulted in 2018 by a 16-year-old boy in a homophobic attack. Instead of prosecuting the boy for a crime, Thomas persuaded the police to apply restorative justice. Thomas met with the boy and explained how the assault had affected him. The boy admitted his guilt and apologised. This is what Thomas said about the experience: 'There are an awful lot of people out there who want to hurt us, but unfortunately for them there is a lot more who want to help us heal so this I hope will be a positive message' (BBC News 2018, tinyurl.com/yc7gvfax).

B2.6 Learning aim B2 – Task 6

The second part of your report for learning aim B will be concerned with methods of modifying criminal behaviour and the effectiveness of these methods – these are covered on the previous spread, this spread and the next spread.

1. **Explain** how Gareth Thomas' experience illustrates the use of restorative justice, with reference to psychological theory. (B.P3)
2. **Assess** the effectiveness of restorative justice with reference to Gareth Thomas' experience. (B.M2)
3. **Evaluate** the impact of restorative justice with reference to Gareth Thomas' experience. (B.D2)

An issue to consider

Schemes such as restorative justice tend not to find favour with the public who often regard them as 'soft options' when compared to alternative punishments such as prison.

Do you agree with this view? Or do you think that the positive outcomes associated with restorative justice outweigh the negatives?

Specification content

B2 Modifying criminal behaviour

Effectiveness and social and ethical implications of methods of modifying criminal behaviour.

● Restorative justice – rehabilitation of offenders, atonement for wrongdoing, victim's perspective.

143

Token economy

Prisoner protest

The *Manchester Evening News* (2017) reported that a prisoner was staging a 60-hour rooftop protest to complain about the lack of conjugal visits in UK prisons. A conjugal visit is a scheduled period in which a prison inmate is allowed to spend several hours with a visitor (usually their spouse or girlfriend/boyfriend). They may engage in sexual intercourse as part of the visit.

Stuart Horner who carried out the protest, was serving life imprisonment for murder in Strangeways Prison, Manchester (pictured above). Horner, who was accused of causing £1m of damage to the prison roof during his sit-in, believes that conjugal visits reduce violence in prison if they are used as part of a system of rewards for good behaviour.

Is Horner right? Some studies in the US, where the idea of conjugal visits originated, have suggested that they do lead to a decrease of sexual and physical violence in prison, as well as helping to maintain family bonds. However, their use is controversial in America, and the number of states that permit these has dropped from 24 to four.

Prisoners enjoying a game of basketball as part of a token economy programme system of rewards.

The use of token economy in prisons

Ever tried to get someone to do want you want by offering them a reward? If the idea of 'you scratch my back and I'll scratch yours' works in everyday life, then why not in prison? Presumably many prisoners quite like the idea of rewards as this may be what drove them to commit crime in the first place!

Token economy aims to manage prisoners' behaviour by establishing a system of rewards.

A learning approach

In the unit on psychological approaches and applications (Unit 1 of our Year 1 'Certificate' book), you studied the *learning approach* to explaining human behaviour. This approach suggests that all animal behaviour, including human criminal behaviour, is learned through *conditioning*. If it has been learned in the first place, then it seems plausible that such behaviour might be *unlearned* by applying the same principles that brought it about in the first place.

This is the philosophy of *token economy* (TE), a form of *behaviour modification*, i.e. trying to modify or change someone's behaviour. The aim is to increase desirable behaviour by rewarding it, and decrease undesirable behaviour by punishing it – in the hope that undesirable behaviours will eventually disappear altogether.

Such TE systems are particularly suited to prison regimes because the environment is highly controlled and therefore rewards can be administered in a careful way. TE can be implemented and coordinated by prison staff, and all inmates are required to play their part in the process.

Operant conditioning

Reinforcement When a behaviour produces a pleasurable consequence from the environment (e.g. a reward) it is likely to be repeated in future. The environment reinforces (strengthens) the behaviour, so this process is called *reinforcement*.

In a TE system, a prisoner who demonstrates desirable behaviour receives a token. Desirable behaviour within prison may take several forms but would include avoiding conflict, following rules, engaging in work and keeping one's cell tidy. Once a prisoner has collected several tokens (the token is a *secondary reinforcer*) these can be exchanged for a reward (the *primary reinforcer*). This may include a phone call to a family member, time in the exercise yard or gym, extra cigarettes or food.

Punishment If a prisoner fails to comply with prison rules and routines then they are *punished* by having their tokens taken away. Thus, inmates learn to associate disobedience with the withdrawal of privileges and will try to avoid this. Each expected behaviour and reward will be explained to the prisoners before the scheme is implemented, and staff must be consistent in the way they apply it.

Incremental change

In a token economy, a target behaviour will be broken down into a series of steps called 'increments'. Each step is rewarded to try to bring about a more general behavioural change.

So, for instance, a target behaviour such as 'learning to work effectively with other inmates' may be broken down into 'supporting others', 'giving positive feedback', etc. All staff who come into contact with prisoners must follow the same regime of selective reinforcement.

Finally, the whole programme can be overseen by prison officials who are able to assess its effectiveness. This assessment should consider whether the token economy scheme has promoted good management of the prison as a whole, as well as the positive effects – assuming there are some – on individual prisoners.

Specification term

Token economy A form of operant conditioning designed to increase desirable behaviour and decrease undesirable behaviour with the use of tokens. Individuals receive tokens immediately after displaying a desirable behaviour. The tokens are collected and later exchanged for a meaningful object or privilege.

Evaluation

Easy and cheap

One strength of token economy in prisons is that it is cheap and easy to implement.

Unlike other methods of modifying behaviour, such as forms of *anger management*, token economy is relatively cheap and straightforward to set up in a prison. There is no need to pay specialist professionals for their services, as existing prison staff can run and manage the system without external support. The only requirement – and this is key – is that the system is applied consistently by all staff, otherwise this could breed resentment among prisoners if they feel some prisoners are receiving 'special treatment'.

This suggests that a token economy system has a benefit for society, as it can be managed within prison budgets.

Recidivism

One weakness of token economy systems is that they may not impact upon *recidivism* rates.

There is little doubt that token economy can facilitate effective management of prisoners whilst they are in the institution, and many studies suggest positive outcomes. However, their long-term *rehabilitative* value has been questioned. A study by Harold Cohen and James Filipczak (1971) found that a token economy group showed more desirable behaviour than a *control group* in an adult prison. Plus, there was also a short-term positive impact on reoffending rates in the first two years of their release. However, an analysis of reoffending rates after three years suggested these had risen, reflecting national statistics.

This suggests that the positive effects of token economy may 'wear off' after release which is detrimental to the individual and wider society.

Token learning

A further weakness of token economy systems is they lead to a kind of passive learning.

As token economies are designed to change just surface behaviour, they don't really encourage the prisoner to reflect more deeply on why they decided to commit crime in the first place. This might mean that treatments that are based on the *cognitive approach* (e.g. anger management), are more likely to modify behaviour in the long-term than *behaviourist* treatments (e.g. token economy). There is also the rather obvious issue that similar systems of reward do not exist on the outside when the offender leaves prison, so that any progress they have made during their sentence may be lost.

This may explain why, as suggested above, the positive effects of token economy tend not to generalise to the real world.

Assessment practice

At the end of learning aim B you must write a report (see pages 133 and 146). This report must be related to a scenario or context. We have used a real-life context.

All British prisons use a type of token economy called the *Incentives and earned privileges scheme* (IEPS). A new arrival in prison is given the status of 'entry prisoner' which allows them certain privileges such as access to TV and visits each month. The prisoner can improve their status through 'good behaviour' (e.g. following prison rules) up to 'standard' and then to 'enhanced'. This allows longer visits, more choice in the canteen, freedom to wear their own clothes, gym use, etc. Higher status only comes from exceeding expectations, not just meeting the minimum requirements of good behaviour. A prisoner's status will also decrease through bad behaviour and can reduce to 'basic' which is below entry level.

B2.7 Learning aim B2 – Task 7

The second part of your report for learning aim B will be concerned with methods of modifying criminal behaviour and the effectiveness of these methods – these are covered on the previous two spreads and this spread.

This activity will help you practise the skills required to write the report in response to your scenario/context.

1. **Explain** how the IEPS illustrates the use of token economies, with reference to psychological theory. (B.P3)

2. **Assess** the effectiveness of token economies with reference to the IEPS. (B.M2)

3. **Evaluate** the impact of token economies with reference to the IEPS. (B.D2)

> You can see an explanation of command terms and the assessment criteria on pages 131 and 146.

An issue to consider

Some people have criticised token economy for being 'manipulative and dehumanising' in that it withholds access to food or exercise as part of punishment.

Is this something you agree with? Or do you think that part of the prison experience should be a suspension of the offender's usual rights?

Specification content

B2 Modifying criminal behaviour

Effectiveness and social and ethical implications of methods of modifying criminal behaviour.

● Token economy based on the principles of behaviourism, used in prisons.

Learning aim B

Assessment guidance

Learning aim B assessment

You are required to produce one or more reports (but not more than three) for the three learning aims in this unit.

The board recommends three reports for Unit 4.

The report can be written or presented as a poster, PowerPoint or other form.

This report can only be completed after you have studied the content of learning aim B as it is a synoptic assessment (see page 131).

Recommended assessment approach

The *Delivery Guide for Unit 4* states that your report (or presentation, poster, etc.) for learning aim B:

- Is likely to be more applied in nature than the report for learning aim A.
- Will involve exploring the different options for punishment/behaviour modification.
- Will conclude with a recommendation of the most suitable option for a particular case.

Assignment briefs

The board supplies suggested assignment briefs which you can use – see *Unit 4 Authorised assignment brief for Learning aim B*.

Your centre can also devise their own assignment brief which should have a vocational scenario/context and a series of tasks to complete.

Vocational scenario	The task (from the assignment brief)
The *Delivery Guide for Unit 4* suggests that the scenario could involve reusing the same case study as used for learning aim A, or creating a new case study.	You need to produce a report on two methods used in the behavioural modification of criminal behaviour and how this may impact on the individual and society as a whole.
	Your report should include the following:
	• Conduct a literary review and **explain** the use of punishment and behaviour modification on criminal behaviour, using psychological theories. (See pass criteria below.)
	• Conduct a literary review and **assess** the effectiveness of behaviour modification and punishment methods on criminal behaviour, using psychological theories. (See merit criteria below.)
	• An **evaluation** on the impact of behaviour modification and punishment of criminal behaviour on the individual and society. (See distinction criteria below.)

Assessment information

Your final report will be awarded a Distinction (D), Merit (M), Pass (P), Near Pass (N) or Unclassified (U).

The specification provides criteria for each level as shown below.

Pass	Merit	Distinction
B.P3 EXPLAIN the use of behaviour modification methods on criminal behaviour, using psychological theories.		
B.P4 EXPLAIN the use of punishments for criminal behaviour, using psychological theories.		
	B.M2 ASSESS the effectiveness of behaviour modification and punishment methods on criminal behaviour, using psychological theories.	
		B.D2 EVALUATE the impact of behaviour modification methods and punishment of criminal behaviour on the individual and society.

See page 131 for an explanation of command terms used for learning aim B.

Marking factors The specification also provides information that an assessor will take into consideration when marking your assignment.

Marking factors	Pass	Merit	Distinction
Different punishment/behaviour modification strategies used in response to criminal behaviour are ...	... explained.	... considered.	... evaluated.
The effect of punishment/behaviour modification strategies on the individual and on society is ...		... included, e.g. the impact on reoffending rates.	... given with detailed analysis, including economic benefits to society and impact on both the criminal and their victim.
Links made between punishment/behaviour modification strategies and ...	... the psychological approaches on which they are based.	... psychological research, including different types of crime and patterns of criminal behaviour.	... detailed, appropriate underlying psychological theories.
Including ...		... some analysis of the methodological limitations of the research.	... a consideration of the validity of supporting research.

Self-review checklist

The list below will help you manage writing your final report.

First draft

Remember this is a *draft*. It is important just to make a start which is what writing a draft is all about – it is a beginning, see 'Blank page syndrome' on the right.

Date to complete first draft:

	Date completed	Explain (B.P3)	Explain (B.P4)	Assess (B.M2)	Evaluate (B.D2)
• In the first grey column enter the completion dates for each section of your report. • As you write each section tick the yellow boxes when you have explained, assessed and evaluated, as appropriate. Ignore the boxes that are crossed through.					
B1 Punishing criminal behaviour					
Imprisonment			✕		
Zero tolerance			✕		
Offender disclosure schemes			✕		
Community sentences, fines and discharges			✕		
B2 Modifying criminal behaviour					
Anger management				✕	
Restorative justice				✕	
Token economy				✕	
References compiled					

Second draft

The next step is to revise your first document. Below is a checklist of things to consider.

Date to complete second draft:

	Date completed
I have checked that I have covered each of the four marking factors (grey column) in the table on the facing page.	
I have gone through and deleted any irrelevant material.	
I have checked that every point has evidence to back it up.	
I have identified long sentences and rephrased them.	
I have checked that each paragraph deals with one idea.	
I have corrected any spelling mistakes.	
I have checked that each paragraph makes reference to the scenario/context.	

Final draft

Read through your completed second draft to polish the report.

Date to complete final draft:

Blank page syndrome*

We all experience it – when you try to start writing something you end up staring at that blank page and can't think where to begin.

You go make a cup of coffee and do a job that has been waiting for you for over a week.

You come back. It's still blank.

It doesn't matter where you begin! That's what a first draft is about. Just write anything – but do write in your own words not chunks copied from the internet or this textbook, otherwise you will forget and they will end up in your final version (see 'Plagiarism' on page 131).

*It's more likely of course to be a blank screen problem.

Essential advice

Learners may not make repeated submissions of assignment evidence.

You may be offered a single retake opportunity using a new assignment. The retake may only be achieved at a Pass.

Under some conditions, and at your centre's discretion, you may be allowed to resubmit your original work in an improved form and will be given 15 days to do so.

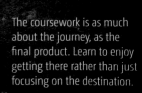

The coursework is as much about the journey, as the final product. Learn to enjoy getting there rather than just focusing on the destination.

Top-down approach

You may wish to read about the aims of profiling on page 152 first.

Ted Bundy

In the 1970s, Ted Bundy travelled across the West Coast of America raping, torturing and murdering young women. The number of women Bundy killed is thought to be over 30 – but could be even higher – with the youngest victim being just 12 years old.

Bundy harboured a long and murderous rage against women. When he was a teenager, he discovered that the person he had been told all his life was his sister was actually his mother (who had given birth to Ted out of wedlock).

Bundy targeted women with long hair parted in the middle, in the image of his college girlfriend who left Bundy devastated when she ended their relationship. His killings followed a grisly pattern. He would rape his victims before beating them to death.

When the full extent of Bundy's crimes was revealed, his many friends and associates were disbelieving. Bundy was charming and highly intelligent. A law school graduate with an outstanding academic record, Bundy was widely regarded as ambitious and successful.

During his criminal trial, Bundy's film star good looks meant that he, perversely, gathered a large female following. After escaping police custody twice, he was finally put to death by electric chair in 1989.

Specification terms

Disorganised serial murderers Murderers who commit spontaneous crimes which show little evidence of planning. They are often socially and sexually incompetent with lower-than-average intelligence.

Organised serial murderers Murderers who show evidence of premeditated planning of the crime. They are typically socially and sexually competent with higher-than-average intelligence.

Top-down approach A method of profiling popularised in the US. It starts with a pre-established typology and 'works down', using evidence from the crime scene and witness accounts, to classify offenders into one of two types of serial murderer.

The FBI approach to offender profiling

The approach to *offender profiling* that is commonly used in the United States came about through the work of the Federal Bureau of Investigation (FBI) in the 1970s. This so-called *top-down approach* (although this term is rarely used nowadays) makes use of evidence gathered from the crime scene to move downwards and create a profile of an offender.

Offenders are then categorised into one of two types – *organised* or *disorganised*. These types provide the police with important information about the potential for further offences and the kinds of interview techniques that will be most successful when the offender is caught.

The FBI interviews

In the 1970s, the FBI began to incorporate insights from psychology to try to understand criminal behaviour. This led to the establishment of the FBI's Behavioural Science Unit to help solve difficult cases, such as serial murder. Part of this work included a series of interviews carried out by John Douglas and Robert Ressler between 1979 and 1983 with convicted criminals. There were 36 interviews in total, all with sexually motivated serial killers such as Ted Bundy (see left). The aim of these discussions was to find patterns in the murderers' backgrounds, personalities and the nature of their crimes.

Hazelwood and Douglas (1980)

Around the same time, Robert Hazelwood and John Douglas (1980) wrote an influential article entitled *The Lust Murderer*. In it, they argued that lust murders are carried out by individuals who kill for reasons of sexual gratification. All such murders are sadistic and involve some kind of mutilation of the victim's body, but some of them are more organised than others. Hazelwood and Douglas proposed the possibility of two distinct lust murderer types: the *organised non-social* type and the *disorganised asocial* type. Broadly speaking, the former is a cunning and manipulative individual who lives some distance from the scene of the crime. The latter is lonely and rejected, and commits spur-of-the-moment attacks in the areas close to where they live.

The organised/disorganised types

Top-down profiling is based on the idea that serial murderers have characteristic ways of working, in that they leave their 'signature' on the victim and the crime scene, which reveals important things about their background, daily routine and personal life.

Organised offenders target their victim, who is nevertheless unknown to them, but usually fits a preferred 'type'. Serial killers have been known to target specific types of victim, such as Bundy's desire for young women with long hair parted in the middle. This may mean stalking an individual for some time to find out when they are most likely to be vulnerable, which may take many weeks of planning. Organised offenders are detached and controlled at the crime scene, leaving behind very little evidence or clues. They are likely to be intelligent, have a skilled job and be in a long-term relationship or married. On the surface, they appear well-adjusted and, for want of a better word, 'normal'.

Disorganised offenders show little evidence of planning and are impulsive. For example, the offender may have intended to rape the victim, but for whatever reason, this spilled over into murder. There may be little attempt to conceal the crime, for example the body is usually found at the scene with no evidence of 'clean-up'. The offender's behaviour shows a general lack of control, suggesting it was random, even frenzied. Disorganised offenders tend to be in unskilled work, have low educational attainment, and may have a history of failed sexual relationships. They often live close to where the body is discovered.

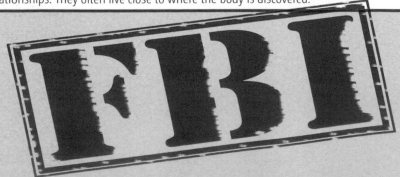

GET ACTIVE Adrian Babb

Between 1986 and 1988, seven attacks on elderly women took place in tower blocks in Birmingham. Women in their 70s and 80s, often infirm, were followed into the lifts by a stocky young man who took them to the same top floor of the tower block, suggesting some element of planning. He would rape the women and then flee.

Consistent patterns seemed to suggest the same man was responsible. In his interactions with the women he appeared confident and at ease. He made no attempt to disguise himself and forensic evidence was found on each occasion. Police eventually arrested Adrian Babb, an attendant at the local swimming pool, where all of Babb's victims were regular visitors.

1. *Do Babb's crimes fit the organised or disorganised typology? Explain your answer.*

2. *Is the distinction between organised and disorganised offences completely clear-cut? Explain your answer.*

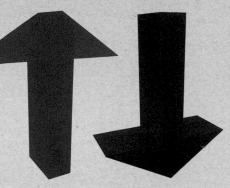

On the next spread we look at the bottom-up approach – starting from the specific and moving to the general.

You can use the bottom-up approach as an evaluation of the top-down approach.

Evaluation

A crime classification manual

One strength of the top-down approach is that it helped to develop the *Crime classification manual*.

The Crime classification manual produced by John Douglas *et al.* in 1992 gathered together all the insights from the FBI interviews and the more general work of the *Behavioural Science Unit* at the FBI. It was reprinted in 2006 and the organised–disorganised distinction survives – though not quite in its original form (see below). The typology continues to be used widely by police departments in the US and most would acknowledge that it has made a positive contribution to the field.

This suggests that the typology approach is a viable method of profiling which continues to prove useful.

Lack of evidence

One weakness of the top-down approach is a lack of evidence for organised and disorganised types.

David Canter and colleagues (2004) analysed police and newspaper reports of 100 murders committed by 100 serial killers in the United States. The researchers were trying to determine whether distinct sub-types of serial killer exist. They used 39 behavioural and psychological characteristics within their analysis. Their findings suggested that there is no clear-cut pattern of characteristics that would support the idea of organised and disorganised categories of killer. The researchers did note a limited group of what could be classed as 'organised features' but none at all for disorganised.

This suggests the basic distinction that forms the basis of the typology approach may have little *validity* in the real world.

Mixed type

A further weakness is that researchers have been forced to concede that most serial killings fall somewhere in the middle.

Most crime scenes where there has been a sexually-motivated murder do not fit neatly within the organised–disorganised distinction and are much more of a mixture of the two different types: the 'mixed crime scene' (Douglas *et al.* 1992). Indeed, this is now recognised in more recent versions of the Crime classification manual (2006) which regards organised and disorganised types as being extreme ends of a continuum, rather than distinct types: 'It should be emphasised that the crime scene rarely will be completely organised or disorganised. It is more likely to be somewhere on a continuum between the two extremes of the orderly, neat crime scene and the disarrayed, sloppy one' (Burgess *et al.* 1986).

This suggests that the difference between the typologies in the top-down model was probably overstated.

Assessment practice

At the end of learning aim C you must write a report containing:

An offender profile based on a case study of a real or imagined event. This should include the different profiling methods and an evaluation of the methods used when creating the profile.

This report must be related to a real or fictitious event. We have used a fictitious event.

> Police were called to a house where they found a body in the kitchen. The victim was a 20-year-old woman with a pale freckled complexion and long fair hair parted in the middle. She was stabbed to death with a single blow to the heart, and there were other stab injuries to her abdomen that formed the pattern of a star. There were no other visible signs of injury. She was carefully placed on the floor with her hands resting on her stomach and bound with a ribbon.

C1.1 Learning aim C1 – Task 1

The first part of your report for learning aim C will be concerned with looking at different profiling methods and evaluating them. These are covered on this spread and the next two spreads plus the spread on pages 158–159.

1. **Produce** an offender profile for the crime above using the top-down approach. (C.P5) (C.M3) (C.D3)

2. **Explain** the top-down approach as you have applied it in your offender profile. Refer to at least one supporting theory. (C.P6)

3. **Explain** at least **two** limitations of the top-down approach as you have applied it in your offender profile. (C.P6)

4. **Assess** your offender profile in terms of use and limitations of the top-down approach. (C.M4) (C.D3)

> **You can see an explanation of command terms and the assessment criteria on pages 131 and 160.**

An issue to consider

The top-down approach was developed, in part, through interviews with convicted serial killers.

Can you think of any issues with this? How might these issues have affected the quality of the information received, and ultimately, the typology approach?

Specification content
C1 Methods of offender profiling
● Top-down US Federal Bureau of Investigation (FBI) approach techniques:
○ Classification of offenders – the organised/disorganised typology of serial murder, Canter *et al.* (2004), the lust murderer, Hazelwood and Douglas (1980).

Bottom-up approach

The Railway Rapist

Between 1975 and 1986 there were 23 women who were raped aged between 15 and 32 at railway stations in and around London. The forensic psychologist David Canter became interested in the case after reading reports in the newspaper. Working alongside two police officers, Canter placed all the cases on a map, so he was able to speculate about where the rapist might live. He also drew up a profile describing the biography of the offender, including his job type and details of his personal life.

Central to Canter's profile was the idea that the offender's behaviour at the scene, and his interactions with victims, said something about his everyday relationships. This was the first British case to use behavioural characteristics to search for an offender alongside evidence gathered from the crime scene. Canter's highly accurate profile reduced the pool of possible suspects from 200 to two (you can see how accurate the profile was in the table at the bottom of the page).

In November 2000, John Duffy who was serving life for the rape and murder of several women, confessed that he was responsible for many more. It also came to light that Duffy had committed some of the rapes with an accomplice – David Mulcahy.

The British approach to offender profiling

The British 'bottom-up' version of *offender profiling* takes a much more psychological and statistical approach than the American FBI *top-down model* described on the previous spread. British profiling has emerged largely through the extensive work of David Canter.

Canter came to the public's attention when he produced a strikingly accurate profile of John Duffy, the Railway Rapist (see left), which eventually led to Duffy's capture. Canter has contributed much to the field of profiling and is largely responsible for making it a more credible and scientific discipline.

Based on psychological theory

One criticism that is often made of the American top-down method of profiling is that it relies too much on 'hunches' and guesswork to make the crime scene fit one of the two typologies. The British model is much more 'data-driven'. There are no preconceptions or fixed types to begin with, the crime scene is taken at face value, and the profile is 'worked up' from there.

The British approach, named *investigative psychology* by Canter himself, tries to get into the mind of the killer. One key assumption is that the *modus operandi* of the offender (how they typically operate) will reflect their personal experiences and *schemas* (a concept explained in Unit 1 of the specification, see our Year 1 'Certificate' book). Understanding this modus operandi can reveal important clues about an offender's motives as well as revealing what they typically do in their everyday life.

Behavioural consistency

Bottom-up profiling uses police databases of historical crimes. The assumption is that offenders are consistent, that repeated patterns of behaviour are likely to occur across crime scenes.

During the profiling process, specific details of an offence (or series of offences), are matched against the database and this may suggest other aspects of their personality and/or likely behaviour, such as being a loner or committing domestic violence.

This 'matching' of the current crime to previous crimes may also inform police of how likely the offender is to strike again. *Statistical* analysis might also reveal whether the person who committed the current crime has committed other similar offences.

Key factors in profiling

Central to investigative psychology, are three key ideas:

Interpersonal coherence The way an offender behaves during the crime, including how they interact with the victim, reflects how they behave in other areas of their life, i.e. there is *interpersonal coherence*. For example, in the Duffy case, Canter pointed out that Duffy's need to dominate women suggested domestic violence within his own marriage – which turned out to be an accurate assumption (see below). It has been noted by Diana Dwyer (2001) that some rapists seek to control and dominate their victims, whilst others are more apologetic. This might tell police how offenders relate to women more generally.

The significance of time and place When and where offences take place allow police to speculate on the offender's likely movements during the day (whether they are employed or unemployed, for instance), as well as where they are living at the time of the crime. The place where crimes are committed is an essential ingredient of *geographical profiling* (see 'Get active' on facing page).

Forensic awareness The extent to which an offender tries to 'cover their tracks' will help determine whether they have had contact with the police before. For instance, someone who tries to remove a fingerprint or conceal a body may suggest some familiarity with the police's investigative procedures.

Canter's profile	True facts about Duffy
Lives in Kilburn/Cricklewood area.	Lived in Kilburn.
Married, no children.	Married, infertile.
Marriage problems.	Separated.
Loner, few friends.	Only two friends (one was his accomplice).
Physically small, unattractive.	5ft 4in with acne.
Martial artist, body builder.	Member of martial arts club.
Needs to dominate women.	Violently attacked his wife.
Fantasies of rape, bondage.	Tied up his wife before sex.

Caught in the act. One strength of bottom-up profiling is that it can be used in cases of burglary.

Evaluation

Evidence of effectiveness

One strength of the bottom-up approach is that evidence supports the effectiveness of the process.

David Canter and Rupert Heritage (1990) conducted an analysis of 66 sexual assault cases. The data was examined using *smallest space analysis*, a statistical technique that identifies *correlations* across different samples of behaviour. Several characteristics were identified as common, such as the use of impersonal language and lack of reaction to the victim. Different individuals display different patterns of these characteristics which may help establish whether two or more offences were committed by the same person. In addition such insights can lead to an understanding of how an offender's behaviour may change over a series of offences.

This supports the merits of the British profiling method.

Wider variety of crime

Another strength of the bottom-up approach is that it has been applied to more offences than the top-down model has.

One of the issues with the top-down approach is that it can only really account for a couple of types of crime. These include serial murder where there is a sexual element (the so-called 'lust murderer') and arson. By contrast, Canter has demonstrated how the bottom-up approach, using insights from geographical profiling (below), can also be used to account for the movements and motivations of serial burglars. This is a strength as burglary is common, and incidents of sexually-motivated murder are still relatively rare (despite their typically higher profile in the media).

This suggests that bottom-up profiling could perhaps be used more often, and for that reason, may be more helpful to police.

Quality of data

One weakness of the approach is the quality of statistical data may sometimes be questionable.

Canter's argument is that bottom-up profiling has the potential to be more scientific than the top-down approach, as it is more grounded in theory and statistical evidence. However, such techniques are only as good as the background data used to inform them. One factor is that statistical data is inevitably based on offenders who have been caught. This may tell us little about the pattern of behaviour related to unsolved crimes. In this way, the assumption of behavioural consistency, on which bottom-up profiling rests, may not necessarily apply in all cases.

This means that the bottom-up approach could struggle to account for crimes that do not fit an anticipated pattern.

GET ACTIVE Geographical profiling

Ever watched a cop show where the police stick pins in a map to denote the location of crime scenes? This is the basis of geographical profiling – another important aspect of the bottom-up approach.

Logically, offenders tend to operate in areas they know well. Serial offenders will often unknowingly create a pattern of crime scenes or body disposal sites that is circular, with the offender's home base in the centre of the pattern. This is *circle theory* (Canter and Larkin 1993).

Spatial awareness of linked crime scenes may provide further insights, such as whether the crime was planned, the mode of transport used and the offender's 'mental map' of the area.

How does geographical profiling reflect the wider aims of bottom-up profiling?

Assessment practice

At the end of learning aim C you must write a report (see pages 149 and 160). This report must be related to a real or fictitious event. We have used a fictitious event.

You should now continue to write your own offender profile. Use the same case you started with on the previous spread. Here is some more information to help you:

Detectives noticed several points of similarity between this crime scene and three others within a ten-mile radius. The pathology reports indicated time of death in all cases was between 9 and 11 am. Also in all cases, there was an attempt to remove evidence from the scene.

C1.2 Learning aim C1 – Task 2

The first part of your report for learning aim C will be concerned with looking at different profiling methods and evaluating them. These are covered on the previous spread, this spread and the next spread plus the spread on pages 158–159.

This activity will help you practise the skills required to write the report in response to your scenario/context.

1. **Produce** an offender profile for the crime above using the bottom-up approach. (C.P5) (C.M3) (C.D3)
2. **Explain** the bottom-up approach as you have applied it in your offender profile. Refer to at least **one** supporting theory. (C.P6)
3. **Explain** at least **two** limitations of the bottom-up approach as you have applied it in your offender profile. (C.P6)
4. **Assess** your offender profile in terms of use and limitations of the bottom-up approach. (C.M4) (C.D3)

An issue to consider

Consider the evidence on this spread and the previous spread.

Of the two methods of offender profiling we have discussed, which do you think would be more successful? Which would be easier for the police to implement? Give reasons for your choices.

Specification content

C1 Methods of offender profiling

- Bottom-up British behavioural evidence analysis approach techniques:
  - Based on key psychological theories.
  - How and why criminal behaviour occurs.
  - Consistencies of offender actions (behavioural consistency).
  - Factors, e.g. interpersonal coherence, significance of time and place, forensic awareness.

Aims of profiling

Thomas Bond and Jack the Ripper

One of the most famous unsolved murder cases in history is the Whitechapel murders during the year of 1888. The name 'Jack the Ripper' came from a signed letter which is now believed to be a hoax. The murderer terrorised women in Whitechapel, an East End area of London. All of the Ripper's five murder victims were prostitutes, and all met their end in the same grisly way – by having their throats cut and their internal organs removed.

Jack the Ripper's identity has never been discovered, and the case has found its way into British history. The term 'ripperology' was even coined to describe the fact that there are over a hundred different accounts of the Ripper's identity that have emerged over the years.

The earliest of all these accounts is often cited as the first attempt to create an offender profile. Thomas Bond was a police surgeon who performed the autopsy on the Ripper's final victim, Mary Jane Kelly. The profile he constructed was based on his examination of Miss Kelly's body as well as the case notes of the other four victims.

As part of his profile, Bond speculated as to the precise nature of the Ripper's attack, and what each murder had in common. He also put forward theories about the probable murder weapon, as well as the killer's background and appearance. He described the Ripper as 'a man of physical strength...of great coolness and daring'. He also suggested that he would likely be 'not quite right in his mind at times'.

Specification term

Offender profiling (also known as criminal profiling) An investigative tool used by law enforcement agencies to identify likely suspects. It has been used by investigators to link cases that may have been committed by the same perpetrator.

Offender profiling

When writing your report, you may wish to begin with the information from this spread to introduce the topic of offender profiling. We have placed it here to match the order of the specification.

Offender profiling has grown steadily in popularity since it was first introduced by the FBI in the 1970s. Offender profiling is an investigative tool that police forces use when solving crimes.

Professional profilers may be called upon to work alongside the police, especially during high profile murder cases. Note that profiling can be used for other crimes too, but is especially relevant to murder inquiries.

As we have seen, there are different approaches – the *bottom-up approach* described on page 150 and the *top-down approach* on page 148. In general profiling involves close examination of a crime scene and analysis of the evidence. Therefore, crime scene data collection is also important, which is discussed on page 156.

The end goal is to draw out a descriptive sketch of the offender, including biographical details such as their age, occupation, family background, etc.

Modern profiling has three main aims which are explained below.

1. Narrowing the range of suspects

The task of the profiler is to offer different *hypotheses* about *who* has committed the crime in question. Following an analysis of all the evidence at their disposal, a profiler will make a social and psychological assessment of the offender. This will include speculating about the offender's personality, age, ethnicity, sex, employment, education and marital status. This can save the police valuable time by reducing the list of suspects that they need to *interview*.

2. Predicting future crimes

It may be that the current crime is part of a larger linked sequence of similar crimes, i.e. they have been committed by a serial killer. Such murderers are often distinguished by their particular ways of working (their *modus operandi*), and the unique features they leave behind at the crime scene (their *signature*).

The times and locations of the crimes are also useful in determining where and how the offender may strike next. This has been referred to as *linkage analysis*.

3. Appropriate interview technique

A final goal of profiling is to suggest the most effective interviewing strategy, once the offender has been arrested. As there are different types of offenders, methods of interrogation must also vary. For instance, not all serial murderers kill for the same reasons, so the police must take account of this when devising interview questions (Holmes and Holmes 1996).

A competent offender profiler will make suggestions about how offenders may react under questioning and how best to extract a confession.

A profile is a representation of something in outline.

Learning aim C is concerned with profiling – variously referred to as psychological profiling, criminal profiling, criminal investigative analysis, crime scene analysis, behavioural profiling, criminal personality profiling, sociopsychological profiling and criminological profiling (Ebisike 2007)!

To be clear, we'll stick with the name on the specification throughout this section – offender profiling.

GET ACTIVE Who are offender profilers?

In the last ten years, profiling in the UK has become a recognised profession. The term *Behavioural Investigative Advisor (BIA)* has replaced 'offender profiler' and the professional and ethical standards of the role are overseen by the Association of Chief Police Officers (ACPO). That said, profilers vary widely in their level of experience and education. Many profilers in this country are individuals with degrees in mental health and forensic psychology.

What skills do you think an effective offender profiler would need?

Is someone nicking my car?

Evaluation

Investigative data

One strength of offender profiling is that it can kick-start an investigation.

Often, in a murder enquiry there may be very few leads for the police to go on. Without a living witness or CCTV evidence, the only physical trace of the offence may be the microscopic evidence left at the crime scene. However, it is likely, through careful analysis, that an experienced offender profiler will still be able to compile enough information for the police to begin their investigation. As we have seen, profilers can offer hypotheses on the characteristics of the offender, the likely weapon, cause of death (which may not necessarily be obvious) and possible sequence of events. This means that the investigation can start with a solid foundation of potentially relevant information.

This suggests that offender profiling can be a positive initial step, assisting the eventual capture of the offender.

Mixed findings

Another strength of profiling is that the police seem to regard it as useful.

The question of whether police officers find offender profiling useful was investigated in a study by Gary Copson (1995). A *survey* of 184 police officers found that 83% claimed that profiling was operationally useful and 92% agreed that they would seek profiling advice again. However, only 14% reported that it helped them solve a case, and a tiny 3% said it actually helped them identify the offender. It may be that offender profiling's primary function is in helping officers to understand more about the case, or in confirming existing lines of enquiry.

This suggests that offender profiling is valued by police but, in and of itself, only occasionally leads to successful outcomes.

Diverse application

One weakness of offender profiling is there is no single agreed framework.

Andreas Kapardis (2017) makes the point that profiling techniques draw on lots of different disciplines, including personality theory, criminality and environmental psychology. Similarly, there are several different approaches to profiling (two of which we have explored on the previous two spreads – top-down and bottom-up profiling). These variations make it difficult to draw general conclusions about the effectiveness of profiling. They also make it difficult to see how profiling could become an essential part of everyday police work if there is little agreement between experts of how it should be applied.

This suggests that profiling may continue to be an investigative technique that the police only rely upon in exceptional circumstances.

Assessment practice

At the end of learning aim C you must write a report (see pages 149 and 160). This report must be related to a real or fictitious event.

You can now 'take a step back' from your offender profile and think about the purpose of it. What is a profile for? What does it achieve and how does it help the forensic psychologist and police officers?

Use this spread to help you consider these questions. By answering the questions below, you can write an introduction to your profile (and continue it using the evaluation spread starting on page 158). This will give readers some idea of the 'overall' uses and limitations of offender profiling.

C2.3 Learning aim C2 – Task 3

The first part of your report for learning aim C will be concerned with looking at different profiling methods and evaluating them. These are covered on the previous two spreads, this spread and the spread on pages 158–159.

This activity will help you practise the skills required to write the report in response to your scenario/context.

1. **Explain** at least **two** ways in which offender profiling can assist forensic psychologists and the police. (C.P6)

2. **Explain** at least **two** limitations of offender profiling in achieving these purposes. (C.P6)

3. **Assess** the aims and purposes of offender profiling. (C.M4)

> You can see an explanation of command terms and the assessment criteria on pages 131 and 160.

An issue to consider

Offender profiling relies heavily on the concept of behavioural consistency, that an offender's behaviour at the crime scene gives clues to their behaviour in everyday life.

Can you see any issues with this assumption? Is there likely to be such a straightforward relationship between the offender's crimes and how they behave in the rest of their life? If not, why not?

Specification content

C2 Offender profiling, purpose and techniques

- Aims of profiling:
  - Narrowing range of suspects.
  - Predicting future crimes, e.g. times, locations.
  - Establishing appropriate techniques for police interviews of suspect.

Building a portrait

Atavistic form

Offender profiling has come a long way since its early origins. An Italian physician, Cesare Lombroso, suggested in his 1876 book, *L'Uomo Delinquente*, that criminals could be identified from their physical features – what he called the *atavistic form*. This is in sharp contrast to today's profilers who are much more likely to focus on the psychological and social characteristics of an offender, rather than what they look like.

Lombroso's central argument was that criminals are a kind of sub-species, a group of individuals who are further back in the evolutionary chain than the rest of us and cannot adjust to the demands of civilised society. Their *untamed wildness* means they struggle to follow society's rules and, as a result, end up committing crime.

Even at the time, this was a controversial proposition. Lombroso claimed that criminals could be marked out by, amongst other things, the shape of their head (cranial structure) and their facial features, alongside other physical abnormalities (such as having extra fingers, toes or nipples!). For instance, murderers would be distinguished by their bloodshot eyes, curly hair and prominent jawline, sexual deviants by their fleshy lips and projecting ears.

Lombroso examined the skulls of many thousands of offenders (like the one in the picture above) – both living and dead – and claimed that he had found support for his theory. Having said that, his argument was undermined by the fact that he failed to compare his sample with a group of non-criminals. When other researchers did this, the differences Lombroso suggested disappeared.

Lombroso's atavistic form theory has long since been discredited – but the idea that certain types of people commit certain types of crime lived on, and has formed the basis of many thousands of offender profiles since.

Building a portrait

We have seen how analysis of crime scene evidence is a vital part of police work. It can help determine how the sequence of events may have happened, as well as what kind of person performed the criminal act. We have also seen how the *offender profiling* process itself is important in narrowing down the range of potential suspects in a criminal investigation.

Offender profiling does not solve crime, but it does mean that the police can begin their enquiries in a more focused manner. Ronald Holmes and Stephen Holmes (1996) have suggested that this is achieved, in the first instance, by developing a psychological and social profile of the likely offender. Investigators make 'educated guesses' about the kind of person they are dealing with, as well as their background and social circumstances.

The psychological portrait

One aspect of profiling focuses on a *psychological portrait* of the offender. This may be needed because the police have very little to go on. There may be little physical evidence at the crime scene, for instance, or no eyewitness accounts. Thus, the investigation needs to start somewhere.

Alternatively, a profile may be developed from what the police already know. For instance, a serial killer who is targeting prostitutes is likely to have had issues with women in the past, or at the very least may know where and how to access prostitutes.

Psychological profiles are usually created using a standard format and are likely to include details of the following.

The age, gender and health of the suspect

According to the Ministry of Justice in 2009, just over one in five of all pre-court and court sanctions were issued to females, which closely mirrors the proportion of all arrests accounted for by females. The numbers of women who commit violent crime however is much smaller, and for very serious crimes such as sexually-motivated murder, it is smaller still. Safe to say then that the gender of the suspect can often be discerned from the nature of the crime.

Exciting recent developments in DNA analysis may reveal other information about the offender. Mahsa Shabani and colleagues (2018) point out that it is now possible to work out the age of an offender from a single drop of blood. The molecular structure of DNA changes as we get older and this allows experts to pinpoint the age of suspects. Similar conclusions can also be drawn from blood samples about the health and physical fitness of the individual.

Habits and behavioural consistency

Behavioural consistency is a key issue in profiling, especially *bottom-up profiling* (see page 150) and is similar to David Canter's concept of *interpersonal coherence*. This is the idea that the way the offender behaves at the crime scene, and in relation to the victim, may reveal crucial details about the offender's daily life, their everyday habits and their mental schemas. Consistent patterns of behaviour across linked crime scenes also allow investigators to understand the development of an offender's criminal career over time.

Personality and intellect

The sum total of profiling is to try and make judgements about what the motivations of this person are, what makes them tick and what drives their behaviour. Handwritten notes, or other forms of communication, could offer clues as to the intellect or educational background of the suspect. Broader conclusions might also be made about their personality. Tying up or restraining a victim, for instance, may indicate a need for control that is reflected in the offender's everyday life.

A psychological profile can put a face (and an age, and a personality) to a suspect.

GET ACTIVE You are the profiler

The body of a woman in her early 20s has been found abandoned in a field. There is severe bruising around the shoulders and neck, and evidence of a sexual assault. A large metal chain has been found around half a mile away. The field backs on to a housing estate next to a building site.

1. *Use your knowledge of profiling to construct a psychological and social portrait of this offender.*

2. *Do you think the crime was premeditated or a 'spur-of-the-moment' act? Explain your answer.*

The social portrait

Psychological profiling is not the complete picture. Investigators will also attempt to make inferences about the social characteristics of the offender, i.e. their status in society, a *social portrait*. Some of these are described below.

Social class, occupation and marital status

The typology approach divides serial killers, rapists and arsonists into *organised* or *disorganised* categories (see page 148). This classification may indicate aspects of social class, occupation and marital status. For example, organised offenders tend to be in high status, skilled work, and are usually married or in a relationship. Disorganised offenders tend to live alone and have lower *socioeconomic status*.

A criminal who has 'cleaned up' the crime scene and removed the body may well be someone who has knowledge of police procedures, or even is in the medical profession.

Ethnicity and religion

The ethnic group the offender belongs to is often determined through DNA analysis if there are no eyewitnesses. Certain kinds of crime, especially terrorism, might indicate a political, ideological or religious motive.

Possible substance abuse

Particular types of crime may also suggest involvement with, or dependence upon, drugs. A study by Anders Håkansson and Virginia Jesionowska (2018) found that perpetrators of violent crime are actually less likely to be drug users than those who commit other forms of crime – apart, that is, from alcohol users. Binge drinking among violent offenders is common. *Substance abuse* is more associated with burglary and theft as a means of financing the habit.

Possible crime history

DNA evidence collected from the crime scene allows investigators to consult *statistical* databases to see if they can find a match (see the next spread for details). Police are able to link a series of crimes together that appear to follow a similar pattern (a technique known as *linkage analysis*).

In the case of serial murder, the offender may distinguish themselves by leaving a trademark 'fingerprint' – in the sense of the offender's *modus operandi*, the way in which they normally behave (they might also leave actual fingerprints too, of course).

There may also be similarities in how the crime was executed. For instance, serial killers may take a souvenir from the victim such as a lock of their hair, an item of clothing or, gruesomely, a body part.

Area where they live

The practice of geographical profiling is discussed on page 151. *Circle theory* proposes that the offender's home base tends to be in the middle of the pattern of crime scene locations. This effect also holds true for serial burglars (Canter and Larkin 1993).

Evidence also suggests that serial offenders, particularly sexually-motivated murderers, often entrap themselves through the body disposal sites they select.

Specification terms

Psychological portrait A description of a person in terms of individual characteristics such as personality, gender, typical behaviours, etc.

Social portrait A description of a person in terms of their interactions with other people. 'Social' refers to interactions between members of the same species.

Assessment practice

At the end of learning aim C you must write a report (see pages 149 and 160). This report must be related to a real or fictitious event. We have used a fictitious event.

Here is some more information about the case you are profiling:
There were no signs of forced entry into the property. In fact the front door was closed but unlocked with the key next to it. The victim had been raped and a variety of sexual acts were forced upon her. There was evidence she had been blindfolded, but the blindfold had since been removed.

C2.4 Learning aim C2 – Task 4

The second part of your report for learning aim C will be concerned with constructing a profile for your own scenario. Some key considerations are covered on this spread and the next spread.

1. **Explain** the process of building a psychological and social portrait of the offender. (C.P6)

2. As part of your offender profile, **produce** a psychological and social portrait applying to the current case. (C.P5) (C.M3) (C.D3)

3. **Explain** and **assess** at least **two** limitations of the portrait-building process as you have applied it in your offender profile. (C.P6) (C.M4)

An issue to consider

In the near future, DNA analysis could reveal many details about the suspect including their age and even their medical history.

Bear in mind that this person has not been found guilty of the crime at this point – are there any ethical issues with this? Or is a suspect always 'fair game' in terms of DNA profiling?

Specification content

C2 Offender profiling, purpose and techniques

● Building a psychological portrait of a suspect, e.g. personality, age, gender, habits, behavioural consistency, intellect, health.

● Building a social portrait of a suspect, e.g. religion, ethnicity, social class, marital status, occupation, possible substance abuse, possible crime history and area where they live.

Problems and issues

Rachel Nickell

On the morning of 15 July 1992, 23-year-old mother-of-one Rachel Nickell was brutally murdered in broad daylight on Wimbledon Common (above). The only witness to the horrific crime was Rachel's two-year-old son, Alex, who was strolling through the park at the time with his mum and the family dog.

Rachel was stabbed many times and sexually assaulted. When Rachel's body was discovered by a passer-by, Alex was unharmed but clinging desperately to her. The Metropolitan Police immediately launched a manhunt.

With assistance from Alex, a photofit was drawn up and a local man, Colin Stagg, was identified as matching the profile. Stagg was unemployed, something of a loner and often seen walking his dog on the common.

There was no forensic evidence linking Stagg to Rachel, but the police were convinced they had found her killer. Under the direction of criminal profiler Paul Britton, the Metropolitan Police set up a 'honey trap'. An undercover policewoman would befriend Stagg and pretend to be romantically interested in him, in an attempt to withdraw a confession.

But Stagg never did confess. Under pressure, Britton and the Metropolitan Police pressed on regardless, and in August 1993, Colin Stagg was charged with Rachel's murder. The judge in the trial, bemused by the lack of evidence he had been presented with, threw the case out and Stagg was acquitted.

In 2002, a decade after the Wimbledon Common murder, new DNA evidence emerged which identified Robert Napper as Rachel's killer. Napper was already serving a life sentence for the murder of Samantha Bisset – another young mother with a striking similarity to Rachel Nickell.

It turned out that whilst the Metropolitan Police were busy pursuing Colin Stagg, Napper had gone on to murder Samantha a year after he had murdered Rachel. It also transpired that Napper had actually been a suspect in the Nickell case, but had been ruled out at an early stage of the enquiry when two junior officers had judged him too tall to fit the profile.

Specification term

Barnum effect The tendency to accept types of information, such as offender profiles or horoscopes, as true even when the information is in fact vague and general enough to apply to a wide range of people or situations.

Problems and issues with offender profiling

Offender profiling is not without its critics. Although there have been many successes using profiling methods, there have also been significant failures (such as the case of Rachel Nickell, described left). Commentators have pointed to several issues and potential problems with the profiling process, and these are described below.

Appropriateness for particular crimes

Ronald Holmes and Stephen Holmes (1996) make the claim that offender profiling techniques only apply to a small number of crimes. This includes where an unknown perpetrator has shown signs of serious *psychopathology* (mental disturbance). This psychopathology is demonstrated through actions such as sadistic torture, slashing/cutting after death, and ritualistic crime.

Such murders are very rare, which limits the scope of offender profiling.

Insufficient empirical investigation

When studies of the success of offender profiling are carried out, they tend to be *surveys* which ask for the police's views on the effectiveness of profiling. Inevitably, these are likely to be *subjective* and/or biased, or not actually based on evidence. For example, a *meta-analysis* of 130 articles on profiling (Snook *et al.* 2007) found that the arguments were based on 'common sense' rather than any scientific evidence.

When profiling is more formally tested, it tends not to come out that well. Laurence Alison *et al.* (2010) analysed 4000 offender profiles and found that around 80% of the claims made in these profiles were unsupported, in the sense that they were not backed up by evidence, and were speculative guesswork.

Reductionist

Every crime scene is different, every killer and victim are different – yet in offender profiling there is an attempt to match crime scenes to former crimes. The *bottom-up approach* depends on the idea of behavioural consistency and using existing *statistical* databases to develop a profile. The *top-down approach* divides all cases of serial murder into just two pre-existing typologies: *organised* and *disorganised*. It may be that both approaches are guilty of a form of *reductionism*, in that they ignore the uniqueness of the situation and focus too heavily on trying to determine the biographical background of the offender.

The Barnum effect

The *Barnum effect* is the view that people often interpret vague and general statements as if they are specific to their own situation. This is the basis of many people's belief in astrology, where the description of an astrological star sign consists of statements that really could fit anyone.

Critics of offender profiling have claimed there is something very similar going on. Profiles are often made up of a series of vague statements that could apply to lots of people and lots of situations. When there is pressure on the police to 'get a result' and make an arrest, they will see what they want to see in a profile, seizing upon some statements and disregarding others.

Ethics

The case of Rachel Nickell is a stark warning of the danger of profiles being misused or misunderstood as part of a police investigation. Paul Wilson and Keith Soothill (1996), in their analysis of the Nickell case, have argued that it raises important questions about the value and appropriateness of the profiling procedure more widely. Clearly, there were *ethical* implications here in the way that an innocent man was pursued and subject to entrapment simply because he 'fitted the description'. The researchers conclude that profilers have a professional responsibility to point out the limitations of profiling – that the process is best described as 'art' rather than 'science'.

Marta wondered, 'Could offender profiling really be nothing more than guesswork?'

Evaluation

Behavioural evidence analysis

One strength of profiling is that new methods are being developed.

A recent development in offender profiling is *behavioural evidence analysis* (BEA), popularised by Brent Turvey (2011) amongst others. BEA attempts to offer a less reductionist approach to profiling. It is more descriptive than alternatives and adopts a much less certain stance in terms of behavioural consistency and predicting the offender's next move. Differences and inconsistencies in linked crime scenes are taken at face value, rather than explained away. Serial offenders are seen as individuals who change and adapt their *modus operandi* (how they typically operate) over a series of crimes, rather than remaining static.

This suggests that offender profiling is an adaptable method and can be adjusted so that it is more useful.

Evidence of the Barnum effect

One strength of the Barnum effect is there is evidence to support it.

In one research study, Laurence Alison and colleagues (2003) showed how senior police officers and forensic psychologists were prepared to believe ambiguous statements about complete strangers if the statements were presented in the form of an offender profile. Despite the fact that participants received different profiles, over 75% rated their profile as at least somewhat accurate and over 50% as very accurate. The researchers took this as evidence of the Barnum effect, that vague and ambiguous statements are judged as factual when presented as an offender profile, even among experts in the field.

This suggests that the Barnum effect may influence how likely police are to accept and act upon a flawed or bogus profile.

Specialist skills

One weakness of profiling is that it appears not to require any real technique.

Anthony Pinizzotto and Norman Finkel (1990) aimed to discover whether professional profilers would be more accurate than laypeople in drawing up profiles from two closed police cases – a sex offence case and a murder case. The *sample* was made up of four professional profilers, 12 detectives, six psychologists and six undergraduates. The written profile produced by each participant was analysed for similarity with the actual offender. It was found that the professional profilers produced more detailed profiles than other participants and were more accurate for the sex offence case especially. However, Pinizzotto and Finkel did conclude that this was the result of the profilers' confidence and experience rather than any exclusive technique they employed.

This suggests that what mainly separates profilers from the general public is their experience in the field.

GET ACTIVE The Boston strangler

Between 1962 and 1964, 13 women were murdered in Boston (Massachusetts, USA). A profile suggested the offender was a male homosexual schoolteacher living alone. When arrested, Albert DeSalvo – who confessed to all 13 crimes – was found to be a heterosexual construction worker living with his family! He was given the name *The Boston Strangler*.

Although DeSalvo was convicted (and was later killed in prison), questions still remain about the Boston Strangler, not least because not all of the women were strangled, and one even died of a heart attack. Experts now believe that it is highly unlikely that DeSalvo murdered all 13 women, if indeed, he murdered any!

Why does this case illustrate some of the limitations of offender profiling?

Assessment practice

At the end of learning aim C you must write a report (see pages 149 and 160). This report must be related to a real or fictitious event.

You can complete your profile by including information covered on this final spread.

In considering these further limitations of offender profiling, refer to specific details in your own profile. Select only a few evaluations that you feel are particularly relevant.

Finally, try to come to a conclusion about which technique you think is more useful and/or effective – top-down or bottom-up, building a portrait or crime scene data collection.

C3.6 Learning aim C3 – Task 6

The third part of your report for learning aim C will be concerned with evaluating different profiling methods. You have already looked at some limitations as part of the assessment practice on pages 149–153.

1. **Explain** at least **two** further limitations of offender profiling in achieving the aims of profiling. (C.P6)
2. **Explain** how these limitations relate to your own profile. (C.P6)
3. **Assess** offender profiling in terms of further problems and issues. (C.M4)

You can see an explanation of command terms and the assessment criteria on pages 131 and 160.

An issue to consider

Overall, how useful is offender profiling as an investigative tool?

Specification content

C3 Limitations of offender profiling

Problems and issues associated with offender profiling, including:

- Appropriateness for particular crimes, e.g. Holmes and Holmes 1996.
- Insufficient empirical investigation.
- Reductionist.
- Police analysis bias – Barnum effect.
- Ethics.

Learning aim C

Assessment guidance

Learning aim C assessment

You are required to produce one or more reports (but not more than three) for the three learning aims in this unit.

The board recommends three reports for Unit 4.

The report can be written or presented as a poster, PowerPoint or other form.

This report can only be completed after you have studied the content of learning aim C as it is a synoptic assessment (see page 131).

Recommended assessment approach

The *Delivery Guide for Unit 4* states that your report (or presentation, poster, etc.) for learning aim C:

- Will be applied to a real or fictitious event.
- Should use different profiling methods to analyse the event.
- Should evaluate which one is most useful to create the profile.

Assignment briefs

The board supplies suggested assignment briefs which you can use – see *Unit 4 Authorised assignment brief for Learning aim C.*

Your centre can also devise their own assignment brief which should have a vocational scenario/context and a series of tasks to complete.

Vocational scenario	The task (from the assignment brief)
The *Delivery Guide for Unit 4* suggests that a scenario might be a real or fictitious event. This could take the form of a report being provided from a profiler to a police team wanting to solve a real or imagined scenario.	You need to produce an offender profile using different profiling methods. Your profile should include the following: • **Produce** an offender profile using different profiling methods. (See pass and merit criteria below.) • **Explain** the techniques applied in your own offender profiles, making reference to their limitations and with reference to supporting theories. (See pass criteria below.) • **Assess** your own offender profile making reference to the use and limitations of the techniques applied, with reference to supporting theories. (See merit criteria below.) • **Produce** a comprehensive offender profile using different profiling methods and justify the effectiveness of the techniques used with the support of theoretical application. (See distinction criteria below.)

Referencing

You must include the details of all references cited in your report. These go in an alphabetical list (by author) at the end of your report.

Author names are always given as last name followed by initial(s). When multi-authored works have been cited, it is important to include the names of all the authors, even when the text reference used was '*et al.*'

Book references

Author name(s), date, book title (in italics), place of publication, publisher. e.g. Offer, D., Ostrov, E. and Howard, K. (1981) *The Adolescent – a psychological self-portrait.* New York: Basic Books.

Journal references

Author name(s), date, article title, journal name (in italics), volume (in italics) and where given issue number (in brackets), page numbers. e.g. MacKay, G. (2002) The disappearance of disability? Thoughts on a changing culture. *British Journal of Special Education*, *29*(4), 159–163.

Internet references

Author name(s), date, article title, source, full date, retrieved from web URL, date of access. e.g. Roller, E. (2016) Your facts or mine? *The New York Times*, 25 October 2016, retrieved from https://www.nytimes.com/2016/10/25/opinion/campaign-stops/your-facts-or-mine.html [Accessed June 2019].

Personal communication

e.g. Robertson, M. (2012) personal communication.

Assessment information

Your final report will be awarded a Distinction (D), Merit (M), Pass (P), Near Pass (N) or Unclassified (U).

The specification provides criteria for each level, shown below.

Pass	Merit	Distinction
C.P5 PRODUCE an outline offender profile using different profiling methods.		
C.P6 EXPLAIN techniques applied in own offender profile, with reference to their use and limitations, and supporting theories.		
	C.M3 PRODUCE a detailed offender profile using different profiling methods.	
	C.M4 ASSESS own offender profile with reference to techniques applied, their use and limitations, and supporting theories.	
		C.D3 PRODUCE a comprehensive offender profile using different profiling methods, giving full justification for effectiveness of techniques used, and supporting theories.

Self-review checklist

First draft

Remember this is a *draft*. So you can write anything, just get thoughts on the page (see 'Blank page syndrome' on page 147). But do not copy anything, even at this stage (see 'Plagiarism' on page 131).

Date to complete first draft:

	Date completed	Produce (C.P5)	Explain (C.P6)	Produce (C.M3)	Assess (C.M4)	Produce (C.D3)
• In the first grey column enter the completion dates for each section of your report. • As you write each section tick the yellow boxes when you have produced, explained and assessed, as appropriate. Ignore the boxes that are crossed through.						
C1 Methods of offender profiling						
Top-down approach						
Bottom-up approach						
C2 Offender profiling, purpose and techniques						
Aims of profiling		✕	✕		✕	
Building a portrait						
Crime scene data collection						
C3 Limitations of offender profiling						
Problems and issues		✕	✕		✕	
References compiled						

Second draft

The next step is to revise your first document. Below is a checklist of things to consider.

Date to complete second draft:

	Date completed
I have checked that I have covered each of the six marking factors (grey column) in the table below.	
I have gone through and deleted any irrelevant material.	
I have checked that every point has evidence to back it up.	
I have identified long sentences and rephrased them.	
I have checked that each paragraph deals with one idea.	
I have corrected any spelling mistakes.	
I have checked that each paragraph makes reference to the scenario/context.	

Final draft

Read through your completed second draft to polish the report.

Date to complete final draft:

Marking factors The specification also provides information that an assessor will take into consideration when marking your assignment.

Marking factors	Pass	Merit	Distinction
Produce offender profile, using UK and US methods which is ...	... simple.	... detailed.	... well-developed, comprehensive.
Profile considers ... psychological and social characteristics.		... a range of ...	... a broad range of ....
The profile ... evidence from the case study to support choices.	... has some ...	... is supported by ...	... is well-supported by ...
Consideration of key psychological research when explaining choices ...	... partial consideration.	... reference made.	... logically reasoned justifications, including reference to key methodologies.
Limitations of the approaches used to produce the offender profile ...	... two relevant limitations covered but not in detail.	... most of the relevant ones considered.	... several suggested, demonstrating a reasoned evaluation.
In addition ...		... some evaluation of how the offender profile could be improved.	... considered arguments on the ethical implications of offender profiling.

Unit 5

Promoting children's psychological development

All of us are parents (Cara, Dave, Rob, Jock and Mark) and, if asked what we hope most for our children, it would be that they grow up happy and contented.

But how do you get there?

➡ *What would you say are the ingredients to becoming a happy, contented adult?*

➡ *What do you think 'society' can do to help achieve this, especially in cases where young people have challenging childhoods?*

Pearson
recommended
assessment
approach

Contents

A report exploring ideas of childhood and theories of development, and their contribution to the understanding and promotion of children's healthy growth, development and mental well-being.

A report linking researched case studies of psychological developmental issues arising from privation/abuse, and approaches used by health professionals to support healthy development in children.

Historical and cultural perspectives on childhood

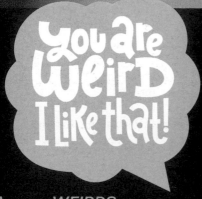

Are we WEIRD?

According to Joseph Henrich *et al.* (2010) we in the UK live in a WEIRD society – Westernised, Educated, Industrialised, Rich and Democratic. We take for granted certain child-rearing and caring practices that elsewhere in the world are looked upon very differently.

One example is the concept of 'spoiling' a child. This is generally frowned upon in WEIRD cultures like ours. So, we have practices such as feeding babies on a schedule rather than on demand and letting them cry instead of picking them up immediately. These are considered 'normal' and are meant to prevent a child getting his or her own way so they learn that not everything comes easily just because they want it (i.e. not 'spoiling' them).

But these practices (and others, such as letting babies sleep in a room by themselves) are seen as strange and potentially harmful in some non-WEIRD societies, even those open to Western influences (e.g. Japan). On the other hand, children on Tonga (a Pacific island) are beaten regularly, even as young as three years. A harsh upbringing is seen as the only way to force children to become socially skilled because they are naturally disobedient and clumsy. Holding back on punishment would only 'spoil' the child.

A mother enriching her baby's experience in the womb – is that a step too far?

Differing perspectives

Historical perspectives

Locke in the 17th century The philosopher John Locke (1632–1704) argued that we are born with no *innate* (inborn) knowledge of the world. He used the latin phrase *tabula rasa* (blank slate) to describe the mind of a newborn baby. Therefore, all our knowledge comes from external sources, i.e. learning and experience (which 'write' on the slate/mind).

Locke recommended an active role for parents in guiding children's development, not through rules and punishment but by encouragement and appealing to the child's reason. Childhood is a time for 'forming the mind', for education and for learning morals and how to behave properly. Early education should be about directing a child's natural tendency to learn and acquire knowledge and virtue.

Rousseau in the 18th century Jean-Jacques Rousseau wrote a novel, *Èmile* (1762), in which he presented children as born good but becoming corrupted by society. Babies are born with natural but undirected and unpolished abilities. His view was a Romantic one of the innocence of childhood, that children had a right to be children (a forerunner to our modern view).

Children should be educated as naturally as possible, preferably in the countryside and without books until adulthood. They should learn from nature, not from teachers, from their own experiences and mistakes and not from the rules of parents. Above all else, childhood should be happy.

Ariès in the 20th century In *Centuries of childhood* (1962), Philippe Ariès argued that 'childhood' is a relatively modern social construction (i.e. it is a recent 'invention' made by different social groups). His central claim was that 'In medieval society the idea of childhood did not exist'. There were no toys or education specifically for children. Instead, children worked alongside adults as soon as they passed infancy. They dressed like adults and were exploited for their labour in the same way. Children were essentially seen as small adults.

By the 17th century a more 'modern' view of childhood appeared. Children came to be seen as different from adults. Middle-class children had their own clothes, interests and ways of thinking. They were no longer seen as mini adults but as children requiring guidance, discipline and education.

Cultural perspectives

Beliefs and norms A widespread belief in WEIRD *cultures* (see left) is that parents should direct children's development from birth (or even before). Therefore, childhood is a 'protected' period, set aside for education not labour.

In some non-WEIRD cultures, three-year-olds are left to their own devices. By eight, children work alongside adults, handling sharp tools and even weapons. Girls are married by the age of 12. All of this is part of a healthy, normal childhood.

Cultural systems WEIRD and non-WEIRD societies represent two different cultural systems, in which adult–child interactions differ. For example, Chinese parents assume a great deal of authority over their children and are entitled to demand respect and obedience, and children usually comply.

In WEIRD societies such as the UK and USA, children are expected to obey their parents but not to the same extent as in China. Individuality is valued and may take the form of disobedience. Ching-Yu Huang and Michael Lamb (2014) noted that the children of Chinese immigrants to the UK were more likely to behave like native English children in not always complying with parental demands.

Religion Spiritual beliefs play an important role in the view of childhood shared by the Beng people of Côte d'Ivoire, West Africa. They believe that before children are born they live in a spirit world closed off to adults. Because this world is so enjoyable, spirits leave it only reluctantly to be born. Families understand that they are lucky to have the spirit join them, and are careful not to do anything that might encourage the spirit to leave. The Beng treat children with great care and even reverence (Gottlieb 1998).

Law The 'age of consent' is the age at which a child is considered by the law to be capable of consenting to sexual activity (and/or marriage). In most WEIRD countries this is 16 years (but not in all, e.g. in Germany it is 14). In non-WEIRD countries there is more variation. In many African countries it is 18, but it is 13 in Japan and 14 in most South American countries. Many countries have no age of consent for homosexuality – it is simply illegal.

Evaluation

Cultural variations in childhood

One strength of the cultural perspective is that it accounts for the existence of a wide range of views of childhood.

For example, in the UK children under 14 years are not legally allowed to supervise other children without adult help, because they are not considered able or competent. However, the Igbo people of Nigeria allow children as young as three to get on with their lives without much adult involvement, including working with sharp tools such as knives and machetes. Both are considered normal aspects of raising children.

These practices represent very different perceptions of what childhood is for and what children are capable of.

Benefits to children

Another strength of the historical perspective is that it highlights how views of childhood have progressed.

For instance, John Locke, Mary Wollstonecraft (an 18th-century philosopher) and others argued that the education of girls and boys should be similar, opposing Rousseau's quite different view. In WEIRD cultures (and many others), children no longer have to engage in unhealthy and dangerous work. Most people in very different cultures would no longer accept the view that 'children should be seen and not heard'.

This shows how a historical perspective can allow us to view how social practices have become more enlightened.

Evidence lacks validity

One weakness of historical perspectives is that Ariès' view lacks *valid* evidence.

According to Linda Pollock (1983), Ariès' evidence for the non-existence of childhood in medieval times is indirect and inconsistent (e.g. portrayals of children in paintings, letters of advice, etc.). When Pollock looked at direct sources such as diaries and newspaper reports, she found that childhood was often seen as different from adulthood. For example, physical punishment of children was common but it was also distinguished from adult punishment. Children could be beaten but not as severely as adults (e.g. servants).

This strongly suggests that childhood was viewed as distinct from adulthood in earlier times.

This Cambodian girl will have learned to use a machete from a very young age to help her work in the countryside. It would be extremely unusual to see a young child in the UK with a tool like this, even in rural areas.

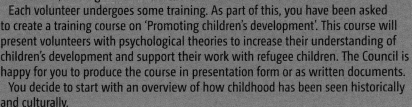

Assessment practice

At the end of learning aim A you must write:

A report exploring ideas of childhood and theories of development, and their contribution to the understanding and promotion of children's healthy growth, development and mental well-being.

This report must be related to a scenario or context. We have used a realistic (but not real) context.

The Refugee Council is the only national charity to support lone refugee children who are seeking asylum in the UK. The Refugee Council has an extensive network of volunteers.

They organise arts, crafts and music groups, mother-and-toddler groups and drop-in centres. They give advice on housing and teach English. They also act as interpreters, counsellors and 'befrienders', looking out for the interests of vulnerable children.

Each volunteer undergoes some training. As part of this, you have been asked to create a training course on 'Promoting children's development'. This course will present volunteers with psychological theories to increase their understanding of children's development and support their work with refugee children. The Council is happy for you to produce the course in presentation form or as written documents.

You decide to start with an overview of how childhood has been seen historically and culturally.

A1.1 Learning aim A1 – Task 1

The first part of your report for learning aim A will be concerned with historical and current social approaches to the nature of childhood – these are covered on this spread and the next spread.

This activity will help you practise the skills required to write the report in response to your scenario/context.

1. **Explain** historical and current social approaches to the nature of childhood. (A.P1)
2. **Analyse** historical and current social approaches to the nature of childhood. (A.M1)
3. **Evaluate** the impact of historical and current social approaches to the nature of childhood. (A.D1)

You can see the assessment criteria on page 190 and an explanation of command terms on page 191.

You can see the assessment criteria on page 190 and an explanation of command terms on page 191.

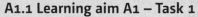

GET ACTIVE Draw a timeline

You can get a clearer picture of the historical perspective on childhood by drawing a timeline. There are dates, events and individuals on this spread you could include.

You could research others yourself, using your favourite search engine. Don't forget to include the ideas themselves, so you can see how they evolved over time.

You can draw the timeline by hand or use commonly-available Office software. There is some advice on how to do that here: tinyurl.com/yygflqpy

An issue to consider

Are there any ways in which children are viewed as small adults today? Can you think of any strengths and limitations to viewing childhood in this way?

Specification content

A1 The nature of childhood

Concepts and perceptions of childhood and their influence on parenting and care practices in modern-day society.

- Historical perspectives of the child, e.g. Locke, Rousseau, Ariès.
- Cultural perspectives, e.g. beliefs, cultural systems, religion, law, norms.

Child-rearing practices and modern-day views of childhood

When are you leaving?

'Adolescence begins in biology and ends in culture' – a quotation from Laurence Steinberg's (2014) book *Age of Opportunity*.

Adolescence used to mean more or less the same thing as the 'teenage' years. But Steinberg believes adolescence nowadays begins at about 10 and ends around 25. Puberty marks the beginning of adolescence – and this now occurs earlier than it used to.

What marks the end of adolescence? Possibly it is the time when you leave the family home, get a job, become financially independent and/or perhaps even marry.

Back in the 1950s, this all happened before the age of 19 for many. Now, young adults are increasingly dependent on their parents because of rising rental costs and unreliable and insecure employment. This means that many people are living with their parents well into their 20s. Even some who go away to university at 18/19 return to the family home at the end of their course. Therefore, the end of adolescence is cultural not biological.

Adolescence may continue to expand because it is influenced by cultural changes that affect economics and society.

The four parenting styles suggested by Baumrind.

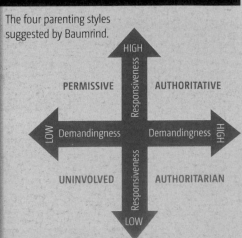

Child-rearing practices

Parenting styles

Diana Baumrind (1978) suggested there are four main *parenting styles*, based on how *responsive* and *demanding* parents are. Baumrind considered *authoritative parenting* superior because it promotes children's healthy development. Children of authoritative parents have good social skills, are self-controlled, creative, academically successful and have high *self-esteem*. However, children of *uninvolved parents* are more likely to behave impulsively and engage in *substance abuse*, etc.

Authoritative parents are highly responsive to their children's needs (warm, loving and supportive). They value independence and expression in their children. They are also very demanding, setting high standards of behaviour. But they are also flexible. In matters of discipline, authoritative parents are democratic and set rational rules in consultation with children.

Authoritarian parents are highly demanding but unresponsive. They value obedience and use power to get it. They view children as needing to be controlled so they meet strict expectations of behaviour. *Authoritarian parents* do not involve children in rule-making ('What I say goes because I said so').

Permissive parents are responsive but undemanding ('indulgent'), passive in dealing with their children, avoiding use of parental power or authority (often for a 'quiet life'). They view discipline as restricting children's freedom and therefore unhealthy for development. They are accepting and supportive of children's wishes and let them have a lot of independence. *Permissive parents* are more like friends than parents.

Uninvolved parents are unresponsive and undemanding ('neglectful'). They have little interest in their children's needs and try to minimise interaction with them. They structure family life around their own interests and do not appear to be bothered about being a parent.

Modern-day views of childhood

Childhood as a social construction

Childhood is a period in development created and defined by society (e.g. by *social norms* and beliefs). There is no fixed perception of childhood – it varies between *cultures* and at different points in history as different meanings are attached to it. Boundaries between stages of development (childhood, adolescence, adulthood) are flexible and can shift.

For example, the definition of adolescence as a time of increasing maturity between childhood and adulthood is historically recent. It is widely believed to begin at puberty when extensive biological, social and psychological changes occur. But the transition to adulthood is much more socially constructed because it has no biological boundary. In WEIRD cultures it is usually 18 years but this is for social rather than biological reasons.

Rationale for the modern view and children's rights

Industrialisation refers to the economic switch from agriculture (farming) to factory production which began in Britain in the 1780s. It meant that the economy required a healthy and educated workforce. This eventually led to laws restricting child labour and protecting children's welfare (e.g. *Prevention of Cruelty to, and Protection of, Children Act* 1889). Higher living standards meant more families could afford for their children not to work. By the time of the Second Industrial Revolution (around 1870), child labour was no longer the 'labour of choice' it had been after the 1780s.

Compulsory education was introduced in 1880, establishing a school leaving age of 10 years. This cemented the view of childhood as a protected period in development – an 'apprenticeship for adulthood'. Children began to be seen as an investment for the future, valued more for what they would eventually become and less for what they already were.

Children's rights were enshrined in laws specifically applied to them – to rescue them from child labour, protect their welfare and prevent exploitation (e.g. legal minimum ages for sex, smoking, drinking, etc.). *The Children Act* of 1989 was a major piece of legislation establishing children's rights. The overriding concern of the courts was now to safeguard children, promote their welfare and take into account their wishes. Parents have responsibilities towards their children, not 'rights'. The Act reinforced the view that children are active participants in society, not passive recipients of adult care.

Permissive parents are usually quite indulgent of their children's desires but probably not this much.

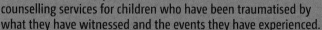

GET ACTIVE Your parents' style

What parenting style do you think your own parents have? What do they think?

1. *Ask your parents to complete the questionnaire from here: tinyurl.com/y4gkhs8c*

2. *Before revealing the outcome, you could give them a brief description of the main styles and ask them for their prediction. Do you agree with it from your own perspective?*

Evaluation

Supporting evidence

One strength is evidence to support the effects of parenting styles on children's development.

According to Donna Hancock Hoskins (2014), adolescents with authoritative parents are less likely to abuse drugs than those with authoritarian, permissive or uninvolved parents. They also have the lowest levels of *depression* and the highest levels of self-esteem, school attendance and educational achievement. Even having just one parent with an authoritative style is more beneficial than having two with the other styles.

These findings show that Baumrind was right to suggest that authoritative parenting leads to more positive outcomes.

Correlation not cause-and-effect

One weakness of the parenting style concept is that it is based on *correlational research*.

The authoritative style is associated with many positive outcomes but these could be explained by other variables that are not considered in the research. A good example is parental monitoring. Parents who use an authoritative style take a close interest in what their children are doing (who their friends are, etc.). They monitor how their children behave, whereas permissive parents do not. So perhaps it is monitoring that explains positive outcomes, not the parenting style as such.

This means we cannot conclude that an authoritative parenting style *causes* beneficial outcomes (or that other styles cause negative ones).

Evaluation

Supporting evidence

One strength is that there is evidence that childhood is a socially constructed concept (i.e. created by each social group).

Children everywhere may pass through the same stages of physical development (puberty, etc.). But this process is defined and understood differently from culture to culture. The boundaries separating childhood, adolescence and adulthood are blurred and vary between cultures (e.g. ages for getting married, criminal responsibility, leaving home or starting work).

There is no universal definition of childhood accepted by all cultures, suggesting a large role for social construction.

Childhood is not just socially constructed

One weakness of modern-day views is that few psychologists accept that childhood is completely socially constructed.

It is true that social context and related factors influence our perceptions of childhood. This is obvious from cultural differences in how children are perceived, treated and raised (as we saw on the previous spread). However, psychologists maintain that childhood is marked by distinct stages of development that are more than just socially defined. For example, as we will see on page 184, Jean Piaget identified several universal stages in how children's thinking develops.

There is a psychological (and biological) reality to child development that is at least as important as social construction.

Assessment practice

At the end of learning aim A you must write a report (see previous spread and page 190). This report must be related to a scenario or context. We have used a realistic (but not real) context.

You learn a little bit more about the work of the Refugee Council. It gives children practical support with housing, schooling, health and other aspects of daily life.

It offers advice and helps refugee children to integrate into communities. It also provides counselling services for children who have been traumatised by what they have witnessed and the events they have experienced.

Because childhood has changed so much over the centuries, you realise that the volunteers will need to understand more up-to-date views. You note that psychologists have been very interested in the different 'styles' parents have in raising children, so you decide to include that alongside how modern views have developed and the reasons why.

A1.2 Learning aim A1 – Task 2

The first part of your report for learning aim A will be concerned with historical and current social approaches to the nature of childhood – these are covered on the previous spread and this spread.

1. **Explain** current social approaches to the nature of childhood. (A.P1)

2. **Analyse** current social approaches to the nature of childhood. (A.M1)

3. **Evaluate** the impact of current social approaches to the nature of childhood. (A.D1)

An issue to consider

If you become a parent, what parenting style do you think you will use?

Specification content

A1 The nature of childhood

Concepts and perceptions of childhood and their influence on parenting and care practices in modern-day society.

● Child-rearing practices, including parenting styles, e.g. permissive, authoritarian.

● Modern-day views of childhood:

○ Childhood as a social construction, e.g. boundaries, childhood, adolescence, adulthood.

○ Rationale for the modern-day view of childhood, e.g. industrialisation, introduction of compulsory education.

○ Children's rights, e.g. Human Rights Act 1998, laws against child labour, child protection; laws applicable to age of consent.

Attachment studies: Lorenz and Harlow

Cuddles

When you were little, did you have a teddy bear or something else to cuddle? My (Cara's) daughter aged 33 still has a soft object called 'ball' that she takes everywhere to help her sleep. In fact she has two – one for home and a smaller one for travelling!

Why do children (and adults) like to have an object to cuddle? It may be that we are hardwired biologically to get comfort from contact with something soft. It is soothing and makes us feel calmer.

The roots of this need for cuddling may lie in attachment. Wanting to be close to something warm and cosy may be a drive to ensure that young animals stay close to a carer and are thus protected. A young animal without this drive might put themselves in danger by wandering away from the safety of a carer.

Specification term

Attachment A close two-way emotional bond between two individuals in which each individual sees the other as essential for their own emotional security. Attachment is important for safety and food (mother and baby stay close together) and independence (a secure attachment enables a child to be more adventurous).

One of the infant monkeys in Harlow's experiment, clinging to the cloth-covered mother while having a drink from the other 'mother'.

Lorenz's study

Aims

Konrad Lorenz (1935) aimed to see what would happen with goslings if the first thing they saw was him rather than their mother goose.

Procedure

Lorenz divided a clutch of gosling eggs into two groups. One group was left with their natural mother while the other eggs were placed in an incubator. When the incubator eggs hatched the first living (moving) thing they saw was Lorenz and they soon started following him rather than their natural mother.

To test this Lorenz marked the two groups to distinguish them and placed them together, with both Lorenz and the natural mother present.

Findings

The goslings quickly divided up, one following their natural mother and the others following Lorenz.

Conclusion

Lorenz used the word *imprinting* to describe what was happening. He suggested that young animals formed an imprint of the first moving object they see after hatching. Imprinting is a process similar to *attachment* in that it binds a young animal to a caregiver in a special relationship.

Critical period and lasting effects

Lorenz claimed that imprinting is restricted to a very definite period of the young animal's life, called a *critical period*. If a young animal is not exposed to a moving object during this early critical period the animal will not imprint.

Harlow's study

Aims

Harry Harlow (1959) wished to investigate what factor mattered most in the development of attachment. In the 1950s people thought that a young animal became attached to its mother because the mother provided food but Harlow thought it might be explained differently. Harlow had been doing research with young rhesus monkeys, separated from their mothers. The young monkeys seemed to form 'attachments' to the nappy liners at the bottom of their cages. He wondered whether attachment was more related to seeking something to cuddle rather than food.

Procedure

There were two wire mothers, each with a different 'head' (see left). One was wrapped in soft cloth. Eight infant monkeys were studied for 165 days. For four monkeys the milk bottle was on the cloth-covered mother, for the other four it was on the wire-only mother (as in the picture).

Findings

All eight monkeys spent most of their time with the cloth-covered mother whether or not this mother had the feeding bottle. Those monkeys who fed from the wire mother would only spend a short amount of time getting milk and then returned to the cloth-covered mother. When frightened all monkeys clung to the cloth-covered mother seemingly for reassurance.

Conclusions

These findings suggest that infants do not develop an attachment to the person who feeds them but to the person offering contact comfort.

Critical period and lasting effects

Harry Harlow and Margaret Harlow (1962) reported that, once the motherless monkeys became adults, they were socially abnormal – they froze or fled when approached by other monkeys. And they did not show normal mating behaviour nor cradle their own babies.

Harlow also found that there was a critical period for these effects. If the motherless monkeys spent time with other, peer monkeys they seemed to recover but only if this happened before they were three months old. Having more than six months with only a wire mother had a permanent effect.

GET ACTIVE Orphan lambs

The concept of imprinting is not very new – farmers have been aware of it for centuries. For example, sheep imprinting involves smell. The baby lamb recognises its mother's smell and vice versa. One common practice to ensure the survival of orphan lambs is to take the fleece from another lamb that died and wrap this around the orphan lamb. This leads the mother of the dead baby lamb to start looking after the orphan lamb, who would no doubt otherwise have died.

How can you use the concept of imprinting to explain this?

Saving the life of an orphan lamb – see left.

Evaluation

A biological mechanism

One strength of Lorenz's study is that it introduced the idea that imprinting (attachment) is biologically-driven.

Lorenz demonstrated that the basis of imprinting is that a young animal is born with a predisposition to stick close to a carer. This has clear survival value for the young animal and would thus be *naturally selected* (the evolutionary process discussed in Unit 1, in our Year 1 'Certificate' book).

This is important because it allowed researchers to understand more clearly the importance of attachment in humans – as a biological survival mechanism (this is discussed on the next spread as part of John Bowlby's attachment theory).

The concept of a critical period

One weakness of this research is that the concept of a critical period may be wrong.

Later researchers have criticised the idea that early imprinting lasts forever and also questioned whether it is really nothing more than an example of rapid learning and does not have long-lasting effects. In fact it is now more commonly called a *sensitive period* in development when learning may occur more easily but not necessarily exclusively during that time period.

This, coupled with the fact that Lorenz's research was with birds, means that it may not be appropriate to try to *generalise* any of Lorenz's ideas to humans.

Evaluation

Application to human behaviour

One strength of Harlow's study is that the value of contact comfort has been demonstrated in humans.

Nathalie Charpak *et al.* (2017) conducted a study with preterm and low-birth-weight babies and their parents. In the 1990s the families were *randomly allocated* to an *experimental* or *control group*. The experimental group of babies were given 'kangaroo care' – constant skin-to-skin contact between baby and mother. Benefits were observed in terms of survival, brain development and the quality of the baby–mother bond. The follow-up study in 2017, 20 years later, found continuing social and behavioural benefits.

This confirms the importance of contact comfort in human development.

A confounding variable

One weakness in Harlow's study is that the two stimulus objects varied in other ways than being cloth-covered or not.

The two heads were also different (see picture on facing page) which acted as a *confounding variable* because it varied systematically with the *independent variable* ('mother' being cloth-covered or not). It is possible that the reason the infant monkeys preferred one 'mother' to the other was because the cloth-covered mother had a more attractive head.

Therefore, the conclusions of this study may lack *validity*.

Assessment practice

At the end of learning aim A you must write a report (see pages 165 and 190). This report must be related to a scenario or context. We have used a realistic (but not real) context.

> The Refugee Council informs you that the volunteers will be working alongside professionals in supporting the refugee children. They have asked you to focus for the time being on the work of teachers, school nurses and people who work in childcare nurseries.
>
> The professionals deal with children who may not have secure emotional attachments with a caregiver, which would have potential negative outcomes for such children.
>
> Psychological studies such as Harlow's and Lorenz's can help professionals to understand the importance of attachment to the healthy development of children.

A2.3 Learning aim A2 – Task 3

The second part of your report for learning aim A will be concerned with how current psychological theories can inform professionals in promoting growth, development and mental well-being in children – these are covered on this spread and the next ten spreads.

1. **Explain** how the studies by Lorenz and Harlow might inform professionals in promoting the healthy growth, development and mental well-being in children. (A.P2)

2. **Analyse** the contribution of Lorenz's and Harlow's studies to the promotion of healthy growth, development and mental well-being in children. (A.M1)

3. **Evaluate** the contribution of Lorenz's and Harlow's studies to the promotion of healthy growth, development and mental well-being in children. (A.D1)

You can see the assessment criteria on page 190 and an explanation of command terms on page 191.

An issue to consider

There are ethical issues related to the research by both Lorenz and Harlow. What are they?

Do you think the benefits justify the costs?

Specification content

A2 Social, emotional and behavioural development

Key principles, application and critique of developmental studies and theories.

● Attachment studies, including Lorenz and Harlow.

Attachment theory: Bowlby

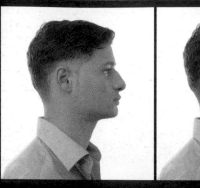

Noses

Have you noticed that fashion models usually have small noses? What is it with small noses? Why is a small nose more attractive than a large nose?

For that matter, fashion models usually also have large eyes and a small chin and a round face.

When people all over the world are asked to rate faces for attractiveness they tend to choose the same features – small nose, big eyes, small chin.

One explanation is that we all tend to have a preference for *baby face* features rather than adult facial features (bigger nose and chin, longer face).

And the explanation for this preference is that we are 'hardwired' to like baby face features because it means we respond to babies with affection and this ensures we are interested in our babies and want to look after them. Any parent who doesn't find their baby attractive (this applies to all mammals) may be more likely to abandon the baby and then the parent's genes are not continued into future generations.

Baby faces, aren't they cute?

The same principles operate in all mammals – very young individuals have larger eyes, a higher forehead, smaller nose and smaller chin than adults.

Not only does this young monkey and cat look cute, but adult monkeys and cats continue to have fairly baby face features – which is why they continue to be seen as cute.

Key concepts of the theory

John Bowlby worked as a psychiatrist in London in the 1930s, treating children with *mental health* problems. He observed that many of the children had experienced frequent and prolonged early separations from their families. This led him to be interested in the negative effects of early separation, which in turn led him to consider the benefits of *attachment*.

Why attachments form

Bowlby (1969) looked at the work of Lorenz and Harlow for ideas and proposed an *evolutionary* explanation – that attachment was an *innate* system that gave a survival advantage. *Imprinting* and attachment evolved because they ensure that young animals stay close to their caregivers and this protects them from hazards.

Social releasers

It is important that attachments are formed in two directions – parents also become attached to their babies and this behaviour has evolved because parents who were not good carers were less reproductively successful and therefore their *genes* were not passed on to subsequent generations.

Bowlby suggested that babies are born with a set of innate 'cute' behaviours (like cooing and gripping) and features (such as large eyes, little chin and a small nose – called a 'baby face'). These behaviours and features encourage attention from adults.

He called these *social releasers* because their purpose is to activate the adult attachment system, i.e. make an adult feel caring and love towards the baby.

A sensitive period

Bowlby proposed that there is a *sensitive period* between 3 and 6 months when attachments are most likely to form in human babies. The baby is maximally sensitive at this time and, if an attachment is not formed, the baby will find it much harder to form one later.

Who becomes the primary attachment figure?

Bowlby proposed that babies are predisposed to form one special attachment – their *primary attachment*. He used the term *monotropy* (leaning towards one person). The primary attachment figure is often the baby's biological mother but not always. It is the person who responds most sensitively to the baby's needs and signals rather than the person who spends most time with the baby.

Secondary attachments

Babies also form many *secondary attachments* that provide an important emotional safety net. For example, many babies would show a preference for their mother if they are upset but, if their mother is absent, could be equally well comforted by their father, grandparent or sibling.

Consequences of attachment

The importance of monotropy is that this one special relationship forms a 'template' for what relationships are like, called an *internal working model*. This model has two consequences:

(1) In the short-term it gives the child insight into the caregiver's behaviour and enables the child to influence their caregiver's behaviour, so that a true partnership can be formed.

(2) In the long-term it acts as a template for all future relationships because it generates expectations about what loving relationships are like. This *continuity hypothesis* proposes that individuals who are strongly attached in infancy continue to be socially and emotionally competent, whereas babies who are not strongly attached have more social and emotional difficulties in childhood and adulthood. In other words there is continuity from infancy to adulthood in terms of emotional type.

Evaluation

Application to childcare

One strength of Bowlby's theory is that it can help to make recommendations about how children can best be cared for when parents are at work.

Many people feel that Bowlby's theory implies that mothers (primary attachment figures) should stay at home to look after their children, because separation would be harmful to their child's development. However, Bowlby offered two answers to this – attachment is about quality and not quantity of care, and secondary attachment figures can offer substitute emotional care. So, the absence of the primary attachment figure need not have negative consequences.

Therefore, the aim for child carers is to focus on the quality of the substitute emotional support. For example, this can be enhanced in a day care setting by having a high staff-to-child ratio (about 1:3 for young children).

Support for the critical period

Another strength is research support for a key principle of Bowlby's theory.

Michael Rutter et al. (2010) have followed a group of 165 Romanian orphans adopted in Britain to assess the developmental effects of a lack of attachment in infancy. Their findings show that those children adopted after the age of six months have found it difficult to form close attachments whereas this is not true for those adopted earlier. (This study is discussed again on page 203.)

This suggests that there is a sensitive period for developing attachment, supporting the biological evolutionary basis of Bowlby's theory – because a sensitive period relates only to biological 'hardwired' mechanisms.

Temperament may be as important as attachment

One weakness is that the long-term effects may be due to innate emotional style (temperament) and not attachment.

Jerome Kagan (1989) argues that some babies are more anxious than others and some more sociable than others as a result of their genetic make-up. These temperamental characteristics affect the formation of attachments in infancy (because it is more difficult to form a close attachment with an anxious baby). These temperamental differences would also affect relationships later in life.

This means that the way an attachment is formed depends on more than just the sensitivity of the mother or other caregiver, illustrating that both *nature and nurture* matter.

Research has found that strongly attached children tend to be more popular at school (Sroufe et al. 2005) and are more likely to form enduring relationships when they are older (Hazan and Shaver 1987). But is this due to attachment – or to innate temperament?

Assessment practice

At the end of learning aim A you must write a report (see pages 165 and 190). This report must be related to a scenario or context. We have used a realistic (but not real) context.

Some of the volunteers at the Refugee Council will be working alongside nursery nurses in supporting the refugee children.

You want the volunteers to understand how John Bowlby's theory of attachment relates to the work of nursery nurses. Nursery nurses care for preschool children (up to about five years) in hospitals, health and community centres and children's centres. The children may or may not have special needs and/or learning disabilities.

Nursery nurses use play to stimulate and develop children's abilities (e.g. intellectual and social). They respond to each child's needs with warmth, care and sensitivity.

A2.4 Learning aim A2 – Task 4

The second part of your report for learning aim A will be concerned with how current psychological theories can inform professionals in promoting growth, development and mental well-being in children – these are covered on the previous spread, this spread and the next nine spreads.

1. **Explain** how Bowlby's attachment theory can inform professionals in the promotion of healthy development and mental well-being of children. (A.P2)

2. **Analyse** how the contribution of Bowlby's attachment theory might inform professionals in the promotion of healthy development and mental well-being of children. (A.M1)

3. **Evaluate** how the contribution of Bowlby's attachment theory might inform professionals in the promotion of healthy development and mental well-being of children. (A.D1)

GET ACTIVE Mono means 'one'

As you have read, one of the key concepts of Bowlby's attachment theory is monotropy. Bowlby argued that a key feature of human infant behaviour is the attachment bond which is formed with one special person – often the child's mother but the primary attachment figure could be a father, older brother or sister, grandparent. Bowlby claimed the formation of this bond was nothing to do with time spent together, it was to do with sensitivity and responsiveness.

Explain what sensitivity and responsiveness might involve and why this might be important in establishing an attachment bond.

An issue to consider

The key feature of Bowlby's theory is that it explains attachment in evolutionary terms – it is a behaviour that is naturally selected because of its survival importance.

To what extent do you agree with this?

Specification content

A2 Social, emotional and behavioural development

Key principles, application and critique of developmental studies and theories.

● Attachment theories, including Bowlby.

Attachment study: Ainsworth

Dog attachment

Dogs evolved from wolves and have adapted to human relationships. Certain behaviours have been naturally selected because they promote this dog–human relationship. One of these behaviours is attachment. There is good reason to believe that dogs are attached to their owners and owners are attached to their dogs. It is a close emotional bond.

A team of Hungarian researchers were the first to investigate this (Topál *et al.* 1998). They adapted Ainsworth's Strange Situation (discussed on this spread) so they could assess the attachments between 51 owners and their dogs – including English setters, Staffordshire terriers, Hungarian Vizslas and some mixed breeds.

Each dog and owner were observed through seven episodes like the ones listed below. The researchers found that the dogs tended to play more and spent more time exploring in the presence of their owners than when with the stranger.

The dogs showed higher levels of contact-seeking when the owner returned compared with the stranger entering.

So, it seems that there is a caregiver–dog relationship similar to that of parents and their babies. In fact, another study investigated and found a relationship between owner's attachment type and their dog's behaviour in the Strange Situation (Wilshaw 2010).

The eight episodes of the Strange Situation procedure (SSP).

Episode		Behaviour assessed
1	Caregiver and baby are introduced to the experimental room.	
2	The baby is encouraged to explore.	Tests exploration and secure base.
3	A stranger comes in and tries to interact with the baby.	Tests stranger anxiety.
4	The caregiver leaves the baby and stranger together.	Tests separation and stranger anxiety.
5	The caregiver returns and the stranger leaves.	Tests reunion behaviour and exploration/secure base.
6	The caregiver leaves the baby alone.	Tests separation anxiety.
7	The stranger returns.	Tests stranger anxiety.
8	The caregiver returns and is reunited with the baby. Stranger leaves.	Tests reunion behaviour.

Ainsworth's studies of attachment

John Bowlby (previous spread) focused on the universality of *attachments*, whereas Mary Ainsworth was particularly interested in how children differed in terms of their *attachment type*.

Early observations and aims

Ainsworth (1967) spent two years observing interactions between 26 mothers and their babies. She noted that some of the mothers were more sensitive to their babies' needs, for example they tended to be able to provide more details about their babies. She also noted that the babies of these mothers tended to cry less and spent more time exploring the area near their mother.

This led Ainsworth to propose the *secure base* concept that high-quality attachment promoted more independent behaviour in babies.

Procedure: The Strange Situation

This early observational research led Ainsworth to try to find a way to measure the nature of attachment systematically. Together with other colleagues she decided that the best way was to put babies and their mothers in a series of slightly stressful situations These would allow the researchers to observe how the babies reacted and mean they could then classify their attachment type. The key behaviours were:

- Secure base and willingness to explore – in a novel environment some babies explore while others cling to their mothers.
- Stranger anxiety – some babies get upset if left with a stranger, but some babies don't particularly mind.
- Separation anxiety – some babies get more upset than others if their mother leaves the room.
- Reunion behaviour – after a separation, some babies enthusiastically greet their mothers, whereas some are rejecting or indifferent.

The *Strange Situation procedure (SSP)* assesses these four behaviours. It takes place in a novel (strange) controlled environment where the baby's responses to eight different episodes (see left) are observed.

Findings and conclusion: Attachment types

Ainsworth *et al.* (1978) combined data from several studies to make a total of 106 American babies and their mothers. The researchers detected three relatively consistent behaviour types.

- *Secure attachment* (Type B) These children explore happily but regularly go back to their mother/caregiver (proximity-seeking and secure-base behaviour). They usually show moderate separation anxiety and moderate stranger anxiety. Securely attached children seek and accept comfort from their caregiver in the reunion stage. In Ainsworth's sample, 66% of the babies were classified as secure.
- *Insecure–avoidant attachment* (Type A) The key behaviour for these children is their avoidance of intimacy and social interaction. They show little or no reaction when their mother/caregiver leaves and they make little effort to make contact when their caregiver returns. Such children are happy to explore with or without the presence of their caregiver. They are also characterised by high levels of anxiousness. In Ainsworth's sample, 22% of babies were classified as insecure–avoidant.
- *Insecure–resistant attachment* (Type C) These children both seek and resist intimacy and social interaction. They show considerable distress when left with a stranger and/or when separated from their caregiver. On reunion, such children display conflicting desires for and against contact, they may angrily resist being picked up while also trying other means to maintain proximity. In Ainsworth's sample, 12% of babies were classified as insecure–resistant.

(You may be wondering why secure attachment is not Type A – it was to avoid the assumption that it was the best type of attachment.)

Evaluation

Important application

One strength is that the SSP has been vital for attachment research.

In order to research the factors that lead to high- or low-quality attachment and to research the consequences of different types of attachment, a measuring tool was required and Ainsworth supplied this. Ainsworth's method of assessing attachment type continues to be the standard test used in studies of attachment. It has also been adapted for use with older children and adults, for example the *adult attachment interview* (AAI).

This illustrates the enormous contribution to understanding baby behaviour that was made by Ainsworth.

Not all types covered

One weakness is that other types of attachment may have been overlooked.

The original research by Ainsworth *et al.* did classify many different subtypes of attachment (such as A1, A2). However, they were all subtypes of the A, B and C categories. Mary Main and Judith Solomon (1990) analysed over 200 SSP videotapes and proposed that there was actually a fourth clear category – the *insecure–disorganised* (type D). This is characterised by a lack of consistent patterns of social behaviour. Such babies lack a coherent strategy for dealing with the stress of separation. A fifth type has also been identified called *disinhibited attachment*, characteristic of children who have experienced severe *privation* (discussed on page 202).

This means that the initial research may have oversimplified a more complex situation and, as such, lacked *validity*.

Cultural bias

Another weakness is that the test may only apply to babies and caregivers in Western *cultures* such as the US.

The SSP is built on Western, *individualist* assumptions about ideals for behaviour. In such cultures independence is valued highly whereas in *collectivist* societies interdependence is expected. In the SSP a baby who appears to be dependent on their caregiver would not be categorised as securely attached. This is demonstrated by research in collectivist cultures such as Japan, where many more infants are classed as insecure than in individualist cultures such as the US (Takahashi 1990).

This means that the SSP is not measuring universal behaviour.

The Strange Situation procedure (SSP) takes place in a controlled room (a laboratory). Caregiver and baby are usually observed through a two-way mirror and/or a video camera records events.

GET ACTIVE Deconstruction

Like you, Rosie is studying Psychology and has just learned about the Strange Situation. She is quite confused about the different types of attachment and can't remember what behaviours go with each type. So, she creates the table below.

Fill in her table using words like 'high' or 'low', 'strong' etc.

	Type A	Type B	Type C
Classification (e.g. secure)			
Proximity-seeking			
Exploration/secure base			
Stranger anxiety			
Separation anxiety			
Response on reunion			

Assessment practice

At the end of learning aim A you must write a report (see pages 165 and 190). This report must be related to a scenario or context. We have used a realistic (but not real) context.

You want the volunteers at the Refugee Council to understand Ainsworth's research into attachment types and appreciate its relevance to health visitors – qualified nurses (or midwives) who have specialist training in child health.

They support women with very young children, who are pregnant or have recently had a baby, in their own homes. They can give parents advice about children's typical and atypical development. A health visitor would be very interested in the type of attachment bond a very young child has with a parent (in most cases the mother). They would be looking for evidence about whether the attachment is secure or insecure.

A2.5 Learning aim A2 – Task 5

The second part of your report for learning aim A will be concerned with how current psychological theories can inform professionals in promoting growth, development and mental well-being in children – these are covered on the previous two spreads, this spread and the next eight spreads.

This activity will help you practise the skills required to write the report in response to your scenario/context.

1. **Explain** how Ainsworth's studies might inform professionals in the promotion of healthy development and mental well-being of children. (A.P2)
2. **Analyse** how the contribution of Ainsworth's studies might inform professionals in the promotion of healthy development and mental well-being of children. (A.M1)
3. **Evaluate** how the contribution of Ainsworth's studies might inform professionals in the promotion of healthy development and mental well-being of children. (A.D1)

An issue to consider

Certain vocations might find it useful to know about the attachment types of children in their care.

Can you think of some such vocations and how they might use the information?

Specification content

A2 Social, emotional and behavioural development

Key principles, application and critique of developmental studies and theories.

● Attachment studies, including Ainsworth.

Ecological models of child development

Community psychologists

Psychology in general focuses on the study of the individual. By contrast, community psychology aims to investigate and promote community well-being and expects this to have a positive effect on individuals who belong to the community.

One of the triggers that led to the development of community psychology was US soldiers returning from World War 2. Many had mental health problems and mental health institutions in the US could not cope with the numbers who required treatment nor were the treatments effective. However, setting up communities for ex-soldiers had a much more positive effect.

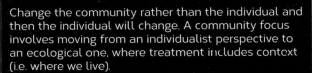

Change the community rather than the individual and then the individual will change. A community focus involves moving from an individualist perspective to an ecological one, where treatment includes context (i.e. where we live).

Another example can be seen in the issue of homelessness. People become homeless in part because of individual-level factors, such as mental illness or not having the skills required to get a job. On the other hand, a community-level perspective would say that people become homeless because of context – lack of jobs or housing. And this informs us about how to intervene – at the context (ecological) level. It might help to provide job training or provide suitable housing rather than focus on the individual.

This may sound obvious with hindsight but often we need a framework to remind ourselves of obvious solutions. The American Psychological Association has a division called the *Society for Community Research and Action* (SCRA, see http://scra27.org).

Specification term

Ecological model An approach to explaining human behaviour that focuses on the interaction between the individual and their environment (ecology). This ecological context is a contrast to a focus solely on individual factors.

Bronfenbrenner's ecological theory

Urie Bronfenbrenner's (1979) *ecological model* focused on the importance of a child's environment as the key influence on development. The word 'ecology' refers to environment or 'context' – and he was especially looking at the social context.

Four systems

A developing child belongs to a series of increasingly larger 'environmental' systems:

Microsystem (meaning 'small'), which includes those human relationships that are most important to the child. The basic unit is the parent–child partnership and the face-to-face interactions the child has on a daily basis with other people – siblings, other family members, peers, teachers and the immediate community (such as day-care centre, local shops). This is nested in the next level (like the Russian dolls below).

Mesosystem (meaning 'middle'), involves interactions between two or more microsystems, such as between home and teachers, or teachers and community, or home and peers. The settings must be those that influence the development of the individual. For example, the benefit a child gains from school depends on the value parents place on education and their cooperation with teachers/the school. This is nested in the next level.

Exosystem (meaning 'outside'), refers to social settings that do not directly include the child but do influence meso- or microsystems and thus affect the child's development. For example, something that might affect the child's parents (financial problems, difficult work colleagues) has an indirect effect on the microsystem. The exosystem also includes, for example, the media, governors of the school, extended family. This is nested in the next level.

Macrosystem (meaning 'large'), this outershell is the belief systems (ideologies) of the *culture* in which the developing child lives. This would include religion, attitudes towards gender equality and social class, and so on. The importance of this layer is to remind us that many social systems are different from our own and it is important to consider this macrosystem when trying to understand a child's development. In particular, the controlled *experimental* approach often used in psychology removes this social context and therefore conclusions may be meaningless.

A bioecological theory

Bronfenbrenner's theory is sometimes called 'bioecological' because at the centre of the ecological systems are the biological characteristics of the child such as their *temperament*, sex (and gender), health and so on. This individual, biological element influences all the other systems.

Time dimension

Bronfenbrenner also added a fifth system – the *chronosystem*. This acknowledges the changes that occur over time both to the child or any of the ecological contexts. As elements change this will affect future development, for example at puberty, the individual level changes and interactions with higher systems will be different from how they were previously. In addition, the time when changes take place interact in different ways with development. For example, parental divorce affects a two-year-old differently from a ten-year-old.

Bronfenbrenner (1979) described the environment as being 'like a set of nested structures, each inside the next, like a set of Russian dolls'.

GET ACTIVE What's your ecology?

Consider the four main systems of Bronfenbrenner's ecology theory.

1. For each system identify **two or more** important interactions that have influenced your development.
2. Identify any of the interactions that you listed which were time-sensitive and explain in what way they were time-sensitive.

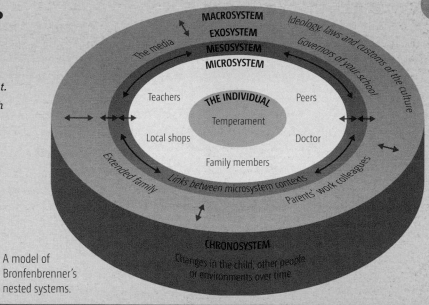

A model of Bronfenbrenner's nested systems.

Evaluation

Application to childcare

One strength of Bronfenbrenner's approach was its application to developing the US *Head Start* programme.

In the 1960s Bronfenbrenner testified to the US congress that the children who grew up in poor environments were destined for failure. They arrived at school already behind their peers. He was invited to develop a government-funded scheme of intensive preschool care, involving both health and education. The scheme was called Head Start and was basically an intervention at the community level. The Head Start programme continues today offering *cognitive*, social and emotional development for over 1 million disadvantaged children and their families every year. It is also concerned with health promotion and check-ups.

This shows how the ecological approach has been translated into valuable community projects.

Changed psychology

Another strength of Bronfenbrenner's theory was that it brought many different disciplines together within psychology.

Psychologists traditionally focused on the individual child and social psychologists focused on social groups. Bronfenbrenner pointed out that it was the interrelationships between systems that matters rather than using a linear model where the different elements are viewed separately. He opened up developmental psychology to understand that the relationships between people, such as between child and parent, were embedded in larger social structures such as community, culture and politics.

This was a novel view and one which had a lasting effect.

Not an empirical theory

One weakness is that it is not a scientific theory.

In order for a theory to be scientific it must be testable, and Bronfenbrenner's theory doesn't easily lead to predictions that can be tested. His descriptions about relationships between the different levels is imprecise, for example he does not explain how family involvement relates to peer involvement in the mesosystem. This situation in part arose because he specifically felt that *laboratory* experiments did not represent the reality of the way complex social systems behave.

This means that, for many psychologists, his theory is at odds with their general approach.

Assessment practice

At the end of learning aim A you must write a report (see pages 165 and 190). This report must be related to a scenario or context. We have used a realistic (but not real) context.

As a psychologist yourself, you are keen for the volunteers at the Refugee Council to understand the work of educational psychologists. They identify children with developmental problems such as learning difficulties, physical disabilities, and social and emotional disorders. They devise interventions and plans to support children's learning, for example advising teachers about how they can adapt their class teaching.

As with all professionals, it is vital that educational psychologists understand that children develop within wider contexts. Therefore, you want the volunteers to appreciate how the work of an educational psychologist can benefit from applying Bronfenbrenner's ecological model.

A2.6 Learning aim A2 – Task 6

The second part of your report for learning aim A will be concerned with how current psychological theories can inform professionals in promoting growth, development and mental well-being in children – these are covered on the previous three spreads, this spread and the next seven spreads.

1. **Explain** how Bronfenbrenner's ecological model might inform professionals in the promotion of healthy development of children. (A.P2)
2. **Analyse** how the contribution of Bronfenbrenner's ecological model might inform professionals in the promotion of healthy development of children. (A.M1)
3. **Evaluate** how the contribution of Bronfenbrenner's ecological model might inform professionals in the promotion of healthy development of children. (A.D1)

An issue to consider

The evaluation points on the left give arguments for and against the usefulness of Bronfenbrenner's theory. Which side of the argument would you defend? And why?

Specification content

A2 Social, emotional and behavioural development

Key principles, application and critique of developmental studies and theories.

● Ecological models, including Bronfenbrenner.

Social identity theory

The jigsaw classroom

In 1970s America, the southern states had been forced to desegregate their schools – it was no longer permissible to have all-white schools. However, in individual classrooms there was considerable hostility between black and white students. Social psychologist Elliot Aronson (1978) was hired to advise the Austin (Texas) school board about how they might diffuse the problem.

Aronson based his approach on psychological research at the time which suggested that involving the two groups of students in shared tasks might reduce intergroup hostility. Such tasks must (a) ultimately benefit both groups and (b) require members from each group to take part in completing the task.

In the jigsaw classroom groups of both black and white students are given a group task (e.g. they have to complete an assignment). The key is that each individual has to prepare a component and share this with the group and only then can the whole group succeed.

The outcome was a reduction in prejudice overall but also all children now expressed a greater liking for outgroup members, i.e. the white children said they liked the black children more than they had expressed at the beginning, and vice versa.

The jigsaw classroom 'forces' ingroup members to get to know outgroup members who then cease to be outgroups!

Specification term

Social identity theory (SIT) The view that your behaviour is motivated by your social identity. A person's self-image has two components: personal identity and social identity. Personal identity is based on your characteristics and achievements. Social identity is determined by the various groups of people to which you belong, your 'ingroups'.

Key concepts of the theory

Henri Tajfel and John Turner (1979, 1986) used *social identity theory* to explain how we develop a sense of self – our *self-concept*. It is based on personal achievements but also based on the various social groups to which we belong. In other words, our social identity has a strong effect on our individual identity.

Desire to belong

Humans (and social animals generally) have a strong desire to be part of a group. Without that urge the species would cease to be a social species.

We like being in a group and dislike feeling isolated. We belong to many different social groups and like the other members of our social groups. Furthermore, we want to be liked by the other members of the social groups, and dislike being rejected by them.

Social categorisation

This sense of our own group means we distinguish between our social groups and other groups – called *ingroups* and *outgroups*. The ingroup is any group to which we see ourselves as belonging and the outgroup comprises anyone who is not part of the ingroup. We may recognise various specific outgroups such as people who support a different football team, or go to a different school, or come from a different part of the country or world.

Social categorisation refers to the separation of individuals into one of these two groups: 'like me' and 'us' (ingroup) or 'not like me' and 'them' (outgroup).

Tajfel and Turner (1979) argue that categorisation is a basic characteristic of human thought and as such we have little control over this automatic sorting process. Without thinking about it we are just aware of many different ingroups and outgroups.

This process of social categorisation begins very early in life and depends on social relations. A baby cannot have a concept of self without having a concept of other. So the self-concept is bound up with social relationships (Durkin 1995).

Self-esteem

A key part of our self-concept is *self-esteem*. This is the respect and admiration we have for ourselves. Level of self-esteem is very important in development – children who have high levels of self-esteem tend to be successful at school, sports and so on (Coopersmith 1968). They are more resilient if things go wrong and tend to be more popular with others than those with low self-esteem. Self-esteem is related to self-confidence.

High levels of self-esteem may come from significant others (such as parents) who give affection and respect to the child, who then internalises these attitudes.

But self-esteem also comes from our group memberships. If the ingroup is successful, that makes everyone in the ingroup feel better about themselves. It affects personal self-esteem. If someone in the group loses a sports match or does something wrong, that makes all the members feel less good.

Ingroup identity may increase during development if self-esteem is damaged – for example, adolescents often feel uncertain about their identity and self-esteem. A way to repair lowered self-esteem is to identify more strongly with a popular and admired ingroup.

Ingroup and outgroup behaviour

Much of our social behaviour is driven by the *motivation* to maintain a positive sense of self. The end result is that all of us do what we can to boost ingroup image and success and reduce the image/success of the outgroup. We exaggerate ingroup successes and exaggerate outgroup failures. We might attribute ingroup successes to effort and attribute outgroup successes to luck.

Why do we feel so depressed when our team loses?

Psychological research and art. Paintings by Klee (above) and Kandinsky (left) were used in Tajfel's study.

Evaluation

Research support

One strength of SIT is support from the mimimal group experiment.

Tajfel (1970) worked with 15-year-old Bristol school boys and asked each boy to choose which of two paintings they like best – one by Wassily Kandinsky or one by Paul Klee. The boys were each then told which other boys selected the same artist – this created ingroups based on very minimal information. Later the boys were engaged in a new task and asked to allocate points to the other boys and were told these points would be exchanged for cash. Tajfel found that more points were awarded to ingroup members than outgroup members. Boys even opted to maximise the difference in points awarded to the ingroup compared with the outgroup, despite the fact that this reduced the total final sum awarded to the ingroup!

This provides strong evidence to support ingroup behaviour.

Explaining and reducing prejudice

Another strength of SIT is that it can be applied to explaining and reducing prejudice.

Identification of ingroups and outgroups leads to negative attitudes (prejudice) about members of outgroups. These *cognitive* processes may lead to discrimination between ingroup and outgroup members, so we think about outgroup members differently and we also may treat them differently. One suggestion to reduce prejudiced behaviour is to break down barriers between in- and outgroups so they accept each other better. This is the purpose of the *jigsaw classroom* (see facing page), which has particularly been used with children. After working on a joint task, members expressed more liking for outgroup members (Aronson 1978).

This shows that SIT can be useful in producing practical applications to serious problems.

SIT doesn't apply to all cultures

One weakness with SIT is that it may be an explanation that only applies to some *cultures*.

Margaret Wetherell (1982) conducted a *replication* of Tajfel's experiment using eight-year-old schoolchildren in New Zealand. She tested both white children and indigenous Polynesian children. The white children behaved as would be predicted by SIT – discriminating in favour of their ingroup (other white children). However, the same was not true for the indigenous Polynesian children who were *significantly* more generous in their allocation of points to outgroup members, i.e. they showed favouritism to the more highly regarded white group rather than their own group. This finding is the opposite to what would be predicted by SIT.

This suggests that the behaviour of some cultural groups (those regarded as *collectivist*) may be less influenced by individual identity.

GET ACTIVE Your social identities

Each of us belongs to many different social groups – some may be very small groups (such as your immediate family or group of close friends) and some may be large (such as the gender you identify with, or your nationality).

1. Draw up a list of at least 20 social groups you identify with.
2. Identify the groups that have the strongest effect on how you perceive yourself (i.e. on your personal identity).
3. Identify the groups that have the greatest effect on how others perceive you.
4. Comment on any differences between the groups identified in 2 and 3.

Assessment practice

At the end of learning aim A you must write a report (see pages 165 and 190). This report must be related to a scenario or context. We have used a realistic (but not real) context.

You decide that the volunteers would benefit from knowing more about social identity theory and especially how it relates to the work of police officers.

Police officers identify and protect children at risk of harm. They have a duty to promote children's welfare in all their work (e.g. children in custody, questioning child witnesses, etc.). Officers frequently have to deal with adolescents who see themselves as being part of a group in conflict with another group. Social identity can help explain gang culture and may be partly behind the rise in knife-related crimes. It may also be an issue for refugee children attempting to integrate into communities in the UK.

A2.7 Learning aim A2 – Task 7

The second part of your report for learning aim A will be concerned with how current psychological theories can inform professionals in promoting growth, development and mental well-being in children – these are covered on the previous four spreads, this spread and the next six spreads.

1. **Explain** how social identity theory might inform professionals in the promotion of healthy development of children. (A.P2)
2. **Analyse** how the contribution of social identity theory might inform professionals in the promotion of healthy development of children. (A.M1)
3. **Evaluate** how the contribution of social identity theory might inform professionals in the promotion of healthy development of children. (A.D1)

You can see the assessment criteria on page 190 and an explanation of command terms on page 191.

An issue to consider

Consider the ingroups you identified in the *Get active* task on the left. Try to list five positive traits and five negative traits of one or two of your ingroups.

Is it more difficult to identify the negative traits than the positive traits? Is that a good thing or a bad thing?

Specification content

A2 Social, emotional and behavioural development

Key principles, application and critique of developmental studies and theories.

- Social identity theory, including Tajfel, Turner.

Learning theories

A bit of gossip and a not-so-happy ending

On this spread we revisit a number of the studies you learned about in Unit 1 (in our Year 1 'Certificate' book). One of which is the study of Little Albert by John Watson and Rosalie Rayner.

Rosalie Rayner holding Little Albert.

Rayner was Watson's graduate student. They became lovers and as a result he was asked to leave the university where he was a professor. They married and Watson then took up an entirely new career for a prestigious New York City firm, applying reinforcement principles to advertising.

In 1928, he wrote a book on childcare – in fact it was the most popular childcare guide of its time: *Psychological care of infant and child.* As good behaviourists, Watson and Rayner believed that parents should focus on the environment in which they raised their children and also believed that parental affection was detrimental to independence, so their two sons were never kissed or cuddled at home.

One son later wrote: 'I honestly believe the principles for which Dad stood as a behaviourist eroded both [my brother] Bill's and my ability to deal effectively with human emotion... and it tended to undermine self-esteem in later life, ultimately contributing to Bill's [suicide] and to my own crisis. Tragically, that's the antithesis of what Dad expected from practising these philosophies' (Smirle 2013).

Specification term

Learning theory A way of explaining behaviour in terms of what is observable and in terms of classical and operant conditioning.

Skinner designed an 'air crib' for his baby daughter. This was a sealed box with a glass window. He claimed this was a way to keep the environment controlled (warm enough for no blankets, sound proof and providing clean air plus built-in toys). But others interpreted it as his attempt to put a baby in a box where he could reinforce desirable behaviours – you can listen to his daughter's comments on YouTube (tinyurl.com/y4rzswhb).

Key concepts of the theories

Learning theories are based on the *learning approach* in psychology, which you studied in Unit 1 of this course (covered in our Year 1 'Certificate' book). In that unit you also learned about the contributions of John Watson, B. F. Skinner, and Albert Bandura. We will look at their contributions again in relation to child development.

Watson and classical conditioning

The concept of *classical conditioning* was first outlined by Ivan Pavlov in his observations of how dogs acquired a salivation response to a bell ringing. The association of an *unconditioned stimulus* (UCS, food) with a *neutral stimulus* (NS, bell) means that the *unconditioned response* (UCR, salivation) became a *conditioned response* (CR) to the bell.

John Watson and Rosalie Rayner (1920) demonstrated how classical conditioning can explain how children learn emotional responses. Working with Little Albert, they showed how fear (UCR) can be associated with a rat (NS) by pairing the rat and a loud noise (UCS). This could then explain how children generally learn emotional responses.

Skinner and operant conditioning

B. F. Skinner (1932) demonstrated *operant conditioning* using rats in a *Skinner box*. He argued that this form of learning offers a powerful explanation of how animals and humans acquire all behaviours. We learn via the consequences of our behaviour. *Reinforcements* may be positive or negative – both *positive* and *negative reinforcement* increase the likelihood of a behaviour being repeated whereas *punishment* decreases the likelihood.

Skinner proposed that children learn everything through reinforcement and punishment. Though he also added the concept of *shaping* as a way to explain how complex behaviours are acquired. Shaping involves reinforcing successive approximations of the behaviour. In other words, you start by reinforcing behaviour that is vaguely what you are seeking, but only continue the reinforcement each time the behaviour becomes a step closer to the target behaviour.

According to Skinner, shaping occurs in the development of *language*. When babies babble they are initially reinforced by adult attention and praise, but this reinforcement only continues if the child produces recognisable words and, later, sequences of words.

Bandura and social learning

Albert Bandura (1962) proposed the most powerful learning explanation of all. He argued that if all learning depends only on direct experience, then the process would be very slow. Instead it is much more likely that children learn through both direct and indirect experience of what others do (*observation*).

Bandura *et al.* (1961) demonstrated this in their study of nursery children who observed an adult *model* interacting with a Bobo doll. The study showed that children who observed the model behaving aggressively were more likely to behave aggressively when they had an opportunity to play with the doll.

Imitation This is *social learning* because we learn through observing the behaviour of others (a social activity) and then *imitating* their behaviour. There are two key elements in imitation:

- *Vicarious reinforcement* – children are much more likely to imitate behaviours that were successful when observed. Bandura *et al.* (1963) repeated their Bobo doll study and compared the effects of different kinds of reinforcement. Those children who saw the model *positively reinforced* were more likely to behave aggressively later than those who saw the model punished or getting no reinforcement. This shows the importance of vicarious reinforcement in imitation.

- *Identification* – children are more likely to imitate people who they identify with, i.e. people they like, admire and/or want to be like. This includes parents, pop stars, teachers and peers. Children tend to imitate same-sex models so young boys tend to imitate their father and/or same-sex friends and the same for young girls.

GET ACTIVE Attachment

On page 170 we described Bowlby's account of attachment formation. Before Bowlby, learning theorists offered their own explanation.

1. *Classical conditioning – food is associated with pleasure and when a mother* feeds her baby the mother becomes a conditioned stimulus. Identify the UCR, NS/CS, and CR in this scenario.*

As the mother now produces a sense of pleasure this is the basis of attachment.

2. *Operant conditioning – being hungry is unpleasant, so when a baby is fed this unpleasantness is reduced. Is this positive or negative reinforcement?*

The mother is acting as the 'reinforcer', so she becomes an attachment figure.

*'The mother' may of course be anyone who is doing the feeding.

Love the one who feeds you. Attachment can be explained through the principles of conditioning, see left. The learning theory account has been called the 'cupboard love' theory because it suggests that attachments are based on food.

Evaluation

Explains a lot

One strength is that learning theories, taken together, can explain many aspects of child development.

Many of the behaviours that children acquire are learned through direct or indirect conditioning – we have mentioned emotion and aggression on the facing page, but you have also studied explanations of how gender behaviours are learned by *modelling* the behaviour of others (Unit 1 in our Year 1 'Certificate' book).

This means that the explanations on the facing page are an important part of understanding development and can be applied to many situations.

Ignores many other influences

One weakness is that learning theories tend to exclude other explanations.

Having said, in the first point of evaluation, that the learning approach can explain many developmental changes, it is also the case that alone these are not sufficient. Skinner in particular held the view that there was no reason to include *cognitive* concepts in order to understand behaviour – however social learning theory (SLT) does just that. In SLT there must be some cognitive element in order to retain expectations of what behaviours will be rewarded.

This means that some learning explanations, such as the classical conditioning of emotions, omit important factors and thus are incomplete explanations. Both cognitive and biological explanations are largely excluded from learning theories.

Ethical issues

A further weakness is that the application of these learning principles may be harmful to development.

Learning theories suggest that one person can manipulate another person's behaviour by deliberately shaping their environment. In fact Skinner wrote a book called *Walden Two* in which he described a supposedly utopian world where the community organisers ('Planners') reinforce behaviours they regard as desirable. This may sound far-fetched but one form of treatment for prisoners and people with *mental health* problems is called *behaviour modification* where people are rewarded for desirable behaviour (see page 244).

This shows that the principles of learning theories could be seen as a way to unethically manipulate a child's development.

Assessment practice

At the end of learning aim A you must write a report (see pages 165 and 190). This report must be related to a scenario or context. We have used a realistic (but not real) context.

Primary school teachers obviously help children to learn. Some of the Refugee Council volunteers are even teaching refugee children to learn English. As children learn some behaviours through behavioural principles, it is useful for primary teachers to have a detailed knowledge of the learning processes underlying children's development.

Since teachers have regular contact with students, they are in a good position to promote their well-being and protect their welfare. For example, they can help children enjoy learning in class and adapt to the individual needs of each child.

A2.8 Learning aim A2 – Task 8

The second part of your report for learning aim A will be concerned with how current psychological theories can inform professionals in promoting growth, development and mental well-being in children – these are covered on the previous five spreads, this spread and the next five spreads.

This activity will help you practise the skills required to write the report in response to your scenario/context.

1. **Explain** how learning theories might inform professionals in the promotion of healthy development and mental well-being of children. (A.P2)

2. **Analyse** how the contribution of learning theories might inform professionals in the promotion of healthy development and mental well-being of children. (A.M1)

3. **Evaluate** how the contribution of learning theories might inform professionals in the promotion of healthy development and mental well-being of children. (A.D1)

An issue to consider

As you have grown up to be who you are today, to what extent do you feel your behaviour has been shaped by the reinforcements and punishments you received from parents and others around you?

To what extent is the development of your behaviour and thoughts shaped by genetic factors?

Specification content

A2 Social, emotional and behavioural development

Key principles, application and critique of developmental studies and theories.

● Learning theories, including Skinner, Watson, Bandura.

Peer status

Sociometry

Peer status is also called *sociometric status* and sociometry refers to measurement (metric) of social relations. Sociometry offers a way to objectively study group behaviour from the inside – in terms of the way group members see themselves.

Individual members in a social group (classroom, office, etc) are asked questions such as:

• Name three individuals in your group who you like most.

• Name three individuals in your group who you like least.

• Name the individual you would most like to sit next to.

A sociogram can be plotted which represents people as nodes and the relationships between them as lines. In some cases arrows are included to indicate the direction of liking.

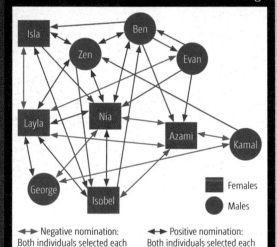

Females
Males

⟷ Negative nomination: Both individuals selected each other.

⟷ Positive nomination: Both individuals selected each other.

⟶ Negative nomination: The individual selected the person the arrow is pointing at.

⟶ Positive nomination: The individual selected the person the arrow is pointing at.

Specification term

Peer status A classification of how much a person is liked or disliked by their equals (peers). It is often measured by asking each member of a group to identify three group members they like most and three who they like least.

Aggressive but smart = controversial child.

$$E = MC^2$$

Key concepts of the perspective

Your 'peers' are those people who are at your level. Therefore, a peer may be someone who is the same age as you or who is your equal, for example, in terms of academic or sporting achievements.

In childhood, peers have an especially strong influence on our behaviour. We may start off, as babies, being influenced by our parents, but when we move to nursery and later to school (especially during adolescence), peers become a major influence on development. We have considered peer influences in other parts of this course, for example peer influence on gender development in Unit 1 (in our Year 1 'Certificate' book). Being part of a peer *ingroup* contributes to our identity and is important for emotional well-being.

Peer status

Peer status is a measurement that reflects the degree to which someone is liked or disliked by their peers as a group. The study of peer status is concerned with the long-term implications of a person's relationship with their peers – which may be one of popularity or rejection.

John Coie and Kenneth Dodge (1988) developed a method to test peer status – children are given a list of the other children in their class and asked to nominate three children they like most and three they like least. This allows researchers to classify children in one of five groups:

• *Popular* children receive many positive nominations.

• *Rejected* children receive many negative nominations and few positive nominations.

• *Neglected* children receive few positive and few negative nominations. These children are not especially liked or disliked by peers, and tend to go unnoticed.

• *Average* children receive an average number of both positive and negative nominations.

• *Controversial* children receive many positive and many negative nominations, i.e. they are liked by quite a few children, but also disliked by quite a few. It may be that such children are quite aggressive but also have good *cognitive* and social abilities and therefore avoid rejection.

A *meta-analysis* of 77 studies concluded that peer statuses tend to be fairly stable throughout childhood and adolescence (Jiang and Cillessen 2005).

Effects on behaviour

Social development

Coie and Dodge collected behavioural data about classmates from peers, teachers and observers and found that, not surprisingly, unpopular children had social difficulties. For example, neglected boys were the most solitary during play and rejected boys showed very little prosocial behaviour (e.g. being kind to others). The researchers also found that both rejected and controversial boys were rated as more aggressive than other boys.

Academic development

Kathryn Wentzel (2005) reports a relationship between peer status and academic success. Research has shown that children who are socially successful (i.e. the popular children) also tend to do better at school than average children.

Intriguingly Wentzel, together with Steven Asher (1995), found that the opposite is true as well. In a study of just over 400 American children in 7th and 8th grade (average age about 12½ years), they found that neglected children also did well academically – these children reported higher levels of *motivation* than average children and teachers described them as more self-regulated learners and more prosocial and better liked by teachers.

Mental health

Kyoung Min Shin *et al.* (2016) studied almost 4000 Korean first-grade students and revisited the same group six years later. They found that children who had peer-relationship problems were more likely to exhibit *depression* or *anxiety* (i.e. *internalising* problems where emotion is directed inwards) when adolescents than those children who were considered popular.

The fact that this is a *longitudinal study* suggests that children who have poor peer relationships in early childhood might be more vulnerable to emotional problems as adolescents.

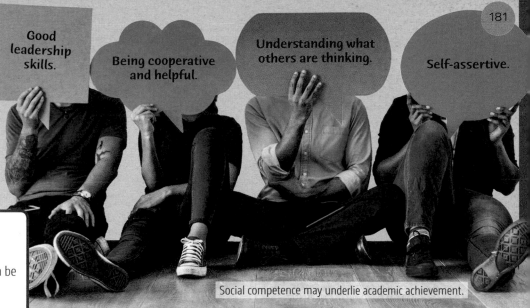

GET ACTIVE Interpreting a sociogram

On the facing page is a sociogram of a group of young people.

1. For each child decide on what peer status might best describe him or her.

2. What conclusions can you draw from your classifications? Identify **at least two**.

3. Look online for more sociograms and repeat the process.

Good leadership skills.

Being cooperative and helpful.

Understanding what others are thinking.

Self-assertive.

Social competence may underlie academic achievement.

Evaluation

Application to increasing status

One strength is that understanding peer status can be used to engineer better friendships.

Given the importance of peer status in academic success and social behaviour, it may help to identify children who are not popular. A teacher is likely to have some idea of the peer relationships in their classroom but using a *sociogram* is more objective. The teacher (or other adult) may use the sociogram to identify certain individuals and discuss social relationships with them. In addition, it may also help to arrange class seating so that more popular (and socially adept) children are sitting next to less popular children – for example, psychologists have found that familiarity increases liking (Zajonc 1968)!

This suggests that testing peer status could improve academic and social outcomes.

Correlational data

One weakness is that the research does not indicate what is cause and what is effect.

In the case of academic success, it might be that being popular creates greater self-confidence and determination, leading to academic success. Or it may be the other way round, that children who are academically successful are admired for such qualities and this makes them more self-confident and popular.

This means that peer status cannot be reliably used as a way to boost academic performance because it may be an effect rather than a cause.

Furthermore, the picture is clouded by the fact that neglected children also achieve academic success.

What does peer status represent?

Another weakness is that assessments of peer status are only made in school.

Sociograms are embedded in one particular social setting, such as the classroom. So, they only tell us about the status of a child in that setting. This is important because children do have other peer relationships outside school, for example with family members or in extracurricular activities which might include children from other year groups.

Therefore, it is difficult to draw any meaningful conclusion about the causes of behaviour (such as aggression or academic success) using peer status of the classroom.

Assessment practice

At the end of learning aim A you must write a report (see pages 165 and 190). This report must be related to a scenario or context. We have used a realistic (but not real) context.

Many of the volunteers you work with often talk to the refugee children, like professional counsellors do. Counsellors provide children with an opportunity to talk with a trained and understanding adult, to help them cope better with their lives (counselling). Counsellors can promote children's healthy development by helping them to cope with stress, for instance. One source of stress for children and adolescents is popularity/rejection by peers. Peer status can have deep effects on development, so it helps counsellors to understand how it affects the children who come to them with problems to discuss.

A2.9 Learning aim A2 – Task 9

The second part of your report for learning aim A will be concerned with how current psychological theories can inform professionals in promoting growth, development and mental well-being in children – these are covered on the previous six spreads, this spread and the next four spreads.

1. **Explain** how knowledge of peer status might inform professionals in the promotion of healthy development and mental well-being of children. (A.P2)

2. **Analyse** how knowledge of peer status might inform professionals in the promotion of healthy development and mental well-being of children. (A.M1)

3. **Evaluate** how knowledge of peer status might inform professionals in the promotion of healthy development and mental well-being of children. (A.D1)

An issue to consider

Cause or effect? Is peer status the cause of various behavioural differences. Or are these differences the cause of peer status?

Specification content

A2 Social, emotional and behavioural development

Key principles, application and critique of developmental studies and theories.

● Peer status, including Wentzel (2005).

Development of mental processes in children

The Sally–Anne task

Here are two children, Sally on the left and Anne on the right. Sally puts a marble in her basket. And then Sally leaves the room.

While Sally is gone, Anne moves the marble to her box.

Sally comes back. Where will she look for the marble?

The answer is 'In the basket'. *We* know the marble is in the box but we also know that *Sally* doesn't know that – we know she thinks it is in the basket. But that is because we understand that other people have their own view of the world.

Young children don't understand this. That's quite a strange idea – children think differently from adults.

Specification terms

Communication The exchange of information between animals within the same species using a variety of signals. Some signals are vocal (involve sound), but some are visual or involve smell.

Language A communication system unique to humans. It consists of a set of arbitrary conventional symbols through which meaning is conveyed. These symbols can be combined in such a way that an infinite number of novel messages can be produced.

Problem-solving The process of finding a solution to a situation that requires action.

What is she thinking? We are not 'mind readers' but we do try to read other people's minds. Social relationships rely on this.

Cognitive development

Cognitive development refers to the way a person's mental abilities change as they get older. The term *cognitive* is used to refer to mental processes, especially: thought processes, understanding the environment, problem-solving, language and communication (the four areas named in the specification).

Thought processes

On the next spread we look at Jean Piaget's theory of cognitive development. One of the most notable features of his theory was the suggestion that children think differently from adults. Before Piaget's theory, the view was that the difference between child and adult thinking lay in the amount that they knew. Piaget claimed that it was not simply a matter of acquiring more knowledge about the world – it was about qualitative differences in thinking that take place as the brain matures. An immature brain cannot think abstractly and also cannot use logical reasoning (Piaget called it 'operations').

Another cognitive psychologist, Jerome Bruner (1966), proposed three ways or modes of thinking which develop sequentially:

- Enactive representation – initially a baby learns to control its body and interacts with its environment *physically* (i.e. actively). This knowledge is encoded in our muscles. We later use this mode of thinking when we learn a new skill such as driving or sailing.
- Iconic representation – develops from the age of one. Information is stored in the form of mental images or even sound or smell images.
- Symbolic representation – develops around the age of seven. Again, like Piaget, Bruner saw this ability to start to think abstractly as an important shift in cognitive development.

Bruner believed that all these modes of representation remain necessary for adults to engage in problem-solving activities – different tasks require different strategies.

Understanding of their environments

A child's environment can be divided into the physical and social world.

Physical environment Understanding the physical environment involves experimentation – testing perception against reality. For example, seeing an object and then touching it or smelling it to see if both physical experiences match. If not, the child's *schemas* about the world need adjusting (more about schemas on the next spread).

Social environment Understanding the social world means being able to understand that other people – just like ourselves – are able to represent the world in their minds. Understanding their internal mental states means we can interpret and predict their behaviour. Such understanding underlies social relationships.

The process begins with an ability to *imitate* other people's expressions. Babies who are less than 72 hours old are able to imitate facial expressions (Meltzoff and Moore 1977). The next step is to understand the intentions of another person. Infants as young as three months will follow a person's gaze to nearby objects, which indicates an understanding of communicative intent (D'Entremont *et al.* 1997).

Theory of mind A distinction is made between knowing, for example, whether someone is happy or sad and knowing about how they experience these emotions. This latter ability is what psychologists call having a *theory of mind* (ToM), i.e. the recognition that other people have thoughts, emotions and intentions of their own. (Note that this is not the same kind of 'theory' as the theories you have been studying in psychology, it is a personal explanation of the world around you.)

ToM first appears around the age of three or four years (Wimmer and Perner 1983). At this time children also start using terms like 'think' and 'know' when referring to others. ToM is assessed using a false belief task such as the *Sally–Anne task* (see top left).

The concept of ToM has been very influential as an understanding of *autism spectrum disorders* (ASD). It is suggested that the inability to understand how others think and feel is a key characteristic of ASD and this is what makes it difficult for some children to interact socially with others.

GET ACTIVE The pendulum problem (Piaget and Inhelder 1956)

Children were asked to discover which factors were most important in determining the swing of a pendulum: the length of the string, the heaviness of the weight or the strength of push.

How would you work out a solution? Try it out and write down your steps.

Problem-solving

There are many different ways to solve problems. We look at a few here and how they relate to development.

Trial and error means trying one solution and, if it doesn't work, trying another. However, the selection of the next task may be *random* or may be systematic. Piaget suggested that a key change during childhood is moving from random methods to more systematic approaches. For example, in the *pendulum task* (see above), Piaget found that children over the age of 11 systematically tested one factor at a time, keeping the others constant. Whereas younger children changed all variables each time hoping to find a solution – a random approach.

However, more systematic approaches aren't always best. Robert Siegler (1976) found that 5-year-olds were 89% correct on a particular problem whereas 17-year-olds, who tended to use a more sophisticated strategy, were only correct 51% of the time on the same problem.

Developing different strategies Bruner (1973) argued that children are natural problem-solvers from their early months, they simply become better as they get older because they have learned a variety of strategies. When faced with a new problem, a child tries out a range of already-encountered strategies.

The role of adults Bruner also suggested that adults play an important role in *scaffolding* children's problem-solving. The adult creates a 'scaffold' (i.e. temporary support), which is gradually withdrawn as the child becomes more able to work independently. For example, when trying to solve a puzzle, the adult may give hints about what to do next but the hints become less specific as the child gets more proficient at that kind of problem. (Scaffolding is explained on page 186.)

Language and communication

Humans *communicate* with facial expressions and gestures but especially using *language*.

Communication Some expressions (e.g. smiling or crying) are recognised in all *cultures*, and therefore must be *innate*. Other expressions or gestures are culture-specific, for example the thumbs up signal means 'OK' in many cultures but is quite rude in others.

Universal sequence The word 'infant' means 'without language' – so infancy ends when a child starts to use language. This is usually around the age of one when children start babbling – making repetitive sounds (e.g. lalala or mama). They then begin to produce single words and quickly move on to two-word utterances. By 2½, children start using more words and also add verb tenses, plurals and other refinements. This order is true for all children, even those who are deaf or who have learning impairments.

Predictable errors There are several types of error that are made which provide insight into the process of language acquisition:

* *Overgeneralisations* – children apply rules to irregular words. For example, they say *tooths* instead of *teeth*, *runned* instead of *ran*. In doing this they are demonstrating that they have understood certain *grammatical* rules – adding an 's' for plurals and adding 'ed' for past tense. They are not copying others because no one would say tooths or runned.

* *Overextension* – children apply one word to a large class, for example using the word *dog* for all animals with four legs.

* *Underextension* – children may sometimes use the name of the class to refer just to one specific example, such as using the word *dog* for a pet but not applying it to other dogs.

On page 188 we will look at theories of how language and communication skills develop in children.

Assessment practice

At the end of learning aim A you must write a report (see pages 165 and 190). This report must be related to a scenario or context. We have used a realistic (but not real) context.

You help out at a Refugee Council centre to get first-hand experience of how children play on their own and together.

This makes you realise that teaching assistants (TAs) need to know how children's thinking develops. Teaching assistants help qualified teachers to plan and deliver lessons in (and out of) the classroom. They help children to work together in groups.

TAs benefit from knowledge of children's thought processes, how they understand their environments, their problem-solving and language/communication. These are all vital topics to help refugee children who find themselves without their parents in a strange country.

A3.9 Learning aim A3 – Task 9

The second part of your report for learning aim A will be concerned with how current psychological theories can inform professionals in promoting growth, development and mental well-being in children – these are covered on the previous seven spreads, this spread and the next three spreads.

1. In relation to each topic on this spread, **explain** what psychologists have learned that might inform professionals in the promotion of healthy development of children. (A.P2)

An issue to consider

One of the persistent questions in development is, which comes first – language or thought? Does a child discover a concept and then learn the word for it or do they learn a word first and then it helps them understand the concept?

Think of your experience learning psychology – do you learn a new term first or do you need to grasp the underlying concept first and then use the term?

Specification content

A3 Cognition, language and communication development

* Development in children of:
  * Thought processes.
  * Understanding of their environments.
  * Problem-solving.
  * Language and communication.

Piaget's theory and the role of adults

Piaget's conservation studies

In this picture, a child is shown two glasses of coloured water. Is the quantity of water the same in both glasses A and B?

In the picture below we pour the water from one glass (A) into a taller, thinner glass (C).

Is the quantity of water in the new glass (C) the same as the other glass (B)?

Young children say no – the level of water is higher and therefore it looks like there is more water.

They are not yet able to conserve the quantity – i.e. they don't understand that quantity can't change.

Specification terms

Adaptation In Piaget's theory, it involves a child changing their schema to meet the demands of new situations or experiences.

Schema A mental package of beliefs and expectations that influence memory.

Stage theory A description of developmental changes in terms of distinct qualitative changes in behaviour from one age to another.

Next stop, *Grand Designs*... a little girl practises her architectural skills in the concrete operational stage with adult guidance.

Key concepts of the theory

Jean Piaget (1954) changed the way that we understand *cognitive development*. On the previous spread we discussed the point that, in Piaget's view, children's thinking doesn't just change *quantitatively* as they get older, it also changes *qualitatively*. When they are young, children actually think in a quite a different way from adults – as shown in the example on the left. This was a revolution in understanding cognitive development.

Schema and schematic development

As part of his theory, Piaget described how we learn new information. We construct more and more detailed and complex mental representations of the world. These representations are stored in the form of *schemas* which you learned about in Unit 1 of this course (in our Year 1 'Certificate' book). A schema is a mental 'package' of knowledge relating to a concept, object, event, etc.

According to Piaget, children are born with a small number of schemas. Gradually these schemas develop, becoming more complex through the process of *adaptation*.

Adaptation

Piaget saw the process of learning as adapting schema to new situations so that we understand it. Adaptation involves *assimilation* and *accommodation*.

Assimilation Let us imagine that a young child has a schema for 'car'. The child knows that you get into a car and other people get into a car and the car makes a noise and it moves. A car is red and shiny. One day the child encounters a blue sports car. This doesn't quite match their existing schema – different colour, only holds two people, makes a new noise, etc. The child's 'car schema' needs to change to take in the new information.

Assimilation takes place when we add new information to our existing schema.

Accommodation On another occasion, the child gets to ride in a tractor – this also moves and is shiny and red but makes quite a different noise and has very large tyres. This requires a big change to the existing car schema – in fact it probably requires the formation of a new schema – a tractor schema.

Gradually, throughout our life span, we develop new schemas. This is how we acquire knowledge about the world.

A stage theory of cognitive development

Piaget suggested that young children are not able to think like an adult. Their brains are simply not mature enough, in the same way as a very young child cannot walk because their muscles and coordination are not mature enough.

As a child gets older, their brain matures (a biological process) and different kinds of thinking become possible. These are described as different stages of cognitive development (thus a *stage theory*). The order of the stages listed below is invariant – they occur in the same order in children all over the world. They also occur at typical ages.

1. Sensorimotor stage (0–2 years) A baby's early focus is on developing coordination between what they see/hear/feel (sensory) and what they can do (motor).

2. Pre-operational stage (2–7 years) The term *operations* means 'logical thinking'. So, children at this stage do not think in an internally consistent logical way. For example, they cannot understand that quantity remains constant even though it may look like more (see conservation demonstration, top left).

3. Concrete operational stage (7–11 years) Children now have better reasoning (e.g. they can conserve). However, these are strictly concrete operations, i.e. they can be applied only to physical objects in the child's presence. Children still struggle to reason about abstract ideas and to imagine objects or situations they cannot see.

4. Formal operational stage (11+ years) Children became capable of thinking abstractly and formally. They are able to focus on the *form* of an argument and not be distracted by its content.

The role of adults in Piaget's theory

Piaget believed that each stage of cognitive development appears through the natural process of ageing. Therefore, in his view, you cannot teach a child to perform certain activities before they are biologically 'ready'. If you try to teach a child before they are ready they may only acquire skills superficially.

However, adults can assist the process through *discovery learning* – providing activities that are age-appropriate and allow a child to discover concepts for themselves. The adult's role is to create an environment which will stimulate children to ask questions and challenge them to develop new schemas.

Unit 3 Health Psycholog - exam 66% - y2
marks   2hr 70 marr

Sep - Dec   Exam Jan

Unit 6 Psychopathology course work 33%
3 written

Dec - Apr

Retackes units may / June

Naughty teddy

Piaget tested conservation with glasses of water (see facing page). He also tested conservation by showing children two identical rows of six counters, equally spaced.

Young children correctly answered that each row had the same number of counters.

Then the top row is spread out so it looks longer.

Pre-operational children answer that there are more counters in the top row.

Enter naughty teddy and a study by James McGarrigle and Margaret Donaldson (1974). The children were shown the two rows of equally-spaced counters and then the teddy jumped out of his box and pushed the counters in one row about, in a haphazard fashion, making it look longer.

This time more of the pre-operational children said the number remained the same (i.e. they conserved). This suggests that Piaget's method underestimated what younger children can do.

Evaluation

Educational application

One strength is that Piaget's ideas about how children learn by forming their own mental representation of the world has had an enormous influence on education.

Since Piaget's ideas became popular in the 1960s, the old-fashioned classroom, in which children sat silently in rows copying from the board, has been replaced by activity-oriented classrooms in which children actively engage in tasks that allow them to construct their own understandings of the curriculum. The major changes happened in the 1960s after Piaget published his theory.

This underlines the huge importance of his theory.

The sample

One weakness is that Piaget's research involved middle-class European children.

Piaget developed his theory from research studies he conducted where he lived – in Switzerland. The children were from European academic families who valued academic abilities. In other *cultures* and social classes, greater value may be placed on, for example, a more basic level of concrete operations (i.e. making things rather than thinking about abstract ideas).

Therefore, his theory may not be universally applicable.

Overestimated children's abilities

Another weakness of Piaget's stage account is that he overestimated what older children are capable of.

Piaget suggested that, by the age of 11 years, children should be capable of logical thinking in an abstract way. In fact, it is doubtful whether many adults are capable of this. One way to test logical thinking is the Wason card selection task devised by Peter Wason (1968, see below). When he tested undergraduate students in London he found that only two out of 16 participants got this right in the abstract version but ten out of 16 solved the same problem if it was given in a concrete form (Manchester, Leeds, car and train).

This suggests that Piaget was over-optimistic about what children of 11 can do.

Assessment practice

At the end of learning aim A you must write a report (see pages 165 and 190). This report must be related to a scenario or context. We have used a realistic (but not real) context.

You introduce the refugee volunteers to the work of school nurses. These professionals see every child (and their parents) within the first school year for a health assessment. They improve children's well-being by helping them to make healthy lifestyle choices (e.g. diet and exercise). School nurses are in a good position to identify children and adolescents with developmental disorders.

They benefit from a good understanding of Piaget's theory of cognitive development. They know the sequence of developmental stages and the appropriate ages associated with them. This helps them to identify the children whose thinking abilities appear to be lagging behind, for example.

A3.10 Learning aim A3 – Task 10

The second part of your report for learning aim A will be concerned with how current psychological theories can inform professionals in promoting growth, development and mental well-being in children – these are covered on the previous eight spreads, this spread and the next two spreads.

This activity will help you practise the skills required to write the report in response to your scenario/context.

1. **Explain** how Piaget's theory (and the role of adults) might inform professionals in the promotion of healthy development and mental well-being of children. (A.P2)
2. **Analyse** how the contribution of Piaget's theory (and the role of adults) might inform professionals in the promotion of healthy development and mental well-being of children. (A.M1)
3. **Evaluate** how the contribution of Piaget's theory (and the role of adults) might inform professionals in the promotion of healthy development and mental well-being of children. (A.D1)

An issue to consider

As you have seen, Piaget believed that children should direct their own learning (active learning) rather than being told what to think and do (passive learning). Does this match your primary school experience?

Do you think active or passive learning is best?

GET ACTIVE Formal operational thinking

There are four cards on the right, each has a letter or digit on the other side of the card.

There is a rule: 'If a card has a vowel on one face, then that card has an even number on the opposite face.'

What card or cards would you turn over to test this rule? (Answer at bottom of page 187.)

Specification content

A3 Cognition, language and communication development

- Key principles and critique of theories of cognition and language, and their application in different situations:
  - Piaget, including schemas and schematic development, adaptation, stage theory of cognitive development.
- Role of adults in supporting and promoting optimal learning and development opportunities.

Vygotsky's theory and the role of adults

Teaching

Theories about the development of thinking (cognition) are obviously important for teaching.

A teacher may decide to create a Vygotskian classroom – where the social context is important, i.e. learning by being led by others. Or the Piagetian classroom – where the emphasis lies in each person actively creating their understanding for themselves rather than being guided by someone else. Both Vygotsky and Piaget valued group work but for different reasons – for Piaget it was the opportunity to be stimulated by others' thinking, for Vygotsky it was more about direct instruction.

You will undoubtedly have experienced a bit of both styles in your own experience of education and can relate the theory to your actual experience.

Specification terms

Internalisation An individual's acceptance of a set of norms and values (established by others) through socialisation.

Scaffolding An approach to instruction that aims to support a learner only when absolutely necessary, i.e. to provide a support framework (scaffold) to assist the learning process.

Zone of proximal development (ZPD) In Vygotsky's theory of cognitive development, the 'region' between a person's current abilities, which they can perform with no assistance, and their potential capabilities, which they can be helped to achieve with the assistance of 'experts'.

Lots of scaffolding going on here.

Key concepts of the theory

Lev Vygotsky (1934) believed that *cultural* influences were the key driving force in *cognitive development*. Such cultural influences come through interactions with others and through *language*.

Elementary and higher mental functions

Vygotsky proposed that children are born with *elementary mental functions*, such as perception and memory. These are transformed into *higher mental functions* (such as use of mathematical systems) by the influence of culture. Elementary mental functions are biological and a form of natural development. Higher mental functions are exclusively human. The role of culture is to transform elementary mental functions into higher mental functions.

Internalisation

According to Vygotsky, every function in a child's cognitive development appears twice: first, on the *social* level (between people), and later on the *individual* level (inside the child) when the knowledge becomes *internalised*.

Zone of proximal development (ZPD)

The ZPD is a key concept in Vygotsky's theory. At any time in your life there are things you know about and know how to do and there are things you don't know about or know how to do. Some of the things you don't know are much too difficult but for some of them you are just about ready for the new understanding or skill. This is your *zone of proximal development* – the region in which you are ready for the learning to take place.

However, to move through the ZPD you need an expert to guide you, someone who can explain a new principle or can demonstrate a new skill and explain it to you.

(Note this is quite different from Piaget's view – Piaget said a child has to be biologically ready for the next step whereas Vygotsky believed that, with assistance, a child can always move on to the next step.)

The role of adults – scaffolding

The concept of *scaffolding* was introduced on page 183. It can be related to the ZPD. Any 'expert' can help a learner to move through the ZPD – all people with greater knowledge than the learner are called 'experts'. Initially, the person interacting with a learner assumes most of the responsibility for guiding the problem-solving activity, but gradually this responsibility transfers to the child.

The expert creates a 'scaffold' (i.e. temporary support), which is gradually withdrawn as the child is more able to work independently.

David Wood and David Middleton (1975) found that successful scaffolding depends on something they called *contingent regulations*. They watched as mothers assisted their three- to four-year-old children to complete a difficult task (assembling a three-dimensional pyramid puzzle).

The mothers responded differently to success and failure on elements of the task. If what their child did was successful the mothers provided fewer explicit instructions (e.g. simply praising the strategy that has just been used). If their child's actions resulted in failure, the mothers provided more explicit instructions (e.g. identifying what particular piece needs to be moved).

In other words, the mothers' responses depended on (were *contingent* on) the child's behaviour.

GET ACTIVE Teaching teachers

Imagine that your job is to teach teachers about psychological theories of cognitive development and how they might apply these theories to what they actually do in the classroom.

Prepare PowerPoint slides giving your student teachers four main points from Piaget and Vygotsky's theories.

Explain how each of your points could be applied in the classroom.

The difference between Piaget and Vygotsky's views may be related to the politics of their environments. Vygotsky wrote from a Russian socialist perspective which believes in the power of community, and thus valued the role of society in the development of the individual. Piaget was a product of individualist European society.

Evaluation

Educational application

One strength of Vygotsky's theory is its application to education.

Vygotsky placed emphasis on how learning is facilitated by collaboration with others. This means working in small groups often varying in ability, where each student helps the others complete tasks – helping each other through the ZPD. *Peer tutoring* is another application of Vygotsky's theory. 'More knowledgeable others' instruct their peers. Many studies have shown that peer tutoring leads to improvements in both tutees' and tutors' academic and social development (e.g. Cohen *et al.* 1982). The concept of scaffolding is also important in education, whereby teachers should support their learners with cognitive structures to assist them, for example giving sentence starters to help writing essays.

This shows how Vygotsky's ideas have been translated into common classroom practices, supported by research studies.

Evidence for the role of culture

Another strength is support from research with animals.

This research illustrates the role of culture in cognitive development. Some psychologists believe that non-human animals possess elementary mental functions which may be transformed into higher mental functions by immersing an animal in human culture. For example, Sue Savage-Rumbaugh (1991) has exposed Bonobo apes (such as Kanzi) to a language-rich culture – the apes are 'spoken' to all the time through the use of symbols that stand for common words. It is debatable as to whether Kanzi could be said to have acquired human language but he is able to *communicate* using this symbol system. (*Language* is discussed on the next spread.)

This shows that higher mental functions (a symbol system) can be transmitted through culture – the apes were able to learn something they couldn't discover for themselves.

Limitations of the social approach

One weakness is that Vygotsky may have overplayed the importance of the social environment (whereas Piaget underplayed social influences).

If social input was all that was needed to advance cognitive development then learning would be a lot faster than it is. Additionally, the emphasis on social factors meant that biological factors were largely ignored in Vygotsky's theory. (In Piaget's theory biological maturation is a key concept.)

This suggests that both Piaget's and Vygotsky's theories have drawbacks and might benefit from being more balanced.

The answer to the Get active on page 185 is A and 7 because if you turn over B and it has an even number you still don't know whether a card with a vowel does or does not have an even number. And same argument for the 4.

Assessment practice

At the end of learning aim A you must write a report (see pages 165 and 190). This report must be related to a scenario or context. We have used a realistic (but not real) context.

You want the refugee volunteers to understand how Vygotsky's theory can help SENCOs in their work. A SENCO is a school's special educational needs coordinator. They help to identify students who have learning difficulties. They also organise teachers and other staff (e.g. teaching assistants) to provide support in and out of class (e.g. adapting learning materials). Like every teacher, a SENCO also promotes learning in all children and adolescents. For instance, they apply Vygotsky's concept of scaffolding every day in their work.

A3.11 Learning aim A3 – Task 11

The second part of your report for learning aim A will be concerned with how current psychological theories can inform professionals in promoting growth, development and mental well-being in children – these are covered on the previous nine spreads, this spread and the next spread.

1. **Explain** how Vygotsky's theory (and the role of adults) might inform professionals in the promotion of healthy development and mental well-being of children. (A.P2)

2. **Analyse** how the contribution of Vygotsky's theory (and the role of adults) might inform professionals in the promotion of healthy development and mental well-being of children. (A.M1)

3. **Evaluate** how the contribution of Vygotsky's theory (and the role of adults) might inform professionals in the promotion of healthy development and mental well-being of children. (A.D1)

> You can see the assessment criteria on page 190 and an explanation of command terms on page 191.

An issue to consider

Piaget said that if you teach a child something before they are ready you prevent them ever fully understanding it.

Vygotsky believed the opposite – it is only with the help of others that our thinking grows.

Which view do you think is better? And why?

Specification content

A3 Cognition, language and communication development

● Key principles and critique of theories of cognition and language, and their application in different situations:

  ○ Vygotsky, including the zone of proximal development (ZPD), internalisation, scaffolding.

● Role of adults in supporting and promoting optimal learning and development opportunities.

Language and communication acquisition and the role of adults

Teaching animals to use language

If asked to define language, you might say it is a communication system unique to humans. However, many researchers have tried to teach non-human animals (parrots, dolphins, chimpanzees and gorillas) to use human language – which, if possible, would mean it isn't unique to humans.

One such chimpanzee was called Nim Chimsky (after Noam Chomsky on the right) but probably the best known was Washoe, a female chimpanzee, raised by Drs Allen and Beatrix Gardner and later by Roger and Deborah Fouts.

As chimpanzee vocal chords do not allow for the production of words, Washoe was taught American Sign Language. Washoe learned to use about 250 signs reliably, and was able to combine these into two- and three-word phrases. Washoe also taught her adopted son, Loulis, to use sign language.

However, not everyone agreed that she truly *understood* language. Computers are able to simulate language but they clearly have no capacity for understanding. In addition, Washoe never developed a regular word order (grammatical use of language).

The jury is still out on whether anyone except humans can actually use *language* as distinct from *communication*.

PS Washoe died in October 2007, aged 42, and had an obituary in the *New York Times*. You can read about her life at www.friendsofwashoe.org

Specification terms

Communication and **Language** See page 182.

What is remarkable is that children learn to speak just by listening to others speaking – whereas all non-human animals have had to be taught very carefully over quite a long period of time.

Theories of language and communication

Three theories are reviewed below representing three different approaches – the *learning approach*, the *biological approach* and the *social approach*.

Skinner and learning theory

B. F. Skinner (1957) claimed that *language* is acquired in the same way as any other behaviour, as a consequence of *operant conditioning* and *reinforcement*. Babbling or random sounds ('mands') are produced by a young child and reinforced by the child getting what it wants, such as a biscuit or parental attention. The child also *imitates* sounds/words and is *positively reinforced*.

Shaping Through the process of *shaping* these sounds come closer and closer to the actual word – initially the child may be reinforced for something that vaguely sounds correct but gradually reinforcement is only given for something closer and closer to the actual word or sentence.

Chomsky and the LAD

Noam Chomsky (1959) proposed that language develops uniquely in humans because we possess a *language acquisition device* (LAD – sometimes called LAS where S stands for *system*) in our brain, which is *innate*. He agreed that imitation and reinforcement are part of learning language but foremost is the human predisposition to generate the rules of language from the words they hear and, using the rules of combinations, be able to generate infinite novel expressions.

Biological and innate Possessing a LAD means that all children inevitably produce language – in the same way as they inevitably learn to walk. They do not need to be taught but develop the ability when biologically ready. All that is needed is exposure to a native vocabulary and then the LAD system generates the rules of *grammar*. 'Grammar' refers to the rules by which words are modified to express, for example, plurals or tenses, and how words are combined into sentences to express meaning. Consider these sentences: 'The cat chased the dog' and 'The dog chased the cat'. They have exactly the same words but the order expresses a different meaning.

A sensitive period A key feature of any innate, biological system is that there is likely to be a *critical* or *sensitive period* for development (as is the case for *attachment*). Chomsky suggested that children who were not exposed to a native vocabulary before the age of 11 would not be able to ever become fluent speakers. The case of Genie (discussed on page 202) was used to support this.

Bruner and the LASS

Jerome Bruner (1983) proposed an innate acquisition system – LASS (*language acquisition support system*). This was not a criticism of Chomsky's LAD/LAS but more of a further development. The LASS emphasised the importance of social meaning in language acquisition. This refers to the social nature of speech – not just the fact that other people are part of the process of language acquisition but also that language plays a key role in social interaction and expression of our *culture*. The language you speak (and accent you use) *communicates* to others what cultural group you belong to.

Chomsky's model would predict that there are no 'stone-age' languages, i.e. languages which are very simple in terms of their construction. The LASS would predict that stone-age cultures should have stone-age languages, because language is a reflection of culture.

The role of adults

Skinner and learning theory Adults and other children who are talking have a role in reinforcement and shaping. It has also been suggested that people use 'baby talk' when speaking to babies (technically called *infant-directed speech*, IDS). IDS is slower, higher in pitch, repetitive, has exaggerated intonation patterns and uses a special vocabulary (e.g. 'tummy') and a simplified grammar (e.g. 'pat the doggie'). This is all aimed to help a young child imitate both words and sentence construction.

Chomsky and the LAD/LAS In this theory, the main role of adults is to expose children to a language so the children can imitate what they hear and generate the rules of the language. If you travel to a foreign country and are exposed to a new language, you would do the same thing. Expert speakers help by correcting mistakes.

Bruner and the LASS Language acquisition is related to *scaffolding*, as with learning generally. An adult (or any 'expert') gives hints and advice as to what is required but gradually this is reduced.

Evaluation

Application to language acquisition

One strength of biological theories of language acquisition is that they explain the importance of the critical/sensitive period.

All theories suggest that children need adult reinforcement and exposure to a rich linguistic environment in order to develop their language abilities. This could especially be applied to deaf children who wish to communicate via sign language. But most particularly, it has been shown that deaf children need to be exposed to sign language as early as possible in order to develop a grammatical version. This is because there is a *critical period* in the development of true language (e.g. Mayberry 2010).

This shows how theoretical understanding can be useful in practice.

Criticism of learning theory

One weakness of Skinner's account of language is that it can't explain how children learn irregularities.

On page 183 we noted that a key characteristic of early speech is the use of *overgeneralisations* such as sheeps and runned. A child cannot learn these through imitation because no adult would use these words so they cannot have been imitated. Imitation is certainly part of the acquisition process but a child must be deducing the rules of grammar from the sentences they hear and using these rules to produce overgeneralisations. Furthermore, according to Skinner, mothers tend to reinforce meaning rather than grammatical structure, which again shows that grammar is not acquired through reinforcement.

This means that Skinner's theory cannot alone account for language acquisition, though it clearly does explain some aspects of language acquisition such as learning speech sounds, vocabulary and accent, and also applies generally to learning other communications – gestures and facial expressions.

Criticism of LAD

One weakness of Chomsky's theory is that there may be no need for a specialised language unit.

Chomsky's views were revolutionary, because they could explain overgeneralisations, linguistic universals, the universal sequence of acquisition, the ease of acquisition even when working on an incomplete sample and the lack of true language in animals. However, Jean Piaget (1970) always argued that human language ability could be seen as one outcome of a general intellectual ability rather than a specific language device – the tendency of the brain to organise information into categories and hierarchies.

This means it is not necessary to introduce the specific LAD mechanism to explain language acquisition. Nevertheless, the production of language is the product of an innate and probably uniquely human ability.

GET ACTIVE A guide for parents

Some parents of young babies get together to record a podcast. They want to help expectant parents understand how their babies and young children will develop/acquire language/communication. They need a psychologist to provide insights into the psychology involved and ask you to step up to the microphone.

Based on what you have learned on this spread and also page 183, write a script suitable for podcasting.

Include some theoretical input – you are a psychologist after all.

PS Why not have a go at the podcast yourself?

Baby sign language

Adults and babies communicate long before language begins. A baby's cry is a form of communication. Some parents use baby sign language to be able to be more specific in their communications. This is not a technical sign language as used by the deaf community. It is taught by making the sign and then doing the activity, for example signing 'food' and then giving food. The baby will start to use the sign themselves. Signs can be made up.

Eat

Finish

Assessment practice

At the end of learning aim A you must write a report (see pages 165 and 190). This report must be related to a scenario or context. We have used a realistic (but not real) context.

The refugee volunteers need to understand how general practitioners of medicine (GPs) promote the healthy development of all children and adolescents.

GPs generally believe that 'prevention is better than cure'. This means they promote children's development by encouraging healthy lifestyles (e.g. diet and exercise) and giving advice. To do this, GPs need to be able to communicate appropriately with children at different stages of development. An understanding of how children acquire language can help with this.

A3.12 Learning aim A3 – Task 12

The second part of your report for learning aim A will be concerned with how current psychological theories can inform professionals in promoting growth, development and mental well-being in children – these are covered on the previous ten spreads and this spread.

This activity will help you practise the skills required to write the report in response to your scenario/context.

1. **Explain** how theories of language/communication acquisition (and the role of adults) might inform professionals in the promotion of healthy development of children. (A.P2)

2. **Analyse** how the contribution of theories of language/communication acquisition (and the role of adults) might inform professionals in the promotion of healthy development and mental well-being of children. (A.M1)

3. **Evaluate** how the contribution of theories of language/communication acquisition (and the role of adults) might inform professionals in the promotion of healthy development and mental well-being of children. (A.D1)

An issue to consider

When do words or expressions count as communication and when do they become language?

Specification content

A3 Cognition, language and communication development

● Key principles and critique of theories of cognition and language, and their application in different situations:
  ○ Language and communication acquisition, including Chomsky, Bruner, Skinner.
● Role of adults in supporting and promoting optimal learning and development opportunities.

Assessment guidance

Learning aim A assessment

For learning aim A you are required to produce a report (which can be written or presented as a poster, Powerpoint or other form).

The report for learning aim A can only be completed after you have studied the content of learning aim A as it is a synoptic assessment (see 'Synoptic assessment' on facing page).

You can, if you wish, combine this report with the report for learning aims B and C but you cannot submit more than two assessments for this unit and no learning aim can be subdivided.

Recommended assessment approach

The *Delivery Guide for Unit 5* states that your report (or presentation, poster, etc.):

- Is likely to be theoretical in nature.
- Will consider how theories of childhood development contribute to the understanding of children's growth and development.

Assignment briefs

The board supplies suggested assignment briefs which you can use – see *Unit 5 Authorised assignment brief for Learning aim A*.

Your centre can also devise their own assignment brief which should have a vocational scenario/context and a series of tasks to complete.

Vocational scenario	The task (from the assignment brief)
The *Delivery Guide for Unit 5* suggests that it would be useful to give learners some suitable stimulus material, perhaps in the form of a case study that will enable them to showcase their understanding.	You need to produce a detailed report that should include the following: • An **explanation** of the historical and current societal (social) approaches to the nature of childhood with an **explanation** of how current psychological theories inform professionals in promoting growth, development and mental well-being in children. (See pass criteria below.) • An **analysis** of the contribution of societal approaches to childhood along with an **analysis** of the psychological theories of child development in the promotion of a healthy childhood. (See merit criteria below.) • An **evaluation** of the impact of societal approaches to childhood and the various theories, backed up by examples to support your understanding of child development in promoting healthy growth, development and mental well-being in children. (See distinction criteria below.)

Assessment information

Your final report will be awarded a Distinction (D), Merit (M), Pass (P), Near Pass (N) or Unclassified (U).

The specification provides criteria for each level as shown below.

Pass	Merit	Distinction
A.P1 EXPLAIN historical and current societal approaches to the nature of childhood.		
A.P2 EXPLAIN how current psychological theories can inform professionals in promoting growth, development and mental well-being in children.		
	A.M1 ANALYSE the contribution of societal approaches to childhood and the psychological theories of child development to the promotion of healthy growth, development and mental well-being in children.	
		A.D1 EVALUATE the impact of societal approaches to childhood and the psychological theories of child development in promoting healthy growth, development and mental well-being in children.

Marking factors The specification also provides information that an assessor will take into consideration when marking your assignment.

Marking factors	Pass	Merit	Distinction
The ways in which children and childhood have been viewed historically are ...	... identified with brief examples.	... identified, including a range of ways.	... discussed in depth.
The influence of cultural or child-rearing practices on modern-day view of childhood is ...	... given including a few examples.	... given including several examples.	... fully-focused and a wide range of examples covered.
The ways in which children's healthy development and learning is promoted is ...	... outlined.	... illustrated with justifiable examples.	... thoroughly evaluated.
Key theories will be covered, including ...	... a few in outline.	... two or more, showing sound understanding.	... a wide range discussed in detail.
The way that children's behaviour may be influenced and the impact on learning and development includes ...	... brief examples.	... appropriate examples.	... supporting examples.
Critique of theories will be ...	... vague and not linked to theorists' work.	... linked directly to theorists' work.	... well-reasoned with sustained judgements.

Self-review checklist

Writing a big report requires organisation and planning. You learned about time management as part of the unit on conducting psychological research (which is in our Year 1 'Certificate' book). Apply those skills to writing your report for this unit.

It is important to set yourself target dates at the outset.

It is also important to write at least two drafts.

First draft

Remember this is a *draft*. So you can write anything (see 'Blank screen syndrome' on page 259). But do not copy anything, even at this stage (see 'Plagiarism' on the right).

Date to complete first draft:

	Date completed	Explain (A.P1)	Explain (A.P2)	Analyse (A.M1)	Evaluate (A.D1)
• In the first grey column enter the completion dates for each section of your report. • As you write each section tick the yellow boxes when you have explained, analysed and evaluated, as appropriate. Ignore the boxes that are crossed through.					
A1 The nature of childhood					
Historical and cultural perspectives on childhood				X	
Child-rearing practices and modern-day views				X	
A2 Social, emotional and behavioural development					
Attachment studies: Lorenz and Harlow				X	
Attachment theory: Bowlby				X	
Attachment study: Ainsworth				X	
Ecological models of child development				X	
Social identity theory				X	
Learning theories				X	
Peer status				X	
A3 Cognition, language and communication development					
Development of mental processes in children				X	X
Piaget's theory and the role of adults				X	
Vygotsky's theory and the role of adults				X	
Language/communication acquisition / Role of adults				X	
References compiled					

Second draft

The next step is to revise your first document. Below is a checklist of things to consider.

Date to complete second draft:

	Date completed
I have checked that I have covered each of the six marking factors (grey column) in the table on the facing page.	
I have gone through and deleted any irrelevant material.	
I have checked that every point has evidence to back it up.	
I have identified long sentences and rephrased them.	
I have checked that each paragraph deals with one idea.	
I have corrected any spelling mistakes.	
I have checked that each paragraph makes reference to the scenario/context.	

Final draft

Read through your completed second draft to polish the report.

Date to complete final draft:

Synoptic assessment

This assessment is synoptic. Synoptic refers to the ability to provide an overview of many different strands of information.

In your assessment you must demonstrate that you can identify and use effectively, in an integrated way, an appropriate selection of skills, techniques, concepts, theories and knowledge from across the whole sector as relevant to this task.

Plagiarism

Plagiarism means to use someone else's work without crediting the source. It means to steal and pass off the words (or ideas) of another as one's own. All the work submitted as your internal assessments must be your own.

We are lucky to have the internet at our fingertips when writing this book and we often cut and paste content into our notes – and it is very easy to forget we have done this. However, we know this can be easily checked and if we were found to have committed plagiarism in our book we would be accused of committing a crime and could be fined or receive a prison sentence for plagiarising someone else's work.

The same is true for you – it is tempting to use something written on a website or in this book and feel 'I can't say it as well as this' and therefore copy it exactly. You cannot do that unless the sentence is in quotes and attributed to the author.

We take great care to ensure that all of our sentences are our own. You must do the same or you will be disqualified from this exam.

Referencing

If you cite any research study or source (such as a website) you need to include this in a list of references at the end of your report.

The conventions for referencing are described on page 160.

Maslow's hierarchy of needs

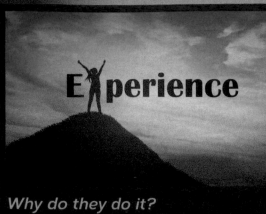

Why do they do it?

Why do people climb mountains, jump out of aeroplanes, try to break the world record for eating jam doughnuts, etc.? Psychologists suggest it is because we are born with an innate drive to try new things, to challenge ourselves to conquer the next level in *Fortnite*, to travel the world ...

There are good evolutionary reasons why we are hardwired to seek new experiences and try to be all we can be. These attributes would be naturally selected because they lead to, for example, exploration of the globe and trying out new ways to build houses or cook food or solve equations – all characteristics which were fundamental to human success.

This drive for new experiences and to be the best is called *self-actualisation*. But not everyone has this drive and, according to Maslow's hierarchy, this is because they have not yet satisfied their lower needs. That doesn't mean this is correct – but it is an interesting idea!

Specification term

Hierarchy of needs Maslow proposed that human behaviour is driven by a variety of different requirements (needs) and that these needs are arranged in a ranked order (a hierarchy from most to least important). The most basic needs are for food and water and the highest needs are for self-fulfilment.

Each to their own needs.

Key concepts of the theory

Abraham Maslow (1954) sought to develop a theory of *motivation* that went beyond physical needs. Psychologists have an interest in what drives people to do what they do, but many early theories of motivation were centred around *physiological* needs. Maslow felt that human motivation goes beyond this – when basic, physiological needs are satisfied humans seek to fulfil other needs, a *hierarchy of needs*.

The hierarchy of needs

The basis of Maslow's theory was a ladder from lower to higher needs. The needs towards the bottom of the hierarchy are *deficiency needs*, because they are designed to reduce inadequacies or deficiencies. These needs are always satisfied first. Needs towards the top of the hierarchy represent *growth needs*.

Basic needs

As you can see from the diagram on the right the lower, basic needs are physiological needs for food, water, warmth, rest, sex, sleep as well as safety needs (level 2).

Level	Need	Category
7	S-A	Self-fulfilment
6	Aesthetic	
5	Cognitive	
4	Esteem	Psychological
3	Love and belonging	
2	Safety	Basic
1	Physiological	

If a person has not satisfied these requirements/needs, then they will be motivated to satisfy them before they can attend to any higher needs. They are called 'prepotent' needs (more powerful when unfulfilled).

For any animal these basic needs are clearly of prime importance for survival, especially for young animals. Human babies are fairly helpless so they cannot, on their own, satisfy these needs. Therefore, certain behaviours are *naturally selected* to assist in satisfying basic needs. For example, *attachment* behaviours (such as a cute face, see page 170) seek to encourage protection and care from adults. Crying is a way to attract attention and signal that food, water, warmth, etc. are needed.

Children who grow up in poverty may remain focused on basic needs.

Psychological needs

Intermediate needs are the psychological ones – the need for other people and friends, and to be liked and loved (level 3) and for respect and esteem from others (level 4).

In developmental terms, seeking attachment is the beginning of satisfying these psychological needs. Attachment is the basis of peer and adult relationships. Children who are securely attached go on to be the ones who are more popular at school (Sroufe *et al*. 2005) and who, in adulthood, have longer-lasting relationships (Hazan and Shaver 1987).

According to Carl Rogers (1951), *self-esteem* (level 4 in the hierarchy) is based on unconditional positive regard from parents or significant others (such as grandparents or teachers). Conditional love refers to affection given if a child behaves in certain ways, such as obedience to parents or being tidy. If the need for self-esteem is not satisfied, a child/adult may remain at this level and may focus on finding alternative ways to develop higher self-esteem.

In adolescence, young people may experience rejection from their family and seek esteem from delinquent groups as a way to foster self-esteem because membership to such groups may be relatively easy.

Self-fulfilment needs

Finally, at the highest level, are needs that are related to achieving goals and growing as a person. This may involve increased knowledge and understanding (cognition). Young children at primary school are excited about exploring and understanding new things. Even older children and many university students maintain a love of knowledge.

At the next level are aesthetic needs, an enjoyment of art or music and of beauty generally. Finally, the peak motivation is *self-actualisation*, the drive for psychological growth and the need to realise your full potential.

The education system focuses on all of these self-fulfilment needs. The main target is academic work but schools are also interested in encouraging students in sports, music, art, cookery, woodworking etc – self-actualisation is not just about academic success.

GET ACTIVE Assess your needs

Maslow (1970) estimated that Americans satisfy about 85% of their physiological needs, 70% of their safety needs, 50% of their belongingness and love needs, 40% of their self-esteem needs, and only 10% of their self-actualisation needs.

There is an online test which can be used to assess where you are in relation to Maslow's hierarchy of needs: go to tinyurl.com/z8dpz and then click 'Next' to complete the questionnaire.

1. *Take the test and record your scores.*

2. *Reflect on the results. How do they relate to what you know about your needs? Did the results surprise you in any way? What do you conclude from the results?*

3. *You could try this questionnaire at various points in the academic year and see if your results change.*

Evaluation

A valuable contribution

One strength is that Maslow's theory has had a powerful and lasting effect in psychology.

In the 1950s, Maslow was one of the first *humanistic psychologists* (see page 218 for a brief discussion). This approach has had a lasting effect on the study of behaviour, in particular the humanistic emphasis on the importance of higher order needs. This was a contrast with the dominant view in the 1950s of *learning theory* which focused on *conditioning* as the way to explain all behaviour, and also Freud's *psychodynamic approach* which used biological drives to explain motivation. Maslow's approach is more wide-ranging because not all of his ideas are mentioned in other theories of motivation or human development, such as self-actualisation.

This demonstrates the value of the theory both in terms of the approach and content.

Not a testable theory

One weakness of Maslow's theory is that it is difficult to test it *empirically*.

There have been a few studies which have provided some support. For example, Joel Aronoff (1967) compared fishermen and cane cutters in the British West Indies. The fisherman had comparatively well-paid jobs but they were often unable to work. Aronoff found that only those whose security and esteem needs were met elsewhere (e.g. from family) chose the more challenging and responsible job of fisherman, as predicted by the hierarchy of needs. However, this was a fairly uncontrolled piece of research. The problem is that the concepts of this theory are difficult to *operationalise* and manipulate.

This means that the theory is not scientific and may have very little predictive power.

The idea of a hierarchy may be wrong

Another weakness is that the concept of a hierarchy may not fit the facts.

There is some question about whether the hierarchy is strictly followed. For example, many sports involve considerable danger (creating safety needs) but participants are motivated by self-fulfilment needs. Many artists are very poorly paid (so they may have trouble paying for food) yet their behaviour is motivated by aesthetic needs.

This means that there may be no actual hierarchy and, with no hierarchy, the theory is little more than an unconnected set of ideas which cannot predict behaviour.

What does a baby need?

Food, water, warmth, safety, love …

But from the beginning they also have a need for knowledge, to understand about the world. However, it is possible that such higher order needs cannot be satisfied when lower order needs are not satisfied, as in the case of children raised in deprived situations (discussed later in this unit).

Assessment practice

At the end of learning aims B and C you must write:

A report linking researched case studies of psychological developmental issues arising from privation/abuse, and approaches used by health professionals to support healthy development in children.

This report must be related to a scenario or context. We have used a realistic (but not real) context.

Several students are studying for qualifications to help them work with children. They decide to get together to start a YouTube vlog on child development. They all hope to produce regular vlogs to help other students in their studies, while also providing useful information for parents and carers.

The first trainee is studying to be an educational psychologist. As a psychologist she recognises that people are motivated by different kinds of needs and this drives healthy development.

She will present the first vlog, so she writes a script explaining, assessing and evaluating the main factors in Maslow's theory.

B1.1 Learning aim B1 – Task 1

The first part of your report for learning aims B and C will be concerned with factors affecting the healthy development of children and the role of professional support – these are covered on this spread and the next four spreads.

This activity will help you practise the skills required to write the report in response to your scenario/context.

1. **Explain** the factors Maslow identified that affect healthy development in children. (B.P3)

2. **Assess** the importance of these contributory factors in the healthy development of children. (B.M2)

3. **Evaluate** the impact of these contributory factors on the healthy development of children. (B.D2)

An issue to consider

Can you think of examples of self-actualisation in yourself and others? Do you think some people aren't interested in such needs because their lower needs are not satisfied?

Specification content

B1 Supporting children's optimal development

● The importance of providing optimal care and conditions to ensure children's healthy growth and development, including:

○ Maslow's hierarchy of needs, e.g. safety, nutrition, friendship, self-esteem.

Personal and biological factors

Maternal stress and 9/11

The stress and anxiety experienced by a pregnant woman can affect a developing foetus' brain and immune system.

On 11 September 2001, terrorists deliberately piloted two aeroplanes into the Twin Towers of the World Trade Center in New York. Thousands of people were killed and many more were traumatised by witnessing the horror of the event. Some of these witnesses were pregnant women, who had much-reduced levels of cortisol (the hormone that increases during stress but decreases during severe stress because it is used up). But their babies also had much-reduced cortisol when they were about one year old. This response in babies has been linked with physical and mental health problems later in life.

This clearly illustrates the interaction between nature and nurture. A feature of the environment (a stressful experience) affects biological processes going on in the womb (brain and immune system), producing negative effects on the baby's development that can last into adolescence and beyond (Yehuda *et al.* 2005).

Specification terms

Nature/nurture The question of whether behaviour is determined more by 'nature' (inherited and genetic factors) or 'nurture' (all influences after conception, e.g. experience). It is not a debate about whether one or the other is determining behaviour but about the contributions of each, as well as their interaction with each other.

Prenatal Before birth, when an embryo/foetus is developing in the womb.

The effects of alcohol on the child's later development can be direct (causing damage to the brain) and indirect (leading to low birth weight, which has further effects).

Personal and biological factors

Prenatal factors

Various factors affect the development of a *prenatal* embryo/foetus. A surprising number are due to *nurture* (i.e. experience/environment) whereas others are due to *nature* (i.e. *genetic*).

Maternal health Rubella (German measles) contracted by a woman just before or during early pregnancy can have devastating consequences for a foetus. A child born with *congenital rubella syndrome* (CRS) is likely to experience vision and hearing problems (deafness in serious cases) and heart disease as well as problems with physical growth (including microcephaly, i.e. small head size). CRS usually also includes intellectual difficulties due to brain damage, resulting in serious learning disabilities.

Diet and lifestyle Women who eat a high-calorie diet (especially 'empty' calories from nutrition-poor foods) often have high-birth-weight babies who may be at greater risk of obesity and *Type II diabetes* as adults (Parsons *et al.* 1999). Conversely, women with low-calorie intake may have low-birth-weight babies. Low birth weight is linked with developmental problems in childhood, such as learning difficulties (Johnson and Breslau 2000). In terms of lifestyle, *stress* during pregnancy may be the single most important influence on *depression* in offspring (Schetter and Tanner 2012). Such babies are also more likely to develop *attention deficit hyperactivity disorder* (ADHD) and have low intellectual ability (Glover 2019).

Addiction and substance abuse Alcohol abuse during pregnancy may lead to *substance abuse* and depression in offspring during adolescence and early adulthood. This is true even at low to moderate levels of alcohol use (Easey *et al.* 2019). Smoking during pregnancy has been linked to poorer school performance and behavioural problems in offspring (Martin *et al.* 2006).

Heredity and genetic disorders Not all *genetically*-caused disorders are inherited (they may be due to a genetic mutation or other abnormality). One example is *Down syndrome*, caused by the presence of a third copy of chromosome 21 (there are usually just two). Children with Down syndrome typically experience delayed physical growth and mild to moderate learning disabilities. An example of an inherited genetic disorder is *Huntingdon's disease*. This causes gradual damage to the brain resulting in memory losses, depression, movement problems and sometimes personality changes.

Biological and health factors

Disability Follow-up studies of children with physical disabilities show that by the time they reach adolescence they have three times the risk of developing a *mental disorder* than people in the non-disabled population (Dekker *et al.* 2002). A physical disability can affect a child's play, for example by restricting their movement so they cannot approach or use toys or interact with other children. This can limit the beneficial effects of play on these children's social and *cognitive development*.

Short-term illness Babies with acute illnesses (e.g. infections) can lose weight through eating less. But this rarely has long-term effects because growth resumes with normal eating, so most babies 'catch up'. Young people who contract glandular fever often become depressed, but again this usually disappears once the infection lifts (White *et al.* 1998).

Long-term medical conditions/illness Chronic (long-term) illnesses can have a serious effect on children's development. For example, a child with *Type I diabetes*, cancer or HIV/AIDS may spend significant time in hospital, missing out on schooling and interaction with friends and family. They may have to make adjustments in daily life (e.g. diet) that mark them out as 'different', increasing their sense of loneliness and isolation. Longer-term outcomes therefore include depression, low *self-esteem*, delayed or disordered social development and educational underachievement. The relationship operates in the other direction as well. Mental disorders make chronic physical conditions more difficult to treat, so the physical disorder often gets worse.

Learning difficulties Children with general learning difficulty (e.g. associated with Down syndrome or *cerebral palsy*) may find it hard to communicate and may even be bullied. These children are more likely to develop mental disorders (e.g. depression) or behavioural problems (e.g. ADHD). Specific learning difficulties (e.g. *dyslexia*) are associated with depression and educational underachievement, even though the child may function well in areas other than those affected by the difficulty.

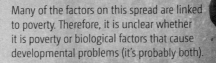

Evaluation

Application to maternal care

One strength is that knowledge of prenatal factors can have real-life benefits.

This is because women who experience any of the prenatal factors on the facing page are more likely to have a baby of unusually low birth weight. By addressing these factors, birth weight can be normalised avoiding several developmental problems in childhood, adolescence and adulthood. For instance, a healthy diet and low-stress lifestyle could partly prevent mental disorders (e.g. depression), poor school achievement, learning difficulties and physical disorders (e.g. diabetes).

This shows that knowledge of the biological mechanism involved (low birth weight) can help us to prevent some problems linked to prenatal factors.

Complex interactions

One weakness of identifying individual causes of developmental problems is that it is too simplistic.

Combinations of factors are much stronger predictors of problems than any individual factor on its own. For example, women who take one drug during pregnancy (e.g. alcohol) may well take others (e.g. nicotine), and may also have a poor diet and experience high levels of stress. Therefore, it is difficult to assess which of these factors matters most. It is far more sensible to assume that they all do, by interacting with each other and with other factors as well.

This suggests that a better practical approach might be to address the environmental contexts that create several issues together rather than target individual factors. This is the ecological approach discussed on page 174.

Issues of causation

Another weakness is that most 'causes' are actually just *correlations*.

There is huge debate over whether prenatal, biological and health factors actually cause developmental problems in childhood. For example, low-birth-weight babies are relatively more likely to experience learning difficulties in childhood. But as many do not, this is not an inevitable outcome. It depends on additional factors, which may be environmental (e.g. quality of postnatal care). So, low birth weight is definitely linked to learning difficulties but may not cause them.

Therefore, we should be extremely cautious about claiming that these factors cause developmental problems when at most they increase the individual's risk.

Many of the factors on this spread are linked to poverty. Therefore, it is unclear whether it is poverty or biological factors that cause developmental problems (it's probably both).

Assessment practice

At the end of learning aims B and C you must write a report (see previous spread and page 210). This report must be related to a scenario or context. We have used a realistic (but not real) context.

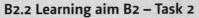

The next vlog to be prepared is going to be organised by a student health visitor. She understands how important prenatal factors are. Her course recently covered how short-term and long-term development can be affected by mother's health and lifestyle, for example.

The trainee health visitor is joined by a student nursery nurse who has been learning on his course about other biological and health factors that affect development.

Nursery nurses often have to care for children with physical disabilities, learning difficulties and medical conditions/illnesses.

These two students present the next vlog.

B2.2 Learning aim B2 – Task 2

The first part of your report for learning aims B and C will be concerned with factors affecting the healthy development of children and the role of professional support – these are covered on the previous spread, this spread and the next three spreads.

This activity will help you practise the skills required to write the report in response to your scenario/context.

1. **Explain** some prenatal/biological/health factors affecting healthy development in children. (B.P3)
2. **Assess** the importance of these contributory factors in the healthy development of children. (B.M2)
3. **Evaluate** the impact of these contributory factors on the healthy development of children. (B.D2)

You can see the assessment criteria on page 210 and an explanation of command terms on page 191.

An issue to consider

You will soon be moving on to look at environmental/social factors. But before you do, think about which factors they might be. How do they relate to the factors on this spread in terms of the nature/nurture debate?

Specification content

B2 Factors impacting children's development, learning and mental health

Personal and biological factors:

● Prenatal factors, e.g. maternal health, diet and lifestyle, addiction, substance abuse, heredity, genetic disorders, nature/nurture.
● Biological and health factors, e.g. disability, long-term medical conditions, short-/long-term illness, learning difficulties.

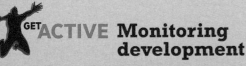

GET ACTIVE Monitoring development

Health practitioners monitor children's development by creating checklists of the different influencing factors, like the ones on this spread. This is a help in a situation where someone (e.g. a psychologist) has a limited time to talk to parents about how their child is developing. It also helps practitioners to identify children who are 'at risk' of developmental problems.

Use the information on this spread to create a checklist.

Include all the relevant prenatal, biological and health factors that could affect a child's development.

You could also include a severity rating instead of just 'yes' or 'no' tickboxes (e.g. a scale of 1 to 5).

Personal and biological factors (continued)

The Millennium Cohort Study (MCS)

This study is being run by the *Centre for Longitudinal Studies* (CLS) at the Institute of Education in London. The researchers recruited more than 18,000 children born in the UK in 2000 and 2001 (and their families). Since then they have collected information on many factors affecting social, cognitive, emotional and behavioural development. The children have been studied at the ages of nine months and then three, five, seven, 11, 14 and 17 years.

The Millennium study is the scientific version of the TV series *Up*. The TV series began in 1964 with a group of children aged seven (*7-Up*). Since then, every seven years, further interviews are filmed with the same 14 people. The most recent series was broadcast in 2019 when the participants had reached 63.

The TV series, the Millennium study and other studies supervised by the CLS are all longitudinal. In the words of the Director of the CLS, Professor Alissa Goodman, longitudinal studies 'follow thousands of babies from birth and periodically across their whole lives, systematically tracing their lifetime experiences and the factors that shape how their lives turn out' (Goodman 2019).

Specification terms

Abuse Treat with cruelty or violence, especially regularly or repeatedly.

Bullying Repeated behaviour, intended to intimidate or hurt someone either physically and/or emotionally.

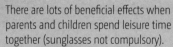

There are lots of beneficial effects when parents and children spend leisure time together (sunglasses not compulsory).

Personal and biological factors (continued)

The specification for Unit 5 lists many different behaviours, some of which are covered elsewhere in this unit: attachment (page 170), friendships (page 180), *parenting styles* (page 166), education and income (next spread). Some factors appear in more than one place, such as friends being classed as both personal and family factors.

Personal, social and emotional factors

Friendship orientations The benefits of friendship are highlighted by the effects of being friendless. Children without friends are more lonely and *depressed* and more likely to be victims of *bullying*. Gaining a friend has many protective effects, not least against bullying. Friendship is beneficial for adolescents who have difficult relationships with their parents. Having a strong friendship with a 'best friend' protects *self-esteem* and makes *depression* less likely (Rubin *et al.* 2008).

Bullying Being a victim of bullying can cause both negative short-term and long-term effects on physical and *mental health*. These include physical injury, depression, anxiety, school adjustment problems, low educational achievement, low self-esteem, and a greater risk of suicide (Smokowski and Kopasz 2005). The children most negatively affected are bully-victims (this refers to children who are both bullies and the victims of bullying). They are part of a bullying group, organised by a ringleader who bullies the other members. They are at greatest risk of mental and developmental problems (Ford *et al.* 2017).

Transitions These are significant *life events* (see page 38 in Unit 3) that represent 'turning points' in development (or in family life). The child makes a psychological adjustment to change, which is potentially stressful. Children from lower *socioeconomic* groups are particularly at risk from the transition to school. This is because they are more likely to start with poorer communication skills that affect their ability to learn. They may quickly disengage from learning, beginning a cycle of low aspirations and underachievement that lasts throughout schooling (Jackson and Cartmel 2013).

Abuse This can be sexual, physical and/or emotional and also includes physical and emotional neglect. Abused children experience a multitude of negative and lasting effects on most areas of development. This includes delayed intellectual, social and emotional development, as well as increased levels of anger and impulsive aggression. Abused children who behave aggressively may be avoided by other children so they then face difficulties in making friends.

Children who are physically and/or sexually abused may use *dissociation* as a way of coping (that is, deliberately becoming 'disconnected' from what is going on around them). This can interfere with memory and learning, resulting in poor school performance.

We will look at the effects of *abuse* again on page 202.

Family factors

Work Parental employment patterns mean that young children may be left in the care of other people. This is a controversial and complex area, but one research finding stands out – the single most important factor influencing the child's development is *quality* of care. High-quality care can be beneficial for a child's *cognitive*, social and emotional development because it is sensitive and responsive to the child's individual needs. But poor-quality care can be damaging, producing low intellectual functioning, depression and *insecure attachments* that lead to later developmental difficulties (e.g. behavioural problems such as ADHD, Waldfogel 2006).

Leisure An important source of psychological health comes from leisure activities. When these are shared by family members, they can protect mental and physical health, increase self-esteem, ward off depression and improve social interaction skills. These benefits arise because shared activities promote family unity and relieve *stress* for both parents and children. They also transmit parents' values – the choice of leisure activity reinforces family norms (e.g. what parents consider valuable for children to experience such as fun, appreciation of art and science, etc.).

Parenting styles We looked at Diana Baumrind's (1978) four main parenting styles on page 166. She argued that an *authoritative style* is usually most beneficial. It promotes self-esteem, independence and social skills in children. These children also experience better mental health, demonstrate high academic achievement and are less likely to abuse drugs. The least desirable parenting style is *authoritarian* because it leads to the opposite outcomes. Interestingly, the children of both *permissive* and *uninvolved parents* are more likely than any others to engage in impulsive behaviours (e.g. aggression) and have relationship difficulties.

Day care for children does not have to negatively impact their development, as long as the carers are sensitive and responsive (see page 171).

Evaluation

Research on long-term effects

One strength is that the long-term effects of personal and family factors have been studied.

Psychologists have conducted studies which follow families and individuals over several years to be able to judge whether the observed effects are lasting ones. Such *longitudinal studies* are needed in order to demonstrate that any changes in, for example, learning abilities and mental health have enduring effects rather than just being short-term responses. For instance, the Millennium Cohort Study (see facing page) has identified several factors (such as family structure, parenting activities) by following children from birth to (currently) age 19 and beyond.

This means we can identify which factors could be causes of long-term developmental problems and direct resources to preventing them or reducing their effects.

Application to preventing negative outcomes

Another strength is that interventions to prevent negative outcomes can be designed based on the factors on this spread (and others).

Interventions must address various factors that exist on different levels (personal, family, etc.). For example, recognising that transitions linked to life events can be stressful for children means psychologists can find ways of making such transitions smoother. At a different 'level' of intervention, families can be supported to cope with pressures of work and home life, again to reduce stress on children.

Therefore, interventions that are 'multidimensional' are more likely to be effective because they target different types of interacting factors.

Associated variables

One weakness is that personal, social and family factors generally occur together.

This makes it hard to understand the separate effects of individual factors on children's development. For example, stressful transitions, neglect of children, low-quality care and an absence of shared leisure nearly always occur together. Children from such households may also be bullied and lack friends. Which of these directly cause children's poor intellectual ability and which are indirectly linked is a very difficult question to answer.

This is a major challenge for researchers to design studies that reveal the true relationships between these factors and developmental problems.

GET ACTIVE Pastoral support

You are a pastoral support worker in a primary school and you run the lunchtime 'friendship club'. There is a six-year-old girl who comes along (we'll call her 'Nicole'). You're concerned about her because she doesn't seem to be making friends. The other children are quite wary of her and tend to avoid her. You speak to Nicole's teachers and find that she is doing poorly in her schoolwork. You are a trained professional with knowledge of what might be causing Nicole's problems, so you make an appointment with the head teacher to discuss her.

1. *You plan to take some notes into the meeting. Briefly write some bullet-pointed sentences outlining the factors you are concerned about.*

2. *For each factor, explain what effect it could be having on Nicole's development.*

Assessment practice

At the end of learning aims B and C you must write a report (see pages 193 and 210). This report must be related to a scenario or context. We have used a realistic (but not real) context.

The next vlog is presented by a student nurse who wants to eventually work in schools. As a school nurse she would see all the new students in their first year of school for a health assessment. She is interested in personal, social and emotional influences on development.

The team's student speech and language therapist also features in this vlog. He is interested in how family-related factors can affect all aspects of a child's development, not just their speech and language.

Taking on these roles, write the scripts to explain, assess and evaluate these two groups of factors.

B2.3 Learning aim B2 – Task 3

The first part of your report for learning aims B and C will be concerned with factors affecting the healthy development of children and the role of professional support – these are covered on the previous two spreads, this spread and the next two spreads.

1. **Explain** some personal/social/emotional and family factors affecting healthy development in children. (B.P3)

2. **Assess** the importance of these contributory factors in the healthy development of children. (B.M2)

3. **Evaluate** the impact of these contributory factors on the healthy development of children. (B.D2)

An issue to consider

Most of the factors on this spread have one damaging effect in common – stress. Think about how each one causes stress for children.

Specification content

B2 Factors impacting children's development, learning and mental health

Personal and biological factors:

- Personal, social and emotional factors, e.g. attachment, friendship orientations, security, bullying, transitions, separations, abuse.

- Family factors, e.g. work, leisure, home life, society, parenting styles, attachments, friends, family, education, income.

Environmental and social factors

Every Child Matters

Government policies are important influences on children's development because they affect how and where public money is spent. Spending reflects a government's political philosophy and social priorities.

Since 2003, all governments have claimed to put the needs of the individual child at the centre of services aimed at children. In 2003, the *Every Child Matters* policy was published. The policy stated that services for children must make sure that every child has opportunities to: stay safe, be healthy, enjoy life and achieve, make a positive contribution, and achieve economic well-being (you can remember these with the acrostic SHEEP: Safe, Healthy, Enjoy, Economic, Positive).

Every Child Matters had a big impact because it applied to schools, local authorities, health and medical services, children's homes, social services, etc. Everything these services do has to meet the five criteria above. It also formed the basis of all legislation passed by the government that affected children.

Just to show how policies influence children's lives, *Every Child Matters* still exists but it is no longer a government priority and there is much less money available for it.

Environmental and social factors

Environmental factors

Housing/location Poor housing can disrupt child development in several ways. Young children cannot explore a dangerous home, which limits their natural curiosity and hampers intellectual development (Eamon 2000). Children living in temporary housing for more than one year are at greater risk of *depression* than other children (Harker 2006). Poor housing may reflect neglect of an area where amenities are non-existent and antisocial behaviour is rife.

Access to amenities Some children have no access to a garden or other open space, which can limit physical development. Children living in rural areas with poor public transport may find it difficult to access a library, sports centre, health clinic, etc. This is also true of children in urban areas where provision has been neglected or cut back. Children with physical disabilities and learning difficulties might also find it harder to access amenities because of lack of support.

Social and political factors

Social class (or *socioeconomic status*) Low parental income creates poverty that affects children's development. Children from households in the bottom 20% of income are 4.5 times more likely to develop a *mental disorder* (e.g. depression) than those in the top 20% (Gutman *et al.* 2015). This type of unequal outcome is known as a *social gradient*.

Children whose parents have low income and low educational attainment (e.g. few or no qualifications) perform worse on tests of *cognitive development* between the ages of 5 and 7 years. This social gradient is often a huge disadvantage to working-class children at the start of their schooling (González *et al.* 2018).

Government policies, services and constraints Government policies related to poverty, inequality and social mobility are especially important as these factors have a major impact on children's development. The *Children Act 2004* implemented legislation (in England and Wales) known as *Every Child Matters* (see panel left).

However, the success of such policies depends on funding. For example, Sure Start (see page 128) was a programme designed to support parents and children throughout the UK. Funding for the programme was slashed by 50% between 2010 and 2018, with further cuts planned.

Cultural factors

Beliefs, values and social norms These influence child-rearing practices and how children are expected to behave towards adults. For instance, children in Western *individualist cultures* are usually raised to be independent and self-assertive. Western norms consider these as valuable social skills. Children who do not develop them are generally seen as socially 'less competent'.

China is a very different culture, a *collectivist* one, in which putting the group before the individual is seen as an important goal of parenting. Therefore, self-control, sensitivity and even shyness are valued and considered signs of maturity and normal development (Chen *et al.* 1992).

Attitudes towards gender These affect the roles that are considered appropriate for boys and girls within a culture. For example, some adults hold stereotyped views of what is an appropriate education for girls and boys. They may believe that maths and sciences are not suited to girls' skills, which are thought to be more 'people-orientated'. This attitude could create a self-fulfilling situation in which girls adjust their ambitions and prospects to match their parents' expectations.

Attitudes towards ethnicity Children often become aware of racist attitudes and stereotypes from the age of five onwards. African American children who are aware of such attitudes about their ethnic group perform worse in school tests. Again, this is a self-fulfilling process. The children experience anxiety associated with the negative stereotypes other people hold of them (e.g. they lack intelligence) and this interferes with their performance (McKown and Strambler 2009).

This girl's ambitions for a career in engineering could be affected when she realises that other people hold stereotyped views about what is a suitable career for her.

Evaluation

Application to reduce risk

One strength is that knowledge of risk factors can create successful early interventions.

For example, Elizabeth Pungello *et al.* (2010) investigated the effectiveness of an intervention into 'high risk' home environments in the early years of children's lives. The intervention was called *Project CARE*, a full-time, high-quality day-care programme for young children. The children in this study attended from the age of nine weeks up to five years old. The researchers followed up the children and found that those in the intervention group (compared with a *control group*) were more likely to graduate from high school, go on to further education and find skilled jobs.

This suggests that understanding risk factors can help create interventions that counteract negative effects on children's development.

Interacting factors

One weakness is that the effects of environmental and social factors are complex.

Many of these factors interact with each other and with other influences to affect children's development. For example, the biological and psychological characteristics of a child partly determine how much they can resist negative social and cultural influences. Social (e.g. class) and cultural influences (e.g. attitudes towards *gender* or *ethnicity*) may trigger an existing predisposition (e.g. *genetic*) or worsen the effects of stressors (e.g. *life events*).

This means that identifying one or two factors as directly causing developmental problems is a gross oversimplification which limits our understanding of the true relationship with social and cultural factors.

Cause and effect

Another weakness is that it is not certain that most of these factors actually cause developmental problems.

Research studies identify *correlations* between, for example, low income and children's social development. There is ongoing debate over how meaningful these correlations are. Children experience most factors indirectly, through their parents' impact on the home environment (e.g. *stress* caused by poverty). Therefore, most studies are not able to identify which are causes.

This means the most we can claim is that environmental and social factors increase children's risk of developmental problems, not that they cause them.

Environmental and social factors often affect children not because they are stressful for the children – but because such factors create stress for their parents.

Assessment practice

At the end of learning aims B and C you must write a report (see pages 193 and 210). This report must be related to a scenario or context. We have used a realistic (but not real) context.

Social workers understand the importance of wider environmental and cultural factors and how they can impact children's development. The student social worker knows that, where there are issues concerning housing and access to amenities, children's development can be affected. He has personal experience of how  *Sure Start* centres can promote positive development. He also appreciates the relevance of government policies and strategies, and how stereotyped attitudes towards ethnicity and gender can hold back some children.

Write the student social worker's script for his vlog presentation on environmental, political and cultural factors.

B2.4 Learning aim B2 – Task 4

The first part of your report for learning aims B and C will be concerned with factors affecting the healthy development of children and the role of professional support – these are covered on the previous three spreads, this spread and the next spread.

This activity will help you practise the skills required to write the report in response to your scenario/context.

1. **Explain** environmental, social/political and cultural factors affecting healthy development in children. (B.P3)
2. **Assess** the importance of these contributory factors in the healthy development of children. (B.M2)
3. **Evaluate** the impact of these contributory factors on the healthy development of children. (B.D2)

GET ACTIVE Placards

Imagine you live in an area which has seen cuts to local services. The *Sure Start* centre has gone, public transport is non-existent and the local library has closed. You have two children who have been affected and many of your friends and neighbours are in the same situation. You band together and form an action group. You decide to carry out a peaceful protest at the offices of the local council. It will be colourful and noisy and there will be banners, posters and placards to wave about.

Based on what you know about environmental and social factors, write down some slogans that could be put onto a placard or poster. They should be short but express factors covered on this spread (and/or previous ones). Here's some examples: 'No Sure Start means no support for our kids' and: 'No parks, nowhere for kids to run around'.

An issue to consider

What do these factors, together with the ones on the previous two spreads, tell us about the roles of nature and nurture?

Specification content

B2 Factors impacting children's development, learning and mental health

Environmental and social factors:

- Environmental impact on health of, e.g. housing, location, access to amenities.
- Social and political factors, e.g. social class, government policies, services and strategies.
- Cultural factors, e.g. the effects of beliefs, values and social norms, attitudes towards gender and ethnicity.

Role of professionals in healthy growth and development

A SENCO

Alice is a special educational needs coordinator (SENCO) in an English primary school with 500 students. She explains her work:

I am a class teacher and deputy head, but am also responsible for the 120 pupils registered with a learning support need. These pupils need additional help to overcome factors that could disrupt their learning.

I deal every day with children who have learning disabilities (e.g. dyslexia), mental health issues (e.g. depression) and behavioural issues (e.g. self-harm, ADHD). Some children have physical disabilities (e.g. cerebral palsy) and medical conditions (e.g. epilepsy). Some pupils have experienced abuse and neglect, a few are in the care of social services and three are traumatised refugees.

I work with other professionals and attend a lot of multi-agency meetings to discuss individual pupils and their needs. A recent meeting involved a pupil's mum, class teacher, educational psychologist and attendance officer, as well as the head teacher. I think that the skill most important to me is communication – as I spend about 70% of the day communicating with pupils, parents, teachers and other professionals.

The greatest joy of my role is that I am providing an advocate for every single child with support needs. Whenever there is a conflict between the needs of the pupil and other factors (funding, attitudes, lack of time, etc.), I work on the side of the pupil.

An educational psychologist will assess a child's development through observation, discussion and testing.

Role of professionals

The focus on this spread is to look at how professionals support healthy development – on page 208 we return to look at the role of professionals but there our focus will be more on their role in supporting children who have experienced forms of *abuse* or *privation*.

Education professionals

Teachers have regular contact with many students, so are in a good position to promote children's well-being and protect their welfare (and all teachers have appropriate training). Teachers must follow school policies concerning child welfare (e.g. reporting concerns within a certain time frame). This is especially important as a child may well choose a teacher to confide in about anything troubling them (*disclosure*).

SENCOs (special educational needs coordinators) are teachers trained and qualified to Masters level in special educational needs (SEN). They are responsible for the everyday operation of the school's SEN policy. Part of this involves identifying students who have learning difficulties, physical disabilities and *mental health* issues. The SENCO then coordinates teachers and other staff (e.g. teaching assistants) to provide support in and out of class.

School nurses are qualified and registered nurses who work in the community with parents, children and teachers. They help train other education professionals to identify children with developmental disorders. They see every child within the first school year for a health assessment, including hearing and vision tests. They improve children's well-being by helping them to make healthy lifestyle choices (e.g. diet and exercise).

Health, social and other professionals

Educational psychologists identify and support children with learning difficulties, physical disabilities, social and emotional disorders and other developmental problems. They identify issues through observation, interviews and assessment (e.g. tests). They devise interventions and plans (e.g. how class teaching can be adapted to support learning). They also provide advice to teachers, parents and children themselves.

General practitioners (GPs) are medically qualified but not usually trained specialists in child health (although some are). A GP can diagnose a disorder in many cases, prescribe medication, provide advice and refer to other professionals.

Social workers are legally obliged to protect and promote the welfare of children who are at risk of harm. A social worker carries out an assessment to identify risks to a child. In most cases they will refer the child/family to another agency for support and/or produce a *child protection plan*. But if a child is at risk of significant harm, the social worker may arrange for a court order to place the child in foster or residential care. Social workers also support children by helping families to discuss their problems, thus reducing *stress*.

Police officers identify and protect children at risk of harm. Some officers have specialist training in child protection. The police are expected to share information with other organisations (e.g. social services) about children at risk and adults who may cause them harm. According to the *Children Act 2004*, the police must keep a child's welfare at the forefront of all their dealings with children (e.g. in custody, questioning child witnesses, etc.).

Midwives support women through pregnancy (antenatal/prenatal), during birth and after birth (postnatal). They can identify issues with women's physical and mental health, but also with the foetus and newborn baby.

Other support services

Charities promote children's welfare and the UK charity with a central role in this is the *National Society for the Prevention of Cruelty to Children* (NSPCC). The NSPCC provide training for professionals (e.g. promoting healthy lifestyles) online and in face-to-face workshops. They have a national network of centres providing direct support for children and families (e.g. *counselling*, workshops for parents). They also run *Childline*, the national phone support service.

Self-help groups exist in the UK to help children and parents 'help themselves' by providing information and other resources. One common way of doing this is by providing space on a website for people to post requests for help and/or advice.

GET ACTIVE Case conference

For this activity, you are going to be a 'one-person case conference'. You are taking the roles of three or four of the professionals described on this spread. You are all meeting in a case conference to discuss an 'at-risk' child and/or family. There are case reports available on the UK government website here: tinyurl.com/y5xpug5o and on the NSPCC's website here: tinyurl.com/y9h49gz2

1. *Choose a case study that interests you most.*
2. *Select **three** roles from this spread and write a paragraph for each role, explaining your view of the case and how you can contribute to the welfare of the child/family.*

A case conference with myself, see left.

Evaluation

A multidisciplinary approach

One strength of professional roles is that different approaches are combined to support children.

This is called a *multidisciplinary approach*. Professionals involved in promoting healthy development and identifying 'at-risk' children have different perspectives on what is best for the child. But all are required by law to put the child first. For example, in cases of learning difficulties, all the involved professionals meet together to discuss a child's needs.

This is necessary because there are so many factors that can influence a child's well-being and development, so professionals working together from different disciplines have a better chance of identifying the different factors that should be considered.

Lack of cooperation

One weakness is that there is sometimes disagreement over roles.

Some cases are so complex that the involvement of many professionals can lead to conflicts. This is one of the reasons why governments produce policies (e.g. *Every Child Matters*) and pass laws (e.g. the *Children Act 2004*) – to make professionals work together more smoothly. Even so, there can be a lack of communication, failure to share information and arguments about roles and responsibilities.

These issues can create tensions within multidisciplinary teams and even lead to problems in recruiting staff, which means children's needs may not be as well-served as they should be.

Role of charities and self-help groups

Another weakness is that not all charities and self-help groups are equally beneficial.

For example, the quality of training provided by groups is highly variable – excellent in some cases and poor in others (and occasionally non-existent). As a result, some volunteers lack expertise or knowledge of children's development, or their knowledge may be out-of-date. This is partly because training provided by charities and self-help groups is not regulated by any national body. There are no standards for quality that have to be achieved.

This means that children may not benefit as much as they could from properly-regulated training provided by reputable support groups.

Assessment practice

At the end of learning aims B and C you must write a report (see pages 193 and 210). This report must be related to a scenario or context. We have used a realistic (but not real) context.

All of the team members are involved in the next vlog presentation. Two other trainees have also joined in – a teacher and a SENCO. There is also a representative from a children's charity to explain their work. As part of their course, each student has done work experience supervised by a practising professional in their discipline. Therefore, they all have a clear idea of what their roles are. They also know how they can support children's healthy development and also identify and help children with developmental problems.

Write brief scripts for each trainee plus the charity worker. Include a section assessing and evaluating the impact and value of professionals (especially in terms of working together as a multidisciplinary team).

B3.5 Learning aim B3 – Task 5

The first part of your report for learning aims B and C will be concerned with factors affecting the healthy development of children and the role of professional support – these are covered on the previous four spreads and this spread.

Note that this final activity for the first part of your report should look more specifically at the various roles of professionals in supporting the healthy development of children.

1. **Explain** the roles of professionals in supporting children and their parents or carers. (B.P4)
2. **Assess** the role of professional support in the healthy development of children. (B.M2)
3. **Evaluate** the impact of professionals in providing support to children and their parents or carers. (B.D2)

An issue to consider

All of the roles discussed on this spread are important. But do any of them stand out for you in taking the leading role in promoting children's healthy development and identifying developmental problems?

Specification content

B3 Professionals involved in supporting children's healthy development

Role of professionals involved in supporting healthy growth and development and their role in the identification and treatment of children with developmental deviations from norms:

- Education, e.g. teachers, support workers, teaching assistants, health visitors, school nurses, special educational needs coordinators (SENCO).
- Health, social and other professionals, e.g. clinical and educational psychologists, general practitioners of medicine (GPs), health workers, social workers, police, psychiatric professionals, midwives, counsellors.
- Other support services, including charities, self-help groups.

Cases and studies of privation and abuse

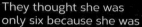

Genie

Genie is the pseudonym of a young girl who walked into a Los Angeles social services department, with her mother, when she was 13½ years old. Her mother was seeking help for her own developing blindness but the authorities focused on Genie.

They thought she was only six because she was so small. It transpired that she had spent most of her childhood locked in a room by her father because he thought she was retarded and not safe anywhere else.

Her father barked at her like a dog and beat her if she made a sound. Genie was tied to a potty during the day and bound in a cot at night.

When she was discovered, she was severely malnourished, physically very small and could not stand straight. She had no social skills and could not speak.

The tragedy of her life continued after she was found. The courts decided that she should be placed in care and one of the psychologists documenting her recovery took her into his own home. However, when the research money ran out and the study ended she was placed with a variety of foster families, including one home where she was further abused (Rymer 1993).

Specification terms

Abuse Treat with cruelty or violence, especially regularly or repeatedly.

Feral child A child who has lived away from humans for a significant period of their childhood.

Privation In the context of development this refers to a lack of emotional care during early life. This may also include a lack of physical care but it is the emotional care which has the most severe effects on psychological development.

Deprivation dwarfism (see next spread). Children who are abused or in institutional care are often physically small. Lack of emotional care leads to high levels of stress hormones which have a negative effect on growth.

Cases of privation and abuse

Case studies are appealing but unscientific. Information is often anecdotal and comes from different and often conflicting sources. We have no way of knowing whether any observed effects were due to *privation/abuse* or whether there were other issues with these children that might explain their later behaviour. However, they provide unique insights into very unusual situations.

Genie

Genie was given a new life at the age of 13½, after many years of emotional privation and abuse (see left). She was studied intensively by psychologists and reportedly formed *attachments* with some of the researchers such as Susan Curtiss (1977), but not lasting ones. Her mother claimed to have always had a relationship with her. She showed all the characteristics of *disinhibited attachment*, a form of *insecure attachment* where children do not discriminate between people they choose as attachment figures. Such children will treat near-strangers with inappropriate familiarity (overfriendliness) and may be attention-seeking.

She also never acquired normal *language*, probably because she was rescued relatively late, long after the *critical period* for language acquisition (if language is not acquired during this time it never is, see page 188).

Czech twins Andrei and Vanya

Jarmila Koluchová (1976, 1991) conducted a case study of identical Czech twin boys. Their mother died shortly after they were born and they were brought up by their stepmother who treated them cruelly, locking them in a wardrobe most of the day and beating them regularly. This continued until they were rescued at the age of seven years. Their physical growth was limited and they were severely intellectually retarded. They could not speak and did not appear to have acquired language.

They then spent two years in an institution with intensive speech therapy, psychotherapy and physiotherapy. Subsequently they were fostered by two sisters who gave them excellent care. By age 14 years the twins had almost 'caught up'. They showed near-typical social, emotional and intellectual development. They later married, had children and pursued successful careers.

It is possible that, at age 7, the twins were young enough to recover, whereas Genie was older when she first received more normal emotional care.

Victor of Aveyron

'Victor' was a 12-year-old boy discovered in a forest near the French town of Aveyron in 1800. He was 'wild', a *feral child*, considered uncivilised and 'mentally deficient' and could not speak. A doctor called Jean Marc Itard took responsibility for Victor and tried to transform him over five years into a civilised human being.

To start with Victor responded well to methods used to teach language to deaf people (even though he wasn't deaf). He acquired some manners and could care for himself. However, Itard was much more pessimistic by 1806. Victor never learned to speak or interact socially, so Itard considered his efforts had failed.

Victoria Climbié

Victoria was aged 8 years when she died in 2000, murdered by her great-aunt and her boyfriend. Victoria's guardians imprisoned her in their apartment, first in Paris and then London. The boyfriend Carl Manning regularly and horrifically abused and tortured Victoria over a 15-month period. She was beaten and tied up for periods of 24 hours or longer.

Child protection and welfare service workers (police officers, social workers, medical staff, etc.) visited Victoria's home but missed several opportunities to identify Victoria as a victim of severe abuse. The professionals repeatedly accepted the adults' explanations for Victoria's injuries (she had 128 injuries on her body when she died).

Victoria's death and the events around it led to the complete reform of children's services in the UK, and directly to the *Children Act 2004* and *Every Child Matters* (see page 201).

Studies of privation and abuse

A number of *longitudinal studies* have looked more systematically at groups of children who have experienced privation. These studies are *natural experiments* where the *independent variable* (privation versus no privation) was not controlled by the researchers.

Hodges and Tizard

Jill Hodges and Barbara Tizard (1989) carried out a study of 65 children placed in an institution for adoption. All of the children were less than four months old at the start of the study. High staff turnover and stated policy meant children could not form a continuous emotional attachment with an adult carer. Over the following years some children were adopted, others returned to their biological families and others remained in institutional care.

At 16 years the adopted children's attachments were similar to those of a *control group* (children raised in their biological families). However, the returned group were less closely attached. All of the ex-institutional children (now adolescents) were less liked, had fewer friends, and were more likely to be bullies than the controls.

The findings show there are long-term permanent damaging effects of early privation on social/peer relationships (although no obvious effects on intellectual development).

Romanian orphans

Michael Rutter *et al.*'s (2010) English and Romanian Adoptees (ERA) study includes 165 Romanian children who spent their early lives in the appalling conditions of Romania's children's homes, with no emotional care. The children's physical, *cognitive*, social and emotional development has been compared with a control group of 52 English children who had never lived in an institution and were all adopted before six months.

At adoption the Romanian children were smaller, lighter and 'intellectually retarded' compared with the control children. At age four years, almost all the Romanian children who were adopted before six months had caught up with the English controls. But there were *significant* physical, social and emotional deficits in the Romanian children who were adopted after six months – these deficits have continued beyond the age of 15 years.

These late-adoption children have shown disinhibited attachment (see facing page) and at ages 11 and 15 continued to show signs of mental retardation. In this study the ability to make comparisons with an early adoption group means that causal conclusions can be drawn.

Why study Romanian orphans? Psychological research in the 1960s (e.g. Bowlby 1969) showed that emotional privation had severe effects on development and since that time institutional care in the West disappeared. In 1989 the Romanian regime of Nicolae Ceauşescu fell and the plight of more than 100,000 orphans was revealed. It provided a new opportunity for psychologists to study the effects of privation.

Assessment practice

At the end of learning aims B and C you must write a report (see pages 193 and 210). This report must be related to a scenario or context. We have used a realistic (but not real) context.

You want to continue doing the vlog on children's development so you invite some experienced professionals to make guest appearances. But there is a different emphasis now. You want the professionals to talk about their roles in tackling privation and abuse to reduce the impact such experiences have on children's healthy development. Your first guest is a speech and language therapist whose role is to develop programmes of intervention and support for young children with speech and language difficulties. Your second guest is a general practitioner of medicine (GP). She is especially interested in the physical, emotional and intellectual effects of privation/abuse. You ask each guest to take one case or study of privation/abuse and present it from their professional point of view. Write the script for each professional.

C1.6 Learning aim C1 – Task 6

The second part of your report for learning aims B and C will be concerned with problems of psychological development in children – this is covered on this spread and the next two spreads.

1. **Explain** problems of psychological development in children. (C.P5)
2. **Explain two** professional approaches to treating dysfunctional psychopathology in children. (C.P6)
3. **Analyse** approaches taken by professionals in the treatment of dysfunctional psychopathology in children. (C.M3)

GET ACTIVE Finding the cause

Imagine you are a clinical psychologist trying to work out the reasons why some children who experience privation go on to have positive long-term outcomes and others don't. The answers may be in the cases and studies on this spread.

1. *What do you think is meant by 'positive long-term outcomes'?*
2. *Which cases/studies demonstrate positive long-term outcomes? What are these outcomes?*
3. *Explain **one** reason why outcomes for some children are positive but negative for others.*
4. *A charity emails you, asking you to explain what they can do to support children who have experienced abuse/privation. Write a brief paragraph in response.*

An issue to consider

What do the studies and cases on this spread tell us about the contributions of nature and nurture to development?

Specification content

C1 Instances of privation and abuse

Privation and abuse, and their impact on children's healthy growth, development and mental health – cases and studies:

- Cases of privation, e.g. Genie and Czech Twins, Victor of Aveyron, Oxana Malaya.
- Cases of abuse, e.g. Victoria Climbié, Liam Fee.
- Studies, e.g. Hodges and Tizard (1989), Romanian orphans.

Sources of privation and abuse

Post-traumatic stress disorder (PTSD)

PTSD is a mental disorder in people who have experienced a frightening or shocking event. Most people recover relatively quickly from such events. However, those who continue to feel stress long afterwards may develop PTSD. The main symptom is extreme anxiety.

People with PTSD often have 'flashbacks' in which they relive the traumatic event, complete with physical symptoms. This can happen during sleep when it takes the form of a nightmare. Young children may wet the bed, have extreme difficulty talking or become very 'clingy'. PTSD has serious effects on a child's daily life, making it difficult for them to concentrate on their schoolwork and disrupting their friendships.

There is a long list of experiences and factors that can cause PTSD in childhood. It occurs in children who are regularly bullied, have been physically and/or sexually abused, have witnessed domestic violence or whose parents have divorced or separated. Children who suffer natural disasters such as earthquakes and floods also commonly experience PTSD, as do children traumatised by war.

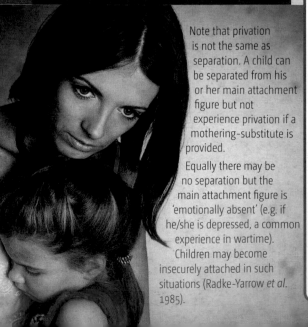

Note that privation is not the same as separation. A child can be separated from his or her main attachment figure but not experience privation if a mothering-substitute is provided.

Equally there may be no separation but the main attachment figure is 'emotionally absent' (e.g. if he/she is depressed, a common experience in wartime). Children may become insecurely attached in such situations (Radke-Yarrow *et al.* 1985).

Psychological sources of privation and abuse

Early separations

Separation (emotionally or physically) from a *primary attachment figure* early in life can result in privation and later negative effects on a child's development. There is evidence of this in Hodges and Tizard's (1989) study and the research with Romanian orphans (see previous spread).

John Bowlby (1944) also demonstrated this in his '44 thieves' study. He studied 88 emotionally-disturbed children. Half of them had been caught stealing (the 44 thieves). The others were a *control group*. Bowlby diagnosed 14 of the thieves as 'affectionless psychopaths'. That is, they lacked normal feelings of affection and shame or a sense of responsibility.

86% of the affectionless thieves had experienced frequent separations before they were two years old. The comparable figure for the other thieves was just 17%. Also, almost none of the control group children experienced early separations, but 39% of the thieving group had.

This and other evidence (such as the Romanian orphan study on the previous spread) shows that disrupted and inconsistent caregiving (e.g. early separations) up to the age of six months can have long-term effects on emotional development.

Physical abuse

The case of Victoria Climbié (previous spread) was one of physical abuse. Her mother's boyfriend regularly tortured Victoria over a 15-month period, beating her and tying her up for 24 hours or longer at a time.

We also saw that Genie was beaten by her father whenever she made a sound. Her physical isolation meant she probably formed no emotional attachments to her parents and no lasting attachments to anyone else (e.g. researchers). Genie never fully recovered from her experience of privation. So, it is likely that she was rescued after the *critical periods* for different aspects of development (i.e. attachment, language acquisition, etc.).

Both cases demonstrate how physical abuse can be a source of severe privation, with longer-term consequences dependent on the age at which the abuse takes place and when it ends.

Environmental sources of privation

Poverty

This is a type of economic privation. The causes of poverty are complex but they include unemployment, poor parental education levels and low income. Poverty is strongly associated with long-term negative effects on intelligence, social skills and *mental health*.

The study of Romanian orphans (previous spread) illustrates poverty as a source of privation. All of the orphans experienced extreme economic privation in their early months or years. The institutions in which they were raised were physical and emotional wastelands in which even the most basic needs were often not met (e.g. food). For the children adopted after the age of six months, the negative effects on their social, emotional and *cognitive development* has persisted into adolescence, even though they were raised in well-off families for more than a decade.

War and PTSD

Joanna Santa Barbara (2006) lists several ways in which war is a significant source of privation for children in many parts of the world.

War disrupts emotional bonds between caregivers and children. Parents have to spend most of their time, energy and attention on survival, or they may be depressed and unable to respond to their children. In extreme cases they may be injured and hospitalised or even killed. In these circumstances, children may be receiving inadequate substitute care.

During wartime children may find themselves in refugee camps with little or no schooling, so they miss out on education. They are also likely to be deprived of opportunities for play and to make friends, both of which are important for social and emotional development.

One powerful way in which war is a source of privation is through its role in causing *post-traumatic stress disorder* (PTSD, see left). Children may experience PTSD after being exposed to traumatic events during conflict. The long-term consequences can be extremely serious and recovery is difficult, not least because the child's society or *culture* is destroyed along with any people or services that provide support (psychologists, counsellors, hospitals, etc.).

Just one of the many 'privations of war' suffered by children in regions of conflict.

Evaluation

Long-term recovery from sources

One strength is that research shows it is possible to recover from early privation.

For example, in the study of Romanian orphans, those orphans adopted after six months experienced multiple and serious negative effects. But when the researchers looked more closely, they discovered that about 20% of these children experienced no negative impacts from the age of six years onwards. They were more resilient than other adoptees (i.e. they were able to overcome the effects of privation).

This means that early separation may not always be a source of privation. Understanding the biological and psychological reasons why these children were resilient could help recovery.

Application to institutional care

Another strength is that research can help improve the lives of children who experience privation.

Research has shown that poor life outcomes are likely when children are placed in large-scale institutional care. Therefore, such places have disappeared in most countries of the world because of psychological research which demonstrated the damage from a lack of emotional care. The process of adoption has also been affected because we now realise how important early adoptions are (before six months).

This shows that understanding how sources of privation impact on children can have practical benefits.

Physical versus emotional separation

One weakness is that understanding 'separation' in terms of physical distance is too simplistic.

For instance, Marian Radke-Yarrow *et al.* (1985) studied severely *depressed* mothers of young children (with a mean age of 32 months). They found that 55% of the children were *insecurely attached*. This compared with only 29% of children in a *control group* of mothers who were not depressed. The depressed mothers were 'psychologically absent' and unable to provide suitable emotional care.

This shows that emotional or psychological separation may be the main source of privation rather than physical separation. Therefore, children who experience privation can be helped by offering substitute emotional care.

GET ACTIVE Applying to cases and studies

Some of the sources on this spread are applied to specific cases of privation/abuse. Here's an opportunity for you to do the same. Read through the cases and studies on the previous spread and think about the types of privation in each one.

1. What does the Hodges and Tizard study and the Romanian orphans study tell us about early separation?

2. Is there any evidence from the cases of Genie and the Czech twins that poverty or PTSD may have played a role in privation?

3. What do you think are the main lessons to be learned from these cases/studies about how privation can be avoided or prevented?

Assessment practice

At the end of learning aims B and C you must write a report (see pages 193 and 210). This report must be related to a scenario or context. We have used a realistic (but not real) context.

In your next vlog you want to explore the sources of privation/abuse experienced by children and encountered by professionals in their work. Your guest professionals this time are a clinical psychologist and a social worker. The clinical psychologist has a lot of experience dealing with children in residential homes, as well as children who have been victims of physical and/or sexual abuse.

The social worker has frequently worked with the poorest families and with child refugees who are escaping conflict in other parts of the world and are placed with families in the UK. You ask your guests to take two sources of privation and discuss them from their professional point of view. Write the script for each professional.

C1.7 Learning aim C1 – Task 7

The second part of your report for learning aims B and C will be concerned with problems of psychological development in children – this is covered on the previous spread, this spread and the next spread.

1. **Explain** some problems of psychological development in children. (C.P5)

2. **Explain two** professional approaches to understanding sources of privation/abuse/dysfunctional psychopathology. (C.P6)

3. **Analyse** approaches taken by professionals to understanding sources of privation/abuse/dysfunctional psychopathology. (C.M3)

An issue to consider

The importance of understanding the sources of privation and abuse is to prevent negative effects before they happen.

Do you feel this is possible? For example, what might people do in war zones to help affected children?

Specification content

C1 Instances of privation and abuse

Sources of privation and abuse:

● Psychological sources of privation and abuse, e.g. early separations, parenting styles, bullying, divorce, death, physical/sexual abuse.

● Environmental sources of privation, e.g. poverty, lifestyle, income, parental education levels, deviance from norms of society, natural disasters, war and its potential effects, e.g. Post-Traumatic Stress Disorder (PTSD).

Effects of privation and abuse

Deprivation dwarfism

Genie and the Czech twins (page 202) were found to be physically unusually small for their ages when they were rescued from their abusers. This is also often true of children in institutional care, such as the Romanian orphans. Psychologists call this condition *deprivation dwarfism*.

Research suggests that deprivation dwarfism is not caused by poor diet or undernourishment but by a lack of emotional care (e.g. Gardner 1972). Even when children receive adequate nutrition in institutions, deprivation dwarfism is still common. It is important to understand this because knowing the true cause has led directly to an effective treatment.

For example, Elsie Widdowson (1951) reported on a group of orphanage children with this severe underdevelopment. They were placed on a regime of dietary supplements but this made no difference. What did make a difference was changing their 'carer' (actually an orphanage supervisor), who was a harsh and unsympathetic person. More sensitive emotional care from the new supervisor was followed by rapid weight gain in the children.

Specification terms

Attachment disorder Physical, psychological and behavioural symptoms due to problems in forming emotional attachments, often caused by privation.

Deprivation dwarfism Children who are abused, neglected or in institutions may be physically underdeveloped due to a lack of emotional attachments.

Disinhibited attachment A type of insecure attachment where children will treat strangers with inappropriate familiarity (overfriendliness) and may be attention-seeking

Dysfunctional psychopathology Mental disorders which lead to abnormal behaviours. 'Dysfunctional' means not operating normally and 'psychopathology' is the scientific study of what causes mental disorders.

There are individual differences in the way that children react to life circumstances. For example, some are naturally more resilient.

The effects of privation and abuse

Disinhibited attachment

Disinhibited attachment was a relatively common effect found in many of the Romanian orphans who were adopted after they were six months old. It is a form of *insecure attachment* (see page 172). The child does not discriminate between people they choose as attachment figures. So, he or she treats near-strangers with inappropriate familiarity (i.e. they are overfriendly) and may be attention-seeking. In extreme cases these are features of *attachment disorder*, a *mental disorder* which is listed in both DSM and ICD. It has been linked to *depression* in adolescence (Moran *et al.* 2017).

Another effect of *privation/abuse* is *deprivation dwarfism* (see left).

Effects on young carers

A young carer is a child 'under 18 who provides primary care for sick, disabled or elderly relatives in the home, usually their own parents' (Fallon 1990). Parents may have a physical illness or *mental disorder* that prevents them from fulfilling their normal parental role. Young carers often therefore experience a process known as *parentification*, the 'expectation that one or more children will fulfil the parental role in the family system' (Barnett and Parker 1998).

Parentification represents a dissolution (removal) of the boundary between childhood/ adolescence and adulthood because the young carer has to grow up too fast. Young carers sacrifice their own emotional and practical needs in favour of the parent's needs, reversing the usual roles. This exposes them to a greater risk of developing a *dysfunctional psychopathology* such as depression.

Parentification is seen by many psychologists as a form of privation. According to Aldridge and Becker (1993), young carers' lives are physically, socially and psychologically restricted. Their school attendance may be poor, they have few friends and social activities are limited because of their responsibilities at home. They also experience a lot of *stress*, not just because of their parent's condition but because of the need to keep the family's situation hidden. This is linked to depression and anxiety.

Effects on prenatal development

Privation/abuse can affect the development of the foetus in the womb (i.e. prenatal effects). This is mainly because privation/abuse experienced by a pregnant woman (e.g. domestic violence) causes high levels of psychological stress.

One indirect effect is that stress increases the risk of outcomes that themselves have negative effects on the baby's development. For example, stress can make premature birth more likely and cause abnormally low birth weight. Low birth weight is strongly linked to later dysfunctional psychopathology (e.g. depression, see page 194). Another indirect effect is malnutrition. A pregnant woman experiencing stress may eat a poor diet, which itself can increase the chances of having a low-birth-weight baby even further.

Prenatal maternal stress also has direct effects because it can change the foetus' biological development. For instance, during maternal stress the foetus is exposed to high levels of stress hormones (e.g. *adrenaline*, see page 46). Constant exposure to stress hormones can alter the foetus' brain development (e.g. low brain volumes, Dancause *et al.* 2011).

Moderating factors

Sources of privation/abuse do not produce the same effects in everyone. The effects depend on moderating factors such as *individual differences*. For example, in the Romanian orphan study over half of the children adopted after six months showed little impairment when they reached adolescence. These children demonstrated a high level of resilience.

Differences in resilience can be explained by *genes*. Jana Kreppner and Edmund Sonuga-Barke (2016) suggest that the experience of privation may have altered brain structures but only in Romanian orphans who had a genetic vulnerability. Non-genetic factors are also involved. Some of the adoptive families may have been more emotionally supportive than others, leading to a greater chance of recovery.

Rutter *et al.* (2010) also argued that some of the Romanian orphans did receive special attention in the institution (perhaps they smiled more). This meant they did have early attachment experiences and would explain why they were able to recover from the effects of privation.

Evaluation

Practical application

One strength is that understanding privation can stimulate ways of avoiding negative effects on development.

For example, young carers face a damaging conflict because they have to meet the needs of their families without disrupting their own social and emotional development. The right kind of support can help to reduce this conflict so that young carers do not have to sacrifice their childhoods. In the UK, authorities are legally obliged to provide services for young carers (e.g. respite care so they can have breaks, and *counselling*).

This shows that providing appropriate support can help to avoid parentification of young carers, or at least transform it into a positive experience.

Privation is only one factor

One weakness is that privation was not the only factor causing negative effects in the Romanian children study.

Emotional privation was undoubtedly associated with negative outcomes, but this does not mean it caused them. The Romanian orphans experienced not only emotional privation but also the terrible physical conditions of the institution. This would have had a negative impact on their health. There was also a serious lack of *cognitive* stimulation, negatively affecting intellectual development.

Therefore, privation alone is probably not the only cause of later effects on development, and may not even be the most important factor.

Outcomes not effects

Another weakness is that many of the 'effects' on this spread may not really be effects at all.

Using the term 'effects' strongly implies that there are identifiable causes. In fact, rather than uncovering causes and effects, most research has found *correlations* between sources and outcomes. For example, poor school attendance is definitely linked to parentification but may not necessarily be caused by it. The fact that there are moderating factors (see facing page) shows that the effects on this spread are not inevitable.

This means that, at most, we can say that there is a greater risk of experiencing these negative outcomes when the sources of privation are present.

The mental health practitioner, Suzette Misrachi (2018), calls parentification a 'license to kill childhood'. Because the young carer is giving care and not receiving it, they 'lose' their childhood and adolescence.

Assessment practice

At the end of learning aims B and C you must write a report (see pages 193 and 210). This report must be related to a scenario or context. We have used a realistic (but not real) context.

You invite back the social worker from the last vlog because he has vast experience of working alongside young carers. He has seen how this role affects the development of children and adolescents, so you would like him to focus on that aspect of his professional work.

Your other guest is a health visitor. She has expertise in the effects of stress on pregnant women and how this can affect the baby's development. She has also worked with parents who are struggling to form strong attachments with their babies.

You ask each guest to consider the effects of privation and present them from their professional point of view. Write the script for each professional.

C1.8 Learning aim C1 – Task 8

The second part of your report for learning aims B and C will be concerned with problems of psychological development in children – this is covered on the previous two spreads and this spread.

1. **Explain** some problems of psychological development in children. (C.P5)
2. **Explain two** professional approaches to understanding sources of privation/abuse/dysfunctional psychopathology. (C.P6)
3. **Analyse** approaches taken by professionals to understanding sources of privation/abuse/dysfunctional psychopathology. (C.M3)

An issue to consider

Some children are born with many more disadvantages than others. If you knew someone in that position, what advice would you give them?

GET ACTIVE Measuring parentification

There is a checklist for measuring parentification on this website: tinyurl.com/y6b2t8ej

If you want to, complete the checklist yourself. A good way to do this is to imagine yourself when you were, say, eight years old. Bear in mind that checklists that appear on websites should be treated as interesting or fun, but not taken too seriously.

Psychologists believe that young carers are more likely to be parentified than children who do not care for family members. Looking at each item on the checklist, do you think this is a reasonable belief? Are there any items that would apply strongly to a young carer?

Specification content

C1 Instances of privation and abuse

Effects of privation and abuse:

- Effects of privation and abuse (e.g. disinhibited attachment, attachment disorder, parenting styles, intellectual delay, deprivation dwarfism) and effects on young carers (e.g. loss of childhood and adolescence, boundary dissolution).
- Effects of privation and abuse on prenatal development, e.g. effects of domestic violence on foetus in utero.
- Moderating factors, e.g. resilience (genetics), substitute attachment figures.

Application and working practice

Troubled Families Programme

The UK government's *Troubled Families Programme* (TFP) was introduced in 2011 to help up to 400,000 families in Britain with the most complex support needs. Children in such families are at risk of a range of problems, from abuse/neglect to the continuation of educational underachievement. A central feature of the programme is the way professionals work together in teams to meet these complex needs.

Children and young people aren't just at risk in families. Young people in care experience particularly negative outcomes (e.g. addiction, mental disorders). Therefore, as part of the TFP, a project in North Yorkshire called *No Wrong Door* was created to keep adolescents out of the care system.

A team of professionals was formed, comprising a police liaison officer, a communications support worker, a life coach and other key workers. This one team provided all the support services for vulnerable adolescents who would otherwise end up in care. As a result, research has shown that many of them stayed longer in education, training and jobs, and were less likely to become involved in crime and substance abuse.

Source: Department for Education (2017)

Specification term

Multidisciplinary workforce A group of professionals from different disciplines (areas) working together, for example education, social care and criminal justice.

Skin-to-skin contact can help to promote the special attachment bond between the main caregiver and baby. This sort of theoretical knowledge is put to practical use by midwives and health visitors.

Application of theories

Theory 1: Bowlby's attachment theory

An *insecure attachment* in infancy can lead to an *attachment disorder* in childhood. This has been linked to the development of a *dysfunctional psychopathology* such as *depression* or *anxiety* (see previous spread).

Midwives can help to prevent dysfunctional psychopathology by giving expectant mothers advice about the importance of attachment. Midwives understand the importance of skin-to-skin contact in the hours immediately after birth. They positively reinforce the mother's responses to the baby, encourage communication and increase her confidence.

Health visitors can help by observing interactions between baby and caregiver in the home environment to look for evidence of a *secure attachment* during the initial *sensitive period* (three to six months). For example, based on Ainsworth's research (page 172), they can see if the baby is confidently exploring their environment and at the same time using the caregiver as a *secure base*. They would encourage any caregiver to respond sensitively to the baby's needs and signals.

Theory 2: Theories of language acquisition

Some children's acquisition of language is delayed or disrupted because they have experienced privation/abuse. This can lead to later development of depression or anxiety because the child cannot communicate effectively.

Speech and language therapists help to treat dysfunctional psychopathology by intervening early to support children with communication disorders. This is based on the idea from Chomsky's theory that there is a sensitive period for the acquisition of *language* (supported by evidence from Genie's experience, see page 202). Possession of a *language acquisition device* (LAD) within the brain means children usually acquire language through exposure. Therefore, therapists encourage parents to use language with their children in everyday contexts as much as possible.

Nursery nurses and **teachers** can help by developing children's language through play. For example, presenting objects to a child for them to name. These activities – as well as reading to children – demonstrate that there is a social context for the development of language, as suggested by Bruner. Learning principles can also be used to *model* the use of language for children to *imitate* (and adults reinforce the correct responses).

Working practice: Multidisciplinary teams (MDTs)

The UK government's definition of *multidisciplinary teams* (MDTs) is: '...professionals from different disciplines in health, community, social care, *mental health*, employment, education, criminal justice and community services who work together to plan services and support for people and families' (King 2018). *The Children Act 2004* requires professionals involved in child protection to work together with the best interests of the child at the forefront of everything they do. Two key professionals on MDTs working with children who face *abuse* are social workers and police officers.

Social workers carry out assessments of families to identify the risk of harm to a child (if they have a child assessment order this can be done without parents' consent). In most cases a child/family is referred to another agency for support and/or a child protection plan is produced. Where a child is in immediate danger the social worker can request he or she be placed in police protection without a court order (but the social worker does not have the power to do this themselves).

Police officers by law can remove a child from the family home if there is immediate risk of harm. Officers with training in child protection investigate criminal cases of abuse.

Features of effective MDTs

An effective MDT has a single leader who manages the work of the team. Each child/family has a named 'key case worker' who is assigned to coordinate support.

Each MDT includes social workers, nursery nurses, health visitors and primary teachers. These professionals are supplemented as needed by specialists in youth crime, *substance abuse* and mental health. They communicate regularly with each other through weekly emails, informal meetings and social media.

The main objective is to break down the barriers between professional groupings that usually hamper communication and sharing of information (a major failing identified by Lord Laming's inquiry into the tragic case of Victoria Climbié, see page 202).

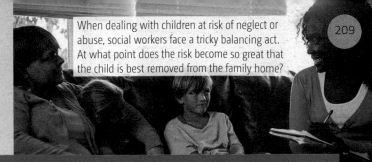

When dealing with children at risk of neglect or abuse, social workers face a tricky balancing act. At what point does the risk become so great that the child is best removed from the family home?

GET ACTIVE Theories and professionals

We covered a wide range of theories in sections A2 and A3. This spread has used attachment and language acquisition as examples, but there are plenty more including Bronfenbrenner, social identity theory, Piaget, Vygotsky and others.

1. Choose **two** theories not covered on this spread.
2. Identify **two** main concepts of each theory.
3. Write **two** sentences explaining how each concept could help a school nurse (or teacher or general practitioner of medicine) in their work. On page 200 there are descriptions of these roles.

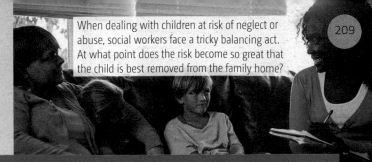

When dealing with children at risk of neglect or abuse, social workers face a tricky balancing act. At what point does the risk become so great that the child is best removed from the family home?

209

Evaluation

Support for attachment and midwives' role

One strength is evidence that midwives can use attachment theory to support pregnant women.

Some women give birth by caesarean section, putting them at risk of attachment difficulties. This is because a caesarean is a major surgical operation that can disrupt initial bond-formation (e.g. pain and discomfort in holding the baby). Midwives help by providing reassurance and advice to increase a mother's confidence in such a situation.

This shows how a professional's knowledge of theory can prevent negative outcomes associated with *insecure attachment*.

Applying theories of language acquisition

Another strength is that applying theories of language acquisition has benefits for children.

For example, many speech and language therapists use Makaton. This is a form of sign language using gestures, facial expressions and body language. Children learn it by using it as much as possible in everyday interactions. This reflects Bruner's view that language is acquired in a social context, for purposeful communication between people.

This shows that a theory can form the basis of an intervention programme to support children with speech and language disorders.

Evaluation

The value of MDTs

A strength of MDTs is that they provide a single point of contact for vulnerable children.

This avoids the problems that used to occur with uncoordinated support services, which saw children being passed 'from pillar to post' with no single agency taking responsibility. Information is now shared between professionals, who have a much clearer picture of a child's support needs and the risks they face.

This level of coordination is highly cost-effective – it makes the work of professionals more beneficial to children at lower cost to the taxpayers who fund it.

MDTs are resource-dependent

One weakness of MDTs is that they are clearly not a complete solution to supporting vulnerable children.

This is shown by the fact that similar cases to Victoria Climbié continue to occur. For instance, in 2017 two-year-old Dylan Tiffin-Brown was murdered by his father, with support services failing to coordinate and missing several opportunities to identify Dylan as 'immediately at risk'.

This suggests that the effectiveness of MDTs may be hampered by lack of government funding and a failure of support services to work together.

Assessment practice

At the end of learning aims B and C you must write a report (see pages 193 and 210). This report must be related to a scenario or context. We have used a realistic (but not real) context.

For your last vlog you will present a mock meeting of a group of professionals working together in a multidisciplinary team. A health visitor, speech and language therapist and nursery nurse have agreed to take part.

They will discuss a fictitious case you have written. It concerns a two-year-old girl living with parents who are both involved in dealing drugs. The father has a previous conviction for domestic violence. The child cries a lot, especially when she cannot see her mother. Her development appears to be delayed, including her acquisition of language. The team is therefore worried that she is at high risk of developing depression and anxiety later on.

C2.9 Learning aim C2 – Task 9

The final part of your report for learning aims B and C will be concerned with problems of psychological development in children and the role of professional support – this is covered on this spread.

1. **Explain two** professional approaches to treating dysfunctional psychopathology (e.g. depression) in children. (C.P6)
2. **Analyse** approaches taken by professionals in the treatment of dysfunctional psychopathology (e.g. depression) in children. (C.M3)
3. **Evaluate** the use of theories of child development in approaches taken by professionals in the treatment of dysfunctional psychopathology (e.g. depression) in children. (C.D3)

An issue to consider

One professional might find a certain theory useful, but another professional often will not.

What do you think are the pros and cons of professionals bringing different theories with them into multidisciplinary teams?

Specification content

C2 Application of theories to working practice

Influence of theories informing privation and abuse on explaining approaches taken by multidisciplinary professional teams, including treatment and preventative measures in everyday practice:

- Use of theories to inform professionals' approach to promote children's healthy development, e.g. midwives and GPs in supporting positive prenatal growth, educationalists, health visitors, school nurses, speech therapists in developing programmes of intervention and support.
- Multidisciplinary working and its role in supporting children experiencing forms of abuse and in promoting positive outcomes for children, parents and carers, e.g. police, social workers, educationalists.

Assessment guidance

Learning aims B and C assessment

You are required to produce a report for each learning aim in this unit. You can, if you wish, combine units but no learning aim can be subdivided. The specification recommends that you combine learning aims B and C.

This report can only be completed after you have studied the content of learning aims B and C as it is a synoptic assessment (see page 191).

Your report can be written or presented as a poster, Powerpoint or other form.

Recommended assessment approach

The *Delivery Guide for Unit 5* states that your report (or presentation, poster, etc.) is likely to:

- Be more applied in nature than for learning aim A.
- Consider developmental issues that arise from privation/abuse and how theories can help us understand the challenges for the child.
- Link the approaches used by professionals to support healthy development.

Assignment briefs

The board supplies suggested assignment briefs which you can use – see *Unit 5 Authorised assignment brief for Learning aims B and C.*

Your centre can also devise their own assignment brief which should have a vocational scenario/context and a series of tasks to complete.

Vocational scenario	The task (from the assignment brief)
It will be useful to have a case study (or case studies) and undertake some analysis/assessment of the child's needs, identifying recommendations that a professional might give. You can take the position of a professional who is managing the case.	Your report should aim to: • **Explain**, **assess** and **evaluate** the impact and importance of contributory factors affecting the healthy development of children and the roles of professional support for parents, carers and healthy development in children. (See pass, merit and distinction criteria below.) • **Explain**, **analyse** and **evaluate** the uses of child development theories in approaches taken by professionals in the treatment of dysfunctional psychopathology in children. (See pass, merit and distinction criteria below.)

Assessment information

Your final report will be awarded a Distinction (D), Merit (M), Pass (P), Near Pass (N) or Unclassified (U).

The specification provides criteria for each level as shown below.

Pass	Merit	Distinction
B.P3 EXPLAIN factors affecting healthy development in children.		
B.P4 EXPLAIN the roles of professionals in supporting children and their parents or carers.		
C.P5 EXPLAIN problems of psychological development in children.		
C.P6 EXPLAIN professional approaches to treating dysfunctional psychopathology in children.		
	B.M2 ASSESS the importance of contributory factors, and the role of professional support, in the healthy development of children.	
	C.M3 ANALYSE approaches taken by professionals in the treatment of dysfunctional psychopathology in children.	
		B.D2 EVALUATE the impact of contributory factors on the development of children and the impact of professionals in providing support to children, their parents or carers.
		C.D3 EVALUATE the use of theories of child development in approaches taken by professionals in the treatment of dysfunctional psychopathology in children.

Marking factors The specification also provides information that an assessor will take into consideration when marking your assignment.

Marking factors	Pass	Merit	Distinction
A report that … the importance of supporting children's optimal development.	… identifies …	… discusses …	… explores …
Including … of one group of personal and biological factors, or environmental and social factors, influencing children's healthy growth and development.	… an outline …	… a detailed account …	… a thorough analysis of the impact…
The report will … the role of professionals in one area, for example education.	… identify …	… make well-defined and reasoned judgements on …	… examine …
Learners will provide … professionals support children's healthy growth and development.	… a few examples of how …	… a broad range of examples of the ways in which …	… well-defined and reasoned examples of how…

See page 191 for an explanation of command terms used for learning aims B and C.

Self-review checklist

The list below will help you manage writing your final report.

First draft

Remember this is a *draft*. So you can write anything, just get thoughts on the page (see 'Blank screen syndrome' on page 259). But do not copy anything, even at this stage (see 'Plagiarism' on page 191).

Date to complete first draft: _____

	Date completed	Explain (B.P3)	Explain (B.P4)	Explain (C.P5)	Explain (C.P6)	Assess (B.M2)	Analyse (C.M3)	Evaluate (B.D2)	Evaluate (C.D3)
• In the first grey column enter the completion dates for each section of your report. • As you write each section tick the yellow boxes when you have explained, assessed, analysed and evaluated, as appropriate. Ignore the boxes that are crossed through.									
B1 Supporting children's optimal development									
Maslow's hierarchy of needs			⊠	⊠	⊠		⊠		⊠
B2 Factors impacting children's development, learning and mental health									
Personal and biological factors				⊠	⊠	⊠	⊠		⊠
Personal and biological factors (continued)				⊠	⊠	⊠	⊠		⊠
Environmental and social factors				⊠	⊠	⊠	⊠		⊠
B3 Professionals involved in supporting children's healthy development									
Role of professionals in healthy growth and development		⊠		⊠	⊠			⊠	
C1 Instances of privation and abuse									
Cases and studies of privation and abuse			⊠	⊠	⊠		⊠	⊠	⊠
Sources of privation and abuse			⊠	⊠	⊠		⊠	⊠	⊠
Effects of privation and abuse			⊠	⊠	⊠		⊠	⊠	⊠
C2 Application of theories to working practice									
Application and working practice			⊠	⊠	⊠		⊠		⊠
References compiled									

Marking factors	Pass	Merit	Distinction
The report will … one form of privation or abuse and consider the relationship to, and impact on, children's healthy growth and development.	… outline a few examples of …	… provide a detailed account of and a wide range of reasoned examples of …	… provide a considered account and evaluation of the impact of …
The report will … that professionals have used knowledge gained from instances of privation or abuse to apply to inform working practice in promoting healthy growth and development in children.	… identify some ways …	… contain a detailed analysis of the ways …	… provide a comprehensive and well-constructed discussion of the ways …
Links, explanations and discussions will be …	… generally accurate, although they may contain some inconsistencies and may be occasionally vague.	… well-considered and include a wide range of reasoned and generally accurate examples.	… thorough and well-supported by accurate and appropriate examples.

Second draft

The next step is to revise your first document. Below is a checklist of things to consider.

Date to complete second draft: _____

	Date completed
I have checked that I have covered each of the seven marking factors (grey column) in the table on the left.	
I have gone through and deleted any irrelevant material.	
I have checked that every point has evidence to back it up.	
I have identified long sentences and rephrased them.	
I have checked that each paragraph deals with one idea.	
I have corrected any spelling mistakes.	
I have checked that each paragraph makes reference to the scenario/context.	

Final draft

Read through your completed second draft to polish the report.

Date to complete final draft: _____

Unit 6

Introduction to psychopathology

Psychopathology is all about psychological (mental) disorders – defining them, understanding and explaining them, preventing and treating them.

➡ You have very likely heard of several mental disorders – make a list of them.

➡ What behaviours do you associate with these disorders? What about thoughts and feelings?

➡ What other words do you associate with mental disorder?

➡ Where does your knowledge come from?

Contents

Pearson recommended assessment approach

A report exploring ways in which psychopathology has been defined, and the changing perceptions and explanations of the way psychopathology is perceived and treated, e.g. a poster or a PowerPoint presentation.

A report that examines:
- Causal factors that can contribute to mental health disorders.
- The different types of mental disorder and their symptoms.
- The approaches used by professionals in treating different mental disorders and their specific roles in diagnosing and treating individuals.

Mental health and well-being

Here is the short answer: Probably not.

Here's the longer answer. It depends on what you mean by 'normal'. Think for a minute about what *you* mean by normal. What can you do if you are normal? How do you behave? How do you think? What do you feel? Can you write a checklist of all the things that make someone normal? What if you can't do, think or feel these things? Does that make you abnormal?

If you're finding this tricky, you're not alone. The finest psychological brains in history have struggled with this one (and still do). We're going to have a look at some of the answers they've come up with. But here's something else to think about. Is there anyone you know who would tick every box on your checklist? Is anyone normal?

The even longer answer to the question takes up this and the next three spreads...

Specification terms

Abnormal behaviour Defined in many ways, but sometimes as 'deviating from normal behaviour'.

Disease A disorder of the body or mind that causes illness.

Mental disorders The collection of illnesses that affect behaviour, thinking and emotions.

Pathology The study of what causes diseases.

Psychopathology Literally 'psychological diseases'. The study of mental disorders (e.g. producing an explanation of depression).

Depression is a well-known mental disorder. The symptoms include an inability to function adequately because of low mood and loss of interest (see page 240).

What is mental health?

Physical health and pathology

We probably all know what the basic signs of physical health are. Blood pressure and body temperature are within a narrow range, skin colour is normal, etc.

These all change when we are ill (or have *ill health* – the term used in Unit 3, see page 10). We often become physically ill because we experience *disease*, such as a viral infection or tumour. The term 'disease' includes any disorder of physical structure or function. The causes of disease are studied in an area of science called *pathology*.

Mental health, psychopathology and mental disorders

Psychopathology is the study of the causes of *psychological* (mental) disorders. We can apply the concepts of health and illness to *mental health* and *mental illness* – in fact the term mental 'disorder' is preferred to mental 'illness' to emphasise the fact that not all mental disorders have a physical basis. In those cases where mental disorder is the result of disease, it is the structure and/or function of the brain and nervous system that is disordered (although other systems are often involved). However, most mental disorders do not have a physical cause.

When we are mentally healthy our minds feel good, we perceive the world clearly, we can enjoy life, and so on. However, when we experience mental disorder this all changes.

As with physical illness, the symptoms of mental disorder are often expressed in behaviour which we can measure – though the behaviour tends to be psychological rather than physical. For example, someone with *depression* feels sad, their sleep patterns and weight change, they don't enjoy things any more, etc. Their behaviour becomes *abnormal*. What 'abnormal' means is very controversial, and we'll explore this issue below and over the next few spreads.

The symptoms are also expressed in what a person thinks and feels, which we can't measure.

What counts as mental health?

According to Marie Jahoda (1958), mental disorder is the absence of mental health (like physical disorder/illness is the absence of physical health). This means we have to work out what good mental health is before we can understand mental disorder. Jahoda looked at research and identified six categories of good mental health:

- Positive self-attitudes, high *self-esteem*, strong sense of identity.
- Capable of personal growth and fulfilling our potential.
- Able to cope with *stress*.
- Independent of others and regulate our own behaviour.
- Perceive reality, including ourselves, accurately.
- Can successfully work, love and enjoy our leisure.

Someone who deviates from one or more of these criteria for ideal mental health could be considered abnormal and potentially mentally disordered.

What counts as abnormal behaviour?

Another way of thinking about *abnormality* was put forward by David Rosenhan and Martin Seligman (1989). They pointed out that most of us can cope with the demands of our everyday lives most of the time. 'Normal' becomes 'abnormal' when someone can no longer do this. So, the person who is failing to function is abnormal – they cannot look after themselves, they go without washing or eating, they struggle to hold down a job, maintain a relationship or communicate with others.

Rosenhan and Seligman suggested that people who cannot function adequately:

- Experience personal distress and/or cause distress to others.
- May lack control and behave unpredictably or irrationally.
- Do not follow rules of interpersonal communication (e.g. they do not maintain eye contact or respect personal space).

GET ACTIVE Mental Health Awareness Week

Mental Health Awareness Week starts on the second Monday in May every year. Your school/college wants to mark the next one with a series of events and you have been asked to join the planning committee to represent BTEC students. As your contribution, on the next inset/CPD day, you will be presenting to teachers on the topic of 'What is mental health?'. As part of your presentation, you focus on Jahoda's categories of mental health.

1. *For each of Jahoda's six categories, write a sentence applying it to a typical student's experience of school/college.*

2. *Again, for each one, suggest **one** way in which that category could be promoted in school/college.*

Problems with definitions

Jahoda's definition is unrealistic

One problem of Jahoda's definition is that it sets an unrealistically high standard for mental health.

Probably everyone fails to meet at least one of the criteria, which means everyone is abnormal. The good news is that this reduces the differences between normal and abnormal people – we are all somewhere on the same scale. On the other hand, it is harder to identify people who would benefit from support or treatment.

Therefore, the problem is that we end up labelling everyone as abnormal and this makes the word meaningless and is probably not very useful.

Difficult to assess personal distress

One problem of Rosenhan and Seligman's definition is that it can be hard to judge whether someone is distressed.

Some people experience the symptoms of a mental disorder and yet appear to be happy (or at least not very distressed). Conversely, plenty of us are distressed from time to time and yet we don't see that as a sign we are abnormal.

Therefore, final judgement about distress is mostly subjective and open to interpretation (and potentially bias).

All definitions depend on culture

One problem for all definitions of abnormality is they are very much related to a person's culture and yet they are used to judge people from different cultures.

Jahoda's criteria for ideal mental health are characteristics that are valued in Western European and North American cultures. These Western cultures emphasise and prioritise the needs of the individual person over those of the group (called *individualist* cultures). In many other cultures group needs come first, such as considering the views of your family when getting married or sharing your money with members of your community. The group functions collectively and thus these are called *collectivist* cultures (e.g. China and India).

This means that Jahoda's approach, and that of Rosenhan and Seligman, are rooted in Western culture and therefore cannot explain abnormality or psychopathology across the whole world.

Assessment practice

At the end of learning aim A you must write:

A report exploring ways in which psychopathology has been defined, and the changing perceptions and explanations of the way psychopathology is perceived and treated, e.g. a poster or a PowerPoint presentation.

This report must be related to a scenario or context. We have used a realistic (but not real) context.

There are several charities in the UK offering support for young people with mental health issues. A new charity has been set up in your local area – HelpingMinds.

They have asked you to run a training session for a group of volunteers on the topic of 'Understanding modern concepts of psychopathology'.

You plan to start by giving the volunteers an in-depth explanation of current definitions of psychopathology in psychology. You should always bear in mind how this will help the volunteers in their work with young people. You must produce a detailed report that will accompany the training session.

A1.1 Learning aim A1 – Task 1

The first part of your report for learning aim A will be concerned with defining psychopathology – various ways to define psychopathology are covered on this spread and the next three spreads.

This activity will help you practise the skills required to write the report in response to your scenario/context.

1. **Explain** how psychopathology is defined in terms of deviation from mental health. (A.P1)

2. **Optional: Explain two or more** problems involved in defining mental health. (A.P1)

The assessment criteria on page 228 show that you are not required to address the problems with the way psychopathology is defined. However, you may choose to include these as part of your explanation.

An issue to consider

Health versus illness. Do we tend to think in terms of mental health or mental disorder? Do we think about physical health or physical illness?

Specification content

A1 Defining psychopathology

Types, characteristics and use of methods for defining psychopathology.

- Mental health and well-being, including pathology, disease, abnormal behaviour, mental disorders and illness, structuring mental disorders (this is covered in the section on classification systems, see page 220).

Statistical definitions of psychopathology

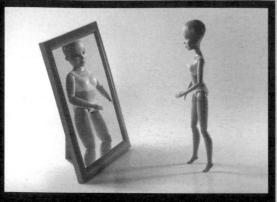

A case of anorexia

Carol is a typical 16-year-old in most ways, but she has anorexia nervosa. She almost always makes a reference to her body size and shape when she talks about herself. She pays a lot of attention to details of her appearance – she thinks she has 'fat eyelids'. She avoids any foods that she thinks will make her 'feel fat'. She frequently skips meals, eating rice cakes to fill up and continue losing weight. She has recently started taking laxatives.

Carol can't see it herself, but her friends tell her she is too thin. She takes no notice and thinks they are just jealous. Her hair is falling out, she bruises easily and has no energy. But her weight is the one thing in her life she can control.

Think about the word *unusual*.

Are Carol's behaviours, thoughts and perceptions unusual? What is unusual about them? How do they differ from 'normal' behaviours, thoughts and perceptions? Is Carol's behaviour *abnormal*?

Specification terms

Deviation from political norms Beliefs, opinions and behaviours that do not match what is considered acceptable by people in power (e.g. government).

Deviation from social norms Concerns behaviour that is different from the accepted standards of behaviour in a community or society.

Deviation from statistical norms Occurs when an individual has a less common characteristic, for example being more depressed or less intelligent than most of the population.

Statistical definitions

Counting how many people do something is an example of using *statistics* and statistics is about numbers. This is one way to define *abnormality*. How often does a behaviour happen? How many people behave like that? Is it common or rare?

Deviation from statistical norms

In terms of statistics, quite a few human characteristics and behaviours are 'average'. This means if we measure a large group of people on a *questionnaire*, most people score in the middle (e.g. the *mean*). The higher the score above and below the mean, the fewer people get that score.

Take intelligence for example. Imagine we ask a lot of people to complete an intelligence (IQ) test and we plot their scores on a graph. It would look a lot like the graph at the bottom of the page. This is called a *normal distribution*. It shows that most people have average intelligence (in the middle where the 'hump' is). Statistically, we could say that they have 'normal intelligence' because they are the majority. So average intelligence is the statistical norm.

But if a behaviour doesn't happen often or not many people do it, then it is statistically infrequent. Such behaviours are abnormal because they are different (deviate) from how most people behave (the statistical norm). So, who are the abnormal people? In the graph, they are in the 'tails' of the distribution at both ends of the curve. These are the people who have very high and very low intelligence – they are abnormal because there are not many of them. They have *deviated from statistical norms*.

Deviation from social norms

Is there more to abnormality than just numbers? Are there any other kinds of 'norms' apart from averages?

Yes there are. Societies have unwritten 'rules' about how people should behave. Most of us observe them most of the time. For example, we are sad at funerals and happy at weddings, we make eye contact when we talk to someone, we keep ourselves clean and tidy, etc. These are *social norms* and anyone who consistently deviates from them is considered abnormal.

Here are some examples: you talk to yourself out loud in public, you yawn in someone's face, you ask a stranger for directions and stand very close to them, you feel sad all the time. A person who does not behave according to social conventions is considered to have *deviated from social norms* and is abnormal.

Deviation from political norms

In some societies, governments decide what views and behaviours are allowed. Some opinions, beliefs and behaviours are therefore abnormal because they deviate from what the people in power consider acceptable – *deviation from political norms*.

Historically in some countries if you expressed deviant views or behaviours you might be diagnosed with a mental disorder. This was often used to deprive people of human rights. For example, in the USA in the 19th century, black slaves who persistently tried to escape could be diagnosed with a mental disorder called *drapetomania* – a perfectly rational and understandable behaviour was turned into a mental disorder.

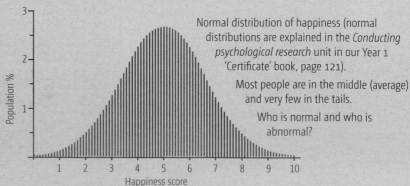

Normal distribution of happiness (normal distributions are explained in the *Conducting psychological research* unit in our Year 1 'Certificate' book, page 121).

Most people are in the middle (average) and very few in the tails.

Who is normal and who is abnormal?

'Horse boy' was first spotted on Google Maps' Street View in 2010. A man in a purple jumper and rubber horse's head has at least twice waited for Google's imaging car to photograph him by the side of the road. Strange behaviour perhaps, eccentric maybe. But is it 'abnormal'?

Was that you in Street View?

Neigh!

Problems with definitions

The behaviour may be desirable

One problem of a purely statistical definition is that it doesn't take into account the desirability of the behaviour or characteristic.

Someone with an IQ score over 130 is just as unusual (statistically) as someone with an IQ below 70. But most people would not view super-intelligence as an undesirable characteristic needing treatment. To use another example, if we say that very happy people are just as abnormal as very unhappy people, then the term abnormal becomes basically meaningless.

Therefore, a definition based just on numbers cannot be used on its own to make a diagnosis of psychopathology.

Cultural relativism

A further problem of the definition is that social norms vary significantly between cultures.

People from one culture often label behaviours of people from other cultures as abnormal because they differ from their own norms. For example, hearing voices is seen as a sign of abnormality in the UK, but people in some cultures regard hearing voices as a fairly usual experience.

This can make diagnosis difficult when the *clinician* (person doing the diagnosing) is from a different culture from the *client*.

Potential for human rights abuses

Another problem is that defining *mental health* and disorders in terms of social norms is open to abuse, especially by political authorities.

Social norms have changed in many countries over the past few decades. This means that being gay, for example, is no longer viewed as a crime or a mental disorder (as it used to be, even in the UK). People in the former Soviet Union (Russia and other states today) who disagreed with how the country was run risked being detained in mental institutions by the state.

Therefore, this definition of mental disorders can be used as an effective way of removing nonconformists from society (Szasz 1974).

GET ACTIVE Eccentric or abnormal?

One challenge to the social norms definition is the concept of eccentricity.

Eccentric people are those whose behaviour is generally thought of as unusual, bizarre, sometimes hard to understand but mostly harmless. Even celebrities or others in the media spotlight have been called eccentric, some even earning the label 'national treasure' or 'lovable'.

On the other hand there are people who live lives that do not match the expectations of the majority in a society, so they may be labelled as abnormal. All of these people are probably deviating from social norms, and yet some are called 'abnormal' and others are considered merely 'eccentric'.

Where do you think the dividing line between eccentric and abnormal lies? What are the differences between the two? Why is this a weakness of the social norms definition?

Assessment practice

At the end of learning aim A you must write a report (see pages 215 and 228). This report must be related to a scenario or context. We have used a realistic (but not real) context.

Once you have explained the concepts of mental health and well-being to the volunteers, you move on to another current definition of psychopathology – the statistical definition.

You decide to include statistical, social and political norms in the training.

Also, as you did for mental health/well-being, you suspect that the volunteers might ask you about any problems with the statistical definitions. So, you may decide to include them.

A1.2 Learning aim A1 – Task 2

The first part of your report for learning aim A will be concerned with defining psychopathology – various ways to define psychopathology are covered on the previous spread, this spread and the next two spreads.

This activity will help you practise the skills required to write the report in response to your scenario/context.

1. **Explain** how psychopathology is defined in terms of deviation from norms (for example, statistical, social and political). (A.P1)

2. **Optional: Explain two or more** problems involved in defining psychopathology in terms of deviation from norms. (A.P1)

You can see the assessment criteria and explanation of command terms on pages 228 and 229.

An issue to consider

Which of the three definitions seems to you to be closest to how you think about mental disorder?

Specification content

A1 Defining psychopathology

Types, characteristics and use of methods for defining psychopathology.

● Statistical definitions, including deviation from norms, e.g. statistical, social and political.

Approaches to defining psychopathology

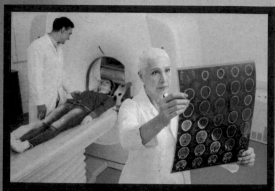

Diagnostic radiography

The biological approach is closely associated with technology that allows us to see what is going on in the brain. This is important because brain activity is linked to psychological and behavioural symptoms, for example some physical disorders of the brain can cause hallucinations. So, scanning the brain can be useful to support a diagnosis.

Diagnostic radiographers are professionals who are trained and qualified to use brain-scanning technology to diagnose disorders. A commonly-used form of scanning is called *functional magnetic resonance imaging* (fMRI). This detects changes in blood oxygen levels in the brain. Areas that are active use more oxygen, so these 'light up' on the scan. The radiographer's job is to prepare the patient, carry out the scan and then help to interpret the results.

Research continues to progress and we are learning more and more about the brain mechanisms involved in mental disorders. The biological approach will become even more important in understanding, diagnosing and treating these disorders.

Specification terms

Biological approach Behaviour is explained in terms of faulty bodily systems, including genes, neurochemistry, neuroanatomy and infection.

Psychological approach Behaviour is explained in terms of a range of mental, emotional and learned factors (e.g. thinking patterns, unconscious processes, learned responses to the environment).

The behavioural approach assumes that everyone who has a phobia must have had a distressing experience with the feared object or situation.

Approaches to defining psychopathology

Broadly speaking, approaches to *psychopathology* are related to physical aspects of the body (biological) or the mind (psychological).

Biological approach

The *biological approach* defines psychopathology in terms of faulty bodily systems. Mental disorder is caused by one or more of the following:

Genes Individual *genes* or collections of genes may be identified in people with a disorder. What probably happens is that some unusual genetic variation causes a malfunction in the brain's biochemistry, so normal levels of *neurotransmitters* are disrupted (see below).

Neurochemistry/neuroanatomy Normal neurotransmitter levels (e.g. of *serotonin* and *dopamine*) can be disrupted by various internal and external factors (genes, brain injury, stress, etc.). For instance, *depression* has been associated with abnormally low levels of the neurotransmitter serotonin. The anatomy (structure) of the brain can be similarly affected (e.g. through injury or disease), with damage causing symptoms of mental disorders.

Infection Exposure to several viruses has been linked to psychopathology. For example, in one study adults who had *schizophrenia* were more likely than non-schizophrenic people to have contracted the Epstein-Barr virus (which causes herpes), probably in adolescence (Dickerson *et al.* 2018).

Neuroscience This is an aspect of the biological approach. Psychologists would like to understand the patterns of brain activity underlying psychopathology. Are there specific brain dysfunctions associated with specific mental disorders? Neuroscience uses techniques such as *brain scanning* (e.g. PET, fMRI) to identify these patterns and link them to symptoms.

Psychological approach

The *psychological approach* views mental disorders as having psychological rather than physical causes, i.e. the origins lie in mental, emotional or learned activity.

Psychodynamic approach Sigmund Freud (late 19th/early 20th centuries) argued that psychopathology is the result of unconscious processes in the mind. These are thoughts and emotions we are unaware of and have no access to, but which can powerfully influence our behaviour and personality. Freud's therapy (*psychoanalysis*) gives a therapist and client insight into the client's unconscious mind, uncovering what was once hidden.

Behavioural approach This approach assumes that psychopathology is behaviour learned in response to the environment. The main learning processes involved are *classical* and *operant conditioning*.

For instance, a person might develop a *phobia* after being bitten by a dog (Mowrer 1947). An association is formed between the fear (*UCR*) and the dog (*NS*). When the person later sees a dog (now a *CS*), they re-experience the fear (*CR*). This is classical conditioning. The person reduces the unpleasant state of fear by avoiding dogs. The relief they feel is negatively reinforcing so avoidance is learned. This is operant conditioning.

Social learning contributes by suggesting that psychopathology can be learned through *imitation* and *vicarious reinforcement*, for instance via the media (e.g. observing another person being scared of a dog).

Cognitive approach Psychopathology is caused by negative and distorted patterns of thinking. For example, some people are vulnerable to depression because they pay more attention to the negative aspects of a situation than the positives. This includes the way depressed people think about themselves. They also blow small things out of proportion and think in ways that are very 'black and white' ('I can never be happy unless...').

Humanistic approach Carl Rogers (1959) proposed that we all have a drive to achieve our full potential, called *self-actualisation*. This is a key characteristic of *mental health*, the ability to accept ourselves, have good relationships with others and find meaning in life. Personal growth is an essential part of being human, developing and changing as a person to become fulfilled and satisfied. This is achieved when our sense of self (the way we see ourselves) is broadly the same as our ideal self (the person we want to be). Self-actualisation is blocked when the gap between actual self and ideal self is too big. This produces feelings of worthlessness and the outcome may be mental disorder.

Problems with the definitions

Biological approach is limited and narrow

One problem with the biological approach is that it is simplistic.

In focusing on physical processes, the biological approach neglects non-biological risk factors that affect an individual's likelihood of developing a mental disorder. For instance, a person may have genes that predispose them to develop a certain mental disorder (called a *diathesis*) but the disorder is only triggered under certain circumstances such as childhood trauma or living in poverty (called *stressors*). This is called the *diathesis-stress model*.

Therefore, the biological approach is a narrow explanation that may limit rather than expand our understanding of psychopathology.

Uncontrollable causes of behaviour

Another problem with the biological approach is that it claims every behaviour is caused by internal factors we have no control over.

For example, brain scanning studies try to match activity in the brain with the individual's characteristics and behaviour. Therefore, uncontrollable brain activity causes the symptoms of mental disorders. Our feeling that we have *free will* to govern our own behaviour is just an illusion.

This means that we could plausibly argue that we have no responsibility for our behaviour, which has serious implications for morality and the legal system.

Psychological approach is fragmented

One problem with the psychological approach is it is a fragmented explanation.

There are several psychological approaches to mental disorders. They include concepts and ideas that are not compatible with each other and in fact are directly contradictory. For instance, the psychodynamic approach focuses on the unconscious mind as the source of mental disorders, whereas the behavioural approach denies the unconscious even exists. In the psychodynamic approach, the aim is to remove the root cause of the disorder, but for the behavioural approach all that matters is changing behaviour (the initial cause is seen as irrelevant).

This means the psychological approach is a much less coherent way to understand and treat mental disorders than the biological approach.

Psychological approach uses vague concepts

Another problem with the psychological approach is that many of its concepts are abstract and vague.

For example, in the psychodynamic approach, it is very difficult to test concepts such as 'the unconscious mind' or 'dream interpretations' because they cannot be defined precisely. Added to this, most humanistic practitioners actively disapprove of the scientific method. For them, it does not matter that we cannot define concepts precisely, because scientific testing misses the point of what it means to be human anyway.

This means that the psychological approach is not seen as being particularly 'scientific' whereas the biological approach is highly scientific.

According to Freud's psychodynamic approach, the mind is like an iceberg – most of it is hidden below the surface. This is the unconscious.

Assessment practice

At the end of learning aim A you must write a report (see pages 215 and 228). This report must be related to a scenario or context. We have used a realistic (but not real) context.

You want to introduce the volunteers to how some approaches in psychology have defined psychopathology.
You choose the biological model. You also select psychological, behavioural and humanistic approaches.
You feel this selection will give the volunteers an appreciation of the wide variety of definitions of psychopathology that psychologists have produced.

A1.3 Learning aim A1 – Task 3

The first part of your report for learning aim A will be concerned with defining psychopathology – various ways to define psychopathology are covered on the previous two spreads, this spread and the next spread.

This activity will help you practise the skills required to write the report in response to your scenario/context.

1. **Explain** approaches to defining psychopathology in terms of biological models/neuroscience, psychological, behavioural and humanistic approaches. (A.P1)

2. **Optional: Explain two or more** problems involved in these approaches to defining psychopathology. (A.P1)

An issue to consider

If you had to choose biological or psychological approaches as the best way to explain psychopathology, which would you select? And why?

Specification content

A1 Defining psychopathology

Types, characteristics and use of methods for defining psychopathology.

● Biological and psychological approaches to defining psychopathology, including biological models (e.g. genes, neurotransmitters) and psychological models (e.g. cognitive, behavioural, humanistic).

GET ACTIVE Similarities or differences

It is useful to get some idea of the similarities and differences between the approaches on this spread.

1. *Draw up a table with the biological approach and one of the psychological approaches as headings across the top.*

2. *In the first row, for each of the two approaches write a sentence summarising the main cause(s) of psychopathology.*

3. *In the next row, write some sentences across the columns to explain one way in which the two approaches are similar.*

4. *Finally in the next row, write some sentences across the columns to explain how the two approaches are different.*

Classification systems

Diagnosing a disorder

Mental disorders are often diagnosed by a medical practitioner called a *psychiatrist*. He or she starts by listening to the *client* (this is the preferred term for someone seeking help, although in medical contexts, they are often called the *patient*).

The psychiatrist wants to know about the client's experiences, their feelings, behaviours and even physical symptoms, as well as the impact of the symptoms on the client's life. This is because just small differences in these things can affect which disorder the psychiatrist diagnoses.

The client might be asked to fill in questionnaires. There are no medical tests to diagnose mental disorders, but the client might still have some tests (e.g. blood tests) because the psychiatrist has to rule out physical disorders. If the client has an eating disorder (such as anorexia), she or he will have their weight and height measured because this is part of the diagnosis.

The psychiatrist might want to see the client again, especially if the diagnosis is complex (they could be experiencing more than one disorder). Once the psychiatrist has narrowed down the choice of disorder by excluding alternatives, they can see which one best 'fits' the presented symptoms.

Specification terms

Classification system Individual items (such as symptoms) are grouped into larger categories (such as specific mental disorders). Such systems are used to identify larger categories.

DSM A classification system published by the American Psychiatric Association. The current version (DSM-5) contains typical symptoms of over 300 disorders and guidelines for clinicians to make a diagnosis.

ICD A classification system produced by the World Health Organization (WHO), used mainly outside the USA. The current version is ICD-10.

DSM

DSM stands for the *Diagnostic and statistical manual of mental disorders*, a large reference book produced by the *American Psychiatric Association* (APA). It divides more than 300 mental and behavioural disorders into 22 different categories.

The disorders are grouped based on their symptoms, *clinical* features and risk factors. It is used by *mental health* practitioners throughout the United States and many parts of the world to decide what *mental disorder* a client has based on the symptoms that are apparent. It is also used to guide research into the causes and treatment of disorders.

History of the DSM

The first version was released in 1952, containing about 60 disorders and based on diagnosing soldiers in World War II. It has been revised and updated several times since, usually to reflect changing perceptions of mental health and illness. For instance, homosexuality appeared in DSM-I as a mental disorder but was removed in DSM-II in 1974. The current version is DSM-5, which was released in 2013 and was the first major revision in 20 years.

DSM-5

Roman numerals were dropped so future minor updates can be released (i.e. 5.1, 5.2, etc.). DSM-5 has three main sections:

Section One Guidance in using the system for diagnosis.

Section Two Disorders are categorised, based on recent research into their underlying causes. They include categories such as *depressive disorders*, *substance-use disorders* and *eating disorders*. A severity rating was introduced (e.g. mild, moderate, severe) to try to improve the *reliability* and *validity* of diagnosis.

Section Three Includes suggestions for disorders to be considered in future revisions (e.g. Internet gaming disorder), which will require further research. This section also includes discussion of how culture affects symptom presentation, communication and diagnosis, in order to reduce *cultural bias*.

ICD

ICD stands for *International classification of diseases*. This is older than the DSM and more widely used (in most places outside the US). Unlike the DSM, the ICD includes categories of physical as well as mental disorders. It offers a 'common language' for practitioners, researchers and policymakers so that data from many countries can be compared effectively.

History of the ICD

The ICD began in 1893 as the *International list of causes of death*. This provided a standard way of collecting data on death and disease (*mortality* and *morbidity*) from around the world. The World Health Organization (WHO) took over this task in 1948 and the first major revision came in 1949 with ICD-6.

ICD-11 was approved in May 2019 but member states will not start using it until 2022. Therefore, ICD-10 is still the commonly-used version and will remain so for the near future.

ICD-10

The system is divided into 22 chapters. The most relevant one is Chapter 5: Mental and Behavioural Disorders. There are 11 sections, each covering a broad category of disorder with each allocated a code starting with F.

For example, one category is 'Mood (affective) disorders', which has the codes F30–F39. Within this, F33 is 'Recurrent depressive disorder'. This is further subdivided to reflect severity (e.g. F33.0 is 'current episode mild', F33.1 is 'current episode moderate', and so on). Each category has a 'left-over' code, such as F33.8 'Other recurrent depressive disorders'.

There are also empty codes for 'future-proofing' – when research identifies disorders that can be placed within the category without recoding everything (e.g. there is no disorder associated with F35–F37).

GET ACTIVE **Write your own clinical checklist**

A practitioner tries to make a neat and tidy diagnosis from the words the client tells her. Classification systems recognise that this is difficult.

How do practitioners make a diagnosis? The answer is through a *clinical interview* with the client, by asking questions to get the client to explain their symptoms. These interviews often use structured checklists, based on the classification systems. Here are some examples: Have you experienced the following symptoms (a list of symptoms is then provided)? How severe were the symptoms? How long did they last?

1. *Look at the ICD-10 criteria for 'Depressive episode' here: tinyurl.com/y5uzezrp*

2. *Write a checklist (like the example above) that a practitioner could use in a clinical interview.*

3. *Repeat this for any other disorder in Chapter V of ICD-10 that you are interested in.*

Problems with DSM-5

Reliability of DSM-5

One weakness of DSM-5 is a low level of agreement between practitioners.

Field trials were conducted to test the reliability of DSM-5 – testing to see if different clinicians gave the same diagnosis to a client. Darrel Regier *et al.* (2013) found that the reliability of diagnosis of several disorders was low. Diagnosis of *depression* had one of the lowest reliability levels of all.

This means that the diagnosis of depression with DSM-5 is unreliable and may therefore be meaningless.

Validity of DSM-5

Another weakness of DSM-5 is that its use for diagnosis may lack validity.

Many psychologists and other practitioners objected in principle to the publication of DSM-5 (for example, Johnstone 2014). The objection is that diagnosing a disorder is meaningless unless it leads to a successful treatment, as is the case for most medical disorders, such as measles.

Therefore, just saying that a certain set of symptoms represent a particular mental disorder is meaningless. (This criticism is not limited to DSM-5, but applies to the whole business of attempting to categorise people as 'mentally disordered'.)

Problems with ICD-10

Reliability of ICD-10

One weakness of ICD-10 is relatively poor reliability.

Alexander Ponizovsky *et al.* (2006) wondered if patients got the same diagnosis when they were reassessed after a period of time. They compared the diagnosis that patients were given when they entered a psychiatric hospital with the one they received when they were discharged. For some disorders (e.g. *personality disorders* and alcohol/drug misuse), reliability was low. For others, reliability was lower for ICD-10 than for the previous version (ICD-9).

This low reliability, especially for some disorders, means that a diagnosis made on one occasion may not be the same at another time or with a different version of ICD.

Validity of ICD-10

Another weakness is that some categories of disorders in ICD-10 lack validity.

This is mainly because many disorders are *co-morbid*, i.e. they frequently 'go together'. For example, some people experience both *schizophrenia* and depression and it is impossible to say which is the 'main' disorder. ICD-10 deals with this by creating another category called *schizoaffective disorder*, a combination of schizophrenia and depression.

The problem is that this is not really a solution – just because they co-occur doesn't make them a new disorder. This challenges the validity of some of the ICD-10 categories.

Assessment practice

At the end of learning aim A you must write a report (see pages 215 and 228). This report must be related to a scenario or context. We have used a realistic (but not real) context.

Finally, for this stage of the training, you want the volunteers to understand how psychologists and other practitioners diagnose mental disorders.

You believe that classifying mental disorders is an important part of how they are defined. Therefore, you decide to explain the two major classification systems DSM-5 and ICD-10.

You include a brief history lesson for each one. More importantly, because you want to explain problems with the systems, you may briefly introduce the volunteers to the concepts of reliability and validity.

A1.4 Learning aim A1 – Task 4

The first part of your report for learning aim A will be concerned with defining psychopathology – various ways to define psychopathology are covered on the previous three spreads and this spread.

1. **Explain** the DSM system in terms of how it defines and classifies psychopathology. (A.P1)

2. **Explain** the ICD system in terms of how it defines and classifies psychopathology. (A.P1)

3. **Optional: Explain two or more** problems involved in the DSM classification systems. (A.P1)

4. **Optional: Explain two or more** problems involved in the ICD classification systems. (A.P1)

> The assessment criteria on page 228 show that you are not required to address the problems with the way psychopathology is defined. However, you may choose to include these as part of your explanation.

An issue to consider

Why do you think there are two major systems for classifying mental disorders?

Can you think of any issues that might arise because of this?

Specification content

A1 Defining psychopathology

Types, characteristics and use of methods for defining psychopathology.

● Classification systems, including Diagnostic and Statistical Manual of Mental Disorders (DSM), International Classification of Diseases (ICD).

Early perceptions / Early biological explanations

Take two leeches, three times a day

Ancient beliefs about the causes of mental disorders produced some strange 'treatments'.

Bleeding and purging (induced vomiting) were popular in ancient Greece and Rome (and in the Middle Ages in Europe). Bleeding was done by tapping veins or using water-dwelling creatures called leeches. These have three jaws which they use to latch onto flesh and suck blood, consuming up to ten times their body weight.

In complete contrast, consider the progressive treatments of the ancient Egyptians. They believed that mental disorders in women were caused by a detached uterus. It would travel around the body and become lodged against some vital organ such as the heart, preventing the heart from working properly. The Greeks later called this disorder *hysteria*, a word still in common use today (although not by psychologists). Egyptian doctors treated women's disorders with strong smells, especially pleasant ones to try and entice the uterus back into place.

Specification terms

Environment The complete set of non-genetic influences on behaviour, including prenatal influences in the womb, family, peers, social and cultural factors, food you eat, etc.

Heredity The genetic transmission of mental and physical characteristics from one generation to another.

Naturalistic explanation In the context of mental disorders, the view that the causes are 'natural' rather than supernatural, i.e. based on activity in the brain/body that can be demonstrated using the scientific method.

The term 'humour' is not just about laughter. Being in a good humour means you are in a good mood. The term comes from the Greek idea of humours – the right mix of black bile, yellow bile, blood and phlegm (that gooey stuff in your throat).

Early explanations for psychopathology

Early perceptions

Ancient views of *mental disorder* were usually supernatural. Evil spirits, demons or witches were considered responsible for behaviours seen as strange or unusual (i.e. abnormal). These demons were thought to control the individual like some kind of puppet.

Demonic possession was also sometimes seen as a punishment, often for the misdeeds of an earlier generation. This was a widespread view in the ancient world, shared by cultures as diverse as Hebrew, Greek and Chinese.

Possession could be treated by making the body an unwelcoming place for a demon to live. A long list of inventive methods of punishing the body included whipping, starving, freezing, boiling, stretching and compressing.

In this context, exorcism may involve using rituals, prayer, loud noises, incense, etc. This approach could be seen as relatively enlightened compared to an alternative method to provide the demon with an escape route by *trephining* (see photo on the facing page).

Early biological explanations

The Greek physician Hippocrates had no time for supernatural explanations. Around 400 BC, he was one of the first to suggest that mental disorders arose out of a failure of the body to perform its natural functioning, i.e. a *naturalistic explanation*. He based his view on a parallel between mental and physical disorders – believing they are similar in that they both have natural causes.

Theory of the four humours The four humours are bodily fluids that Hippocrates believed determined behaviour, personality and both physical and mental functioning: black bile, yellow bile, blood and phlegm. Mental disorders occur when the natural balance of these humours is lost and one humour predominates.

This was the basis of Hippocrates' classification of mental disorders into three main types – *mania*, *melancholia* and *phrenitis* (a 'fever of the brain'). For example, he believed melancholia (now called *depression*) is caused by excess black bile from the spleen and mania is due to excess yellow bile from the gallbladder. Classification into categories still underlies modern approaches to diagnosing mental disorders such as *DSM* and *ICD* (see previous spread).

Hippocrates later identified brain injury or disease as causes of mental disorder, an idea that was developed by another Greek physician (Galen) some 500 years later. Hippocrates also argued that as mental disorders had physical causes they should be treated by physical means. Some of these treatments were dangerous (e.g. bloodletting), but others were enlightened and humane (e.g. lifestyle changes such as diet and exercise). The naturalistic view continues today in the *medical model* (discussed on the next spread).

Heredity and environment

Most psychologists accept that mental disorders are caused by a combination of two factors – *heredity* (i.e. *genes*) and the *environment* (e.g. peer and family influences). Exactly how these factors contribute to behaviour is sometimes known as the *nature/nurture debate*. This has its roots in philosophy.

Environment In 1690 the philosopher John Locke argued that we are born with no inherited characteristics or abilities. He used the Latin phrase *tabula rasa* ('blank slate') to describe the human mind at birth. Our personality, behaviour, abilities, etc. all develop as we learn from our experience of the world (experience 'writes' on the 'slate', so our minds are no longer blank). This view in psychology is called *empiricism* and is now closely associated with the *behaviourists*.

Heredity In 1874 Sir Francis Galton argued that nature plays the predominant role in determining behaviour. We are born with certain abilities and characteristics. Some of these are immediately evident, but most of them develop over time in a process called *maturation*. But the capacity to develop is present at birth. In other words these abilities are *innate*, so this view in psychology is known as *nativism*.

The current view is that it is impossible to separate the effects of heredity and the environment. Both are involved in any given mental disorder, but they interact in order to have their effects. For example, some people's genetic make-up predisposes them to be susceptible to developing depression. But whether it actually develops or not depends on *environmental* factors that trigger the predisposition (you may recognise this as the *diathesis-stress model*).

Evaluation

Basis of later developments

One strength of the naturalistic explanation is that it paved the way for later *biological approaches*.

Hippocrates' theory of the four humours was wrong. However, the principle that physical dysfunction of the body underlies mental disorders was far-sighted. In particular, his identification of the brain as the source of mental disorder was so far ahead of its time that it took 500 years before others rediscovered it.

This naturalistic way of thinking about mental disorders was revolutionary at the time and led eventually to effective treatments.

Stigma

One weakness of ancient beliefs is that they created stigma (mark of disgrace) relating to mental disorders.

Mental disorder in ancient Greece was seen as shameful. Hippocrates observed that when people experienced early symptoms they would often run away and hide because otherwise their families would suffer the consequences. In the Middle Ages, people were shunned, isolated, locked up, restrained and cruelly treated. Even today there is sometimes stigma attached to having a mental disorder or someone with a mental disorder in your family.

This means people are discouraged from getting help because they believe others will think worse of them.

Inhumane treatments

Another weakness of early perceptions is that they tended to lead to inhumane treatments.

This was partly because of the stigma associated with those early perceptions. When people with mental disorders were seen as deserving of punishment rather than pity, it became very easy to treat them badly. This is what happened with some of the appalling treatments such as bloodletting and trephining.

This meant that far from being helped, many people with mental disorders died from the treatments they were subjected to.

This ancient skull belonged to a member of the Paracas people of Peru (about 2500 years ago). It clearly shows trephination holes (see facing page). Interestingly it also shows evidence of skull elongation. The Paracas forced babies' heads to develop like this as a sign of social status.

Assessment practice

At the end of learning aim A you must write a report (see pages 215 and 228). This report must be related to a scenario or context. We have used a realistic (but not real) context.

HelpingMinds were very pleased with your first training session. You were such a hit that they have invited you back. The volunteers realised that as there are different modern definitions of psychopathology, views have probably changed over time.

So, they would like to know more about the historical aspects. As the volunteers were so keen on understanding the problems with definitions last time, you decide to include analysis and evaluation as well as explanations in the training.

You start at the beginning, historically-speaking, with early views about psychopathology and also how they were treated. You also realise that this is a good opportunity to introduce the concepts of heredity and environment.

A2.5 Learning aim A1 – Task 5

The second part of your report for learning aim A will be concerned with the origins of psychopathology – these are covered on this spread and the next two spreads.

This activity will help you practise the skills required to write the report in response to your scenario/context.

1. With reference to early perceptions, **explain** how views of psychopathology have developed over time. (A.P2)
2. **Analyse** the historical development of psychopathology from ancient beliefs through to views on heredity and environment. (A.M1)
3. **Evaluate** how psychopathology has been viewed historically, from ancient beliefs through to views on heredity and environment. (A.D1)

> Analysis and evaluation are required for the remaining three spreads of learning aim A.

An issue to consider

What sort of stigma surrounds mental disorders today? How is it reflected in the language that some people use about people with mental disorders?

Have you or your friends encountered this?

GET ACTIVE Heredity, environment and diathesis-stress

Genes operate in some ways like switches. When a gene is 'switched on' it contributes to the development of whatever characteristic, ability or behaviour it is involved in. But it cannot do this when it is 'switched off'. Minae Niwa *et al.* (2013) found that chronic stress experienced in adolescence can disrupt the functioning of a single gene, DISC1. This gene is involved in several types of mental disorder (including depression and schizophrenia).

1. *How does this study help us to understand the nature/nurture debate?*
2. *How does the finding relate to the diathesis-stress hypothesis?*

Specification content

A2 Origins of psychopathology

Characteristics and traits of historical definitions, approaches to, and understanding of, psychopathology and the impact on modern-day societal perceptions.

- Early perceptions, e.g. ancient beliefs, demonology and treatments, exorcism rituals, cultural differences.
- Early biological explanations, including naturalistic, heredity and environment.
- Classifications, e.g. mania, melancholia.

The medical model

The Pox

To the English, it was the French Disease. To the French, it was the Italian Disease. To the Italians, it was the English Disease. To all of them, it was the Pox.

Today we know exactly what syphilis is: a four-stage, sexually transmitted disease caused by the bacterium *Treponema pallidum*, fatal if untreated. But until the end of the 19th century the cause was unknown. An Austrian psychiatrist, Richard von Krafft-Ebing, thought it was caused by a 'germ' and set out to prove it.

At a time when there were no tests, no ways of seeing the brain in living people, there was only one method Krafft-Ebing could use. A symptom of early syphilis is the presence of sores on the genitals. Krafft-Ebing harvested infectious material from these sores and injected it into patients who had symptoms of a mysterious mental disorder. He suspected that the same germ caused both the sores and the disorder. None of the patients with the mental disorder developed the sores, which could only mean one thing – they had already had the disease and now they were immune.

Krafft-Ebing was proved right when researchers were eventually able to observe the bacterium under a microscope. But he was right in a much bigger sense – he had proved that a mental disorder could be caused by a physical disease.

Specification terms

General paresis of the insane (GPI) Mental symptoms associated with the final (tertiary) stage of syphilis.

Medical model Mental disorders are seen as physical disorders with physical causes (e.g. brain disease) and should be treated by physical means (e.g. drugs).

Psychiatry A branch of medicine involving diagnosis and treatment of mental disorders. A psychiatrist is medically trained whereas a psychologist isn't.

Somatogenic hypothesis The view that mental or psychological symptoms are caused by physical dysfunctions of the body. Soma = body.

The medical (disease) model of mental disorders

The first truly scientific approach to treating mental disorders was the *medical model*. The basic assumption is that what we call *mental disorders* are in fact physical disorders. That is, the causes are physical and include brain injury, *neurochemical* disturbances, disease, etc. In other words mental disorders should be treated in the same way as physical disorders because the causes are the same.

The model also assumes that, even if the current state of our knowledge is unclear, further research will eventually uncover these physical causes. For instance, in *depression* the symptoms may be psychological but the cause is likely to be some disruption of the brain's neurochemistry, probably linked to *genes*.

A practitioner identifies symptoms and uses these to diagnose a disorder (a medical approach). It follows that the most effective treatment is also physical, usually drugs because they 'correct' the brain's faulty neurochemistry.

General paresis of the insane

In Victorian Britain people with mental disorders were mostly placed in large institutions called asylums. By the late 19th century, about 20% of all the men in asylums were being given the diagnosis of *general paresis of the insane* (GPI). Patients were usually in their 30s and 40s. Their symptoms included a staggering walk, weakness of the muscles and delusions of grandeur (e.g. believing they were a historically important person, or wealthy and powerful). Because there was no treatment inmates eventually died within days or months.

Noting the distribution of the disease, some practitioners suspected GPI was somehow linked with the sexually transmitted disease called syphilis. This turned out to be correct – GPI was the outcome of an untreated syphilis infection that had reached the central nervous system. Today we call it tertiary syphilis (or neurosyphilis). When the bacterium causing syphilis was treated with penicillin in the 1920s, GPI was all but wiped out.

Somatogenic hypothesis

The treatment of GPI marked a triumph for the medical approach to mental disorders. In this case psychological symptoms were shown to have a physical cause in the body (the brain and nervous system). A physical treatment was therefore required to remove the symptoms. This is the basis of the *somatogenic hypothesis* – somatogenic means 'of the body'.

The start of the 20th century saw a renewed interest in the *naturalistic explanation* that went back to the ancient Greeks (e.g. Hippocrates, see previous spread). In 1883, a German medical doctor called Emil Kraepelin realised that symptoms of mental disorders (just as with physical symptoms) occur together in clusters. He called these clusters *syndromes*. Once he had identified syndromes, he was then able to label them and create a system for classifying them. This was the basis of the *ICD* and *DSM* systems we covered on page 220.

Research inspired by the somatogenic approach focused on discovering physical treatments for mental disorders, such as drug treatments (see page 250).

Psychiatry

This is a branch of medicine that diagnoses and treats mental disorders. It is practised by *psychiatrists* who are medically-qualified doctors. *Psychiatry* therefore operates on assumptions that are somatogenic (see above). In contrast, psychologists who work in the field of *mental health* and illness are also highly qualified, but they are not medics and are much less likely to be tied to the somatogenic approach and are less likely to treat mental disorders using psychological therapies.

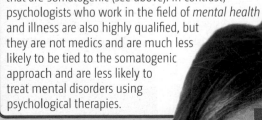

The medical model is very keen on labelling people.

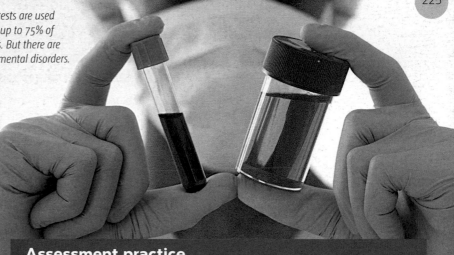

Blood and urine tests are used to help diagnose up to 75% of physical disorders. But there are no such tests for mental disorders.

Evaluation

Reduces stigma

One strength of the medical model is that it reduces the stigma associated with mental disorders.

Hippocrates believed people with mental disorders should not be held responsible for their behaviour. Viewing mental disorders as illnesses is arguably a relatively humane approach. It is not the patient's fault they are ill, any more than it would be if they had measles. Historically the alternatives saw the patient as guilty of something or otherwise morally defective.

Therefore, the medical model has a valuable aim – to avoid blame and just try to treat the patient.

Labelling

One weakness of the medical model is its enthusiasm for labelling people.

This is reflected in classification systems that are based on the medical approach (e.g. DSM and ICD). These systems allow a vast number of labels to be applied to patients with little understanding of why. Labelling has consequences for a patient. For example, people labelled with a mental disorder face discrimination in the jobs market.

This is ironic – the model has reduced the stigma of mental disorders, but at the same time its labelling of patients has made life more difficult for them.

Lack of validity

Another weakness of the model is that the parallel with physical disorders may not be valid.

Diagnosis of physical disorders is based on a well-established understanding of the causes of the disorder (called *aetiology*). For instance, a doctor who diagnoses *diabetes* can confirm this with a blood test because the physical causes of the disorder are well understood. This is not true of mental disorders. Despite decades of research, the physical causes of most mental disorders are still not properly understood.

This means there is no objective physical test that can confirm the psychological diagnosis for any mental disorder.

GET ACTIVE What's your humour?

Hippocrates' humour theory was somatogenic because it suggested mental disorders had a physical cause – an imbalance of bodily fluids. The details were wrong but the principle became the basis of the medical model. We each have a personality type based on our balance of humours. So, there are four types – choleric, melancholic, phlegmatic, sanguine. Which are you?

1. *Complete the online temperament test here: tinyurl.com/y7dmpdym*

2. *Does your result match your own view of yourself?*

3. *Special question for Harry Potter fans (and anyone else who fancies it): apparently, the four houses of Hogwarts are based on the four temperaments. How?*

Assessment practice

At the end of learning aim A you must write a report (see pages 215 and 228). This report must be related to a scenario or context. We have used a realistic (but not real) context.

You decide to introduce the volunteers at HelpingMinds to the medical model of psychopathology.

You think it is important that they appreciate how the model explains psychopathology in terms of physical causes because this is a view that is very central today.

Therefore, you trace the medical model from the understanding and treatment of general paresis through to the somatogenic hypothesis and the creation of psychiatry as a branch of medicine.

You know that the volunteers will want to assess the model, so you include its strengths and weaknesses as well. The volunteers and their friends have experienced stigma and labelling, so they are especially interested in these ideas.

A2.6 Learning aim A1 – Task 6

The second part of your report for learning aim A will be concerned with the origins of psychopathology – these are covered on the previous spread, this spread and the next spread.

This activity will help you practise the skills required to write the report in response to your scenario/context.

1. With reference to the medical model, **explain** how views of psychopathology have developed over time. (A.P2)

2. **Analyse** the historical development of psychopathology in terms of the medical model. (A.M1)

3. With reference to the medical model, **evaluate** how psychopathology has been viewed historically. (A.D1)

> You can see the assessment criteria and explanation of command terms on pages 228 and 229.

An issue to consider

The medical model encourages us to see people with mental health issues as 'patients'. What are the benefits and drawbacks of this?

Specification content

A2 Origins of psychopathology

Characteristics and traits of historical definitions, approaches to, and understanding of, psychopathology and the impact on modern-day societal perceptions.

- Medical or disease model, including general paresis, somatogenic hypotheses, psychiatry.

Asylum and community care models

Community care

People with mental disorders have historically been treated very poorly. For a long period they were ignored and neglected, left to fend for themselves in a world where most could not function. Later in history, they were perceived as a threat and therefore locked away and chained up for the safety of society. Very rarely were they ever helped to get better.

About 200 years ago this changed, as we discuss on this spread, and well into the 20th century, big institutions (asylums) were seen as the best places to treat people with serious mental disorder. Then, in the 1950s, new drugs were developed that helped to keep symptoms under control. This meant that many patients could be treated in more everyday environments such as their own homes.

Many asylums fell into disrepair as the 'community care' approach gradually took hold (including the one pictured above in Denbigh, Wales). Between 1955 and 2017 the number of places available in mental hospitals in England and Wales fell from 150,000 to 19,000 (which ironically means there is now a shortage).

Specification terms

Asylum A large institution in which people with mental (and physical) disorders were placed, sometimes for restraint and control but also to try to treat them.

Bethlem Hospital The first asylum in London, used to lock up people with mental disorders.

Community care model Promotes treatment of clients in homes (their own or residential), away from large impersonal institutions.

Milieu therapy Clients live within a respectful environment ('milieu') that is structured to provide therapy (e.g. learning social interaction skills).

Moral treatment 18th/19th-century movement promoting respectful and humane treatment in asylums to help people recover and be released.

Token economy A form of operant conditioning designed to increase desirable behaviour and decrease undesirable behaviour with the use of tokens. Individuals receive tokens immediately after displaying a desirable behaviour. The tokens are collected and later exchanged for a meaningful object or privilege.

Asylum and community care

The treatment of people with *mental disorders* moved from the ancient practices described on page 222 to something more modern – placing people together in huge institutions (*asylums*). This in turn eventually gave way to the *community care model* in the 20th century.

Bethlem Hospital

Bethlem Hospital, London was opened in 1547. It was the first institution of its kind in Europe. It was a place where the 'insane' were locked away (for public safety), with no attempt to treat or even care for them.

In the 18th century, Bethlem was given a nickname by the locals: *Bedlam*, a word we still use today for a place of chaos, madness and confusion. Inmates were usually confined at Bedlam until they died, when they were buried in a mass grave in Liverpool Street.

Philippe Pinel and moral treatment

Philippe Pinel, painted on the side of a building in Paris.

In the 1790s, Philippe Pinel was head of an asylum for men in Paris. His view was that people with mental disorders should be given respect and moral guidance (hence a *moral treatment*). Pinel viewed the hospital's inmates as ill rather than wicked. So, he removed their chains and allowed them to exercise. Many patients improved and several were released.

The moral treatment movement was supported in Britain by William Tuke, a Quaker and wealthy tea merchant. In 1796 he opened an asylum for the mentally ill in York (the 'York Retreat'). Patients were treated with kindness and respect, and could work, live and talk with each other.

Moral treatment received a boost in the UK in 1845 when the County Asylums Act was passed. Asylums had to be provided in every county in England and Wales and many took their lead from the York Retreat. New asylums were built in the countryside. The aim of moral treatment was not to keep inmates locked up for public safety but to make them better so they could be released.

Milieu therapy

'Milieu' is a French word which basically means 'social environment'. *Milieu therapy* is a comprehensive therapy because the client lives within the milieu. The client's environment is carefully structured so that everything that happens is therapeutic (i.e. it contributes towards the client's growth and development).

For example, clients learn and practise social interaction skills. This means they focus outwardly rather than withdrawing into themselves. They do so within an environment of mutual respect, cooperation and communication. The policies and 'rules' of the milieu are decided by therapists and clients together. Clients have the freedom to make their own decisions, but they also have to accept the responsibilities that come with that freedom.

Token economy (TE)

By the mid-20th century, the *behavioural approach* was dominant in psychology. *Behaviourists* set about applying principles of the approach to various practical situations, including treatment of mental disorders. *Token economy* was first used by Teodoro Ayllon and Nathan Azrin (1968) with patients who had been hospitalised with a mental disorder for an average of 16 years.

This treatment is based on *operant conditioning*, specifically the concept of *secondary reinforcement*. When an object is associated with a reinforcer, it can take on reinforcing properties itself. For instance, as we saw on page 52, a smoking-related cue (e.g. a lighter or ashtray) can become associated with the pleasure of smoking. When the smoker sees the lighter, they feel some of the rewarding pleasure associated with smoking – the lighter has become a secondary reinforcer.

In a TE, an object such as a plastic disc (the 'token') is given to a client whenever they perform a target behaviour (a desirable behaviour such as getting dressed). Tokens have no value in themselves but can be exchanged for a primary reinforcer, something with tangible value such as food. Ayllon and Azrin's patients improved *significantly* using this treatment.

A 'straitjacket'. A patient's arms were strapped to their body to restrain them. These devices were still being used in some institutions in the 1990s.

Evaluation

Supporting evidence

One strength of token economy is evidence showing it is effective.

Faith Dickerson *et al.* (2005) reviewed 13 studies of TEs used with chronic *schizophrenia* patients. Eleven studies found that TEs significantly benefitted patients. Target behaviours improved as a result of treatment, including self-care, social interaction and work activities. The greatest benefit was found in higher quality studies, suggesting effectiveness of TEs is real.

This shows that there is an effective treatment based on learning principles that can be applied in a community setting.

Lack of support

One weakness of milieu therapy is a lack of evidence showing it works.

Gordon Paul and Robert Lentz (1977) compared milieu therapy with TE and 'treatment-as-usual' (TAU). They *randomly allocated* 84 individuals with chronic schizophrenia to one of these three groups. TE was superior to milieu therapy on a number of measures, including time spent in hospital and amount of medication needed. In the TE group, 89.3% participants improved, compared with 46.4% in the milieu group. This trend continued in a six-month follow-up.

This shows that milieu therapy is an inferior treatment for chronic disorders and that TE is a better choice.

Ethical issues

One weakness of some therapies, such as token economy, is that there are *ethical issues*.

Such issues centre around control and manipulation of behaviour. TEs have been criticised for undermining patients' human rights. Patients have to 'earn' items and privileges that in other circumstances are considered theirs by right (their own property, social contact, etc.). The most obvious violations of patients' rights are now legally unacceptable.

This explains why token economies have fallen out of favour, despite evidence of their effectiveness.

Assessment practice

At the end of learning aim A you must write a report (see pages 215 and 228). This report must be related to a scenario or context. We have used a realistic (but not real) context.

You know the volunteers at HelpingMinds are interested in how psychopathology has been treated historically.

So you decide to include an explanation of the concepts of asylums and community care in the training session.

You start with the Bethlem Hospital, move on to Philippe Pinel's work in Paris and then explain two examples of treatments under the heading of 'community care'.

You include strengths and weaknesses to help with analysis and evaluation of historically recent treatments – milieu therapy and token economies. The obvious question the volunteers will want to address is, 'Do community care models work?'.

A2.7 Learning aim A1 – Task 7

The second part of your report for learning aim A will be concerned with the origins of psychopathology – these are covered on the previous two spreads and this spread.

This activity will help you practise the skills required to write the report in response to your scenario/context.

1. With reference to asylum and community care, **explain** how views of psychopathology have developed over time. (A.P2)

2. **Analyse** the historical development of psychopathology in terms of the concepts of asylum and community care. (A.M1)

3. With reference to the concepts of asylum and community care, **evaluate** how psychopathology has been viewed historically. (A.D1)

An issue to consider

Treating people in the community (home, small clinics) is common these days. What do you think are the benefits compared to treatment on a psychiatric ward in a big hospital?

Specification content

A2 Origins of psychopathology

Characteristics and traits of historical definitions, approaches to, and understanding of, psychopathology and the impact on modern-day societal perceptions.

● Asylum and community care models, including Bethlem hospital, Philippe Pinel, moral treatment, milieu therapy, token economy.

Learning aim A

Assessment guidance

Learning aim A assessment

For learning aim A you are required to produce a report (which can be written or presented as a poster, PowerPoint or in another form).

The report can only be completed after you have studied the content of learning aim A as it is a synoptic assessment (see facing page for an explanation).

You can, if you wish, combine this report with the report for learning aims B and C but you cannot submit more than two assessments for this unit and no learning aim can be subdivided.

Recommended assessment approach

The *Delivery Guide for Unit 6* states that your report (or presentation, poster, etc.) needs to:

- Explore ways in which psychopathology has been defined.
- Look at the changing perceptions of mental disorder.
- Explain how psychopathology has been treated.

Assignment briefs

The board supplies suggested assignment briefs which you can use – see *Unit 6 Authorised assignment brief for Learning aim A.*
Your centre can also devise their own assignment brief which should have a vocational scenario/context and a series of tasks to complete.

Vocational scenario	The task (from the assignment brief)
The *assignment brief* suggests that a scenario might involve writing a *literature review* related to the definitions for, perceptions of and attitudes towards mental disorders. The *Delivery Guide for Unit 6* notes that the report for Section A is likely to be more theoretical than other reports for this unit, though it also suggests that you could additionally use a case study.	You need to produce a detailed report that shows how understanding and perceptions of psychopathology have developed over time. Your report should include the following: • An **explanation** of the ways in which psychopathology is defined. (See pass criteria below.) • An **explanation** of how perceptions of psychopathology have developed over time. (See pass criteria below.) • An **analysis** and an **explanation** of the historical development of concepts of psychopathology. (See merit criteria below.) • An investigative literature review which **evaluates** how psychopathology has been viewed historically. (See distinction criteria below.)

Assessment information

Your final report will be awarded a Distinction (D), Merit (M), Pass (P), Near Pass (N) or Unclassified (U).

The specification provides criteria for each level as shown below.

Pass	Merit	Distinction
A.P1 EXPLAIN ways in which psychopathology is defined.		
A.P2 EXPLAIN how perceptions of psychopathology have developed over time.		
	A.M1 ANALYSE the historical development of the concept of psychopathology.	
		A.D1 EVALUATE how the concept of psychopathology has been viewed historically.

Marking factors The specification also provides the following information that an assessor will take into consideration when marking your assignment.

Marking factors	Pass	Merit	Distinction
Report is ...	... mostly accurate.	... detailed.	... comprehensive.
The ways psychopathology is defined and explained are ...	... identified.	... illustrated.	... explored.
Uses examples of approaches in psychopathology ...	... appropriate.	... a range.	... wide-ranging.
Discussion of origins of psychopathology from early to modern is ...	... included.	... explored.	... thorough and well-reasoned.
Critical thinking is applied to discussions ...	... sometimes personal views not evidence.	... some.	... considered.

The coursework is as much about the journey as getting there, so learn to enjoy getting there instead of focusing on the destination.

Self-review checklist

Writing a big report requires organisation and planning. You learned about time management as part of the unit on conducting psychological research (which is in our Year 1 'Certificate' book). Apply those skills to writing your report for this unit.

It is important to set yourself target dates at the outset.

It is also important to write at least two drafts.

First draft

Remember this is a *draft*. So you can write anything, just get thoughts on the page (see 'Blank screen syndrome' on page 259). But do not copy anything, even at this stage (see 'Plagiarism' on the right).

Date to complete first draft:	

	Date completed	Explain (A.P1)	Explain (A.P2)	Analyse (A.M1)	Evaluate (A.D1)
• In the first grey column enter the completion dates for each section of your report. • As you write each section tick the yellow boxes when you have explained, analysed and evaluated, as appropriate. Ignore the boxes that are crossed through.					
A1 Defining psychopathology					
Mental health and well-being			☒	☒	☒
Statistical definitions of psychopathology			☒	☒	☒
Approaches to defining psychopathology			☒	☒	☒
Classification systems			☒	☒	☒
A2 Origins of psychopathology					
Early perceptions				☒	☒
Early biological explanations				☒	☒
The medical model				☒	☒
Asylum and community care models				☒	☒
References compiled					

Second draft

The next step is to revise your first document. Below is a checklist of things to consider.

Date to complete second draft:	

	Date completed
I have checked that I have covered each of the five marking factors (grey column) in the table on the facing page.	
I have gone through and deleted any irrelevant material.	
I have checked that every point has some evidence to back it up.	
I have identified long sentences and rephrased them.	
I have checked that each paragraph deals with one idea.	
I have corrected any spelling mistakes.	
I have checked that each paragraph makes reference to the scenario/ context.	

Final draft

Read through your completed second draft to polish the report.

Date to complete final draft:	

Referencing

If you cite any research study or source (such as a website) you need to include this in a list of references at the end of your report.

The conventions for referencing are described on page 160.

Command terms used in this unit

The assessment criteria for learning aims A, B and C use the following command terms:

Analyse = A methodical and detailed examination, breaking down a topic.

Assess = Consider factors that apply to a specific situation, come to a conclusion.

Discuss = Identify and investigate all aspects of an issue or situation.

Evaluate = Consider strengths/weaknesses, come to a conclusion.

Explain = State and then justify or give an example.

Synoptic assessment

This assessment is synoptic. Synoptic refers to the ability to provide an overview of many different strands of information.

In your assessment you must demonstrate that you can identify and use effectively, in an integrated way, an appropriate selection of skills, techniques, concepts, theories and knowledge from across the whole sector as relevant to this task.

Plagiarism

Plagiarism means to use someone else's work without crediting the source. It means to steal and pass off the words (or ideas) of another as one's own. All the work submitted as your internal assessments must be your own.

We are lucky to have the internet at our fingertips when writing this book and we often cut and paste content into our notes – and it is very easy to forget we have done this. However, we know this can be easily checked and if we were found to have committed plagiarism in our book we would be accused of committing a crime and could be fined or receive a prison sentence for plagiarising someone else's work.

The same is true for you – it is tempting to use something written on a website or in this book and feel 'I can't say it as well as this' and therefore copy it exactly. You cannot do that unless the sentence is in quotes and attributed to the author.

We take great care to ensure that all of our sentences are our own. You must do the same or you will be disqualified from this exam.

Essential advice

Learners may not make repeated submissions of assignment evidence.

You may be offered a single retake opportunity using a new assignment. The retake may only be achieved at a Pass.

Under some conditions, and at your centre's discretion, you may be allowed to resubmit your original work in an improved form and will be given 15 days to do so.

Prenatal, biological and health factors

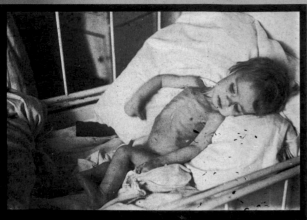

Hongerwinter

This is what the people of the Netherlands call the 'hunger winter' of 1944 to 1945 when the Nazis blocked food supplies to the part of the Netherlands they occupied in the Second World War.

Up to this point, the diet of people in the country had been reasonable. But that changed during the Hongerwinter. By April 1945 the average calorie intake was about 500 kcal per day – this was starvation level, and 22,000 people died as a result.

Women who were pregnant during this time had babies that were well below normal birth weight. Because the health of the population was being monitored, these babies were followed up until they became adults. Researchers found that they were twice as likely to develop schizophrenia as adults who had not been born at the height of the famine.

A study of survivors of the Great Chinese famine of 1959–1961 (which killed up to 45 million people) found similar results.

Specification terms

Learning difficulties A significantly reduced ability to understand new or complex information and to learn new skills.

Nature/nurture The question of whether behaviour is determined more by 'nature' (inherited and genetic factors) or 'nurture' (all influences after conception, e.g. experience). It is not a debate about whether one or the other is determining behaviour but about the contributions of each, as well as their interaction with each other.

Prenatal Before birth, when an embryo/foetus is developing in the womb.

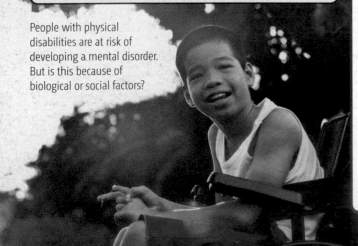

People with physical disabilities are at risk of developing a mental disorder. But is this because of biological or social factors?

Prenatal, biological and health factors

Prenatal factors

There are some factors that occur during *prenatal* development that have been related to the development of a mental disorder later in life.

Health A mother's general state of health has been linked to mental disorders in offspring. For example, people whose mothers have flu during pregnancy have an increased risk of *schizophrenia* in adulthood (Blomström *et al.* 2016). A similar link with schizophrenia has been found for maternal *diabetes* and infection of the mother by *toxoplasma gondii* (a parasite in cat faeces).

Stress during pregnancy may be the single most important influence on mental disorders in offspring and has been linked to *depression* (Schetter and Tanner 2012).

Diet A pregnant woman's diet may have an indirect effect because poor nutrition in pregnancy can cause low birth weight in her baby. Low birth weight has been linked to the later appearance of several mental disorders including schizophrenia (Rifkin *et al.* 1994). The effect depends on stage of pregnancy. A poor diet in the first trimester (three months) has the most negative outcomes.

Addiction Alcohol abuse during pregnancy may lead to *substance abuse* and depression in offspring during adolescence and early adulthood (even at low to moderate levels of use, Easey *et al.* 2019). Women who smoke during pregnancy may have babies with low birth weight, linked to mental disorders developed later. The same relationship exists for other drugs including heroin.

Genetic factors Some physical disorders (e.g. *cystic fibrosis*) are known to have a large *genetic* component. Adults with cystic fibrosis have a much increased risk of developing depression. Similar links with depression exist for several other genetic disorders. This could mean that genes for physical disorders play some role in the development of depression. Or more likely it means that genetic disorders make some people more vulnerable to depression (this is an example of the *nature/ nurture* interaction).

Biological and health factors

Short-term disorders Young people who contract *glandular fever* often become depressed until the infection lifts (White *et al.* 1998). Some research also indicates there may be a link between infection by the streptococcus bacterium in childhood and the development of *obsessive-compulsive disorder* later (Vogel 2018).

Measles can cause 'measles encephalitis'. This can occur if an unvaccinated child develops measles that infects the brain during the rash phase. Encephalitis means that the brain becomes inflamed and swells. This is potentially very dangerous, and 10–15% of patients die with a further 25% experiencing permanent brain damage resulting in deafness and/or intellectual retardation.

The encephalitis can cause further disorders. For example, Hashimoto Hiroshi *et al.* (2003) reported the case of a 46-year-old woman with measles encephalitis that recurred over a period of years. She had symptoms similar to schizophrenia, especially auditory *hallucinations* (voices), and *delusions* concerning bodily sensations (e.g. feelings of burning) as well as depression.

Long-term disorders Physical disability is a significant factor in depression, especially in females and older people. Follow-up studies of children with physical disabilities show that by the time they reach adolescence they have three times the risk of developing a mental disorder than people in the non-disabled population (Dekker *et al.* 2002). However, the reasons for this are probably not 'biological' and more to do with the social consequences of having a disability (e.g. social isolation, greater difficulty in accessing services).

People with *learning difficulties* often have *mental health* problems, in many cases more than one issue. According to Eric Emerson and Chris Hatton (2007), rates of mental disorder are *significantly* higher for young people with learning difficulties in 20 out of the 28 categories of ICD-10 (including schizophrenia, *anxiety disorders*, depression and *bipolar disorder*).

 GET ACTIVE Monitoring children's mental health

You are a qualified nurse who is part of a team of health visitors. Your role is to support families with a recently-born child, and to monitor the child's development, health and well-being.

You first visit each family not long before the birth. What you find out during that visit helps to prioritise the families that need more support. Your visit will only last about 30 minutes so you need to gather a lot of information in a short time. Your team decides that a checklist will help you to identify the factors that might negatively affect the child's well-being.

Use the information on this spread to create the checklist.

Include all the relevant prenatal, biological and health factors that could affect the child's well-being.

You could also include a severity rating instead of just 'yes' or 'no' tickboxes (e.g. a scale of 1 to 5).

Women who smoke during pregnancy often have babies of abnormally low birth weight. These babies may well have mental disorders later on. Therefore low birth weight is directly linked to mental disorders and drug use is indirectly linked.

Evaluation

Plausible mechanism

One strength is that there is a likely biological explanation for the greater risk of mental disorders.

Many of the factors outlined on this spread are linked to mental disorders because they affect the body's stress response (see page 46). When the mother or young child experiences stress, the hormone *cortisol* is produced. Cortisol may have damaging effects on the developing brain, interfering with normal processes. Stress also suppresses the *immune system*, which may lead to inflammation of brain tissues.

Therefore, it is through the stress response that prenatal, biological and health factors may be linked to mental disorders.

Complex interactions

One weakness of identifying individual causes of mental disorders is that it is too simplistic.

According to Mark Fraser (1997), combinations of factors are much stronger predictors of mental disorders than any individual factor on its own. For example, women who take one drug during pregnancy (e.g. alcohol) may well take others (e.g. nicotine), and may also have a poor diet and experience high levels of stress. Therefore, it is difficult to assess which of these factors matters most. It is far more sensible to assume that they all do, by interacting with each other and with other factors as well.

This suggests that full understanding and treatment of mental disorders is only possible by considering the complex ways in which their causes interact.

Issues of causation

Another weakness is that most 'causes' are actually just *correlations*.

Anita Thapar and Michael Rutter (2009) point out that there is huge debate over whether prenatal, biological and health factors actually *cause* mental disorders. For example, people with learning difficulties are relatively more likely to become depressed. But this is not inevitable and depends on additional factors such as the severity of the learning difficulty. So, having a learning difficulty is definitely linked to depression but may not cause it.

Therefore, we should be extremely cautious about claiming that these factors cause mental disorders when at most they increase the individual's risk.

Assessment practice

At the end of learning aims B and C you must write:

A report that examines:

- **Causal factors that can contribute to mental health disorders.**
- **The different types of mental disorder and their symptoms.**
- **The approaches used by professionals in treating different mental disorders and their specific roles in diagnosing and treating individuals.**

This report must be related to a scenario or context. We have used a realistic (but not real) context.

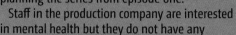

A TV production company wants to make a major new series about mental health in the UK in the 21st century. You have been asked to be the psychological consultant, involved in planning the series from episode one.

Staff in the production company are interested in mental health but they do not have any expertise. So, you have to produce a detailed report, explaining the academic basis of each programme.

You start with an in-depth look at the many factors that cause mental disorders – prenatal, biological and health factors.

B1.1 Learning aim B1 – Task 1

The first part of your report for learning aims B and C will be concerned with causal factors that can contribute to mental disorders – these are covered on this spread and the next two spreads.

1. **Discuss** prenatal/biological/health factors that may lead to mental disorders in individuals. (B.P3)
2. **Assess** prenatal/biological/health factors that may contribute to mental disorders. (B.M2)
3. **Evaluate** the impact of prenatal/biological/health factors that may contribute to mental disorders. (B.D2)

An issue to consider

Which of the factors on this spread could be explained by the damage caused by the body's stress response?

Specification content

B1 Causal factors associated with mental disorders

Types and impact of primary causes that can be used to understand risk for later psychopathology:

- Prenatal factors, including environmental factors (e.g. health, diet, addiction) and genetic factors.
- Biological and health factors, including short-term disorders (e.g. measles) and long-term disorders (e.g. disabilities, learning difficulties).

Family and environmental factors

Adverse Childhood Experiences – ACES

Not so ACE

The *Adverse childhood experiences* (ACE) study was set up by Vincent Felitti and Robert Anda in 1993. Felitti originally wanted to know why so many people dropped out of an obesity prevention programme he was running. In 1985 he interviewed nearly 300 of the ex-participants to find out why they had left. He was stunned to discover that many of them had been sexually abused when they were children.

Childhood abuse is one of the adverse childhood experiences that Felitti thought could potentially cause mental disorders in later life. So, he and Anda set up a study (ACE) to find out the long-term impact of childhood experiences.

One of their lasting contributions has been the development of the ACEs score. Most people experience one ACE in their lives, but a substantial number experience multiple ACEs. So Felitti and Anda assigned one point to each category of ACEs that participants had experienced up to the age of 18. They found that 43% of participants had an ACE score of two or more. Only one-third had no ACEs at all (Felitti 1993).

The researchers were then able to link ACE scores to later mental and physical disorders and have been following up participants ever since.

Specification terms

Attachment A close two-way emotional bond between two individuals in which each individual sees the other as essential for their own emotional security. Attachment is important for safety and food (mother and infant stay close together) and independence (a secure attachment enables a child to be more adventurous).

Life events Significant and relatively infrequent experiences/occasions in people's lives that cause stress. They are stressful because we have to expend psychological energy coping with changed circumstances.

Parenting style A representation of the degree to which parents respond to their children's needs/personalities and the degree to which they make demands on their children.

Urbanicity – crowded, polluted, noisy city environments cause stress and have been related to schizophrenia.

Family and environmental factors

Family factors

Home life and parenting styles Many psychologists believe *parenting style* has two main elements. *Parental care* refers to a child's perception that their parents express warmth, affection and concern. *Parental control* refers to the child's perception that parents are overprotective, interfering and authoritarian. The key feature of the two elements is how the child *perceives* them. This may be very different from 'reality' or from what parents intend. High parental control and low parental care are associated with *depression* and *eating disorders* in later life (Parker and Gladstone 1996).

Attachments Some childhood *attachment* bonds are *insecure*, meaning that the child's main caregiver does not provide reliable emotional support (see page 172 for detailed discussion). These insecure attachments are also associated with depression and eating disorders in adulthood (Lee and Hankin 2009). Insecure attachment also plays a role in *personality disorders* – for instance an *avoidant attachment* type is a risk factor for adult *antisocial personality disorder* (Steptoe 2011).

Transitions and significant life events Transitions within the family include *significant changes* from one state to another, such as separation/divorce and arrival of a new family member. Transitions are therefore significant *life events* (see page 38) within the context of the family. Effects on adolescents of a transition to a single-parent or 'blended' family are generally negative and linked to *substance abuse* and depression (Langenkamp and Frisco 2008). But, as usual, the effects depend on other factors. For instance, divorce has much less impact on *mental health* if the relationship between mother and adolescent is emotionally close and thus provides support (Garber *et al.* 1997).

Abuse Research overwhelmingly shows a strong association between childhood experiences of abuse and adult mental disorders. Abuse can be sexual, physical and/or emotional and also includes physical and emotional neglect. The ACE study (see left) clearly shows that abused and neglected children are at least twice as likely to experience depression, substance use, anxiety disorders and self-harm in adolescence and adulthood. How severe the mental disorder is depends on when the abuse began and how long it lasted.

Environmental factors

Housing There is some evidence that poor housing conditions can negatively affect mental health. Uncomfortable and dangerous housing (e.g. damp, structural problems) can damage physical health (e.g. can cause lung problems). It also creates *stress*, which becomes more damaging to mental health over time. The worse the conditions are, the greater the stress and the more severe the mental disorder (Evans 2003).

Children who have lived in temporary housing for more than a year are more likely than other children to have symptoms of depression (Harker 2006). Housing is linked to the wider influences of poverty and location. Poor housing may reflect the neglect of an area where amenities are non-existent and antisocial behaviour is rife.

Access to amenities and funding This refers to whether facilities are available to allow daily tasks such as shopping, recreational activities, getting medical treatment, or even enjoying a garden or other green space. People who cannot access such amenities experience stress, which threatens their mental health. This is most likely in rural areas where lack of public transport makes it much harder to travel to places where amenities are available. It is also a risk in urban areas where provision has been neglected. People with physical disabilities and *learning difficulties* might also find it harder to access amenities because of lack of support.

Amenities and services require money which may be reduced by governments through cuts in public spending. This includes services dedicated to improving mental health. For example, the Royal College of Psychiatrists warned in 2018 that the money available to mental health services in England and Wales was lower than it had been in 2012.

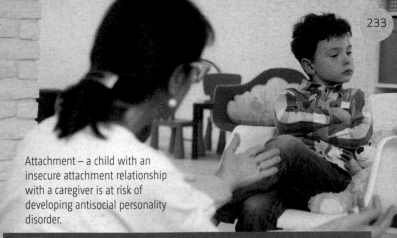

GET ACTIVE Monitoring children's mental health

Imagine you are a social worker whose role is to support families through difficult times and especially to safeguard the well-being of children.

One of your cases is a family with multiple problems. There are two children under the age of five and you are concerned that issues within the family will affect their mental health. There are also environmental factors placing stress on the family, making the children more 'at risk'. Your manager has asked you for a brief report outlining your concerns.

1. *Write a report of two paragraphs (about 150 words each) – one paragraph about causal factors within the family and another about environment-related issues.*

   Include a specific example for each factor that concerns you.

2. *Your manager wants you to give your opinion about whether the children might be affected in the long term. Write two or three sentences on this.*

Attachment – a child with an insecure attachment relationship with a caregiver is at risk of developing antisocial personality disorder.

Evaluation

Long-term effects

One strength is that research has supported the view that family and environmental factors do have long-term effects.

For example, psychologists have conducted studies which follow families and individuals over several years. These are necessary to see how experiences in childhood translate into mental disorders in adolescence or adulthood. Some of these studies were reviewed by Scott Weich *et al.* (2009). They found that abuse of children within the family strongly predicted *clinical depression* in adolescence and adulthood for both males and females.

These *longitudinal studies* mean we can identify which factors really could be causes of mental disorders and which are just risk factors.

Role of psychological processes

One weakness is that the impact of family and environmental factors depends on psychological processes.

For example, according to Peter Kinderman *et al.* (2013), family-related factors and life events cause depression when the individual blames themselves, otherwise the impact is minimal. Therefore, how the person perceives or thinks about family and environmental factors influences how these factors affect mental health. This partly explains why individuals differ so much in their responses to the same factors. Some develop severe mental disorders and others are affected by family/environmental factors to a much lesser extent.

This shows that the links between causal factors and mental disorders are highly complex and not yet fully understood.

Associated variables

Another weakness is that family and environmental factors interact with other associated variables that generally occur together.

This makes it hard to assess the separate impacts of these factors on mental health. For example, early research showed that children from non-traditional families (single-parent, blended) had worse mental health outcomes as adults than children from traditional families (Cherlin and Furstenberg 1994). However, later studies controlled the effects of associated variables (poverty, housing, parental mental health) and found there were no differences (Golombok 2015).

This is a major challenge for researchers to design studies that can account for the effects of associated variables and reveal the true relationships between daily/environmental factors and mental disorders.

Assessment practice

At the end of learning aims B and C you must write a report (see pages 231 and 258). This report must be related to a scenario or context. We have used a realistic (but not real) context.

Episode two of the TV series continues the investigation of causal factors, moving on to family and the environment.

Your report will provide detailed information about what the factors are and how they might affect mental disorders.

But just as with episode one, you will also provide an evaluation of the factors in terms of their strengths and weaknesses.

The production company furthermore wants you to make an assessment and draw a conclusion about the importance of family and environmental factors.

B1.2 Learning aim B1 – Task 2

The first part of your report for learning aims B and C will be concerned with causal factors that can contribute to mental disorders – these are covered on the previous spread, this spread and the next spread.

This activity will help you practise the skills required to write the report in response to your scenario/context.

1. **Discuss** family/environmental factors that may lead to mental disorders in individuals. (B.P3)

2. **Assess** family/environmental factors that may contribute to mental disorders. (B.M2)

3. **Evaluate** the impact of family/environmental factors that may contribute to mental disorders. (B.D2)

> You can see an explanation of the command terms on page 229 and the assessment criteria on page 258.

An issue to consider

What do the family/environmental factors on this spread and the prenatal/biological factors on the previous spread tell us about nature and nurture?

Specification content

B1 Causal factors associated with mental disorders

Types and impact of primary causes that can be used to understand risk for later psychopathology:

● Family factors, e.g. home life, parenting styles, attachments, transitions, significant life events, abuse.

● Environmental, e.g. housing, location, access to amenities, funding.

Social, political and cultural factors

Culture and Cotard's syndrome

Yasir Abbasi is a British Muslim with family origins in South Asia. She is also a psychiatrist, a medical doctor who specialises in diagnosing people with mental disorders. In 2016 she described one of her earliest cases, of a young girl from a similar background to herself.

The girl was diagnosed as having severe depression with *Cotard's syndrome*, a bizarre delusion in which the person believes they are dead. The girl was being treated on a hospital ward for people with mental disorders. She wanted Abbasi to let her use the internet so she could see her own grave.

The girl's family believed she was possessed by a demon and therefore wanted her to be treated by a traditional spiritual healer. Eventually a compromise was reached and the girl continued to get hospital treatment and recovered.

As Abbasi comments, 'This was my first exposure, as a psychiatry trainee, to cultural issues entwined with mental health problems in England... I learned it was important to make sure we listened to and respected all views before coming to a decision.'

Source: *The Guardian* (2016)

Specification terms

Ethnicity Socially-defined grouping of people based mainly on physical features (e.g. skin colour) but not based on genuine biological differences.

Gender The label of being male or female.

Social class Broadly an individual's socioeconomic status (e.g. working, middle, upper class), partly determined by their income and level of education.

Social norm Something that is standard, usual or typical of a social group (small or large group of people).

'I have learned not to be ashamed or embarrassed by my mental health problems' (*Mind* 2019).

Social, political and cultural factors

Social and political factors

Social class, education and income *Social class* (or *socioeconomic status*) is judged partly in terms of education level and income of self and/or parents. In the early 2000s, children from households in the bottom 20% of income were three times more likely to develop a mental disorder than those in the top 20% (Green *et al.* 2005). A decade later, the gap had widened to 4.5 times (Gutman *et al.* 2015). This unequal distribution of mental disorders is known as a *social gradient*.

People with low educational attainment (e.g. few or no qualifications) are more at risk of developing a range of *mental disorders* such as *depression* (Mirowsky and Ross 2003). This is true regardless of job status or income.

Policies Government policies can influence the *mental health* of the population because they determine spending priorities. The *Health and Social Care Act* (2012) enshrined the concept of 'no health without mental health'. Mental health was given the same priority as physical health ('parity of esteem'). In 2015, the *Five Year Forward View for Mental Health* included improved access to psychological therapies. Mental health was included as part of the national measure of well-being. This means mental health has to be taken into account when the government decides its priorities and creates policies.

Services and strategies The services that can be provided for people with mental disorders is constrained by funding. An extra £2 billion was allocated to fund mental health services in the five years after 2018. However, the King's Fund organisation (2018) argue that much of this money is not reaching front-line services and is being used to compensate for spending cuts elsewhere. This is thought to hit child and adolescent services particularly hard. Therefore, progress towards 'parity of esteem' has been very slow.

Cultural factors

Beliefs, values and social norms may influence attitudes towards mental disorders and therefore affect how people with mental health problems describe their symptoms to a practitioner. For example, British Bangladeshis often describe their physical symptoms but not their emotional ones, unless questioned further. This would affect any diagnosis.

A practitioner unfamiliar with *cultural* differences may overlook symptoms and make the wrong diagnosis. For instance, a Western clinician may not realise that a British Bangladeshi patient describing a 'headache' or 'pains all over' is actually describing their experience of depression and not a physical disorder.

There are also cultural differences in views about shame that may affect mental health. A group of charities looked at the beliefs of a community in north-west London with South Asian origins (Time to Change 2010). A common view was that mental disorder reflects badly on the whole family. Families protect individual members from 'community gossip' but also isolate individual members from social contact. Viewing mental disorders as shameful has serious consequences, e.g. a lack of sympathy and support, failure to get treatment or treatment delay, resulting in a worsening of symptoms.

Gender In most Western cultures, *gender role stereotypes* suggest that men should not show psychological 'weakness'. This attitude has discouraged many men from expressing their emotions, talking about their mental state and seeking help for a range of mental disorders. One of the consequences has been a very large *gender* difference in cases of suicide.

Gender stereotypes also negatively impact on women's mental health. Western standards of feminine beauty are involved in the development of *eating disorders*. The media presents an ideal body shape that most women cannot live up to without damaging their mental health.

Ethnicity also has negative effects. For example, refugees and asylum seekers, who are the target of prejudice due to their *ethnicity*, experience social isolation, limited access to services, and so on. This creates *stress* and creates or worsens mental disorders.

An example of this is the prevalence of *schizophrenia* in British African-Caribbean people, who are diagnosed with the disorder nine times more often than white people (Fearon *et al.* 2006). This could be due to either *stereotype*-influenced diagnosis or ethnic-related stress.

Evaluation

Wider focus

One strength of considering social and cultural causes is that they undoubtedly contribute to the development of many mental disorders.

Anthony Marsella (2003) argues that we should view 'society as a patient'. A person's mental health is strongly affected by factors in the external environment. For example, refugees and migrants experience racism and discrimination, people in lower socioeconomic groups experience stress linked to job loss and poor housing. Social changes have been accompanied by very large increases in depression and anxiety.

This focus provides a useful balance to the narrow view that mental disorders are mostly caused by individual characteristics.

Interacting factors

One weakness is that the effects of social and cultural factors are complex.

Many of these factors interact with each other and with other influences. For example, the biological and psychological characteristics of an individual partly determine whether they will develop a mental disorder. Social factors (e.g. class) and culture-related influences (e.g. attitudes towards gender or ethnicity) may trigger an existing predisposition (e.g. *genetic*) or worsen the effects of stressors (e.g. *life events*).

This means that identifying one or two factors as directly causing mental disorders is a gross oversimplification which limits our understanding of the true relationship with social and cultural factors.

Social drift or social causation?

Another weakness is that social class differences may not be a cause of mental disorders but an outcome.

Many people experience mental disorders as a result of important life events (e.g. relationship breakdown, job loss, eviction from home). These people may end up in neighbourhoods that are stressful, socioeconomically deprived and with limited access to services. Their children may miss out on educational opportunities. Therefore, the experience of mental disorder causes a 'drift' into lower socioeconomic status.

This is a controversial argument and not all psychologists agree, but it does highlight the fact that social factors are not always the cause of mental disorders – they may be effects.

GET ACTIVE Charity report

You work for a small mental health charity in a part of the country that has high levels of deprivation and many families of South Asian origin. You conducted some interviews with people in the area to find out how issues such as class, education, gender, racism and stress affect their mental health. You have to prepare an 'executive summary' for the charity's board of directors. This is a very short report which summarises the findings of the interviews and makes recommendations for using the charity's resources.

Prepare the summary by:

1. Using the information on this spread to outline the main mental health challenges faced by the different communities in the area.

2. Making recommendations about how the charity can address these challenges.

Assessment practice

At the end of learning aims B and C you must write a report (see pages 231 and 258). This report must be related to a scenario or context. We have used a realistic (but not real) context.

Episode three of the TV series discusses the social, political and cultural factors involved in mental disorders.

In the programme, you want to explore the impact of people's background on their mental health.

So, you consider differences in class, culture, gender and ethnicity, as well as the effect of government policies.

You decide to include some carefully-selected statistics and examples to illustrate some of these factors.

However, as the relationship between these factors and mental disorders is complex, it will be important to provide an assessment and evaluation.

B1.3 Learning aim B1 – Task 3

The first part of your report for learning aims B and C will be concerned with causal factors that can contribute to mental disorders – these are covered on the previous two spreads and this spread.

This activity will help you practise the skills required to write the report in response to your scenario/context.

1. **Discuss** social/political/cultural factors that may lead to mental disorders in individuals. (B.P3)
2. **Assess** social/political/cultural factors that may contribute to mental disorders. (B.M2)
3. **Evaluate** the impact of social/political/cultural factors that may contribute to mental disorders. (B.D2)

Living in deprived areas with limited access to services is linked to poor mental health. But what is the direction of cause and effect – social drift or social causation?

An issue to consider

Which two social/political factors would you regard as the most critical factors associated with mental disorders?

Specification content

B1 Causal factors associated with mental disorders

Types and impact of primary causes that can be used to understand risk for later psychopathology:

● Social and political factors, e.g. social class, education, income, policies, services and strategies.
● Cultural factors, e.g. beliefs, values and social norms, attitudes towards gender and ethnicity.

Personality disorders / Self-injury

Professor Marsha Linehan

Marsha Linehan is a Professor of Psychology at the University of Washington in Seattle, USA.

By the time she was 17, Linehan self-harmed repeatedly. She was admitted to a hospital for people with mental disorders and incorrectly diagnosed with schizophrenia. She spent two years there, described in her notes as 'one of the most disturbed patients in the hospital'.

Linehan then began her academic career in psychology, starting with evening classes. She created a therapy to help people who – like herself – wanted to die, the very worst cases ('supersuicidal', she called them). It was only when she was 68 that she publicly revealed she had been diagnosed with a personality disorder. She decided to do this because it brought hope to others (she said 'I cannot die a coward').

Linehan has an unusual perspective as both a psychologist and someone with a personality disorder herself. She recognises that she has been manipulative, needy, dangerously impulsive and self-destructive. But she has vastly increased our understanding of personality disorders, saved lives and these days she says, 'I'm a very happy person now'.

Source: Mental Healthy

Specification terms

Non-suicidal self-injury disorder (NSSID) A disorder in which a person intends to damage their body tissues (e.g. by cutting) but does not intend to kill themselves.

Personality disorder (PD) An enduring collection of inflexible behaviour patterns that disrupt normal interactions, therefore causing problems in relationships.

Someone with a Cluster A personality disorder takes serious offence very easily and is not prepared to 'forgive and forget'.

Personality disorders

A *personality disorder* (PD) is a condition that affects the whole personality, i.e. it relates to behaviour patterns that are enduring and affect the whole person and the way they interact with the world, and especially with other people.

Someone with a PD has an inflexible personality which means they respond in very similar but inappropriate ways in different situations (whereas most of us adapt our behaviour to suit the situation).

PD often emerges in early childhood and may be due to inherited factors or social experiences, but sometimes is only apparent later in life. It may continue for the rest of the person's life unless treated. In most cases (but not all), the disorder brings the person a great deal of distress and difficulty functioning in everyday life.

Key symptoms The category of PD appears in both *DSM*-5 and *ICD*-10 (see descriptions of these diagnostic systems on page 220). DSM-5 identifies the following four defining features of PD:

1. **Distorted thinking patterns** The exact pattern of thinking depends on the specific type of PD, but can include distrusting others, thinking both well and badly of others (e.g. thinking they are perfect one day and the worst example of humanity the next), 'black-and-white' thinking, perceiving others to be either 'for you' or 'against you'.

2. **Problematic emotional responses** Some people with a PD may experience their own emotions intensely and are very sensitive to the emotions of others. Other people with a PD have no emotional responses, even in situations where most people would feel them. People with a PD do not regulate their emotions, or adapt their responses to the situation.

3. **Impulse control difficulties** Most people can control their impulses (e.g. controlling anger) and match it to the situation. In PD, impulse control is either over-regulated or under-regulated. Some people with a PD are tightly controlled, so they never try new things or express views or emotions. Others cannot inhibit their impulses even when the impulses are socially unacceptable.

4. **Interpersonal difficulties** The three issues outlined above cause difficulties in most relationships. It is unusual for someone with a PD to maintain a meaningful and rewarding relationship because they are unable to adapt their behaviour.

Types of PD

Both DSM-5 and ICD-10 distinguish ten or more different types of PD. They are sometimes grouped into three clusters based on similarities:

Cluster A: suspicious types One example of this type of PD is *paranoid personality disorder* (DSM-5 and ICD-10) The main characteristics are distrust and suspicion of other people. The person with a PD assumes others wish them harm and so they interpret neutral or friendly behaviour as hostile. They may be pathologically jealous in relationships. They insist their rights have priority, hold grudges and may attack anyone they perceive as a threat.

Cluster B: emotional and impulsive types DSM-5 includes *antisocial personality disorder* in this category. Someone with antisocial PD does not consider the feelings of others. They will lie, cheat, manipulate and use violence in order to deny other people their rights. A lack of self-control means they act impulsively without planning ahead or considering the consequences (which can include being sacked, losing relationships, causing accidents and being imprisoned). People with antisocial PD usually do not feel remorse (although they are capable of faking it).

Cluster C: anxious types One example of this is *avoidant personality disorder* (DSM-5 and ICD-10). People with avoidant PD are inhibited, feel inadequate, inferior and anxious, and are highly sensitive to criticism (which they perceive everywhere). They believe others dislike them, deservedly so because they are not worthy. Despite this, they have a strong desire to be liked. Because they constantly fear rejection they avoid social situations and generally shun people, so they have few opportunities to improve their social skills. This means they often come across to others as shy, withdrawn or aloof.

Non-suicidal self-injury

Non-suicidal self-injury disorder (NSSID) is perhaps more commonly known as self-harming, i.e. intentionally inflicting damage to one's own body tissue without intention of suicide.

There are several ways in which someone with NSSID will self-harm, including burning, severe scratching, punching, biting and preventing wounds from healing. The most common form is cutting, which occurs in up to 70% of cases and is used more often by females than males (who generally turn to burning and punching). Self-harming is more common in adolescents than in adults. Up to 18% of adolescents may self-harm at any one time, and 5.9% of adults (Wester *et al.* 2016).

The person's intentions are central to the disorder. Self-harming is deliberate and intended to cause damage.

Key symptoms NSSID is not currently a disorder in ICD-10. It has been included in DSM-5, but only as a condition requiring further study. Key features from DSM-5 include:

- **Self-harming behaviour** In using their chosen method, the self-harmer intends to cause damage to their body's tissues (bruising, bleeding, scarring). But the damage is not intended to be life-threatening because the person is not attempting suicide. For a diagnosis of NSSID, self-harming behaviour must occur on at least five days in the past year.

- **Specific expectations** The person carries out the self-harming behaviour to, for example, relieve negative feelings (e.g. *stress*) or to resolve a problem in a relationship.

- **Not socially sanctioned** Any behaviour that is socially or culturally accepted cannot be counted as self-harm (so picking at a scab, biting nails, getting tattooed or pierced are not self-harming behaviours).

- **Distress/functioning** The person experiences significant personal distress or has difficulty functioning in everyday life.

NSSID and suicide

There are two main differences between NSSID and suicide.

First, unlike people who attempt suicide, people who harm themselves do not intend to die. In fact, part of the diagnosis of NSSID is that self-harm is a coping mechanism. Self-harming increases positive feelings and reduces negative ones.

Second, this means that the methods that self-harmers use are less drastic than those used in attempted suicides. The damage caused by methods such as cutting and punching are not life-threatening. For example, self-harmers who cut themselves almost always avoid blood vessels.

On the other hand, there are ways in which NSSID and suicide/attempted suicide are closely related. People who self-harm are at greater risk of later suicide. NSSID is a significant predictor of suicidal behaviour. Between 50% and 80% of self-harmers also attempt suicide (Kerr *et al.* 2010). Also, although self-harmers do not intend to kill themselves, they do have persistent thoughts about suicide (suicidal ideation).

This is Elaine Davidson, at the time of this picture the 'most pierced person in the world' (6,725 piercings).

This might seem excessive in our culture, but it is not self-harm.

Assessment practice

At the end of learning aims B and C you must write a report (see pages 231 and 258). This report must be related to a scenario or context. We have used a realistic (but not real) context.

For episode four of the TV series you take a slightly different approach. You now want to look in detail at some specific mental disorders.

You decide there are six disorders that are highly relevant to life at the start of the 21st century. The first two are personality disorders and self-injury.

At this stage, the production company just want you to give a detailed description of the types and characteristics of these disorders. It is especially important to be clear about personality disorders because there are several types of these.

You will look in greater detail at one of the six disorders in the last episode.

B2.4 Learning aim B2 – Task 4

The second part of your report for learning aims B and C will be concerned with the different types of mental disorder and their symptoms – these are covered on this spread and the next two spreads.

This activity will help you practise the skills required to write the report in response to your scenario/context.

1. **Explain** the characteristics of personality disorders. (B.P4)
2. **Explain** the characteristics of non-suicidal self-injury disorder. (B.P4)

An issue to consider

What are the benefits and drawbacks to diagnosing a condition such as a personality disorder or non-suicidal self-injury? Consider it from the individual's perspective and society's perspective.

Specification content

B2 Types and characteristics of mental disorders
- Personality disorders, including suspicious, emotional and impulsive, anxious.
- Non-suicidal self-injury.

GET ACTIVE Reality TV

Imagine you are a researcher on a reality TV programme. You have to find 12 people to take part in a series, in which all the contestants live together. The producers want the programme to avoid psychologically damaging those involved. Your job is to stop two types of applicant getting through – vulnerable people who are prone to self-harming, and people who see taking part as a chance to control others.

1. For each type, list the characteristics you would look out for.

2. How would you assess each applicant?

3. Write an email to the producers explaining how you intend to proceed.

Psychotic disorders / Anxiety disorders and OCD

Joey Ramone

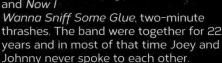

Joey, Dee Dee, Tommy, Johnny. The Ramones launched punk rock in New York City in 1974.

They were famous for songs like *Blitzkrieg Bop* and *Now I Wanna Sniff Some Glue*, two-minute thrashes. The band were together for 22 years and in most of that time Joey and Johnny never spoke to each other.

Joey was the singer and he first had symptoms of schizophrenia when he was 20. He started to hear voices that weren't there. This frightened him so much he began to distrust everyone, including his mother. He became increasingly angry and hostile, until one day he threatened his mother with a knife.

Joey admitted himself to a psychiatric hospital in New York. He stayed for a month and was diagnosed with paranoid schizophrenia. Although he recovered enough to leave hospital, form a band, launch punk rock and have a critically acclaimed career, Joey struggled with his symptoms all his life. He died in 2001 of prostate cancer, aged 55.

Specification terms

Agorophobia An irrational fear of leaving home and going out in public.

Anxiety disorder A group of mental disorders characterised by levels of fear and apprehension disproportionate to any threat.

Obsessive-compulsive disorder An anxiety disorder characterised by obsessions and/or compulsive behaviour.

Phobia An anxiety disorder characterised by an irrational fear of an object or situation. The central symptom is intense anxiety when encountering the phobic stimulus.

Psychosis Severe mental disorder where a person's thought processes and emotions are so impaired that they have lost contact with external reality.

Schizophrenia spectrum A set of severe psychotic disorders sharing certain symptoms including delusions, hallucinations and disordered thinking.

Social phobia Extreme fear of being judged or even looked at by other people.

Specific phobia Fear is linked to a particular class of objects such as spiders or heights.

Schizophrenia and other psychotic disorders

Schizophrenia, and psychotic disorders in general, are characterised by the fact that a person has difficulty distinguishing between what is real and what isn't, often experiencing *hallucinations* and *delusions*. *Psychosis* is contrasted with other disorders such as *anxiety disorders* (facing page) and *depression* (next spread). In these disorders there is much more contact with reality.

Schizophrenia

Schizophrenia affects about 1% of the world's population, is more common in men than women and tends to develop in early adulthood. About 25% of people with schizophrenia have a single episode and recover completely. Another 25% never recover, and the other 50% experience a cycle of recurrent episodes followed by improvement.

The spectrum concept was introduced in *DSM-5*. It recognises that schizophrenia is one disorder that shares symptoms with several other psychotic disorders (e.g. *schizoaffective disorder*). Therefore, there are similarities and overlaps between related disorders, as well as differences.

Diagnosis and key symptoms For a diagnosis of schizophrenia using DSM-5, a person must have at least two of the four key symptoms below. One of these has to be either delusions, hallucinations or disorganised thought/speech.

1. **Thought insertion/withdrawal/broadcast** The person believes their thoughts are not their own, but are placed there by an external source. Or they may feel their thoughts are being taken out of their minds against their will, or broadcast for everyone to hear.
2. **Hallucinations** These are clear perceptions the person experiences without any external stimulus. For example, they might hear voices when no one else is present. The voice is experienced as coming from outside the person and is different from their own 'inner thoughts' (it could be commenting on the person's behaviour or appearance, often critically). Hallucinations can be auditory, visual, olfactory (smell) or somatosensory (bodily sensations).
3. **Delusions** These are irrational beliefs that are not changed by conflicting evidence. A person who has a delusion may behave in ways that seem rational to themselves but which are bizarre to others.
4. **Disorganised thought/speech** Determined from how the person uses language. For example, they may skip between unrelated ideas in the same sentence (*derailment*). Or they may string words together randomly (*word salad*). They may even make up new words, usually by blending existing ones (*neologisms*). This use of language means it is hard to follow the person's train of thought, making communication very difficult.

For a diagnosis to be made, symptoms must have been present for a significant amount of time in a one-month period. There has to be continuous disturbance of everyday functioning for at least six months.

ICD-10 distinguishes between positive and negative symptoms. Positive symptoms are experiences that occur in schizophrenia but not usually in most people's existence, e.g. delusions and hallucinations. Negative symptoms involve a loss or reduction of some usual ability or behaviour, e.g. a lack of motivation or interest (*avolition*).

Other psychotic disorders

DSM-5 includes *catatonia* as an 'other psychotic disorder' whereas ICD-10 includes this as a subtype of schizophrenia.

People diagnosed with catatonia experience disturbances of movement. This could be *catalepsy*, an extreme form of immobility so the person hardly moves at all for hours or even days. Or they allow themselves to be placed in a posture which they maintain for long periods (*waxy flexibility*).

Schizophrenia is often wrongly described as 'split personality' or 'multiple personality'. *Multiple personality disorder* is a very different disorder.

Anxiety disorders

Anxiety disorders are characterised by an excessive amount of worry or unease such that it prevents a person from functioning normally (e.g. going to work, having satisfying interpersonal relationships, etc.).

Phobia

A *phobia* is an irrational fear of an object, place or situation. The fear is irrational because it is out of proportion to the danger involved. Phobia is classified as an anxiety disorder because the main response to the stimulus is *anxiety*. DSM-5 and ICD-10 recognise three major types of phobia – *specific phobias*, *social phobia* and *agoraphobia*.

Key symptoms All phobias share several features:

- **Behavioural features** A common response is panic (e.g. crying, running away, freezing). Another is avoidance. Someone with a phobia will go to a lot of effort to avoid the stimulus (e.g. staying out of rooms or buildings). This seriously interferes with everyday activities, education, etc.

- **Emotional features** The main emotional response is anxiety, basically a *stress* response (unpleasant state of high *physiological* arousal). The happens even just thinking about the phobic stimulus (or something associated with it).

- **Cognitive features** A phobia is often accompanied by *cognitive distortions* (e.g. perceiving ear lobes as disgusting or believing that the aeroplane you are flying on is bound to crash).

Specific phobias are irrational fears of highly specific objects, situations or activities. They include specific animals, heights, enclosed spaces, belly buttons, public toilets, flying, injections... (the list is lengthy).

Social phobia is an extreme fear of being scrutinised by other people. A person with social phobia is afraid of being looked at, spoken to or evaluated in public. They go to extreme lengths to avoid social situations and, when in social situations, experience hand tremors, feeling sick or even a panic attack.

Agoraphobia is an intense fear of leaving home and venturing into the outside world. People with agoraphobia are anxious in crowds and public places, even if other people are taking no notice of them.

Obsessive-compulsive disorder (OCD)

In the past, OCD was classed as an anxiety disorder but both DSM-5 and ICD-10 now place it in a separate category. However, anxiety is still considered the central feature of OCD. Anxiety can arise from both *obsessions* (persistent thoughts) and/or *compulsions* (behaviours that are repeated over and over again). Compulsions are a response to obsessions and the person believes the compulsions will reduce anxiety. Most but not all individuals experience both obsessions and compulsions.

Obsessions are unpleasant, intrusive and unwanted thoughts. They include common themes such as ideas ('Germs are everywhere'), doubts ('I've forgotten to turn the tap off'), impulses ('I just want to swear') and images (brief mental pictures that are usually sexual or violent). The obsessions are irrational and the person is aware of this.

Compulsions are repetitive behaviours (e.g. handwashing, checking, putting things in order). They are not enjoyable or useful, but have 'rules' that the person has to follow rigidly. Engaging in compulsive behaviours reduces the anxiety associated with obsessive thoughts. However, compulsions are excessive and do not resolve the issues behind the obsessive thoughts.

Acrophobia

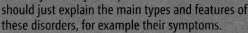
An issue to consider

People often have the wrong idea of what schizophrenia is. How has your own view changed after reading this?

Specification content

B2 Types and characteristics of mental disorders

- Schizophrenia spectrum and other psychotic disorders.
- Phobias or anxiety disorders, including specific phobia, social phobia, agoraphobia, obsessive-compulsive disorder (OCD).

GET ACTIVE Classifying phobias

Because the number of potential specific phobias is so vast psychologists have tried to group them together. One suggestion is that there are four categories – animals, natural environments, blood/injection/injury, situations.

1. Use these as headings for a table. Write down some examples under each heading.

2. Go to tinyurl.com/yegwsm5 to find out their scientific names (you don't have to remember them).

Depression / Eating disorders

Famous people

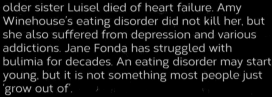

Diana Princess of Wales,
Lady Gaga,
Karen Carpenter,
Amy Winehouse,
Jane Fonda,
Allegra Versace...

There is a very long list of famous women who have had an eating disorder. Eliana Ramos was a model from Uruguay who died aged 18 from a heart attack associated with anorexia. This was just a few months after her older sister Luisel died of heart failure. Amy Winehouse's eating disorder did not kill her, but she also suffered from depression and various addictions. Jane Fonda has struggled with bulimia for decades. An eating disorder may start young, but it is not something most people just 'grow out of'.

Many people experience more than one at a time. This is *co-morbidity*, the ways in which disorders frequently occur together. Depression is unsurprisingly co-morbid with many other disorders, because having almost any kind of mental disorder can cause a person to become depressed.

Specification terms

Bipolar disorder A mood disorder in which the person switches between a depressed state and a manic state (high energy, euphoria, excitement).

Clinical depression Low mood beyond everyday sadness, severe enough to be diagnosed as a disorder.

Depressive disorder A mental disorder characterised by low mood and low energy.

Eating disorders Mental disorders in which the main feature is disruption of feeding behaviour with restriction of energy intake (anorexia) or control of body weight through repeated bingeing and purging (bulimia).

A person with bipolar disorder is optimistic in the manic state ('half full') and pessimistic in the depressed state ('half empty').

Depression

Depression is referred to as *depressive disorder* in both *DSM*-5 and *ICD*-10. In the latter it is included under the category of mood disorders (i.e. emotional disorders) which further contains *bipolar disorder* (or bipolar affective disorder, 'affect' meaning emotion).

Almost everyone experiences feelings of sadness from time to time. But these do not usually interfere with everyday life and recovery is quick. When these feelings become severe and persistent (accompanied by other symptoms), then the person may be experiencing *clinical depression* (i.e. it has been diagnosed as a *mental disorder*).

Depressive disorder

About 20% of us will experience clinical depression at some point in our lives. It is diagnosed twice as often in women as in men, and found in all cultures. Although classified as a mood disorder, depression also affects behaviour, thinking and the body.

Key symptoms

ICD-10 identifies mild, moderate and severe depression. The three key symptoms are listed below. Mild depression is diagnosed if at least two of these symptoms are present, plus two/three others described in the 'other' list. Moderate depression is diagnosed if five or six symptoms are present and severe for seven or more.

- **Depressed mood** Low mood most of the day, which doesn't vary from day to day. Indicated by either subjective report (e.g. feels sad, hopeless) or observation made by others (e.g. appears tearful).
- **Loss of interest and enjoyment** Markedly diminished interest or pleasure in all, or almost all, activities most of the day, nearly every day (as indicated by either subjective account or observation).
- **Reduced energy levels** A feeling of lethargy which may make a person withdraw from work, education and social life. In extreme cases this can be so severe that the person cannot get out of bed.

The other symptoms include:

- **Bodily symptoms** Appetite changes (increase or decrease), leading to weight gain or loss (more than 5% in one month). Sleep patterns may be disrupted so the person sleeps a lot more or less than usual.
- **Cognitive symptoms** People with depression experience negative thoughts. They blame themselves, or feel guilty or unworthy. They have a pessimistic outlook on life, focusing on negative experiences. Poor concentration and a lack of *self-esteem* are common in depression. Some people may have recurrent thoughts of death or suicide (although without a specific plan).

Bipolar disorder

In bipolar disorder, a person switches between two extreme mood (affective) states – *mania* and depression.

Manic episode A person's mood is euphoric and excited. Their energy and activity levels increase dramatically. They may have over-ambitious plans and ideas. But they lose judgement, which can sometimes lead them into taking risks (for example, spending and debt). Some people eat and sleep very little during a manic episode, which can last between two weeks and four or five months.

Depressive episode An individual usually recovers completely from a manic episode before eventually shifting into a depressive state (as outlined above). This usually lasts longer than the manic episode (about six months) and may be mild, moderate or severe. *DSM*-5 recognises a form of bipolar disorder called *rapid cycling*, in which the person switches between manic and depressive episodes at least four times in 12 months.

ICD-10 diagnosis When a client sees a practitioner, they may be presenting symptoms of mania or depression. This means it is not unusual for a client to be first diagnosed with depression and then only later with bipolar disorder if they experience an episode of mania (perhaps years later). For a diagnosis, episodes of mania and depression must be repeated (i.e. at least two of each). People differ a great deal in the length of episodes, how often they occur and the length of time between them.

GET ACTIVE Identifying eating disorders

Schools and colleges must appoint a member of staff to be the 'special educational needs coordinator' (SENCO). Imagine you are a SENCO and one of your roles is to help teachers support students who have mental health difficulties. A teacher has emailed you because she is concerned that one of her students may have an eating disorder. The teacher doesn't feel she knows enough about eating disorders to be sure. She would like you to outline what she should be looking for.

Write an email to the teacher briefly explaining the signs and symptoms of eating disorders likely to be found in a student.

Body size and shape are distorted in anorexia, and this significantly affects how some individuals value themselves.

Eating disorders

The term *eating disorders* is a general label given to a range of syndromes in which disrupted feeding/eating is the main feature. Both ICD-10 and DSM-5 recognise two major types – *anorexia nervosa* and *bulimia nervosa*.

Anorexia nervosa (AN)

AN overwhelmingly affects females. Between 1.7% and 3.6% of women are diagnosed with AN at some point in their lives, compared with 0.1% of men (Dahlgren *et al.* 2017). AN has the highest mortality rate of all mental disorders. For women with AN, their probability of death is almost six times greater than it is for women without AN (Arcelus *et al.* 2011).

Key symptoms

- **Restriction of energy intake** Someone with AN limits their calorie intake so much that their body weight is significantly low, defined by ICD-10 as 'maintained at least 15% below expected... or BMI (body mass index) is 17.5 or less'.

- **Fear of weight gain/interfering behaviours** The person feels 'intense fear of gaining weight or becoming fat' (DSM-5). This leads to behaviours such as self-induced vomiting (purging) or excessive exercise. It also involves constant dieting, which may have a ritualistic element (e.g. eating food of only one colour).

- **Disturbed experience of body weight/shape** The person has a distorted perception of their own body weight or shape. How they feel about themselves (*self-esteem*) depends excessively on their weight and/or shape. Their perception is so disturbed that they may fail to realise how seriously low their weight is.

ICD-10 diagnosis All of the above symptoms are required for a diagnosis. However, there is a fourth symptom in ICD-10 which is highly controversial. The individual must experience disruption of their hormones. In females this shows itself as *amenorrhoea* (absence of periods) and in males as 'loss of sexual interest and potency'. This is controversial because it is *gender-biased* (and was dropped from DSM-5).

Bulimia nervosa (BN)

BN is less common than AN, with about 1–1.5% of the population diagnosed at any one time (Hail and Le Grange 2018). As with AN, mortality rates are relatively high but the gender gap is narrower, with a higher proportion of males diagnosed than for AN.

Key symptoms

- **Preoccupation with food** Someone with BN thinks about eating a lot and experiences strong cravings for food. When they lose control of their resistance, they embark on a binge in which a much larger amount of food is consumed in a shorter period of time than usual (e.g. eating a whole pack of biscuits).

- **Control of body weight** The person tries to control their eating but overcompensates. They may use self-induced vomiting, appetite-lowering drugs, excessive exercise or starvation. Because of the repeated binging and purging, the person maintains a fairly stable body weight (although usually on the low side). This is why weight loss is not part of the diagnosis of BN.

- **Fear of fatness** People with BN have a dread of becoming fat. Therefore, the individual will set a minimum weight to prevent this, but their threshold is usually below a healthy weight.

ICD-10 diagnosis All of the above symptoms are required for a diagnosis. The practitioner should be aware that BN is often a sequel to AN. Someone with AN may appear to recover, perhaps over a long period of time. They gain weight and their periods return. But they become trapped in a cycle of overeating and vomiting in order to maintain their body weight.

Psychodynamic therapy

In learning aim C1 you are required to consider approaches to the treatment of one disorder – we have focused on depression throughout C1 except for behavioural therapies.

Sigmund Freud
(1856–1939)

Unleash your creativity

There is a technique described on this spread that writers use to help them 'warm up' or 'unblock' their minds. It is called *free association* and Sigmund Freud used it to understand his clients' unconscious minds. They would speak their thoughts out loud, but this is a written version.

Here's what to do if you want to give it a go:

Write down everything that comes into your mind. Don't worry about spelling or grammar or even meaning – it doesn't have to make sense at this stage. Don't try to edit or censor your thoughts – in this activity you are definitely writing for yourself, you probably wouldn't want to show it to anyone else. The key thing is to get your thoughts down on paper as quickly and 'purely' as possible.

Give yourself a time limit and set an alarm. Once the time is up, you could go back and correct spellings, etc. Read through what you've written. Although it might seem a bit nonsensical, can you spot any thread that runs through it? Is there an idea or thought that connects each sentence with the next?

Specification terms

Dream analysis A client free associates around images from a dream as the analyst offers interpretations about what the images really (unconsciously) mean.

Free association A psychodynamic technique in which a client speaks their thoughts out loud without altering them and the analyst makes connections between the thoughts.

Psychodynamic therapy An approach to treatment of mental disorders that assumes that the causes of psychopathology are hidden in the unconscious mind and must be made conscious so they can be worked through.

Transference A client transfers their feelings of love and hate for their parents/others onto the analyst.

Freud's psychodynamic therapy

On page 218 we looked briefly at Freud's approach to understanding mental disorders (*psychopathology*). He based his treatment on the idea that the causes of mental disturbance are hidden from the person, in their *unconscious*.

The unconscious mind

The unconscious mind is the part of the mind we are unaware of but which powerfully influences our behaviour and personality. Memories of loss and anger in childhood are too disturbing to be recalled, so they are hidden away in the unconscious – this is called *repression*, an active process of forgetting. We are not aware of these memories, but they continue to affect us, resulting in mental disorders such as *depression* and *anxiety*.

Psychoanalysis aims to bring these repressed memories back to the surface (into consciousness) where a client can recognise and deal with them. There are three main techniques used to do this.

Free association

Psychoanalysis is known as a 'talking therapy' for good reason. A client is encouraged to speak their thoughts out loud without altering or censoring them. They express any thought that comes to them, no matter how irrelevant or trivial it might seem. This is valuable because, without knowing it, the client is expressing thoughts that are connected (i.e. 'associated'). The more freely they do this the better, thus *free association*.

For instance, a client might talk for hours about their childhood before mentioning an event that made them feel angry or sad, a parent leaving perhaps. This key piece of material might help to unlock or make sense of everything else the client has said. The job of the analyst is to listen carefully to the client's thoughts and identify the associations between them. This will give the analyst insight into the unconscious memories that underlie the associations.

Freud saw the analyst as an 'archaeologist of the mind', someone who digs into history and exposes it. As the client continues to talk, the analyst offers conclusions (interpretations) about what is causing the client's problems. Because this is likely to be painful, it is natural for the client to disagree. She or he might then avoid talking about their parents, for example – but what the client doesn't say is just as interesting to the analyst as what they do say.

Transference

As the therapy progresses, *transference* may occur. The client's feelings about, for example, his or her parents are hard for them to accept. So, they transfer them onto the analyst. These feelings can be very powerful.

To begin with, transferred feelings are usually positive, so the client feels intense emotional connection to the analyst (as they felt towards a much-loved parent). But later in the transference process these feelings gradually become negative. The client behaves towards the analyst as if they are someone they despise (e.g. a hated parent).

Transference can hinder therapy, because the client might become withdrawn and stop saying what comes into their mind. But part of the therapy involves working through transferred feelings rather than ignoring them. The analyst has to guard against transferring their own strong feelings onto the client. This is *countertransference*.

Dream analysis and interpretation

The source of the client's mental disorder is in the unconscious mind. But dreams offer a way of gaining access to the unconscious. The dreams we have (e.g. the images in them) express what is in the unconscious but in a symbolic form. The dream you can describe to your friends is called the *manifest content*. This disguises the real meaning of the dream, which is called the *latent content*.

Dream analysis reverses this process – the analyst removes the disguise by interpreting the symbols, revealing the true meaning of the dream. This can be done through free association. For instance, perhaps the client dreamed about a queen. The client talks around the topic of 'queen' and the analyst offers several different interpretations of what this might mean (e.g. the queen represents the client's mother). In discussing the analyst's interpretations, the client's responses become part of the process – how did he or she react to each suggestion?

Evaluation

Research evidence

One strength of Freud's therapy is that it can be effective.

Peter Fonagy (2015) *randomly allocated* 129 individuals with depression to either a psychodynamic treatment group or a standard treatment group (CBT plus medication). Treatment lasted 18 months for both groups. At a follow-up two years after the end of treatment, Fonagy found that the psychodynamic treatment group showed *significant* decreases in symptoms of *depression*. In fact, 44% were so improved that they no longer met the diagnostic criteria for depression. This compared with 10% in the standard treatment group.

Therefore, there is some research evidence that Freud's therapy can help improve symptoms in the long term.

Depends on client

One weakness of the therapy is that it only appears to benefit a certain 'type' of client.

William Schofield (1964) interviewed 377 psychodynamic therapists about their 'ideal client'. He coined the acronym YAVIS to describe these clients. Psychodynamic therapy is most likely to benefit people who are 'youthful, attractive, verbal, intelligent and successful'. Therefore, people who do not match these categories are unlikely to benefit. For example, given what we know about the nature of the 'talking therapy' (e.g. free association), clients who are not easily able to express what they are thinking are unlikely to improve after treatment.

Therefore, Freud's therapy is a limited and narrow approach to treating mental disorders.

Long-term commitment

Another weakness is that psychodynamic therapy is a long-term and expensive commitment.

A therapist and client must rake over the same ground repeatedly, to get more clarity on the unconscious causes of the client's disorder. This was confirmed in a study by Volker Tschuschke *et al.* (2007) of long-term psychodynamic treatment in Germany. A total of 450 clients were treated by 28 very experienced therapists for two years. The longer the treatment took the better the outcomes (i.e. improved symptoms).

This shows that Freud's therapy is not a 'quick fix' and may only benefit clients who are prepared to commit to a lengthy and costly process.

Youthful, attractive, verbal, intelligent, successful? Maybe. If so, then psychodynamic treatment might work for them.

GET ACTIVE 'I have a dream...'

Perhaps you've seen those books or websites about how to interpret your dreams. They tell you what symbols really mean. But dream interpretation in Freud's approach is not 'one size fits all'. The meanings of symbols that you dream about depend on what you associate with them. So, try this.

1. *You need to remember a dream. Write one down as soon as you wake up, in as much detail as possible.*

2. *Break up the dream into four or five main elements.*

3. *Free associate for each element for 30 seconds each. Record yourself, play it back and write it down.*

4. *Can you see any connections within the passages? Are they helping you to work out what the latent content of the dream is?*

Lying down with the therapist just out of sight frees a client to speak their thoughts.

Assessment practice

At the end of learning aims B and C you must write a report (see pages 231 and 258). This report must be related to a scenario or context. We have used a realistic (but not real) context.

The UK government has set up a commission to improve access to NHS treatments for young people with mental disorders. The Prime Minister has asked you to provide psychological expertise.

You will make a presentation to government ministers and the head of NHS mental health services. This will be a detailed explanation and evaluation of the main treatments provided by the NHS.

You plan to start the presentation with the psychodynamic therapy. You make another executive decision – you will choose one mental disorder to illustrate all the treatments.

C1.7 Learning aim C1 – Task 7

The third part of your report for learning aims B and C will be concerned with treatments for different mental disorders – these are covered on this spread and the next five spreads.

This activity will help you practise the skills required to write the report in response to your scenario/context.

1. **Explain** the psychodynamic therapy as a treatment for **one** mental disorder. (C.P5)

2. **Evaluate** the importance of the psychodynamic therapy as a treatment for **one** mental disorder. (C.D3)

An issue to consider

What do you see as Freud's most important contribution to psychopathology?

Specification content

C1 Approaches to the treatment of mental disorders

Characteristics of approaches and methods used in the treatment of mental disorders.

● Psychodynamic therapy, including Freud, e.g. free association, transference, dream analysis.

Behavioural therapies

Phobias at work

If you were offered your dream job, would you accept it if it meant facing your biggest fear? If you had a fear of heights, would you work in a tall building? If you were afraid of social spaces, would you work in a city?

Rohit is intensely afraid of speaking in public, but he works as an IT consultant and part of his job involves giving presentations. This is a big struggle as he experiences huge anxiety before and during them. He sometimes has to take days off work to recover. His greatest fear is looking stupid in front of everyone. Rohit's career has suffered because he has avoided applying for similar jobs, even though he is otherwise an excellent consultant.

Maya is a stage manager for a major theatre company. But she is *acrophobic* – she has an extreme fear of heights. It makes her job very difficult because she has to climb ladders, lighting rigs and scaffolds. Like Rohit, she manages to disguise her fear so that nobody really notices. But the cost is high because she feels terrible a lot of the time in a job she loves.

Both stories have happy endings. Rohit and Maya undertook one of the therapies described on this spread and overcame their phobias. But their experience is surprisingly common.

(Based on a number of case studies.)

Behavioural therapies

Behavioural therapy is based on the principles of *learning theory* – learning new responses through *conditioning*.

Systematic desensitisation (SD) and exposure therapy

If a *phobia* can be learned through conditioning then it can be unlearned through *counterconditioning*. *Systematic desensitisation* (SD) is a therapy based on this idea. This is where learning a new response (relaxation) to the phobic stimulus (e.g. dog) replaces the previously learned response (fear/*anxiety*). This works because of *reciprocal inhibition*. It is not possible to experience fear and relaxation at the same time – one emotion inhibits the other.

SD has three phases. First an *anxiety hierarchy* is constructed by the client and therapist. This is a list of situations from least to most anxiety-producing (e.g. from looking at a picture of a dog all the way up to being in a roomful of dogs). Second, *relaxation training* teaches the client to relax deeply, perhaps through breathing exercises. The final stage is *exposure* where the client works through the anxiety hierarchy (from the bottom) while using relaxation techniques.

Flooding

Flooding is also based on conditioning. There is no build-up using a hierarchy. Instead the client is immediately exposed to the phobic stimulus (e.g. a roomful of dogs). The client is flooded with anxiety but, as they cannot escape, the anxiety eventually subsides. This is *extinction* – the learned fear response is extinguished (disappears) because the CS (e.g. a dog) is encountered without the UCS (e.g. pain of being bitten). This may take place over a number of long sessions.

Behaviour modification (BM)

Behaviour modification aims to change behaviour (modify it) using principles of *operant conditioning* and *positive* and *negative reinforcement*.

Behaviour analysis At the beginning of therapy, a therapist assesses the client to discover the exact *environmental* stimuli that have caused (and maintain) his or her current behaviour. This is called *behaviour analysis*, looking at past experiences of positive and negative reinforcements.

Take the example of a *depressed* client who has lost his or her job. The behavioural approach suggests that depression happens because of fewer positive reinforcements. Losing your job leads to a loss of many rewarding daily experiences (meeting people, financial rewards). Withdrawing from social interaction maintains symptoms through negative reinforcement because the client feels relief at not interacting socially. They are trapped in a vicious circle of feeling low, avoiding interaction, reduced positive reinforcement and feeling even lower.

Daily diary The aim of BM is to break this vicious circle. Clients keep a daily diary to track their activities and note the link between low activity and low mood. They identify and plan enjoyable activities, especially ones involving relationships. Activities are scheduled a week at a time to provide realistic, specific and measurable goals to positively reinforce social behaviour.

Shaping *Response shaping* rewards behaviours that get closer and closer to the desired target behaviour. For example, a goal of 'go to the pub with a group of friends' is broken down into a series of steps (start with 'phone one friend to arrange a date'). Each step is rewarded as it is achieved, 'shaping' the behaviour in the desired direction.

Behavioural self-control training (BSCT)

In BSCT, an individual consciously decides to exert control over their own behaviour. This disrupts the 'automatic' nature of many learned behaviours, including those underlying substance abuse. For example, an individual makes themselves aware of the cues that can trigger cravings (e.g. for alcohol) or they learn strategies to deliberately refuse unwanted drinks.

Specification terms

Aversion therapy is covered in Unit 3, page 88.

Behaviour analysis A therapist's assessment of a client to discover what stimuli have caused and maintain his or her current behaviour (e.g. past positive and negative reinforcements).

Behaviour modification (BM) The use of operant conditioning techniques to change the frequency of desired behaviours.

Behavioural self-control training (BSCT) A form of training in which a client decides to deliberately take charge of their own behaviour.

Behavioural therapy Any treatment for mental disorders based on the principles of learning theory.

Conditioning Means 'learning', includes operant and classical conditioning.

Counterconditioning Being taught a new association that is the opposite of the original association, thus removing the original association.

Extinction When a conditioned stimulus (CS) and an unconditioned stimulus (UCS) have not been paired for a while, the CS ceases to elicit the conditioned response (CR).

GET ACTIVE Your own anxiety hierarchy

You may not suffer from a phobia but perhaps you do have a fear of something (heights, for example, or perhaps you're a bit wary of snakes, dogs, whatever). You can get a useful insight into systematic desensitisation by creating your own anxiety hierarchy.

1. *Thinking of your own fear (or just any common phobia), decide on the target behaviour. What is the goal of therapy? Perhaps it's to stand on top of a tall building without being afraid to approach the edge. Or to stroke a dog, or pick up a snake.*

2. *What is the first step in the hierarchy – that is, the least scary situation? Perhaps it involves a photo or a written description.*

3. *Now think of five or six more situations, each one a bit more scary than the last, ending with the target behaviour.*

If the cause of a phobia is not tackled, then the symptoms could just reappear later. A fear of dogs might resurface as a fear of cats.

Evaluation

Research support

One strength of behavioural therapies is evidence that behaviour modification is effective.

David Richards *et al.* (2016) compared CBT with a form of behaviour modification called behavioural activation (BA). They *randomly allocated* clients with depression to the two treatments. CBT was provided by experienced therapists, but BA was provided by less experienced 'junior mental health workers'. Despite this, BA was just as effective as CBT. There were no *significant* differences in outcomes between the two therapies after 12 months.

This suggests that behaviour modification is a desirable alternative to treat depression as it is more effective and also simpler and cheaper than CBT.

Wide application

Another strength of behavioural therapies is that they suit a range of clients.

This is mainly because clients do not have to reflect on their thought processes (which is required in many other therapies). This benefits people with *learning difficulties* for example, who may have trouble understanding the requirements of other therapies. Behavioural therapies on the other hand are relatively straightforward because they aim to change behaviour rather than thinking. Behaviours are more specific and easier to identify ('speak every day to someone on the phone') than thought processes ('write down your irrational thoughts').

This means that behavioural therapies can bring relief from symptoms of depression and *anxiety disorders* to people who do not benefit from other therapies.

Symptom substitution

One weakness is that behavioural therapies focus only on removing symptoms.

These therapies do not tackle the root causes of mental disorders, such as childhood experiences, past trauma, irrational thoughts, etc. So, the chances are that symptoms will reappear later. They could take another form, so one symptom is simply substituted by another. The client has short-term relief only and the disorder itself remains, requiring future further treatment, adding to costs financially and in terms of human misery.

Therefore, it seems that there is more to treating a mental disorder than just temporarily removing symptoms – the causes need to be dealt with too.

Assessment practice

At the end of learning aims B and C you must write a report (see pages 231 and 258). This report must be related to a scenario or context. We have used a realistic (but not real) context.

You plan to move on to behavioural therapy in your presentation. The Secretary to the commission reminds you that your explanation must be fairly detailed, even though there are many behavioural therapies.

You also need to give an evaluation of the therapy in terms of its strengths and weaknesses. The commission members are hoping you will come to a conclusion about the usefulness of these therapies.

C1.8 Learning aim C1 – Task 8

The third part of your report for learning aims B and C will be concerned with the treatments for different mental disorders – these are covered on the previous spread, this spread and the next four spreads.

This activity will help you practise the skills required to write the report in response to your scenario/context.

1. **Explain one or more** behavioural therapies as a treatment for **one** mental disorder. (C.P5)

2. **Evaluate** behavioural therapy as a treatment for **one** mental disorder. (C.D3)

You can see an explanation of the command terms on page 229 and the assessment criteria on page 258.

An issue to consider

Is it enough for a therapy just to focus on symptoms of a disorder? Are other therapies better at dealing with underlying causes?

Specification terms

Flooding A behavioural therapy in which a phobic client is exposed to an extreme form of a phobic stimulus in order to reduce anxiety triggered by that stimulus.

Reciprocal inhibition In exposure therapy, a client cannot experience fear and relaxation at the same time (they inhibit each other).

Response shaping A process of modifying behaviour by reinforcing successive approximations to a desired behaviour.

Systematic desensitisation (SD) and exposure therapy A behavioural therapy designed to reduce an unwanted response, such as anxiety, to a stimulus. SD involves drawing up a hierarchy of a client's anxiety-provoking situations, teaching the client to relax, and then exposing them to anxiety-creating situations.

Specification content

C1 Approaches to the treatment of mental disorders

Characteristics of approaches and methods used in the treatment of mental disorders.

● Behavioural therapies, e.g. conditioning, behaviour modification, behaviour analysis, extinction, flooding, counterconditioning, systematic desensitisation, exposure therapy, reciprocal inhibition, aversion therapy (covered in Unit 3, page 88), functional analysis, response shaping, behavioural self-control.

Cognitive therapies

Arguing with myself

One of the therapies on this spread encourages clients to argue with themselves.

The idea is that if you have an irrational thought, you should not welcome or entertain it because that is what makes you feel bad (anxious or depressed). Instead you should dispute the thought by arguing with yourself. Here are some ways to dispute (silently, or out loud is fine).

Scientific dispute: 'So, you think you're going to fail that exam in three months' time? How do you know that's going to happen? Have you failed it before? No, you haven't. Is it too late to do anything about it? No, it isn't because it's not for three months. What are you worrying about?'

Functional dispute: 'OK, so you're worried you didn't do very well in the exams you sat last week. Is there anything you can do about it? Is thinking about it making you feel better or worse?'

Logical dispute: 'So, you think you're going to fail everything? Does that even make sense? Just because you feel you did badly in one exam, does it follow that you'll do badly in all of them?'

Specification terms

Acceptance and commitment therapy (ACT) A client stops controlling their thoughts and feelings and becomes involved in meaningful life activities.

Cognitive behavioural therapy (CBT) A method for treating mental disorders based on both cognitive and behavioural techniques. From the cognitive viewpoint the therapy aims to deal with thinking, such as challenging irrational thoughts. The therapy also includes behavioural techniques such as skills training and using reinforcement.

Cognitive therapy A treatment for psychological disorders that focuses on replacing negative irrational thoughts/beliefs with positive rational ones.

Mindfulness-based cognitive therapy (MBCT) Version of CBT incorporating mindfulness techniques such as guided meditation.

Rational emotive behaviour therapy (REBT) Involves identifying irrational thoughts/beliefs/ feelings and challenging them through argument and confrontation (disputing).

Cognitive therapies

Cognitive therapies are based on the *cognitive approach* in psychology, so they focus on what a person is thinking. When a person has a mental disorder the assumption is that it is due to irrational thinking. The pathway to recovery is to challenge the irrational thoughts.

Rational emotive behaviour therapy (REBT)

Albert Ellis (1962) proposed one of the most influential cognitive therapies, *rational emotive behaviour therapy*.

Identifying irrational thoughts The starting point for the therapist and client is to identify irrational thoughts/feelings/beliefs. Examples include *utopianism* (life should always be fair), *'I-can't-stand-it-itis'* (if something doesn't go perfectly it's a disaster) and *musterbation* ('I must be perfect, I must succeed, I must be the most attractive'). A client holds these beliefs rigidly but can never live up to them, so they are bound to feel depressed.

Challenging irrational thoughts The therapist then challenges the client's irrational beliefs, using various techniques such as *disputing*. The therapist is confrontational, passionate and argumentative ('How do you know that?' or 'What's your proof?'). This is because disputing isn't just a cognitive exercise – it must engage emotions as well.

Emotion REBT was initially called *rational therapy*, and then Ellis added the E because he recognised that the problems were *emotional*. Therefore, for example, disputing is confrontational to engage emotions.

Cognitive behavioural therapy (CBT) Ellis later added *behaviour* (REBT) because ultimately the problems express themselves as behaviours. This developed his therapy into an example of *cognitive behavioural therapy*.

A therapist, for example, may also work to encourage a depressed client to be more active and engage in enjoyable activities. This is called *behavioural activation* which will provide more evidence for the irrational nature of beliefs.

Mindfulness-based cognitive therapy (MBCT)

This is a combination of CBT and a more recent approach called *mindfulness*. Its aim is to prevent *relapse* into *depression*. The client learns skills that they can apply when they start to feel low, so 'everyday sadness' does not turn into *clinical depression*.

CBT This aspect of therapy identifies and challenges negative thought patterns and replaces them with rational positive ones.

Mindfulness A client is encouraged to pay attention to their thoughts and feelings as they experience them (e.g. through meditation). This means not worrying about the future or the past and not judging their thoughts/feelings. The aim is to disrupt negative thoughts before they are able to affect feelings and cause the client to spiral down into depression.

Techniques The techniques used in MBCT help a client to be aware of themselves and what they are feeling. A popular one is a guided meditation called the *body scan*. The client focuses their attention on each part of their body, starting at the toes and working upwards. They become aware of the physical sensations and notice how each part of the body feels, without making any judgements or trying to change anything.

Acceptance and commitment therapy (ACT)

The basis of ACT is the idea that fighting emotions can make them worse. For example, people who are depressed often feel ashamed or guilty because they are depressed. So, they have a 'double burden'.

ACT teaches the client to accept their thoughts and feelings, to stop struggling to control them. As part of the therapy, the client also commits to getting involved with other meaningful activities in their lives.

Cognitive therapies often involve group sessions at some point. Clients can benefit from hearing about each other's experiences.

Yoga is a technique used in some mindfulness-based cognitive therapies. It helps a client focus on physical sensations rather than their anxieties or worries.

Evaluation

Flexibility

One strength of most cognitive therapies is that they are flexible.

For example, there are many different forms of CBT which use a wide range of strategies and techniques. Although the basic approach is always the same (to challenge and replace irrational thoughts), the techniques can be selected to suit the individual and his or her disorder. So, some techniques are more useful in treating depression, others are better with OCD or *phobias*. There is a vast variety of mindfulness exercises that can be used as part of MBCT and ACT. A related benefit is that these therapies can be effective within a few weeks or months rather than over years (and at great expense).

This increases the chances that cognitive therapies can be successful for improving individuals' symptoms.

Active and future-oriented

Another strength is that cognitive therapies are long-term treatments in which the client is fully involved.

There is a strong 'self-help' element to all of the cognitive therapies on this spread. The client is actively involved in planning the therapy and in working through it. For example, they complete homework assignments, engage in role play, develop skills, learn more about their disorder and the role of irrational thinking, etc. They are equipped with techniques such as disputing, meditation and body scan to help them cope with future *stress*.

This means the client is more able to avoid relapse because they think more rationally and can put into practice the skills they have learnt.

Exaggerates role of cognitive factors

One weakness of cognitive therapies is their overemphasis on cognitive factors.

The cause of mental disorder is located in the client's distorted thinking. This ignores wider social contexts such as the role of the family or social forces. This approach risks placing too much responsibility on the individual for their symptoms, 'blaming' them for their disorder. Those who do not improve are seen as not trying hard enough or not being prepared to accept responsibility.

This means cognitive therapies may not be useful when only changing the situation will improve the client's symptoms.

GET ACTIVE Fight your ANTs

Do you tend to think negative thoughts automatically? A technique called the *dysfunctional thought record* can help you to identify *automatic negative thoughts* (ANTs) and consider what to do about them.

This is just one of many exercises that focuses on the cognitive distortions that underlie mental disorders. Whenever you notice you are having ANTs (e.g. about exams), write down:

1. *The ANT itself (e.g. 'OMG I'm going to fail').*

2. *How you felt when you had the ANT.*

3. *Positive thoughts as alternatives to the ANT ('I'm going to nail it'). Write down as many as you can.*

4. *How do you feel now?*

Assessment practice

At the end of learning aims B and C you must write a report (see pages 231 and 258). This report must be related to a scenario or context. We have used a realistic (but not real) context.

You intend to move on to cognitive therapies for the third part of your presentation. You are aware that cognitive therapies are the most widely used psychological treatments in the NHS.

However, it appears that the commission members are uncertain about the main features of the different cognitive therapies. So, you will need to be very clear on this point in your explanation.

Your evaluation is also important. Because cognitive therapies are used so often, the commission members want to know if they are useful.

One member believes that the most useful therapies are the most flexible ones. He is hoping you might be able to provide some guidance on this point.

C1.9 Learning aim C1 – Task 9

The third part of your report for learning aims B and C will be concerned with the treatments for different mental disorders – these are covered on the previous two spreads, this spread and the next three spreads.

This activity will help you practise the skills required to write the report in response to your scenario/context.

1. **Explain one or more** cognitive therapies as a treatment for **one** mental disorder. (C.P5)

2. **Evaluate** cognitive therapies as a treatment for **one** mental disorder. (C.D3)

An issue to consider

There are three cognitive therapies on this spread. Apart from being 'cognitive' can you think of what else they have in common?

Specification content

C1 Approaches to the treatment of mental disorders

Characteristics of approaches and methods used in the treatment of mental disorders.

● Cognitive therapies, e.g. rational emotive behaviour therapy (REBT), cognitive behavioural therapy (CBT), mindfulness–based cognitive therapy (MBCT), acceptance and commitment therapy (ACT).

Family systems therapy

A troubled family

The Bowen Center website describes a family who undertook family systems therapy.

Martha and Michael had been happily married for two years when Martha became pregnant for the first time. During her pregnancy, Martha expressed how anxious she was about becoming a mother and whether she would be 'good enough'. Michael was reassuring but also began to view Martha as being 'childlike'.

The months after their baby, Amy, was born were hard for Martha. She was very anxious and Michael spent longer at work and become more critical of Martha's coping abilities. Martha invested all her emotions in Amy, withdrawing from Michael but reacting strongly whenever he criticised her.

As Amy grew up she demanded more and more from Martha. Sometimes Martha and Michael agreed that Amy's selfishness was the 'problem' in the family. But whenever Michael was critical of Amy, Martha took her side. Martha and Amy were so bound up together that Michael sometimes wondered where one ended and the other began.

So, at various times, Martha, Amy and Michael were seen as the 'problem' in the family.

Source: The Bowen Center website

Specification term

Family systems therapy Treats an individual's mental disorder by changing patterns of interaction within the whole family. Encourages members to differentiate from each other and operate as individuals with their own needs.

Triangling in FST. Not this kind of triangle though.

Family systems therapy (FST)

Family systems therapy is based on a theory by Murray Bowen (1978). He argued that every family is a social system and each one has its own structure and ways of communicating.

Mental disorders and the family system

Bowen believed that *mental disorders* are caused by *fusion* – family members are too close emotionally and so fail to see themselves as individuals with their own needs, desires etc. Fusion occurs in order to keep the family stable. If one member was to emotionally withdraw to take care of their own needs, this would disrupt the whole family.

Each member faces a difficult balancing act – to remain emotionally connected to the family but also to function as an individual (this is called *differentiation*). The family member who is least differentiated is the one most at risk of developing a mental disorder, especially *depression*.

Family relationships are dysfunctional because of *reactivity*. This is the way members respond to each other immediately, being instantly emotional because they are too closely involved.

The process

Therapy involves the whole family and not just the individual with a mental disorder. The aim of FST is to help family members become more differentiated from each other. Each one needs to be less emotionally dependent, stop blaming others for their unhappiness and take more responsibility.

FST does not try to change family members but to change how they relate to each other. In a sense the 'client' is not the individual members but the system of relationships. There are two main elements.

- **Educating** clients to understand how the mental disorder of one member is caused by relationship patterns within the family system.
- **Strategies and techniques** such as *detriangling* (below) are used to increase differentiation of family members and counteract the tendency they have to pull closer together. This reduces *anxiety* and increases each member's responsibility for themselves.

Role of the therapist

The therapist is valuable because he or she is completely differentiated from the client family. But they do not have 'the cure' to hand on a plate while the family just waits for it to arrive. The therapist must bring the family to a point where its members can take 'responsibility for its own change' (Bowen 1978).

Therefore, it is very important the therapist does not get drawn into family conflicts and resists 'taking sides'. This is harder than it sounds because in FST couples do not communicate directly with each other, at least to begin with. Discussion and conversation passes through the therapist, to 'defuse' the emotional reactions and provide a calm environment.

Detriangling

This is the main technique in FST. Its aim is to prevent family members *triangling* each other. When a couple are in emotional conflict, one partner may try to drag a third member (e.g. a child or parent) into the conflict to provide support – this is a triangle. This third member becomes depressed because the *stress* and tension of their position in the triangle is too much for them to cope with.

Bowen believed that triangling can be difficult to identify in normal circumstances but is much more obvious in times of stress (e.g. when one family member is experiencing a mental disorder).

The therapist helps to detriangle the family by becoming the third member themselves. But crucially, the therapist responds non-emotionally and non-anxiously to the dynamics of the triangle. At this point, family members are helped to communicate directly with each other in neutral, non-emotional ways that do not reinforce the triangle. For example, by refusing to discuss another family member behind their back, or changing the subject or even standing up for the other family member.

GET ACTIVE Comparing therapies

Comparing therapies can help you to understand them better. We have looked in detail at four types of psychological therapy so far – psychodynamic, behavioural, cognitive and family systems (there is also counselling to come on page 252). There is a skill to making comparisons. You need to explain how two therapies are similar or how they are different. The key word is how – this is more than just describing a feature of one therapy and a feature of another. You have to bring them together to genuinely compare them.

1. Identify **one** area in which you can compare the four therapies (e.g. the techniques they use).

2. Take **two** of the therapies and explain how they are similar in this area.

3. Take the other **two** therapies and explain how they are different.

4. Identify another area and repeat this process.

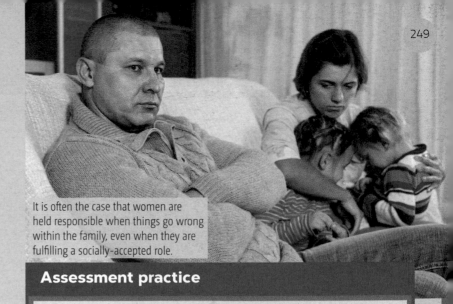

It is often the case that women are held responsible when things go wrong within the family, even when they are fulfilling a socially-accepted role.

Evaluation

A more holistic approach

One strength of FST is that it treats the whole family rather than just the individual.

FST recognises that mental disorders often develop in a context, e.g. the family. Treating an individual as if they were not part of this social system is a limited way of helping them. This is because even if the client is helped, the risk of *relapse* is still great as long as they continue to be part of their (unchanged) family. Instead, FST aims to change patterns of interaction within the family, addressing the dysfunctional context in which the disorder developed.

This is more effective in the longer term because relapse is less likely when the whole family's way of interacting is changed.

Minimises individual dysfunction

One weakness of FST is that it does tend to underplay the individual's disorder.

It could be argued that in highlighting the overall influence of the family system, the individual's concerns become lost. What matters to the individual who is depressed, more than anything else, is that they feel better. But improving the individual client's symptoms is seen by family systems therapists as secondary to changing family interactions. Also, there is a tendency in FST to assume that symptoms will improve automatically once the family is functioning well.

This lack of focus on the individual experiencing the mental disorder means there is a risk of making their symptoms worse rather than better.

Feminist criticism

Another weakness is that there is some evidence of *gender bias* in FST.

Deborah Luepnitz (1988) noted that the pioneers of FST (e.g. Bowen) were all men. They thought that mothers and fathers contributed differently to family dysfunction, with mothers being handed most of the 'blame'. They held mothers mostly responsible for creating destructive triangles in the family, while appearing to give fathers a 'free pass'. The mother's role in many families, even now, is to be the main emotional supporter of their partners and children. In fact women are often raised to fulfil this role, putting other people's needs before their own.

Therefore, as FST views this behaviour as fusion, mothers are seen as an obstacle to differentiation whereas fathers generally are not.

Assessment practice

At the end of learning aims B and C you must write a report (see pages 231 and 258). This report must be related to a scenario or context. We have used a realistic (but not real) context.

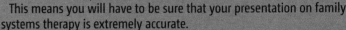

You decide that the fourth treatment in your presentation will be family systems therapy.

You have looked into the backgrounds of the commission members.

You know that Baroness Triangle is an expert on this therapy. Apparently she has been through it herself and was a personal friend of its creator.

This means you will have to be sure that your presentation on family systems therapy is extremely accurate.

The commissioners would like some information about the main concepts associated with the therapy. However, they want you to focus on the process – how the therapy is actually conducted.

You decide to describe the process using the example of detriangling to explain how the therapy works.

C1.10 Learning aim C1 – Task 10

The third part of your report for learning aims B and C will be concerned with the treatments for different mental disorders – these are covered on the previous three spreads, this spread and the next two spreads.

This activity will help you practise the skills required to write the report in response to your scenario/context.

1. **Explain** family systems therapy as a treatment for **one** mental disorder. (C.P5)

2. **Evaluate** family systems therapy as a treatment for **one** mental disorder. (C.D3)

> You can see the explanation of the command terms on page 229 and the assessment criteria on page 258.

An issue to consider

Family systems therapy is not suitable for everyone. Some members of a family may resist involvement.

How could you encourage such members to take part?

Specification content

C1 Approaches to the treatment of mental disorders

Characteristics of approaches and methods used in the treatment of mental disorders.

● Family systems therapy, e.g. relationship dynamics within the family.

Drug therapies

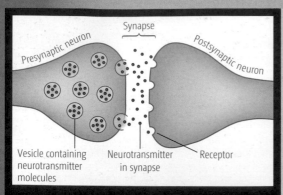

Synapse
Presynaptic neuron
Postsynaptic neuron

Vesicle containing neurotransmitter molecules
Neurotransmitter in synapse
Receptor

How synapses work

The diagram above is of a synapse, an extremely tiny gap between two neurons. There are hundreds of these at the ends of every neuron, connecting the neuron with many, many other neurons.

But as you can see the connection isn't physical – neurons do not touch, so the communication between them is chemical. The chemicals are called neurotransmitters.

Neurons operate electrically. The electrical signal comes down the presynaptic neuron (the neuron before the synapse). This causes synaptic vesicles (containing neurotransmitter molecules) to move towards the neuron's membrane and eject the neurotransmitter into the synapse.

The molecules drift across the very narrow synapse and combine with the receptor sites on the postsynaptic neuron. When enough molecules have done this, the electrical signal continues in the postsynaptic neuron. Any leftover neurotransmitter is either recycled or another chemical comes along and destroys it.

Drugs treat mental disorders by interfering with this process in ways that are described on this spread.

Specification terms

Drug therapy Treatment involving drugs, i.e. chemicals that have a particular effect on the functioning of the brain or some other body system. In the case of mental disorders such drugs usually affect neurotransmitter levels.

Named drugs defined in the index/glossary.

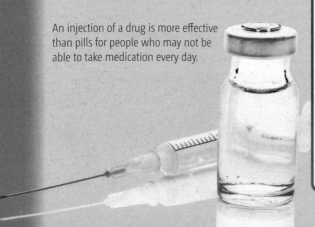

An injection of a drug is more effective than pills for people who may not be able to take medication every day.

Drug therapies

Antidepressant drugs

These *antidepressant drugs* are all based on the theory that people with *depression* do not have enough of the *neurotransmitter serotonin* in their brains. Increasing serotonin improves the individual's mood and there are several ways of doing this. The main antidepressants in order of discovery are:

Tricyclic antidepressants The most obvious way to increase serotonin is to stimulate neurons to produce and release more into the *synapses* between them – which is how *tricyclics* work. They increase levels of *noradrenaline* as well, which is also thought to help depressed people feel better. However, tricyclics have serious side effects so others were developed.

Monoamine oxidase inhibitors (MAOIs) These drugs use another way of boosting brain serotonin levels. Serotonin that is left over in the synapses is normally destroyed by a chemical called *monoamine oxidase*. Therefore, one way to keep serotonin active in the brain is by stopping monoamine oxidase from destroying it. So *monoamine oxidase inhibitors* inhibit (prevent) the normal function of monoamine oxidase so that more serotonin stays in the synapses. The result is improved mood in many people with depression.

Selective serotonin reuptake inhibitors (SRRIs) These drugs (e.g. trade name Prozac) are the most commonly used antidepressants in the UK. Another way the brain gets rid of leftover serotonin is by recycling it. It is 'hoovered up' by the neuron that produces it – this is called *reuptake*. *Selective serotonin reuptake inhibitors* stop reuptake from happening which allows serotonin to 'hang around' the synapse for longer so more gets used (see diagram on left).

Serotonin noradrenaline reuptake inhibitors (SNRIs) Noradrenaline (or *norepiniphrene* in the USA) is another neurotransmitter involved in depression. *Serotonin noradrenaline reuptake inhibitors* inhibit the reuptake of both serotonin and noradrenaline, so more stays in the synapses to be used.

Anxiolytic drugs

Anxiolytic drugs reduce anxiety. Two common types are *benzodiazepines* and *beta blockers* which we covered in detail on page 80 (Unit 3).

Antipsychotic drugs

Psychotic disorders include *schizophrenia spectrum disorders* (see page 238). Some people take antipsychotics for a limited time and don't get any return of symptoms. Others, however, need to take them for the long term, possibly the rest of their lives, otherwise risk symptoms reappearing.

One theory suggests that schizophrenia may be caused by too much activity in the brain of the neurotransmitter *dopamine*. Therefore, antipsychotic drugs mostly work by reducing dopamine in two distinctly different ways.

Typical antipsychotics (TAs) These are older drugs, first developed in the 1950s and include *chlorpromazine*. *Typical antipsychotics* (TAs) are dopamine *antagonists*. This means they stop dopamine from attaching to neurons in the brain by blocking it. This reduces the activity of dopamine, stabilising its effects throughout the brain and reducing symptoms such as *hallucinations*.

Atypical antipsychotics (AAs) These are newer 'second generation' drugs, although they have been around since the 1970s. *Atypical antipsychotics* (AAs) are more effective than TAs and have fewer side effects. One example of an AA is *clozapine*. This drug blocks dopamine but not as strongly as chlorpromazine does. But clozapine also affects two other neurotransmitters – it increases serotonin and reduces *glutamate*.

This combined effect on three neurotransmitters seems to be effective. It reduces the symptoms of schizophrenia, improves the person's mood and increases their cognitive functioning (e.g. memory and language). For this reason it is often prescribed for people who are at risk of suicide (between 30% and 50% of people with schizophrenia attempt suicide at some point).

Clozapine is the 'gold standard' of drug treatment for schizophrenia, especially because it is useful for people who have not responded to other drugs.

GET ACTIVE Making the patient aware

Antidepressants are mostly prescribed by general practitioners (i.e. your family doctor at the local medical practice). A patient might have ten to fifteen minutes in an appointment to explain their symptoms before the GP decides to prescribe the drugs.

Because antidepressants do not work for everyone, it is very important the GP understands the individual patient in front of them. Patients often expect the drugs to start working immediately, but none of them do. This is just one piece of information that a GP should make a patient aware of. There are others too.

Your task is to prepare an attractive and easy-to-understand information sheet that a GP could give to a patient. The sheet should focus on five key points that a patient needs to know. For each point you should write two or three sentences.

Here are two sources to help you:

tinyurl.com/y9ocfeja

tinyurl.com/yy6cvjlf

Evaluation

Research evidence

One strength is evidence that drug treatments work.

For instance, Andrea Cipriani *et al.* (2018) reviewed 522 trials of 21 antidepressants. Although there were some differences in effectiveness between them, all 21 drugs were better than a *placebo* in reducing symptoms. Stefan Leucht *et al.* (2013) conducted a similar review of 15 antipsychotic drugs (212 trials). Again, all drugs were *significantly* more effective than a placebo in reducing symptoms of schizophrenia (the most effective was *clozapine*).

This shows that almost all drugs can be reasonably effective in improving symptoms of mental disorders.

Side effects

One weakness of drug treatments is that they have side effects.

Typical antipsychotics produce a wide range of side effects including dizziness, stiff jaw and weight gain. A serious long-term effect is *tardive dyskinesia*, involuntary movements of facial muscles producing grimacing, blinking and lip smacking. A serious side effect of clozapine is *agranulocytosis*, which is a lowered number of white blood cells (involved in the immune response). People taking this drug must have regular blood tests to monitor for signs of this effect. Side effects of SSRIs and SNRIs include agitation, loss of appetite and low sex drive. A serious effect is *serotonin syndrome*, associated with seizures and loss of consciousness.

The problem with side effects is that the person may stop taking their medication, risking the return of symptoms.

Symptoms not causes

Another weakness is that drugs relieve symptoms of mental disorders but do not tackle their causes.

For example, an antidepressant stabilises the brain's serotonin system, but only for as long as the person takes the drug. There is a reasonable chance that symptoms such as low mood will improve (though that is not guaranteed for everyone). But the cause of the depression remains, and this could be *environmental*, e.g. a *stressor*. It could be argued that if the individual's mood does improve, this demotivates them from tackling the environmental stressors that may be causing their disorder.

This means the benefits of drugs are limited in the longer term, which is why a psychological therapy may be more useful.

251

Drug treatments often reduce the symptoms of mental disorders, but only for as long as the drugs are taken.

Assessment practice

At the end of learning aims B and C you must write a report (see pages 231 and 258). This report must be related to a scenario or context. We have used a realistic (but not real) context.

The fifth treatment in your presentation is going to be drug therapies.

The head of NHS mental health services is particularly interested in what you have to say about this treatment.

You realise this is probably because she is a medical doctor and drug therapy is closely tied to the biological approach.

However, some commission members are concerned about the widespread use of drugs to treat mental disorders, so you remind yourself to include both strengths and weaknesses in your evaluation.

C1.11 Learning aim C1 – Task 11

The third part of your report for learning aims B and C will be concerned with the treatments for different mental disorders – these are covered on the previous four spreads, this spread and the next spread.

This activity will help you practise the skills required to write the report in response to your scenario/context.

1. **Explain one or more** drug therapies as a treatment for **one** mental disorder. (C.P5)
2. **Evaluate** drug therapies as a treatment for **one** mental disorder. (C.D3)

An issue to consider

On balance, would you recommend a drug therapy to a friend who was experiencing prolonged depression?

Specification content

C1 Approaches to the treatment of mental disorders

Characteristics of approaches and methods used in the treatment of mental disorders.

● Drug therapies, e.g. antidepressant drugs, anxiolytic drugs, antipsychotic drugs, tricyclic antidepressants, monoamine oxidase inhibitors (MAOIs), selective serotonin reuptake inhibitors (SSRIs), benzodiazepines, serotonin-norepinephrine reuptake inhibitors (SNRIs).

Humanistic therapies

'Tell me all about it'

In an article called 'Help is where you find it', Emory Cowen (1982) interviewed people who counselled clients as part of their day-to-day jobs. He wanted to know which occupations involved listening to clients' personal and emotional problems.

To almost no one's surprise, Cowen found that people are most likely to confide in their hairdresser. Hairdressers make excellent informal counsellors. They even use similar techniques to those used by the professionals. A good counsellor-hairdresser will listen actively, try to understand how their client is feeling (empathise) and boost their client's self-esteem (by telling them how great they are).

Cowen's conclusion was that hairdressers are doing a great job of keeping a huge proportion of mental health issues from ever reaching the professionals.

Specification terms

Computerised CBT (CCBT) Delivering cognitive behavioural therapy online via devices such as tablets, usually prepackaged CBT programmes.

Counselling A form of therapy that aims to increase a client's self-esteem through unconditional positive regard from the therapist. Striving to achieve conditional love blocks the ability to self-actualise.

e-therapy (online therapy) Delivering any form of therapy over the internet, with or without therapist support, often via an app.

NHS therapies will increasingly be 'going digital' in the coming years.

Counselling

Counselling is one of several 'talking therapies' (such as *psychoanalysis*, page 242, and *cognitive behavioural therapy*, page 246).

Client-centred

Carl Rogers (1959) was the first to introduce client-centred counselling. A central feature is that generally the client does most of the talking, much more so than in other talking therapies. The therapist tries to reflect back thoughts and emotions. This low level of involvement is because the client is regarded as the expert on their own condition. Thus, the therapy is non-directive, and the client is encouraged towards the discovery of their own solutions within a therapeutic atmosphere that is warm, supportive and non-judgemental.

The therapist's role

For Rogers, an effective therapist should provide the client with three things: genuineness, empathy and *unconditional positive regard*. This support aims to increase the person's feelings of self-worth, so that a client can accept all the aspects of themselves. Only in doing so can they begin to deal with those characteristics that are undesirable – the characteristics that 'are not like me' or incongruent.

Wider influence

Rogers' work transformed psychotherapy and introduced a variety of counselling techniques. In the UK and the US, similar counselling skills are practised, not only in *clinical* settings, but throughout education, health, social work and industry. It is the basis of many helplines where the focus is less on advice and more on enabling a person to recognise their own solutions.

Client-centred therapy has been praised as a forward-looking and effective approach that focuses on present problems rather than dwelling on the past. However, much like psychoanalysis, it is best applied to the treatment of 'mild' psychological conditions, such as anxiety and low self-worth.

Other humanistic methods of therapy

In general, therapy is conducted face-to-face between two individuals or in a group. However, modern technologies offer other possibilities.

Phone and online counselling

Some people prefer not to see a counsellor face-to-face, in which case telephone or online counselling can help them to be more willing to express their feelings. Communicating in writing (in emails or online) gives some clients the chance to think more deeply – they find it easier and more liberating than talking.

Computerised CBT (CCBT)

CCBT is a way of delivering *cognitive behavioural therapy* via laptops or smartphones. Some standard 'prepackaged' CCBT programmes exist, for example *Beating the Blues* to treat *depression* and *Stressbusters* for school-aged people. These are designed to be completed without direct therapist support (although contact details may be given).

Face-to-face CBT has transferred relatively smoothly to an online format for three main reasons: it has an educational element which can be presented, it includes many exercises/tasks for the client to carry out to understand their distorted thought patterns, and there is a major skill development element which does not require personal contact.

The UK's *National Institute of Health and Care Excellence* (NICE) recommends CCBT as a 'first step' treatment for *depression* (on its own or with medication), before considering other approaches if it is not effective for individual clients.

e-therapy / online therapy

CBT is just one type of therapy that can be delivered online. Other types are being provided as device-based or web-based apps with as much online therapist support as the client prefers. The NHS website provides a list of currently recommended 'mental health apps', some available for free and some for a cost. For example, SilverCloud is an eight-week programme to help manage *stress*, *anxiety* and depression which clients complete at their own pace.

e-therapies are 'low intensity' because they are less confrontational, which means a client is more likely to stick with them. They are also easier to access.

Evaluation

A useful approach

One strength is that the counselling approach has a wide appeal and application.

It has been adapted for many different settings such as schools and hospitals, and for a range of different situations, such as finding the right job or marriage guidance. It also requires much less training than many other therapies as its effectiveness depends a lot on what any good listener can offer (e.g. the trust and warmth of the client-counsellor relationship, though a trained counsellor has highly-developed additional skills).

This means that the therapy can offer positive effects and benefits to a wide range of people.

Limited application

One weakness is that the therapy is not useful for more severe mental disorders.

Counselling is best applied to the treatment of 'mild' psychological conditions, such as anxiety and low self-worth. It is also only valuable to individuals who wish to express themselves and are willing to do so. For example, it is less useful for people with *schizophrenia*, a disorder in which communication is impaired. These clients are less able to express their thoughts, feelings and goals in an understandable way.

This limits the benefits of counselling to people who are most likely to be helped by almost any 'talking therapy'.

Evaluation

Highly flexible

One strength of all these other methods of therapy is their flexibility.

They can include a wide variety of techniques to help the client. They can be used with individuals, couples, and groups both large and small. Duration can be from 15 minutes to an hour or more per 'session', for a few weeks or longer. Online modes can come with or without therapist support, with the client deciding which they would prefer.

This flexibility means therapy can be tailored to the individual client's needs, which helps them to see the relevance of it to their own problems and makes it more likely to be effective.

Ethical issues

One weakness is that these methods of therapy are not as well-regulated as some of the other therapies we have covered.

For instance, unlike the titles 'psychologist' and 'general practitioner', anyone can call themselves a 'counsellor' or 'psychotherapist'. Especially online, there are concerns that untrained, unqualified and unregulated 'practitioners' are seeking (and gaining) business from people with mental disorders. Even qualified and experienced counsellors are not necessarily trained in how to deliver therapy online.

This means that the chances of a client's symptoms being made worse are much greater in e-therapy than in face-to-face traditional counselling.

GET ACTIVE App-based therapies

Find out more about e-therapy or CCBT packages available online.

The NHS Mental health apps library is part of the NHS website. You can find it here: tinyurl.com/y5zb6ejx. Choose three or four apps to investigate further. Use your knowledge of online and face-to-face therapies to answer these questions:

1. *Which mental health disorders do the apps claim to help with?*
2. *Identify **one** way in which the apps address cognitive factors.*
3. *Identify **one** way they address behavioural factors.*
4. *The NHS only lists 'evidence-based' apps. What do you think this means?*

> Not sure if this counselling does help...

Anyone can call themselves a 'counsellor'. There are registers that reputable counsellors can sign up to, but this is voluntary.

Assessment practice

At the end of learning aims B and C you must write a report (see pages 231 and 258). This report must be related to a scenario or context. We have used a realistic (but not real) context.

The final treatments in your presentation will be counselling and 'other modes'. All the commission members are very interested indeed in 'other modes'. 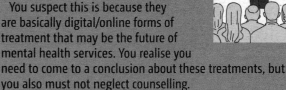 You suspect this is because they are basically digital/online forms of treatment that may be the future of mental health services. You realise you need to come to a conclusion about these treatments, but you also must not neglect counselling.

C1.12 Learning aim C1 – Task 12

The third part of your report for learning aims B and C will be concerned with the treatments for different mental disorders – these are covered on the previous five spreads and this spread.

This activity will help you practise the skills required to write the report in response to your scenario/context.

1. **Explain** counselling as a treatment for **one** mental disorder. (C.P5)
2. **Evaluate** counselling as a treatment for **one** mental disorder. (C.D3)
3. **Explain one or more** other methods of treatment for **one** mental disorder. (C.P5)
4. **Evaluate** other methods of treatment for **one** mental disorder. (C.D3)

An issue to consider

Think of a time when someone tried to help you by just listening to how you were feeling. Did it help?

Why do you think it did or didn't help?

Specification content

C1 Approaches to the treatment of mental disorders

Characteristics of approaches and methods used in the treatment of mental disorders.

● Humanistic therapies, e.g. counselling, computerised CBT (CCBT), e-therapy/online therapy.

Diagnosis and treatment by professionals

Child and Adolescent Mental Health Services (CAMHS)

CAMHS/Healthy Young Minds

'The support I received from CAMHS was invaluable and I do not know where I would be without it. I now study Health and Social Care and hope to study Psychology at university' (*YoungMinds* 2019).

CAMHS is the NHS' Child and Adolescent Mental Health Services. Students in full-time education who are experiencing mental health problems might be referred to CAMHS to be assessed and treated. A CAMHS team will usually be made up of people in the professional roles described on this spread. A young person could be referred to the services by a parent, teacher, GP or social worker. The *YoungMinds* charity produces a guide which breaks the CAMHS process down into three steps:

- Assessment – at your first appointment you get a chance to explain your mental health concerns and what could be causing them. The professional you speak with might make a diagnosis at this point.

- Treatment and support – if CAMHS can help, you will be given a treatment plan indicating the kind of therapy, how it will be delivered and how long it lasts.

- Review and ending treatment – your therapist discusses your progress with you and together you decide when your treatment can end.

Specification term

Mental health professionals Qualified and trained individuals involved at various points in the process of identifying, diagnosing and treating mental disorders. Their behaviour and quality of work is regulated by national bodies (e.g. the *British Psychological Society*).

Diagnosis and treatment by professionals

Professionals involved in diagnosing and treating disorders

As most people with *mental disorders* are treated outside hospital, care is provided by a *community mental health team* (CMHT).

Psychiatrists are medically-qualified doctors who have chosen to specialise in *mental health*. They diagnose mental disorders using *DSM/ICD* classification systems. They provide physical treatments such as drug therapy. Some *psychiatrists* are trained in psychological therapies such as CBT or *psychoanalysis*.

Clinical psychologists are trained to diagnose and treat mental health problems. They provide a range of psychological therapies such as CBT and *behaviour modification*, individually or in groups.

Neurologists are medically-qualified doctors. They play a specialist role in diagnosing and treating people who experience psychological symptoms as a result of a physical disorder of the brain or nervous system.

General practitioners (GPs) are usually the first point of contact. They are medically qualified but not specialists in mental health. GPs may diagnose disorders, prescribe medication, provide advice and recommend support groups. GPs refer patients to other services, e.g. social worker or mental health provider.

Mental health workers

Mental health nurses (MHNs) are qualified nurses who are registered with the Nursing and Midwifery Council and have specialist training. Some MHNs work inside hospitals (e.g. on psychiatric wards) but many work in the community. They visit clients in their homes, in GP surgeries and in community health clinics. They monitor a client's progress, the effects of medication and therapy and their general health. Some have further training so they can provide therapy.

Case managers are usually senior nurses or social workers and are responsible for coordinating other professionals in their care of several clients ('cases'). They would be unlikely to have direct contact with clients but monitor how the care is provided, especially in the community.

Social workers can give practical advice about housing, benefits, health care and so on. They also give emotional support. Some are specialised psychiatric social workers, who can provide *counselling* and/or therapy.

Paediatricians are medically-qualified doctors specialising in children's health and illness. A child mental health paediatrician provides advice about child and adolescent clients (e.g. creating treatment plans). They have an important role in promoting mental health and ensuring it is seen to be just as important as physical health by professionals ('parity of esteem').

Occupational therapists (OTs) help clients to carry out practical everyday activities that may have been disrupted by a mental disorder. This could involve support with specific skills (e.g. writing, managing *anxiety*) or helping to build self-confidence in their social relationships, work, etc. OTs work in psychiatric units, residential units, GP surgeries and often visit clients at home.

Counsellors provide a talking treatment to help clients cope better with their lives (see previous spread). This can be individually or in groups, often in GP surgeries or health centres. They may specialise in specific issues such as anxiety or grief. Many counsellors also work outside the NHS, for voluntary organisations.

Professionals in educational organisations

Health visitors are qualified nurses (or midwives) who have specialist training in child health. Health visitors support women with very young children, and women who are pregnant or have recently had a baby, and visit them at home. They can give clients advice and information about mental disorders (especially postnatal depression) and refer them to more specialist services.

School nurses are qualified and registered nurses who work with parents and children. They are in a unique position to help train other education professionals (e.g. teachers) to identify mental health issues in young people.

Special educational needs coordinators (SENCOs) are teachers who are trained and qualified to Masters level in special educational needs (SEN). They are responsible for the everyday operation of the school's SEN policy. Part of this involves identifying students who have mental health issues, providing support for them and referring them to specialist services.

Speech and language therapists (SLTs) help clients who experience communication problems as part of their mental disorder (e.g. *schizophrenia*, anxiety). SLTs can also help clients who experience eating and swallowing difficulties as an outcome either of their disorder or their medication.

Mental health nurses are highly trained and qualified professionals on the 'front line' of client care.

Evaluation

Combined approaches to care

One strength of professional input into care is that different approaches are combined.

This is because clients are looked after by community mental health teams (CMHTs) and not individuals. This is called the *case management approach*. The professionals in CMHTs have different roles and bring different approaches to treatment. For example, GPs and psychiatrists have a medical perspective, involving drug treatments. Psychologists and nurses on the other hand are more likely to use psychological therapies and counselling.

This means that people with complex mental health needs can get the right support, whereas in the past they may not have been able to access appropriate services.

Funding issues

One weakness is that some organisations argue that government funding is not high enough.

The charity *YoungMinds* points out that the government in 2015 committed to providing an additional £1.4billion over five years. But increased demand means that there is a mental health crisis in the UK. One consequence has been that identification and intervention do not happen soon enough (i.e. in schools) and CAMHS receives only 8% of all mental health funding.

The relative lack of funding, at a time when there are greater demands on services, make it very hard for professionals to carry out their roles effectively.

Lack of clarity over roles

Another weakness is that the responsibilities of different professional roles are sometimes unclear.

For example, GPs and psychiatrists are both involved in diagnosis and this can lead to conflict. In recent years GPs have become more central and psychiatrists have shifted to a 'consultation' role, supporting teams rather than managing or coordinating them. It is also the case that some teachers and volunteer supporters have not received training in mental health issues, so may not be completely sure what their roles are.

This means there is a real danger that clients can 'fall through the cracks' of mental health services, not getting the help they need because practitioners are unclear about their roles and responsibilities.

GET ACTIVE Jade's story

Up until she was 14, Jade was happy at school, loved her family and had lots of friends. Then one night she felt lower than she'd ever felt before, but had no idea why. After two weeks of this, Jade's mood suddenly shifted and she felt incredibly happy. She felt the world was a wonderful place and she could do anything she wanted. Then, a couple of days later, her mood returned to something more normal. But not long after that she declined again. Jade was on an emotional rollercoaster for two years before her mum took her to see…

1. *Who do you think Jade's mum took her to see, and what might have happened?*

2. *Choose **four** other professionals and explain their roles in the diagnosis and treatment of Jade's disorder.*

Assessment practice

At the end of learning aims B and C you must write a report (see pages 231 and 258). This report must be related to a scenario or context. We have used a realistic (but not real) context.

The use of treatments is very closely linked to the people who carry them out. Therefore, the commissioners ask you to write an in-depth report about the roles of various professionals and support groups in treating mental disorders.

Again, you decide to focus on one disorder. The commissioners want you to analyse how professionals contribute to treatment. They also want you to evaluate their roles in terms of strengths and weaknesses.

C2.13 Learning aim C2 – Task 13

The third part of your report for learning aims B and C will be concerned with the specific roles of professionals in diagnosing and treating individuals – these are covered on this spread and the next spread.

This activity will help you practise the skills required to write the report in response to your scenario/context.

1. **Discuss** the role of professionals involved in diagnosing and treating **one** mental disorder. (C.P6)

2. **Analyse** the ways professionals can contribute to the treatment of **one** mental disorder. (C.M3)

3. **Evaluate** the importance of the role of professionals in treating **one** mental disorder. (C.D3)

An issue to consider

There are lots of professional roles on this spread and they are all important.

Which do you think may be the most important and why?

Specification content

C2 Mental health professionals

Purpose and role of professionals and organisations in the diagnosis and treatment of mental disorders.

● Diagnosing and treating disorders, e.g. psychiatrists, psychologists, neurologists, general practitioners in medicine (GPs).

● Mental health workers, e.g. mental health nurses, case managers, social workers, paediatricians, occupational therapists, counsellors.

● Professionals in educational organisations, e.g. health visitors, school nurses, special educational needs coordinators (SENCOs), speech and language therapists.

Support groups

Every year the national mental health charity *Mind* runs a festival called *Peerfest*.

Peerfest is open to anyone who wants to celebrate or learn more about peer support. (Peer support is when people use their shared experiences to support each other and improve their mental health and well-being.) At Peerfest, ideas are shared and those attending can learn from each other. This includes small support groups from different parts of the country who set up stalls and explain what they do. Here are some examples of groups from Peerfest 2018:

Core Sport supports people with severe and enduring mental health problems, helping them socialise with others through physical exercise, such as gym, swimming, dance and yoga. 70% are from ethnic minority groups. 'You meet lots of friends. You'll probably find out something about yourself you probably didn't know and it helps give you confidence in what you do.'

Mindful Mums is a weekly walking group of expectant and new mothers who meet up and share experiences: 'When I've been sleep deprived and have felt isolated, it can be so hard to get perspective on things, but it's genuinely helped me to stay sane through my maternity leave.'

Source: *Mind* (2018)

Specification term

Support group (also called self-help or peer support group) An organisation usually involving volunteers and sometimes including professionals. They provide non-medical support to people with mental health problems (e.g. information, advice, training, campaigning for better services).

'We won't give up until everyone experiencing a mental health problem gets support and respect' (*Mind* 2019).

Support groups

There are many groups in the UK offering support for people with *mental health* problems and for their families and friends. Many are registered charities and some are national organisations with a regional and local structure. Some are run independently and others work with health services, GPs and other agencies such as Housing Associations.

What support groups provide

Support groups (sometimes called self-help or peer support groups) can provide:

- **Practical information and advice** This is provided through websites and printed materials. Most support websites have sections aimed at separate groups – a section for the client themselves, one for friends/peers, another for parents/family.
- **Face-to-face support** Some bigger charities organise face-to-face support from professionals and volunteers, usually in groups. These can be specialist support groups, for example for people with *eating disorders* or *depression*, etc. Some are for people supporting friends or family members. Support groups are not alternatives to treatment – they are additional or often a first step on the road to professional help.
- **Online/phone/text support** *Counselling*, advice, emotional support and a friendly ear do not have to be given face-to-face. Helplines are increasingly popular and are staffed by professionals or trained volunteers. Again, the bigger charities offer support in a variety of languages and specialisms (e.g. a self-harm helpline). Most support groups these days also have a social media presence.
- **Crisis support** Many charities offer 24-hour support to people experiencing a mental health crisis. Their websites feature a button on the home page offering 'urgent help now'. The client can then be referred to emergency services or put through to a helpline.
- **Training** This is provided by some support groups. Workshops help volunteers, friends and family members to develop their skills to support people with mental health problems. They can take place in schools, colleges, universities, workplaces, GP surgeries and so on. Some charities also offer employment training for people with mental health problems who have found it hard to get back into work.
- **Housing** This is provided by some charities. This could be residential and/or nursing home accommodation with a focus on care and support, in some cases 'around the clock'. This prevents homelessness and hospital readmissions (common outcomes for some people with mental health issues), providing stability in a therapeutic environment.
- **Campaigning** A key role of support groups is to bring mental health issues to the attention of the wider public and attract more resources for mental health services. Charities also aim to reduce the stigma that still surrounds mental health problems. Some support groups have an advisory board made up of academics, practitioners and sometimes celebrities. These provide advice about programmes, strategies and campaigns. Campaigns are sometimes explicitly political and aim to change government policy. So, some organisations have political links with government ministers through members of parliament, for example.

Mind

Mind is a leading mental health charity in the UK, providing information and advice via its website and print publications. It has a membership network of donors, fundraisers and volunteers. It raises funds through its high street shops, selling donated clothes, books, furniture, etc. *Mind* is also a classic campaigning organisation. It is politically involved, aiming to improve services for people with mental health problems in areas such as employment, housing and legal rights. The President of *Mind* is Stephen Fry.

YoungMinds

This major charity specialises in providing information, advice and support to children and young adults. Their priorities are to help young people cope with mental health problems and to monitor the negative impact of social media, school stress and unemployment. *YoungMinds* campaigns for funding for CAMHS (see page 254), the NHS's Child and Adolescent Mental Health Services. CAMHS is many young people's main experience of mental health services.

Evaluation

Benefits of support groups

One strength of support groups is that they have unquestionably helped a great many people.

They have saved lives, improved people's quality of life, provided practical assistance (including housing and jobs). On a wider scale, support groups have educated the public about the importance of mental health, addressed the stigma surrounding mental disorders, helped to change government policy and protected and enhanced the rights of people with mental health problems.

This suggests that support groups have a very important and beneficial role to play in providing mental health care services in the UK.

Supporting the NHS

Another strength of support groups is that they benefit the NHS in several ways.

For example, their websites provide useful (and accurate) information about mental health and disorders. Some groups work closely with NHS practitioners, which means standards of training are high and volunteers are able to support clients. This frees time for professionals to see others with perhaps more complex issues. Charities can attract funding that would not have reached the NHS without their campaigning and efforts.

This means financial burdens on the NHS are significantly decreased by the donations of time and money that groups receive from supporters.

Inconsistent quality

One weakness is that not all support groups are equally beneficial or effective.

For example, the quality of training provided by support groups is highly variable – excellent in some cases and poor in others. As a result, some volunteers lack sufficient expertise or knowledge of mental health issues, or their knowledge may be out-of-date. Part of the reason for this is that training provided by mental health support groups is not regulated by any national body. There are no standards for quality that have to be achieved.

This means that clients may not be benefitting as much as they could from properly-regulated training provided by reputable support groups.

Many homeless people have mental health problems. Being homeless makes it much harder to access support services, so providing housing makes a real difference.

GET ACTIVE Lend a hand (or ear)

Here's a suggestion that will definitely help you to 'get active'.

Are you interested in pursuing psychology at university? What about making it a career? Or perhaps you want to help people? It can be very hard to get relevant 'work experience', so why not do some voluntary work for a mental health support group? It's very fulfilling and you'll be doing a lot of good. In the meantime, here are the addresses of a few mental health support groups.

www.giveusashout.org

www.themix.org.uk

www.time-to-change.org.uk

www.rethink.org

Take a look at them and for each one write down:

1. *One* of their stated aims.

2. *One* of the services they offer.

Assessment practice

At the end of learning aims B and C you must write a report (see pages 231 and 258). This report must be related to a scenario or context. We have used a realistic (but not real) context.

Finally, the commission is keen to promote the involvement of groups, organisations and charities in providing support for people with mental disorders.

Your report will discuss what these groups are, their aims and objectives and what they do.

You decide to use two examples of specific groups to illustrate your report.

The commission Secretary has hinted that if your work is approved there is a good chance you will get a damehood or knighthood in the Queen's birthday honours list.

C2.14 Learning aim C2 – Task 14

The third part of your report for learning aims B and C will be concerned with the specific roles of professionals in diagnosing and treating individuals – these are covered on the previous spread and this spread.

This activity will help you practise the skills required to write the report in response to your scenario/context.

You can see the explanation of the command terms on page 229 and the assessment criteria on the next spread.

1. **Evaluate** the importance of organisations in supporting people with mental disorders. (C.D3)

An issue to consider

Support groups offer a considerable amount of support! But perhaps they are doing the NHS's job, on the cheap... Do you think support groups are a good thing or a bad thing?

Specification content

C2 Mental health professionals

Purpose and role of professionals and organisations in the diagnosis and treatment of mental disorders.

● Support groups, e.g. Mind, Rethink Mental Illness, YoungMinds.

Learning aims B and C

Assessment guidance

Learning aims B and C assessment

You are required to produce a report for each learning aim in this unit. You can, if you wish, combine units but no learning aim can be subdivided. The specification recommends that you combine learning aims B and C.

This report can only be completed after you have studied the content of learning aims B and C as it is a synoptic assessment (see page 229).

Recommended assessment approach

The *Delivery Guide for Unit 6* states that your report (or presentation, poster, etc.) needs to:

- Explore causal factors that contribute to mental disorders.
- Describe different mental disorders.
- Consider approaches used by professionals in treating mental disorders and their roles.

Assignment briefs

The board supplies suggested assignment briefs which you can use – see *Unit 6 Authorised assignment brief for Learning aims B and C*.

Your centre can also devise their own assignment brief which should have a vocational scenario/context and a series of tasks to complete.

Vocational scenario	The task (from the assignment brief)
You are required to focus on one disorder so your scenario might be a case study of your selected disorder.	Your report should include the following: • A **discussion** of causal factors related to mental disorders. (See pass criteria below.) • An **explanation** of the characteristics of **one** mental disorder, and an **assessment** and **evaluation** of the contribution of causal factors to that disorder. (See pass/merit/distinction criteria below.) • An **explanation** of treatments for that disorder (with reference to associated characteristics) and a **discussion** of the role of professionals in that treatment. (See pass criteria below.) • An **analysis** and **evaluation** of the role of professionals and treatments in that disorder. (See merit/distinction criteria below.)

Assessment information

Your final report will be awarded a Distinction (D), Merit (M), Pass (P), Near Pass (N) or Unclassified (U).

The specification provides criteria for each level as shown below.

Pass	Merit	Distinction
B.P3 DISCUSS different causal factors that may lead to mental disorders in individuals.		
B.P4 EXPLAIN the characteristics of one form of mental disorder.		
C.P5 EXPLAIN appropriate treatments for one form of mental disorder.		
C.P6 DISCUSS the role of professionals involved in diagnosing and treating one mental disorder.		
	B.M2 ASSESS causal factors that contribute to one mental disorder in relation to its associated characteristics.	
	C.M3 ANALYSE the ways in which professionals can contribute to the treatment of individuals with one form of mental disorder.	
		B.D2 EVALUATE the impact of causal factors that contribute to one mental disorder in relation to its associated characteristics.
		C.D3 EVALUATE the importance of the role of professionals and organisations, and treatments for one mental disorder.

See page 229 for an explanation of command terms used for learning aims B and C.

Marking factors The specification also provides information that an assessor will take into consideration when marking your assignment.

Marking factors	Pass	Merit	Distinction
A report that shows understanding/assessment of risk factors that impact on mental health/wellness and can be used to identify the onset of later mental disorders …	… generally accurate.	… reasoned.	… thorough.
Focus on …	… mental disorders.	… a type of mental disorder.	… a single type of mental disorder.
Discussion of characteristics and links between characteristics and earlier risk factors …	… generally accurate, some examples of risk factors.	… examples considered, well-structured and logically presented.	… wide range considered, logical and reasoned.
Examples of approaches to treatment for one mental disorder, and assessment of how they are administered/used …	… included, some inconsistencies and errors.	… a range that is mostly appropriate and accurate.	… detailed, clear and accurate understanding.
Professionals/organisations involved in diagnosing, treating and supporting individuals with mental disorders …	… some considered.	… considered account of at least two.	… detailed consideration of range of professionals.

Self-review checklist

The list below will help you manage writing your final report.

First draft

Remember this is a *draft*. So you can write anything, just get thoughts on the page (see 'Blank screen syndrome' on right). But do not copy anything, even at this stage.

Date to complete first draft:

- In the first grey column enter the completion dates for each section of your report.
- As you write each section tick the yellow boxes when you have discussed, explained, assessed, analysed and evaluated, as appropriate. Ignore the boxes that are crossed through.

	Date completed	Discuss (B.P3)	Explain (B.P4)	Explain (C.P5)	Discuss (C.P6)	Assess (B.M2)	Analyse (C.M3)	Evaluate (B.D2)	Evaluate (C.D3)
B1 Causal factors associated with mental disorders									
Prenatal, biological and health factors			✗	✗			✗	✗	✗
Family and environmental factors			✗	✗			✗	✗	✗
Social, political and cultural factors			✗	✗			✗	✗	✗
B2 Types and characteristics of mental disorders									
Personality disorders			✗	✗	✗	✗	✗	✗	✗
Self-injury			✗	✗	✗	✗	✗	✗	✗
Psychotic disorders			✗	✗	✗	✗	✗	✗	✗
Anxiety disorders and OCD			✗	✗	✗	✗	✗	✗	✗
Depression			✗	✗	✗	✗	✗	✗	✗
Eating disorders			✗	✗	✗	✗	✗	✗	✗
C1 Approaches to the treatment of mental disorders									
Psychodynamic therapy		✗	✗		✗	✗	✗	✗	
Behavioural therapies		✗	✗		✗	✗	✗	✗	
Cognitive therapies		✗	✗		✗	✗	✗	✗	
Family systems therapy		✗	✗		✗	✗	✗	✗	
Drug therapies		✗	✗		✗	✗	✗	✗	
Humanistic therapies		✗	✗		✗	✗	✗	✗	
C2 Mental health professionals									
Diagnosis and treatment by professionals		✗	✗	✗	✗	✗	✗	✗	✗
Support groups		✗	✗	✗	✗	✗	✗	✗	✗
References compiled									

Second draft

The next step is to revise your first document. Below is a checklist of things to consider.

Date to complete second draft:

	Date completed
I have checked that I have covered each of the five marking factors (grey column) in the table on the facing page.	
I have gone through and deleted any irrelevant material.	
I have checked that every point has evidence to back it up.	
I have identified long sentences and rephrased them.	
I have checked that each paragraph deals with one idea.	
I have corrected any spelling mistakes.	
I have checked that each paragraph makes reference to the scenario/context.	

Final draft

Read through your completed second draft to polish the report.

Date to complete final draft:

Blank screen syndrome

We all experience it – when you try to start writing something you end up staring at that blank screen and can't think where to begin.

It doesn't matter where you begin! That's what a first draft is about. Just write anything – but do write in your own words not chunks copied from the internet or this textbook, otherwise you will forget and they will end up in your final version (see 'Plagiarism' on page 229).

Stop copying

The best strategy is to close your textbook and just write what comes to mind.

Then open your textbook and see what extras you might add. Close the book and add them.

Never write with your book open (or the text on the screen) – it is difficult not to copy.

Unit 7

Applied sport psychology

What motivates us to play sport?

➡ *Make a list of the reasons people play sport.*

➡ *Do elite level sport players have a different set of motivations from those of us who play recreationally?*

➡ *Where does our motivation come from?*

➡ *Is it intrinsic or extrinsic – from within or from others?*

Contents

Pearson recommended assessment approach

A report on the key principles of psychological theories relating to motivation, self-confidence, arousal and anxiety, and how they can be applied to understand the experiences and performances of athletes. Learners can use case studies from professional sports performers or their own experience of competing in sport.

A programme of recommended psychological interventions to address the needs of a selected sportsperson.

Need achievement theory

Motivation exists on a continuum

Some of us are motivated to take part in sport at the elite level such as the swimmer above. The rest of us may prefer to swim recreationally once a week at our local pool or simply to splash around in the shallow end.

What we need to consider is *why* – why are there such individual differences in motivation? Lots of us enjoy sports because we like spending time with our friends and it helps us stay fit and active. For others, participating in sport is important because it fulfils our need to achieve and be successful.

If you participate in sport you will recognise the thrill when you beat your 'personal best' or when your team wins. However, you will also know that a lot of hard work and effort in training underpins those successes. Time spent practising is by no means as much fun as competing.

So understanding what *motivates* us to keep training hard is of real interest to sport psychologists.

Specification terms

Motivation Refers to the forces that 'drive' your behaviour. It encourages an animal to act. For example, hunger is a basic drive state which pushes an animal to seek food. Winning a match may drive you on to greater success, i.e. it motivates you.

Need achievement theory Explains an individual's desire to take part in sport because of a need to achieve success and avoid failure.

Defining motivation

Motivation explains what causes people to behave in a particular way. It is the drive or incentive or stimulus to act. Motivation to take part in sport can include wishing to improve our skills, having fun with friends, experiencing excitement, achieving success and/or developing fitness.

Key concepts of the theory

David McClelland (1961) and Jack Atkinson (1974) suggested that the reason why people engage in sport is the need to achieve something, called *achievement motivation*.

Some performers want to succeed in sport for the pride and satisfaction in performing well (*NACH, need to achieve* – described on page 280) whereas others seem to want to succeed only to avoid failure and the associated feelings of shame or humiliation (*NAF, need to avoid failure*). We all have aspects of both NACH and NAF, but it is the difference between the two motives that makes up our achievement motivation.

Need achievement theory suggests that five factors contribute to how likely performers are to engage in sport:

1. **Personality factors** People who are high achievers are motivated by the need for success but low achievers are motivated by the avoidance of failure.

2. **Situational factors** This includes the *probability of success* (e.g. which could be determined by the amount of training undertaken) and the *incentive value of success* (e.g. the experience of a golfer beating a strong opponent would have great value).

3. **Resultant tendencies** Personality and situational factors combine to show how people approach situations, called *resultant tendencies*. For example, a high achiever would prefer a challenging situation where the probability of success is high and there is value in being successful.

   However, low achievers are motivated by fear of failure and so prefer situations where there is a high probability of success (such as an easy opponent), or very unrealistic challenges (such as playing against a better opponent where losing is expected).

4. **Emotional reactions** This describes the player's emotional focus. Do they focus on the feelings of pride and satisfaction associated with success or on shame associated with failure? High achievers tend to focus on achieving success and low achievers focus on avoiding failure.

5. **Achievement behaviour** This is the combination of the above factors and relates to the motivation shown by the player. For example, high achievers are highly motivated to take on challenges whereas low achievers avoid risky or challenging situations and seek easy or impossible wins.

GET ACTIVE Michael Jordan's motivation

'I've missed over 9000 shots in my career, I've lost almost 300 games. 26 times I've been trusted to take the game's winning shot and missed. I've failed over and over and over again in my life. And that is why I succeed' (*Nike Culture: The Sign of the Swoosh*, 1998).

In this quote from a Nike advertisement, the famous American basketball player, Michael Jordan, shows how he turned it around for himself with sheer grit and determination.

Jordan was scrapped from his high school basketball team because at 5'11" he was deemed too short and lacked the skills to play even at high school level. However, Jordan never gave up and focused on the principle of 'I can accept failure but I cannot accept not trying'. Jordan went on to become the best player in the history of the sport.

How does need achievement theory explain Michael Jordan's success? What personality factors does he show? What is the situation that determines his motivation? How do the resultant tendency explain how he approached his challenging situation? Describe his emotional reactions and how all these factors culminate in his achievement behaviour.

Important note
Learning aim A covers ten theories. Learning aim B revisits all ten theories and applies them to sporting environments. Before you write your report you will therefore have plenty of time to understand the theories.

Evaluation

Explains high and low achievers

One strength of need achievement theory is that it explains why people are likely to engage in sport and can be considered as a low achiever or a high achiever.

For example, people who are low achievers are described as having a fear of failure and so they take on tasks that are very difficult or very easy so that they avoid feelings of shame should they lose. On the other hand, high achievers seek out challenges so that they experience pride and satisfaction when they win.

This suggests that players who have a need to avoid failure will be successful at a low level whereas players with a need to achieve will be successful at a higher level.

Helpful for coaches

Another strength is that this approach can be used by sports coaches because it shows how they can manipulate training situations.

Achievement motivation explores how people with a high versus a low *need to achieve (NACH)* vary in terms of their personality dispositions, motivational drive and task selection in sporting situations. This information is useful for coaches because they can give players practice tasks that focus on achievement, for example mastering techniques where they receive lots of positive reinforcement rather than avoiding failure.

This suggests that creating a positive motivational climate in training sessions is important for coaches in developing high achievers in their team.

Difficult to measure

One weakness of the theory is that it is difficult to reliably measure the need to achieve and the need to avoid failure.

For example, sports performers have to self-report their attitudes using questionnaires and it may be difficult to consistently interpret the scores of the NACH and NAF concepts. Additionally, some people choose risky sports such as rock climbing and others less risky sports such as bowls.

This would suggest that need to achieve and need to avoid failure may differ between sports but also between individuals, and that these concepts cannot reliably predict participation or performance in sport.

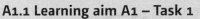

GET ACTIVE — It's not just about the money

Elite footballers are often criticised for being paid too much, for example Harry Kane was reputedly paid up to £200,000 per week. But what keeps players such as Harry Kane motivated once they are financially secure?

For many of them, money no longer becomes a factor for why they play sport. They want to play and to win because they enjoy the sport and the level of competition that challenges them in their professional career.

1. *What are the personality and situational factors of a sportsperson such as Harry Kane that keeps them motivated to train and perform each week?*

2. *What effect do these factors have on the sportsperson's emotional reactions?*

Assessment practice

At the end of learning aims A and B you must write:

A report on the key principles of psychological theories relating to motivation, self-confidence, arousal and anxiety, and how they can be applied to understand the experiences and performances of athletes. Learners can use case studies from professional sports performers or their own experience of competing in sport.

This report must be related to a scenario or context. We have used a real-life context.

Steph Houghton has been one of the captains of the England women's football team and Manchester City. She has overcome several serious injuries during her career, including a broken leg. She has won trophies and titles with Manchester City, Arsenal and Leeds and in 2019 captained England to a World Cup semi-final.

Former Leeds United WFC manager, Rick Passmore, said, 'Steph was always first on the training pitch and last off... even when injured she'd be with us, carrying the water, putting the balls out... She's a very proud individual so I'm sure she had her tears away from the club, but when she was at training, whether in a boot or on crutches, she was there all the time.'

Former Arsenal WFC manager, Laura Harvey, also said, 'We were getting a player who was really hungry to be better... she wanted to be coached.'

Source: *These Football Times* (2018)

A1.1 Learning aim A1 – Task 1

The first part of your report for learning aims A and B will be concerned with theories of motivation in sport – these are covered on this spread and the next two spreads (and again in learning aim B).

This activity will help you practise the skills required to write the report in response to your scenario/context.

You can see the assessment criteria and explanation of command terms on page 298.

1. **Explain** how Steph Houghton's behaviour supports the need achievement theory of motivation in sport. (A.P1)

2. **Discuss** the extent to which need achievement theory can account for changes in Steph Houghton's motivation. (A.M1)

3. Using Steph Houghton's experience as an example, **evaluate** how need achievement theory explains changes in motivation in sportspeople. (A.D1)

An issue to consider

Do you think motivation in sport is best explained by our personality characteristics or by the sporting situation in which we find ourselves?

Or is it a combination of both?

Specification content

A1 Theories of motivation in sport

- Definition of motivation: the direction and intensity of one's effort (Sage 1977).
- Need achievement theory (Atkinson 1974, McClelland 1961):
  - Personality factors.
  - Situational factors.
  - Resultant tendencies.
  - Emotional reactions.
  - Achievement behaviour.

Achievement goal theory

What drives Ronaldo?

One of the best footballers of his generation, Cristiano Ronaldo has revealed that the desire to become the best player in the world inspires him to improve his playing.

'I am as hungry as I have ever been,' he says, adding that 'I haven't broken so many records by accident. They're there to be broken, and breaking records motivates me to train and be even better. I have the ambition to always improve.'

So for Ronaldo his motivation is all about trying to be the best and setting realistic goals for himself.

'I will keep working hard to achieve it but it is within my capabilities.'

Source: *The Daily Express* (2017)

Specification terms

Achievement goal theory Explains motivation in terms of targets to be achieved.

Outcome or ego orientation People with an outcome or ego orientation believe their natural ability determines their success because it increases their belief in how good they are.

Task orientation Such people believe the effort they put into a task is likely to be rewarded with success.

Consider the motivational climate in this practice session. The way in which the golf coach creates a mastery climate means that the golfer is able to focus on improving his swing technique and ball flight.

Key concepts of the theory

This theory from Joan Duda and Howard Hall (2001) is based around two personality orientations: *task orientation* and *outcome* or *ego orientation*.

- **Task-orientated** athletes are likely to be motivated to take part in sport because they enjoy it and they prefer tasks that give them the opportunity for self-improvement. This would explain why Ronaldo (left) is willing to work hard in order to break so many footballing records.
- **Outcome or ego-orientated** athletes participate because they see sport as an opportunity to favourably compare themselves with others and show that they have superior ability. They prefer tasks that allow them to look good in comparison to other athletes.

Personality

These different orientations are basically about your *personality*.

For example, task-orientated athletes are far more likely to take on challenging tasks. This allows them the opportunity to see how well they have developed their skills due to their persistence and practice.

In contrast, ego-orientated people are much more interested in showing how good they are in comparison to other athletes. Therefore, they tend to choose much easier tasks so they can be seen to be successful.

When athletes train for their sport, those who are task-orientated are less likely to give up in comparison to ego-orientated athletes. This might be expected because we know that they believe that their success is determined by the amount of effort they put in. In contrast, ego-orientated people believe that their success is due to their natural ability and not just their efforts.

Situation-specific goal achievements

We have seen that people have personality orientations: task orientation and outcome/ego orientation. However, we may be able to explain *motivation* based on the interaction of the situation we find ourselves in and our personality.

Goal involvement explores motivation to see if people have different goals in specific situations. For example, as part of a training session, an ego-oriented golfer who we might expect to be only interested in the outcome, may believe the improvement in their chipping is due to hours spent on the practice ground.

Therefore, the *motivational climate* can contribute to how task- or ego-oriented a person might be.

- **Mastery climate** is where a coach gives supportive comments when an athlete persists in the face of challenges, helps others to improve through teamwork and tries to improve on the athletes' personal targets.
- **Competitive climate** uses competition and comparison between athletes, and high achievers will be more highly rewarded.

GET ACTIVE Coaching for motivation

Coaches and PE teachers should always try to create an environment to encourage the best performance from their team or players. The motivational climate is really important in developing determination based on enjoyment and well-being – intrinsic motivation (see next spread).

For beginners or less able players, a competitive climate can have a negative effect on players' self-esteem.

Imagine you are a rugby coach. Describe how you might design practice sessions to create a mastery environment for a group of year 7 players.

To help, you could speak to the PE staff at your school or college to get their thoughts. It may even be possible to work with them to help design and run a rugby practice or lesson.

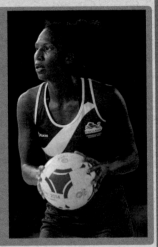 GET ACTIVE Motivation for elite sport

It is interesting to look at the influences that coaches, parents and peers have on the motivation of elite athletes.

Coaches tends to perform the key roles of leadership, instruction and evaluation of performance.

Parents are most important in terms of the way they support participation and learning. This can be through buying equipment and arranging weekend activities around sport but also the satisfaction and pride they show in their son or daughter.

Peer motivation tends to be encouraging and challenging of each other as well as fostering confidence – 'you can beat this guy'.

List some examples of the things a coach, parent or peer might say to give encouragement to a sportsperson.

Evaluation

Can be applied to practical settings

One strength of *achievement goal theory* is that it provides an effective approach for *sport psychologists*.

A psychologist would treat a task-oriented player differently from an ego-oriented one. For example, a task-oriented snooker player might be given tasks for improvement based on the number of long pots they make during their hours spent practising on the snooker table. On the other hand, an ego-oriented snooker player might be given a less experienced opponent to play against and simply compare scores.

This suggests understanding personality orientation is useful to motivate different kinds of players.

Helpful for coaches

Another strength is that achievement orientation can be used by sports coaches to create flexible training sessions where specific situations require different goals.

For example, a mainly ego-oriented performer may sometimes need to show involvement in a training task that requires practice and perseverance. This requires a switch to task-orientation. Knowing about the two different orientations means the coach can encourage flexibility in someone who may prefer to stick to ego-orientation.

This suggests that the motivational climate created by coaches is central to developing a healthy blend between ego and task orientations and that they can both exist in the same person.

Does not explain motivation for all sports

One weakness of achievement goal theory is that some sports require a very ego-based orientation and perhaps are less suited to task-oriented people.

For example, some martial arts such as Taekwondo are based very much on competition and winning.

This would suggest that motivation to play sport may depend on the type and characteristics of the sport rather than the motivation of the sportsperson.

Assessment practice

At the end of learning aims A and B you must write a report (see pages 263 and 298). This report must be related to a scenario or context. We have used a real-life context.

Serena Guthrie was a member of the England netball team that won gold in the 2018 Commonwealth Games. She moved from England in 2014 to play in Australia and New Zealand. Guthrie went for the challenge of playing with and against the best in the world: 'It's such tough competition (in Australia/New Zealand), it keeps you accountable week-in, week-out. You have to always be at your best.'

Guthrie is known as one of the fastest players in the sport, the result of intensive daily training. Looking forward to the World Cup in Liverpool in 2019 (in which England made it to the quarter-finals), she said, 'One player doesn't make a team, all 12 players do… There are so many great, genuine people in our team who want to do the best for each other. That's rare to find in team sport, to have everybody working to achieve so highly…' (bbc.co.uk, 2019).

A1.2 Learning aim A1 – Task 2

The first part of your report for learning aims A and B will be concerned with theories of motivation in sport, covered on the previous spread, this spread and the next spread (and again in learning aim B).

This activity will help you practise the skills required to write the report in response to your scenario/context.

1. **Explain** how Serena Guthrie's comments and experience support the achievement goal theory of motivation in sport. (A.P1)

2. **Discuss** the extent to which achievement goal theory can account for changes in Serena Guthrie's motivation as a sportsperson. (A.M1)

3. **Evaluate** how changes in Serena Guthrie's motivation can be explained by achievement goal theory. (A.D1)

An issue to consider

Do you think achievement goals in motivation are different between recreational level and elite level sport?

Specification content

A1 Theories of motivation in sport

- Achievement goal theory (Duda and Hall 2001):
  - Task orientation.
  - Outcome or ego orientation.

Self-determination theory

Why does the 'fire' burn so brightly?

Coaches are often heard saying that sports performers at the elite level are really driven, that they are hungry or obsessed with being successful. What makes the 'fire' burn more brightly for these highly motivated athletes such as Usain Bolt?

Elite sport environments are characterised by a focus on winning, medals and large financial rewards – these are called 'external' or extrinsic factors because they come from outside rather than inside the person.

Usain Bolt's journey to worldwide stardom started at the 2008 Olympic Games in Beijing where he won the 100 m, 200 m and 4 × 100 m, all in world record times.

He repeated these gold medal performances at the Olympic Games in London 2012 and Rio 2016. He also won golds at the same events at the World Championships in Berlin 2009, Moscow 2013 and Beijing 2015.

Was Usain Bolt's participation intrinsically or extrinsically motivated?

Specification terms

Amotivation An absence of any drive at all, i.e. no motivation to participate or be competent in an activity.

Autonomy Freedom from external control.

Competence The ability to do something successfully.

Extrinsic motivation Participating in sport for a reward or praise. The drive to continue comes from outside (external).

Intrinsic motivation Participating in sport for its own sake and wanting to play well. The drive to continue comes from inside you (internal).

Relatedness Feeling a connection to other things (e.g. people or events).

Self-determination theory Explains motivation in terms of a person's inborn psychological needs, seeing internal rather than external influences as more important.

Flow is a special case of intrinsic motivation. It is that sensation that sportspeople feel when they are totally involved in an activity, i.e. are on 'automatic pilot'.

Key concepts of the theory

Edward Deci and Richard Ryan's (2000) theory considers both *intrinsic* and *extrinsic motivation*, i.e. focusing on the extent to which people are 'driven' to take part in sports either from internal (intrinsic) drives or external (extrinsic) factors.

Individual needs

There are a number of different innate psychological needs. *Autonomy* is the extent to which sports performers feel it is their choice to participate in an activity without pressure to do so by parents or teachers. *Relatedness* is the need that sports performers have to feel accepted by others and to play sport because they form meaningful relationships with teammates or coaches. *Competence* is the belief that sports performers have that they can achieve desired outcomes, for example completing a triathlon.

Intrinsic (internal) motivation

In the case of intrinsic motivation people play sport for its own sake. Performers often say that their motivation stems from a desire to learn and improve skills, for the fun of taking part and to persist at the challenges that sport provides. For example, when children or adults learn new techniques such as parallel turns to allow them more easily to move from skiing a blue piste to more difficult red slopes.

Intrinsic motivation has three components:

1. **Knowledge** where a performer shows the need to learn new skills in order to develop performance.
2. **Accomplishment** enables a performer to demonstrate what they can do.
3. **Stimulation** provides a performer with the physical sensation of experiencing a task that gives them feedback to improve future performance.

Extrinsic (external) motivation

Self-determination theory also explains that extrinsic motivation (for example, the gold medals won by Usain Bolt, described on the left) drive behaviour but, more importantly, can encourage performers to move from a point where they have no drive to play sport, called *amotivation*, towards intrinsic motivation where sport is played for sheer pleasure.

However, this shift from extrinsic to intrinsic depends on the extent to which athletes can regulate or control their own behaviour and show autonomy.

There are four types of extrinsic motivation that can be spread along a continuum from external regulation to integrated regulation.

- **External regulation** – participation is carried out to please others (e.g. a coach or parent) or for a reward (e.g. the prestige of being a multiple Olympic champion such as Usain Bolt).
- **Introjected regulation** – an athlete performs to avoid feelings such as guilt or anxiety. They may also perform sport to feel good about themselves.
- **Identified regulation** – performers take part because they accept the benefit of participating in sport and recognise its value as a way to maintain friendships.
- **Integrated regulation** – an athlete considers performing as important as a personal goal. This is the most internalised form of extrinsic motivation and is closest to intrinsic motivation when motivation becomes self-determined. As such, we might consider whether there were occasions when Usain Bolt (after he had already won a gold medal) competed to try and break world records and not simply to win gold medals.

GET ACTIVE Creating autonomous performers

Olivia is a trainee PE teacher who has read that giving choice or autonomy to students in lessons helps their well-being and makes them more likely to persist in activities and practices.

Imagine you have been sent to advise Olivia on how to structure her lessons so that her pupils have more choice.

1. *What ideas should Olivia consider in order to increase intrinsic motivation and engagement in healthy, physical activity? You might consider whether she should include more game-play situations with rewards for the winners to develop extrinsic motivation. Or whether she should try to remove amotivation.*

2. *Does it matter whether the pupils like the choices they are given by Olivia?*

Providing players with the choice of which skills they practise, such as tackling, is important to help them develop the intrinsic motivation to improve.

Evaluation

Usefulness for PE teachers

One strength of *self-determination theory* is that it helps PE teachers provide autonomy support for their students.

For example, research by Behzad Behzadnia *et al.* (2018) has shown that PE teachers who provide students with choices and options, and are empathetic to what their students are thinking, are likely to increase intrinsic motivation in their students.

This shows that it is valuable for PE teachers to be need-supportive to help students' autonomous motivation and increase positive educational outcomes.

Understanding the performer

Another strength of self-determination theory is that it helps coaches understand what drives performers.

Such understanding helps to develop engagement with training sessions and match practices. For example, a hockey coach can tailor a training session to a player who wishes to spend time improving their dribbling or passing skills. In turn, the player will then be more willing to invest time and effort in developing these skills as they appreciate that the practice session has been designed for them.

This suggests that coaches can use the ideas of self-determination theory to create more effective training environments that are productive and stimulating for the players.

Rewards destroy intrinsic motivation

One weakness of self-determination theory is that using extrinsic rewards such as medals may actually reduce intrinsic motivation.

For example, an extrinsically motivated gymnast may only take part in order to please their parents or coach and so is less likely to strive for personal goals. If they were intrinsically motivated they are more likely to focus on the development of their skills and take on challenging vaults or floor routines. Ultimately this will lead to better performance.

This suggests that it is a mistake for parents and/or a coach to focus on extrinsic motivators.

Assessment practice

At the end of learning aims A and B you must write a report (see pages 263 and 298). This report must be related to a scenario or context. We have used a real-life context.

Andy Murray is arguably Britain's greatest ever tennis player. But early in his career he split from a number of coaches before achieving his greatest successes with Ivan Lendl, a champion tennis player. They formed a close and stable coaching relationship. When Murray lost in the Australian Open final in 2011, he stayed up all night with Lendl and the rest of his team, working out what he could do to improve next time.

In an interview with *The Guardian* newspaper he said, 'I can totally understand how parents who are very pushy take the enjoyment out of it, but that was not my experience... You need to love winning, you can't just hate losing. It's too negative... To play at a time when [other great players] are around obviously makes things difficult but it also makes your achievements mean more. That's why you put the work in' (*The Guardian*, 2010).

A1.3 Learning aim A1 – Task 3

The first part of your report for learning aims A and B will be concerned with theories of motivation in sport, covered on the previous two spreads and this spread (and again in learning aim B).

1. **Explain** how Andy Murray's behaviour and comments support the self-determination theory of motivation in sport. (A.P1)
2. **Discuss** the extent to which self-determination theory can account for changes in Andy Murray's motivation. (A.M1)
3. **Evaluate** how the self-determination theory explains changes in Andy Murray's motivation. (A.D1)

An issue to consider

Why do you think the way rewards are perceived by a performer is critical in determining whether intrinsic motivation increases or decreases?

Specification content

A1 Theories of motivation in sport
- Self-determination theory (Deci and Ryan 2000):
  - Individual needs for autonomy, relatedness and competence.
  - Intrinsic motivation – internal, knowledge, accomplishment, stimulation.
  - Extrinsic motivation – external, introjected, identified, integrated.
  - Amotivation.

Vealey's multidimensional model of sport confidence

The sports physiotherapist

Athletes require high level performance with demands placed upon their body that push their muscles, joints and bones to the limit. Sports physiotherapy deals with injuries related to sports people and helps athletes recover from sporting injuries, and provides education and resources to prevent further problems.

A physiotherapist must complete an approved degree level qualification or degree apprenticeship and be registered with the *Health and Care Professions Council.* Courses differ but all involve a lot of practical work with patients.

Sports physiotherapists usually have sport-specific knowledge that addresses acute, (short-term) chronic (long-term) and overuse injuries. They must also show an aptitude for caring for others.

When an injury occurs in sport, immediate attention is given to the part of the body that is affected – this is the physical part of the job. However, psychological challenges are also present and it is important to look at the types and sources of confidence used by athletes to help recovery and performance.

Specification terms

Multidimensional model of sport confidence Explains the relationship between trait sport confidence and state sport confidence. The updated model additionally included factors, sources, constructs and consequences of sport confidence.

Self-confidence The belief performers have that they will be successful.

" Call it a hunch....but I don't think he feels too confident! "

Defining self confidence

Self-confidence can be explained as the belief that you can successfully perform a desired behaviour (Weinberg and Gould 2015).

In the context of sport, Robin Vealey (1986) describes this as the belief or degree of certainty individuals possess about their ability to be successful in sport.

Key concepts of the model

The original sport-specific model of self-confidence developed by Robin Vealey (1986) conceptualises sport confidence in terms of two components:

- *Trait sport confidence (SC-trait)* The perceptions an individual has in their ability to be successful in sport, for example scoring a hundred in cricket.
- *State sport confidence (SC-state)* The perceptions an individual has at a particular moment about their ability to be successful in sport, for example this might include how quickly they recover from a particular injury.

The model also included a *competitive orientation* construct that explains individual differences in defining success in sport as either win or goal orientation. For example, performers may experience *motivation* from winning either because of feelings of satisfaction (win orientation) or developing goals through their own technical standards (goal orientation).

An updated model

Vealey (2001) later created a more integrated model of SC-trait and SC-state to include a broader perspective of how sport confidence works, involving factors, sources, constructs and consequences.

Factors influencing sport confidence There are different factors influencing SC-state in sport. It may come from social and organisational factors, such as the pressure of international competition which might increase or decrease self-confidence. A factor that would influence SC-state would be *personality* characteristics, such as *extroversion* (being very outgoing). Gender and age are also important factors, for example men may be more confident in some sports and older people might have more confidence because of past successes.

This confidence has an impact upon athletes' *affect* (enjoyment), *behaviour* (performance) and *cognitions* (SC-state). For example, the worry of Olympic competition can make SC-state unstable and fleeting (Gould *et al.* 1999).

Sources of sport confidence

- *Achievement* provides confidence for performers through *mastery* of skills and demonstrations of ability by outperforming opponents.
- *Self-regulation* gives confidence through physical and mental preparation for the competition ahead.
- *Social climate* can provide confidence if it is positive and achievement-nurturing. For example, support and leadership from coaches or physiotherapists and watching others perform successfully can provide confidence. Feeling comfortable in a competitive environment and belief that luck is on your side helps performers feel they will be successful.

Constructs of sport confidence

- *Cognitive efficiency* helps performers' confidence as they believe they can mentally focus and make effective decisions to perform successfully.
- *Physical skills and training* provides performers with a degree of certainty about their ability to execute the physical skills necessary to perform successfully.
- *Resilience* helps performers regain focus and bounce back from poor performance and injury setbacks to perform successfully.

Consequences of sport confidence Sport confidence is seen as a 'mental modifier' that continually influences how performers feel, think and behave before, during and after performance (Vealey 2001).

A person's expectations of success can affect confidence in their performance.

You can see the assessment criteria and explanation of command terms on page 298.

GET ACTIVE Girls active – attitudes and actions

In 2017, *Women in Sport* and the *Youth Sport Trust* published a survey of over 26,000 students from secondary schools in England and Northern Ireland. They found that 82% of girls understood the importance of an active lifestyle but only 56% of girls felt it was an important part of their life. Barriers such as competition, body image and low confidence were all put forward as possible reasons why girls do less physical activity than boys.

Using your knowledge of Vealey's sources and constructs of self-confidence, explain how teachers can improve the self-confidence of girls so that they can benefit from an active lifestyle.

You could also consider role models and friends, relevance of PE to girls and the design of PE lessons.

Evaluation

Improvements in self-confidence can be measured

One strength is that Vealey used her predictions to measure sources of self-confidence.

Vealey tested her model on 666 high school, college and adult sports performers, using questions to measure SC-trait, SC-state and competitive orientation. She found, for example, that mastery of skills was a key source in creating self-confidence.

This shows the value of the theory in being able to investigate sources of self-confidence.

Nature of the task

One weakness of the model is that it doesn't apply to all situations.

Research has shown that self-confidence has less impact when the task is a novel or unfamiliar one. Sandra Moritz *et al.* (2000) found that performers have lower levels of SC-state when they do not understand the demands of the task. For example, beginner golfers are often unclear about how to swing the club properly and so are less capable of predicting successful performance, i.e. low in self-confidence.

This suggests that coaches' explanations of technique are important in building confidence in performers.

Elite vs non-elite

A further weakness is that the confidence-performance relationship also appears to be stronger for elite rather than non-elite performers.

A *meta-analysis* of 48 studies by Tim Woodman and Lew Hardy (2003) found national or international performers' self-confidence was higher than that of state or regional performers. At national/international (elite) levels performers will have greater proficiency than those at lower levels. This in turn means that elite level performers can make more accurate judgements about their degree of success. And this further creates high self-confidence.

This shows us that proficiency (being elite versus being non-elite) plays an important role in self-confidence.

Assessment practice

At the end of learning aims A and B you must write a report (see pages 263 and 298). This report must be related to a scenario or context. We have used a real-life context.

Dame Katherine Grainger is a rower. As of 2019 she held five Olympic medals, the most of any British female Olympian at that time.

She won a silver in the double sculls at the 2016 Rio Olympics, by which time she was 40, unusually old for a rower. But just weeks before, she and her rowing partner Vicky Thornley had been left out of the squad.

Grainger took a two-year break after the 2012 London Olympics. She found it hard to return and lost form, which affected her self-confidence during that period. Yet she still believed that she would win a medal on the day: 'We just had to hold our nerve... it proves what a great working relationship [we have] to come out with a result like that'.

Another rower, James Cracknell, said Grainger and Thornley won silver in Rio by 'backing themselves in a way no one else backed them.'

Source: *espn.co.uk* (2016)

A2.4 Learning aim A2 – Task 4

The second part of your report for learning aims A and B will be concerned with theories of self-confidence in sport, covered on this spread and the next one (and again in learning aim B).

1. **Explain** how Katherine Grainger's experience and comments support the multidimensional model of sport confidence. (A.P1)

2. **Discuss** the extent to which the multidimensional model of sport confidence can account for changes in Katherine Grainger's sport confidence. (A.M1)

3. **Evaluate** how the multidimensional model of sport confidence explains changes in Katherine Grainger's sport confidence. (A.D1)

An issue to consider

There is a relationship between self-confidence and performance prior to an event but it is not a strong relationship.

Why do you think this may be? Are there other factors that affect performance? Are measures of self-confidence sensitive enough?

Specification content

A2 Theories of self-confidence in sport

- Definition of self-confidence: belief that you can successfully perform a desired behaviour (Weinberg and Gould 2015).
- Vealey's multidimensional model of sport confidence (1986, 2001):
  - Factors influencing sport confidence.
  - Sources of sport confidence.
  - Constructs of sport confidence.
  - Consequences of sport confidence.

Bandura's self-efficacy theory

Charity bungee jumping

The bungee jumper stood on the lip of the bridge 192 metres in the air, with a bungee cord strapped to her. After overcoming her fear, she dived head first off the platform.

It is the ultimate act of free will. The bungee jumper had to internally command herself to 'jump' despite her body's strong instinct to back away from the ledge.

Research by Surjo Soekadar in 2018 focused on the brain activity associated with bungee jumpers' free will. He found that approximately one second before jumping, the brain has already given the command. So the next time you find yourself in a bungee jumping harness or simply standing at the edge of a cold swimming pool trying to work up the nerve to take the plunge, remember the moment you tell yourself to jump, because your brain has already given the command.

In deciding to jump, a person has to actively work against their survival instincts and as Soekadar says, 'nobody can tell me that we don't need free will to do this'.

But what makes you think you could do it? That's what self-efficacy is all about.

Specification terms

Athletic performance Carrying out a specific physical activity.

Efficacy expectations Judgements about how successfully a performer can perform a task. This contrasts with outcome expectations which relate to the consequences of a successful performance.

Emotional arousal A state of heightened physiological activity.

Performance accomplishments Previously successful experiences.

Self-efficacy theory A person needs both belief and competence to successfully carry out a performance.

Verbal persuasion Encouragement used by teachers, coaches and peers to influence performers.

Vicarious experience Observing others engaging in a task that performers themselves have never executed.

Key concepts of the theory

Self-confidence (defined on previous spread) refers to the strength of belief to carry out an activity. However, according to Albert Bandura, the concept of self-confidence fails to include the important role of perceived competence.

Bandura (1977, 1986) introduced the term *self-efficacy* to describe the certainty *and* competence a performer has to successfully carry out a performance that will win a trophy or produce performance satisfaction. Self-efficacy is concerned with the judgements of what a performer can do with the skills he or she possesses rather than the skills themselves. It can be considered as a situationally-specific form of self-confidence.

Source of self-efficacy

Bandura's *self-efficacy theory* (1997) suggests that personal efficacy stems from four principal sources of information:

1. Performance accomplishments These provide the most dependable source of self-efficacy information because they are based on personal mastery experiences, such as using video playback of a successful penalty. If these experiences have previously been perceived as successes, this will raise personal efficacy expectations. In contrast, if past experiences have been perceived as failures, this will lower a performer's expectations.

2. Vicarious experience Self-efficacy information is also gained by *vicarious* (second-hand) experiences, for example observing or imagining others engaging in a task that performers themselves have never performed. The less experience a performer has with a task or situation, the more they will rely on others' experiences to assess their own capabilities. (You learned about *vicarious reinforcement* as part of the social learning approach in Unit 1 of our Year 1 'Certificate' book.)

3. Verbal persuasion Coaches and teammates often try to convince a performer that they 'can do it' to influence self-efficacy. However, this is not seen as being a powerful tool and the extent of such persuasive influences on self-efficacy depends on the credibility, status and expertise of the coach.

4. Emotional arousal Some athletes may interpret increases in their physiological arousal as an indication that they cannot perform the skill successfully, whereas others may interpret this state as being a sign that they are ready for performance. Bandura suggests that performers use such indicators of physiological arousal, for example their levels of fatigue and fitness, to gauge self-efficacy for an activity.

Seeing someone else perform a movement may encourage you to believe you can do it.

Efficacy expectations

Bandura distinguishes between *efficacy expectations* and *outcome expectations*. Efficacy expectation is a judgement of a performer's ability to perform at a certain level, whereas outcome expectation pertains to their judgement of the likely consequences of such a performance. For example, the belief a runner has to complete a marathon in less than two hours is an efficacy judgement. On the other hand the anticipated social recognition, money and the self-satisfaction created by such a performance are outcome expectations.

Athletic performance

A performer's judgement of their capability to perform at given levels affects their choice of activities, effort and persistence, their thinking, and their emotional reactions in demanding or anxiety-provoking situations.

Bandura concludes that self-efficacy is a major determinant of success in sport but only when people have sufficient incentives to act on their self-efficacy and when they possess the necessary skills to carry out successful performance. It is how these sources interact that determines *athletic performance*.

As part of your course you have learned about *social learning theory* – Bandura's original theory about how we learn by observing models and then *modelling* the behaviour. Coaches and PE teachers model sports techniques and their demonstrations to increase self-efficacy by transferring certainty and competence for successful performance.

Evaluation

Self-efficacy can be measured

One strength of the theory is that self-efficacy can be measured.

Richard Ryckman and colleagues (1982) developed the *Physical self-efficacy scale* to measure perceived physical ability and physical self-presentation confidence (jointly these indicate the confidence a person has in being able to perform physical skills). The participants also performed two physical tasks: a reaction-time task and a movement coordination task. The researchers found a significant correlation between the overall perceived physical self-efficacy and performance, and also between the perceived physical ability scores and performance.

This suggests that self-efficacy can successfully predict performance in physical activity.

Global vs task-specific

A further strength is that research supports the distinction between general and specific measures of physical self-efficacy.

Edward McAuley and Diane Gill (1983) found that task-specific measures of self-efficacy in gymnastics areas such as vault, beam, bars, and floor exercise are a much better predictor of gymnastics performance than the global measure of physical self-efficacy such as the Physical self-efficacy scale.

This supports the idea that specific measures of self-efficacy have greater explanatory and predictive power than global measures.

Problems with correlations

One weakness of the self-efficacy theory is that supporting research is only correlational.

The research by McAuley and Gill (above) used the physical self-efficacy scale to measure self-efficacy in women's intercollegiate gymnasts. The women's self-efficacy scores were correlated with their performance scores for the vault, bars, balance beam, and floor exercise. The findings showed significant correlations for the relationship between self-efficacy and gymnastic performance. However, this does not show that self-efficacy caused better performance. There might be another variable involved, such as decreased anxiety.

This correlational nature of the evidence undermines the view that self-efficacy enhances performance.

Assessment practice

At the end of learning aims A and B you must write a report (see pages 263 and 298). This report must be related to a scenario or context. We have used a real-life context.

Ellie Simmonds is a swimmer. She won multiple medals across three Paralympic Games.

She knew from a very young age that she had great potential in the pool and quickly acquired a taste for winning. Aged ten, Simmonds won all the races she entered at the British Junior Championships. At 13 she was the youngest British competitor at the Beijing Paralympics.

As a child, Simmonds trained with able-bodied swimmers, doing exactly what they did. She competed against them too, but there came a point when her dwarfism put her at a disadvantage, so she switched to disability swimming.

Training for Tokyo 2020, she has complete trust in her coach Billy Pye: 'he understands how I think and what I respond to' (*girlguiding.org.uk*, 2017).

A2.5 Learning aim A2 – Task 5

The second part of your report for learning aims A and B will be concerned with theories of self-confidence in sport, covered on the previous spread and this one (and again in learning aim B).

1. **Explain** how Ellie Simmonds' experience and comments support Bandura's self-efficacy theory of self-confidence in sport. (A.P1)
2. **Discuss** the extent to which Bandura's self-efficacy theory can account for changes in Ellie Simmonds' self-confidence in sport. (A.M1)
3. **Evaluate** how Bandura's self-efficacy theory explains changes in Ellie Simmonds' self-confidence in sport. (A.D1)

ᴳᴱᵀ ACTIVE Self-efficacy helps adherence

Imagine you are an instructor at your local fitness centre. You have to design a six-week programme of exercise sessions for 18–25-year-olds. You plan to use your knowledge of Bandura's self-efficacy theory to encourage over-60s to participate and stick to your exercise programme.

1. *What experiences of exercise or physical activity might your participants have had previously?*
2. *How might you demonstrate the new exercises?*
3. *What types of encouragement might you give to ensure the participants adhere to the programme?*
4. *How might you manage their efficacy expectations during the programme?*

An issue to consider

A highly successful sport performer, such as the tennis player Roger Federer or footballer Lionel Messi, will have high self-efficacy. What happens when they experience an occasional loss of a set or match? To what extent do you think this will affect their levels of self-efficacy?

Specification content

A2 Theories of self-confidence in sport

● Bandura's self-efficacy theory (1977, 1986, 1997):
  ○ Performance accomplishments.
  ○ Vicarious experiences.
  ○ Verbal persuasion.
  ○ Emotional arousal.
  ○ Efficacy expectations.
  ○ Athletic performance.

Drive theory and Inverted U hypothesis

Three Lions on a shirt

England's win over Colombia in a penalty shootout at the 2018 World Cup in Russia, laid to rest a personal ordeal for England manager Gareth Southgate – who had missed a vital penalty 22 years earlier in the semifinals of Euro '96 against Germany. In his autobiography, Southgate describes himself as the man who shattered a nation's dream.

Penalty shootouts are often described as a lottery, yet the England manager strongly disagrees. 'Definitely, it's not about luck. It's not about chance. It's about performing a skill under pressure.'

This time Southgate already had his five designated penalty-takers drawn up and the back-up options. England's players even took *psychometric tests* before the tournament to identify the best psychological profile to be first choice picks.

Southgate explains that he has looked at how to approach a shootout, making sure there is calm and that they take control of the situation. 'We have to be prepared physically and mentally to go to extra time and beyond if that's what it takes' (*The Guardian*, 2018).

Specification terms

Anxiety Feelings or thoughts that can have a negative impact on sport performance.

Arousal Raised levels of physiological functions such as increased blood pressure and muscle tension.

Drive theory Explains motivation as a simple linear relationship between increasing arousal and improved performance.

Inverted U hypothesis Explains motivation as a curvilinear relationship where increasing arousal leads to improved performance up to a point and then higher arousal leads to a decline.

The point of optimal arousal varies between sports. Sports such as darts, that require complex, coordinated movements, need low levels of arousal for optimal performance. Other sports, such as rugby, need higher levels of arousal for simpler, larger muscle movements.

Defining arousal and anxiety

Arousal refers to a physiological (body) and mental state of readiness. The terms *arousal, excitement* and *stress* are often used interchangeably, and can all be defined in terms of activation of the nervous system, as we explain in Unit 3 on Health psychology (see pages 11 and 46). The physiological response to stress ends with the production of *adrenaline*, which has the effect, for example, of increasing heart rate. Stress (and arousal) also has effects on mental activity, such as sometimes a better ability to focus attention.

Sport performers who are optimally aroused are therefore those who are physically and mentally ready to perform.

Anxiety is related to arousal (and excitement and stress). It has both trait and state components. *Trait anxiety* is an enduring characteristic of someone's *personality*, for example someone may be characteristically nervous. It is stable which means that a person behaves like this throughout their life. *State anxiety* refers to temporary feelings of worry in a particular situation.

Key concepts of the theories

The specification identifies five explanations for arousal and anxiety. We start with two of them on this spread.

Drive theory

Clark Hull's (1943) *drive theory* suggests that as arousal increases so will performance, a *linear* (straight line) relationship. However, this affects experts and beginners differently. At any time the 'dominant response' is the response that comes most easily and quickly.

- For experts, when arousal is high, they can still produce a well-learned skill accurately.

- For beginners the skill is not well-learned so their dominant response is less accurate (or correct).

However, even elite level performers make mistakes under pressure, as we have seen with Gareth Southgate's missed penalty (on left). The increased pressure created by the 'sudden death' nature of the penalty shootout resulted in over-arousal, performance dropped and the penalty was missed.

So we might suggest that arousal only benefits sport performance up to a certain point, after which the athlete becomes over-aroused and their performance decreases. This leads us to our second explanation.

The inverted U hypothesis

The *inverted U hypothesis* (Yerkes-Dodson 1908) is so-called due to its shape (see right).

It suggests that a gradual increase in a performer's arousal levels will lead to a gradual

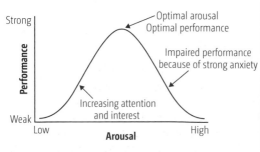

increase in performance – but only up to an optimal point.

At this point any further increases in arousal will lead to a gradual decline in performance.

If arousal is either too high or too low, performance will drop. Ideally, performers will aim for optimal levels of arousal where performance will be at its highest. This optimal level is usually a moderate level of arousal.

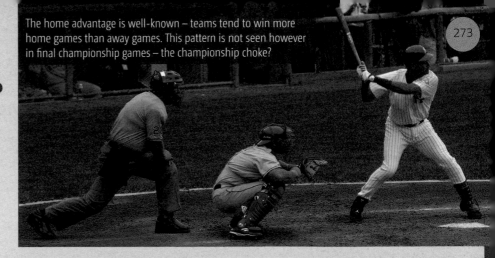

The home advantage is well-known – teams tend to win more home games than away games. This pattern is not seen however in final championship games – the championship choke?

^{GET}ACTIVE The championship choke

This phrase has been coined to explain decreases in sport performance under pressure. When the stakes are high, the biggest fear for any player is that they will choke. Psychologist Roy Baumeister found that in baseball's World Series, teams tend to win when they are playing at home in early games in any season but lose decisive, final home games.

This pattern occurs even when the home team has the opportunity to win the championship. This has also been found in semi-final and championship series in professional basketball.

1. *What factors could contribute to why the championship choke might exist?*

2. *Do you believe that choking involves some element of over-arousal? Can the championship choke be explained by drive theory or the inverted U hypothesis?*

Evaluation

Improvement on drive theory

One strength of the inverted U hypothesis is that, unlike drive theory, it does explain declines in performance when athletes are under extreme pressure.

For example, penalty takers such as Gareth Southgate do miss when facing increased levels of arousal. Whereas drive theory would suggest that they would score because performance should increase as arousal increases (Harmison 2011).

This suggests that the inverted U hypothesis has greater application to sport than drive theory and can be used by coaches to achieve optimal arousal.

Oversimplification

One weakness of the inverted U hypothesis is that it oversimplifies the complex interaction between performers' arousal and their sport performance.

For example, it is difficult to quantify high or low arousal and so a player would struggle to optimise their arousal when faced with a challenging routine.

This suggests that, although players should perform a warm up to raise arousal levels, they will find it difficult to measure or maintain optimal arousal levels during performance.

Simple or complex tasks

Another weakness is that the inverted U hypothesis doesn't explain different kinds of tasks.

Joseph Oxendine (1970) claims it fails to explain differences in optimal arousal for simple or complex tasks. For example, complex tasks such as golf putting need a lower optimal arousal level than simple tasks such as running that require higher levels for optimal arousal.

This suggests that as the optimal level of arousal can vary between sports, coaches need to personalise their players' preparations for performance in order to optimise arousal.

Assessment practice

At the end of learning aims A and B you must write a report (see 263 and 298). This report must be related to a scenario or context. We have used a real-life context.

Eric Bristow was a five-time world darts champion when he was struck down by 'dartitis', a disturbance of a player's fine motor movements. In Bristow's case, it meant he could not let go of the dart he was throwing. It could be described as darts' version of 'choking'.

Although not fully understood, it may be linked to anxiety and over-arousal. Bristow himself put it down to an 'extreme fear of missing'. The irony of Bristow's dartitis was it got worse the more effort he put in because he became more anxious. Knowing that he could not release the dart smoothly no matter what he did increased his arousal even further.

A3.6 Learning aim A3 – Task 6

The third part of your report for learning aims A and B will be concerned with theories of arousal and anxiety for sports performance, covered on this spread and the next three spreads (and again in learning aim B).

1. **Explain** how Eric Bristow's experience of dartitis supports the inverted U hypothesis of arousal and anxiety in sport. (A.P2)

2. **Discuss** the extent to which the inverted U hypothesis can account for changes in Eric Bristow's arousal and anxiety levels. (A.M1)

3. **Evaluate** how the inverted U hypothesis explains changes in arousal levels in the case of Eric Bristow. (A.D1)

An issue to consider

Gareth Southgate's England penalty takers focused on controlling the situation in order to score under pressure. The attendance at the stadium was over 44,000 people. To what extent do you think the crowd affects penalty takers?

Consider other factors that can create pressure on performers.

Specification content

A3 Theories of arousal and anxiety for sports performance

● Psychological definitions of arousal and anxiety.

● Drive theory (Hull 1943) – linear relationship between arousal and performance.

● Inverted U hypothesis (Yerkes and Dodson 1908) – curvilinear relationship between arousal and performance.

Multidimensional anxiety theory

Laura Townsend

PE teachers need to have the ability to enthuse and engage with their pupils and effectively communicate sports techniques and strategies. But PE is more than just performance. It is also about developing healthy living for all pupils, including positive mental health, and creating self-confidence that can be transferred to all walks of life.

Having joined Clacton County High School as a trainee PE teacher just three years before, Laura Townsend was voted Pearson 'Teacher of the year' for 2018. Her qualities include a unique, innovative and passionale teaching style that complements her enthusiastic PE teaching.

Laura organises regular engagement events including the 'This Girl Can' assault courses (see below) and 'Colour Runs' that involve students, staff and parents. The Colour Run is the most unique 5 km colour fun run in the world where runners start the day in a white T-shirt and get covered from head to foot in a rainbow of colours at four Colour Zones.

Laura inspires students daily to reach beyond their expectations and achieve more. Clearly an outstanding practitioner, coach, mentor and guide for all her pupils, the broader life of her school would not be the same without Laura.   Adapted from *teachingawards.com* (2018)

This Girl Can is a Sport England campaign to get women and girls moving, regardless of shape, size and ability. Celebrating being active no matter how they look or how well they do, participants overcome any negative expectations of success due to cognitive anxiety in order for them to successfully take part and complete this assault course.

Key concepts of the theory

On this spread we look at the third explanation of *arousal* and *anxiety*, the *multidimensional anxiety theory* from Rainer Martens *et al.* (1990).

(This is now the second multidimensional model you have studied. On page 268 we discussed Vealey's multidimensional model of sport confidence. It's just a popular phrase meaning there is more than one dimension!)

State and trait components of anxiety

The theory makes a distinction between different aspects of anxiety. In the context of sport:

- *Trait anxiety* (A-trait) is a performer's tendency to be anxious in evaluative situations such as during competition. This is an enduring aspect of their *personality*.
- *State anxiety* (A-state) reflects our current level of anxiety and can vary from one situation to another such as the 'This Girl Can' assault courses and colour runs (see left).

Performers high in A-trait are more likely to perceive situations as threatening and respond with more intense levels of state anxiety than performers with low A-trait.

State anxiety is multidimensional

The multidimensional anxiety theory is, in particular, interested in the different levels (dimensions) of state anxiety. At any time a performer may be experiencing both of these at different levels:

Cognitive anxiety (cog A-state) is the mental component of anxiety characterised by a fear of failure, negative expectations of success and negative self-evaluation. This may occur, for example, when students tackle an assault course and doubt their ability to complete it.

Somatic anxiety (som A-state) is an individual's perception of their physiological (body) response that stems from arousal and shows itself for example as sweaty palms or rapid heart rate.

Behavioural outcomes

The multidimensional anxiety theory predicts that performance is likely to decrease as *cognitive anxiety* increases (a negative *linear* relationship).

With *somatic anxiety*, the theory predicts an inverted U relationship. As somatic arousal increases so does performance to an optimal point but any further increases in somatic anxiety will lead to a decrease in performance.

The negative effects of both cognitive and somatic anxiety may manifest as poor posture, lethargic movement or playing safe. The role of a coach or teacher (such as Laura) is to help students overcome these effects of anxiety.

Specification terms

Behavioural responses The way we respond to cognitive and somatic anxiety in our performance.

Cognitive anxiety The negative thoughts we have about our performance.

Multidimensional anxiety theory Explains state anxiety as having two components, cognitive and somatic anxiety, each influencing performance differently.

Somatic anxiety Our physiological symptoms of anxiety, such as butterflies in the stomach.

State anxiety Our current level of anxiety, an emotional state characterised by apprehension and tension.

Trait anxiety A predisposition to perceive certain situations as threatening and to respond to the situation with varying levels of state anxiety.

Evaluation

Anxiety can be measured

One strength of the multidimensional theory of anxiety is that the different components can be measured using the *Competitive state anxiety inventory* (CSAI-2).

The inventory measures cog A-state, som A-state and self-confidence with nine statements each, such as 'I am nervous'. Performers rate each statement on a 4-point scale, where 0 is 'not at all' and 4 is 'very much so'. The final score in each category is between 9 and 36 and can be used by coaches to identify, for example, which performers experience high state anxiety so they can provide interventions to control anxiety in order to maximise performance (Martens *et al.* 1990).

This means that the theory provides a useful way to quantify anxiety and use that to improve performance.

Individual differences

Another strength of the multidimensional theory of anxiety is that it allows coaches to identify how different performers respond to anxiety so they can tailor training programmes to individual needs.

Two tennis players may both experience arousal before a match but one responds with mainly cog A-state, the other player with mainly som A-state. The first player may respond to the arousal by having concerns about the effectiveness of their serve, which is a cognitive response, whereas the second player may respond to the arousal by experiencing butterflies in their stomach (a somatic response).

This suggests that it is important for coaches to understand how each form of anxiety shows itself in different performers so they can maximise performance (Martens *et al.* 1990).

Interactions between cognitive and somatic anxiety

One weakness of the multidimensional theory of anxiety is that it does not consider possible interactions between different components of anxiety (Craft *et al.* 2003).

For example, hockey players may perform better with moderate levels of som A-state when cog A-state is low rather than when cog A-state is high.

This suggests that the multidimensional theory of anxiety only provides coaches and *sport psychologists* with a limited understanding of the effect of anxiety on performance.

Answers on the CSAI-2 are given on a scale of 1–4 where 4 is very anxious. But there are several problems with data collected like this – does it actually represent what people experience? Do some people lie? Do some over-estimate their anxiety, or underestimate it?

Assessment practice

At the end of learning aims A and B you must write a report (see pages 263 and 298). This report must be related to a scenario or context. We have used a real-life context.

Victoria Pendleton retired in 2012 as one of Britain's greatest ever cyclists and Olympians. But in 2008, she explained the anxieties she experienced in a sport she dominated. Talking about the Beijing Olympics (where she won a gold medal), she said, 'I was an emotional wreck beforehand because, while I was happy for everyone else, I was apprehensive about my ride. I worried that I would be the one person who let down the team. So winning was just a relief. And even that felt like a complete anticlimax' (*The Guardian*, 2008).

On other occasions, she has talked about 'The Curse' – being the favourite to win and the expectations that come with it: 'It's exciting but it's also added pressure. It churns away in my stomach at times... It makes me feel anxious just thinking about it' (*skysports.com*, 2010).

A3.7 Learning aim A3 – Task 7

The third part of your report for learning aims A and B will be concerned with theories of arousal and anxiety for sports performance, covered on the previous spread, this spread and the next two spreads (and again in learning aim B).

1. **Explain** how Victoria Pendleton's experiences and comments support the multidimensional anxiety theory of arousal and anxiety in sport. (A.P2)

2. Referring to Victoria Pendleton's comments, **discuss** the extent to which multidimensional anxiety theory can account for changes in arousal levels. (A.M1)

3. Referring to Victoria Pendleton's comments, **evaluate** how the multidimensional anxiety theory explains changes in arousal levels. (A.D1)

GET ACTIVE Love or loathing?

Some children can't wait to run off their energy in physical education lessons, but for others, PE is the most dreaded time of the school day. They may be embarrassed about their lack of athletic ability or self-conscious about their weight and/or changing body. Fear of PE can keep children from enjoying school and embracing a healthy lifestyle.

Imagine you are a PE teacher with some children in your class who experience anxiety during PE lessons. What strategies would you use to make your lessons as inclusive as possible so that all children feel comfortable to take part and achieve?

You could consider their level of skills, the extent to which they enjoy physical contact activities or their level of fitness.

An issue to consider

What do you think is the relationship between self-confidence and performance in sport? Additionally, do you think that self-confidence is closely linked to cognitive anxiety or somatic anxiety?

Specification content

A3 Theories of arousal and anxiety for sports performance

- Multidimensional anxiety theory (Martens *et al.* 1990):
  - State and trait components.
  - Cognitive, somatic and behavioural components.

Catastrophe theory

Jennifer Savage, Performance psychologist

If you've watched sports, you've seen the following scenario: With seconds on the clock and the game tied, a player needs to make one free throw to win the game. They take a deep breath, focus, shoot – and score!

Have you then wondered how they did it, with the crowd roaring, under such pressure? It's possible they have been working with a *performance psychologist* whose job is to focus sportspeople on the *mental* aspect of achievement. Often behind the scenes, they are vital in helping individual players or even entire teams realise their potential.

Performance psychologists such as Jennifer Savage (above) help performers through various mental strategies, such as visualisation and relaxation techniques to achieve their full potential by coping with the pressures of competition. However, as practitioners, performance psychologists can only facilitate performance up to a certain point – then it's up to the performers themselves.

Top level competition can create high cognitive anxiety which can have catastrophic consequences on performance unless performers are able to control it.

Specification term

Catastrophe theory Explains when cognitive anxiety is high and increases in arousal beyond optimal levels create a rapid decline in performance.

Even if cognitive anxiety is high, the process of hysteresis is likely to occur too late to help once the baton has been dropped at a relay changeover.

Key concepts of the theory

This is the fourth of our explanations for *arousal* and *anxiety*.

Lew Hardy (1990, 1996) developed a theory which he had originally proposed with John Fazey (1988). They had noticed that when performers became over-aroused, their performance did not follow a gradual decline as proposed by the *inverted U hypothesis*.

Instead Hardy and Fazey pointed to a large, catastrophic fall in performance from which it would be difficult to recover. For example, over-arousal might lead a runner to drop the baton in a world championship relay race, a situation which would lead to utter disaster.

On the previous spread, you studied the *multidimensional anxiety theory* which explains that *state anxiety* has two components: *cognitive* and *somatic anxiety* which influence performance differently. You will recall that somatic anxiety is an individual's perception of their physiological response that stems from arousal.

However, *catastrophe theory* suggests it is cognitive anxiety that is the vital 'splitting factor' that determines whether or not the effect of arousal is a smooth and small decline or whether the effect is large and catastrophic.

- **Low cognitive anxiety** Cognitive anxiety refers to your mental state. When a performer is experiencing low cognitive anxiety, physical (somatic) arousal and performance show a weak inverted U relationship.

- **Low physiological arousal** 'Physiological' refers to your body, your somatic state. When physiological arousal is low the theory predicts that cognitive anxiety will have a positive relationship with performance – as cognitive anxiety increases so does performance.

- **High physiological arousal** When there is high physiological arousal, cognitive anxiety will have a negative relationship with performance – as cognitive anxiety increases performance will decrease.

- **High cognitive anxiety** When cognitive anxiety is high any increases in physiological arousal will lead to a catastrophic drop in performance.

A summary		Cognitive anxiety	
		Low	High
Physiological arousal	Low	As cognitive anxiety increases so does performance.	OK
	High	As cognitive anxiety increases performance decreases.	Catastrophic drop in performance.

Predictions of catastrophe theory

Once a catastrophic drop in performance has occurred, a large reduction in physiological arousal is needed in order to return performance to pre-catastrophe levels.

Prediction 1 When a performer's cognitive anxiety is high the path of their performance differs according to whether physiological arousal is increasing or decreasing.

This is called *hysteresis*. When arousal is increasing, performance will increase and when arousal is decreasing, performance will decrease. Hysteresis does not occur when cognitive anxiety is low.

Prediction 2 When physiological arousal and cognitive anxiety are both high, performance will either be catastrophic or excellent and an average level of performance is unlikely to occur.

This is because the performer will either be performing on the cusp of optimal arousal or they will tip over the threshold and experience a steep decline in performance. Thus it is a fine line between a perfect relay run with clean changeovers and someone dropping the baton.

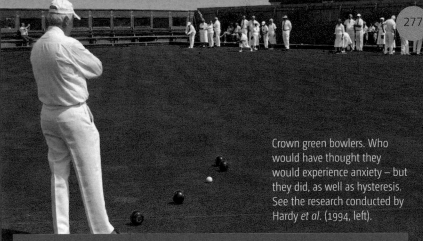

Crown green bowlers. Who would have thought they would experience anxiety – but they did, as well as hysteresis. See the research conducted by Hardy *et al.* (1994, left).

Evaluation

Interaction of anxiety and arousal

One strength is that catastrophe theory does account for the interactive effects of cognitive anxiety and physiological arousal on performance, in particular when task difficulty is high.

Tara Edwards *et al.* (2002) interviewed eight elite sportsmen aged 19–28 years old who participated in sports such as canoe slalom. The participants described catastrophic declines in performance such as, 'It was in the middle of the course and that's where I took the touch, I took the penalty and along with those doubts and suddenly bang, that was like, it was a big wound and I would say it takes, what 5 to 10 seconds to recover, too late'. These declines happened alongside the performers' reported increases in cognitive anxiety and, to a lesser extent, arousal.

This suggests that performers must understand how to control cognitive anxiety if they are to prevent catastrophic declines in performance.

Difficult to test

One weakness of catastrophe theory is that its complexity has made it difficult to test in competitive situations.

Therefore, the solution is to test it in rather artificial situations. For example, research carried out by Lew Hardy and Gaynor Parfitt (1991) involved eight female basketball players. Players were required to perform an artificial set-shooting task the day before an important competition (high cognitive anxiety) and the day after the competition (low cognitive anxiety). Performers carried out a shuttle run task to simulate the physiological arousal experienced in a basketball match. The findings showed that performance on the set-shooting task was lower the day before competition than the day after competition.

This would appear to support catastrophe theory but the nature of the tasks makes the findings difficult to apply to competitive sport situations.

Sampling bias

A further weakness of the theory is that participant samples have tended to be small.

For example, the research carried out by Lew Hardy *et al.* (1994) used a sample of just eight crown green bowlers and as we have seen above Hardy and Parfitt (1991) used a sample of eight basketball players.

This makes it difficult to generalise the findings as support for catastrophe theory and the claim that hysteresis does occur in all sport performers.

Assessment practice

At the end of learning aims A and B you must write a report (see pages 263 and 298). This report must be related to a scenario or context. We have used a real-life context.

Scott Boswell was a cricketer whose career high point was playing for Leicestershire in the C&G Trophy final in 2001. Boswell's expectations were high, he was looking forward to the best day of bowling in his life. His first over of the final was fine. But the first ball of his second over was wide, and the third and the fourth... he bowled six wides in eight balls. It was almost as if he had forgotten how to bowl.

He said in an interview in 2013: '[The batsman] looked as though he was 50 yards away. He was like a tiny dot...I just couldn't let go of the ball. I wanted to get on with it, so I began to rush. The more I panicked, the more I rushed' (*The Guardian*, 2013). Boswell was sacked two weeks later. He couldn't bowl a straight ball for nearly ten years.

A3.8 Learning aim A3 – Task 8

The third part of your report for learning aims A and B will be concerned with theories of arousal and anxiety for sports performance, covered on the previous two spreads, this spread and the next spread (and again in learning aim B).

1. **Explain** how Scott Boswell's experience and comments support the catastrophe theory of arousal and anxiety in sport. (A.P2)
2. **Discuss** the extent to which catastrophe theory can account for changes in Scott Boswell's arousal levels. (A.M1)
3. **Evaluate** how catastrophe theory explains changes in Scott Boswell's arousal levels. (A.D1)

GET ACTIVE Measuring your anxiety levels

On the previous spread we mentioned the *Competitive state anxiety inventory-2* (CSAI-2) which is relevant to this spread as well.

1. *Arrange for your class to complete the CSAI-2 online (see tinyurl.com/ycyu5m4n).*
2. *You will get three scores from each person, for cognitive anxiety, somatic anxiety and self-confidence. Plot two scattergrams:*
   - *Cognitive anxiety and self-confidence.*
   - *Somatic anxiety and self-confidence.*
3. *It would be expected that there would be negative relationships, with a stronger negative relationship for cognitive anxiety than somatic anxiety. Do your results support this?*

An issue to consider

The theories of arousal and anxiety that we have looked at make predictions about how they might affect performance. However, they tell us little about why performers get anxious.

Consider the effects of teammates, the audience, opposing team members, the performer's own skill levels or even the media. Which ones probably have the greatest effect?

Specification content

A3 Theories of arousal and anxiety for sports performance
- Catastrophe theory (Hardy 1990, 1996) – increases in arousal can lead to a sudden decrement in performance rather than a gradual decline.

Reversal theory of arousal

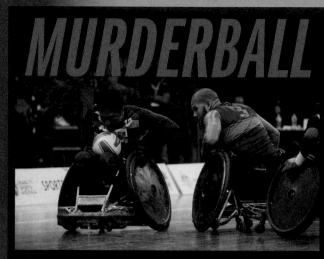

The Academy Award nominated film *Murderball* is considered one of the most engaging sports films ever. Thrilling and adrenaline-pumping, the documentary film focuses on the US quad rugby team (now called wheelchair rugby) who took part in the 2004 Paralympics. Wheelchair rugby is performed by players in custom-built wheelchairs which have metal side plates added to them.

Murderball follows the team from how they feel during their training until they make their appearance, winning the bronze medal.

Mark Zupan, captain of the team, said breaking his neck 'was the best thing that ever happened to me. I have an Olympic medal. I've been to so many countries I would never have been, met so many people I would never have met. I've done more in the chair ... than a whole hell of a lot of people who aren't in chairs' (*Washington Post*, 2005).

Do players interpret the high arousal levels that stem from this full contact sport as anxiety or excitement?

Specification term

Reversal theory of arousal Explains how an individual can change their interpretations of arousal depending on their state of mind.

Arousal too low.

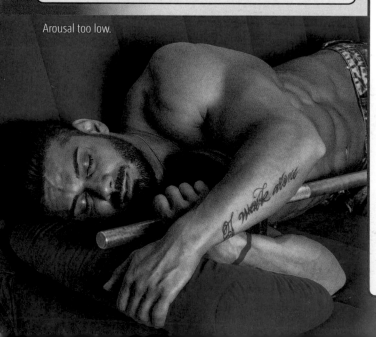

Key concepts of the theory

We now arrive at the final explanation for *arousal* and *anxiety*.

Reversal theory of arousal was put forward by John Kerr (1985) as a broad theory of *motivation*, emotion and *personality* but here we will only look at the way it is used by *sport psychologists* to explain anxiety.

Reversal theory differs from *drive theory* and the *inverted U hypothesis* as it suggests that performance is affected by the way in which performers *interpret* arousal levels as anxiety or not. This interpretation depends on their current mental state, what is known in reversal theory as a *metamotivational state*.

A metamotivational state is a frame of mind which comes in one of two forms:

Telic (serious) state Performers are motivated to achieve something meaningful and look at how this can contribute to longer term goals. In the *telic state*, low arousal is seen as pleasant relaxation but high arousal as unpleasant anxiety.

Paratelic (playful) state Performers are motivated to be spontaneous and enjoy what they are doing and do not concern themselves with future consequences. In the *paratelic state* high arousal is seen as pleasant excitement but low arousal as unpleasant boredom.

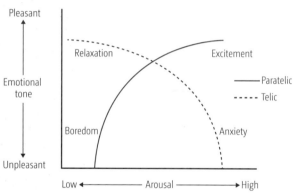

The relationship of telic (red dotted line) and paratelic (blue solid line) states in reversal theory.

Impact on performance

The emotional response (tone) of the performer depends on their preferred level or arousal, either in the telic or paratelic state.

Telic state In the telic state, where there is a preference for low arousal, performance should be optimal when arousal is low. Performers become anxious if they interpret events such as competition as threatening, which thereby raises arousal levels.

However, they become pleasantly relaxed when a task is completed and arousal falls, for example achieving training goals prior to an important competition.

Paratelic state In the paratelic state, where there is a preference for high arousal, performance should be optimal when arousal is high. Performers become pleasantly excited as they get more emotionally involved and aroused, such as when wheelchair rugby athletes complete a 'lap of honour' around the arena after their victory in an Olympic final.

This happens because the performers are able to interpret the arousal as excitement rather than anxiety or boredom.

Overall

Reversal theory differentiates between 'felt' and 'preferred' arousal.

- Performance should be better when there is no difference between the arousal levels a performer felt and the level they *preferred*.

- Performance will be worse when there is a difference (higher or lower) between the preferred and actual felt level of arousal.

Researchers found that slalom canoeists, whose felt levels of arousal matched their preferred levels, performed at their best (Males and Kerr 1996).

GET ACTIVE The triathlete

Imagine you are a triathlete at the 2020 Tokyo Olympics. You have to combine a 1.5 km swim with a 40 km bike ride, followed by a 10 km run. Of course you have no control over the conditions that may well change over the duration of the race.

1. Use your knowledge of reversal theory to explain the possible changes you may experience in telic and paratelic states during the race.

2. You may wish to consider your 'felt' and 'preferred' levels of arousal.
   - Could your arousal levels change over the duration of the race?
   - How would you interpret these changes?
   - What may be the reasons for changes in your arousal levels?
   - To what extent do you think you would be able to control your arousal levels?

Evaluation

Dominance can be measured

One strength is that telic and paratelic states can be measured and so reversal theory can be tested.

The *paratelic dominance scale* and the *telic state measure* were used by Jamal Bindarwish (2004) to differentiate between participants in a dart-throwing task. Findings showed that participants were more serious-minded in the long-throwing *condition* whereas they tended to be more playful-minded during the short-throwing condition.

This suggests that reversals from telic-to-paratelic states do occur.

Risk takers

Another strength is that telic/paratelic states have been shown to influence people's preference for participation in risky sports.

Research by John Kerr and Sven Svebak (1989) found that serious (telic-dominant) individuals are more likely to choose safe endurance-based sports, such as long-distance running, while playful (paratelic-dominant) individuals are more likely to participate in risky explosive sports such as surfing or rock-climbing.

This suggests that we may be able to predict people's involvement in risky sports based on the extent to which they seek arousal.

States for optimal performance

One weakness of reversal theory is that, as yet, there is no obvious evidence that specific metamotivational states are related to optimal performance.

Often performers can be successful when operating in either the telic or paratelic state. Research by Joanne Thatcher *et al.* (2011) used ten telic-dominant and ten paratelic-dominant participants on an exercise bike task. The researchers found no relationship between performance outcome and the telic or paratelic states. Similarly, Jamal Bindarwish and Gershon Tenenbaum (2006) found no relationship in a dart-throwing task between telic- or paratelic-dominant participants and performance.

This suggests that the relationship between the telic and paratelic states and performance has not been demonstrated.

Assessment practice

At the end of learning aims A and B you must write a report (see pages 263 and 298). This report must be related to a scenario or context. We have used a real-life context.

Usain Bolt is the fastest runner of all time. He won eight gold medals, setting several world records. For a period of more than ten years, he won almost every race he entered and the lack of truly tough competition meant he became complacent and bored. Bolt's early career was marked by a lack of seriousness, and he was criticised by some for being 'lazy'. He decided early on that he would do all he could to never experience nerves before a big race. He did this by focusing at the starting line on just the race.

Bolt was known for bringing a sense of fun to competition, for example by popularising the 'Lightning Bolt' and pleasing crowds with his pre-race antics. He sometimes gave a lap of honour before the race as well as after.

A3.9 Learning aim A3 – Task 9

The third part of your report for learning aims A and B will be concerned with theories of arousal and anxiety for sports performance, covered on the previous three spreads and this spread (and again in learning aim B).

1. **Explain** how Usain Bolt's experiences support the reversal theory of anxiety in sport. (A.P2)

2. **Discuss** the extent to which the reversal theory can account for changes in Bolt's anxiety in sport. (A.M1)

3. **Evaluate** how the reversal theory explains changes in Bolt's anxiety in sport. (A.D1)

An issue to consider

Think about the factors that may trigger reversals between telic and paratelic states.

What effect would a change in the environmental situation have on a performer's interpretation of arousal or indeed how frustrated a performer may become by remaining in the same state?

Would performers naturally reverse between states over time once they become satisfied in one state?

Specification content

A3 Theories of arousal and anxiety for sports performance
- Reversal theory of arousal (Kerr 1985, 1997) – impact of individual interpretation of arousal on performance.

Need achievement theory

True Grit

Have you seen the film? Not to be missed. One of the great characters of all time, it features 'Rooster' Cogburn (played by John Wayne in the original films and Jeff Bridges in a more recent remake). Mattie, aged 14, hires Cogburn to find her father's killer, because she hears he has 'true grit'. In the end Mattie also shows that she is Cogburn's equal.

The character trait of grit has been extensively researched by psychologist Angela Lee Duckworth and her colleagues (2007). She defines grit as extreme perseverance and passion for long-term goals.

'True grit' may be an important factor in sport performance.

Specification terms

Mastery Comprehensive knowledge or skill in an activity.

Need to achieve (NACH) An individual's desire for accomplishment and mastery of skills.

Need to avoid failure (NAF) An individual's motivation to avoid shame and negative feelings.

Task persistence The ability to perform despite distractions, physical or emotional discomfort or lack of immediate success.

Roger Federer's 20 Grand Slam titles (as of 2019) suggest he has a high NACH personality and true grit.

The theory

In learning aim A1 (page 262), we looked at David McClelland (1961) and Jack Atkinson's (1974) *need achievement theory* of why people engage in sport. They identified people's *need to achieve* and perform well (*NACH*) and their *need to avoid failure* and the associated feelings of shame or humiliation (*NAF*).

On this spread we will investigate the interrelationship of *need achievement theory* with the actions and reactions of people in sport (their *personality*) and high-pressure competitions (*situational*).

Applying the theory

The interaction between personality (NACH or NAF) and situational factors allows us to predict how a performer will react in sporting situations. These behaviours are called *resultant tendencies*.

Impact on task persistence

Performers with high NACH are likely to have already achieved success and probably want to feel the sense of pride again and strive for more success. They tend to select tasks that require perseverance. For example, when Roger Federer (high NACH) played tennis against Novak Djokovic (also high NACH) in the 2019 Wimbledon final they both maintained their motivation through five intensely long and gruelling sets – but they were motivated to persist in search of yet more victory.

In contrast performers with a high NAF do not see things this way. They tend to prefer unrealistic challenges that do not require them to exert much effort. For example, if a local darts club player challenged the 2019 world champion Michael Van Gerwen, he would not expect to win and therefore would be more likely to give up at the first sign that things were not going well – there would be little incentive to persist and show any grit in trying to achieve a win.

Impact on mastery

Mastery means being able to develop the skills required for high performance sport. Performers with high NACH are willing to persevere when the going gets tough. For example, rugby goal kickers such as England's Owen Farrell spend hours practising in the endless pursuit of perfection. Whereas performers high in NAF shy away from the commitment needed to develop the mastery of skills and tactical knowledge.

Choice of competitions/opponents

The *incentive value of success* is important in understanding the choice of opponents for NACH and NAF performers. The motives of high NACH performers are to strive for success and to experience pride and satisfaction in winning. Therefore, they are likely to choose challenging yet not unbeatable opponents. For example, England's netballers as Commonwealth champions would relish playing against world champions Australia.

However, performers with high NAF are motivated by fear of failure and choose opponents where they have a high *probability of success* regardless of the value this provides. What is important is avoiding feelings of shame and embarrassment. For example, a club squash player choosing to play the weakest player in the club to ensure a victory. In some situations high NAF performers may choose to play against much better opponents but these would be occasions when there is little shame in losing.

Effect of being evaluated

The effect of being judged, for example by an audience or the coach, is often stressful creating both *arousal* and *anxiety*. You learned about the effects of arousal on page 272 onwards.

High NACH players perform better when stressed because they have developed well-learned skills. In addition high NACH players perform better when being evaluated as they are used to challenging, risky situations that create stress. Therefore, they have learned how to cope with stress.

High NAF performers will experience more anxiety in stressful situations partly because their skills are less well-learned but also because of their fear of failure, an example of *cognitive state anxiety*.

NACHOS

GET ACTIVE NACH or NAF

From the following list of NACH or NAF statements, identify which ones are NACH and which are NAF.

- *A 200 m swimmer who sees fourth place as a temporary setback and will work harder to achieve a medal next time.*
- *A footballer who is happy playing recreational football.*
- *A gymnast who will try out a new release-and-catch move on the bars.*
- *A rugby player who does not like to take conversions in case they miss.*
- *Ideal people to coach to a higher level.*

Evaluation

Builds self-efficacy

One strength is that understanding achievement motivation in sport is useful.

When performers are motivated to improve their task mastery it can increase levels of *self-efficacy*. For example, a badminton player's drive to master a smash takes hours of practice but will then increase their self-efficacy. This then affects their ability to perform at a higher level and willingness to play against tough opponents (Feltz 1988).

This shows that insights into NACH can lead to better performance.

Helpful for coaches

Another strength is that achievement motivation theory can be helpful for coaches.

Coaches should try to identify which performers are high NAF so they can turn them into high NACH performers. They can do this by looking for the traits of high NAF, such as lack of persistence, shying away from commitment, low aspirations in choice of competitors and poor performance when anxious. The coach then focuses on each of these areas to produce 'true grit'.

This suggests that the theory has some practical value.

Subjective perceptions

One weakness in trying to apply achievement motivation to sport is that a performer's (and coach's) perceptions of their motivations are subjective.

For example, the task persistence and mastery of a tennis player can be assessed as high or low against their own standards or can be judged more objectively against the norms of other tennis players (Nicholls 1984). So a tennis player might show improvements against their own standards, but a gain in mastery alone does not indicate high achievement motivation in comparison to others.

This means that that the assessment of achievement motivation lacks usefulness.

Naff.

Assessment practice

At the end of learning aims A and B you must write a report (see pages 263 and 298).

This report must be related to a scenario or context. We have used a real-life context.

> You can see the assessment criteria and explanation of command terms on page 298.

Read again about the footballer Steph Houghton on page 263. The key quotation about her comes from Laura Harvey, former Arsenal WFC manager: 'We were getting a player who was really hungry to be better... she wanted to be coached' (*These Football Times*, 2018).

Think about why Steph Houghton was so hungry and keen to be coached. How would this impact on her task persistence, her mastery of skills and the prospect of playing against the best in the world?

B1.10 Learning aim B1 – Task 10

The first part of your report for learning aims A and B will be concerned with theories of motivation in sport, covered earlier in this unit (pages 262–267) and again on this spread and the next two spreads.

This activity will help you practise the skills required to write the report in response to a scenario, such as the one above.

1. **Explain** how need achievement theory accounts for Steph Houghton's footballing performance. Refer in your answer to her motivation and self-confidence. (B.P3)

2. **Discuss** need achievement theory in terms of how Steph Houghton's motivation and self-confidence impact on her footballing performance. (B.M2)

3. In terms of its strengths and weaknesses, **evaluate** how need achievement theory accounts for Steph Houghton's footballing performance. Refer in your answer to the relationship between her motivation and self-confidence and arousal levels. (B.D2)

An issue to consider

Do you think it is possible for a performer with high NAF characteristics to develop the characteristics of a high NACH performer?

Specification content

B1 Motivation theories in sporting environments

- Need achievement theory (Atkinson 1974, McClelland 1961):
  - Impact of levels of achievement motivation on task persistence and mastery.
  - Choice of competitions/opponents for high need to achieve (NACH) and high need to avoid failure (NAF) athletes.
  - Effect of being evaluated on performance of high and low achievers.

Achievement goal theory

Jerry Rice

In American football, the gold standard for work rate always belonged to San Francisco 49ers' wide receiver Jerry Rice.

Almost every day the assistant coach with the 49ers, Jim Mora, watched Rice's gruelling training regime and showed other players the video recordings of Rice's practices and then challenged them to be like Rice.

'Nobody matched up with him,' Mora said of Rice, 'His work ethic was legendary' (*Seattle Times*, 2007).

For Jerry Rice the importance of training was to improve his performance against his own standards rather than competing against others. By working against his own very high standards Rice turned himself into one of the greatest pass catchers in the history of the game.

Specification terms

Optimal performance The highest level of performance that can be achieved.

Persistence Continuing to perform or train despite difficulty.

Work ethic The principle that hard work is intrinsically worthy of reward.

See page 264 for other definitions.

Only one of these 100 m sprinters will win the race but those with a task orientation will focus on their own time and judge their performance against their personal best.

The theory

Achievement goal theory proposed by Joan Duda and Howard Hall (2001) is based around two personality orientations: *task orientation* and *outcome* or *ego orientation* (also discussed in learning aim A1, page 264).

Task-orientated performers are likely to be motivated to take part in sport because they enjoy comparing their current and previous performances and focusing on personal improvement. However, ego-orientated performers focus on comparing their performance with, and defeating, others.

Applying the theory

Sport psychologists argue that the value of a *task orientation* is that it improves three important factors in performance: *work ethic*, *persistence* and *optimal performance*.

Work ethic

When a performer is task-oriented their primary focus is on *mastery* of the task in hand not on the outcome nor on competition with others. For example, Jerry Rice's (left) focus was on practising the skills required to improve. Rice's pass-catching achievements can be attributed to his interest in learning and self-development.

Performers with a task orientation have a focus on improving their skills with little or no concern for the outcome. The result is a strong work ethic.

Persistence

Task-oriented performers' perceptions of success in the pursuit of mastery are based on their own standards and so Jerry Rice felt able to spend hours mastering his catching skills comparing his improvement against himself. His determination to continue practising a particular drill with his quarterback shows the benefits of his task orientation.

If task-oriented performers believe that high effort is necessary to produce improvement they apply high effort and persist until it pays off.

Optimal performance

Task orientation can protect performers from disappointment and frustration when their performance is surpassed by others. Performers often have little control over opponents' performance but by focusing on their own work ethic, persistence and personal standards, they are able to demonstrate a high degree of control over their own performance and thus can reach the highest standards – their optimal or best performance.

For example, when two sprinters such as Cameron Burrell and Noah Lyles race against each other and focus on their own time (task orientation) they focus on their *perceived* competence and not on comparing their performance with others (outcome orientation). This encourages persistence to continue to improve towards optimal performance even when they lose.

Drawbacks of adopting an outcome/ego orientation

Outcome/ego-oriented performers have more difficulty in maintaining high perceived competence. They judge success by how they compare with others but cannot necessarily control others' performance. Such comparisons lower *motivation* to persist when the sportsperson is faced with difficulties.

Joan Duda (1993) suggests that performers with low perceived competence do not adapt to losing situations well and make excuses, reduce efforts and even give up.

For example, golfers drawn to play against each other cannot directly control the others' performance as they play the course. If the golfer who loses has an outcome/ego orientation, they may blame their loss on the wind moving the ball or the ball having a bad bounce and ending up in the rough grass, making the next shot more difficult. If this continues, the golfer may become frustrated and their motivation to try and overcome their difficulties may be lowered.

In sport it does not require a poor performance or mistakes to experience failure but if this happens persistently the helpless performer has thoughts of overwhelming incompetence.

Know the feeling?

Task orientation is the solution!

Evaluation

Task orientation can be measured

One strength in applying achievement goal theory is that it can be measured.

Diane Gill and Thomas Deeter (1988) developed the *sport orientation questionnaire* to measure performers' motivation orientations either as goal (task), win (outcome or ego) or competitiveness. They found that males score higher for competitiveness and win/outcome-orientation than females but females score higher for goal/task-orientation. Their overall findings suggest that performers see goal/task-orientation as more important than win/outcome-orientation.

This shows that achievement goal theory provides a useful tool for analysing successful and less successful orientations.

Useful for sport psychologists

Another strength is that applying achievement goal theory can help sport psychologists.

For example, François Cury *et al.* (1997) showed that outcome/ego-oriented sport performers have low perceived competence and are not willing to invest in training in order to overcome prior failure. Sport psychologists can use this information to correct behaviours when performers reduce their efforts or make excuses by emphasising a mastery climate (see page 264).

This suggests that by setting task goals that focus on mastery and downplaying outcome goals, performers can avoid a defeatist attitude.

It's not fair play

One weakness of applying achievement goal theory is that it may create unsporting behaviours.

For example, research by John Nicholls (1989) has pointed to problems when performers are identified by coaches as high outcome/ego orientation with low perceived ability. Nicholls suggests that such performers are more likely to engage in cheating and intent to injure in order to achieve their outcome goals at all costs.

This suggests that coaches should ensure performers' outcome orientation behaviours are directed within the rules of the sport.

GET ACTIVE Helpless and hopeless

Chris has all the characteristics of an outcome/ego performer. He has little persistence and a poor work ethic when it comes to practising badminton in PE lessons. He does not want to attempt new skills and if he does, he just says he is no good so why should he even try.

1. *Imagine you are Chris' PE teacher. What would you do to help Chris to develop task-oriented behaviours?*
2. *What would the PE staff at your school or college suggest?*
3. *How do their answers compare to the theories discussed on this spread?*

Assessment practice

At the end of learning aims A and B you must write a report (see pages 263 and 298). This report must be related to a scenario or context. We have used a real-life context.

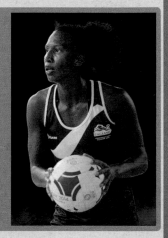

Read again about the netballer Serena Guthrie on page 265. The key quotation comes from Guthrie herself: '...one player doesn't make a team, all 12 players do... There are so many great, genuine people in our team who want to do the best for each other' (bbc.co.uk, 2019). Guthrie travelled around the world to live and work where she could compete against the best.

Think about whether Guthrie is task-oriented, ego/outcome-oriented or both. What impact does this have on her work ethic, persistence and likelihood of optimal performance?

B1.11 Learning aim B1 – Task 11

The first part of your report for learning aims A and B will be concerned with theories of motivation in sport, covered earlier in this unit (pages 262–267) and again on the previous spread, this spread and the next spread.

1. **Explain** how achievement goal theory accounts for Serena Guthrie's netball performance. Refer in your answer to her motivation and self-confidence. (B.P3)
2. **Discuss** achievement goal theory in terms of how Serena Guthrie's motivation and self-confidence impact on her netball performance. (B.M2)
3. In terms of its strengths and weaknesses, **evaluate** how achievement goal theory accounts for Serena Guthrie's netball performance. Refer in your answer to the relationship between her motivation and self-confidence and arousal levels. (B.D2)

An issue to consider

Do you think having a task orientation in sport can have drawbacks in any way?

Specification content

B1 Motivation theories in sporting environments
● Achievement goal theory (Duda and Hall 2001):
  ○ Value of a task orientation on work ethic, persistence and optimal performance.
  ○ Drawbacks of a sportsperson adopting an outcome or ego orientation.

Self-determination theory

Marcel Hirscher

Austrian skier Marcel Hirscher (above) has won multiple accolades including seven consecutive overall World Cup globes, two Olympic golds and six world titles. At 29, he has dominated the men's technical events since making his World Cup debut in 2007 at the age of 18.

Despite this he insists that his motivation remains sky-high. You might think after all those successes he has less need to achieve. 'The motivation for me is that I can be active in this sport at such a high level that I would never achieve in any other sport. Also, the real fascination has been and always will be the joy of racing' (AFP, 2019).

So what is it about ski racing that meets Hirscher's needs for self-determination so that he continues to be motivated to ski? That's what this spread aims to explain.

Specification terms

See page 266 for definitions.

A primary goal in elite sport is to win. However, the focus on winning often associated with elite sport can undermine intrinsic motivation and promote extrinsic motivation.

The theory

In learning aim A1 (page 266), we discussed Edward Deci and Richard Ryan's (2000) theory that considers both *intrinsic* and *extrinsic motivation*.

Intrinsically motivated performers play sport from a desire to learn and improve skills and to take on the challenges that sport provides. Extrinsic motivation stems from playing sport to please others and the tangible rewards on offer, e.g. financial reward or medals.

What is interesting and important is to understand the impact on performers if they shift from extrinsic to intrinsic motivation.

Applying the theory

Participation in sport meets individual needs

Taking part in sport should provide people with some of the elements of a 'good life', i.e. should improve your well-being. It does this by satisfying three key needs:

1. *Autonomy* means freedom from external control, which provides a sense of well-being. Performers who feel it is their choice to participate in an activity are experiencing autonomy. They are in an intrinsically controlled state, controlling their own behaviour and this makes them feel good.

For example, competing in situations that involve task *mastery* gives a person a sense of intrinsic control and autonomy, as in the example of Hirscher (on the left).

2. *Relatedness* is a feeling of connection to other people. Working closely with a coach over many years and also working with team members can provide performers with this sense of relatedness and should foster 'feelings of belongingness'. Both of these are important for our sense of well-being and both satisfy the need for relatedness.

For example, Hirscher and his coach Michael Pircher have worked together in many major championships, and thus have a strong sense of relatedness.

3. *Competence* is the belief that sports performers have that they can achieve desired outcomes.

For example, Hirscher feels competent when perfecting turns, showing personal improvement, overcoming the challenges presented by different slalom courses and mastering a skill that requires high amounts of effort.

Importance of self-determined behaviour

Behaviour that is self-determined (i.e. it is autonomous) has other benefits that contribute to well-being.

Impact on persistence The more self-determined a performer's *motivation*, the more persistent they are and less likely to give up.

For example, Luc Pelletier *et al.* (2001) found that self-determined motivation at the start of a swimming season was associated with higher levels of *persistence* 10 and 22 months later.

Coping with stress Self-determined motivation helps performers cope with stress as they are able to maintain control over their performance thereby reducing *cognitive anxiety*.

Peak performance High-achieving performers are focused on mastery of their own performance which increases *self-efficacy*. This leads to more positive outcomes and a better quality of sporting experience and peak performance (Deci and Ryan 2000).

Impact of extrinsic rewards on intrinsic motivation

Extrinsic rewards may weaken the intrinsic motivation of performers. Praise or medals may make you feel good but it means that, in the future, you seek those rewards as your motivator rather than your intrinsic desire to achieve and master tasks.

On the other hand, for some performers, extrinsic rewards can also maintain or strengthen intrinsic motivation. If a reward is viewed as informing performers positively about their ability, then the rewards will likely foster internal satisfaction and intrinsic motivation.

Evaluation

Useful for coaches

One strength is that understanding the benefits of intrinsic motivation is helpful for coaches.

For example, effective coaching can influence the intrinsic motivation of performers and help performers feel like they control their own behaviour even with the presence of extrinsic rewards, such as money or medals. By recognising performers' specific contributions to practice or the team, the coach will be positively informing performers about their ability. The more performers experience competence and success due to their own actions and skills, the greater their intrinsic motivation.

This suggests that coaches should provide specific feedback to performers that fosters feelings of satisfaction and promotes participation.

Gender differences in motivation

Another strength is that the concepts of intrinsic and extrinsic motivation may provide insight into gender differences.

Luc Pelletier *et al.* (1995) used the *sport motivation scale* to measure intrinsic and extrinsic motivation, and consider gender differences. They tested 593 university performers (319 males and 274 females) recruited from different sports such as basketball and swimming. The researchers found that female performers scored higher than males for intrinsic motivation.

This suggests that gender does play a role in self-determined forms of motivation.

Coaching predisposition

One weakness of applying the theory is it assumes that all coaches prefer to coach in a way that gives performers control and autonomy.

For example, Clifford Mallett (2005) argues that some coaches prefer a coach-centered approach rather than an athlete-centered approach. He suggests it can take two years before coaches can feel comfortable in letting their performers have control of aspects such as training content, times and venues.

This suggests some coaches may have to adapt their style of coaching to enable performers to develop intrinsic motivation.

Assessment practice

At the end of learning aims A and B you must write a report (see pages 263 and 298). This report must be related to a scenario or context. We have used a real-life context.

Read again about the tennis player Andy Murray on page 267. The key quotation for you to consider comes from Murray himself: 'You need to love winning, you can't just hate losing. It's too negative... That's why you put the work in' (*The Guardian*, 2010).

Consider whether Andy Murray was mostly intrinsically or extrinsically motivated. Bear in mind that he suffered serious injury and recovery from surgery during his career.

How does his involvement in tennis satisfy his needs for autonomy, relatedness and competence? Is his behaviour self-determined and how does this impact on his performance?

B1.12 Learning aim B1 – Task 12

The first part of your report for learning aims A and B will be concerned with theories of motivation in sport, covered earlier in this unit (pages 262–267) and again on the previous two spreads and this spread.

1. **Explain** how self-determination theory accounts for Andy Murray's tennis performance. Refer in your answer to his motivation and self-confidence. (B.P3)

2. **Discuss** self-determination theory in terms of how Andy Murray's motivation and self-confidence impact on his tennis performance. (B.M2)

3. In terms of its strengths and weaknesses, **evaluate** how self-determination theory accounts for Andy Murray's tennis performance. Refer in your answer to the relationship between his motivation and self-confidence and arousal levels. (B.D2)

GET ACTIVE Swimming for motivation

Swimming is a rigorous competitive sport that involves a considerable amount of discipline, hours of practice, and sustained focus. Competitive swimming can be approached in an autonomy-supportive way to help create intrinsically motivated performers.

Explain how you as a coach would create an autonomy-supportive motivational climate for your swimmers.

You may wish to consider the purpose of the practice sessions, individual swimmers' targets, improving stroke technique and race strategies.

An issue to consider

Do you think it is more difficult for coaches to develop autonomy, competence and relatedness in performers involved in team sports than those taking part in individual sports?

Specification content

B1 Motivation theories in sporting environments

● Self-determination theory (Deci and Ryan 2000):

○ Participation in sport meets individual needs for autonomy, relatedness and competence.

○ Importance of self-determined behaviour and its impact on persistence, ability to cope with stress and produce peak performance.

○ Impact of extrinsic rewards on intrinsic motivation.

Vealey's multidimensional model of sport confidence

Tiger Woods

Tiger Woods was the top ranked golfer in the world for most of the years between 1999 and 2010. However, that all fell apart after his many problems off the course, including the collapse of his marriage and several serious back surgeries. Tiger looked like he had lost all his self-confidence.

Self-confidence in sport is often seen as a fickle quality – it appears to come and go at whim. However, in April 2019 Tiger had regained his with a staggering win at the Masters at Augusta, Georgia. Finding a way to regain his self-confidence must have been a key part of this success – trait or state?

Specification terms

Affect Experiencing emotions and feelings.

Behaviour Range of actions made in conjunction with the environment.

Cognition The mental processes of acquiring knowledge and understanding.

Sport confidence See self-confidence, page 268.

High self-confidence (cognition) affects how you feel (low anxiety) and how you behave (a perfect 10).

The model

In learning aim A2 (page 268), we looked at how Robin Vealey's (1986) *multidimensional model* describes *sport confidence* as the belief or degree of certainty individuals possess about their ability to be successful in sport.

She conceptualises sport confidence either as *trait* (SC-trait) or *state* (SC-state) sport confidence. SC-trait is the general perception an individual has of their ability to be successful in sport. SC-state is the perception at any particular moment about their ability to be successful. SC-state impacts on performance through feelings, thoughts and actions.

Applying the model

Different levels of sport confidence

Effects of high sport confidence A survey of 335 performers from 35 sports identified high SC-state as one of the most useful mental skills that contributes to sporting success (Durand-Bush *et al.* 2001). SC-state allows performers to remain focused on the task, and those performers who possess a strong belief in their ability to perform successfully might be more able to perform optimally under pressure (Hays *et al.* 2009).

Effects of low sport confidence Performers experiencing low SC-state in sport tend to be unsuccessful. SC-state comes in part from SC-trait (i.e. general perceptions of ability) but is also affected by immediate factors. For example, if a performer has been injured this will lower current SC-state.

Also, Rainer Martens (1990) has highlighted the role of high SC-trait – this can create high expectations of success which in turn creates *cognitive anxiety* which then damages state self-confidence (SC-state).

Consequences of sport confidence

SC-state can influence *affect*, *behaviour* and *cognition*, and these three elements are inter-related.

Affect Performers high in SC-state enjoy competition. Their emotional state is positive, they can be relaxed and calm. Any nervousness that may be present is transferred into feelings of excitement to be playing. For example, international rugby players report relishing the challenge of the upcoming match.

However, performers with low SC-state tend to be nervous and perform poorly under pressure. They may not enjoy playing and often become frustrated and angry.

Therefore, affect influences behaviour and also changes how the performers think (cognition) about the likelihood of their success.

Behaviour Poor past performances can have a debilitating effect on SC-state (cognition). For example, a cricketer who has been out for a series of low scores will have reduced SC-state.

Previous good performances can create high SC-state, for example a basketball player who has been successful with their last ten free throws will have high SC-state for their next attempt.

Poor preparation and coaching can create low SC-state and this appears to be more prevalent in female elite performers who may rely on social support networks supplied by coaches. By contrast, male elite performers may derive SC-state from, for example, a belief in their coach setting correct training sessions (Hays *et al.* 2009).

Therefore, behaviour impacts beliefs (cognition) as well as how the performers feel (affect) about the likelihood of their success.

Cognition Performers with high SC-state (cognition) appear committed to their decisions and make decisive movements. This can result in them believing they can dictate tactics to the opposition and displaying increased effort (behaviour) in their performance.

On the other hand, performers who have low sport confidence tend to lack *persistence* to compete effectively (behaviour) against their opponent and this influences how much they enjoy what they are doing (affect).

Therefore, cognition impacts how sports people perform (behaviour) as well as the emotions performers experience (affect).

Confident performers (such as Serena Williams, left) tend to be better able to deploy good tactics to make their opponent struggle.

Evaluation

Useful for coaches

One strength of the multidimensional model is that sources that weaken self-confidence can be identified.

Interviews carried out with world class performers by Kate Hays *et al.* (2009) highlighted the primary factors responsible for reducing pre-competition confidence. They found that 79% of performers thought that poor performances reduced self-confidence and in particular 85% of women thought poor preparation contributed to low self-confidence.

This shows how behaviour influences both affect and cognition and suggests that coaches should create pre-competition routines that focus on these two sources to increase performer confidence.

Problem solvers

Another strength of the multidimensional model is it highlights the differences in how performers overcome obstacles.

Confident performers (high SC-trait) tend to be more skilled and effective in using cognitive resources necessary for sporting success. For example, confident performers remain focused on finding tactical solutions, such as a tennis player hitting the ball to an opponent's weaker backhand. Less confident performers however are more likely to focus on their own lack of ability as the reason why they are unable to beat an opponent (Bandura and Wood 1989).

This shows that the model can explain real-world observations.

Gender differences

One weakness of Vealey's theory is that sources of confidence are different for men and women.

For example, Hays and colleagues (2009) report that the threat of playing a good opponent could create a vulnerability in women that is not experienced by men. Women derive confidence from a perceived competitive advantage, such as seeing their competitors perform badly whereas men simply believe they are better than their opponents.

This suggests that the predictions of the theory do not equally apply to all people, and coaches must learn to apply different sources of confidence in order to build confidence in male and female performers.

GET ACTIVE ABC categories

From the following list of responses to competition, identify which ones are related to affect or behaviour or cognition as consequences of high sport confidence.

1. *Confident body language.*
2. *Excited.*
3. *Happy.*
4. *Self.*
5. *Increased effort.*
6. *Committed to decisive movements.*
7. *Enjoyment.*
8. *Task.*
9. *Relaxed.*
10. *Outcome.*
11. *Automatic.*
12. *Knowledge.*

Assessment practice

At the end of learning aims A and B you must write a report (see pages 263 and 298). This report must be related to a scenario or context. We have used a real-life context.

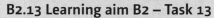

Read again about the rower Katherine Grainger on page 269. The key quotation for you to think about comes from James Cracknell: Grainger and Thornley won silver by 'backing themselves in a way no-one else backed them' (*espn.co.uk*, 2016).

Consider the level of self-confidence required to do this, especially after returning from a break and overcoming loss of form.

What were the effects of Grainger's confidence on her affect, behaviour and cognition?

B2.13 Learning aim B2 – Task 13

The second part of your report for learning aims A and B will be concerned with theories of self-confidence in sport, covered earlier in this unit (pages 268–271) and again on this spread and the next spread.

1. **Explain** how the multidimensional model of sports confidence accounts for Katherine Grainger's rowing performance. Refer in your answer to her motivation and self-confidence. (B.P3)

2. **Discuss** the multidimensional model of sports confidence in terms of how Katherine Grainger's motivation and self-confidence impact on her rowing performance. (B.M2)

3. In terms of its strengths and weaknesses, **evaluate** how the multidimensional model of sports confidence accounts for Katherine Grainger's rowing performance. Refer in your answer to the relationship between her motivation and self-confidence and arousal levels. (B.D2)

> You can see the assessment criteria and explanation of command terms on page 298.

An issue to consider

We have looked at high and low sport confidence but do you think sport performers can ever be 'over-confident'?

If so, what factors might contribute towards over-confidence in sport?

Specification content

B2 Self-confidence theories in sporting environments

- Vealey's multidimensional model of sport confidence (1986, 2001):
  - Impact of different levels of sport confidence on sports performance.
  - Consequences of sport confidence on sports performance – relationship between affect, behaviour and cognition.

Bandura's self-efficacy theory

Judy Murray

Judy Murray, mother of tennis player Andy Murray, is a world-class tennis coach. She has developed a world-class tennis academy in her home town of Dunblane, Scotland. It aims to bring strong benefits to Scottish sport, helping in the development of elite competitors, while also providing facilities for the community.

The academy sets out an amazing vision for facilities that will help young people be active and love tennis with all the passion that she does.

Judy has high expectations and when coaches have high expectations this helps to develop the sense of self-efficacy that performers need to be successful.

Specification terms

See page 270 for definitions.

Ricky Ponting's previous performance accomplishments at batting will give him high self-efficacy, i.e. belief in his own competence.

The theory

Albert Bandura (1977, 1986) introduced the term *self-efficacy* as a form of self-confidence that is specific to particular situations. You learned about his theory in learning aim A2 (see page 270).

Self-efficacy refers to feelings of certainty *and* competence about successfully carrying out a performance. These judgements about how successfully a sportsperson can perform a task are called *efficacy expectations*.

Applying the theory

Manipulating sources of self-efficacy

The way in which performers can improve their efficacy expectations is to manipulate the four sources of self-efficacy discussed on page 270.

1. Performance accomplishments provide the most reliable basis for judgements on self-efficacy because they are based on mastery experiences. A coach can help a sports person experience the feeling of successful performance.

For example, a gymnastics coach can use tactics such as guiding the gymnast through a complicated floor routine. In this way the coach can reinforce the performer's mastery of gymnastic techniques leading to increased efficacy expectations in the performer.

2. Vicarious experience PE teachers and coaches often use demonstrations or *modelling* to help performers learn new skills that increase performers' sense of mastery. Coaches like Judy Murray (left) ensure that the quality of demonstrations is high. For example, making sure they demonstrate complex skills, such as a tennis serve, from different angles. When young tennis players observe a good demonstration, this increases their expectations of success.

For elite performers, self-modelling can be achieved by repeatedly observing the correct or best parts of their own past performance captured on video, and using that as a model for future performance. This increases efficacy expectations for elite performers as the technique is already well-learned.

3. Verbal persuasion Persuasive techniques are widely used by coaches, in attempting to influence performers' perceptions of self-efficacy.

For example, a tennis coach such as Judy Murray can provide feedback to her tennis players about their performances. Providing positive feedback to performers has been shown to boost their self-efficacy and improve performances (Wells *et al.* 1993).

4. Emotional arousal A performer's physiological and emotional state provides an indication of their efficacy expectations.

For example, rugby players' *arousal* levels can be manipulated by a coach's pre-match preparation, providing players with positive *affect* (emotion) such as feelings of exhilaration about the upcoming match. This suggests that expectations of success can be influenced by how players feel about their performance.

Influence of expectations of success

Self-efficacy can have a powerful influence on performance. When performers expect to be successful, their self-efficacy will be high and this leads to improved performances. For example, Edward McAuley (1985) studied female gymnasts watching a team member complete a difficult move on the parallel bars. The observers experienced reduced *anxiety* and their subsequent performance improved, suggesting watching their team member helped convince them that they too could accomplish this move.

As you might expect, low self-efficacy tends to result in poor sports performance. For example, a cricket player watching a teammate struggling against a fast bowler on a bouncy pitch might approach her own innings with an expectation that she too will fail. However, a cricket player might not improve if she sees a teammate playing well but she believes her teammate is much more skilled than herself.

It is important to recognise that the presence of sources of self-efficacy do not automatically change self-efficacy in performers. What is important is how performers interpret the information associated with that source.

GET ACTIVE Effective coaching

You have learned that sources of self-efficacy interact to increase the expectancy of success in sport. Imagine you are a basketball coach teaching free-throw shooting to a group of players aged 11–13. You want to give them a demonstration of how to be successful before they practise.

How would you apply Bandura's self-efficacy theory in order to help your demonstration and improve the efficacy expectations of the group when they practise?

You could consider their previous basketballing experience, use of video technology, the nature of any feedback you may give to the players and how nervous the children may be at taking free throws in front of their peers.

Fans help boost the self-efficacy of a Tour de France cyclist on the long climb up to L'Alpe d'Huez.

Evaluation

Useful for coaches

One strength of Bandura's self-efficacy theory is that it can help coaches improve performance in sport.

Christie Wells *et al.* (1993) arranged for coaches to give false feedback to weightlifters. Some participants (the 'light' group) were told they had lifted less than they actually did (which would enhance their sense of self-efficacy as they feel they have room to improve) and others (the 'heavy' group) were told they had lifted more. In a later trial, the light group improved more than the heavy group.

This shows that self-efficacy does change performance.

Which source to choose?

One weakness of Bandura's self-efficacy theory is deciding which source of self-efficacy is most appropriate to use.

Sporting situations provide performers with a range of self-efficacy sources and each one may be interpreted differently by each performer and thus have a different influence on their performance. For example, football players often have pre-game butterflies and this may lower self-efficacy. This can be countered by *vicarious experience* (seeing someone else who is calm) or by verbal persuasion (a positive team talk from the coach) – but it is difficult to predict which will work for any one individual.

This suggests that understanding sources of self-efficacy in itself is not helpful in increasing performers' expectations of success.

Task difficulty

Another weakness is that the influence of Bandura's self-efficacy theory depends on the performers' perceived difficulty of the task.

Performance accomplishments have the most influence over self-efficacy. For example, when an ice skater completes a difficult jump that requires a lot of effort such as a triple axel, it will increase their self-efficacy more than if they completed an easier jump such as a double salchow.

This suggests that more attention needs to be paid to the power of each source of influence and also to how the different sources of self-efficacy interact.

Assessment practice

At the end of learning aims A and B you must write a report (see pages 263 and 298). This report must be related to a scenario or context. We have used a real-life context.

Read again about the swimmer Ellie Simmonds on page 271. The key feature of her experience is her clear knowledge and vision of her own abilities, which is shared by her coach Billy Pye: 'he understands how I think and what I respond to' (*girlguiding.org.uk*, 2017).

Consider how Ellie Simmonds' self-efficacy as a successful swimmer might have been influenced by performance accomplishments, vicarious reinforcement, verbal persuasion and emotional arousal. How would her expectations of success have affected her performance?

B2.14 Learning aim B2 – Task 14

The second part of your report for learning aims A and B will be concerned with theories of self-confidence in sport, covered earlier in this unit (pages 268–271) and again on the previous spread and this spread.

1. **Explain** how Bandura's self-efficacy theory accounts for Ellie Simmonds' swimming performance. Refer in your answer to her motivation and self-confidence. (B.P3)

2. **Discuss** Bandura's self-efficacy theory in terms of how Ellie Simmonds' motivation and self-confidence impact on her swimming performance. (B.M2)

3. In terms of its strengths and weaknesses, **evaluate** how Bandura's self-efficacy theory accounts for Ellie Simmonds' swimming performance. Refer in your answer to the relationship between her motivation and self-confidence and arousal levels. (B.D2)

An issue to consider

Self-efficacy makes a difference to performance.

Do you think this difference will be greater when opponents are physically well-matched or when one player is more skilful than another?

Specification content

B2 Self-confidence theories in sporting environments

● Bandura's self-efficacy theory (1977, 1986, 1997):

○ Manipulating sources of self-efficacy to increase a sportsperson's expectations of success.

○ Influence of expectations of success on sports performance.

Drive theory and Inverted U hypothesis

The Burnley Express

Bowler Jimmy Anderson, known as the *Burnley Express* (above), has a personal need to perform consistently at the highest level.

Researchers Richard Thelwell and Ian Maynard (2000) asked 198 county-level English cricketers to identify the variables they considered to have the most important effect on their performance. Optimum level of arousal emerged in the top four factors, important to both batsmen and bowlers. The other top factors were self-confidence, a pre-match routine and following a performance plan.

So optimal levels of arousal are seen as important but are poor performances due to under- or over-arousal?

Specification term

Ideal performance state (IPS) A person's mental and physiological state during peak performance.

See page 272 for other definitions.

The theories

In learning aim A3 (page 272) we explored how sport performers who are physically and mentally ready to perform can be described as optimally aroused.

Two explanations for this were discussed. First, Clark Hull's (1943) *drive theory* explained the relationship between *arousal* and *performance* as being *linear* – as arousal increases, so does performance.

The second explanation, the *inverted U hypothesis*, looked at the arousal-performance relationship as being a *curvilinear* one (Yerkes-Dodson 1908). Increases in a performer's arousal levels create a gradual increase in performance up to an optimal point. Any further increases in arousal lead to a gradual performance decline.

Applying the theories

Arousal-performance relationship

Drive theory If a performer's arousal levels are low, their performance would be expected to be low. The performer is neither physiologically nor psychologically ready, for example heart rate or concentration levels may be too low. This would make it difficult for a basketballer, for example, to focus on the position of teammates and opponents when trying to complete a pass leading to an interception.

As arousal levels increase, drive theory suggests that performance increases even under the highest pressure. For example, a world-class bowler such as Jimmy Anderson (left) bowling in a crucial Ashes cricket test against Australia would be predicted to perform at their best. However, when we watch sport, we see that this is not always the case and occasionally even expert bowlers such as Jimmy Anderson bowl badly under intense pressure. Therefore, the inverted U hypothesis suggests there is an optimal point of arousal/anxiety and after that performance decreases.

Inverted U hypothesis This hypothesis agrees with drive theory that, if a performer's arousal is too low, there will be a detrimental effect on performance. This is known as the warm-up decrement. All performers should carry out a warm-up to ready themselves for performance. As their arousal increases so gradually does their performance. For example, rugby forwards run through their lineout moves so they are ready to perform them at their optimum once the game starts.

However, any further increases in arousal will lead to a performance decrement. For example, a hockey player experiencing over-arousal may not control a pass properly because they have lost concentration and may be distracted by an opponent attempting a tackle.

Ideal performance state

The *ideal performance state* (IPS) in sport is a term coined by Dr Jim Loehr where performers are 'in the moment' and performing at an automatic level, without need for conscious thought and direction. They feel totally in control and focused on the task (Williams and Krane 2001).

Demand of the task The IPS depends on the demands that the task places on the performer. Complex decision-making tasks (e.g. playing fly-half in rugby) need a lower optimal arousal level than simple tasks (e.g. weightlifting) that require higher levels for optimal arousal. So, there is an inverse relationship between demands of decision-making and arousal levels.

Type of task A rugby tackle is an example of a task that requires large muscle movements (gross motor skills). The IPS for such tasks is high arousal levels. Fine motor skills, such as throwing darts, require smaller, more precise muscle movements and therefore lower levels of arousal for the IPS. Again, there is an inverse relationship, this time between precision of muscle movements and arousal levels.

Skill level of performer Highly skilled performers, such as the bowler Jimmy Anderson, are able to maintain their ideal performance state at higher levels of arousal than less skilled cricketers, as they can perform at an automatic level because their skills are well-learned. This is a linear relationship between skill set and arousal levels.

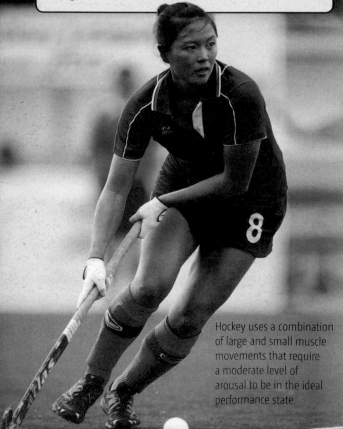

Hockey uses a combination of large and small muscle movements that require a moderate level of arousal to be in the ideal performance state.

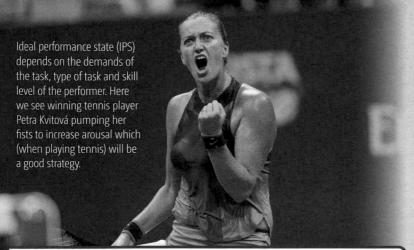

Ideal performance state (IPS) depends on the demands of the task, type of task and skill level of the performer. Here we see winning tennis player Petra Kvitová pumping her fists to increase arousal which (when playing tennis) will be a good strategy.

Evaluation

Useful for coaches

One strength of understanding the impact of arousal on performance is that it is useful for coaches to help optimise performers' abilities.

For example, a tennis coach who understands the relationship between arousal and the ideal performance state (IPS) can help a player develop positive physical responses such as fist pumping when they win a point. The demands of tennis require moderate levels of arousal but highly skilled players such as Kvitová (above) can perform under high arousal conditions created by large audiences.

This shows how IPS varies from player to player and suggests that an understanding of the IPS is a very useful real-world application.

Not always gradual

One weakness of the inverted U hypothesis is that changes in performance are not always gradual.

For example, once arousal has reached an optimal level, it is unlikely that any increases or decreases in arousal will lead to gradual incremental changes in performance. John Fazey and Lew Hardy (1988) observed that declines in performance often resemble a sudden, catastrophic drop rather than a gradual decline (see pages 276 and 294).

This means that there are problems in applying the inverted U hypothesis to real-life sporting situations.

An overly simple explanation

Another weakness is that arousal is not the only factor in *optimal performance*.

For example, personality factors have been shown to be important. Research by Daniel Landers and Stephen Boutcher (1998) highlights that extrovert performers generally have higher levels of optimal arousal than introverts. So an extrovert is already at a high level of arousal which means for a sport involving fine muscle movements (e.g. darts), an extrovert requires especially lower levels of arousal to be successful.

This suggests that personality type is useful in order to understand the impact of optimal levels of arousal on sport performance.

GET ACTIVE Not going swimmingly

Freddy, an Olympic freestyle swimmer has told his coach that he often worries about his ability to get into his ideal performance state before semi-finals and finals compared to qualifying rounds. In particular he is concerned about his ability to tumble-turn effectively under pressure.

Imagine you are Freddy's coach. Consider how you would use your knowledge of the inverted U hypothesis of arousal to explain to Freddy why he has these concerns.

You should include information about the demands of the task, the type of task and Freddy's skill level.

Assessment practice

At the end of learning aims A and B you must write a report (see pages 263 and 298). This report must be related to a scenario or context. We have used a real-life context.

Read again about the darts player Eric Bristow on page 273. He explained his dartitis as an 'extreme fear of missing'. This points very clearly to a link between performance and arousal/anxiety.

Think about the impact of arousal and anxiety on Bristow's declining darts performance. What about the 'ideal performance state'?

Bristow was one of the best darts players ever, and yet even he could do little to counter his dartitis. Was that because he could no longer be 'in the moment'? Was he 'overthinking'?

B3.15 Learning aim B3 – Task 15

The third part of your report for learning aims A and B will be concerned with theories of arousal and anxiety in sport, covered earlier in this unit (pages 272–279) and again on this spread and the next three spreads.

1. **Explain** how the drive theory/inverted U hypothesis accounts for Eric Bristow's darts performance. Refer in your answer to his arousal and anxiety levels. (B.P4)

2. **Discuss** the drive theory/inverted U hypothesis in terms of how Eric Bristow's arousal and anxiety levels impact on his darts performance. (B.M2)

3. In terms of its strengths and weaknesses, **evaluate** how the drive theory/inverted U hypothesis accounts for Eric Bristow's darts performance. Refer in your answer to the relationship between his motivation and self-confidence and arousal levels. (B.D2)

An issue to consider

When performers are in the ideal performance state they often talk about being 'in the zone'. Others describe sporting experiences as being in a 'flow state'.

Do you think you have to experience flow before you enter 'the zone'?

Specification content

B3 Arousal and anxiety theories in sporting environments

● Drive theory (Hull 1943): relationship of increases in arousal to performance.

● Inverted U hypothesis (Yerkes and Dodson 1908):

○ Increases in arousal lead to increases in performance, then after a certain point further increases will lead to a performance decrement.

○ Ideal performance state (IPS) where arousal level matches demand of task, including dependency on type of task and skill level of performer.

Multidimensional anxiety theory

Is surfing dangerous?

If you have ever surfed or even body-boarded you will know that it can be tremendous fun. The rewards of riding the waves are great but so are the dangers.

The sea can be a dangerous place even for professionals. Powerful currents and waves can be enough to overcome even the strongest swimmers. A surfboard can become a projectile very quickly and surfers take care to avoid being entangled in their leash.

Competitive surfers such as Lakey Peterson (above) use mental preparation to overcome those elements of anxiety that may reduce performance levels – while maintaining the focus to perform well. Anxiety can be a good or a bad thing.

Specification terms

See page 274 for definitions.

Not a sign of worry in the world. Cognitive A-state under control. Tick. Somatic A-state under control. Tick. SC-state high. Tick.

The theory

Multidimensional anxiety theory was introduced in learning aim A3 (see page 274). In this theory Rainer Martens *et al.* (1990) suggested that there are both state and trait components of *anxiety*.

Trait anxiety (A-trait) is a performer's tendency to be anxious in competitive situations. This is an enduring aspect of their *personality*. In contrast, *state anxiety* (A-state) reflects our current level of anxiety.

Applying the theory

State and trait components

Performers with state anxiety (A-state) are likely to show signs of apprehension and tension. For example, when a figure skater is in a high A-state before going on the ice their body is 'aroused' and produces *adrenaline* (see page 46), which has the effect of, for example, increasing heart rate and making you sweat more.

A-state is a temporary state whereas, in contrast, trait anxiety (A-trait) is part of a performer's personality. Performers who have high A-trait are more likely to perceive dangerous situations and competitions as threatening and then respond with more intense levels of A-state than performers with low A-trait. In other words, A-state is influenced by A-trait.

Cognitive and somatic anxiety

Multidimensional anxiety theory includes different dimensions of A-state – *cognitive state anxiety* (cog A-state) and *somatic anxiety* (som A-state). The former concerns a performer's *mental* state and the latter is their perception of their *physiological* (body) state.

Increases in cog A-state *negatively* affect performance Cognitive anxiety represents performers' thinking about their performance. When cog A-state is low, this means performers have few concerns about their performance. However, if cog A-state is high then all performers, even low A-trait performers, are affected. For example, if Lakey Peterson (left) has to deal with bigger waves, then her cog A-state will increase which can negatively affect her surfing despite her usual low levels of A-trait.

Indeed all performers may sometimes have anxieties – maybe because of a weakness in their technique or because they are playing against a strong opponent. This will cause cog A-state to increase. For example, in football if a defender has to play against a very good attacker such as Harry Kane they would be concerned about how they will stop him scoring. At such a time, when cog A-state is high, there is a negative effect on performance and all performers tend to play poorly.

Increases in som A-state *positively* affect performance – up to a point Somatic anxiety is the perception a performer has of their symptoms of arousal and anxiety such as sweaty palms. When som A-state is low, performance will be weak but as som A-state increases, so does performance. For example, if a surfer experiences butterflies in their stomach before surfing their som A-state will increase. This will have a positive effect on their performance – but only up to an optimal point.

Any further increases in som A-state will lead to a decrease in performance as there is an inverted U relationship between som A-state and performance.

Inverse relationship between cognitive anxiety and self-confidence

Martens also included Vealey's views on self-confidence in his theory (see page 286). He predicted that when cog A-state is low, state self-confidence (SC-state) will be high. Performers will have few concerns over their performance and they will have a high expectancy of success. For example, Lakey Peterson will expect to be able to surf safely and carry out all her planned moves with self-confidence – but only when she is experiencing low cog A-state.

If performers have lots of concerns and are apprehensive about how they will perform, their cog A-state will be high. It follows that their SC-state will be low as they will not expect to be successful. For example, if the surfer Lakey Peterson is concerned about difficult wave conditions or feels she has not prepared well for a competition then the multidimensional model predicts she will be high in cog A-state and low in SC-state.

When Gareth Bale's cog A-state is low we would expect his self-confidence (SC-state) to be high and this obviously leads to the ability to defy gravity.

Evaluation

Useful for coaches

One strength of multidimensional anxiety theory is that coaches can recognise which performers suffer from high cognitive state anxiety (cog A-state).

This is useful for coaches as it allows them to predict which performers will have low self-confidence. For example, a cricket opening batsman may experience high cog A-state before a test match with concerns about being out for a duck (without scoring a run) against a team with good fast bowlers. This would reduce their levels of self-confidence and expectations of success.

This suggests that coaches can help by providing performers with interventions to control their anxiety and increase self-confidence in order to maximise performance (Martens *et al.* 1990).

Time

A further strength of multidimensional anxiety theory is that it shows how different dimensions of anxiety can be tracked over time.

Performers' levels of cog A-state tend to remain high in the days before competition but fall at the start of the game (Martens *et al.* 1990). For example, England rugby players may have concerns about the tactics of the Welsh team but once they see them play, England adapt to them successfully and their cog A-state reduces.

Som A-state however, remains low in the days before performance and only begins to increase within six hours of kick off. Once again as the match starts, som A-state falls.

This insight is useful to coaches and players in coping with the differing dimensions of anxiety before competition.

Imperfect relationship

One weakness of multidimensional anxiety theory is that the relationship between state and trait anxiety is not perfect.

A high A-trait performer should respond to competitive situations with a high A-state reaction. However, there are situations where this relationship doesn't hold true. For example, an elite/experienced volleyball player who is high A-trait may not perceive a club match as worrying and so their A-state will be low. Also, some high A-trait performers learn coping skills to help them reduce their A-state during competition (Weinberg and Gould 2015).

This suggests that there are individual explanations for how performers respond with anxiety to competitive situations.

Assessment practice

At the end of learning aims A and B you must write a report (see pages 263 and 298). This report must be related to a scenario or context. We have used a real-life context.

Read again about the cyclist Victoria Pendleton on page 275. The key quotation for you to consider comes from Pendleton herself: 'I was an emotional wreck [before the Beijing Olympics]...winning was just a relief...a complete anticlimax' (*The Guardian*, 2008). But also remember that Pendleton went on to win the gold medal in her big race.

Is it possible to identify state and trait components of anxiety in Victoria Pendleton's experience? Is there evidence of cognitive and somatic anxiety in what Pendleton says? What impact might such anxiety have had on her performance, given that she did win gold?

B3.16 Learning aim B3 – Task 16

The third part of your report for learning aims A and B will be concerned with theories of arousal and anxiety in sport, covered earlier in this unit (pages 272–279) and again on the previous spread, this spread and the next two spreads.

1. **Explain** how the multidimensional anxiety theory accounts for Victoria Pendleton's cycling performance. Refer in your answer to her arousal and anxiety levels. (B.P4)

2. **Discuss** the multidimensional anxiety theory in terms of how Victoria Pendleton's arousal and anxiety levels impact on her cycling performance. (B.M2)

3. In terms of its strengths and weaknesses, **evaluate** how the multidimensional anxiety theory accounts for Victoria Pendleton's cycling performance. Refer in your answer to the relationship between her arousal and anxiety levels. (B.D2)

An issue to consider

Multidimensional anxiety theory suggests that state anxiety (A-state) is influenced by trait anxiety (A-trait).

Can you think of any other factors in sport that might affect a performer's levels of A-state?

GET ACTIVE State or trait?

Here are several statements that performers use to describe their feelings towards competition in sport.

Identify which statements are related to A-state or A-trait.

1. I feel nervous.
2. I feel self-confident.
3. Before I compete I feel calm.
4. I feel comfortable.
5. When I compete I worry about making mistakes.
6. I feel at ease.
7. Just before competing my heart beats faster.
8. I feel uneasy before I compete.
9. I have self-doubts.
10. My body feels tense.

Specification content

B3 Arousal and anxiety theories in sporting environments

● Multidimensional anxiety theory (Martens *et al.* 1990):
  ○ State and trait components.
  ○ Increases in cognitive anxiety negatively affect performance.
  ○ Increases in somatic anxiety positively affect performance.
  ○ Inverse relationship between cognitive anxiety and self-confidence.

Catastrophe theory

Jean van de Velde

The 18th hole of the final round in the 1999 Open golf championship at Carnoustie, Scotland.

Leading by three strokes and standing on the 18th tee at the 499-yard par four final hole, Jean van de Velde needed just a double bogey six to claim the title.

What followed can only be described as a comedy of errors. Van de Velde hit the ball into a spectator grandstand, then knocked an approach shot into the Barry Burn, wading into the water to hit it before deciding against that idea. He finally scored a seven to scrape into a play-off that was eventually won by Paul Lawrie.

Jean van de Velde's mistakes went down in dubious history. The key to unlocking why he made them is understanding the relationship between arousal and cognitive state anxiety.

Specification terms

Aggression Behaviour that is intended to cause psychological or physical injury.

Attentional focus Performers concentrate on either internal or external cues.

Choking Decrease in sport performance under pressure.

Muscle tension The semi-contraction of muscles due to stress.

Under extreme pressure even experienced players like John Terry can choke (because they experience high arousal and cog A-state) and miss a vital penalty.

The theory

Lew Hardy (1990, 1996) and John Fazey (1988) developed a *catastrophe theory* that predicts the interactive relationships between *cognitive anxiety*, *arousal* and *performance* (described earlier on page 276).

The key to catastrophe theory is understanding the role of *cognitive state anxiety* (*cog A-state*) – it is a vital 'splitting factor'. When there is *low* cog A-state, increased arousal leads to a gradual decline in performance. But if there is *high* cog A-state, increased arousal leads to a large and catastrophic decline in performance.

Applying the theory

The phrase *choking* was used by Roy Baumeister (see page 273) to explain the patterns of behaviour that cause decreases in sport performance under pressure.

Choking due to high cog A-state

Cog A-state (discussed on the previous spread) can be used to explain choking in sport (Weinberg and Gould 2015). High cog A-state can be created by high expectations of success, as in the case of Jean van de Velde (left).

Catastrophe theory predicts when cog A-state is high any increases in a performer's physiological arousal (e.g. increased heart rate) lead to conditions where they choke and experience a catastrophic drop in performance. So any increases in Van de Velde's heart rate at that time would interact with his high cog A-state and account for the steep decline in his performance on the final approach shots to the 18th green.

Characteristics of performers experiencing choking

When choking occurs, arousal (*anxiety*) is high and performers have problems with *attentional focus*, *muscle tension* and *aggression*. The outcome is poor performance.

Attentional focus Changes in attentional focus are one of the key characteristics of performers who experience high arousal (Weinberg and Gould 2015). Instead of focusing externally on the cues from the sporting environment (e.g. the ball or the opponent's movements), attention is switched internally with a narrow focus on the performer's worries about losing (cog A-state).

Additionally high arousal reduces a performer's flexibility to change their attentional focus as the situation requires. Catastrophe theory suggests that high cog A-state leads to a sharp decline in performance when arousal levels increase and this can lead to choking.

Muscle tension Changes in muscle tension are also one of the characteristics that occur when performers are highly aroused. Robert Weinberg and Daniel Gould (2015) suggest a gymnast who experiences increased muscle tension might allow an early mistake of falling off the balance beam to upset her and this causes additional errors later in the routine – a large decline in performance consistent with catastrophe theory.

Aggressive behaviour Leonard Berkowitz's (1993) cue-arousal theory proposed that frustration increases arousal, and this is felt as anger. This anger creates a readiness for aggression which is then expressed if a cue or suitable target is present. For example, poor performance by an ice hockey player can lead to frustration (experienced as anger) towards an opponent (who acts as a cue). This results in aggression, such as high-sticking or body-checking. This aggression is then penalised by time spent in the penalty box and finally a decline in performance – choking.

Poor performance This is a result of the characteristics of performers who experience choking in sport. They perform badly because they tend to have high cog A-state which affects their mental focus. For example, a golfer such as Jean van de Velde may rush their pre-shot routines and fail to focus on cues such as the strength and direction of the wind that are relevant to the shot. Performance is also affected by feelings of fatigue through high levels of arousal. These characteristics often lead to problems with timing and coordination in movements, e.g. Jean van de Velde's golf swing.

Take care

So many similar but different concepts:
- A-trait
- Cog A-state
- Som A-state
- Arousal
- Anxiety

Make sure you understand the differences.

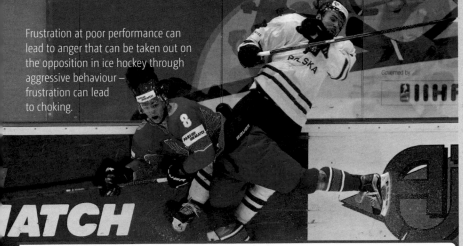

Frustration at poor performance can lead to anger that can be taken out on the opposition in ice hockey through aggressive behaviour – frustration can lead to choking.

Evaluation

Useful for coaches

One strength of understanding catastrophe theory for coaches is that they can intervene to help performers control arousal and cognitive state anxiety (cog A-state) levels.

For example, one golfer may experience muscle tension due to heightened arousal and a coach can use *muscle relaxation techniques* to improve performance. Whereas thought control techniques may be better for another golfer who may experience high cog A-state. Using these techniques reduces the likelihood of catastrophic declines in performance as they control arousal and cog A-state.

This shows how coaches can tailor their interventions to suit the arousal/anxiety levels of individual performers.

All performers

One weakness of applying catastrophe theory is that it may not be relevant to all performers or sports.

Research has so far been carried out on limited participant samples and a small range of sports. For example, Lew Hardy *et al.* (1994) and Lew Hardy and Gaynor Parfitt (1991) have investigated the application of catastrophe theory to only eight crown green bowlers and basketball players respectively. This has made it difficult to claim there is a consistent effect of cog A-state under high levels of arousal for all sports.

This suggests that coaches need to be wary of generalising the predictions of catastrophe theory.

Recognising high cog A-state

Another weakness of applying catastrophe theory is that coaches need to be able to recognise the signs of increased cog A-state.

For example, only 25% of American college cross-country coaches could accurately predict and recognise their runners' cog A-state levels. Even coaches who could recognise cog A-state effectively found the task difficult and worked hard to learn about their performers (Hanson and Gould 1988).

This suggests that coaches need to be aware of the symptoms of high arousal and cognitive state anxiety so they can apply their understanding of catastrophe theory to provide effective interventions.

GET ACTIVE To choke or not to choke – that is the question

A basketball team is losing by two points with two seconds left. Bob has a 90% free-throw success rate and has two free throws to win the game. He scores the first shot but misses the second and the team lose.

Jane is winning the last set in a tennis match 5–4 but double faults and loses the game to even the score to 5–5. However, she goes on to win the next two games to win the match.

Did Bob choke when he missed the second free throw? Did Jane choke when she double faulted?

Use your understanding of catastrophe theory to explain these two scenarios. Consider the impact of cognitive state anxiety and arousal.

Assessment practice

At the end of learning aims A and B you must write a report (see pages 263 and 298). This report must be related to a scenario or context. We have used a real-life context.

Read again about the cricketer Scott Boswell on page 277. He was brutally honest about what happened to him: '[The batsman]...was like a tiny dot... The more I panicked the more I rushed' (*The Guardian*, 2013).

Would it be fair to describe Boswell's performance decline as 'catastrophic'? He seems to have gone from a great bowler to a terrible one in the space of just a few balls.

Could this be fairly described as 'choking'? If so, can we explain Boswell's performance in terms of attentional focus, muscle tension and degree of aggression?

B3.17 Learning aim B3 – Task 17

The third part of your report for learning aims A and B will be concerned with theories of arousal and anxiety in sport, covered earlier in this unit (pages 272–279) and again on the previous two spreads, this spread and the next spread.

1. **Explain** how catastrophe theory accounts for Scott Boswell's cricketing performance. Refer in your answer to his arousal and anxiety levels. (B.P4)

2. **Discuss** catastrophe theory in terms of how Scott Boswell's arousal and anxiety levels impact on his cricketing performance. (B.M2)

3. In terms of its strengths and weaknesses, **evaluate** how catastrophe theory accounts for Scott Boswell's cricketing performance. Refer in your answer to the relationship between his motivation and self-confidence and arousal levels. (B.D2)

An issue to consider

Catastrophe theory predicts a sudden, steep decline in performance.

Do some sports lend themselves more to recovering from this than others?

Specification content

B3 Arousal and anxiety theories in sporting environments

- Catastrophe theory (Hardy 1990, 1996):
  - Choking due to the impact of high cognitive anxiety.
  - Characteristics of a sportsperson experiencing choking.
  - Impact of high arousal levels on attentional focus, muscle tension and aggressive behaviour.

Reversal theory of arousal

The pursuit of vertigo

Some people deliberately seek out high arousal situations such as rock climbing where they can 'pursue vertigo'. This means they love the thrill and element of danger attached to the sport.

Other people tend to be arousal avoiders and stay as far away from heights as possible as they create that head-spinning sensation of vertigo.

Research by Tanja Kajtna *et al.* (2004) showed that people who take part in high-risk sports such as rock climbing tend to be emotionally stable. This means that external events have little influence on their arousal and anxiety levels and they remain relaxed in all situations.

The key may lie in how a person *interprets* arousal.

Specification terms

Negative emotion Undesirable feelings such as nervousness, fear or aggression.

Positive emotion Desirable feelings such as hope, pride and inspiration.

Reversal theory of arousal See page 278.

How do ski-fliers interpret the arousal from speeds of 65 mph on the in-run before take-off and landing over 200 m down the mountain as excitement? They must be paratelic!

The theory

In learning aim A3 (page 278) we looked at how John Kerr (1985) explained that performance is affected by the way in which performers *interpret* arousal levels as anxiety or not.

This interpretation depends on the performer's current mental state, either telic (serious) or paratelic (playful).

Reversal theory explains how an individual can change (reverse) their interpretations of arousal depending on their state of mind.

Applying the theory

A sportsperson's response to physiological (body) *arousal* may be positive or negative, depending on certain *personality* characteristics.

Reversal theory differentiates between 'felt' and 'preferred' arousal. 'Felt arousal' is the arousal actually experienced by a performer (e.g. worked up or emotional) whereas 'preferred arousal' refers to the level of arousal the performer would rather experience.

Arousal interpreted as a *positive* emotion

Telic state A performer in the *telic state* is described as serious and motivated by *achievement*. When they have *low* levels of felt arousal they interpret the arousal as a *positive emotion*.

For example, a netballer in a serious frame of mind who is experiencing low arousal will feel relaxed when they are on court. Playing netball is a pleasant experience for them.

Performers in this telic state and experiencing low arousal are also described as future-oriented and they look to channel their felt arousal towards meaningful, long-term goals such as improving their netball shooting and passing.

Paratelic state When a performer is in the *paratelic state* they are described as 'playful', enjoying the process in the moment. They interpret *high* levels of felt arousal as positive. Performers in this state are mainly characterised as task-oriented and focused on the present. For example, a rock climber whose focus is on finding the next foot- or handhold, will succeed because the task is associated with the excitement they feel.

Levels of high arousal in this state are seen as positive because performers enjoy the experience of becoming better at, for example, their climbing skills. Therefore, performers tend to seek out the arousal associated with improving skills.

Arousal interpreted as a *negative* emotion

Telic state A performer in the telic state who experiences *high* levels of felt arousal interprets that arousal as a *negative emotion*, e.g. *anxiety*. Performers in a telic state can be mainly characterised as serious and goal-oriented. For example, a swimmer who is focused solely on winning their race (telic state) will interpret high levels of felt arousal negatively and become anxious. This may cause them to lose focus on the quality of their swimming technique and this will interfere with winning the race.

High arousal in the telic state is associated with anxiety and so performers tend to avoid arousal.

Paratelic state A performer in the paratelic state who experiences *low* levels of felt arousal interprets that arousal as a negative emotion, e.g. boredom. Performers in the paratelic state tend to enjoy immediate pleasure. For example, a rugby player who is spontaneous (paratelic state) and experiences low levels of felt arousal may interpret their structured passing practice as boring because they prefer to practise their skills in a less rehearsed way. This may cause them to find the practice unenjoyable.

Low arousal in the paratelic state is seen as negative due to lack of enthusiasm when practising, for example, their rugby passing and so performers tend to seek arousal.

Felt versus preferred arousal

As we have seen, a sportsperson in the telic state who has low *felt* arousal experiences positive emotions and therefore, when in the telic state, the *preferred* arousal level is low.

By contrast a performer in the paratelic state experiences positive emotions when experiencing high *felt* arousal and therefore their *preferred* arousal is high as they interpret it as excitement and enjoyment.

Marathon fun runners in a paratelic state are likely to perceive high levels of arousal from the crowd as excitement.

Evaluation

Useful for coaches

One strength of applying reversal theory is that it gives coaches an increased understanding of a performer's experience of sport.

Reversal theory offers the potential to explain, predict and manage a range of problematic sporting situations. For example, Jonathan Males *et al.* (1998) suggest that the golfer Greg Norman's disastrous final round in the 1996 Masters Tournament can be explained by a paratelic to telic state reversal that brought increased anxiety and an inappropriate focus on the future outcome of the tournament.

This suggests that coaches should provide sport psychology interventions to help sportspeople cope with state reversals.

Elite vs non-elite

Another strength of reversal theory is that it predicts that there is a difference in telic and paratelic states between elite and non-elite performers.

For example, John Kerr (1985) suggests that elite performers are more likely to experience telic rather than paratelic orientation. This is because elite level sport requires a serious attitude towards performance. There is also a need for long-term planning of training in order to master skills.

This means that when elite performers experience high levels of arousal they are more likely to interpret it as leading to negative emotions and anxiety, and interfering with winning.

Use of questionnaires

One weakness of reversal theory is it relies on self-report of arousal states and this may not be accurate.

An example of such research is a study by Jonathan Males and John Kerr (1996) who used a questionnaire (self-report) to investigate pre-event emotion in a canoe slalom competition. They found that performers recalled significant unpleasant emotions prior to both their best and worst performances throughout the season. However, reversal theory suggests that a performer's state can change dramatically in a short time and therefore the emotions that were subsequently recalled may not have been correctly assigned to good and bad performances.

This suggests that reversal theory has methodological problems that limits its usefulness to sports coaches.

GET ACTIVE Telic or paratelic dominance

Serious (telic-dominant) performers are more likely to choose safe endurance-based sports while playful (paratelic-dominant) performers are more likely to participate in risky explosive sports.

From the following list of sporting activities identify which ones are likely to suit telic-dominant or paratelic-dominant performers.

1. *Long-distance running.*
2. *Cross-country skiing.*
3. *Weight-lifting.*
4. *Marathon running.*
5. *Motocross.*
6. *White water kayaking.*
7. *Swimming.*
8. *Rowing.*
9. *Karate.*
10. *Downhill mountain biking.*

Assessment practice

At the end of learning aims A and B you must write a report (see pages 263 and 298). This report must be related to a scenario or context. We have used a real-life context.

Read again about the sprinter Usain Bolt on page 279. Everyone knows Bolt was a truly great athlete. But his approach to his sport seemed casual. What was Bolt's state of mind when he was training and competing? How do you think this reflected his physiological arousal? Clearly his approach worked.

Was Bolt able to interpret his physiological arousal in a way that improved his performance? Perhaps his apparently casual behaviour was a way of experiencing low arousal in a telic state.

B3.18 Learning aim B3 – Task 18

The third part of your report for learning aims A and B will be concerned with theories of arousal and anxiety in sport, covered earlier in this unit (pages 272–279) and again on the previous three spreads and this spread.

1. **Explain** how the reversal theory of anxiety accounts for Usain Bolt's sprinting performance. Refer in your answer to his arousal and anxiety levels. (B.P4)

2. **Discuss** the reversal theory of anxiety in terms of how Usain Bolt's arousal and anxiety levels impact on his sprinting performance. (B.M2)

3. In terms of its strengths and weaknesses, **evaluate** how the reversal theory of anxiety accounts for Usain Bolt's sprinting performance. Refer in your answer to the relationship between his motivation and self-confidence and arousal levels. (B.D2)

An issue to consider

Do you think that performers experience consistent telic or paratelic states when engaging in different sports?

Specification content

B3 Arousal and anxiety theories in sporting environments

- Reversal theory (Kerr 1985, 1997):
  - Characteristics of a sportsperson who interprets arousal as a positive emotion.
  - Characteristics of a sportsperson who interprets arousal as a negative emotion.

Assessment guidance

Recommended assessment approach

The *Delivery Guide for Unit 7* states that your report (or presentation, poster, etc.) for learning aims A and B:

- Is concerned with the key principles and application of psychological theories relating to motivation, self-confidence, arousal and anxiety.
- Uses EITHER case studies of professional sports performers OR learners can assess their own experiences of sporting performance and competition.

Assignment briefs

The board supplies suggested assignment briefs which you can use – see *Unit 7 Authorised assignment brief for learning aims A and B*.

Your centre can also devise their own assignment brief which should have a vocational scenario/context and a series of tasks to complete.

Vocational scenario	The task (from the assignment brief)
The *Delivery Guide for Unit 7* suggests that a scenario could use psychological theories to address a number of key questions in sport psychology such as 'why do certain performers (or teams) seem to choke under pressure?', 'Why are some teams so successful?', 'Is it all about talent or about attitude?', 'Why do some performers perform better with an audience?'.	You need to produce a detailed report that provides an understanding of the importance of psychological theories in sport, and an investigation into how these theories can be applied to sporting situations. Your report should include the following: - An **explanation** of the key principles of theories that highlight motivation, self-confidence, arousal and anxiety in sport. (See pass criteria below.) - An **evaluation** and **discussion** of the extent to which psychological theories can explain change in sporting individuals. (See merit and distinction criteria below.)

Synoptic assessment

This assessment is synoptic. Synoptic refers to the ability to provide an overview of many different strands of information.

In your assessment you must demonstrate that you can identify and use effectively, in an integrated way, an appropriate selection of skills, techniques, concepts, theories and knowledge from across the whole sector as relevant to this task.

Essential advice

Learners may not make repeated submissions of assignment evidence.

You may be offered a single retake opportunity using a new assignment. The retake may only be achieved at a Pass.

Under some conditions, and at your centre's discretion, you may be allowed to resubmit your original work in an improved form and will be given 15 days to do so.

Assessment information

Your final report will be awarded a Distinction (D), Merit (M), Pass (P), Near Pass (N) or Unclassified (U).

The specification provides criteria for each level as shown below.

Pass	Merit	Distinction
A.P1 EXPLAIN key principles of theories of motivation and self-confidence in sport.		
A.P2 EXPLAIN key principles of theories of arousal and anxiety in sport.		
B.P3 EXPLAIN how motivation and self-confidence factors impact on sports performance.		
B.P4 EXPLAIN how arousal and anxiety levels impact on sports performance.		
	A.M1 DISCUSS the extent to which psychological theories can account for changes in motivation, self-confidence and arousal levels of sportspeople.	
	B.M2 DISCUSS how motivation, self-confidence, arousal and anxiety levels impact on sports performance.	
		A.D1 EVALUATE how far psychological theories can account for changes in motivation, self-confidence and arousal levels in sportspeople.
		B.D2 EVALUATE the impact on sports performance of the relationship between motivation, self-confidence and arousal levels.

Command terms used in this unit

The assessment criteria for learning aims A, B and C use the following command terms:

Explain = State and then justify or give an example.

Discuss = Identify and investigate all aspects of an issue or situation.

Evaluate = Consider strengths/weaknesses, come to a conclusion.

Produce = Apply knowledge to a plan or report.

Self-review checklist

First draft

Remember this is a *draft*. So you can write anything, just get thoughts on the page (see 'Blank page syndrome' on page 309). But do not copy anything, even at this stage (see 'Plagiarism' on page 309).

Date to complete first draft:

- In the first grey column enter the completion dates for each section of your report.
- As you write each section tick the yellow boxes when you have explained, discussed and evaluated, as appropriate. Ignore the boxes that are crossed through.

	Date completed	Explain (A.P1)	Explain (A.P2)	Explain (B.P3)	Explain (B.P4)	Discuss (A.M1)	Discuss (B.M2)	Evaluate (A.D1)	Evaluate (B.D2)
A1 and B1 Theories of motivation in sport									
Need achievement theory				X	X				
Achievement goal theory				X	X				
Self-determination theory				X	X				
A2 and B2 Theories of self-confidence in sport									
Vealey's multidimensional model				X	X				
Bandura's self-efficacy theory				X	X				
A3 and B3 Theories of arousal and anxiety for sports performance									
Drive theory / Inverted U hypothesis		X		X					
Multidimensional anxiety theory		X		X					
Catastrophe theory		X		X					
Reversal theory of arousal		X		X					
References compiled									

Writing a big report requires organisation and planning. You learned about time management as part of the unit on conducting psychological research (which is in our Year 1 'Certificate' book). Apply those skills to writing your report for this unit.

It is important to set yourself target dates at the outset.

It is also important to write at least two drafts.

Second draft

The next step is to revise your first document. Below is a checklist of things to consider.

Date to complete second draft:

	Date completed
I have checked that I have covered each of the four marking factors (grey column) in the table below.	
I have gone through and deleted any irrelevant material.	
I have checked that every point has evidence to back it up.	
I have identified long sentences and rephrased them.	
I have checked that each paragraph deals with one idea.	
I have corrected any spelling mistakes.	
I have checked that each paragraph makes reference to the scenario/ context.	

Final draft

Read through your completed second draft to polish the report.

Date to complete final draft:

Referencing

If you cite any research study or source (such as a website) you need to include this in a list of references at the end of your report.

This list should be in alphabetical order. The conventions for referencing are described on page 309.

Marking factors The specification also provides information that an assessor will take into consideration when marking your assignment.

Marking factors	Pass	Merit	Distinction
Psychological explanations of how motivation, self-confidence and arousal levels impact on the performances of sportspeople ...	... examples of psychological factors.	... theories plus strengths and limitations, and a balanced argument.	... detailed knowledge of range of theories including evaluation and reasoned assessment.
Linked to examples ...	... some relevant.	... wide range in different sporting situations.	... highly relevant.
Link between theories and examples ...	... appropriate but generic.	... consistently relevant.	... logical and thorough.
How changes in one factor can impact positively or negatively on one or more other factors ...	... some interpretation.	... shown, plus impact on sports performance.	... clearly reasoned assessment of how psychological factors impact on sports performance.

This coursework is as much about the journey as the final product. Learn to enjoy getting there rather than just focusing on the destination.

Performance profiling

Mind the gap

Those of you familiar with the London Underground will be aware of *minding the gap* between the platform and the train.

Sportspeople also have to mind the gap. This time it is the gap between their current perceptions of performance and their ideal level of performance.

Developing an understanding of the strengths and weaknesses of performance plays an important role in being able to improve performance.

Performance profiling is one way in which performers can assess their own performance and adapt to help bridge the gap.

A circular target performance profile for a golfer. Each slice covers one construct. The rings numbered from 2 to 10 represent the assessment of the construct – for example, for flexibility seven rings are shaded which means the player has scored their performance in terms of flexibility as 7 out of 10.

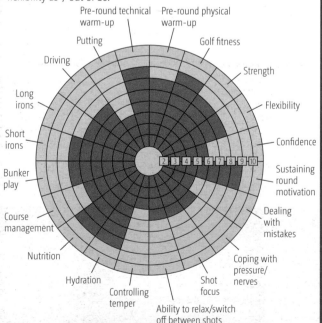

The story so far

In learning aim A1 we looked at *motivation* as a cause for people taking part in sport. You will recall that this may be due to a performer's *achievement motivation*, how their *personality* affects their sport/task selection and/or the extent to which they are 'driven' by intrinsic or extrinsic factors.

In learning aim B1 we developed this to show the interrelationship of these theories with the actions and reactions of performers in sport and high-pressure competitions.

Over the next two spreads we will look at how coaches and performers can use and apply motivational techniques to improve performance in different sporting contexts.

Performance profiling

Richard Butler and Lew Hardy (1992) introduced *performance profiling* as an assessment strategy which aims to put the performer at the heart of their performance development. The performance profile takes the form of a circular target or column chart (see diagram on left).

Process

Step 1 – Introduction In the first step, the coach/psychologist introduces the technique.

Step 2 – Eliciting constructs In the second step, psychological constructs (qualities) that underpin successful performance are identified. For example, ten possible psychological constructs important to performance might be: motivation, arousal, anxiety, self-confidence, self-efficacy, controlling aggression, personality, use of imagery, attention and leadership.

Further constructs can be identified for technical, physical and tactical categories. For example:

- Technical category examples in tennis could include smooth ball toss or wrist snap during a serve that are important aspects of technique for good performance.
- Physical category examples could include constructs such as speed, agility or flexibility that are vital in helping the performer get into the correct position to play the shot.
- Tactical category examples could include serve to the backhand or playing at the net or baseline and involve strategic decision-making.

The performer and psychologist and/or coach discuss the constructs important for successful performance in the target sport/position and also consider the performer's perceived strengths and weaknesses. They then produce an appropriate personalised list drawing from the four main categories (psychological, technical, physical and tactical).

Importantly, at this stage, each construct must be defined so that, should the performer wish to rerate themselves at a later date, it can be done with consistency.

Step 3 – Assessment of constructs Later on the performer self-assesses their ability in each of their chosen performance constructs. Performers typically rate their current perception of their ability for each construct via a scale of 1 (lowest possible ability) to 10 (ideal level of performance). The coach can also assess performers' constructs so any discrepancies can be discussed.

Uses

Performance profiling allows coaches to monitor performance. In doing so they can maximise the performer's motivation to improve and adhere to the training intervention.

Utilising results from assessment A simple calculation can be carried out to find a 'discrepancy score' between current and ideal performance (also a coach versus performer discrepancy can be calculated). Higher discrepancies indicate areas that may need to be addressed through training or other intervention. Additionally the completed profile provides a useful visual display of the performer's perceived strengths and weaknesses.

Areas resistant to change Performers may be resistant to change in some areas of their performance. This may be because they perceive a construct to be of relatively low importance. For example, a cricketer who believes that their throwing ability is not as important as catching or bowling may be unwilling to spend time improving it.

Assessing your own strengths and weaknesses is particularly important for sports such as gymnastics because the movements are so complex.

Evaluation

Construct importance

One strength of performance profiling is that it highlights which constructs are most important to performance.

For example, Daniel Gucciardi and Sandy Gordon (2009) suggested that each profile construct that a performer identifies is restricted by the number of situations to which it is applicable, e.g. the construct 'preparation for competition' is only relevant to one situation (normal training). The construct/situation interaction can be assessed by creating a table with constructs along the top and situations down the side. You then tick boxes where each construct is relevant to a situation. The higher the number of situations in which the construct can be applied, the more important that construct is to the performer's development.

This means that performers can identify which constructs they need to focus on developing.

Performer-centred

A further strength of performance profiling is that it supports *self-determination theory* of motivation.

This approach to motivation suggests that motivation will be higher if determined by the performers themselves. Performance profiling enables a performer to enhance their perceptions of *autonomy*. Furthermore, when used within a group setting, performance profiling encourages teammates to discuss performance and could help increase perceptions of *relatedness*. Finally, employing the profile to monitor progress could improve perceived competence as performers see their profile ratings increase over time.

This shows how performance profiling can instil greater *intrinsic motivation* which will help adhere to future training interventions.

Lack of sporting awareness

One weakness of performance profiling is that some populations of performers may lack sufficient sporting awareness to self-assess performance effectively.

For example, young or novice sport performers may lack sufficient knowledge to identify appropriate qualities/constructs for their sport or position. This would result in profiles that lack the required depth and/or construct accuracy that would be expected of their position or sport.

This suggests that coaches must be wary in such situations and may benefit from asking young or inexperienced performers to choose from a pre-prepared list of constructs.

GET ACTIVE Eliciting constructs

We have listed ten psychological constructs (on facing page) that can be used for performance profiling. We have also listed some examples of technical, physical and tactical constructs.

Using sports of your choice generate a list of ten technical, ten physical and ten tactical constructs that could be used for performance profiling.

Sport 1 ten technical constructs...

Sport 2 ten physical constructs...

Sport 3 ten tactical constructs...

Assessment practice

At the end of learning aim C you must write:

A report on a programme of recommended psychological interventions to address the needs of a selected sportsperson.

This report must be related to the student's own needs or to a known sportsperson.

The experience of Andy Murray (see page 267) demonstrates the importance of motivation in sports performance.

Zane is an amateur squash player who has had some success at county level. He wants to take the next step and see if he can compete at national level. But he and his coach are both concerned that Zane's motivation is not strong enough for him to progress much further. Looking again at Andy Murray's experiences, think about how performance profiling might help Zane.

C1.1 Learning aim C1 – Task 1

The first part of your report for learning aim C will be concerned with psychological interventions to influence the motivation of sportspeople, covered earlier in this unit on pages 262–267 and 280–285, and also on this and the next spread.

You can see the assessment criteria on page 308 and explanation of command terms on page 298.

1. **Produce** an outline programme of performance profiling to address Zane's motivation level. (C.P5)

2. **Explain** how performance profiling would benefit Zane. (C.P6)

3. **Produce** an analysis of the suitability of performance profiling to address Zane's motivation level. (C.M3)

4. In terms of its strengths and weaknesses, **produce** an evaluation of the suitability of performance profiling to address Zane's motivation and self-confidence and arousal levels. (C.D3)

An issue to consider

We have argued that performance profiling is more effective for experienced performers rather than beginners as experienced performers have a better awareness of their own performance.

But do you think performance profiling would be more effective for individual or for team sports?

Specification content

C1 Psychological interventions to influence motivation of sportspeople.

Key principles, strengths, limitations and uses of motivational techniques applied in different sporting contexts.

- Performance profiling – uses and process, including:
  - Eliciting constructs – ten psychological factors important to performance.
  - Assessment of constructs.
  - Utilising results from assessment.
  - Areas resistant to change.

Goal setting

Smart car

The Smart Car began with Nicolas Hayek, the man who invented Swatch watches. He wanted to make a small car that would be fuel efficient, environmentally responsible and easy to park in small spaces. Clearly from that point of view this car is smart.

Cars require a great deal of detailed planning to design and build. Initial ideas need to be discussed and prototypes tested before the final design is approved and built.

We can see similarities in how performers are motivated to improve their sport performance. First there need to be initial discussions with the coach and then skills need to be learned and practised before the final performance is successful.

In order to build a car or remain motivated to improve sport performance, goals need to be set. This can be done using SMART(S) goals.

Actually SMART is an acronym for Swatch Mercedes Art.

Specification term

Goals In sport, goals are the aim of a performer's action.

HE HASN'T QUITE YET MASTERED THE ART OF THE DIVING HEADER.

Alexander Aldorino

The story so far

On the previous spread we looked at one motivational technique (performance profiling) used by coaches and performers to improve performance in different sporting contexts. On this spread we look at goal setting, another motivational technique.

A *goal* can be seen as what the performer is trying to accomplish. It is the object or aim of an action.

Goal setting

Edwin Locke and Gary Latham (2002) proposed the *goal setting theory of motivation*. By breaking down a general goal into a number of smaller and more specific goals, coaches and performers can make the desired outcomes appear less intimidating and more achievable. Thus, goal setting theory is helpful in improving *motivation*.

Setting specific goals is also an effective strategy for improving motivation in individual performers. It can also affect team performance – if each performer is motivated to achieve their individual goals, the combined effect is that it helps the team achieve its overall goals.

Timescale for goals

- **Short-term goals** can be used to give a performer a specific measure of progress and achievement. For example, a rugby player who made eight tackles in a match may then set out to make ten tackles during the next match.

- **Medium-term goals** can help develop performance over a longer period of time, such as a month. For example, a basketball player who had a goal of running 3 km in training at the start of the season could increase this to 4 km at the end of the first month's training.

- **Long-term goals** provide performers with an overview of what they are trying to achieve. For example, a golfer may want to win a major championship or become the best player in the world by topping the PGA rankings.

Types of goals

Performers set goals at the start of the season and work towards and monitor them. Goals are evaluated at the end of the season. Performers may have a number of different types of goal that may be discussed with their coach:

- **Performance goals** focus on present standards of performance compared with previous performances. Levels of success are judged in terms of skill mastery or beating a personal best. For example, a javelin thrower throwing further than before.

- **Process goals** are what performers have to do in order to achieve the required improvement in performance. For example, a runner keeping a training log of practice sessions.

- **Outcome goals** are an objectively-defined standard to achieve. For example, aiming to be in the top five in a marathon.

- **Mastery goals** are where performers strive for improvement over their previous best performance. For example, a 100 m sprinter wishing to run their fastest time.

- **Competitive goals** are where performers are focused on winning in sport competition.

Principles of goal setting (SMARTS)

Performers set and check progress against their goals with their coach.

Specific – goals are as precise and detailed as possible.

Measurable – a method is selected so current performance can be quantified to determine the amount of improvement required.

Action-orientated – performer identifies the actions needed to reach their goal.

Realistic – the goal is achievable yet challenging.

Time-bound – there is a date set by when the goal is to be achieved.

Self-determined – the goal is personal and satisfies intrinsic aspirations.

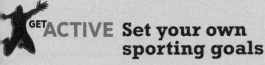

GET ACTIVE Set your own sporting goals

Apply the types and principles of goal setting to your own sport performance.

1. *Identify one short-term goal, one medium-term goal and one long-term goal.*

2. *Give an example for each of the five types of goal in the context of a sport you take part in.*

3. *Explain how each of the six principles of SMARTS goal setting could help you achieve one of the goals identified in question 2.*

Whatever the sport, it is always good to keep your target in sight in order to remain motivated to achieve it.

Evaluation

Practical

One strength of goal setting theory is that it is relatively easy to apply.

For example, a tennis player and his coach can use *performance profiling* (see previous spread) to identify strengths and weaknesses in performance. Goals for improvement can then be steered using the SMARTS principles. There are time implications for coaches and players in meeting to discuss and agree targets, i.e. it uses a lot of their time. However, such activity is a very important part of the coaching process because these processes are vital if performance is to be improved.

This shows how goal setting can be a key part of the coaching process.

Improves intrinsic motivation

A further strength of goal setting theory is that it helps satisfy the drive to participate in sport for its own sake and wanting to play well.

An example of this is that performers often say their motivation stems from a desire to learn and improve skills and to persist with the challenges that sport provides. SMARTS principles enable a performer to set goals that are meaningful to them. For example, a darts player might set a *mastery goal* to average a score of ninety each time they throw three darts. This is likely to satisfy self-determination needs – as discussed in *self-determination theory* (page 266 and 284): feeling accepted by others (*relatedness*), achieving desired outcomes (*competence*), and choosing to participate (*autonomy*).

This shows how goal setting can help performers create tasks which will satisfy their *intrinsic motivation* needs.

Using ineffective strategies

One weakness with goal setting is, paradoxically, goal attainment.

For example, a cricketer's success at achieving their goals will naturally increase their own and their coach's satisfaction. This satisfaction can lead them to continue to use their previously successful strategies to reach even higher future goals. However, as Edwin Locke and Gary Latham (2006) suggest, this may often lead to the use of strategies that are not actually effective for the future goals.

This suggests that not only do goals need to be continually re-evaluated but strategies to meet those goals need to be reviewed in order to achieve improved performance.

Assessment practice

At the end of learning aim C you must write a report (see pages 301 and 308). This report must be related to the student's own needs or to a known sportsperson.

In different ways, the experiences of Steph Houghton and Serena Guthrie (pages 263 and 265) demonstrate the importance of motivation in sports performance.
Dani is a volleyball player. Her team is becoming increasingly successful and they are set to win their league and be promoted. Everyone in the team is enthusiastic about the next season, even though it will require a bigger commitment (more matches and travelling and a lot more training). But there are question marks over Dani's motivation. The team's coach is concerned that Dani is not 'hungry' enough for success or committed enough to make the necessary sacrifices. Looking again at the experiences of Houghton and Guthrie, think about how performance profiling might help Dani.

C1.2 Learning aim C1 – Task 2

The first part of your report for learning aim C will be concerned with psychological interventions to influence the motivation of sportspeople, covered earlier in this unit on pages 262–267 and 280–285, and also on the previous spread and this spread.

This activity will help you practise the skills required to write the report in response to your scenario/context.

1. **Produce** an outline programme involving goal setting to address Dani's motivation level. (C.P5)

2. **Explain** how goal setting would benefit Dani. (C.P6)

3. **Produce** an analysis of the suitability of goal setting to address Dani's motivation level. (C.M3)

4. In terms of its strengths and weaknesses, **produce** an evaluation of the suitability of goal setting to address Dani's motivation level. (C.D3)

An issue to consider

'Don't think it, ink it'!

Why do you think it is important that goals are written down by performers and coaches in order to maintain motivation for sport performance?

Specification content

C1 Psychological interventions to influence motivation of sportspeople

Key principles, strengths, limitations and uses of motivational techniques applied in different sporting contexts.

● Goal setting:
  ○ Timescale for goals – short, medium, long term.
  ○ Types of goals – performance, outcome and process, mastery and competitive.
  ○ Principles of goal setting – specific, measurable, action-orientated, realistic, time-bound, self-determined (SMARTS).

Imagery and self-talk

Dr. Krista Munroe-Chandler

Dr. Krista Munroe-Chandler is recognised for her work in the psychology of sport. She is a full professor in the Faculty of Human Kinetics at the University of Windsor, Canada. Her research interests include imagery use in sport and exercise as well as youth sport development. She works with performers of all ages, levels, and sport helping them to achieve their personal performance goals.

In one study, Munroe-Chandler *et al.* (2008) looked at the use of imagery in young Canadian soccer players.

They used motivational general-mastery (MG-M) imagery where elite and recreational football players pictured themselves coping in difficult situations and mastering those circumstances.

The researchers showed that MG-M imagery use was an effective way of improving self-efficacy and self-confidence.

Specification terms

Imagery Use of words or pictures to describe ideas or situations.

Self-talk Intentional statements that we say to ourselves.

The use of imagery is important when completing complex movements that require precision.

The story so far

In learning aim A2 you learned about the *multidimensional model of sport confidence*. Robin Vealey (1986) described *self-confidence* in the context of sport as the belief or degree of certainty individuals possess about their ability to be successful in sport. In learning aim B2 you developed this to apply self-confidence theories to sporting environments.

On this spread we look at how *imagery* and *self-talk* can be used to increase self-confidence of sportspeople.

Imagery

The term *imagery* is used to describe the structured mental practice techniques used to create or recreate an *athletic performance* (Vealey and Greenleaf 1998).

Types

Imagery takes two forms.

* *Internal imagery* involves imagining yourself performing a task, feeling the performance and experiencing being in the situation.
* *External imagery* is seeing yourself performing the task, watching yourself on film, from the outside.

Internal and external imagery are used equally amongst all players. As skill level increases so does the use of imagery.

Applications

Imagery is best used amongst elite performers who are able to imagine the required technique being carried out perfectly. It is used in addition to physical practice. Imagery is a skill that can be improved through practice.

Paul Holmes and Dave Collins (2001) devised PETTLEP representing a seven-point checklist of guidelines to be used to create an imagery intervention. This technique can be used to improve self-confidence. For example:

Physical – A golfer imagines holding his or her club and standing in a tray of sand.

Environment – A figure skater uses photographs of the ice arena to imagine their routine.

Task – A biathlete imagines exact elements of their rifle-shooting routine.

Timing – A hurdler imagines their activity in real time, as timing is vital to their stride pattern.

Learning – A diver focuses on the more refined elements of the dive after becoming competent in the basic shapes.

Emotion – A soccer player includes all the nerves or excitement in their image before taking a penalty.

Perspective – A basketball player imagines how someone else might see them completing a free-throw shot.

Self-talk

Positive self-talk is a cognitive technique where performers give themselves messages to improve their self-confidence (Vealey 2007).

Types

Cognitive or *instructional self-talk* focuses on the technical aspects of performance. For example, a tennis player might say 'high ball toss' as they are serving, or a basketball player might say 'wrist, centre' when shooting. The intention is to increase the likelihood of success, which in turn increases self-confidence.

Motivational self-talk includes phrases or words designed to increase self-confidence. For example, an 800 m runner approaching the final lap might say 'you can do this, stay strong'.

Uses

Positive self-talk can be used at any time before, during or after a performance. The self-talk words and phrases can be devised by players themselves to be meaningful. The technique and its use can be reviewed with a coach. It is useful for coaches to understand the different types of self-talk so they can personalise the intervention to the performer's needs.

Positive self-talk can help gymnasts by building an expectancy of success through improved self-confidence.

Evaluation

Time efficient

One strength of imagery is that it makes an efficient use of time for performers.

Fatma Kerkez and colleagues (2012) suggest that imagery can be practised in any location and at any time and when weather conditions make it difficult for physical practice. For example, an athlete can imagine a race as they travel to the event and a cricket batsman can imagine facing a fast bowler when play is stopped due to bad light. Additionally imagery can be used when a performer is injured and cannot take part in normal training sessions.

This shows that imagery can help deal with a problem before a performer faces it and imagery can also break the monotony of training.

Best for cognitive control

One weakness of imagery is that it is most effective when skills are under conscious control.

Deborah Feltz and Daniel Landers (1983) suggest that sporting activity that involves decision-making and tactics can benefit most from the use of imagery – for example, a gymnastic floor routine that involves a performer carrying out a long sequence of moves or sports such as basketball that have tactical strategies. This is because these skills contain a cognitive component. Imagery is less effective for other skills, such as weightlifting that have few tactical requirements.

This shows that imagery has restricted uses.

Evaluation

Adaptable

One strength of self-talk is that the technique can take different forms.

Activities that need timing and accuracy, such as a somersault, benefit from instructional self-talk. Performers can 'guide themselves' through the movement, for example saying 'tight tuck' to improve self-confidence. Whereas motivational self-talk can be used by performers to boost their confidence during a challenging task, such as the final set of a tennis match.

This means that self-talk is a technique that can be used in a variety of sports.

Not all self-talk is positive

One weakness of self-talk is that it can be negative as well as positive.

For example, Antonis Hatzigeorgiadis and Stuart Biddle (2008) found that cross-country runners who had negative thoughts, such as 'I am not going to achieve my goals' or 'Other runners are better than me', had increased anxiety and reduced performance.

This suggests that self-talk is not always to be encouraged and self-defeating or over-evaluating types of self-talk should be avoided.

Assessment practice

At the end of learning aim C you must write a report (see pages 301 and 308). This report must be related to the student's own needs or to a known sportsperson.

Dame Katherine Grainger (page 269) took a break of two years from rowing and she lost form on her return. By her own admission her performances were poor. Despite all this, she was still confident of winning a medal at the Rio Olympics in 2016.

Mariko is a talented amateur boxer who won many bouts early in her career and once came second in the National Championships at her weight. At one time she was considered a serious prospect for a Commonwealth Games medal. But other commitments mean she has not been able to spend time training. Her performances have declined drastically and her self-confidence has been badly dented. Looking again at the experience of Katherine Grainger, think about how imagery and self-talk might help Mariko.

C2.3 Learning aim C2 – Task 3

The second part of your report for learning aim C will be concerned with psychological interventions to influence the self-confidence of sportspeople, covered earlier in this unit on pages 268–271 and 286–289, and also on this spread.

1. **Produce** an outline programme involving imagery and self-talk to address Mariko's motivation level. (C.P5)
2. **Explain** how imagery and self-talk would benefit Mariko. (C.P6)
3. **Produce** an analysis of the suitability of imagery and self-talk to address Mariko's motivation level. (C.M3)
4. In terms of its strengths and weaknesses, **produce** an evaluation of the suitability of imagery and self-talk to address Mariko's motivation level. (C.D3)

An issue to consider

Do you think performers who are low in trait anxiety are more likely to use positive self-talk than performers who have high trait anxiety?

Specification content

C2 Psychological interventions to influence self-confidence of sportspeople

Key principles, strengths, limitations and uses of techniques to influence self-confidence applied in different sporting contexts.

- Imagery – types and applications.
- Self-talk – types and uses.

Relaxation and energising techniques

The Boss

Bruce Springsteen's hit song *Born to run* is an exuberant and lively ballad in which Springsteen invokes one of his favourite metaphors – the car as an engine of escape from the many disappointments that seem to constrain young, working-class Americans.

It appeared on the playlist of quarterback Peyton Manning, five-time NFL *Most Valuable Player*. Manning also listened to *The Stroke* by Billy Squier before walking out at the Mile High stadium in Denver.

Many sportspeople use music in diverse ways in order to achieve a certain level of focus and concentration before a game.

Listening to upbeat music before competition can certainly generate enthusiasm and the emotion needed to increase arousal levels that performers need for optimal performance (Bishop *et al.* 2007).

Specification terms

Energising techniques Methods that will create higher levels of activity.

Mind-to-muscle techniques Cognitive processes involved in relaxation, such as thinking and visualising to reduce muscle tension.

Progressive muscular relaxation (PMR) Tensing and then relaxing muscles repeatedly to reduce tension overall.

Relaxation techniques Methods that help a person become more calm and reduce levels of pain, anxiety and stress.

A 'pep talk' from Manchester City manager Pep Guardiola!

The story so far

In learning aim A3 you learned about theories of *arousal* and *anxiety*. Performers who are optimally aroused are physically and mentally ready to perform. In learning aim B3 you developed this understanding to investigate how these theories explain performance in sporting environments.

   On this spread we look at how *relaxation* and *energising techniques* can be used to influence arousal in sportspeople so that they are ready to perform optimally.

Relaxation techniques

Relaxation techniques reduce arousal and help performers cope with the demands of competition in sport.

Mind-to-muscle techniques

Mind-to-muscle techniques involve a focus on the *cognitive* (mental) processes involved in relaxation. For example, *autogenic training* is a self-hypnotic method where attention is focused inwards and away from external stimuli (similar to the process of hypnosis). This leads to producing the desired sensation in the body. Common practices include performers making self-suggestions such as 'my right arm is heavy and warm' or 'my heartbeat is becoming calm and regular'. Autogenic training can help performers to reduce arousal and achieve relaxation of the body and mind.

Progressive muscular relaxation (PMR)

PMR is another mind-to-muscle technique where a performer learns to become more sensitive to *muscle tension* as an indicator of arousal. PMR is a whole-body technique that works by the performer alternately contracting a muscle for four to six seconds then relaxing it. The performer works through muscles progressively, usually starting from the lower body to the upper body. For example, a rifle shooter may use PMR prior to a competition, starting with muscle groups in the fingers, then the arm and moving up to the shoulder muscles.

   The main goal of PMR is for the performer to learn to recognise unwanted muscle tension and then to relax the muscle to remove this tension and to be aware of how this reduces arousal.

Breathing control

Breathing techniques to reduce arousal such as *centring*, focus on regulating breathing and are usually most applicable prior to or during competition. The performer takes slow, deep breaths, centring their attention on a specific area of the body such as the navel. They may repeat a calming word such as 'relax, relax'. This technique is a way of countering the increased breathing rate and negative thoughts that can be present during competition or high arousal-inducing activities such as rock climbing.

Energising techniques

Sometimes performers appear to be under-aroused and require increased arousal.

Pep talks

Many coaches use a pep talk from motivational speakers or former 'greats' to give their players a 'lift' or to increase arousal before a big game. Ideally pep talks should be short and simple. Coaches should give one to two final pieces of strategic or instructional information to help performers reach optimal arousal.

Listening to music

Music can be a great source of energy prior to competition, as described above left. It is not unusual to see football players arriving at a stadium with headphones listening to their favourite bands, e.g. the Spanish goalkeeper David de Gea listens to metal and rock bands like Slipknot and Metallica. Performers tend to choose music that has inspirational lyrics, is associated with past success or is characterised by a strong beat to increase arousal.

Energising imagery

Imagery use is another way of generating positive feelings and arousal. Energising imagery involves visualising a performance that creates powerful feelings of activation and arousal in the performer. For example, a 100 m sprinter might imagine a cheetah running swiftly across the plains of Africa or a swimmer imagines moving through the water like a shark.

GET ACTIVE Top of the Pops

We all have our favourite music to listen to when we are working or in the car.

Use your knowledge of energising techniques for optimal arousal to come up with your top ten pieces of music that would influence your sport performance.

For each of the pieces of music explain your choice in terms of, for example, the beat, your identification with the lyrics or artist, whether you wish to be energised or relaxed and any family or peer influences on your choice of music.

Performers report that listening to music leads to improved mood, increased arousal, and increased visual and auditory imagery (Bishop *et al.* 2007).

Evaluation

Helps control arousal

One strength of breathing techniques (such as centring) is that they are easy to apply.

For example, Carolyn Savoy (1993) used centring as part of an intervention package with an elite-level female basketball player. Centring was taught during the off-season and the player applied it throughout the playing season. Savoy monitored the performer using observations and interviews and reported decreases in the performer's arousal levels.

This suggests that breathing control techniques can be relatively easy to apply to control arousal in sport.

Time efficient

One weakness of progressive muscular relaxation (PMR) is that performers find it difficult to use during competition.

For example, a typical PMR session takes thirty minutes and, while this may be reduced to ten minutes with practice, even this is difficult to achieve during a competition (Weinberg and Gould 2015).

This suggests that PMR can be a valuable technique to use *between* performances but not *during* performances.

Evaluation

Effective

One strength of techniques such as energising imagery is that they do work, increasing arousal and well-being.

Cecilie Thøgersen-Ntoumani *et al.* (2012) asked 499 Greek adults aged 50–84 years to evaluate the imagery they used before exercising. The participants said that imagery gave them a feeling of being alive, invigorated and possessing enthusiasm and energy.

This suggests that energising techniques have the intended effect and can be used by coaches and performers in order to influence arousal levels.

Individual differences

One weakness of energising techniques such as pep talks is that they may not suit all performers.

For example, pre-game preparation is individual to each performer and so a motivational pep talk designed to increase arousal might be detrimental to a performer who is already experiencing high levels of arousal.

This suggests that coaches should consider the individual requirements of performers when attempting to energise their team's arousal.

Assessment practice

At the end of learning aim C you must write a report (see pages 301 and 308). This report must be related to the student's own needs or to a known sportsperson.

The experience of Victoria Pendleton (page 275) demonstrates the roles of arousal and anxiety in sports performance.

Ewan is an amateur curler. He is a skilled performer in a sport that needs precision and nerves of steel. Recently however he has found it hard to let go of the stone on the ice at just the right moment. He always feels the urge to hold on to it for a fraction of a second too long. This means his team's performance has plummeted. Ewan is feeling the pressure of being the one responsible which is making his problem worse. Looking again at the experience of Victoria Pendleton, think about how relaxing and energising techniques might help Ewan.

C3.4 Learning aim C3 – Task 4

The third part of your report for learning aim C will be concerned with psychological interventions to influence the arousal of sportspeople, covered earlier in this unit on pages 272–279 and 290–297, and also on this spread.

1. **Produce** an outline programme of relaxation and energising techniques to address Ewan's motivation level. (C.P5)

2. **Explain** how relaxation and energising techniques would benefit Ewan. (C.P6)

3. **Produce** an analysis of the suitability of relaxation and energising techniques to address Ewan's motivation level. (C.M3)

4. In terms of its strengths and weaknesses, **produce** an evaluation of the suitability of relaxation and energising techniques to address Ewan's motivation level. (C.D3)

An issue to consider

While there are a range of techniques that influence arousal, performers respond to each of them differently.

What factors should performers take into account when choosing relaxation and energising techniques?

Specification content

C3 Psychological interventions to influence arousal levels of sportspeople

Key principles, strengths, limitations and uses of arousal control techniques applied in different sporting contexts.

- Relaxation techniques, including progressive muscular relaxation, mind-to-muscle techniques, breathing control.
- Energising techniques, including pep talks, listening to music, use of energising imagery.

Assessment guidance

Learning aim C assessment

You are required to produce one or two reports for the three learning aims in this unit (but not more than two).

It makes most sense to combine learning aims A and B, and then do C separately. No learning aim can be subdivided.

The report can be written or presented as a poster, PowerPoint or other form.

This report can only be completed after you have studied the content of learning aim C as it is a synoptic assessment (see page 298).

Recommended assessment approach

The *Delivery Guide for Unit 7* states that your report (or presentation, poster, etc.) for learning aim C:

- Should primarily focus on recommending psychological interventions for sport performance.
- Should address the student's own needs or those of a selected sportsperson.
- Should include an assessment of the strengths and limitations of motivational techniques for a number of sporting contexts.

Assignment briefs

The board supplies suggested assignment briefs which you can use – see *Unit 7 Authorised assignment brief for learning aim C*.

Your centre can also devise their own assignment brief which should have a vocational scenario/context and a series of tasks to complete.

Vocational scenario	The task (from the assignment brief)
The *Delivery Guide for Unit 7* states that learners must be given enough time to do their own independent research on their own or the chosen sports performer and to write up a detailed programme of recommended interventions to address their own, or their sports performer's, needs. This may involve looking at examples of programmes written by professional sport psychologists, and taking a look at their relative success and failure in their chosen field.	Produce a detailed programme that provides an: • **Outline** and **explanation** for a recommended and suitable programme. (See pass criteria below.) • **Analysis** of the motivation, self-confidence, and arousal levels that may impact on that individual. (See merit criteria below.) • **Evaluation** and intervention that addresses the needs of a selected sportsperson. (See distinction criteria below.)

Assessment information

Your final report will be awarded a Distinction (D), Merit (M), Pass (P), Near Pass (N) or Unclassified (U).

The specification provides criteria for each level as shown below.

Pass	Merit	Distinction
C.P5 PRODUCE an outline programme of recommended psychological interventions to address the performance needs of a selected sportsperson.		
C.P6 EXPLAIN the suitability of the programme to benefit a selected sportsperson.		
	C.M3 PRODUCE a programme of recommended psychological interventions for a selected sportsperson, analysing their suitability in addressing performance needs.	
		C.D3 PRODUCE a detailed programme of recommended psychological interventions for a selected sportsperson, evaluating their suitability in addressing performance needs.

Marking factors The specification also provides information that an assessor will take into consideration when marking your assignment.

Marking factors	Pass	Merit	Distinction
Produce a programme to address the sports performance needs of a selected sportsperson, that uses ...	... appropriate psychological interventions.	... a range of psychological interventions.	... in-depth knowledge of the principles that underpin a range of psychological interventions and how they work together to improve sports performance.
This includes ...		... justifications as to why certain interventions have been selected and not others.	... evaluation of the effectiveness of the interventions by drawing out and expanding on the strengths and limitations of each, and make judgements about their value.
Give recommendations based on information they have collected, matching specific interventions to the needs of the chosen sportsperson ...	... included.	... and explain how and when each intervention should be practised and learned in relation to an event or competition.	... and show an awareness of what psychological skills are needed to enable sportspeople to use each intervention effectively.

Self-review checklist

The list below will help you manage writing your final report.

First draft

Remember this is a *draft*. So you can write anything, just get thoughts on the page (see 'Blank page syndrome' below). But do not copy anything, even at this stage (see 'Plagiarism' on the right).

Date to complete first draft:	

	Date completed	Produce (C.P5)	Explain (C.P6)	Produce (C.M3)	Produce (C.D3)
• In the first grey column enter the completion dates for each section of your report. • As you write each section tick the yellow boxes when you have explained and produced a programme.					
C1 Psychological interventions to influence motivation of sportspeople					
Performance profiling					
Goal setting					
C2 Psychological interventions to influence self-confidence of sportspeople					
Imagery and self-talk					
C3 Psychological interventions to influence arousal levels of sportspeople					
Relaxation and energising techniques					
References compiled					

Second draft

The next step is to revise your first document. Below is a checklist of things to consider.

Date to complete second draft:	

	Date completed
I have checked that I have covered each of the three marking factors (grey column) in the table on the facing page.	
I have gone through and deleted any irrelevant material.	
I have checked that every point has evidence to back it up.	
I have identified long sentences and rephrased them.	
I have checked that each paragraph deals with one idea.	
I have corrected any spelling mistakes.	
I have checked that each paragraph makes reference to the scenario/context.	

Final draft

Read through your completed second draft to polish the report.

Date to complete final draft:	

Blank page syndrome*

We all experience it – when you try to start writing something you end up staring at that blank page and can't think where to begin.

It doesn't matter where you begin! That's what a first draft is about. Just write anything – but do write in your own words not chunks copied from the internet or this textbook, otherwise you will forget and they will end up in your final version (see 'Plagiarism' above).

*It's more likely of course to be a blank screen syndrome.

Plagiarism

Plagiarism means to use someone else's work without crediting the source. It means to steal and pass off the words (or ideas) of another as one's own. All the work submitted as your internal assessments must be your own.

We are lucky to have the internet at our fingertips when writing this book and we often cut and paste content into our notes – and it is very easy to forget we have done this. However, we know this can be easily checked and if we were found to have committed plagiarism in our book we would be accused of committing a crime and could be fined or receive a prison sentence for plagiarising someone else's work.

The same is true for you – it is tempting to use something written on a website or in this book and feel 'I can't say it as well as this'. You cannot do that unless the sentence is in quotes and attributed to the author.

We take great care to ensure that all of our sentences are our own. You must do the same or you will be disqualified from this exam.

Referencing conventions

You must include the details of all references cited in your report. These go in an alphabetical list (by author) at the end of your report.

Author names are always given as last name followed by initial. When multi-authored works have been cited, it is important to include the names of all the authors, even when the text reference used was '*et al*'.

Book references

Author name(s), date, book title (in italics), place of publication, publisher.
e.g. Offer, D., Ostrov, E. and Howard, K. (1981) *The Adolescent – a psychological self-portrait*. New York: Basic Books.

Journal references

Author name(s), date, article title, journal name (in italics), volume (in italics) and where given issue number (in brackets), page numbers.
e.g. MacKay, G. (2002) The disappearance of disability? Thoughts on a changing culture. *British Journal of Special Education*, *29*(4), 159–163.

Internet references

Author name(s), date, article title, source, full date, retrieved from web URL, date of access.
e.g. Roller, E. (2016) Your facts or mine? *The New York Times*, 25 October 2016, retrieved from https://www.nytimes. com/2016/10/25/opinion/ campaign-stops/your-facts-or-mine.html [Accessed June 2019].

Personal communication

e.g. Robertson, M. (2012) personal communication.

Index/Glossary

A-state See state anxiety. 274–5, 292–5

A-trait See trait anxiety. 274, 292–4

abnormal behaviour Defined in many ways, but sometimes as 'deviating from normal behaviour'. 214–15

abnormality A comparison with what is 'normal' or typical behaviour. Normality can be defined statistically or in terms of socially acceptable behaviour. 118, 194, 214–17

absolute discharge A defendant is found guilty of a charge but no punishment is imposed because it is deemed unnecessary or inappropriate. See also conditional discharge. 138

abuse Treat with cruelty or violence, especially regularly or repeatedly. 54–5, 57, 64–5, 67, 88, 95, 100, 105, 116, 125, 128–9, 132–3, 135–7, 155, 163, 166–7, 193–7, 199–200, 202–11, 217, 230, 232–3, 241, 244

acceptance and commitment therapy (ACT) A client stops controlling their thoughts and feelings and becomes involved in meaningful life activities. 246–7

accommodation A form of learning that takes place when we acquire new information that changes our understanding of a topic to the extent that we need to form one or more new schemas and/or radically change existing schemas in order to deal with the new understanding. 184

achievement goal theory Explains motivation in terms of targets to be achieved. 261, 264–5, 282–3, 299

achievement motivation A person's desire to master skills, attain high standards and generally to succeed at their chosen targets. 262–3, 281, 300

acute stress A threat requiring an immediate response. 46–9, 66, 68, 81–2

adaptation In Piaget's theory, it involves a child changing their schema to meet the demands of new situations or experiences. 46–7, 66, 110, 184–5

adaptive Any physical or psychological characteristic that enhances an individual's survival and reproduction, and is thus likely to be naturally selected. Such characteristics are passed on to future generations. 46–7, 66, 68, 88, 93

addiction A mental health problem in which an individual takes a substance or engages in a behaviour that is pleasurable but eventually becomes compulsive with harmful consequences. 9–35, 50–65, 67, 69, 71–2, 79–95, 103–109, 121, 138, 142, 194–5, 208, 213, 230–31, 240–41

ADHD See attention deficit hyperactivity disorder. 194, 196, 200

adherence reminders Techniques of 'nudging' patients into following medical advice (e.g. box to organise pills). 102, 105

adoption studies Genetic factors are implicated if adopted children are more similar to their biological parents with whom they share genes (but not environment) than to their adoptive parents with whom they share environment (but not genes). Environmental factors are implicated if the reverse is true. 114–15

adrenal cortex The outer region of the adrenal glands. 46–7, 66

adrenal glands Small glands located on top of each kidney. Various hormones are produced including adrenaline and noradrenaline and corticosteroids (e.g. cortisol). 46–7

adrenal medulla The central region of the adrenal gland. 46–7, 66, 72, 80

adrenaline A hormone produced by the adrenal glands which is part of the human body's acute stress response. It is also a neurotransmitter. 11, 42, 44, 46–8, 60, 62–3, 65–8, 72, 80, 100, 104, 106, 111, 120–21, 206, 250, 272, 278, 292

adrenocorticotrophic hormone (ACTH) A hormone produced in response to stress by the pituitary gland which then stimulates the adrenal cortex which then produces cortisol. 46–7, 66, 68

adult attachment interview A method used to assess attachment type of adults using a series of questions such as, 'I'd like you to try to describe your relationship with your parents as a young child if you could start from as far back as you can remember.' This stimulates the adult to recall and evaluate attachment-related memories. The answers are scored for what they indicate about attachment relationships. 173

aetiology Studying the causes of a disorder. 225

affect Experiencing emotions and feelings. 11, 19, 36, 49, 73, 101, 107, 111, 195, 199, 231, 233, 235, 287

affectionless psychopathy A behaviour disorder in which the individual has no ability to experience shame or guilt and lacks a social conscience. This means that they may find it 'easier' to commit crimes. 128, 204

aggression Behaviour that is intended to cause psychological or physical injury. 66, 113, 116–19, 124–5, 131, 140–41, 179, 181, 196, 294–6, 300

agonist A drug that has the same effect as a naturally-produced neurotransmitter. 90–91, 105, 107, 140, 250

agorophobia An irrational fear of leaving home and going out in public. 238

agranulocytosis A severe reduction in white blood cells. As white blood cells are vital in the body's immune response this may be life-threatening. 251

amenorrhoea The absence of a menstrual period in women of reproductive age. 241

American Psychiatric Association (APA) The main professional organisation for psychiatrists in the United States. It aims to ensure humane care and effective treatment for all people with mental illnesses. 220

amotivation An absence of any drive at all, i.e. no motivation to participate or be competent in an activity. 266–7, 278–9

amygdala A small region of the brain which is responsible for detecting fear and preparing an animal for emergency events. It is associated with memory, emotion, sleep, arousal and the fight or flight response. 57, 67, 69, 113, 118–19, 131

anger management Therapy that involves identifying the signs that trigger anger as well as learning techniques to calm down and deal with the situation in a positive way. The aim of anger management is not to prevent anger but to recognise it and manage it. 92, 94, 105, 113, 140–41, 145, 147

anorexia nervosa (AN) An eating disorder characterised by self-induced weight loss, fear of gaining weight and disturbances of body image. 216, 241

antagonist A drug that prevents the effects of a naturally-produced neurotransmitter. 90–91, 105, 107, 140, 250

antidepressant A group of drugs which increase the production of serotonin and/or noradrenaline, and reduce symptoms of depression. 11, 90, 100–101, 105, 107, 250–51

antigens Any foreign body such as bacteria or viruses that creates an immune response and usually leads to the production of antibodies (proteins produced by the body to fight antigens). 48, 66

antipsychotic drugs Drugs used to reduce the intensity of symptoms, in particular the positive symptoms, of psychotic conditions such as schizophrenia. 250–51

antisocial personality disorder A mental health condition where a person has a repeated pattern of manipulating the behaviour of other people or violating their rights. Often leads to crimes against people. 232–3, 236

anxiety Feelings or thoughts that can have a negative impact on sport performance. 12, 20, 26–7, 31, 40, 42, 50, 54–6, 58, 60, 62, 64–7, 69, 73, 76, 80–86, 94, 98, 103–105, 107, 111, 140, 172–3, 180, 194, 196, 198, 204, 206, 208–209, 213, 230, 232, 235, 238–9, 242, 244–5, 248, 250, 252–4, 259, 261, 263, 266, 270–80, 284, 286, 288, 290–300, 305–307

anxiety disorder A group of mental disorders characterised by levels of fear and apprehension disproportionate to any threat. 65, 67, 103, 213, 230, 232, 238–9, 245, 259

anxiety hierarchy In systematic desensitisation, the identification of situations that create anxiety. The hierachy starts with the least threatening and progresses through increasingly more anxiety-provoking situations. 244–5

anxiolytic drugs A medication that reduces anxiety, i.e. anti-anxiety. 250–51

arousal Raised levels of physiological functions such as increased blood pressure and muscle tension. 9–10, 13, 26, 28–9, 31, 42, 53, 60–62, 66–7, 69, 76–7, 80, 83, 86, 94, 104, 106–107, 109, 118, 140, 239, 261, 263, 270–81, 283, 285, 287–301, 306–309

assimilation A form of learning that happens when new information radically changes our understanding of a topic. One or more new schemas are formed and/or existing schemas are changed drastically to cope with the new understanding. 184

associative evidence Information (evidence) that can link elements of a crime scene to a potential offender, e.g. fingerprints found at the crime scene can link the location to the offender. 156

asthma A long-term condition where a person experiences difficulty breathing at certain times. 16–17, 30, 32, 39, 66, 71, 107

asylum A large institution in which people with mental (and physical) disorders were placed, sometimes for restraint and control but also to try to treat them. 165, 213, 224, 226–7, 229, 234

atavistic form A biological approach to offending that attributes criminal activity to the fact that offenders are genetic throwbacks or a primitive sub-species ill-suited to conforming to the rules of modern society. Such individuals are distinguishable by particular facial and cranial characteristics. 154

atherosclerosis A build up of fats and chlosterol (plaque) on the walls of the arteries. It eventually restricts blood flow from the heart or plaques may break off and block arteries, both of which may cause a stroke. 48–9, 66

athletic performance Carrying out a specific physical activity. 270–71, 304

attachment A close two-way emotional bond between two individuals in which each individual sees the other as essential for their own emotional security. Attachment is important for safety and food (mother and baby stay close together) and independence (a secure attachment enables a child to be more adventurous). 128, 163, 168–73, 179, 188, 191–2, 196–7, 202–204, 206–209, 232–3

attachment disorder Physical, psychological and behavioural symptoms due to problems in forming emotional attachments, often caused by privation. In ICD-10 there is a distinction between the inhibited form (reactive attachment disorder, RAD) and the disinhibited form (disinhibited attachment disorder, DAD). DSM-5 lists only RAD. 206–208

attachment type Refers to whether a person is securely or insecurely attached, i.e. the way you relate to others in the context of intimate relationships. 172–3, 232

attention deficit hyperactivity disorder (ADHD) A condition characterised by inattention, impulsiveness and motor hyperactivity which is inappropriate for a child's age. May continue into adolescence and adulthood. 194

attentional focus Performers concentrate on either internal or external cues. 294–5

attribute/attribution The process of explaining the causes of your own or someone else's behaviour. 18–19, 30, 32, 55, 131, 140–41, 176, 191–2, 229, 282, 309

atypical antipsychotics (AAs) Drugs for schizophrenia (a psychotic disorder) developed after typical antipsychotics. They typically target a range of neurotransmitters such as dopamine and serotonin. Examples include Clozapine and Risperidone. 250

authoritarian parents A type of parenting style involving high demandingness and low responsiveness. 166

Authoritative parents A type of parenting style involving high demandingness and high responsiveness. 166–7

autism spectrum disorders (ASD) A classification that unites a range of different disorders that share similar characteristics, such as difficulty in social relationships and difficulty in understanding what is in other people's minds. 'Low' functioning autism is at one end of the spectrum and 'high' functioning Asperger syndrome at the other end. 182

autogenic training A form of psychotherapy which is derived from hypnosis. A person aims to enter a hypnotic-like trance state and relax deeply. 306

automatic negative thoughts (ANTs) An example of dysfunctional, irrational thinking which is hard to control. Negative ideas about yourself just appear and won't go away. 247

autonomic nervous system (ANS) Transmits information to and from internal bodily organs. It is 'autonomic' as the system operates involuntarily (it is automatic). It has two main divisions: the sympathetic and parasympathetic nervous systems. 46–7, 66, 80, 82, 104, 106

autonomy Freedom from external control. 266–7, 284–5, 301, 303

average children Those who receive a moderate number of positive and a moderate number of negative nominations when their peers are asked to say who they like most and least. See peer status. 180

aversion therapy A behavioural treatment based on classical conditioning. A maladaptive behaviour is paired with an unpleasant stimulus such as a painful electric shock. Eventually, the behaviour is associated with pain without the shock being used. In covert sensitisation the aversive stimulus is not real but imagined. 9, 52–3, 67, 72, 88–9, 105–109, 244–5

aversive drug A drug that has the effect of causing a person to avoid a situation or substance if the situation/substance is associated with the aversive drug, e.g. disulfiram (Antabuse). 88, 90, 107

avoidant personality disorder A mental disorder listed in both DSM and ICD, characterised by social anxiety, feelings of inferiority and extreme sensitivity to rejection. This means such people tend to avoid social interaction. 236

avolition A symptom of schizophrenia where a person shows a lack of goal-directed behaviour and a lack of concern for what is going on around them. 238

B cells A type of white blood cell (leucocyte) that contributes to the body's immune response. B cells recognise certain antigens and secrete appropriate antibodies. 48, 66, 68

Barnum effect The tendency to accept types of information, such as offender profiles or horoscopes, as true even when the information is in fact vague and general enough to apply to a wide range of people or situations. 158–9

Beck depression inventory (BDI) A psychological test to assess the degree of depression an individual is experiencing. The original version contained 21 questions on how the person has been feeling in the last week. Each question has a set of at least four possible responses, for example (0) I do not feel sad, (1) I feel sad, (2) I am sad all the time and I can't snap out of it, (3) I am so sad or unhappy that I can't stand it. 100–101

Bedlam See Bethlem Hospital. 226

behaviour Range of actions made in conjunction with the environment. 9–10, 12–19, 21–37, 39, 41–5, 48, 50–52, 55–65, 67, 69, 71, 74–9, 82, 84–5, 87–110, 113–55, 158–9, 163, 166, 168–82, 184, 186, 188, 190–94, 196, 198, 200, 202, 206, 212–20, 222–3, 225–7, 230, 232, 236–42, 244–7, 249, 252–4, 259, 262–3, 266–9, 271, 274–5, 280, 283–7, 294–5, 297

behaviour analysis A therapist's assessment of a client to discover what stimuli have caused and maintain his or her current behaviour (e.g. past positive and negative reinforcements). 244–5

behaviour modification (BM) The use of operant conditioning techniques to change the frequency of desired behaviours. 113, 144, 146, 179, 244–5, 254

behavioural activation (BA) A therapy for depression focusing on encouraging patients to engage in those activities they are avoiding. The goal of the intervention is to increase environmental reinforcement. 245–6

behavioural addiction Occurs when someone compulsively continues a behaviour and experiences withdrawal when they stop it. 9, 12–13, 15, 17, 19, 21, 23, 25, 27, 29–30, 32, 35, 58–65, 67, 71, 88

behavioural consistency The tendency for people to behave in the same way as they have in the past, i.e. make similar decisions and act in a similar manner. 150–51, 153–5, 158–9

behavioural evidence analysis (BEA) A form of profiling that seeks objective information from the crime scene – descriptions of the scene, physical evidence, details of the victim. It aims to focus on the individual case rather than making deductions from similar cases and offenders. 151, 159

behavioural responses The way we respond to cognitive and somatic anxiety in our performance. 274

Behavioural Science Unit A department of the FBI in the US, where people from different disciplines (psychology, criminology, sociology etc) worked together to understanding criminal thinking and behaviour. Now called the Behavioural Research and Instruction Unit. 148–9

behavioural self-control (BSCT) A form of training in which a client decides to deliberately take charge of their own behaviour. 244–5

behavioural therapy Any treatment for mental disorders based on the principles of learning theory. 9, 92–3, 95, 101–103, 105–106, 110, 244–7, 252

behaviourist An approach to explaining behaviour in terms of what is observable and in terms of learning theory (classical and operant conditioning). 140, 145, 178, 222, 226

benzodiazepines (BZs) Drugs used to reduce anxiety. They attach to receptors of the neurotransmitter GABA, enhancing its effects. 80–81, 104, 106, 111, 250–51

beta blockers (BBs) Drugs used to reduce anxiety. They attach to beta-receptors in the cells of the heart and other parts of the body that are usually stimulated during sympathetic arousal. They prevent adrenaline having such a strong effect. 80–81, 104, 106, 111, 250

beta-adrenergic receptors Enable the hormones adrenaline and noradrenaline to attach to the heart and blood vessels and stimulate them. The receptors are the locations where the attachment takes place like putting a key in a lock. 80

Bethlem Hospital The first asylum in London, used to lock up people with mental disorders. 226–7

biofeedback A method of stress management that turns physiological processes (such as heart rate) into signals that a client then learns to control. Clients do this by applying the techniques they have learned, such as relaxation and breathing exercises. 9, 82–3, 104, 106–107, 109, 111

biological approach Behaviour is explained in terms of faulty bodily systems, including genes, neurochemistry, neuroanatomy and infection. 9, 50–51, 67–9, 71, 114, 116, 188, 218–19, 223, 251

biomedical Applying the understanding of biology or technology to treatment of illness. 10–11, 30, 32

biopsychosocial An interdisciplinary approach to health and illness, including understanding from biology, psychology as well as social-environmental influences. 10–11, 30, 32

bipolar disorder A mood disorder in which the person switches between a depressed state and a manic state (high energy, euphoria, excitement). 230, 240–41

body scan A technique used as part of mindfulness-based cognitive therapy to provide mindful awareness of your bodily sensations. All parts of the body are considered and any that are tense are focused on. 246–7

bottom-up approach An approach to offender profiling favoured in the UK. Investigators work upwards from evidence collected at the crime scene to develop hypotheses about the likely characteristics, motivations and social background of the offender. 113, 149–52, 158, 161

bottom-up profiling Criminal investigators work up from evidence collected from the crime scene to develop hypotheses about the likely characteristics, motivations and social background of the offender. 150–51, 153–4

brain scan A technique used to investigate the structure or functioning of the brain by taking images of the living brain. This makes it possible to match regions of the brain to behaviour by asking participants to engage in particular activities while the scan is done. Brain scans are also used to detect brain abnormalities such as tumours. Examples: CAT scan, PET scan, MRI scan, fMRI scan. 10, 30, 218–19

British Psychological Society (BPS) The representative body for psychologists and psychology in the UK, which aims to promote excellence in psychology, raise standards of training and practice in psychology, and increase public awareness of psychology. 254

broken windows theory Proposes that signs of crime and antisocial behaviour create an urban environment that encourages further crime. 134

bulimia nervosa (BN) An eating disorder in which an individual regularly engages in excessive (binge) eating followed by compensatory behaviour such as self-induced vomiting or misuse of laxatives (purge). People with bulimia typically do not become as thin as those with anorexia and also feel more out of control. 241

bullying Repeated behaviour, intended to intimidate or hurt someone either physically and/or emotionally. 125, 196–7, 205

bupropion An antidepressant that blocks noradrenaline and dopamine. 90–91, 105, 107

Cambridge study in delinquent development Longitudinal prospective study of 411 males. The aim was to describe the development of criminal and delinquent behaviour in inner-city males and investigate how much it could be predicted in advance. The participants were followed from age 8 to 32. 128

cardiovascular disorder (CVD) Any disorder of the heart (cardio) or blood vessels (vascular), including blood vessels in the brain (e.g. stroke). 45, 48–9, 66, 97, 102

case management approach Involves coordinating multiple services to provide one individual with customised support. Different professionals must collaborate, monitor and evaluate the care they provide. 255

case study The detailed study of one case (such as a family or a football team or a festival). It involves the use of mixed methodologies. 96, 113, 118, 130, 146, 149, 161, 190, 201–202, 210, 228, 258

catalepsy Rigidity of the body, posture is fixed, lack of responsiveness and there is decreased sensitivity to pain. 238

catastrophe theory Explains when cognitive anxiety is high and increases in arousal beyond optimal levels create a rapid decline in performance. 261, 275–7, 294–5, 299

catatonia A state of immobility accompanied by a lack of responsiveness (stupor). The person may remain in the same position for extended periods of time. 238

CDH13 gene Produces adhesive proteins in the brain. Low levels of CDH13 have been linked to substance abuse, and, in a small number of studies, to violent behaviour. 116

central nervous system (CNS) Consists of the brain and spinal cord, where complex decisions are made. 80, 104, 106, 224

central route The recipient processes the content of the message because they are interested, motivated and cognitively able. 78–9, 104, 106

centring A breathing technique to reduce stress. It is claimed to be an ancient visualisation technique whereby the person focuses on the physical sensations related to stress (tense muscles, rapid breathing and heart rate, sweaty palms) and then imagines that they are all the result of energy flowing through the body. Then you mentally redirect this energy to the centre of your body, providing inner calm. 306–307

cerebral palsy A group of lifelong movement disorders that appear in early childhood. Symptoms include poor coordination and tremors, and sometimes speech and sensory difficulties. 194, 200

child protection plan A strategy constructed by the local authority and child care professionals to set out how an abused child can be kept safe. 200, 208

child sex offender disclosure scheme Often called 'Sarah's Law'. Allows parents or carers to formally ask for information about any person that has contact with their child (or a child close to them) if they are concerned that the person may pose a risk. 136

chlamydia A sexually transmitted bacterial infection. There are often no symptoms but when untreated can cause further medical conditions. 14, 30

chlorpromazine (trade name e.g. Largactil) A first generation (typical) antipsychotic drug. It is an antagonist of D2 dopamine receptors and also D3 and D5 receptors. 250

choking Decrease in sport performance under pressure. 273, 294–5

chronic stress A threat that continues over weeks and months. 46, 48–9, 66, 68, 81, 106, 223

chronosystem 'Chronos' means 'time'. One of the five systems in Bronfenbrenner's ecological systems theory. It refers to life changes and transitions over time. 174–5

circle theory A form of geographical profiling, whereby the location of an offender's home base can be identified by drawing a circle around all crime scenes. The home base tends to be in the middle of this circle. 151, 155

Clare's Law See domestic violence disclosure scheme. 136–7

classical conditioning Learning by association. Occurs when two stimuli are repeatedly paired together – an unconditioned (unlearned) stimulus (UCS) and a new 'neutral' stimulus (NS). The neutral stimulus eventually produces the same response that was first produced by the unlearned stimulus alone. 52–3, 57, 60–61, 67–9, 72, 88–9, 105–106, 178–9, 218, 244

classification system Individual items (such as symptoms) are grouped into larger categories (such as specific mental disorders). Such systems are used to identify larger categories. 213, 215, 220–21, 225, 229, 254

client A person who uses a professional service. In mental health treatment the term 'client' is preferred to 'patient' because it implies a more equal relationship between therapist and person being treated. There is more of an assumption of a passive role in the term 'patient' than 'client'. See patient. 27–8, 37, 56, 72, 82–5, 87–9, 91–5, 102, 104–105, 108, 110, 116, 217–18, 220–21, 226, 240, 242–9, 252–7

clinical Refers to medical practice. 79, 99, 201, 203, 205, 220–21, 233, 240–41, 246, 252, 254

clinical depression Low mood beyond everyday sadness, severe enough to be diagnosed as a disorder. 233, 240–41, 246

clinical interview A form of semi-structured or unstructured interview similar to the kind of interview used by a GP when determining a medical diagnosis. There are some fairly set questions but many questions are related to the answers given. 221

clinician A health care professional who works directly with people/clients/patients. 217, 220–21, 234

clozapine (trade name e.g. Clozaril) A second generation (atypical) antipsychotic drug. It is mainly used to treat people with schizophrenia who have not responded to other drugs. 250–51

co-morbid The occurrence of two illnesses or conditions together, for example a person has both schizophrenia and a personality disorder. Where two conditions are frequently diagnosed together it calls into question the validity of classifying the two disorders separately. 64–5, 67, 100–101, 105, 107, 221, 240

cog A-state See cognitive anxiety. 274–5, 292–5

cognition/cognitive The mental processes of acquiring knowledge and understanding. 9, 47, 54–5, 58–9, 61, 63–5, 67–9, 71, 74, 78–9, 84–6, 92–3, 95, 98–9, 101–107, 109–110, 113, 122–4, 130–31, 140–41, 163, 145, 175, 177, 179–180, 182–9, 191–2, 194, 196, 198, 203–204, 207, 213, 218–19, 239–240, 246–7, 249–250, 252–3, 259, 268, 270, 274–7, 280, 284, 286–7, 292–5, 304–306

cognitive anxiety The negative thoughts we have about our performance. 274–7, 284, 286, 292–5

cognitive approach 'Cognitive' refers to 'mental processes' (for example thoughts, perceptions, attention) and how they affect behaviour. The approach using cognitive concepts to explain behaviour. 9, 54–5, 58–9, 64–5, 67, 69, 71, 110, 123, 140–41, 145, 218, 246

cognitive behavioural approach A way of understanding behaviour by using both cognitive and behaviour (learning theory) concepts. 84, 104

cognitive behavioural therapy (CBT) A method for treating mental disorders based on both cognitive and behavioural techniques. From the cognitive viewpoint the therapy aims to deal with thinking, such as challenging irrational thoughts. The therapy also includes behavioural techniques such as skills training and using reinforcement. 9, 84, 92–5, 101–103, 105–107, 109–110, 243, 245–7, 252–4

cognitive bias A distortion of attention, memory and thinking. It arises because of how we process information about the world, especially when we do it quickly. This can sometimes lead to irrational judgements and poor decision-making. 58–9, 67–9, 140

cognitive development A general term describing the development of all mental processes, in particular thinking, reasoning and our understanding of the world. Cognitive development continues throughout the lifespan but psychologists have been particularly concerned with how thinking and reasoning develops through childhood. 123, 182, 184–7, 194, 198, 204

cognitive distortion Faulty, biased and irrational ways of thinking that mean we perceive ourselves, other people and the world inaccurately and usually negatively. 59, 95, 107, 239, 247

cognitive efficiency The term 'cognitive' refers to mental activity, so cognitive efficiency is about the qualitative increases in knowledge gained in relation to the time and effort invested in doing this – the ratio of outcome to effort. 268

cognitive state anxiety See cog A-state. 280, 292–5

cognitive therapy A treatment for mental disorders that focuses on replacing negative irrational thoughts/beliefs with positive rational ones. It differs from cognitive behavioural therapy because the latter involves some element of behavioural techniques. 110, 246–7

collectivist culture People who place more value on the 'collective' (i.e. the other group members) rather than each individual being most focused on themselves. Collectivist cultures also value interdependence rather than independence. 43, 173, 215

communication The exchange of information between animals within the same species using a variety of signals. Some signals are vocal (involve sound), but some are visual or involve smell. 16, 74–5, 77, 84, 94, 104–105, 110, 142, 154, 160, 163, 182–9, 191, 196, 200–201, 208–209, 214, 220, 226, 238, 250, 253–4, 309

community care model Promotes treatment of clients in homes (their own or residential), away from large impersonal institutions. 213, 226–7, 229

community mental health team (CMHT) Support people who have complex mental health problems to enable them to live in the community rather than in an institution. The team may consist of psychiatrists, psychologists, community psychiatric nurses, social workers and occupational therapists. 254–5

community sentence A punitive sentence requiring a convicted person to perform unpaid work for the community as an alternative to imprisonment. The precise length and nature of the activity will be determined by the court. 113, 138–9, 147

competence The ability to do something successfully. 14, 48–9, 181, 266–7, 270–71, 282–5, 288, 301, 303

competitive orientation The extent to which an individual is prepared to compete and to strive to achieve a performance goal. 268–9

Competitive state anxiety inventory 2 (CSAI-2) A set of 27 statements measuring cognitive and state anxiety (cog A-state and som A-state) and self confidence. There are nine statements for each of the three constructs. Each item is rated on a scale of 1 to 4 where 1 = not at all and 4 = very much so. 275, 277

compulsions Behaviours or mental acts that are repeated over and over again. In obsessive-compulsive disorder compulsions are performed to reduce the anxiety experienced from obsessions. A person feels they must perform the behaviours or mental acts otherwise something dreadful might happen, i.e. they are compelled to do it. 239

compulsive shopping An uncontrollable desire to shop and buy items, leading to spending a lot of time and money on the activity. 62–5, 67, 69

computerised CBT (CCBT) Delivering cognitive behavioural therapy online via devices such as tablets, usually prepackaged CBT programmes. 252–3

concordance rate A measure of similarity (usually expressed as a percentage) between two individuals or sets of individuals on a given trait. 114–15

conditional discharge A defendant is found guilty of a charge but punishment is not given unless a further offence is committed within a specified period. See also absolute discharge. 138

conditioned cues (secondary reinforcer) Smoking is a primary reinforcer because it is rewarding. Anything associated with smoking (e.g. a lighter) takes on the same properties but is then called a secondary reinforcer. In the future the lighter predicts the reward and is thus a conditioned (learned) cue that indicates pleasure will follow. 52–3, 60–61, 67, 69

conditioned response (CR) The response produced by the CS on its own. A new association has been formed so that the NS now produces the UCR (which is now called the CR). 88, 178, 244

conditioned stimulus (CS) A stimulus that only produces the desired response after pairing with the UCS. 178–9, 244

conditioning Means 'learning', includes operant and classical conditioning. 52–3, 56–7, 60–61, 63, 67–9, 72, 82, 88–9, 104–106, 120, 144, 178–9, 188, 193, 218, 226, 244–5

conditions In an experiment, the different levels of the independent variable are called 'conditions'. In an independent groups design each group of participants takes part in one condition. In a repeated measures design each participant experiences all conditions. 16–17, 30, 43, 53, 67, 71, 88, 99–100, 102–103, 115, 138, 147, 193–5, 200, 203, 207, 229, 232, 252–3, 279, 291–2, 294, 298, 305

conflict When two or more things have competing demands, creating a clash. 12–13, 30, 32, 42–3, 66, 68, 94, 105, 144, 172, 177, 200–202, 204–205, 207, 238, 248, 255

confounding variable A special class of extraneous variable because it changes systematically with the independent variable (IV). This means that we cannot be sure that any change in the dependent variable was due to the IV. In fact the confounding variable is acting as another IV. 29, 31, 115, 169

congenital rubella syndrome (CRS) A condition that is likely to include deafness, eye abnormalities and congenital heart disease and may also involve small head size, liver problems and intellectual disability. This occurs in infants whose mothers had rubella (German measles) in the 28 days before conception or during the first 26 weeks of their pregnancy. 194

content analysis A kind of observational study in which behaviour is observed indirectly in written or verbal material such as books, diaries or TV programmes. 58, 67

contingent regulations A regulation is an instruction from mother to child that regulates the child's behaviour. It is contingent if it is less explicit than the previous regulation. 186

continuity hypothesis The belief that an infant's attachment type persists through childhood and adulthood so that, for example, emotionally secure infants continue to be emotionally secure, trusting and socially confident adults whereas the opposite is true for insecure infants. 170

continuous reinforcement A reinforcement (e.g. a reward) is delivered after every single target behaviour. 60–61, 67, 69

control The extent to which any variable is held constant or regulated by a researcher. 29, 172, 174, 193, 203, 233

control group In an experiment with an independent groups design, a group of participants who receive no treatment. Their behaviour acts as a baseline against which the effect of the independent variable (IV) may be measured. 45, 83, 85, 89, 93, 99, 101–102, 105, 119, 123, 141, 145, 169, 199, 203–205

controversial children Those who receive many positive and many negative nominations when their peers are asked to say who they like most and least. See peer status. 180

copycat crime A criminal act that is based on or inspired by a previous crime (real or fictional). 124

coronary heart disease The arteries that supply blood to the heart become narrowed by a build up of fatty material. This may eventually lead to a blockage and a heart attack. 44, 46, 48

correlation (correlational analysis) A method used to assess the degree to which two co-variables are related. The measurement of each co-variable must be quantitative and continuous, such as using rating scales and scores on a psychological test. 16–17, 20, 23–5, 28, 30–31, 33, 37–40, 66, 68, 73, 75, 99, 105–107, 151, 167, 181, 195, 199, 207, 231, 271

corticotropin releasing factor (CRF) A hormone produced by the hypothalamus in response to stress. The presence of CRF triggers a response in the pituitary gland that activates the longer term response to stress (the HPA system) that results in the production of cortisol. 46–7, 66, 68

cortisol An important hormone produced by the adrenal cortex. It helps the body to cope with stressors by controlling how the body uses energy. Cortisol suppresses immune system activity. 46–8, 66, 68, 73, 194, 231

cost-benefit analysis An individual weighs up the balance between the perceived benefits of changing behaviour and the perceived barriers (obstacles to change). 14–15, 30, 47, 58–9, 67, 69, 96–7, 105

counselling A form of therapy that aims to increase a client's self-esteem through unconditional positive regard from the therapist. Striving to achieve conditional love blocks the ability to self-actualise. 20–21, 30, 139, 167, 181, 200, 207, 249, 252–6

counterconditioning Being taught a new association that is the opposite of the original association, thus removing the original association. 88, 105, 244–5

countertransference In psychoanalysis, the analyst's emotional reaction to the client's feelings. 242

CR See conditioned response. 46–7, 66, 68, 105, 174–5, 178–9, 194, 218, 244

credibility Believability. In order to be believable something must also be valid – and all the other features expected in scientific research (replicable, reliable, falsifiable as well as objective and generalisable). 15, 26, 29–30, 37, 74–5, 104, 106, 270

crime classification manual A system for organising data about violent crime into groups: homicide, arson/bombing, rape/sexual assault, non-lethal crimes, computer crimes, cybercrime and internet child sex offenders as well as looking at methods of killing and issues in crime (e.g. wrongful convictions). Each classification (e.g. homicide) is then further subdivided into categories (e.g. 120 Personal cause homocide, 122 Domestic homocide, 122.02 Staged domestic homocide). 149

critical period The time within which a behaviour (such as attachment) must form if it is to form at all. 128, 168–9, 171, 189, 202, 204

cross-contamination Contamination means to make something less pure. This may occur because something nearby is transferred from one substance to another. 157

CS See conditioned stimulus. 52, 156–7, 178–9, 196, 218, 244, 275, 277

CSAI-2 See Competitive state anxiety inventory. 275, 277

CSI effect The exaggerated expectations of what forensic science can do, created by TV programmes such as CSI: Crime Scene Investigation. 157

cue exposure with response prevention (CERP) A behavioural therapy used with people who have OCD. A client faces increasingly anxiety-provoking situations (exposure) and waits until their anxiety subsides. At the same time the client is prevented from engaging in their usual compulsive response. This enables the learned association between obsessions and compulsions to be unlearned. 57, 67, 69, 72, 92

cue reactivity Cravings and arousal can be triggered in, for example, gambling addicts when they encounter cues related to the pleasurable effects of gambling (e.g. sounds of a fruit machine). 60–62, 67

cultural bias Refers to a tendency to ignore cultural differences and interpret all phenomena through the 'lens' of one's own culture. 173, 220

culture Refers to the norms and values that exist within any group of people. 10, 14–15, 18, 30, 43, 62–3, 66, 68, 87, 104, 160, 164–7, 173–5, 177, 183, 185–8, 198, 204, 215, 217, 220, 222, 234–5, 237, 240, 262, 309

curvilinear A consistent relationship between two variables which is not linear (in a line). For example, two variables increase together up to a point and then one continues to increase as the other decreases (a U-shaped curve). 75–7, 99, 104, 106, 272–3, 290

cystic fibrosis An inherited disorder in which the lungs and digestive system become clogged with sticky mucus which causes breathing and digestion difficulties. 230

daily hassles The relatively minor but frequent aggravations and annoyances of everyday life that combine to cause us stress, such as forgetting where you have put things and niggling squabbles with other people. 9, 30, 40–42, 66, 68–9, 71, 73

deficiency needs In Maslow's hierarchy of needs, D-needs arise because something is lacking (deficient). 192

delusions Fixed beliefs that are resistant to change and implausible to people. 224, 230, 238

demographic variable The characteristics of a population and an individual, such as age, sex, education level, income level, marital status, occupation, religion. 14–16, 30, 32, 103

dependence (salience) is indicated either by a compulsion to keep taking a drug/continue a behaviour (psychological dependence) or indicated by withdrawal symptoms (physical dependence). 12–13, 30, 34, 50–52, 54–5, 67, 81, 104, 155, 166, 168, 173, 178, 196, 232

depression See clinical depression. 20–21, 30, 36, 40, 42, 54–5, 62, 64–7, 69, 73, 81, 90, 99–102, 105–107, 120–21, 128, 167, 180, 194–6, 198, 200, 206, 208–209, 213–14, 218, 221–4, 230–35, 238, 240–48, 250–52, 254, 256, 259

depressive disorder A mental disorder characterised by low mood and low energy. 220, 240–41

deprivation dwarfism Children who are abused, neglected or in institutions may be physically underdeveloped due to a lack of emotional attachments. 202, 206–207

derailment A characteristic of schizophrenia, where a person's speech consists of a sequence of unrelated or only remotely related ideas – like a train going off the rails. 238

deterrence The act of discouraging offending through fear of the consequences. 132–3, 137

detriangling In family systems therapy, 'detriangling' aims to make all communications between members of the triangle open so that conflicts can be resolved and the 'third' person is protected from being the go-between.' See triangling. 248–9

deviation from political norms Beliefs, opinions and behaviours that do not match what is considered acceptable by people in power (e.g. government). 216

deviation from social norms Concerns behaviour that is different from the accepted standards of behaviour in a community or society. 216

deviation from statistical norms Occurs when an individual has a less common characteristic, for example being more depressed or less intelligent than most of the population. 216

diabetes See Type I diabetes and Type II diabetes. 15, 26, 32, 96, 99–103, 107, 194–5, 225, 230

Diagnostic and statistical manual of mental disorders (DSM) A classification system published by the American Psychiatric Association. The current version (DSM-5) contains typical symptoms of over 300 disorders and guidelines for clinicians to make a diagnosis. 100, 220

diagnostic radiographer A trained professional who uses X-ray, ultrasound and other scanning techniques to look inside a person's body and identify (diagnose) what is wrong in terms of injuries or illness. 218

diathesis-stress model Behaviour is explained as the result of an underlying vulnerability (diathesis) and a trigger, both of which are necessary for the behaviour to be shown. 114–15, 129, 219, 222

differential association model A social explanation for criminality which identifies what is learned (criminal attitudes as well as actual techniques), how it is learned (observation and imitation) and from whom (significant others, such as family members and friends). 113, 126–8, 131

differentiation Distinguishing between two or more things or people. 248–9

discharge A type of sentence where no punishment is imposed, and the court's guilty verdict is revoked, resulting in a non-conviction. 113, 138–9, 147, 221

discovery learning Piaget applied his theory of cognitive development to education, and proposed that children learn best by constructing their own knowledge when placed in novel situations, i.e. discovering things about the world for themselves. 184

disease A disorder of the body or mind that causes illness. 10, 12, 14–15, 30, 43–4, 46–50, 66, 76–7, 79, 84–5, 96–7, 99–100, 102, 107, 129, 194, 214–15, 218, 220–22, 224–5

disinhibited attachment A type of insecure attachment where children treat strangers with inappropriate familiarity (overfriendliness) and may be attention-seeking. 173, 202–203, 206–207

disorganised asocial type One explanation for 'lust murders' (homocides that involve erotic satisfaction). The disorganised asocial type is chaotic in all aspects of their life and lack normal relations with other people (don't make conversations with people, lonely and victims are usually unknown). Contrast with organised non-social type. 148

disorganised serial murderers Murderers who commit spontaneous crimes which show little evidence of planning. They are often socially and sexually incompetent with lower-than-average intelligence. 148

disputing A technique used by cognitive therapists to challenge a client's irrational thoughts, e.g. 'Where is the evidence for this?'. 246–7

dissociation A feeling of being disconnected from yourself and lacking conscious control of your identity. 196

disulfiram (trade name e.g. Antabuse) Alcohol is normally broken down by an enzyme. If this enzyme is inhibited, the chemical acetaldehyde builds up and causes unpleasant effects such as throbbing head, nausea/vomiting, sweating – experienced as a hangover. Disulfiram is a medical drug which inhibits the breakdown of acetaldehyde, causing a hangover. It is used in aversion therapy for the treatment of alcohol addiction. 88–90, 105–106

dizygotic (DZ) twins Develop from two fertilised eggs. DZ twins share, on average, about 50% of their genes. They are as similar as any pair of siblings. 50, 114

domestic violence disclosure scheme Often called 'Clare's Law'. The police have the power to disclose information about a person's history of violence or abuse (relating to previous convictions or charges) in order to prevent further crime. 136–7

dopamine A neurotransmitter that generally has an excitatory effect and is associated with the sensation of pleasure. Unusually high levels are associated with schizophrenia and unusually low levels are associated with Parkinson's disease. 50–52, 56–7, 62, 67–9, 90, 105, 107, 218, 250

dopamine reward system A collection of structures in the brain, called the mesocorticolimbic circuit. Information travels from the ventral tegmental area (VTA) to the nucleus accumbens (NA) to produce the neurotransmitter dopamine. Additionally a second part of the circuit goes from the VTA to the prefrontal cortex producing dopamine. 52, 56, 62, 67, 90

double-blind Neither the participant nor researcher conducting the study are aware of the research aims or other important details of a study, and thus have no expectations that might alter a participant's behaviour. 100–101, 105, 107

Down syndrome A mental and physical disorder caused by an innate but not inherited genetic condition. It is also referred to as 'Trisomy 21' because it is caused by the presence of a third chromosome in pair 21. Individuals with Down syndrome have distinctive facial features, mental retardation and some physical defects, such as heart or gastrointestinal problems. Behaviourally, such children are thought to be very affectionate. 194

drapetomania A suggested category of mental disorder, used to explain why some enslaved Africans tried to escape from their owners. The condition was (supposedly) due to overfamiliar owners who treated their slaves as equals. 216

dream analysis A client free associates around images from a dream as the analyst offers interpretations about what the images really (unconsciously) mean. 242–3

drive theory Explains motivation as a simple linear relationship between increasing arousal and improved performance. 261, 272–3, 278, 290–91, 299

drug therapy Treatment involving drugs, i.e. chemicals that have a particular effect on the functioning of the brain or some other body system. In the case of mental disorders such drugs usually affect neurotransmitter levels. 80–81, 83, 106–107, 251, 254

DSM See Diagnostic and statistical manual of mental disorders (DSM). 100, 206, 220–22, 224–5, 236–41, 254

dysfunctional psychopathology Mental disorders which lead to abnormal behaviours. 'Dysfunctional' means not operating normally and 'psychopathology' is the scientific study of what causes mental disorders. 163, 203, 205–210

dysfunctional thought record (DTR) A technique used in cognitive behavioural therapy where a client, as part of their homework, keeps a log of any automatic negative thoughts and identifies how strongly they believe in them and also considers the rational response and how strongly they believe in that. 247

dyslexia A learning difficulty related to problems with reading and writing. It is not related to intelligence. 194, 200

DZ twin See dizygotic twins. 50–51, 67–8, 115

e-therapy (online therapy) Delivering any form of therapy over the internet, with or without therapist support, often via an app. 252–3

eating disorders Mental disorders in which the main feature is disruption of feeding behaviour with restriction of energy intake (anorexia) or control of body weight through repeated bingeing and purging (bulimia). 100, 213, 220, 232, 234, 240–41, 254–6, 259

ecological model An approach to explaining human behaviour that focuses on the interaction between the individual and their environment (ecology). This ecological context is a contrast to a focus solely on individual factors. 163, 174–5, 191

ecological validity The extent to which a research finding can be applied beyond the research setting. Often research settings are highly controlled and contrived situations and people may not behave in the same way in their everyday lives. 59, 67

efficacy expectations Judgements about how successfully a performer can perform a task. This contrasts with outcome expectations which relate to the consequences of a successful performance. 28, 270–71, 288–9

ego orientation See outcome/ego orientation. 264–5, 282–3

elaboration-likelihood model A theory of persuasion that states the impact of a message on attitude/behaviour change depends on whether the recipient processes the message through the central route or the peripheral route. 9, 78–9, 104, 106–107, 109

electromyogram (EMG) A test that is used to record the electrical activity of muscles. Active muscles produce electricity. 82

elementary mental functions In Vygotsky's theory of cognitive development, those innate cognitive abilities either present at birth or which develop with no instruction, such as basic memory processes and attention. Distinguished from higher mental functions. 186–7

emetic A substance that causes vomiting. 88, 105, 107

emotional arousal A state of heightened physiological activity. 28, 31, 60, 140, 270–71, 288–9

emotional support Focused on what a person is feeling – the anxiety associated with stress and trying to find ways to reduce those feelings. 86–7, 104, 111, 171, 232, 249, 254, 256

empiricism The view that knowledge can only come through direct observation or experiment rather than by reasoned argument or beliefs. 222

endorphins (contracted from endogenous morphine) A protein that acts as one of the body's natural painkillers (endogenous opioid) by inhibiting the release of substance P, a neurotransmitter involved in the transmission of pain. Produced in response to pain but also may be released during high intensity exercise. 57, 67

energising techniques Methods that will create higher levels of activity. 261, 306–307, 309

environment The complete set of non-genetic influences on behaviour, including prenatal influences in the womb, family, peers, social and cultural factors, food you eat, etc. 10–11, 18, 21, 30, 38, 40, 42–4, 50–53, 56, 60–62, 65–7, 73, 84–5, 91–2, 105, 112, 114–15, 129, 139, 144, 153, 163, 172, 174–5, 178–9, 182–4, 187, 189, 194–5, 198–9, 204–205, 208, 210–11, 213, 218, 222–3, 226, 231–3, 235, 239, 244, 248, 251, 256, 259, 261, 263–4, 266–8, 279–97, 302, 304, 306

esteem support Helping someone to attach greater value to themselves so they view their abilities with greater confidence. 86–7, 104, 110–11

ethical issue A dilemma about right and wrong. The dilemma arises because researchers wish to investigate behaviour to benefit our understanding of people and improve our world, but there are costs to participants. 47, 88–9, 105, 155, 169, 179, 227, 253

ethnicity Socially-defined grouping of people based mainly on physical features (e.g. skin colour) but not based on genuine biological differences. 21, 30, 152, 155, 198–9, 234–5

evolution The changes in inherited characteristics in a biological population over successive generations. 47, 154, 166, 169–71, 184, 189, 192, 223

experiment A research method which demonstrates causal relationships. All experiments have one (or more) independent variable (IV) and one (or more) dependent variable (DV). 25, 27, 31, 33, 37, 43, 46, 54, 84, 104, 107, 110, 125, 134, 168–9, 172, 174–5, 177, 182, 203

experimental group The group in an independent groups design who receive the experimental treatment as distinct from the control group. 169

externals See external locus of control. 18–21, 30

external coping resources A distinction is made between external and internal coping resources, i.e. ways of dealing with stress. External methods include other people as well as time, money and positive life events. 11

external locus of control Individuals who feel that their behaviour and/or thoughts are controlled by factors other than their personal decisions and/or action, such as being controlled by luck, fate or the behaviour of other people. 18–19

extinction When a conditioned stimulus (CS) and an unconditioned stimulus (UCS) have not been paired for a while, the CS ceases to elicit the conditioned response (CR). 244–5

extrinsic motivation Participating in sport for a reward or praise. The drive to continue comes from outside (external). 266–7, 284–5

extroversion Outgoing, externally-oriented people who enjoy risk and danger because their nervous systems are under-aroused. 120–21, 268

Eysenck personality questionnaire (EPQ) Self-report test of personality developed by Eysenck. It measures three personality dimensions: extraversion–introversion, neuroticism–stability and psychoticism–normality (the earlier EP1 only measured the first two dimensions). The full version has 100 yes/no questions. 120

Eysenck's theory of criminality A person who scores highly on measures of extroversion, neuroticism and psychoticism is cold and unfeeling, and is likely to engage in crime. 120–21, 125

family studies A means of assessing the contribution made by genetic factors by comparing an individual to people closely related (such as parents) and less closely related (such as grandparents). 114–15

family systems therapy Treats an individual's mental disorder by changing patterns of interaction within the whole family. Encourages members to differentiate from each other and operate as individuals with their own needs. 213, 248–9, 259

fear arousal theory of persuasion The impact of a message on attitude/behaviour change depends on the extent to which it arouses fear in the recipient. Moderately fear-arousing messages are more persuasive than high-fear or low-fear messages. 9, 76–7, 104, 106–107, 109

feral child A child who has lived away from humans for a significant period of their childhood. 202

fight or flight response The way an animal responds when stressed. The body becomes physiologically aroused in readiness to fight an aggressor or, in some cases, flee. 66

fine An amount of money that a court of law or other authority decides must be paid as punishment for an offence. The amount of a fine can be determined case by case, but there are also standard penalties for particular offences. 138

five-factor model A theory of personality which proposes that personality can be broken down into five key traits represented by the letters OCEAN: openness to experience, conscientiousness, extroversion, agreeableness and neuroticism. 121

flooding A behavioural therapy in which a phobic client is exposed to an extreme form of a phobic stimulus in order to reduce anxiety triggered by that stimulus. 244–5

free association A psychodynamic technique in which a client speaks their thoughts out loud without altering them and the analyst makes connections between the thoughts. 242–3

free will The view that our behaviour is determined by our own decisions (will) rather than by other forces, such as genes/neurotransmitters (biological approach) or conditioning (learning approach). 219, 270

frontal areas The part of the brain just behind the forehead, also called frontal lobes. This region is responsible for motor function, problem-solving, memory, language, initiating action, judgement, impulse control and social behaviour. 56, 62, 69

functional magnetic resonance imaging (fMRI) A type of brain scan. Uses radio waves to measure blood oxygen levels in the brain. Those areas of the brain that are most active use most oxygen and therefore blood is directed to the active area. 218

fusion The process of combining two or more things to produce a new whole. 16, 81, 226, 248–9

GABA (gamma-aminobutyric acid) A neurotransmitter that inhibits the activity of neurons in most areas of the brain. 80, 104, 106

gambler's fallacy The mistaken belief that, if something happens more fequently than usual during a given time period, it will then happen less frequently later (or vice versa). 28, 67, 69

gender The label of being male or female. 14–15, 20–21, 30, 47, 63, 66–9, 76, 87, 103–104, 107, 109, 117, 119, 121, 123–5, 154–5, 174, 177, 179–180, 198–9, 234–5, 241, 249, 268, 285, 287

gender bias When considering human behaviour, bias is a tendency to treat one individual or group in a different way from others. In the context of gender bias, psychological research or theory may offer a view that does not justifiably represent the experience and behaviour of men or women (usually women). 68, 249

gender role stereotype An expectation about the behaviours and attitudes that are considered appropriate for one gender and inappropriate for the other. 234

general adaptation syndrome Selye's explanation of stress – the body responds in the same way to any stressor: alarm reaction, resistance and exhaustion. 46–7, 66

general deterrence One aim of imprisonment is to discourage others from committing a crime, not just to discourage the individual who committed the crime, i.e. general as opposed to individual deterrence. 132

general paresis of the insane (GPI) Mental symptoms associated with the final (tertiary) stage of syphilis. 224

generalisability/generalise The extent to which findings and conclusions from a particular investigation can be broadly applied to the population. This is made possible if the sample of participants is representative of the population. It also depends on good internal and external validity. 18–19, 21, 30, 66, 75, 79, 103–105, 140, 145, 169, 277

genes/genetic A unit of inheritance. Genes consist of chemical instructions (DNA) which tell your body what proteins to manufacture – and basically that is what you are, a huge number of proteins. Genes are inherited from parents and contribute to the development of an individual's characteristics. 10, 13, 18, 30, 32, 50–51, 57, 65, 67–9, 107, 112, 114–17, 124, 127, 129, 170–71, 179, 194–5, 199, 206–207, 218–19, 222–4, 230–31, 235

geographical profiling In forensic psychology, a form of the bottom-up approach to profiling based on the principle of spatial consistency: that an offender's operational base and possible future offences are revealed by the geographical location of their previous crimes. 150–51, 155

glandular fever A virus that affects mainly young people, symptoms include extreme tiredness, sore throat and fever which may last for up to three weeks and may take another month to feel completely well. 194, 230

glutamate The principal excitatory neurotransmitter in the brain, involved in most aspects of normal brain function including cognition, memory and learning. 250

goal involvement One of the key constructs in achievement goal theory, which reflects the focus of achievement behaviour at a particular moment in time. 264

goal setting theory of motivation Suggests that better task performance can be achieved by setting specific and challenging goals, i.e. it is focused on different kinds of goals such as performance or mastery goals. 302

goals In sport, goals are the aim of a performer's action. 264–8, 278, 280, 283, 296, 302–305

grammar The way words are put together to produce meaning. Every language has a set of rules to be followed. 188–9, 242

growth needs In Maslow's hierarchy, the needs can be divided into deficiency needs and growth needs. The latter are related to the desire to develop (grow) as an individual. 192

hallucinations Perceptual experiences which do not correspond with reality. 218, 230, 238, 250

Hamilton rating scale for depression (HAM-D) A scale to assess depression. It is not a self-report measure. Instead a clinician rates the individual on 17 or 29 items (depending on which version is used, for example 'Depressed mood' score 0 for absent, 1 for sadness, 2 for occasional weeping, 3 for frequent weeping and 4 for extreme symptoms. 100–101

hardy personality A personality factor used to explain why some people seem able to thrive in stressful circumstances. It consists of commitment, challenge and control. 44–5, 66, 68, 110

Hassles and uplifts scale A self-report measure of the stress associated with everyday irritations (hassles) and of the small pleasures of daily life that are thought to partly offset the negative effects of hassles (uplifts). 40, 66

Hassles scale A self-report measure that only assesses everyday irritations (hassles). See Hassles and uplifts scale. 40–41, 66, 73

Head Start An American enrichment programme started in 1965 as a catch-up summer school programme for low-income children before they started primary school. Later expanded to, for example, promote healthy prenatal outcomes, healthy families and offer intervention services for infants, toddlers and children up to age 5. 175

health Health is a positive state, in which we can face the challenges of life, overcome stress, achieve our goals and fulfil our potential. This applies to our whole lives and not just our physical state. Ill health is any deviation from this. 8–42, 44–6, 48–50, 52, 54–8, 60, 62, 64, 66, 68–80, 82, 84, 86, 88, 90, 92, 94, 96–8, 100–106, 108, 110, 125, 128, 133, 138, 153–5, 163–7, 169–71, 173–5, 177, 179–81, 183, 185, 187, 189–90, 193–201, 203–204, 207–11, 213–15, 217–18, 220, 224–5, 229–36, 241, 243, 245, 251–9, 265, 267–8, 272, 274–5

health belief model Predicts the likelihood of behaviour change. The key factors are perceived seriousness, perceived susceptibility, cost-benefit analysis, demographic variables, cues to action and self-efficacy. 9, 14–17, 30, 32–3, 35

hemisphere The forebrain (largest part of the brain) is divided into two halves or hemispheres. 119

heredity The genetic transmission of mental and physical characteristics from one generation to another. 194–5, 222–3

hierarchy of needs Maslow proposed that human behaviour is driven by a variety of different requirements (needs) and that these needs are arranged in a ranked order (a hierarchy from most to least important). The most basic needs are for food and water and the highest needs are for self-fulfilment. 163, 192–3, 211

higher mental functions In Vygotsky's theory of cognitive development, those cognitive abilities which require some input from others, such as mathematics and language. Distinguished from elementary mental functions. 186–7

Hopkins symptom checklist A self-report list of 58 items. Each item represents symptoms commonly reported by patients and people using the checklist to indicate which symptoms they have experienced. The list is scored on five underlying symptom dimensions (somatisation, obsession-compulsion, interpersonal-sensitivity, anxiety and depression). 40

hostile attribution bias A tendency to assume that someone else's behaviour has an aggressive or antagonistic motive when it is actually neutral. 140–41

Hovland-Yale theory of persuasion Whether a message persuades people to change their behaviour depends not just on the message itself (the communication) but on who gives it (the communicator) and who receives it (the recipients). 9, 74–5, 106

HPA system See hypothalamic-pituitary-adrenal (HPA) system. 46–7, 66, 68

humanistic An approach to understanding behaviour that emphasises the importance of subjective experience and each person's capacity for self-determination. 193, 213, 218–19, 252–3, 259

Huntingdon's disease An inherited disease that stops parts of the brain working properly. The symptoms first start to appear after the age of 30 and then gradually worsen until they cause death. 194

hyperactivity Being abnormally overactive – constantly moving, easily distracted, impulsive and may be aggressive. 119, 128, 194

hypertension High blood pressure, which puts a strain on the blood vessels and heart. May lead to a heart attack or cause other problems such as kidney disease or dementia. 96, 105, 107

hypothalamic-pituitary-adrenal (HPA) system The body's response to a chronic (long-term) stressor. The hypothalamus triggers the pituitary gland to release the hormone ACTH which in turn stimulates release of cortisol from the adrenal cortex. 46

hypothalamus A small subcortical brain structure which plays a major role in the body's stress response and maintaining a state of balance (homeostasis) by regulating many of its key processes such as heart rate and body temperature. 46–7, 66, 118

hypothesis A statement of what a researcher believes to be true. In order to test such a statement, it must be clearly operationalised. 30, 76, 86, 104, 106, 129, 170, 223–5, 261, 272–3, 276, 278, 290–91, 299

hysteresis Literally means 'lagging behind'. Hysteresis describes the different effects of physiological arousal on performance under conditions of high cognitive anxiety. As physiological arousal increases, performance also improves up to a point until it catastrophically drops. At that point physiological arousal is damaging and needs to be reduced for performance to recover. 276–7

I-can't-stand-it-itis One of the types of irrational belief proposed by Ellis to explain depression. This is the person's view that the situation is totally intolerable and cannot be dealt with, a belief that is not reasonable because we all do learn to cope with any situation. 246

ICD See International classification of disease. 12, 30, 206, 220–22, 224–5, 230, 236–41, 254

ideal performance state (IPS) A person's mental and physiological state during peak performance. 290–91

identification The individual temporarily goes along with the norms and roles of the group because they see membership as part of their identity. 26, 57, 62–3, 69, 177–8, 201, 223, 255, 307

ill health (illness) Any deviation from the healthy state. (See health) 9–11, 13–16, 30, 32, 35–6, 38–46, 48–9, 66, 68–9, 71, 73, 96, 100, 116, 138, 174, 194–5, 206, 214–15, 220, 224–5, 254, 257

illusion of control The mistaken belief of having a special ability to influence the operation of chance outcomes. 58–9, 67, 69

imagery Use of words or pictures to describe ideas or situations. 261, 300, 304–307, 309

imitation Occurs when a learner reproduces the behaviour they observed being demonstrated by a model. It is more likely to occur when the observer identifies with the model. 25, 47, 62, 113, 124–6, 128, 146, 149, 151, 153, 155, 157–61, 165, 178, 187–9, 218, 299, 301, 303, 305, 307–308

immune system The body's defence against invading antigens ('foreign bodies'). Its activity can be suppressed by stress, reducing its activity and effectiveness. 8, 46, 48–9, 66, 68, 73, 194, 231

immunosuppression Stress can cause illness by preventing the immune system from working efficiently and carrying out its usual task of identifying and destroying pathogens. 48

imprinting An innate readiness to acquire certain behaviours during a critical or sensitive period of development. 168–70

imprisonment Being held captive. 113, 116, 132–5, 138–9, 142, 144, 147

incapacitation Preventing further crime by physically isolating an offender. 132

incentive value of success In need achievement theory, this is a function of the subjective probability of success (how likely success will be). The higher the probability of success, the lower the value (and vice versa). 262, 280

independent variable (IV) A factor that is directly manipulated by the experimenter in order to observe the effect of different conditions on the dependent variable(s). 43, 169, 203

individual deterrence See general deterrence. 132

individual differences The characteristics that vary from one person to another. People vary in terms of their intelligence, emotional type, resilience and so on – two key individual differences are personality and gender. 131

individualist cultures People who value the rights and interests of the individual. This results in a concern for independence and self-assertiveness. People tend to live in small families unlike collectivist societies. This is typical of Western cultures, in contrast to many non-Western cultures that tend to be collectivist. 43, 66, 173, 198, 215

industrialisation The degree to which an agricultural economy is replaced by industry (manufacture of goods and related services). 166

infant-directed speech (IDS) Sometimes called 'baby talk', characterised by a sing-song pattern of intonation, slower speech rate and shorter sentences. Some sounds may be emphasised and words simplified. 188

ingroup Any social group to which you belong, as distinct from the outgroup. 176–7, 180

inherited Passed to you from previous generations. 67, 113–17, 131, 194, 222, 230, 236

innate Literally means 'inborn', a product of genetic factors. 48, 66, 68, 128, 164, 170–71, 183, 188–9, 192, 222, 266

insecure attachment Develops as a result of the caregiver's lack of sensitive responding to the infant's needs. May be associated with poor cognitive and emotional development. 196, 202, 206, 208–209, 232–3

insecure–avoidant attachment (Type A) An attachment type characterised by low anxiety but weak attachment. In the Strange Situation this is shown by low stranger and separation anxiety and little response to reunion – an avoidance of the caregiver. 172

insecure–disorganised attachment (Type D) An attachment type characterised by a lack of any consistent pattern, for example the infant reacts to separation sometimes by being indifferent and sometimes with great distress. 173

insecure–resistant attachment (Type C) An attachment type characterised by strong attachment and high anxiety. In the Strange Situation this is shown by high levels of stranger and separation anxiety and by resistance to being comforted at reunion. 172

institutionalisation A deficit in social and life skills that comes about after a long period in an institution such as a prison. 132–3

instrumental support Practical help such as lending money, cooking a meal, providing information. 86–7, 104, 106, 111

intention-behaviour gap The difference between making an explicit decision to change behaviour and actually implementing that change. 25

intermittent explosive disorder A type of control or conduct disorder characterised by explosive and destructive rages which are out of proportion to the situation at the time. 118–19

internal coping resources A distinction is made between internal and external coping resources, i.e. ways of dealing with stress. Internal methods include personal characteristics such as resilience, confidence and optimism. 11

internal locus of control Individuals who feel that ultimately they have control over their behaviour and/or thoughts, rather than being controlled by luck, fate or the behaviour of other people. 18, 21, 45, 84, 94, 104–105

internal working model The mental representations we have of our attachment to our primary attachment figure. They are important in affecting our future relationships because they carry our perception of what relationships are like. 170

internalisation An individual's acceptance of a set of norms and values (established by others) through socialisation. 186–7

internalising Refers to mental health problems where negative emotion is directed inwards rather than outwards towards another person. This includes phobias and anxiety disorders. 180

internals See internal locus of control. 18–21, 30, 32

International classification of diseases (ICD) A classification system produced by the World Health Organization (WHO), used mainly outside the USA. The current version is ICD-10. 12, 220

interpersonal coherence To 'cohere' is to be consistent, and this is a key principle of bottom-up profiling – the way an offender behaves at a crime scene, and their interactions with the victim, suggests important details about their life, work and relationships more generally. 150–51, 154

interview A 'live' encounter (face-to-face or on the phone) where one person (interviewer) asks questions to assess an interviewee's thoughts and/or experiences. Questions may be pre-set (structured interview) or may develop during the interview (unstructured interview) or a mixture (semi-structured interview). 16–17, 20, 30, 66, 102, 107, 117, 123, 148–9, 152–3, 173, 196, 200, 221, 232, 235, 243, 252, 267, 277, 287, 307

intrinsic motivation Participating in sport for its own sake and wanting to play well. The drive to continue comes from inside you (internal). 264, 266–7, 284–5, 301, 303

inverted U hypothesis Explains motivation as a curvilinear relationship where increasing arousal leads to improved performance up to a point and then higher arousal leads to a decline. 261, 272–3, 276, 278, 290–91, 299

investigative psychology A form of bottom-up profiling that matches details from the crime scene with statistical analysis of typical offender behaviour patterns based on psychological theory. 150

irrational thoughts Ideas and beliefs that do not have logical basis in reality. 58–9, 61, 67, 92–3, 102, 105, 118, 140, 245–7

jigsaw classroom A cooperative learning technique where a group of students are mutually dependent on each other to achieve individual success. 176–7

killer T cells See memory T cells. 48, 66, 68

Kohlberg's stages of moral development A theory describing the way people think about right and wrong, and how this thinking changes as a child gets older. Kohlberg identified different levels of thinking based on people's answers to moral dilemmas. 122–3

laboratory (lab) Any setting (room or other environment) specially fitted out for conducting research. A lab is not the only place where scientific experiments can be conducted. It is, however, the ideal place for scientific experiments because it permits maximum control. Labs are not used exclusively for experimental research, for example controlled observations are also conducted in labs. 59, 107, 173, 175

language A communication system unique to humans. It consists of a set of arbitrary conventional symbols through which meaning is conveyed. These symbols can be combined in such a way that an infinite number of novel messages can be produced. 84, 98–9, 105, 151, 163, 178, 182–9, 191, 197, 202–204, 208–209, 220, 223, 238, 250, 254–6, 287

language acquisition device (LAD) (or LAS) A proposed part of the human brain which explains why children (or adults) can produce the rules of a native language just by listening to people speak. 188–89, 208

language acquisition support system (LASS) An extension of the concept of LAD to include the social role of others in helping a child to acquire language by, for example, using infant-directed speech. 188

latent content Freud suggested that a dream has both manifest content (the actual content of the dream) and latent content (what the dream symbolises). 242–3

learning approach A collective term for ways to explain behaviour based on conditioning (classical and operant). This also includes social learning theory. 9, 52–3, 56–7, 60–63, 67–9, 71–2, 92, 114, 125, 144, 178–9, 188, 270

learning difficulties A significantly reduced ability to understand new or complex information and to learn new skills. 85, 128, 175, 187, 194–5, 198, 200–201, 230–32, 245

learning theory A way of explaining behaviour in terms of what is observable and in terms of classical and operant conditioning. 60–61, 113, 124–6, 128, 131, 140, 179, 188–9, 193, 244, 271

leucocytes Another name for white blood cells, the cells that form the basis of the body's immune response. One type is lymphocytes which include natural killer cells, T cells and B cells. 48, 66

Ley's cognitive model The model suggests that patients may not adhere to treatment because they lack understanding of medical advice, cannot recall it accurately and/or they are dissatisfied with their interaction with their practitioner. 98–9, 105, 107

life events Significant and relatively infrequent experiences/occasions in people's lives that cause stress. They are stressful because we have to expend psychological energy coping with changed circumstances. 9, 20, 30, 36, 38–41, 48–9, 57, 66, 68–9, 71–3, 196–97, 199, 232–3, 235

limbic system Subcortical structures in the brain (including the hypothalamus and amygdala) thought to be closely involved in regulating emotional behaviour including aggression. 118

linear In a straight line, which would describe a perfect correlation between two variables. 75–7, 99, 104, 106, 175, 272–4, 277, 290

linkage analysis In relation to crime, the assumption that offenders behave in a similar way across a series of crimes and seeking to identify such a pattern in a number of crimes. 152, 155

literature review A systematic consideration of what other people have written or said about your chosen research topic. The word 'literature' refers to books, magazines, websites, TV programmes, etc. 228

Locard's exchange principle The principle that an offender will bring something to a crime scene and also take something from it. Both can be used as forensic evidence. 156

locus of control Refers to the sense we each have about what directs events in our lives. Internals believe they are mostly responsible for what happens to them (internal locus of control). Externals believe it is mainly a matter of luck or the influence of other people or other outside forces (external locus of control). 9, 18–21, 30, 32–3, 35–6, 45, 84, 94, 104–105

longitudinal study Any research that takes place over months and years so that the effects of time (age) can be studied. 128, 180

lymphocytes A type of leucocyte (white blood cell) which forms the basis of the body's immune response. Includes natural killer cells, T cells and B cells. 48, 66, 68

mania Mental disorder characterised by great excitement, grandiose ideas, overactivity, delusions and inappropriate behaviours (such as inappropriate irritability, social behaviour, sexual desire). 171, 203–207, 216, 222–3, 240

manifest content See latent content. 242

MAO-A See monoamine oxidase (MAOs) 116, 129

MAOA gene Regulates the production of monoamine oxidase A (MAO-A) which, amongst other things, regulates the breakdown of serotonin in the brain. People who have a low-activity MAOA gene have high levels of serotonin which is associated with aggressive behaviour. 116–17, 129

mastery Comprehensive knowledge or skill in an activity. 26–7, 31, 37, 264, 268–70, 280–84, 288, 302–304

maternal deprivation The loss of emotional care during early childhood (the first two to three years). The proposed effects include delinquency, intellectual problems and an inability to understand the emotions of other people. 128–9

maturation The process of ripening. A change that is due to innate factors rather than learning, for example the onset of puberty is due to maturation. 187, 222

mean The arithmetic average. Add up all the values and divide by the number of values. 83, 216

median The central value in a set of data when values are arranged from lowest to highest. 25, 31

medical model Mental disorders are seen as physical disorders with physical causes (e.g. brain disease) and should be treated by physical means (e.g. drugs). 213, 222, 224–5, 229

Megan's Law The US version of Sarah's law (see child sex offender disclosure scheme). 137

melancholia A feeling of deep sadness. A symptom of depression. One of the three categories of mental disorder described by the Greeks. 222–3

memory T cells A type of white blood cell (leucocyte) that contributes to the body's immune response. Memory T cells (or T cells) have 'learned' to recognise certain antigens and secrete appropriate antibodies. 48, 66

mental disorders The collection of illnesses … thinking and emotions. 10, 30, 100, 185, 19… 217–26, 228, 230–59

mental health Refers to psychological and e… being. 10, 12, 28, 30, 54, 79, 133, 138, 153, 1… 194–200, 203–204, 207–208, 211, 213–15, 21… 229–35, 241, 243, 245, 251–9, 274

mental health professionals Qualified and tr… involved at various points in the process of ide… and treating mental disorders. Their behaviour an… work is regulated by national bodies (e.g. the British … Society). 213, 254–7, 259

mental illness An old-fashioned term for mental disorders … distinct from physical disorders). They are experienced in the m… but may have physical symptoms. The preferred term now is ment… health problems to avoid the implication that a person is 'ill' with a 'disease'. 116, 174, 214

meta-analysis The results of several studies that have addressed similar aims are combined. Statistical methods are used to produce an effect size to express overall trends. A 'review' of research does not involve a statistical analysis. 16–17, 24–5, 30, 143, 158, 180, 269

metamotivational state The word 'meta' implies that one higher level is interpreting a lower level. Therefore, in reversal theory, at any one time one state (telic or paratelic) is dominating motivation. 278–9

milieu therapy Clients live within a respectful environment ('milieu') that is structured to provide therapy (e.g. learning social interaction skills). 226–7

Mind A mental health charity that aims to provide advice and support to empower anyone experiencing a mental health problem. They also campaign to improve services and promote understanding. 215, 223, 225, 227, 234, 246, 254–7, 300, 306

mind-to-muscle techniques Cognitive processes involved in relaxation, such as thinking and visualising to reduce muscle tension. 306–307

mindfulness Focusing exclusively on experiences occurring in the present moment, in a non-judgemental and accepting way. 246–7

mindfulness-based cognitive therapy (MBCT) Version of CBT incorporating mindfulness techniques such as guided meditation. 246–7

model People who have qualities we would like to have and we identify with, thus we model or imitate their behaviour and attitudes. 26, 51–2, 60, 62, 84, 94, 110, 124–6, 178, 208, 288

modelling Either an observer imitates the behaviour of a model or a model demonstrates a behaviour that may be imitated by an observer. 51, 94, 105, 107, 124–6, 179, 271, 288

modus operandi A particular way of doing something, often unique to an individual. 150, 152, 155, 159

monoamine oxidase (MAO) A group of enzymes (MAO-A and MAO-B) that speed up the oxidation of monoamines, resulting in the removal of oxygen. The end result is deactivation of a monoamine neurotransmitter which has been linked to various mental disorders such as schizophrenia and depression. 116, 250–51

monoamine oxidase A MAO-A, see monoamine oxidase. 116

monoamine oxidase inhibitors (MAOIs) A class of drugs that prevent the action of MAO. There are very significant risks if MAOIs are taken in combination with other drugs (for example amphetamines) or foods (for example tryptophan which is used by the body to produce serotonin). 250–51

monotropy Mono means 'one' and indicates that one particular attachment is different from all others and of central importance to the child's development. 170–71

monozygotic (MZ) twins Develop from one fertilised egg (zygote) and are genetically identical. 50, 114

mood alteration Changing a person's emotional state. May be caused by addictive drugs and behaviour. 12–13, 30

mood disorder A group of mental disorders where the main symptoms are emotional, such as depression and bipolar disorder. 55, 65, 67, 240

moral reasoning The process by which an individual draws upon their own value system to determine whether an action is right or wrong. 122–3

moral treatment 18th/19th-century movement promoting respectful and humane treatment in asylums to help people recover and be released. 226–7

morbidity The condition of being unhealthy. 220, 240

mortality The number of deaths in a population. 220, 241

motivation Refers to the forces that 'drive' your behaviour. It encourages an animal to act. For example, hunger is a basic drive state which pushes an animal to seek food. Winning a match may drive you on to greater success, i.e. it motivates you. 26, 56, 61, 67, 76, 78, 81, 83, 85, 95, 100, 105, 121, 150–51, 154, 176, 180, 192–3, 238, 260–68, 272, 278–85, 287, 289, 291, 295, 297–309

nal climate The psychological environment that the eates by designing sessions which provide instructions dback that will help to motivate the athletes in training and etition. 263–5, 285

vational toxicity An addict's drive is focused on thoughts and naviours related to their addiction at the expense of all other ings, and therefore this motivation is harmful (toxic). 56, 67

multidimensional anxiety theory Explains state anxiety as having two components, cognitive and somatic anxiety, each influencing performance differently. 261, 274–6, 292–3, 299

multidimensional model of sport confidence Explains the relationship between trait sport confidence and state sport confidence. The updated model additionally included factors, sources, constructs and consequences of sport confidence. 261, 268–9, 274, 286–7, 299, 304

multidisciplinary workforce A group of professionals from different disciplines (areas) working together, for example education, social care and criminal justice. 208

multiple personality disorder A type of mental disorder where two or more relatively independent personalities exist in one person. The separate personalities have become 'dissociated' from each other. The disorder is also called 'dissociative personality disorder'. Dissociation may occur as a consequence of stress. 238

muscle relaxation technique A method to reduce muscle tension. For example, first tense particular muscle groups (e.g. neck muscles), then release the tension and note how the muscles feel when you relax them. 295

muscle tension The semi-contraction of muscles due to stress. 272, 294–5, 306

musterbation One of the types of irrational belief proposed by Ellis to explain depression. The tendency to think that certain things must occur or must be done. 246

MZ twins See monozygotic twins. 50–51, 68, 114–15

naloxone (trade name e.g. Narcan) A medication used to block the effects of opioids. It is an antagonist of opioid receptors especially the mu-opioid receptor. Adminstered by injection or nasal spray. 90–91

naltrexone (trade name e.g. Vivitrol) A medication primarily used to manage alcohol or opioid dependence. It is an antagonist of opioid receptors especially the mu-opioid receptor and thus reduces the pleasurable effects of alcohol/opioids. 90–91, 105, 107

National Institute on Drug Abuse (NIDA) An American organisation seeking to support worldwide scientific investigation of the causes and consequences of drug use and addiction. 135

nativism The view that behaviour is innate rather than acquired by learning. 222

natural experiment An experiment where the independent variable has varied as a consequence of some other action rather than the researcher's manipulation, such as comparing children who have spent time in hospital with children who haven't. 203

natural killer (NK) cells A type of white blood cell (leucocyte) that contributes to the body's immune response. NK cells are critical to the innate immune system and recognise 'stressed' cells even if there are no antibodies. 48–9, 66, 68

naturalistic explanation In the context of mental disorders, the view that the causes are 'natural' rather than supernatural, i.e. based on activity in the brain/body that can be demonstrated using the scientific method. 222–4

naturally selected The major process that explains evolution whereby inherited traits that enhance an animal's reproductive success are passed on to the next generation and thus 'selected', whereas animals without such traits are less successful at reproduction and their traits are not selected. 169, 171–2, 192

nature/nurture The question of whether behaviour is determined more by 'nature' (inherited and genetic factors) or 'nurture' (all influences after conception, e.g. experience). It is not a debate about whether one or the other is determining behaviour but about the contributions of each, as well as their interaction with each other. 194–5, 222–3, 230

need achievement theory Explains an individual's desire to take part in sport because of a need to achieve success and avoid failure. 261–3, 280–81, 299

need for cognition (NFC) A personality characteristic, the extent to which a person engages in and enjoys cognitive activity such as thinking and problem-solving. 78–9, 104, 106

need to achieve (NACH) An individual's desire for accomplishment and mastery of skills. 262–3, 280–81, 284

need to avoid failure (NAF) An individual's motivation to avoid shame and negative feelings. 262–3, 280–81

negative emotion Undesirable feelings such as nervousness, fear or aggression. 12, 54, 62, 67, 119, 296–7

negative reinforcement In operant conditioning, a stimulus that increases the probability that a behaviour will be repeated because it leads to escape from an unpleasant situation and is experienced as rewarding. 50, 52–3, 56–7, 60–63, 67–9, 72, 76, 104, 106, 178–9, 244

neglected children Those who receive few positive and few negative nominations when their peers are asked to say who they like most and least. See peer status. 180–81, 232

neologism A new word or phrase. 238

neurochemistry Relating to substances in the brain and other parts of the nervous system that regulate psychological functioning. 10, 218, 224

neuron The basic building block of the nervous system. Neurons are nerve cells that process and transmit messages through electrical and chemical signals. 50, 56, 67, 80, 90, 107, 250

neuroticism The degree to which a person experiences the world as distressing, threatening and unsafe. It is an overreactive response to threat. 120–21

neurotransmitter Chemical (e.g. serotonin) in the brain and nervous system that transmits signals from one neuron to another across synapses. 46, 50, 80, 90, 116, 218–19, 250

neutral stimulus (NS) Any stimulus that does not produce the desired response. It becomes a conditioned stimulus after being paired with the UCS. 52, 88, 178

nicotine regulation model An explanation for smoking addiction, that addicted smokers continue to smoke to maintain a steady level of nicotine in their body and thus avoid withdrawal effects. 50–51

nicotine replacement therapy (NRT) A medically approved method of taking nicotine without having to use tobacco. Therefore, it is a method used to quit smoking. 90–91, 105, 107

non-adherence Patients sometimes do not follow ('stick to') medical advice. If they decide to do this after careful consideration, this is rational non-adherence. 96–9, 101–102, 105, 107

non-suicidal self-injury disorder (NSSID) A disorder in which a person intends to damage their body tissues (e.g. by cutting) but does not intend to kill themselves. 237

noradrenaline A hormone and a neurotransmitter that generally has an excitatory effect, similar to adrenaline. The hormone is produced by the adrenal gland. Americans use the term norepinephrine. 46–7, 68, 80, 100, 250

norepinephrine The American term for noradrenaline. 251

normal distribution Occurs when certain variables are measured, such as IQ or the life of a light bulb. Variables such as these are distributed so that most of the scores are clustered around the mean, median and mode. 68.26% of the scores should lie within one standard deviation of the mid-point. 216

NS See neutral stimulus. 52, 178–9, 218

nucleus accumbens (NA) A part of the mesolimbic pathway, the reward pathway of the brain. There is one in each hemisphere. 50–51, 56–7, 62, 67–9, 90, 105

observation Actively attending to and watching (or listening to) the behaviour of others (models). 33, 51, 53, 60, 63, 66, 114, 124–6, 128, 172, 178, 200, 240, 287, 307

observational learning Learning through imitation, a key concept in social learning theory. 53

obsessions Recurrent, intrusive thoughts or impulses that are perceived as inappropriate or forbidden. They may be frightening and/or embarrassing and are experienced as uncontrollable, leading to anxiety. 238–9

obsessive-compulsive disorder (OCD) An anxiety disorder characterised by obsessions and/or compulsive behaviour. 238–9

OCD See obsessive-compulsive disorder. 213, 230, 238–9, 247, 259

offender disclosure schemes Members of the community can apply to the police if they suspect someone they have come into contact with has a criminal record. Police may then disclose the information to the applicant. This covers child sexual offences to protect children at risk, as well as people who may be in danger of domestic violence. 136–7

offender manager (probation officer) Supervise offenders who have been released from prison under licence (i.e. on probation) and aim to provide support and interventions to reduce the risk of reoffending. 138

offender profiling (also known as criminal profiling) An investigative tool used by law enforcement agencies to identify likely suspects. It has been used by investigators to link cases that may have been committed by the same perpetrator. 159, 161

operant conditioning A form of learning in which behaviour is shaped and maintained by its consequences: reinforcement (positive or negative) or punishment (positive or negative). 52, 56–7, 60, 63, 67, 72, 82, 104, 106, 144, 178–9, 188, 218, 226, 244

operationalise Defining variables so that they can easily be tested. 193

operations The term used in Piaget's theory of cognitive development for internally consistent, logical mental rules, such as rules of arithmetic. 182, 184–5

optimal performance The highest level of performance that can be achieved. 272, 279, 282–3, 291, 306

orbitofrontal cortex (OFC) Located in the prefrontal cortex and involved in decision-making. 119

organised non-social type One explanation for 'lust murders' (homocides that involve erotic satisfaction). The organised non-social type is orderly and tends to display compulsive thinking and behaviour, bright and socially competent. They plan their murders and the crime scene is usually controlled. Contrast with disorganised asocial type. 148

organised serial murderers Murderers who show evidence of premeditated planning of the crime. They are typically socially and sexually competent with higher-than-average intelligence. 148

outcome/ego orientation People with an outcome or ego orientation believe their natural ability determines their success because it increases their belief in how good they are. Contrast with task orientation. 264–5, 282–3

outcome orientation See outcome/ego orientation. 264–5, 282–3

outcome expectations See efficacy expectations. 270

outgroup Any social group to which you do not belong, as distinct from the ingroup. 176–7

overextension Expanding something too far. In relation to language, using one word/phrase to cover more than its specific meaning. For example using 'mummy' to describe all women. 183

overgeneralisation In relation to language development, assuming one rule applies to every instance. For example forming past tenses by adding 'ed' to every verb (e.g. runned, swimmed). 183, 189

paranoid personality disorder (PPD) An enduring characteristic of a person's behaviour, characterised by a mistrust of others, quick to anger, and believing that others have hidden motives or are out to harm you (paranoia). See personality disorder. 236

parasympathetic branch/parasympathetic nervous system A division of the autonomic nervous system (ANS) which supervises 'rest and digest' functions of the normal resting state of the body. The parasympathetic branch is de-activated when the hormone adrenaline triggers the activity of the sympathetic branch of the ANS. 46, 66, 68

paratelic state In a playful state, motivations are proactive (not reactive), behaviour-oriented (not goal-oriented) and process-oriented (not end-oriented). The telic state is the opposite. 278–9, 296–7

parental care See parental control. 232

parental control The consistent ways in which parents raise their children. Includes parental care (e.g. expressed warmth) and parental control (e.g. overprotectiveness). 232

parentification A role reversal, where a child has to act as the parent to their mother, father and/or siblings. 206–207

parenting style A representation of the degree to which parents respond to their children's needs/personalities and the degree to which they make demands on their children (e.g. expect certain standards of behaviour, obey rules). 166–7, 196–7, 205, 207, 232–3

Parkinson's disease A long-term degenerative disease which affects the motor system. It begins with mild shakes, slowness and difficulty walking, symptoms which get progressively worse. It is associated with low levels of dopamine in the brain. There is no cure for the disease but raising dopamine levels may help using the drug L-DOPA. 50

partial reinforcement schedule When a behaviour is reinforced only some of the time it occurs (e.g. every tenth time or at variable intervals). 60

pathology The study of what causes diseases. 151, 158, 163, 203, 205–210, 212–36, 238, 240, 242–4, 246, 248, 250, 252, 254, 256, 258

patient Orignally means 'one who suffers' and patiently tolerates treatment by an expert. The term 'client' is now preferred to emphasise the more equal and active role played by a person receiving therapy. See client. 16, 44–5, 52, 57, 75, 81, 89, 96–103, 105, 107, 218, 220–21, 224–7, 230, 234–6, 251, 254, 268

peer status A classification of how much a person is liked or disliked by their equals (peers). It is often measured by asking each member of a group to identify three group members they like most and three who they like least. 163, 180–81, 191

peer tutoring An effective form of learning, whereby someone at your own age level (a peer) guides learning. Vygotsky recognised that peers can be potential 'experts' (individuals with greater knowledge) and also saw learning as a collaborative process, all children working together for the general good rather than competing against each other for individual gain. 187

pendulum task A person is given some string and a set of weights and asked to work out whether length of the string, heaviness of the weight or strength of the push is most important in determining the speed of the swing of the pendulum. 183

perceived behavioural control How much control a person believes they have over their own behaviour. 22–5, 31–3

performance accomplishments Previously successful experiences. 270–71, 288–9

performance profiling An assessment strategy to improve factors important to performance. 261, 300–303, 309

peripheral route The recipient attends to non-content factors (e.g. attractiveness of the source) because they are uninterested in the message or do not have the cognitive ability to process it. 78–9, 104, 106

permissive parents A type of parenting style involving low demandingness and high responsiveness. 166–7

persistence Continuing to perform or train despite difficulty. 109, 264, 270, 280–86

personal attitudes The balance of a person's favourable and unfavourable attitudes about their behaviour. 22–5, 31–3, 36

personality Patterns of thinking, feeling and behaving that differ between individuals. These are relatively consistent from one situation to another, and over time. 9, 44–5, 47, 66, 68–9, 71, 73, 110, 112, 120–21, 128, 150, 152–5, 194, 213, 218, 221–2, 225, 232–3, 236–8, 242, 259, 262–5, 268, 272, 274, 278, 280, 282, 291–2, 296, 300

personality disorder (PD) An enduring collection of inflexible behaviour patterns that disrupt normal interactions, therefore causing problems in relationships. 213, 221, 232–3, 236–8, 259

personification Giving a non-human animal or object human attributes. 58–9, 67

Peterborough Youth Study Participants were about 2000 white working-class adolescents (14–15 years) in the Peterborough area of England. The aim was to determine young people's involvement in crime and attitudes towards it. Participants were asked questions such as 'If you were caught shoplifting and your mother or father found out, would you feel ashamed?' and 'As far as you know have any of your friends beaten someone up?'. 128

phobia An anxiety disorder characterised by an irrational fear of an object or situation. The central symptom is intense anxiety when encountering the phobic stimulus. 28, 31, 33, 65, 85, 218, 238–9, 244–5, 247

phrenitis An inflammation of the brain, specifically the membranes covering the brain (the meninges). Symptoms range from a headache and fever to paralysis and death. 222

physical self-efficacy scale (PSE) Self-efficacy is the degree to which you are confident in your own abilities, so physical self-efficacy is your confidence in your physical abilities. Respondents rate items such as 'I have excellent reflexes' and 'I am not agile and graceful' (strongly agree to strongly disagree). 271

physiological Relating to bodily functions. 9–13, 15, 17, 19, 21, 23, 25, 27, 29–30, 32, 35, 42, 46–7, 50–57, 60, 66–9, 71, 76, 80–83, 85–91, 93, 95, 100–101, 103–109, 111, 192–3, 239, 270, 272, 274, 276–7, 288, 290, 292, 294, 296–7

physiological addiction Dependence on a substance, shown when an addict gives it up and experiences withdrawal symptoms. 9, 12–13, 15, 17, 19, 21, 23, 25, 27, 29–30, 35, 50–57, 67, 71

pituitary gland Called the master gland of the body's hormone system because it directs much of the hormone activity. 46–7, 66, 68

placebo A treatment that should have no effect on the behaviour being studied, it contains no active ingredient. Therefore, it can be used to separate out the effects of the independent variable (IV) from any effects caused merely by receiving any treatment. 81, 89, 91, 100–101, 104–105, 111, 251

popular children Those who receive many positive and few negative nominations when their peers are asked to say who they like most and least. See peer status. 180–81

positive correlation As one co-variable increases so does the other. For example, the number of people in a room and noise are positively correlated. 16–17, 20, 24–5, 28, 30–31, 38–40, 66, 68, 73

positive emotion Desirable feelings such as hope, pride and inspiration. 296–7

positive reinforcement In operant conditioning, a stimulus that increases the probability that a behaviour will be repeated because it is pleasurable. 52–3, 56–7, 60–63, 67–9, 82, 106, 244, 263

post-traumatic stress disorder (PTSD) Disabling reaction to stress following a traumatic event. The response does not always appear immediately after the event. The reactions are long-lasting, and include: reliving the event recurrently in flashbacks and dreams, emotional numbness and general anxiety which may result in lack of concentration. 204

pre-conventional level The first level of Kohlberg's stage theory. It is characterised by childlike immature reasoning which has also been observed in the adult criminal population. 122–3

prenatal Before birth, when an embryo/foetus is developing in the womb. 119, 194–5, 200, 206–207, 209, 213, 222, 230–31, 233, 259

primary appraisal A person's evaluation of whether an event is a threat or an opportunity. Secondary appraisal is when the person evaluates their ability to cope or take advantage of the situation. 40, 68

primary attachment The person who has formed the closest bond with a child, often the preferred person the child will seek for comfort. This is usually a child's biological mother but other people can fulfil the role. 170–71, 204

primary reinforcer/reinforcement Things that are innately reinforcing, such as food or warmth. 52, 67, 144, 226

primary research Information collected by a researcher specifically for the purpose of the current study. 97, 107

prisonisation Accepting the culture and lifestyle of prison society. 139

privation In the context of development this refers to a lack of emotional care during early life. This may also include a lack of physical care but it is the emotional care which has the most severe effects on psychological development. 117, 128–9, 163, 173, 193, 199–200, 202–11, 235

proactive aggression Behaving in a threatening, hostile manner in order to achieve a goal. It is a means to an end. Contrast with reactive aggression. 118

probability of success The likelihood of achieving a predetermined goal. 262, 280

probation The court places an offender under supervision instead of serving time in prison. Sometimes, the term 'probation' only means a community sentence. In other cases, probation also includes supervision of those conditionally released from prison on parole. 130, 138–9

probation officer See offender manager. 138

problem-solving The process of finding a solution to a situation that requires action. 182–3, 186

progressive muscular relaxation (PMR) Tensing and then relaxing muscles repeatedly to reduce tension overall. 306–307

prosocial Behaviour which is beneficial to other people, and may not necessarily benefit the helper. 134, 180

psychiatrist A medically-trained doctor who has specialised in treating people with mental health problems. 118, 128, 170, 220, 224, 232, 234, 254–5

psychiatry A branch of medicine involving diagnosis and treatment of mental disorders. A psychiatrist is medically trained whereas a psychologist isn't. 224–5, 234

psychoanalysis A form of psychotherapy, originally developed by Sigmund Freud, that is intended to help patients become aware of repressed feelings and issues by using techniques such as free association and dream analysis. 218, 242, 252, 254

psychodynamic approach/therapy An approach to treatment of mental disorders that assumes that the causes of psychopathology are hidden in the unconscious mind and must be made conscious so they can be worked through. 193, 213, 218–19, 242–3, 259

psychological approach Behaviour is explained in terms of a range of mental, emotional and learned factors (e.g. thinking patterns, unconscious processes, learned responses to the environment). 111, 113, 124, 130, 144, 146, 218–19

psychological portrait A description of a person in terms of individual characteristics such as personality, gender, typical behaviours, etc. 154–5

psychometric test A set of questions or tasks that assess some aspect of psychological functioning, such as intelligence or personality. 272

psychopathology Literally 'psychological diseases'. The study of mental disorders (e.g. producing an explanation of depression). 158, 163, 203, 205–210, 212–36, 238, 240, 242–4, 246, 248, 250, 252, 254, 256, 258

psychosis/psychotic disorder Severe mental disorder where a person's thought processes and emotions are so impaired that they have lost contact with external reality. 213, 238–9, 250, 259

psychoticism A personality characterised by aggressiveness, hostility and lack of empathy for others. May be related to high levels of testosterone. 120–21

PTSD See post-traumatic stress disorder. 204–205

punishment The consequence of a behaviour is unpleasant, making the behaviour less likely to be repeated. 113, 120, 122–3, 132–4, 136–9, 143–6, 164–5, 178–9, 222–3

punitive punishment A form of discipline that is intended to be harsh (even draconian) and it is the harshness that should discourage further criminal behaviour. 132–3

questionnaire Respondents record their own answers. The questions are predetermined (i.e. structured). 18–22, 24–5, 27, 30–33, 36, 38, 41, 45, 49, 63, 73, 76, 83, 103, 107, 120–21, 128, 167, 193, 216, 220, 263, 283, 297

random A method that ensures that each item has an equal chance of being selected, i.e. there is no predictable pattern. 54, 59, 76, 91, 95, 100–103, 105, 148, 169, 183, 188, 227, 238, 243, 245

random allocation An attempt to control for participant variables in an independent groups design which ensures that each participant has the same chance of being in one condition as any other. 100, 102, 105

randomised controlled trial Test of the effectiveness of a treatment in which participants are placed into the treatment or control group using a chance (random) technique to balance out pre-existing differences between them. 101–102

rapid cycling A characteristic of bipolar disorder where some individuals alternate between depression and mania more quickly than usual (more than four times in 12 months). 240

rapid smoking A form of aversion therapy used to stop smoking where a person is asked to puff very quickly on a cigarette so that the experience is extremely unpleasant. 52

rational emotive behaviour therapy (REBT) Involves identifying irrational thoughts/beliefs/feelings and challenging them through argument and confrontation (disputing). 246–7

reactive aggression Aggression that occurs as a response to a real or perceived threat. This is distinct from proactive aggression which is designed to achieve a particular goal. 118–19

reactivity The speed and magnitude of a person's response to another person or situation (such as responding to another family member). 60–62, 67, 248

rebound effect When something comes back at you. In relation to addiction, using a drug to solve a problem ultimate makes the problem worse. 54

recall bias A self-serving memory that exaggerates the benefits of a behaviour and minimises the costs. 58–9, 67

recidivism When a convicted criminal reoffends. 132–3, 139, 141, 143, 145

reciprocal inhibition In exposure therapy, a client cannot experience fear and relaxation at the same time (they inhibit each other). 244–5

reductionist In some psychological theories human behaviour is explained in terms of individual variables such as genes or the action of neurotransmitters (the biological approach), or in terms of conditioning (the learning approach) or independent and dependent variables (the experimental approach). Some people feel this is a better way to understand how the system works whereas others prefer a more holistic approach, combining all the contributory influences. 158–9

rehabilitation The reintegration of an offender into society. 117, 132–3, 139, 141–3

reinforcement A behaviour is followed by a consequence that increases the probability of the behaviour being repeated. 18–19, 26–7, 31, 33, 37, 50, 52–3, 56–7, 60–63, 67–9, 72, 76, 82, 92, 102–106, 120, 124–5, 144, 178–9, 188–9, 218, 226, 244, 246, 263, 270, 289

rejected children Those who receive few positive and few negative nominations when their peers are asked to say who they like most and least. See peer status. 180

relapse Reverting to addiction after a period of giving up. 12–13, 28–32, 34, 50–65, 67, 69, 84–5, 89–90, 92–5, 104–107, 246–7, 249

relatedness Feeling a connection to other things (e.g. people or events). 266–7, 284–5, 301, 303

relaxation techniques (relaxation training) Methods that help a person become more calm and reduce levels of pain, anxiety and stress. 244, 276, 295, 306–307

reliability Consistency of a measuring tool, including a psychological test. 19, 30, 32, 220–21

replication Repeating an observation or study to confirm the original finding. 77, 104, 177

repression To push unpleasant thoughts into the unconscious. In psychoanalytic theory, the conscious rational part of the mind (the ego) 'defends' itself from uncomfortable emotions to maintain stability. Repression is one form of ego defence which buries uncomfortable emotions in the unconscious mind. 242

resilience The ability to cope in challenging situations. 11, 30, 206–207, 268

response bias A tendency for interviewees to respond in the same way to all questions, regardless of context. This would bias their answers. 41, 66, 68

response shaping A process of modifying behaviour by reinforcing successive approximations to a desired behaviour. 244–5

rest and digest See parasympathetic branch/parasympathetic nervous system. 46, 66

restorative justice An approach to justice which aims to reduce and atone for offending behaviour as well as address the needs of the victim. It involves reconciliation between offender and victim, as well as the wider community. 113, 142–3, 147

resultant tendencies In need achievement theory, the outcome of an interaction between personality (high or low need for achievement and need to avoid failure) and situational factors (such as the difficulty of a match). Such outcomes affect task persistance and choice of opponents. 262–3, 280

retrospective Looking backwards, to the past. 41, 66, 68

reuptake Presynaptic vesicles release neurotransmitters into the synaptic cleft. Some of these are used by postsynaptic receptors but any neurotransmitters that remain in the cleft are reabsorbed (i.e. taken up again) by the transporter located on the presynaptic neuron for later use. 250–51

reversal theory of arousal Explains how an individual can change their interpretations of arousal depending on their state of mind. 261, 278–9, 296, 299

review A consideration of a number of studies that have investigated the same topic in order to reach a general conclusion about a particular hypothesis. 16–19, 23–25, 27–33, 37–38, 43, 48, 53, 63, 67–68, 77, 81, 87, 91, 93, 96–97, 101, 103–105, 107, 227, 233, 251

role conflict Occurs when an employee (e.g. middle manager) faces competing demands as a result of their responsibilities in the workplace. This causes stress and can lead to dissatisfaction, illness and absenteeism. 42–3, 66, 68

role model See model. 51–3, 56–7, 62–3, 67, 124–6, 269

salience The extent to which something is noticeable or important. 12–13, 30, 32

Sally–Anne task A method to assess theory of mind using a story about two dolls (Sally and Anne). Sally does not know that Anne has moved her marble while she was out of the room. A person with a theory of mind therefore says that Sally will look in the original place. Very young children and children with autism spectrum disorder (ASD) typically say she will look in the place they know the marble is, displaying a lack of theory of mind. 182

sample A group of people who take part in a research investigation. The sample is drawn from a (target) population and is presumed to be representative of that population, i.e. it stands 'fairly' for the population being studied. 21, 30, 39, 66, 79, 103–105, 107, 114, 159, 172, 185, 189, 277, 295

SAM system See sympathomedullary (SAM) system. 46–7, 66, 68

Sarah's Law See child sex offender disclosure scheme. 136–7

SC-state See state sport confidence. 268–9, 286, 292–3

SC-trait See trait sport confidence. 268–9, 286–7

scaffolding An approach to instruction that aims to support a learner only when absolutely necessary, i.e. to provide a support framework (scaffold) to assist the learning process. 183, 186–8

schedule of recent experiences (SRE) A self-report checklist to assess the life events a person has experienced as a measure of stress. A respondent selects events that have occurred in a specific time period from a list of 43 (sometimes 42 if Christmas is excluded). For each event the person lists how many times it has happened and this is multiplied by a mean value for the item (e.g. the life event 'a major change in sleeping habits' has a mean value of 16 whereas 'Taking on a steep mortgage' has a mean value of 31). The SRE was the precursor to the social readjustment rating scale (SRRS). 38–9, 41, 66

schema A mental package of beliefs and expectations that influence memory. 150, 154, 182, 184–5

schizoaffective disorder A mental disorder with symptoms of both schizophrenia (e.g. hallucinations) and mood disorder (e.g. depression or mania). 221, 238

schizophrenia A psychotic disorder characterised by positive symptoms such as delusions, hallucinations and disorganised thinking, speech and movement. Negative symptoms may also be present, for example lack of emotion or speech. 50, 218, 221, 223, 227, 230, 232, 234, 236, 238–9, 250–51, 253–4

schizophrenia spectrum A set of severe psychotic disorders sharing certain symptoms including delusions, hallucinations and disordered thinking. 238–9, 250

secondary appraisal See primary appraisal. 40, 66, 68

secondary attachment The closest emotional bond is with a primary attachment figure. Additional support is available from secondary attachment figures who provide an emotional safety net. 170–71

secondary reinforcement Takes place when the thing that acts as a reinforcer has become associated with something of biological significance, such as money which is associated with being able to buy food. 226

secondary reinforcer The item that is providing a reward because of its association with a primary reinforcer. For example food is a primary reinforcer. If food is associated with money then money becomes a secondary reinforcer. 52–3, 60, 67, 69, 144, 226

secondary research Research using information that has already been collected by someone else and so pre-dates the current research project. In psychology, such data might include the work of other psychologists, or government statistics. 97, 105, 107

secure attachment (Type B) Generally thought of as the most desirable attachment type, associated with psychologically healthy outcomes. In the Strange Situation this is shown by moderate stranger and separation anxiety and ease of comfort at reunion. 168, 172, 196, 202, 206, 208–209, 232–3

secure base Secure attachment provides a sense of safety to enable exploration and independence. 172–3, 208

selective serotonin reuptake inhibitors (SRRIs) An antidepressant group of drugs that increase available amounts of serotonin in the synaptic cleft by preventing their reabsorption by the transmitting (presynaptic) neuron, and thus increasing the amount of serotonin to stimulate the postsynaptic neuron. 250–51

self-actualisation The desire to grow psychologically and fulfil one's potential – becoming what you are capable of. 192–3, 218

self-concept The self as it is currently experienced, all the attitudes we hold about ourselves. 64, 86, 176

self-confidence The belief performers have that they will be successful. 27, 37, 176, 181, 254, 261, 263, 268–71, 274–5, 277, 281, 283, 285–93, 295, 297–300, 304–305, 308–309

self-determination theory Explains motivation in terms of a person's inborn psychological needs, seeing internal rather than external influences as more important. 261, 266–7, 284–5, 299, 301, 303

self-efficacy A person's confidence in being able to do something. Such confidence generates expectations and these act as self-fulfilling prophecies. 9, 11, 14–17, 24, 26–31, 33, 35, 37, 52–3, 67, 69, 86, 94, 104–105, 107, 109, 261, 270–71, 281, 284, 288–9, 299–300, 304

self-efficacy theory A person needs both belief and competence to successfully carry out a performance. 9, 27–9, 31, 33, 35, 37, 261, 270–71, 289, 299

self-esteem The feelings that a person has about their self-concept. 20–21, 27, 30–31, 37, 54, 64–65, 67, 69, 74–75, 86–87, 89, 100, 104, 106–107, 166–7, 176, 178, 192–4, 196, 214, 240–41, 252, 264

self-medication model Views addiction as a way of relieving current feelings of distress caused by past experiences of trauma. How we perceive or think about the trauma and distress is a cognitive process. 54–5, 64, 67, 69

self-regulation Controlling one's own behaviour and emotions. 54, 67, 268

self-report Any method to gather data by asking people questions. 17, 25, 29–31, 39, 41–2, 45, 51, 63, 66–7, 103, 105, 128, 263, 297

self-talk Intentional statements that we say to ourselves. 84, 103–104, 140, 261, 304–305, 309

sensation-seeking Searching for experiences and feelings that create excitement and sensory pleasure. Such experiences may be new, complex and dangerous. 121

sensitive period A biologically-determined period of time during which an animal is most likely to acquire certain behaviours. This is in contrast to the concept of a 'critical period', which suggests a more finite period during which change can take place. 169–71, 188–9, 208

serotonin A neurotransmitter with widespread inhibitory effects throughout the brain. It has a key role in aggressive behaviour. 80, 90, 100, 104, 106, 116, 218, 250–51

serotonin noradrenaline reuptake inhibitors (SNRIs) Similar to SSRIs except noradrenaline levels are increased at the synapse instead of serotonin. 250

serotonin syndrome A range of symptoms such as high body temperature, agitation, tremor, sweating, dilated pupils and diarrhoea which result from taking drugs that increase levels of serotonin. 251

shaping A concept in learning theory to explain how complex behaviours are acquired. Initially rewards are given for very simple behaviours but gradually rewards are witheld until increasingly complex behaviours are performed, progressively becoming closer and closer to the desired behaviour. For example, an animal can be taught to perform a complex trick by first being rewarded for just looking at their owner, then for standing still and looking and so on. 178–9, 188, 244–5

significant A statistical term indicating that the research findings are sufficiently strong to enable a researcher to reject the null hypothesis under test and accept the alternate hypothesis. 18–20, 38–41, 48, 61, 63, 65, 68, 74, 76, 78, 83, 87, 89, 91, 93, 95, 97, 99–102, 105, 133, 177, 226–7, 230, 237, 243, 245, 251, 257, 271

skills training A form of therapy in which clients learn specific abilities to help them cope with high-risk situations. Such abilities include assertiveness, verbal and non-verbal social skills and anger management. Training uses a range of techniques including group discussion, modelling and role play. 9, 92, 94–5, 102, 105, 107, 109, 246

Skinner box An operant conditioning chamber, laboratory apparatus used to study the effects of rewards and punishments on animals using food pellets (as rewards) or electrified floor (as punishment). 178

sleeper effect A delayed effect, for example a person may see an advertisement on the TV which has no immediate effect on their behaviour but at a future time it does. 74, 104, 106

smallest space analysis (SSA) A statistical technique used to identify common patterns of behaviour from a database of crime scenes and offender behaviours. These patterns can then be used to distinguish between different kinds of crime and produce a likely offender profile based on a particular crime scene. 151

snowball sampling Current participants recruit further participants from among people they know. 59, 67

social approach Explanations based on the real or imagined influence of other people. This includes cultural influences. 10, 124, 165, 167, 187–8, 190

social categorisation Putting people into social groupings based on their shared characteristics (e.g. ethnicity). 176

social class Broadly an individual's socioeconomic status (e.g. working, middle, upper class), partly determined by their income and level of education. 155, 174, 185, 198–9, 234–5

social climate A person's perception of the atmosphere created by a group of people. 268

social desirability bias A tendency for respondents to answer questions in such a way so as to present themselves in a 'better light'. 19, 21, 25, 29–31, 33, 45, 51, 63, 66–8, 103

social gradient In relation to health, the observation that people from higher socioeconomic groups have better health compared to those from lower socioeconomic groups. 198, 234

social identity theory (SIT) The view that your behaviour is motivated by your social identity. A person's self-image has two components: personal identity and social identity. Personal identity is based on your characteristics and achievements. Social identity is determined by the various groups of people to which you belong, your 'ingroups'. 163, 176–7, 191, 209

social learning theory (SLT) A way of explaining behaviour that includes both direct and indirect reinforcement, combining learning theory with the role of cognitive factors. 113, 124–6, 128, 131, 179, 254, 271

social norm Something that is standard, usual or typical of a social group (small or large group of people). 134, 166, 198–9, 216–17, 234–5

social phobia Extreme fear of being judged or even looked at by other people. 238–9

social portrait A description of a person in terms of their interactions with other people. 'Social' refers to interactions between members of the same species. 155

social readjustment rating scale (SRRS) A self-report checklist measure of the stress associated with 43 life changes. Each one is linked with a number of Life Change Units (LCUs) reflecting the degree of readjustment needed to cope with the change (e.g. 'Divorce' is 73 LCUs). 38–9, 41, 48, 66, 71

social releasers A social behaviour or characteristic that elicits a caregiving reaction. 170

social support People cope with stressful situations by seeking help from their friends, family and acquaintances. 9, 11, 30, 32, 47, 86–7, 104, 106–107, 109, 111, 286

socialisation The process by which individuals learn the social behaviours of their culture. The 'social behaviours' include morals, values, social skills, norms, language and so on. 120, 186

socio-demographic Social characteristics of a population (demo = 'the people'), for example, age, gender, level of education, occupational status. 103

socioeconomic status A measure of a person's economic and social position in relation to others, based on their or their family's income, education, and occupation. 155, 198, 234–5

sociogram A pictorial illustration of the connections between people, illustrating the interpersonal relationships. 180–81

som A-state See somatic anxiety. 274–5, 292–4

somatic anxiety Our physiological symptoms of anxiety, such as butterflies in the stomach. 274–7, 292–3

somatogenic hypothesis The view that mental or psychological symptoms are caused by physical dysfunctions of the body. Soma = body. 224–5

specific phobia Fear is linked to a particular class of objects such as spiders or heights. 238–9

specificity The quality of something being matched to a particular characteristic or outcome. 54–5, 67, 69

sport confidence See self-confidence. 261, 268–9, 274, 286–7, 299, 304

sport motivation scale (SMS) A self-report questionnaire of intrinsic and extrinsic motivation, and also amotivation (lack of either intrinsic or extrinsic motivation). There were 28 statements about why a person practises their sport (such as 'For the pleasure I feel in living exciting experiences' and 'Because it allows me to be well regarded by the people I know'). Each answer is rated on a scale of 1 to 7 where 7 = corresponds exactly. 285

sport psychologist Work with athletes, coaches, teams and organisations to improve individual and team performance and increase motivation. They also promote participation in exercise generally. 262, 265, 275, 278, 282–3, 308

SSP See Strange Situation procedure. 172–3

stage theory A description of developmental changes in terms of distinct qualitative changes in behaviour from one age to another. 122–3, 184–5

standardised procedures The procedures used in any study should be the same for each participant. If the procedures differ between participants this would act as a confounding variable, affecting the validity of the study. Also, if procedures were not consistent this would reduce the reliability of the study. 29, 31

state anxiety Our current level of anxiety, an emotional state characterised by apprehension and tension. 272, 274–7, 280, 292–5

state sport confidence (SC-state) Sport confidence is the degree of certainty an individual has in their ability to be successful in sport. State sport confidence relates to confidence at a particular moment whereas trait sport confidence refers to an innate predisposition. 268

statistics A method of collecting, summarising and analysing data for the purpose of drawing some conclusions about the data. 78–9, 137–9, 145, 216, 235

stereotype Fixed views of other people based on their perceived membership of a social category. 109, 128, 198–9, 234

Strange Situation procedure (SSP) A research technique used to assess attachment type in babies under the age of 1 year. The key behaviours of interest are separation anxiety, reunion behaviour, stranger anxiety and use of the secure base. Similar measures have been developed to use with older children and adults. 172–3

stress A physiological and psychological state of arousal that arises when we believe we do not have the ability to cope with a perceived threat (stressor). 8–33, 35–50, 54–7, 64–9, 71–3, 75, 80–95, 97, 100, 104–111, 114–15, 118–20, 129, 133, 138, 140–42, 172–3, 181, 194–7, 199–200, 202, 204–207, 214–15, 218–19, 222–3, 230–37, 239, 247–8, 251–2, 256, 272, 280, 284–5, 294, 306

stress inoculation training (SIT) A stress management technique which helps individuals develop coping skills and then exposes the individual to moderate amounts of anxiety to enable practice of coping. 9, 81, 84–5, 104, 106–107, 109–111, 140–41, 177

stress management Techniques to reduce the effects of stress, such as high blood pressure, anxiety and tension. 9, 80–87, 104, 106–107, 109, 111, 140

stressor Any feature of the environment that causes a stress response, including factors associated with work, everyday minor hassles and major changes in our lives. 10–11, 20–21, 30, 32, 38–9, 41–4, 46–9, 57, 66, 68, 73, 81–6, 94, 104, 110–11, 118, 199, 219, 235, 251

subjective norms An individual's belief about whether people who matter to them approve or disapprove of their behaviour. 22–5, 31–3

subjectivity The tendency for a researcher to perceive or interpret information from a personal perspective, resulting in bias. The opposite of objectivity. 17

substance abuse Occurs when someone uses a drug for a bad purpose, i.e. to get 'high' rather than as a 'real' form of medication. Distinct from misuse where a person uses a drug in the wrong way or for the wrong purpose. 100, 116, 133, 155, 166, 194–5, 208, 230, 232, 241, 244

substance-use disorder A mental disorder, where a person fails to be able to control the use of a legal or illegal drug (which includes alcohol and nicotine). 220

support group (also called self-help or peer support group) An organisation usually involving volunteers and sometimes including professionals. They provide non-medical support to people with mental health problems (e.g. information, advice, training, campaigning for better services). 27, 201, 213, 254–7, 259

survey Any method to gather data by asking people questions. 20, 50, 107, 153, 158, 269, 286

sympathetic branch/sympathetic nervous system A division of the autonomic nervous system (ANS) which activates internal organs for vigorous activities and emergencies, such as the 'fight or flight' response. It consists of nerves that control, for example, increased heart rate and breathing, and decreased digestive activity. The sympathetic branch works in opposition to the parasympathetic branch of the ANS. 46, 72, 80, 82–3, 104

sympathomedullary (SAM) system The body's response to an acute (short-term) stressor. The hypothalamus triggers the sympathetic nervous system which causes the adrenal medulla to release adrenaline and noradrenaline. This is the fight or flight response. 46–7, 66, 68

synapse The junction between two neurons. This includes the presynaptic terminal, the synaptic cleft and the postsynaptic receptor site. 250

syndrome A set of symptoms that often occur together. 46–7, 64, 66, 131, 147, 161, 191, 194, 211, 224, 229, 234, 241, 251, 259, 299, 309

synoptic A summary view, drawing together many different perspectives. 130–31, 146, 160, 190–91, 210, 228–9, 258, 298, 308

systematic desensitisation (SD) and exposure therapy A behavioural therapy designed to reduce an unwanted response, such as anxiety, to a stimulus. SD involves drawing up a hierarchy of a client's anxiety-provoking situations, teaching the client to relax, and

then exposing them to anxiety-creating situations. 28–9, 31, 182, 204–205, 244–5

tardive dyskinesia Condition with involuntary, repetitive and jerky body movements, including grimacing, sticking out the tongue or smacking of the lips. It can develop as a side effect of medication, most commonly antipsychotic drugs. 251

task orientation Such people believe the effort they put into a task is likely to be rewarded with success. Contrast with outcome/ego orientation. 264–5, 282–3

task persistence The ability to perform despite distractions, physical or emotional discomfort or lack of immediate success. 280–81

telic state In a serious state, motivations are reactive (not proactive), goal-oriented (not behaviour-oriented) and end-oriented (not process-oriented). The paratelic state is the opposite. 278–9, 296–7

temperament Emotional type, such as being outgoing or reserved, moody or cheerful. 171, 174–5, 225

tend and befriend An adaptive response to stress for females, resulting in protection of offspring (tending) and relying on the social group for mutual defence (befriending). In contrast with the more male response of fight or flight. 47, 66

testosterone A hormone from the androgen group that is produced mainly in the male testes (and in smaller amounts in the female ovaries). Associated with aggressiveness. 120–21

theory of mind (ToM) Our awareness that other people have thoughts, emotions and intentions of their own (i.e. they have minds). Thought to be involved in social and communicative behaviour, but impaired in people with autism/ASD. 182

theory of planned behaviour Changes in behaviour can be predicted from our intention to change, which in turn is the outcome of personal attitudes towards the behaviour in question, our beliefs about what others think, and our perceived ability to control our behaviour. 9, 22–5, 31–6

time urgency Trying to do too many things at once, always in a hurry and watching the clock. A characteristic of Type A behaviour. 44

token economy A form of operant conditioning designed to increase desirable behaviour and decrease undesirable behaviour with the use of tokens. Individuals receive tokens immediately after displaying a desirable behaviour. The tokens are collected and later exchanged for a meaningful object or privilege. 113, 144–5, 147, 226–7

tolerance A reduction in response to a drug, so that the addicted individual needs more to get the same effect. 12–13, 30, 32, 50–51, 67, 113, 134–5, 147

top-down approach A method of profiling popularised in the US. It starts with a pre-established typology and 'works down', using evidence from the crime scene and witness accounts, to classify offenders into one of two types of serial murderer. 113, 148–9, 151–2, 158, 161

trait anxiety A predisposition to perceive certain situations as threatening and to respond to the situation with varying levels of state anxiety. 272, 274, 292–3, 305

trait sport confidence (SC-trait) See state sport confidence. 268

transference A client transfers their feelings of love and hate for their parents/others onto the analyst. 242–3

trauma The experience of severe distress following a terrible or life-threatening event, either something that happened to you or witnessing it happen to someone else. 54–5, 64–5, 67, 69, 129, 133, 142, 167, 194, 200, 204–205, 219, 245

trephining Making a hole in the skull of a living person, thought to have been used to treat health problems such as epilepsy or alleviate mental health problems. 222–3

triangling In family systems therapy, the family is seen as a social system often consisting of triangles – three people interacting. Often one person in this triangle is supporting emotional conflict between the other two and thus becomes depressed/anxious themselves. See detriangling. 248

tricyclic antidepressants (TCAs) (e.g. clomipramine, trade name e.g. Anafranil) and imipramine (trade name e.g. Tofranil) An older class of antidepressants that block serotonin and noradrenaline transporters. They continue to be used but newer SSRIs etc. are preferred because an overdose can be serious. 250–51

twin studies If a particular behaviour is more genetic than environmental we would expect MZ twins to show a higher concordance rate than non-identical (DZ) twins (who share about 50% of their genes). MZ stands for monozygotic meaning 'one egg' whereas non-identical twins come from two eggs – dizygotic. 50–51, 114–15

Type A personality Describes someone who is competitive, time urgent (e.g. impatient) and hostile in most situations. Research has linked this personality type to coronary heart disease (CHD). 44–5

Type B personality Describes someone who is laid-back, relaxed and tolerant of others in most situations (i.e. the opposite of Type A). 44–5

Type I diabetes A serious lifelong condition caused because the body cannot produce insulin and therefore this has to be taken regularly (usually by injection). Insulin is needed to allow glucose into your body's cells. Too much or too little glucose in the bloodstream is fatal. 15, 26, 194

Type II diabetes As with Type I diabetes, the condition is related to abnormal levels of glucose. In this case high levels of glucose (e.g. from a high-calorie diet) mean that insulin production is damaged and eventually the body starts producing less. The condition can be treated by healthier eating. 96, 103, 194

typical antipsychotics (TAs) The first generation of antipsychotic drugs, having been used since the 1950s. They work as dopamine antagonists and include chlorpromazine. 250–51

UCR See unconditioned response. 105, 178–9, 218

UCS See unconditioned stimulus. 52, 178, 244

unconditional positive regard Providing affection and respect without any conditions attached. 192, 252

unconditioned response (UCR) An unlearned response to an unconditioned stimulus. 88, 178

unconditioned stimulus (UCS) Any stimulus that produces a response without learning taking place. 178, 244

unconscious The part of the mind that we are unaware of but which continues to direct much of our behaviour. 82, 218–19, 242–3

underextension In relation to language, using a word/phrase for just one object when it actually applies to a whole category. For example, using the word 'dog' for a family pet and not realising the same term applies to all dogs. 183

uninvolved parents A type of parenting style involving low demandingness and low responsiveness. 166–7, 196

uplifts scale See hassles and uplifts scale. 40, 66

utopianism The pursuit of an ideal and perfect world. One of the types of irrational belief proposed by Ellis to explain depression. 246

validity Refers to the 'trueness' or 'legitimacy' of data collected. 16, 19, 30, 32, 39, 41, 43, 45, 51, 59, 66–7, 71, 75, 77, 97, 99, 103, 105, 115, 123, 125, 130, 146, 149, 165, 169, 173, 220–21, 225

variable reinforcement schedule In operant conditioning when a reward is delivered at intervals that change each time rather than, for example, every tenth trial. 60–61

ventral tegmental area (VTA) An area of the brain rich in dopamine and serotonin neurons, part of two major dopamine pathways: the mesocortical and mesolimbic pathways. 50–51, 56, 67–9, 90

verbal persuasion Encouragement used by teachers, coaches and peers to influence performers. 26–7, 270–71, 288–9

vicarious experience Observing others engaging in a task that performers themselves have never executed. 26–7, 270–71, 288–9

vicarious reinforcement Occurs when a learner observes a model's behaviour being reinforced (rewarded). 26–7, 31, 33, 37, 52–3, 56, 60, 62–3, 67–9, 106, 124–5, 178, 218, 270, 289

war on drugs A term first used by President Nixon in the 1970s. The war on drugs is a campaign, led by the US government, on drug prohibition, with the aim of reducing the illegal drug trade in America. The initiative includes a set of drug policies that are intended to discourage the production, distribution and consumption of illegal drugs. 134–5

waxy flexibility A symptom of schizophrenia and also bipolar disorder, where a person remains in an immobile position and has a reduced response to stimuli. 238

Western Collaborative Group Study (WCGS) A research project that began in 1960 to test the hypothesis that Type A behaviours is a cause of coronary heart disease (CHD). At the outset 3524 men aged 39–59 from California were enrolled. Their medical histories were followed up 2, 4.5, 8.5 and 22 years later to assess incidence of CHD and mortality. 44

withdrawal A set of symptoms that develop when the addicted person abstains from or reduces their drug use. 12–13, 30, 50–54, 56–7, 62–5, 67, 69, 81, 90, 104–105, 144, 238

word salad An unintelligible mixture of seemingly random words, a form of speech characteristic of schizophrenia. 238

work ethic The principle that hard work is intrinsically worthy of reward. 282–3

YoungMinds A UK charity concerned with young people's mental health, trying to support and empower both children and their parents. 254–7

zero tolerance An approach to law enforcement that involves consistent and aggressive policing of what is sometimes referred to as 'petty crime'. The aim is to reduce antisocial behaviour and decrease fear of crime amongst the general public. 113, 134–5, 147

zone of proximal development (ZPD) In Vygotsky's theory of cognitive development, the 'region' between a person's current abilities, which they can perform with no assistance, and their potential capabilities, which they can be helped to achieve with the assistance of 'experts'. 186–7

Acknowledgements

p236 Photograph of Marsha Linehan, reproduced with the kind permission of Jed Share; p256 Peerfest logo reproduced with the kind permission of the Peerfest partnership hosted by Mind, peersupport@mind.org.uk; p276 Photograph of Jennifer Savage, reproduced with kind permission; p304 Photograph of Dr. Krista Munroe-Chandler, reproduced with kind permission.

Picture credits

Cover © PremiumVector / Shutterstock

Shutterstock ©: p3 Rosapompelmo; p6 bomg, Subbotina Anna, Rocketclips, Inc., igorstevanovic, Tatyana Dzemileva, KDdesignphoto; p7 Simone van den Berg, Carla Francesca Castagno, studiostoks, Suwin; p8–9 Naeblys; p10 Sabelskaya, Ljupco Smokovski; p11 Salienko Evgenii; p12 Dejan Stanic Micko, WAYHOME studio; p13 Antonio Guillem; p14 Yayar scentio BH; p15 domnitsky; p16 Nagy-Bagoly Arpad, yurakrasil; p17 Monkey Business Images; p18 Ulf Wittrock, Monkey Business Images; p19 Lipskiy; p20 jorgen mcleman, Scorpp; p21 Syda Productions; p22 NEIL ROY JOHNSON, tale; p23 Milan Ilic Photographer, p24 Nokuro, Monkey Business Images; p25 Dmitry Lobanov; p26 This Is Me, MilanMarkovic78; p27 Dreams Come True; p28 pikselstock, DenisProduction.com; p29 frantic00, rui vale sousa; p31 Salienko Evgenii, Milan Ilic Photographer, WAYHOME studio; p34 aslysun, matkub2499; p35 Phovoir; p37 OSTILL is Franck Camhi; p38 Pretty Vectors, Shtonado; p39 GlebSStock; p40 BY213, paulzhuk; p41 Happy monkey; p42 Vlue, fizkes; p43 ndphoto; p44 Mr Doomits, Jonah_H; p45 eelnosiva; p46 bluefish_ds, rohaizadabu; p48 BCFC, Juan Gaertner; p50 Luis Molinero; p52 Minerva Studio, Haoka; p53 vchal; p54 Blankids, Fabio Dien; p55 colies; p56 monticello, Nomad_Soul; p57 AndreyCherkasov; p58 jamesclark1991, Lucian Milasan; p59 ivector; p60 Barry Barnes, Wpadington; p61 gabriel12; p62 studiostoks, s_bukley; p63 Artisticco; p64 Nomad_Soul, Dima Zel; p65 pixelrain; p66 Happy monkey, Jonah_H; p70 Chris Harvey; p71 Alextype; p74 lev radin, Black Jack; p75 Tap10; p76 Memo Angeles, MoonRock; p77 Antonio Guillem; p78 WAYHOME studio; p79 JStone; p80 pathdoc; p81 kuzmaphoto, Image Point Fr; p82 Kirill Kurashov, Ljupco Smokovski; p83 Malt Digital Agency; p84 Christian Bertrand, DFree; p85 Yuriy Golub; p86 Mono Studios, Goritza; p87 Budimir Jevtic; p88 redpip1984, igorstevanovic; p89 Vova Shevchuk; p90 Dean Drobot, Nicole Lienemann, Image Point Fr; p91 alexskopje; p92 R-Type, Jacob Lund; p93 Michelle Patrick; p94 pickingpok, chuchiko17; p95 HieroGraphic; p96 Raihana Asral, Nata Kotliar; p97 Bukhta Yurii; p98 Klara Viskova, Robert B. Miller; Alexander Raths; p100 Yaoinlove, Sherry Yates Young; p101 B-D-S Piotr Marcinski; p102 Chaowalit Seeneha, kamui29; p103 CHAjAMP; p104 Ljupco Smokovski; p105 Vova Shevchuk; p108 iQoncept, fizkes; p109 anystock; p112–3 Lightspring; p114 Mr Doomits, Olesia Bilkei; p116 Africa Studio, Crystal Eye Studio; p117 Phat1978; p118 CLIPAREA l Custom media; p119 trattieritratt; p120 ilikeyellow, Iakov Filimonov; p122 Photographee.eu, Malysheva Anastasiia;; p124 Beanbeardy, Olena Yakobchuk; p125 Pavel L Photo and Video; p126 Lotus_studio, Robert A. Mansker; p127 Billion Photos; p129 Sarunyu L; p131 igorstevanovic; p132 Thanawan Wisetsin, M-SUR; p134 Prilutskiy, Pro_Foto; p135 pryzmat; p136 Edw, StepanPopov; p137 Pavlo S, Cookie Studio; p138 Chris Jenner, Lia Koltyrina; p139 everything possible, Frederic Legrand - COMEO; p140 GoncharukMaks, Victor Moussa; p141 CURAphotography, DFree; p142 simkoe; p143 BOKEH STOCK; p144 Lorna Munden, Joseph Sohm; p145 LightField Studios; p147 I'm friday, Anna Om; p148 atm2003, Ford Contributor; p149 Yes - Royalty Free; p150 nature photos; p151 Brian A Jackson, Fer Gregory; p152 Pyty, Skocko; p153 Pressmaster; p154 D-VISIONS, dny3d; p155 Alive_art; p156 pikselstock, PRESSLAB; p157 Scott Donkin; p158 eric laudonien, p159 Marijus Auruskevicius; p162–3 ESB Professional; p164 Sveta Evglevskaia, Syda Productions; p165 Robert C. Bergdorf, Procyk Radek; p166 SpeedKingz; p167 Valery Sidelnykov, Procyk Radek; p168 Ermolaev Alexander; p169 FiledIMAGE; p170 luanateutzi, Eric Isselee, Olhastock; p171 EugeneShchegolsky, Robert Kneschke; p172 Pressmaster; p174 John Gomez, itsmejust, Yulia Vasilyeva; p175 mirzavisoko; p176 AimPix, katatonia82; p177 Everett - Art, Drop of Light; p179 Sorapop Udomsri, wavebreakmedia; p180 aslysun; p181 Rawpixel.com, Monkey Business Images; p182 MAZM MAZM; p183 Stefan Malloch, Monkey Business Images; p184 Serhiy Kobyakov; p185 Kidsada Manchinda, Arjan Ard Studio; p186 imtmphoto, Daxiao Productions; p187 StunningArt, fizkes; p188 MarclSchauer, Robert Kneschke; p189 Tyler Olson; p191 igorstevanovic; p192 Guitarfoto studio, alexkich; p193 Monkey Business Images, fizkes; p194 Alfredo Cerra, Pixel-Shot; p195 Olesia Bilke, SpeedKingz, p196 Leremy, altanaka; p197 Rawpixel.com, adriaticfoto; p198 Elizaveta Galitckaia, Dmytro Zinkevych; p199 Iakov Filimonov, kurhan; p200 wavebreakmedia, Photographee.eu; p201 ESB Professional, Monkey Business Images; p202 HTWE; p203 aslysun; p204 fizkes, Billion Photos; p205 Ruslan Shugushev, Anna Nahabed; p206 Kristina Ismulyani, SergiyN; p207 Vladislav Filatov, Monkey Business Images; p208 Michael D Brown, shurkin_son; p209 Monkey Business Images, Billion Photos; p212–13 Ana Ado; p214 Krasimira Nevenova, tommaso79; p215 Aquarell; p216 Tatyana Dzemileva, Ollyy; p217 patronestaff; p218 Dmytro Zinkevych, Helen Sushitskaya; p219 aurielaki; p220 SeventyFour, Lightspring; p221 StockSmartStart; p222 Martin Pelanek, Asier Romero; p223 TravelStrategy; p224 TisforThan, vectorfusionart; p225 JPC-PROD; p226 Clem Hencher-Stevens, EQRoy; p227 Sergio Foto; p228 Nella; p229 igorstevanovic; p230 AnnGaysorn; p231 SpeedKingz, Rido; p232 joyfull; p233 Photographee.eu, Rido; p234 serdjophoto, shipfactory; p235 Rido, Jonny Essex; p236 Tero Vesalainen; p237 nevenm, Rido; p238 Michael715, Doucefleur; p239 Vilkas Vision, Rido; p240 spatuletail, mypokcik; p241 ayelet-keshet, Rido; p242 vkilikov; p243 VGstockstudio, jesadaphorn, Andrew Rybalko; p244 fizkes; p245 SasaStock, jesadaphorn; p246 LightField Studios, Pressmaster; p247 Maksym Fesenko, jesadaphorn; p248 Freeograph, Maria Sbytova; p249 Iakov Filimonov, jesadaphorn; p250 pogonici; p251 cigdem, jesadaphorn; p252 Zoriana Zaitseva, verbaska; p253 ivector, jesadaphorn; p254 Khakimullin Aleksandr; p255 Monkey Business Images, A. and I. Kruk; p256 Roman Samborskyi; p257 Andrey_Popov, A. and I. Kruk; p259 Farknot Architect; p260–1 Dziurek; p262 Maxisport; p264 cristiano barni, Isogood_patrick; p265 Paolo Bona, p266 Petr Toman, GEORGID; p267 Corepics VOF, Neale Cousland; p268 SpeedKingz; p269 CWA Studios, landmarkmedia; p270 Ariane Vermeersch, Anna Furman; p271 fizkes, Featureflash Photo Agency; p272 Marco Iacobucci EPP, Shane Doran; p273 Eugene Parciasepe; p274 Peliken, coxy58; p275 Lubo Ivanko, Mitch Gunn; p276 vectorfusionart; p277 witchcraft; p278 Travability Images, ArtOfPhotos; p279 Petr Toman, Ververidis Vasilis; p280 Neale Cousland; p281 Callahan, Africa Studio; p282 Denis Kuvaev; p283 Master1305; p284 Goran Jakus, Oleksandr Osipov; p285 Neale Cousland, Aleksandr Markin; p286 Hafiz Johari, Mitch Gunn; p287 Leonard Zhukovsky, landmarkmedia; p288 Marc Pagani Photography, Mitch Gunn; p289 Featureflash Photo Agency; p290 mooinblack; p291 lev radin; p292 LouisLotterPhotography, Herbert Kratky; p293 katatonia82, Mitch Gunn; p294 Mitch Gunn; p295 katatonia82; p296 Greg Epperson, krumcek; p297 Melinda Nagy, Ververidis Vasilis; p299 Romolo Tavani; p300 dade72; p301 Aspen Photo; p302 Grzegorz Czapski; p303 Carlos Caetano; p304 Diego Barbieri; p305 sportpoint; p306 Jack Fordyce, Oleh Dubyna; p307 Yuricazac; p309 I'm friday

Alamy ©

p168 © Science History Images / Alamy Stock Photo; p177 World History Archive / Alamy Stock Photo; p203 Mike Abrahams / Alamy Stock Photo; pp265, 283 Allstar Picture Library / Alamy Stock Photo; pp273, 291 Allstar Picture Library / Alamy Stock Photo; p280 TCD/Prod.DB / Alamy Stock Photo; p282 ZUMA / Alamy Stock Photo; p288 WENN Rights Ltd / Alamy Stock Photo; p290 Action Plus Sports Images / Alamy Stock Photo; p294 Allstar Picture Library / Alamy Stock Photo

Cartoonstock ©

p33 kkin240; p268 thln20; p302 aaon26

Getty Images ©

pp121, 123, 125 Donaldson Collection / Contributor; p202 © Bettmann / Contributor

Topfoto ©

pp115, 117, 119, 125, 127, 129, 133 © TopFoto; p128 © PA Photos / TopFoto; p135 © National Pictures / TopFoto; p143 © PA Photos / TopFoto; p262 The Image Works / TopFoto; pp277, 295 PA Photos / TopFoto

Creative Commons licence

p118 Charles Whitman; p128 Jon Venables and Robert Thompson; p133 John McVicar / Nationaal Archief; p178 Rosalie Rayner; p230 Huizinga collectie hongerwinter – NIOD Institute for War, Holocaust and Genocide Studies – 217098; pp263, 281 Steph Houghton © Katie Chan

Other illustrations © Illuminate Publishing